A Fisheries Guide to
Lakes and Ponds
of Connecticut
Including the Connecticut River and Its Coves

Principal Authors

Robert P. Jacobs

Eileen B. O'Donnell

Preface

Edward C. Parker, Chief, Bureau of Natural Resources

Cartography

William B. Gerrish

Contributing Authors

Peter J. Aarrestad

George W. Benz

Stephen R. Gephard

Michael Humphreys

Bruce W. Hunter

William A. Hyatt

David R. Molnar

Brian D. Murphy

Nancy M. Murray

Eric C. Schluntz

Richard J. Van Nostrand

Library of Congress Cataloging-in-Publication Data

Jacobs, Robert Paul.

A fisheries guide to lakes and ponds of Connecticut, including the Connecticut River and its coves / principal authors, Robert P. Jacobs, Eileen B. O'Donnell ; preface, Edward C. Parker ; cartography, William B. Gerrish ; contributing authors, Peter J. Aarrestad ... [et al.].

p. cm. -- (DEP bulletin ; no. 35)

Includes bibliographical references (p.   ).

ISBN 0-942085-11-6

1. Fishing--Connecticut--Guidebooks. 2. Lakes--Connecticut--Guidebooks. 3. Connecticut--Guidebooks. I. O'Donnell, Eileen B., 1955- II. Title. III. Series.

SH477 .J33 2002

799.1'2'09746--dc21   2002025689

Additional copies may be purchased from the DEP Store

79 Elm Street, Hartford, Connecticut 06106-5127

http://dep.state.ct.us

PHONE: (860) 424-3555 FAX: (860) 424-4088

Paper: ISBN 0-942085-11-6

Cloth: ISBN 0-942085-12-4

DEP Bulletin 35

A Fisheries Guide to
Lakes and Ponds
of Connecticut
Including the Connecticut River and Its Coves

CONNECTICUT DEPARTMENT OF
ENVIRONMENTAL PROTECTION

The Honorable John G. Rowland
Governor of Connecticut

Arthur J. Rocque, Jr.
Commissioner

David K. Leff
Deputy Commissioner

Edward C. Parker
Chief, Bureau of Natural Resources

William A. Hyatt
Director, Inland Fisheries

Allan N. Williams
Consulting Publisher, Environmental and Geographic Information Center

Mary Crombie, Acorn Studio
Book Design

David P. Wakefield Jr.
Copy Editor

Albert Obue
Cover Photo

This book is dedicated to the late Jim Moulton,
whose leadership helped to make the
Statewide Lake and Pond Electrofishing
Survey possible, but who was denied
the chance to see its fruition.

Jim began a 30-year career with the DEP Fisheries Division in 1970. He started off as a regional field biologist and later became Assistant Director for Inland Fisheries and eventually Manager of Inland Fisheries. Jim was the leader of the Inland Fisheries Program for nearly 20 years and during his tenure, he worked tirelessly to improve fishing opportunities for Connecticut anglers. Under Jim's leadership, we created new fisheries for northern pike and walleye, renovated trout hatcheries, initiated a habitat protection program, created special Trout and Bass Management Areas, started the Connecticut Aquatic Resources Education Program (CARE), and initiated statewide surveys that led to the development of new and innovative trout and bass management plans. When Jim Moulton began his career, our state had little to offer freshwater anglers. Thirty years later, Connecticut is recognized as having some of the finest freshwater fishing in the East.

Table of Contents

Acknowledgements   ix

Map of Connecticut with Site Locations   x

Preface   xiii

Lake and Pond Ecology   1

    The Lake Environment   1
    Lake Productivity and Classification   3
    Food Chains/Webs   4
    The Concept of Balance in Lake and Pond Fisheries   4
    Density-Dependent Growth and Stockpiling of Fish Populations   5
    Effects of Balance vs. Imbalance on Lake Ecosystems   5
    Causes of Imbalance in Fish Populations   5
    Fish Habitat   7
    Habitat Alteration   8
    Aquatic Vegetation   9
    Major Groups of Aquatic Plants   9
    Endangered Animals and Plants   12
    Introduced Animals and Plants   12
    Fish Parasites   15
    Common Parasites of Connecticut Freshwater Fishes   16
    Fish Kills   18
    Common Causes of Natural Fish Kills   19
    Contaminants in Fish   19

Lake and Pond Fisheries Management   21

    History of Fisheries Management in Connecticut 21
    Coldwater Fisheries Management   22
    Warmwater Fisheries Management   24
    Potential Management Tools for Warmwater Fisheries   25
    Physical Management Tools   25
    Fishing Regulations   30

Life Histories of Common Lake and Pond Fishes   33

    Gamefish   33
    Panfish   40
    Catfish   45
    Forage Fishes   48
    Other Fish Species   50

Descriptions and Maps of Lakes and Ponds 53

Field Methods 53

How to Use This Section 56

Site	A.K.A.	Town	Page
Alexander Lake		Killingly	58
Amos Lake		Preston	60
Anderson Pond	(Blue Lake)	North Stonington	62
Aspinook Pond		Lisbon/Griswold/Canterbury	64
Avery Pond		Preston	66
Babcock Pond		Colchester	68
Ball Pond		New Fairfield	70
Bantam Lake		Litchfield/Morris	72
Bashan Lake		East Haddam	74
Batterson Park Pond		Farmington/New Britain	76
Beach Pond		Voluntown/Exeter (RI)	78
Beachdale Pond		Voluntown	80
Beseck Lake		Middlefield	82
Bigelow Pond		Union	84
Billings Lake		North Stonington	86
Black Pond		Meriden/Middlefield	88
Black Pond		Woodstock	90
Bolton Lake, Lower		Bolton/Vernon	92
Bolton Lake, Middle		Vernon	94
Bolton Lake, Upper		Coventry/Tolland/Vernon	96
Bolton Notch Pond		Bolton	98
Breakneck Pond		Union/Sturbridge (MA)	100
Burr Pond		Torrington	102
Candlewood Lake		Brookfield/Danbury/New Fairfield/ New Milford/Sherman	104
Cedar Lake		Chester	112
Chamberlain Lake		Bethany	114
Colebrook River Reservoir		Colebrook/Sandisfield/Tolland (MA)	116
Congamond Lake	(South, Middle, North Ponds)	Suffield/Southwick (MA)	118
Coventry Lake	(Wangumbaug Lake)	Coventry	120
Crystal Lake		Ellington/Stafford	122
Crystal Lake		Middletown	124
Dodge Pond		East Lyme	126
Dog Pond		Goshen	128
Dooley Pond		Middletown	130
Eagleville Lake		Coventry/Mansfield	132
East Twin Lake	(Washining Lake)	Salisbury	134
Gardner Lake		Bosrah/Montville/Salem	136
Glasgo Pond		Griswold/Voluntown	138
Gorton Pond		East Lyme	140
Great Hill Pond		Portland	142
Green Falls Reservoir		Voluntown	144
Halls Pond		Ashford/Eastford	146
Hampton Reservoir		Eastford/Hampton	148

Site	A.K.A.	Town	Page
Hatch Pond		Kent	150
Lake Hayward	(Shaw Lake)	East Haddam	152
Higganum Reservoir		Haddam	154
Highland Lake		Winchester	156
Holbrook Pond		Hebron	158
Hopeville Pond		Griswold	160
Horse Pond		Salem	162
Lake Housatonic		Derby/Monroe/Oxford/Seymour/Shelton	164
Howells Pond		Hartland	168
Jurovaty Pond	(Bishop Swamp)	Andover	170
Keach Pond	(Peck Pond)	Putnam/Thompson/Burrillville (RI)	172
Lake Kenosia		Danbury	174
Killingly Pond		Killingly/Glocester (RI)	176
Lake of Isles		North Stonington	178
Lantern Hill Pond		Ledyard/North Stonington	180
Lake Lillinonah		Bridgewater/Brookfield/New Milford/ Newtown/Roxbury/Southbury	182
Little Pond	(Schoolhouse Pond)	Thompson	186
Long Pond		Ledyard/North Stonington	188
Maltby Lakes (1, 2 & 3)		Orange/West Haven	190
Mamanasco Lake		Ridgefield	194
Mansfield Hollow Reservoir	(Naubesatuck Lake)	Mansfield/Windham	196
Mashapaug Lake		Union/Sturbridge (MA)	200
Lake McDonough	(Compensating Reservoir)	Barkhamsted	202
Messershmidt Pond		Deep River/Westbrook	204
Millers Pond		Durham	206
Mohawk Pond		Cornwall/Goshen	208
Mono Pond		Columbia	210
Moodus Reservoir		East Haddam	212
Moosup Pond		Plainfield	216
Morey Pond		Ashford/Union	218
Mount Tom Pond		Litchfield/Morris/Washington	220
Mudge Pond	(Silver Lake)	Sharon	222
North Farms Reservoir		Wallingford	224
Norwich Pond		Lyme	226
Pachaug Pond		Griswold	228
Park Pond		Winchester	232
Pataconk Lake	(Russell Jennings Pond)	Chester	234
Pataganset Lake		East Lyme	236
Pickerel Lake		Colchester/East Haddam	238
Pine Acres Lake		Hampton	240
Powers Lake		East Lyme	242
Quaddick Reservoir		Thompson	244
Quinebaug Lake	(Wauregan Reservoir)	Killingly	248
Quonnipaug Lake		Guilford	250
Rainbow Reservoir		East Granby/Windsor	252
Red Cedar Lake		Lebanon	254
Rogers Lake		Lyme/Old Lyme	256

Site	A.K.A.	Town	Page
Roseland Lake		Woodstock	258
Lake Saltonstall		Branford/East Haven	260
Saugatuck Reservoir		Easton/Redding/Weston	262
Shenipsit Lake		Ellington/Tolland/Vernon	264
Silver Lake	(Peat Works Pond)	Berlin/Meriden	266
South Spectacle Lake		Kent	268
Squantz Pond		New Fairfield/Sherman	270
Stillwater Pond		Torrington	272
Tyler Lake		Goshen	274
Uncas Lake	(Hog Pond)	Lyme	276
Lake Waramaug		Kent/Warren/Washington	278
West Branch Reservoir	(Hogsback Reservoir)	Colebrook/Hartland	282
West Hill Pond		Barkhamsted/New Hartford	284
West Side Pond		Goshen	286
West Thompson Reservoir		Thompson	288
West Twin Lake	(Washinee Lake)	Salisbury	290
Winchester Lake		Winchester	292
Wononscopomuc Lake	(Lakeville Lake)	Salisbury	294
Wood Creek Pond		Norfolk	296
Wyassup Lake		North Stonington	298
Lake Zoar		Monroe/Newtown/Oxford/Southbury	300

Descriptions and Maps of Connecticut River Sites

306

Site	A.K.A.	Town	Page
Conn. River Mainstem (North)		Enfield to Windsor	306
Conn. River Mainstem (Central)		Hartford to Portland	310
Wethersfield Cove		Wethersfield	314
Keeney Cove		East Hartford/Glastonbury	316
Crow Point Cove	(White Oak Cove)	Wethersfield	318
Wrights Cove	(Pecausett Pond)	Portland	320
Conn. River Mainstem (South)		Haddam to Lyme	322
Salmon Cove		East Haddam	326
Chapman Pond		East Haddam	328
Hamburg Cove		Lyme	330

Glossary of Scientific Terms

333

Appendix

336

General References

348

Index

349

Acknowledgements

Supervision — Special thanks to David Leff, Ed Parker, Ernie Beckwith, Jim Moulton and Bill Hyatt for supervision and guidance on the many facets of work that led to this publication.

Aquatic Vegetation Survey — We'd like to thank Nancy Murray, often assisted by Bruce Hunter, for her many hours in the field conducting the lake and pond aquatic vegetation surveys and identifying all plant samples.

Lake Mapping — Thanks to Bruce Hunter, often assisted by Nancy Murray, who was responsible for all of the depth-mapping field work. Thanks to Tim Wildman who worked on the Connecticut River mainstem maps and digitized the lake-depth data for many of the other maps. Special thanks to Bill Gerrish for his artistry in creation of the maps.

Contributing Authors — We thank the following people for written contributions to various sections of the publication: Pete Aarrestad (Fish Habitat, Warmwater Fisheries), George Benz (Fish Parasites), Steve Gephard (Connecticut River), Mike Humphreys (Introduced Plants and Animals), Bruce Hunter (Angler Access), Bill Hyatt (Connecticut River, Fish Contaminants), Dave Molnar (Connecticut River), Brian Murphy (Fish Kills), Nancy Murray (Aquatic Vegetation, Introduced Plants and Animals), Eric Schluntz (Coldwater Fisheries, Introduced Predators), and Rick Van Nostrand (Fish Parasites).

Photos — Most photos in this publication were taken by Fisheries staff. Credit for parasite photos goes to George Benz, Ash Bullard, Stephen Curran and Ronnie Palmer. The aerial photo of Lake Chamberlain was provided by the South Central Connecticut Regional Water Authority. The cover photo of Upper Bolton Lake was taken by Albert Obue.

Fish Sampling — Many thanks to DEP Fisheries Division personnel who worked tirelessly over the years on the Statewide Lake and Pond Electrofishing Survey and other fish sampling that contributed to this publication. They included: Pete Aarrestad, George Babey, Tim Barry, Ernie Beckwith, Jim Bender, Tom Bourret, Bill Gerrish, Neal Hagstrom, Mike Humphreys, Bill Hyatt, Rick Jacobson, Gerald Leonard, Ed Machowski, Dave Molnar, Jim Moulton, Bob Orciari, Tony Petrillo, Chuck Phillips, Eric Schluntz, Tim Wildman and all of our dedicated seasonal research assistants who through the years have spent many tedious hours for this project both in the office and the field.

Reviewers — Thank you to our reviewers, who included almost all of the Fisheries and other DEP personnel listed above, as well as: George Benz, Kevin Blados and the DEP Parks Division, Mary DiGiacomo-Cohen, Charles Fredette, Bruce Hunter, Chuck Lee, David Leff, Rick Lewis and the DEP Law Enforcement Division, Nancy Murray, Ed Parker, and Mike Payton and the DEP Boating Division. Special thanks to David Wakefield, our copy editor for the project.

Funding — Sincere thanks to the U.S. Fish and Wildlife Service for funding the Statewide Lake and Pond Electrofishing Survey and other research and management projects that provided the information presented in this book. Additional thanks to the Fisheries Advisory Council (FAC) in procuring funding for this publication and for their ongoing efforts on behalf of the Connecticut DEP and its fisheries programs.

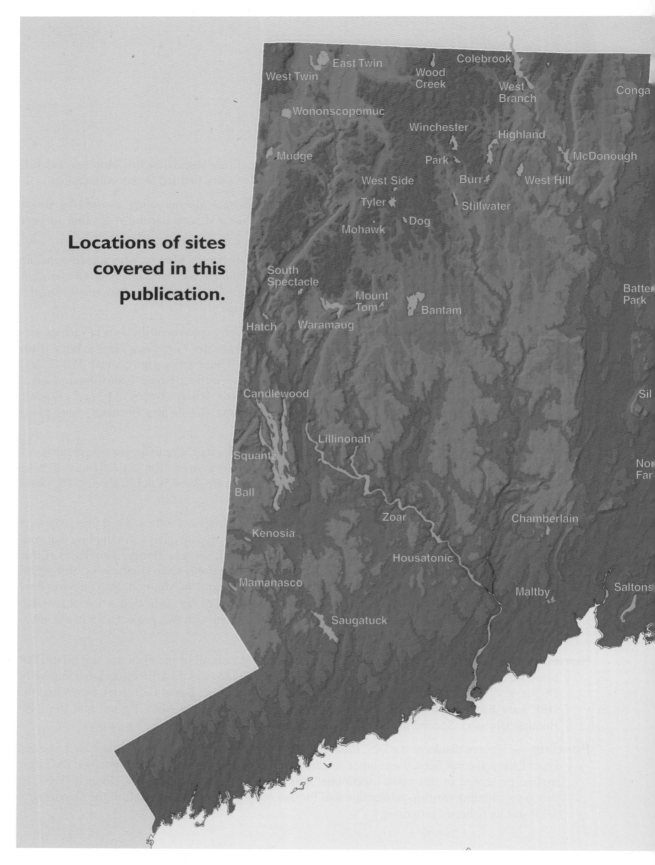

Locations of sites covered in this publication.

East Twin
West Twin
Wood Creek
Colebrook
West Branch
Conga
Wononscopomuc
Winchester
Highland
Mudge
Park
McDonough
West Side
Burr
West Hill
Tyler
Stillwater
Mohawk
Dog
South Spectacle
Batter Park
Mount Tom
Bantam
Hatch
Waramaug
Candlewood
Sil
Lillinonah
Squantz
Nor Far
Ball
Kenosia
Zoar
Chamberlain
Mamanasco
Housatonic
Maltby
Saltons
Saugatuck

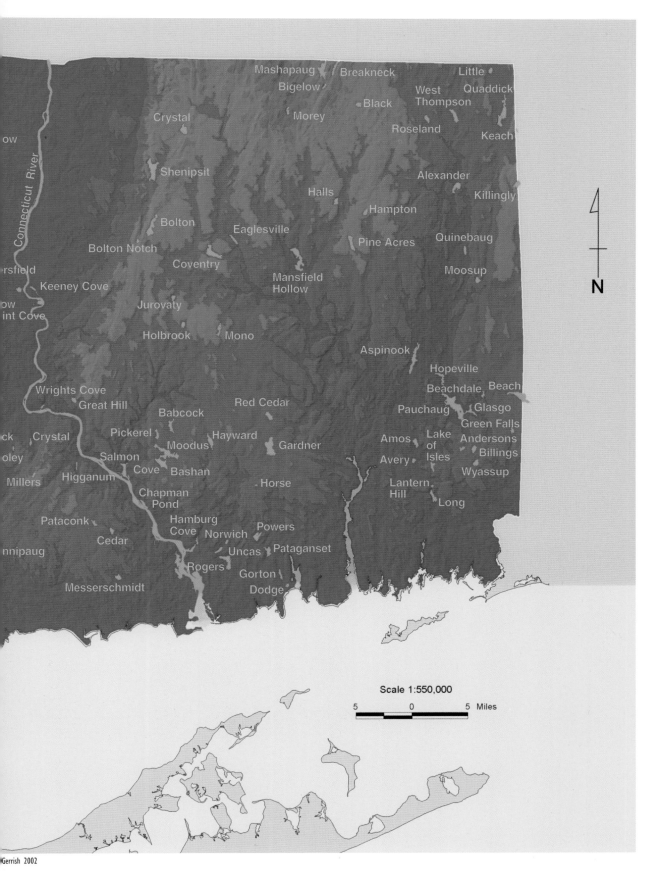

Mashapaug   Breakneck   Little
Bigelow   West   Quaddick
Black   Thompson
Crystal   Morey   Roseland   Keach
Connecticut River
Shenipsit   Alexander
Halls   Killingly
Hampton
Bolton   Eaglesville   Quinebaug
Pine Acres
Bolton Notch
rsfield   Coventry   Moosup
Keeney Cove   Mansfield
ow   Jurovaty   Hollow
int Cove
Holbrook   Mono
Aspinook
Hopeville
Wrights Cove   Beachdale   Beach
Great Hill   Red Cedar   Glasgo
Babcock   Pauchaug   Green Falls
ck   Crystal   Pickerel   Hayward   Amos   Lake   Andersons
oley   Moodus   Gardner   of   Billings
Salmon   Avery   Isles
Millers   Cove   Bashan   Wyassup
Higganum   Horse   Lantern
Chapman   Hill   Long
Pataconk   Pond
Hamburg   Powers
Cedar   Cove   Norwich
nnipaug   Uncas   Pataganset
Rogers   Gorton
Messerschmidt   Dodge

N

Scale 1:550,000

5   0   5 Miles

Preface

Connecticut is blessed with an abundance of lakes and ponds. Most of these water bodies were created over 11,000 years ago during the last ice age when runoff from retreating glaciers filled the holes that had been left in our landscape. In addition to natural lakes and ponds, many water bodies were added to the Connecticut landscape during the industrial revolution and the growth and development of our modern day society. Many impoundments on our rivers and streams were created to meet the water supply needs of textile mills, and more recently, to generate electricity, address potable water supply needs and to control flooding.

Connecticut now has over 425 major lakes, ponds, reservoirs and impoundments covering more than 56,000 acres. These water bodies provide plentiful opportunities for residents and visitors to participate in a variety of recreational activities including fishing, ice-fishing, boating, swimming and diving. It is no wonder that so many people can be found enjoying Connecticut's lakes and ponds during every season of the year. More than 200,000 people fish on our lakes and ponds each year and even greater numbers participate in various boating activities.

The purpose of this book is to provide the latest information on 113 of Connecticut's major public lakes and ponds, and ten locations on the Connecticut River. I have confidence this guide will prove to be an invaluable source of information for anglers, boaters, educators, lake shore residents, lake associations, consultants or anyone interested in nature or the ecology of freshwater lakes and ponds. The format, by design, is easy to read and non-technical. It includes depth contour maps, maximum and minimum water depths, water clarity, thermal stratification, lake productivity, aquatic vegetation, and information on fish populations and their habitat. Anglers will be particularly interested in information on fishing quality and where to catch the big ones. Boaters and anglers alike will benefit from updated information on public access.

Naturalists and anglers will find the chapter on lake and pond fisheries management practices, life histories of common lake and pond fishes, and lake and pond ecology to be enlightening. I anticipate that readers will be left with a heightened understanding and renewed respect for the many creatures that inhabit these waters. Even the parasites will be seen through new eyes! We are also proud to be able to include many beautiful prints of individual fish species by renowned artist Joseph Tomelleri, who is considered by many to be the best fish illustrator in the world.

This publication is the culmination of over 20 years of sampling, monitoring and data evaluation by DEP Fisheries biologists. It will replace the last version, "A Fishery Survey of the Lakes and Ponds in Connecticut", which was published in 1959. Although the 1959 book has been out of print for many years, it was and still is one of the most requested publications ever produced by DEP.

I'm confident that this book will add to your appreciation and enjoyment of Connecticut's lakes and ponds and provide a greater understanding of our fish populations and the environment on which they depend for survival. Anglers will find the new and updated information invaluable for improving fishing success and for finding new angling opportunities to explore.

Good luck and good fishing!

Edward C. Parker
Chief, DEP Bureau of Natural Resources

LAKE AND POND ECOLOGY

The Lake Environment

Water. All living things, especially aquatic plants and animals, owe their existence to the unique physical and chemical properties of water. It is a perfect medium for life because it can exist as either a liquid or a gas at the moderate temperatures found on Earth. Aquatic organisms live in it and, like humans, are mostly made of it.

Water is also an excellent transportation medium. It transports nutrients from place to place, both on a planetary scale and within the bodies of living things.

One of the most remarkable characteristics of water that allows aquatic life to exist is that, unlike almost all other substances, water is lighter as a solid (ice) than as a liquid. If ice were denser than water, it would first form on the bottoms of lakes and oceans, allowing them to freeze solid during winter. Because ice is lighter than water, it floats on the surface of lakes, providing an insulating layer of protection for aquatic plants and animals during winter.

Thermal Stratification. Water is densest (weighs the most) at about 39° F. Both warmer and colder water weigh less. For this reason, lakes with sufficient depth "thermally stratify" during the summer. This means that lake water separates into discrete layers according to temperature, with the warmest (lightest) water at the surface and the coldest (densest) layer at the bottom. This phenomenon has vast implications for fish, especially those like trout that require cool water and high levels of dissolved oxygen to survive.

Spring and Fall. During spring and fall, water temperatures, and therefore densities, are similar throughout the water columns of lakes. Wind action and changing water temperatures cause surface waters to mix with deeper water, resulting in what are called the spring and fall "turnovers" (usually during March and October in Connecticut). During these times, dissolved oxygen levels are usually high throughout the water column because deep lake water is constantly mixing with shallow water that is being oxygenated through contact with the surface as well as through photosynthesis by algae and other aquatic plants. Fish can thrive in all areas of a lake during these times because the shallow water is not too warm and the deep water has sufficient oxygen.

Summer. As summer warms the surface of a lake, it becomes less dense than the cooler water beneath and stratifies to a point at which wind action can no longer readily mix the water

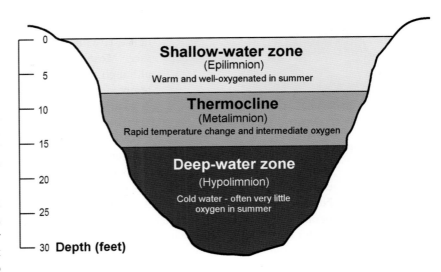

Thermal and chemical stratification of a "typical" Connecticut lake during summer.

layers. Most Connecticut lakes with depths greater than 20 feet stratify into three zones during the warmest months of summer. Below is a description of what happens in a "typical" Connecticut lake during July through September:

- **The Shallow-Water Zone.** The water from the surface to a depth typically of around 12 feet (called the epilimnion) has good sunlight penetration. This both warms the water and allows algae and other aquatic plants to produce oxygen. This layer of water has more than enough oxygen for fish, but is unfortunately too warm for many fish species. For this reason, many warmwater fish, such as adult bass and sunfish, prefer to stay in cooler, deeper water during the heat of the summer day and venture into the shallows only during morning, evening or night, when the water is slightly cooler. Coldwater fish, such as trout, cannot survive long in warm water and typically avoid the shallows altogether during summer.

- **The Thermocline.** In this layer (the metalimnion), usually between 12 and 25 feet, water temperature declines rapidly with depth. Usually, there is still enough light penetration for photosynthesis to occur and provide the oxygen necessary for fish survival. In most Connecticut lakes, this is the only zone that has both high enough oxygen and low enough temperature to support trout during the summer.

- **The Deep-Water Zone.** The deepest water in most Connecticut lakes (the hypolimnion) typically contains little or no oxygen during late summer. Here, bacterial decomposition of organic matter uses up oxygen, while light penetration is so low that oxygen-producing plants cannot exist. Most fish species can survive in this zone only for short periods during summer.

Although most deep Connecticut lakes thermally stratify during the summer, there is considerable variation among lakes in the amount of oxygen available in deeper water. This is usually dependent on water clarity and productivity (trophic classification) of a lake. Some lakes with very clear water and low productivity retain moderate oxygen levels throughout the summer, whereas many turbid lakes retain oxygen only in the surface layers and cannot support coldwater fish species at all during summer.

Many fish species remain active during winter, although their metabolisms slow down when water temperatures are low.

Winter. During winter, surface ice prevents the wind from mixing lake waters. For the most part, this is a benefit to fish because it provides an insulating layer that prevents the deeper water from becoming too cold. The bottom waters of deep lakes remain around 39° (the temperature at which water is densest) with lighter, colder water staying closer to the surface. Most warmwater fish remain relatively active at 39°, although their metabolisms are much slower than at higher temperatures. In very shallow lakes, temperatures approach freezing throughout the water column, which slows warmwater-fish metabolisms to the point of near-hibernation.

When a lake is covered with ice, it can no longer acquire oxygen through contact with the air. The only oxygen available to fish and other aquatic animals is that which is residual from the previous fall and that created by photosynthesizing plants using the little light that passes through the ice and snow. Normally, these low oxygen levels are sufficient, because fish require less oxygen at low temperatures. During severe winters, ice and snow may block all penetrating sunlight for weeks. Under these conditions, "winter kills" sometimes occur in very shallow ponds because there is not enough residual oxygen for fish to survive. Larger fish are typically more susceptible to a winter kill because of their greater oxygen needs.

Lake Productivity and Classification

When referring to aquatic systems, the term "productivity" can be used either generally or specifically, depending on context. "Lake productivity" generally refers to a lake's capacity to support plants and animals, whereas "fish productivity" refers specifically to a lake's capacity to support fish. A lake's productivity depends on the amount of nutrients (chemicals such as phosphorus and nitrogen that plants need to grow) that have washed in from the watershed.

Limnologists (scientists who study lakes) have developed a trophic classification system to describe lake productivity:

- **Oligotrophic** lakes are usually younger water bodies and/or have small watersheds and very low nutrient input. They typically have rocky or gravelly bottoms, have clear water due to low levels of algae and suspended sediment, and support relatively low densities of plants and animals. Bottom waters are usually well oxygenated during summer because high water transparency allows photosynthesis to occur and there is less decaying plant material to use up the oxygen.

- **Eutrophic** lakes are older water bodies and/or have large watersheds with high nutrient input. The water is typically turbid from dense algal growth. They usually have dense beds of aquatic plants and high fish densities. Bottom waters are typically low in oxygen, because a greater volume of decaying detritus uses up oxygen while turbidity prevents photosynthesis.

- **Mesotrophic** lakes are those that are somewhere between oligotrophic and eutrophic.

Eutrophication. Lakes naturally progress from oligotrophic to eutrophic as they age. Most of our natural lakes were formed by the scouring action of the glaciers 15,000 years ago. It is the fate of all lakes to slowly fill with sediments from tributary streams and organic matter. Given enough time, every natural lake becomes shallower and more eutrophic, eventually transforming into a marsh or bog. Many lakes in Connecticut are naturally eutrophic. These are older water bodies, usually low in a watershed or with large drainage areas. It is natural for these types of waters to have high densities of algae and rooted aquatic plants.

The process of eutrophication can be greatly accelerated by increased nutrient input resulting from human activity, a process known as "cultural eutrophication." When excessive nutrients are washed into a lake, plant growth will often become excessive in response. Overly dense algae or macrophytes (larger aquatic plants) can reduce oxygen levels in deeper water by preventing light penetration. Decomposition of overabundant plant material also uses up greater amounts of oxygen than is natural, and results in accelerated filling of lake bottoms. Excessive plant growth can also interfere with recreational activity such as swimming and boating. Common sources of excess nutrients are failing septic systems, farm and lawn fertilizers, waterfowl droppings, and organic matter from eroded sediment that results from poorly managed farms, construction sites or timber harvesting.

When excessive nutrients are washed into a lake, plant growth will often become excessive in response.

Lake residents and the general public often seek in-lake methods to control or eliminate excessive "weed" growth, but in doing so they often are only temporarily treating the symptoms, not the cause of the problem. Only through cooperative watershed management can nutrient input from these "nonpoint" sources be permanently controlled. Control measures involve such things as properly maintaining septic systems, preventing soil erosion and direct storm runoff, maintaining plant buffers (riparian zones) around lake shorelines, using safe agricultural and timber-harvesting practices, and reducing lawn-fertilizer use. More details on watershed management can be found in the Department of Environmental Protection publication, "Caring for Our Lakes — Watershed and In-Lake Management for Connecticut Lakes," available from the DEP Bookstore, 79 Elm Street, Hartford, CT 06106-5127; telephone, 860-424-3555.

Food Chains/Webs

The word "ecosystem" refers to all of the plants and animals in that system and all of the internal and external forces that affect their survival. In general, all living things in lake or pond ecosystems are either directly or indirectly dependent on each other. The simplest metaphor for describing these relationships is that of a "food chain."

At the bottom of the food chain are the primary producers (plants) that, through photosynthesis, convert sunlight and nutrients into energy usable by animals. Aquatic plants come in the forms of algae (small to microscopic plants) and macrophytes (larger, multicellular plants). The plants are grazed on by invertebrate animals such as insect larvae, snails and zooplankton (nearly microscopic animals). These small invertebrates are fed on by small fishes that are in turn preyed upon by larger, predatory fishes. Ultimately, all fishes that are not directly preyed on end up as food for scavengers, such as crayfish or turtles, or decomposers such as bacteria and fungi.

Each link in the food chain is also referred to as a trophic level, with prey species (such as shiners and alewives) at lower trophic levels being more numerous than predators (such as bass and pickerel) at the higher levels. Although the concept is simple, the trophic interactions that occur among lake and pond organisms are usually quite complex. For example, there are generally many microhabitats (shallow water, open water, bottom zones, etc.) within individual lakes that are often occupied by different ages and types of plants and animals. The food chain within lake and pond systems is thus more accurately described as a "food web," with each species interacting with an array of other species, but with all ultimately being connected by this web of interdependency.

The Concept of Balance in Lake and Pond Fisheries

Every successful species of plant or animal has evolved strategies to optimize survival. Predatory species such as bass and pickerel have evolved to become efficient predators. They are larger and faster than the species they prey on and have developed unique physical and behavioral characteristics (such as the pickerel's teeth and ambush behavior) that assure they can acquire more energy through the food they capture than they expend to capture it. In response, prey species have evolved structures (such as spines) and behaviors (such as schooling or hiding in heavy cover) to help avoid capture by predators. Any Connecticut fish species, including predators such as bass and pickerel, can fall prey to larger fishes when they are young. For this reason, an almost universal survival technique among fish species is to produce many more young than would be needed to sustain their populations if no predators existed. Thus, a balance has evolved between predators and prey.

A "balanced" fish population has enough small forage fish to sustain good numbers of large predatory gamefish and enough gamefish to prevent small fish from becoming overabundant.

From a fisheries standpoint, a fish community is in a desirable state of balance when there are enough small fish to sustain a fishable population of large gamefish and enough large gamefish to prevent smaller fish from becoming overabundant. Conversely, a fish community that lacks desirable balance (or is imbalanced) has few large predators, high densities of slow-growing, smaller fish and consequently poor fishing.

Density-Dependent Growth and Stockpiling of Fish Populations

Lakes and ponds are inherently unstable environments. Changes in weather and seasons can cause drastic fluctuations in water level, temperature and chemistry. Because of this, such things as fish spawning success can be extremely variable. In response to uncertain external conditions, fish have evolved internal mechanisms to help regulate their populations. One such mechanism is density-dependent growth. When fish densities are low and available food levels high, fish will capitalize by growing very rapidly. When fish (and many other cold-blooded animals) become overabundant or food becomes scarce, they respond by growing more slowly. This circumvents the danger that they could deplete their food supply, which could lead to starvation and possible population collapse. This adaptive strategy ensures that fish populations can survive until either food or predator abundance increases and balance is restored.

When warmwater fisheries become imbalanced, density-dependent growth often aggravates the situation. For example, a decline in numbers of large bass due to harvest by anglers often results in an increase in numbers of forage fish, which include small panfish as well as young bass. High densities of small fish competing for a limited food supply causes their growth rates to decline. It then takes much longer for both the panfish and the bass to achieve sizes that would be of interest to anglers. The end product is a condition called stockpiling — an overabundance of small, slow-growing fish and few large ones. The most extreme situation occurs when overcrowding is so great that fish become stunted. In these cases, fish grow so slowly that they never reach sizes desired by anglers. Stunting is more common in small ponds where fish abundance is very high, but predators and food are limited.

Effects of Balance vs. Imbalance on Lake Ecosystems

Predator densities can have a cascading effect on a lake ecosystem. A fish population that is in a desirable state of balance contains high densities of large predatory gamefish. High predation rates result in lower abundance of small fish, which improves their growth rates. Small fish feed heavily on zooplankton; therefore, zooplankton numbers will be high when the number of small fish is kept low. Zooplankton feed on algae; therefore, abundant zooplankton will lower algal density. Low algal density leads to greater water transparency. Table 1 lists the typical effects of balanced vs. imbalanced fish populations on lakes.

TABLE I
Effects of balanced vs. imbalanced fish populations on lakes.

BALANCED	IMBALANCED
Higher densities of large gamefish	Lower densities of large gamefish
Lower densities of small gamefish and forage fish	Higher densities of small gamefish and forage fish
Faster fish growth rates	Slower fish growth rates
Higher densities of large zooplankton	Lower densities of large zooplankton
Lower densities of algae	Higher densities of algae
Clearer water	More turbid water

Causes of Imbalance in Fish Populations

Many factors may contribute to imbalance in warmwater fish populations. Most, however, fall under one of three major categories: excessive angler harvest, habitat limitations, or undesirable species composition.

Excessive Angler Harvest. This is the major cause of imbalance in most lake and pond fish communities. A comparison of fish populations in Connecticut's public lakes to those in its water supply reservoirs provides an excellent illustration of the effects angling can have on fish-community balance. Most of the state's water supply reservoirs are closed to angling. Barring other factors, their fish populations should, therefore, be in "natural" states of balance. Indeed, most water supply reservoirs sampled during the Statewide Lake and Pond Electrofishing Survey are excellently balanced from the standpoint of angling quality. They contain higher densities of large, fast-growing fish and lower densities of small fish than are typically found in lakes open to fishing. It is likely that the high density of large predatory fish in the unfished reservoirs thins out the smaller fish. Reduced numbers of small fish then results in improved growth rates.

Angling tends to selectively remove larger fish, because very small fish are not normally caught by anglers and, if caught, are seldom kept. Selective removal of larger predatory fish by anglers can cause increases in numbers of small panfish. As previously discussed, greater numbers of small fish competing for a limited food supply can result in reduced growth rates. The heavier the angler harvest rate, the more imbalanced a fishery tends to become. The result of excessive angler harvest is a poor-quality fishery with few large gamefish and often too many small, slow-growing panfish.

Angler harvest affects lake balance through selective removal of larger fish from a population.

Angler harvest can also affect fish populations in a couple of ways on a genetic level. First, angling tends to selectively remove more aggressive and faster-growing fish from a population. This is because aggressive fish are easier to catch and fast-growing fish are the quickest to become large enough to be caught. The slower growing, less aggressive fish that remain are the only ones that can pass on their genes to succeeding generations. These less aggressive, slower-growing gamefish that anglers do not harvest may also be less effective predators and, therefore, less able to control overabundant panfish populations.

Angler harvest also tends to cause fish populations to spawn at a younger age and smaller size. This in itself is not necessarily a problem, except that fish that spawn early don't usually grow as large as fish that wait a year or two to spawn. The reason for this is that fish face a trade-off: They can either invest most of their energy into growth of reproductive organs or into growth of body tissue. This means that fish grow quickly until they are sexually mature, but much more slowly afterward. The strategy of most fishes is to grow quickly to a large size that is safe from most predators. Only after this period of fast growth do they become sexually mature; they can then reproduce for several seasons in relative safety before dying. The problem is that anglers tend to remove these faster-growing fish before they can reproduce. Subsequently, a heavily fished population becomes sustained primarily by those individuals that mature quickly and spawn at a smaller size.

Fish that are removed from a lake by angling can no longer pass their genes on to the next generation. Through the selective pressures described above, angler harvest tends to "breed" fish populations that are slower growing, less aggressive and spawn at a smaller size.

Habitat Limitations. In the absence of human influence, larger lake systems naturally tend toward balance, with large predators being relatively common and fish growth rates optimal. Systems that have marginal habitat (such as very small ponds), are nutrient poor (as are many small streams) or are inherently unstable (e.g., very shallow ponds or lakes with extreme water-level fluctuations) may not be physically able to support many large predators. Desirable balance may thus be unattainable in such systems. Even in some larger lakes and ponds, habitat idiosyncrasies may influence balance in fish communities. Excessive fish recruitment (production of too many young fish) can occur in lakes that have unusually large areas of ideal spawning or nursery habitat. For example, sunfish prefer to spawn on sandy bottoms in shallow water; thus lakes with large, sandy shoal areas may provide so much sunfish spawning habitat that the population easily becomes overabundant. Conversely, spawning success may be limited where spawning habitat is lacking. Beds of aquatic vegetation are good nursery habitat for young fish. Lakes that are completely vegetation-choked, however, provide young fish too much protection from predators. In this situation, predator growth rates suffer because they cannot forage effectively and juvenile fish growth also suffers due to their overabundance.

Undesirable Species Composition. Native fish communities in lakes tend to be naturally balanced because resident species have evolved to coexist over a long period of time. However, most of our dominant lake and pond fish species have been introduced. Thus, fish populations may tend toward imbalance in some lakes because the resident fish species did not evolve together (at least not in that particular combination or environment). Some introduced species, such as largemouth bass and bluegill, have been very beneficial, providing new angling opportunities and adding diversity to Connecticut lake ecosystems. Others, such as landlocked white perch and alewives, have been "too successful" and have often become overabundant due to their prolific reproductive capabilities and the inability of resident predators to control their numbers. The result among landlocked white perch populations is that they often become stunted. Dense alewife populations influence fish-community balance because they severely reduce zooplankton densities that the larvae of most fish species depend on for survival.

Restoring Balance to Fish Populations. In a habitat-limited population, options for enhancement are also limited and often focus on management of the habitat itself. Among fish communities that contain prolific species such as white perch or alewives, often the only practical way to attain desirable balance is to introduce additional predatory fish, such as northern pike or walleye, that are capable of controlling the abundance of these forage fish. More commonly, balance can be achieved by protecting larger resident predatory gamefish, like bass and pickerel, through such angling regulations as slot or minimum length limits. All of these options are described in detail under the section "Lake and Pond Fish Management."

Fish Habitat

Habitat refers to all of the physical and biological things that fish live in or around. It includes the lake bottom, objects or structure where fish feed or hide from predators, and, of course, the lake water itself. Some fish species can thrive in a wide range of habitats, while others are very specific in their needs. Bluegill and pumpkinseed sunfish, for example, will survive in the smallest of murky ponds as well as in large, clear reservoirs. Trout, on the other hand, are much more limited in their habitat choices because they require cold,

Submerged rocks, aquatic vegetation and sticks all provide good fish habitat.

well-oxygenated water to survive. The quality of a fishery is often dependent on the quality of fish habitat.

Lake and pond fish can be placed into one of three rough categories — coldwater fish, coolwater fish and warmwater fish. In general, coldwater fish are those that require colder water and higher dissolved-oxygen levels to survive. Warmwater fish are those that thrive best in warmer water and typically do not require high oxygen levels. Coolwater fish are those that fall somewhere in-between. Table 2 illustrates general habitat requirements for common adult fish species in the three categories. It is important to realize that most fish species use different habitats during different life stages. For example, younger bluegills typically occupy very shallow water, whereas older adults spend much more time in deeper water. Also, many adult fish that spend time inshore during the spring and fall will retreat to cooler, deeper water during summer to avoid high water temperatures.

TABLE 2
General habitat requirements of common Connecticut lake and pond fishes.

Species	Preferred Temperature	Lethal Temperature	Minimum DO* Required	Typical Physical Habitat Preferred
Coldwater Fish				
Brown trout	54-63°	81°	4ppm	Offshore open water
Brook trout	54-63°	79°	4ppm	Near tributary streams
Rainbow trout	54-64°	79°	5ppm	Nearshore open water
Coolwater Fish				
Northern pike	68-75°	86°	2ppm	Inshore near vegetation
Walleye	68-75°	84°	2ppm	Rocky points, outside edges of vegetation
Warmwater Fish				
Largemouth bass	77-86°	97°	2ppm	Inshore near vegetation or structure
Smallmouth bass	68-82°	95°	2ppm	Inshore near rocky structure
Sunfish	68-86°	97°	2ppm	Inshore near vegetation or structure
Chain pickerel	70-86°	98°	2ppm	Inshore near vegetation
Crappie	75-86°	95°	2ppm	Outside edges of vegetation, near dead trees, deeper water in summer
Yellow perch	54-70°	85°	2ppm	Inshore during cool weather, offshore in summer
Bullhead	66-84°	95°	<1ppm	Inshore over muddy bottom
Channel catfish	79-86°	93°	2ppm	Deeper water near structure

* Dissolved oxygen (parts per million). NOTE: Lethal temperatures and oxygen levels are dependent on each other — i.e., fish need more oxygen at higher water temperatures.

Habitat Alteration

Lakefront property owners very often initiate "beautification" efforts along shorelines without an appreciation of how such efforts may adversely affect fish habitat. Unfortunately, an all-too-common activity is the wholesale conversion of diverse natural shoreline habitat into homogenous artificial habitat. Replacing natural terrestrial vegetation (trees, shrubs and ground covers) with manicured lawns is one example. This practice typically results in increased nutrient runoff from the fertilized lawns and the loss of overhanging vegetation, which provides important cover for fish in shallow water. Overhanging branches also provide spawning habitat for some species. In addition, shoreline vegetation is used by a variety of animals (insects, amphibians, birds, etc.) that contribute directly or indirectly to the health of fish populations. Dead trees and other debris that fall into nearshore water provide shelter and feeding stations for young fish and other animals, but much of this natural habitat is unwittingly "cleaned up" by lake residents.

Construction of waterfront retaining walls can also destroy shoreline fish habitat. Retaining walls are commonly built out of concrete, stone with mortared joints, or timber sheet piles. The resulting structures lack the hiding places used by small fish that were originally present among the rocks and shoreline vegetation. In addition, naturally rocky or vegetated shorelines dissipate waves caused by storms or boat traffic. Solid retaining walls simply deflect this wave energy, which churns up the shallow water bottom, obliterating potential hiding places for small fish. Artificial beaches can also adversely affect fish habitat. They destroy the natural lake bottom, reduce local productivity, and contribute to eutrophication through the annual addition of sand, which accelerates the sedimentation of lake bottoms.

Another common practice that can adversely affect habitat is water-level manipulation. Young fish of many species can suffer severe loss of nursery habitat when lakes are drawn down (see discussion under Physical Management Tools). In addition, methods to reduce or eradicate nearshore submerged and emergent vegetation can have similar adverse effects (see discussion under Aquatic Vegetation).

Important Notice: Activities conducted within and adjacent to wetlands and watercourses in Connecticut are regulated by municipal Inland Wetlands and Watercourse commissions in accordance with the Inland Wetlands and Watercourses Act (CGS 22a-36 to 22a-45, inclusive). Contact your town hall for further information.

Aquatic Vegetation

Aquatic plants are critical components to healthy lake ecosystems and fish populations.

Aquatic plants are extremely important to lake ecosystems because they provide the food, shelter and oxygen (a byproduct of photosynthesis) necessary to the survival of fish and other lake animals. Microscopic algae and larger aquatic plants (macrophytes) form the base of the food web in lakes and ponds. Algae provide food for zooplankters, which are themselves eaten by almost all fish species during their larval stages. Many aquatic insects and other invertebrates feed on or lay their eggs and rear larvae on the stems, leaves or roots of aquatic plants. These invertebrates are also food for fishes.

Aquatic plants serve as fish habitat in a number of ways. Fish species such as yellow perch and chain pickerel lay their eggs on nearshore vegetation, while golden shiners broadcast their eggs over deeper submerged beds of vegetation. Small fish use aquatic plant beds as nursery areas where they feed on invertebrates and find cover from predators. Predatory fish, like bass and pickerel, wait in ambush in or cruise the edges of weedbeds in search of small fish, frogs and other prey.

Turtles, snakes and frogs feed and find cover in aquatic plant beds. Waterfowl, wading birds and shorebirds eat aquatic plants and/or the animals that congregate among them. Emergent plants provide camouflage and protection for birds. Aquatic plants rooted in shallow water and along the pond margin provide protection from shoreline erosion. Aquatic plants can also enhance water quality, because they remove excess nutrients and impurities from the water.

Major Groups of Aquatic Plants

The three major categories of aquatic macrophytes that grow in Connecticut lakes are floating plants, submerged plants and emergent plants. Plants in each of the three categories are described below. See Appendix 4 for a complete list of important Connecticut aquatic plants.

Floating plants have leaves that float on the surface of the water. Many also have leaf stalks (or petioles) that are in the water column and underground stems (or rhizomes) and roots that are in the bottom substrate.

White water-lily, top. Yellow pond-lily, bottom.

- **White water-lily** has large leaves (4 to 12 inches) that resemble a pie with one piece missing. The distinctive flowers have numerous white petals.

- **Yellow pond lily** has leaves 4 to 10 inches long that are nearly heart-shaped and flowers that are small and yellow. The stems grow from thick underwater rhizomes that are anchored in the mud in shallow water.

- **Watershield** has elliptical leaves with a stem attached to the center of the leaf. The underwater stems are covered with a clear, thick, slippery coating.

- **Floating heart** has heart-shaped leaves that are 1 to 3 inches long and attached to long, thin stems. Small white flowers appear in July through September.

- **Duckweed** is a tiny (generally less than 0.25 inch in diameter), spherical, free-floating plant that is usually found in large numbers. There are several types of duckweed, which are very difficult to distinguish from each other. A similar plant, **watermeal**, often co-occurs with duckweed, but the leaves are oval and much smaller.

- **Water shamrock** is a fern with floating leaves that are 1.5 to 2 inches wide and look like four-leaf clovers or shamrocks.

- **Water chestnut** is a rooted, annual aquatic plant with triangular floating and feather-like submerged leaves (0.75 to 5 inches wide). Its black, spiny fruits wash ashore and can inflict a painful wound if stepped on. It forms dense floating beds that can make boating, swimming and other recreational activities nearly impossible. This aggressively invasive species was recently discovered in several coves of the Connecticut River.

- **Floating-leaved pondweed** (*Potamogeton natans*) and **spotted-stem pondweed** (*Potamogeton pulcher*) have floating leaves and are worthy of note in this category. Several other pondweeds also have floating, but smaller leaves.

Submerged Plants grow mostly underwater, though some may have floating leaves or flowering/fruiting structures that emerge slightly above the surface.

- **Pondweeds** are a large and diverse group of alternate-leaved plants, of which 28 species have been reported in Connecticut. Seven pondweed species are on the State Endangered Species List and one is a non-native invasive species. The pondweeds can be split into several subgroups: those with floating leaves and narrow underwater leaves, those with floating leaves and wide underwater leaves, those without floating leaves and having narrow underwater leaves, and those without floating leaves and having wide underwater leaves.

- **Mud plantain** has a pale yellow-green color and is frequently mistaken for a pondweed. It can be distinguished from the pondweeds by its strap-like leaves, which do not have a midrib (major central vein).

- **Water nymph (*Naiad*)** has small, narrow, linear leaves that are opposite or appear almost whorled. Flowers and fruits are found in leaf axils and are very small.

- **Water milfoil** has leaves that are highly dissected, meaning that the leaf segments are less than 0.04 inch wide. The flower and fruits of all but one species are found on terminal spikes that emerge above the water. Eight species are reported in Connecticut; three are on the State Endangered Species List and two are non-native invasive species.

Almost everyone in New England has heard of Eurasian water milfoil. Many lake associations have initiated management activities to control this species, which can form thick beds from the lake bottom to the surface. Variable-leaved water milfoil is another very aggressive non-native invasive species.

• **Tapegrass** gets its name from its strap-like leaves, which look like tape and are up to 6 feet long and 0.25 to 0.5 inches wide. The female plant sends up a long, often spiraled stem that supports the tubular flower and fruit. This plant is typically found in large beds that spread by underground stems.

• **Coontail** has highly branched, narrow leaf segments packed tight around the stem, creating, with a little imagination, the look of a raccoon's ringed tail, thus its common name.

• **Fanwort** has submerged, dissected leaves with leaf segments that are wider than those of water-milfoil and which also have a petiole. These leaves spread out and take the shape of a fan. Floating leaves that look like a diminutive watershield can be found on some plants. In late summer and early autumn, small white flowers can be found in abundance floating on the surface of the water. This plant is a very aggressive non-native invasive species.

Fanwort.

• **Waterweed** has small, sessile, deep green leaves that appear more rounded than those of water nymph.

• **Bladderwort** has very dissected leaves that have bladders. This very distinctive morphological feature of the group is used to capture tiny aquatic invertebrates. Some species have yellow bi-labiate (two-lipped) flowers while others have purple bi-labiate flowers. The flowers appear on "stems" that emerge above the surface of the water.

• **Submerged burreed** resembles tapegrass, with long strap-like leaves, but can be distinguished from tapegrass by its thickened midrib, which runs the length of the leaf.

• **Filamentous Algae.** Some algae are large enough to form dense beds on the bottoms of lakes. The beds often rise to the surface, where they form slimy, bubbly, floating rafts or mats. **Stonewort** (*Nitella*) and **musk grass** (*Chara*) are commonly encountered forms of filamentous algae with thread-like whorled leaves that resemble vascular plants. They appear almost translucent, with a pale green color. *Chara* can be distinguished by having ribbing or raised lines on its stem, whereas *Nitella* is smooth.

Emergent Plants grow in shallow water along the shoreline or other shoal areas. Some emergent species, like sedges and spikerush, may also be found submersed.

• **Pickerelweed** has elongated, upright, heart-shaped leaves and a spike of purple flowers.

• **Arrowleaf** has emergent leaves that are sharply pointed, resembling the head of an arrow. Delicate three-petaled, white flowers appear in late summer.

• **Burreed** has spherical fruits with many points protruding from them, giving the appearance of a small sea urchin. It has long, narrow, upright leaves when it is emergent. When burreed is submergent, its leaves are flaccid and frequently mistaken for tapegrass.

• **Pipewort** is a small (1 to 10 inches tall) plant of sandy shorelines. It has a rosette of pointed leaves that grows

Pickerelweed.

underwater and a long straight stalk with a button-shaped knob at the end. This button is actually the flower and fruit of the plant.

- **Purple loosestrife** is a non-native invasive plant that grows in all types of wetlands, including the shores of lakes, ponds and rivers. It is a tall plant with many large spikes of attractive purple flowers.

- **Smartweed** has spikes, or racemes, with numerous small flowers that grow in the leaf axils or at the ends of the stems. There are many different species, with flowers that can be pink, white or pale green. The leaves range from long and narrow to broad. The stems appear to have swollen "joints" where the leaves branch off from the stem.

Endangered Animals and Plants

Primarily due to human influence over the past 300 years, some native plants and animals have become extinct. Specific causes for extinction include habitat destruction or modification, replacement by exotic invasive species, exploitation, disease, and predation. In 1989, Connecticut enacted the State Endangered Species Act. The goal of the act is to ensure that human activities allow for the conservation, protection, restoration and enhancement of rare plant and animal species. At the time of writing, the State Endangered Species List contained 12 mammal species, 54 birds, 11 reptiles, 6 amphibians, 143 invertebrates (insects, mollusks etc.) and 352 plant species. Native plants and animals on the list are categorized as either: a) Endangered — in danger of extirpation from the state, with no more than five occurrences statewide; b) Threatened — likely to become endangered and having no more than nine occurrences statewide; or c) Species of Special Concern — having a restricted range or habitat in the state, having a low population level, or being in such high demand that unregulated taking could cause the population to become threatened or endangered.

At time of publication, only six fish species were on the State Endangered Species List:

- Endangered: Shortnose sturgeon (also on the Federal Endangered Species List), American brook lamprey and burbot.
- Threatened: Atlantic sturgeon and banded sunfish.
- Special Concern: Longnose sucker.

For more information concerning State Endangered Species, refer to the DEP website (http://dep.state.ct.us).

Introduced Animals and Plants

The plant and animal assemblages of Connecticut lakes and ponds have been strongly influenced by more than a century of intentional and accidental introductions of non-native species. As recently as 15,000 years ago, Connecticut was completely covered by glacial ice. This may be one of the reasons that the state has relatively few native freshwater animal species. Low species diversity may also be an important reason why many introductions have been so successful.

In most of our lakes, the entire food web is now dominated by non-native species. Many aquatic plants, all of our crayfish and many of our snail species are non-native. More than half of the fish species in Connecticut lakes today are non-native (see Appendix 3 for a list of Connecticut lake and pond fish species). Populations of many non-native species became established throughout the state over one hundred years ago, and it is now more appropriate to consider these fishes naturalized and resident as opposed to "exotic." Moreover, the physi-

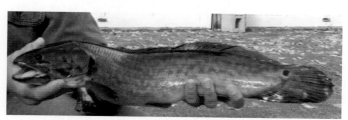

It is unclear when or how bowfin were introduced into Connecticut waters. Populations exist in the Connecticut River and in Scoville Reservoir, Wolcott.

cal/chemical characteristics of our lakes have been greatly altered with changes in land use by humans. This makes it impractical, and in most cases impossible, to restore native ecosystems in Connecticut lakes and ponds.

Introduced Fish Species. Before introductions by humans, the communities of native gamefish and panfish species in Connecticut lakes were limited to chain pickerel, yellow perch, pumpkinseed sunfish, redbreast sunfish, brown bullhead and, in some lakes, brook trout. Native rough fish and forage fish species included golden shiner, white sucker, creek chubsucker, banded killifish, redfin pickerel, and American eel.

Since the mid-1800s, numerous non-native species have been introduced with the intention of creating new recreational fisheries. Many of the coldwater species were not able to establish reproducing, self-sustaining populations in Connecticut due to habitat restrictions. Unsuccessful attempts at introduction included species such as lake trout, cutthroat trout, chinook and coho salmon, landlocked Atlantic salmon and round whitefish. Many warmwater species became well established, however. The most successful introductions were those of largemouth bass, smallmouth bass, black crappie, rock bass, bluegill sunfish, white perch, white catfish, common carp, and landlocked alewives. Other warmwater species have also become established, but were probably introduced accidentally along with other stocked fish or released from bait buckets. These include bowfin, green sunfish, yellow bullhead and goldfish.

Benefits of Planned vs. Dangers of Unplanned Introductions. Despite the fact that Connecticut lakes are now dominated by non-native plants and animals, introductions of new species are still capable of upsetting the balance of aquatic ecosystems. When introductions are carefully planned and consideration is given to all of the likely impacts, changes can be beneficial. Conversely, poorly planned or inadvertent introductions can be disastrous. Some of the most beneficial and successful fisheries management actions have involved stocking non-native predators such as bass and trout. In many waters, stocking these top-level predators has generated extremely popular fisheries by increasing the conversion of small forage fish into desirable sport and food fish, while producing additional benefits such as controlling over-abundant forage species and improving panfish growth rates.

Other planned and unplanned introductions have had mixed or negative results. Exotic plants and animals can be extremely prolific when transplanted to a new environment that does not contain the predators, diseases or competitors that would normally keep their numbers in check. Some invasive species, such as Eurasian water milfoil, variable leaf milfoil and fanwort, are capable of out-competing and eventually eliminating many native species. Noteworthy "newcomers" that have become recently established in Connecticut lakes and may prove troublesome include zebra mussels (*Dreissena polymorpha*), apple snails (*Cipangopaludina chinensis*), water chestnut (*Trapa natans*), eutrophic water-nymph (*Najas minor*), Hydrilla (*Hydrilla verticillata*) and Brazilian waterweed (*Egeria densa*). The following case histories provide two examples of the potential dangers of introducing exotic species into the aquatic environment.

The walleye is a highly beneficial introduced species. It provides exciting fishing opportunities while exerting predatory control on overabundant panfish populations.

- **Landlocked Alewives** were stocked into many Connecticut lakes during the 1960s and 1970s. This prolific herring species was introduced to strengthen the food chain by providing a link between microscopic zooplankton, on which alewives feed, and open-water predatory gamefish that thrive on a diet of alewives. This strategy proved very successful in producing large trout and salmon fisheries throughout North America and holdover brown trout fisheries in a few Connecticut lakes. There is a downside to introducing alewives, however. In many lakes, they become so abundant that they alter the structure of the plankton community, because they feed only on larger zooplankters. Reduction of large zooplankton affects other fish species that rely heavily on zooplankton during their first year of life. Because zooplankters feed on algae, reducing zooplankton numbers also may result in increased algal abundance, thus reducing water clarity. Reduced water clarity, aside from being less aesthetically pleasing, can also cause oxygen levels to decline in deeper water, thereby reducing trout habitat. Reduced water clarity can also cause changes in the distribution of rooted vegetation and associated animal communities. Alewives consume fish larvae and the zooplankton that these larvae need to survive. As a result, abundant alewife populations can reduce and, in some cases, completely eliminate natural reproduction of other fish species (for example, walleye in some other states). On top of all this, alewives tend to be an unstable forage base because they are prone to dramatic winter die-offs, which result in erratic population fluctuations.

Alewives can outcompete and eliminate other planktivorous fish species from a lake. In the early 1990s, alewives were illegally introduced into East Twin and Wononscopomuc Lakes. These deep, cold lakes were managed for kokanee salmon and supported unique and thriving fisheries for this species. Kokanee have similar feeding habits to alewives and rely almost exclusively on large zooplankton. Kokanee completely disappeared from both lakes within a few years of alewife introduction. Connecticut's last remaining kokanee fishery is in West Hill Pond. This fishery would disappear as well if alewives were introduced. There is no practical method to eliminate alewives once they are established in a large water body. Recognizing their negative impacts, the DEP discontinued alewife stocking in the 1970s. To further prevent the spread of this species, it is now illegal to use alewives for bait in many waters, particularly in lakes managed for other planktivores like kokanee and smelt.

• **Zebra Mussels** are native to Europe and first appeared in the United States in the Great Lakes, probably having been accidentally introduced via the ballast water of

Zebra mussels encrusting a rock from East Twin Lake, Salisbury.

ships. Since the initial introduction, this opportunistic, invasive species has spread to many new locations, mostly through unintentional transfer on boats and trailers and by way of interconnected waterways. Zebra mussels are extremely prolific, forming dense carpets of shells that often cover every inch of available hard substrate. They have caused a variety of problems, ranging from clogging water-intake pipes and fouling boat hulls and motors, to causing major ecological shifts in aquatic ecosystems. They can have direct and indirect effects on a wide range of plant and animal species. When abundant, filter-feeding zebra mussels remove a great deal of the plankton from the water column. This redirects the flow of nutrients and energy away from fish and other animals that use the water column and increases the energy flow to the benthic community (organisms living on the lake bottom). In addition, zebra mussels may hamper and possibly eliminate other mollusks by attaching to their shells and interfering with locomotion, respiration and feeding. Also, the nature and suitability of the lake bottom for various organisms change as live zebra mussels and dead shells accumulate.

Zebra mussels were first reported in Connecticut during the fall of 1998 in East Twin Lake. The ultimate effect on the lake's fish community is difficult to predict; however, a decrease in sport-fishing quality for at least some species is likely. As of this writing, zebra mussels have not been identified in any other Connecticut waters. Fortunately, the water chemistry in most Connecticut lakes is unsuitable for zebra mussels. Nonetheless, efforts are under way to prevent the spread of zebra mussels by educating boaters and anglers about the negative impacts of this species and precautions that can be taken to avoid spreading them (see below). There is no known method to control or eliminate zebra mussels once they are established in a lake.

Preventing the Spread of Invasive Plants and Animals. Prevention is the key to keeping invasive species from getting established in new locations. No one should introduce aquatic plants or animals into any water body without authorization from the Connecticut DEP. It is extremely important that well-meaning anglers not transplant fish or plants from one lake to another. This could result in damage to the fisheries, ecosystem balance and/or genetic integrity of resident fish populations. A permit is needed to legally import or stock fish into Connecticut waters (contact DEP's Fisheries Division for details).

The following simple suggestions can help to prevent the spread of harmful invasive species:

Before leaving a boat launch:

1. Completely drain all water from the boat, including bilge water, live wells and engine cooling systems.
2. Inspect your boat, trailer and equipment. Remove and discard all aquatic plants and animals.
3. Rinse boat, trailer and equipment with tap water.
4. Leave live bait behind! Give it to someone fishing the same water body or dispose of it in a suitable container.

Fish Parasites

A parasite is an organism that lives on or in another organism. Parasites live at the expense of their hosts and generally cause at least some minimal degree of harm to them. Hosts typically provide parasites with food and security, and more often than not, parasites act as petty thieves whose insults are not life-threatening. Although it may surprise some, the presence of a mix of parasites is generally an indication of a healthy environment. Parasites play an important role in maintaining healthy ecosystems by removing weak hosts from populations. This can help keep fish and other organisms from becoming overabundant and it can also help to ensure that only strong individuals will pass on their genes to succeeding generations.

Parasitism is such a successful lifestyle that there are far more species of parasites on Earth than there are non-parasites. Almost any organism may serve as a host for parasites, and even parasites can have parasites! Freshwater fishes make great hosts for parasites, and most fish are probably infected by one or more of these freeloaders. Although widespread as a group, individual parasite species tend to be picky regarding the hosts they infect and the places on or in the host's body that they inhabit.

Most parasites are too small or too few in number to be easily seen by anglers. However, anglers may sometimes notice worms inside their catch, or tiny parasites skittering across the body of their fish or dangling nastily from the fish's mouth or eyes. Hence, anglers often ask, "Can I eat the fish?" The simple answer is, "Yes, if you thoroughly cook the fish before eating it." In fact, most parasites that infect freshwater fishes pose no threat to humans even if consumed alive. However, there are a handful of fish parasites that can survive inside humans, and a few of these are considered health hazards under unusual circumstances. Therefore it is not recommended to eat freshwater fish raw. Thoroughly cooking fish kills all parasites. For aesthetic reasons, people typically choose to cut obvious worms or cysts out of fish or discard infected sections before cooking.

Common Parasites of Connecticut Freshwater Fishes

Protozoans. Except for bacteria and viruses, protozoans are usually the most common parasites found on freshwater fishes. Protozoans are single-celled organisms, and certainly not all are parasites. Those that can infect fishes are often found externally on the skin or gills. However, some protozoans are able to invade the gut and other internal organs of fishes. They are usually too small to see with the naked eye, but some (such as members of the genus *Heteropolaria*) live in large colonies that look like tufts of cotton. Under normal circumstances, protozoans do not cause significant damage to fish populations. Common types of protozoan parasites that infect freshwater fishes in Connecticut are *Ichthyobodo*, *Ichthyophthirius*, *Trichodina*, *Chilodonella*, *Capriniana*, and *Heteropolaria*.

Monogenetic Flukes (flatworms). These small, flat parasitic worms often infect the skin, fins, or gills of freshwater fishes. However, a few species routinely inhabit the insides of fishes — in the urinary bladder, for example. These worms typically cause little damage to their hosts when infections are light. They attach to the host by using a posterior sucker equipped with powerful hooks or clamps. Most of these worms are too small to be easily seen unaided, and so usually go undetected by anglers. Each worm contains both male and female reproductive organs, and they reproduce sexually, either producing live young or eggs. The juveniles develop directly into adults without the need for an intermediate host. Many species of these flatworms infect freshwater fishes in Connecticut. *Gyrodactylus*, *Ligictaluridus*, and *Octomacrum* are types that can commonly be found on various lake and pond fishes.

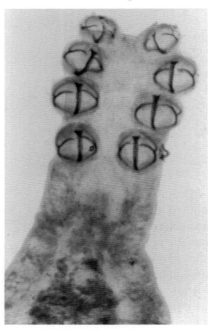

Close-up of the clamp-like attachment structures of Octomacrum *sp., a gill-dwelling flatworm.*

Digenetic Flukes (flatworms). Unlike monogenetic flukes, these flatworms typically live inside their hosts — the gut, eyes, body cavity, musculature, brain, heart and blood vessels, and gonads are just a few common spots. In addition, digenetic flukes typically exhibit complex life cycles that require one or more intermediate hosts before the final host is infected. Although digenetic flukes display remarkable variations in life cycles, virtually all species pass through mollusks (such as snails or mussels) at some point early in their lives. Fish become infected with these worms when they eat infected mollusks, when they are penetrated by parasites that have left mollusks, or when they eat another prey item, like a crayfish or small minnow, that is infected with the parasites. Some species of these parasites are found only as larvae in fishes, while others are found only as adults. Examples of digenetic flukes that live as adults in lake and pond fishes in Connecticut are *Crepidostomum*, *Bunodera*, *Azygia*, *Alloglossidium*, and *Macroderoides*.

Digenetic flukes that are found only as larvae in their fish hosts often mature into adults in fish-eating birds or mammals. The larvae of this type of fluke usually encyst in the tissues of a fish and remain relatively dormant until a bird or mammal eats the fish. The color or type of these obvious cysts yields the common names of these infestations, examples of which are: white grub (*Posthodiplostomulum*), eye grub (*Diplostomulum*), black spot (*Neascus*) and yellow grub (*Clinostomum*). Digenetic flukes that use fish as an intermediate host and require that the fish be eaten by a predator to complete their life cycle usually have a greater effect on their hosts than do other flukes. In fact, they can sometimes affect the behavior of a fish so that it is more likely to be captured by a predator (a good strategy for parasites with this type of life history). For example, fish that are heavily infected with yellow grub swim more slowly than uninfected fish, and fish infected with eye grubs may become blind. Either handicap makes them easier for predators, such as fish-eating birds, to capture.

Tapeworms. Tapeworms are common parasites of freshwater fishes. Adult tapeworms are long, ribbon-like and usually quite visible to the naked eye. Viewed up close, they are composed of a head region followed by many repeating reproductive segments. Species that infect freshwater fishes typically attach with some type of head sucker to the inside of a fish's gut. Tapeworms have no digestive tract; they directly absorb nutrients from their hosts like a sponge. Generally, each segment of a tapeworm contains both male and female reproductive organs, making long tapeworms veritable egg factories. Tapeworms can occur as larvae or adults in fishes, and they have complex life cycles. Fishes become infected with tapeworms when they eat other organisms (for example, small crustaceans or fishes) that are infected with tapeworm larvae. Likewise, some birds and mammals become infected with tapeworms by eating fishes that contain tapeworm larvae.

Head region of a tapeworm, Bothriocephalus *sp., from the intestine of a fish.*

Ligula intestinalis and *Proteocephalus ambloplitis* are tapeworms that are commonly found in Connecticut lakes. *Ligula* can be found as a long, robust larva in several fish species. This parasite matures in a fish-eating bird, with copepods (tiny crustaceans) and fish serving as intermediate hosts. It can become so large that it virtually fills the body cavity to the point where small or heavily infected fish appear to have a potbelly. These worm-filled fishes are probably easier for fish-eating birds to see and capture. *Proteocephalus ambloplitis*, the bass tapeworm, is known to sometimes cause problems for smallmouth and largemouth bass populations. This tapeworm lives as an adult in the intestine of a bass, which acquire the parasite by eating forage fish infected with tapeworm larvae. Forage fish get the tapeworm larvae by eating copepods that have fed on tapeworm eggs that were passed in bass feces. Most tapeworm infections do not cause substantial harm to fish. However, heavy infections can rob hosts of significant amounts of valuable nutrients when the worms out-compete the fish for food in its gut. This can lead to health problems such as emaciation, anemia and, occasionally, reproductive failure.

Roundworms and Thorny-Headed Worms. Roundworms and thorny-headed worms are both common parasites of Connecticut's freshwater fishes. The two groups look superficially alike to the naked eye — relatively long, unsegmented and cylindrical — but are quite dissimilar when viewed under a microscope. One difference is that roundworms have guts, while thorny-headed worms lack a digestive tract. Also, thorny-headed worms have a "thorny head," while roundworms are described as having "lips." Roundworms can live as both larvae and adults in a variety of locations in fishes, while thorny-headed worms are most commonly found as adults in the digestive tracts of their fish hosts.

Both groups have separate sexes and complex life cycles. Fishes become infected with these parasites when they eat other animals (for example, small crustaceans) that are infected with parasite larvae. Eggs of adult roundworms that reside in a fish's gut are passed through the feces. Roundworms that live in the flesh of fish often lay their eggs through small holes that they bore through the fish's skin. Fish typically become infected when they eat invertebrates that have eaten the parasite's eggs. Some roundworms use fish as a second intermediate host, developing into a larval stage in the fish. If the correct fish, bird or mammal eats the infected fish, the larva will develop into an adult to complete the life cycle. Sometimes fish can seem virtually riddled with these parasites; however, infections are usually light and inconsequential. Roundworms such as *Capillaria catenata* and *Camallanus oxycephalus*, and thorny-headed worms such as *Pomphorhynchus bulbocolli* and *Octospinifer macilentus* are commonly found in Connecticut lake and pond fishes.

Leeches. Leeches are well-known and common external parasites that typically feed on blood. They are segmented worms, related to earthworms, that are easily seen as adults on the skin, fins, gills, and in the mouths of freshwater fishes. They attach to their hosts primarily by using a powerful posterior sucker. However, they can move about efficiently in an inchworm-like fashion by alternately using their posterior and oral suckers. Leeches contain both male and female reproductive organs and reproduce sexually. Some leeches that infect fishes brood their eggs in cocoons that are attached to the leech's body while they are still on the fish, while others leave the fish to deposit a cocoon elsewhere. Like most other parasites, leeches do not cause significant health problems for fish unless they are found in great numbers or unless they attach to very small fish. Besides the obvious ill effects caused by blood feeding, leeches can transmit disease-causing viruses, bacteria and protozoans. *Myzobdella* and *Piscicola* are two common groups of leeches that can be found on freshwater fish in Connecticut.

Parasitic Crustaceans (copepods and branchiurans). Several types of copepods, including species of *Lernaea*, *Ergasilus*, *Salmincola*, and *Achtheres*, can infect freshwater fish in Connecticut. These copepods are highly variable in shape, with members of *Lernaea* appearing more like worms than crustaceans to the naked eye. Parasitic copepods attach to the outside of fish, with some species deeply embedding their bodies into one spot on their hosts for the duration of their adult lives. While on the host, they can feed on a variety of materials, including blood, skin cells, and mucus; however, they seldom cause significant health problems. Like all crustaceans, parasitic copepods must pass through a series of life stages before they reach adulthood. Typically, the adult female produces eggs that hatch into free-swimming larvae. The larvae pass through a series of developmental stages before they can attach to a fish and mature into an adult. The sexes are separate and reproduction is sexual. Like other parasites, parasitic copepods are usually picky regarding what fishes they will infect and where on the host they will reside. Representatives of *Ergasilus* are often found on the fins and the gills; members of *Salmincola* and *Achtheres* can be found in the mouth or on the gills; and members of *Lernaea* are typically embedded in the musculature of fish, with the posterior portion of their bodies protruding like half-driven nails.

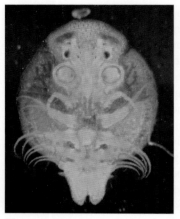

The parasitic crustacean Argulus *sp. feeds on the skin and mucus of fish.*

Branchiurans, sometimes referred to as freshwater fish lice, look superficially similar to some parasitic copepods. They are flat and possess compound eyes. They have four pairs of efficient swimming legs and one pair of legs that serve as powerful suckers to help them attach to their fish hosts. To facilitate feeding, they use a stinger to repeatedly inject the fish with compounds that externally begin the digestion process. Fish lice are excellent swimmers and can detach from one fish and reattach to another. They move about the surface of their hosts feeding on skin and mucus, but unless their numbers are great, they do little significant damage. Like parasitic copepods, branchiurans reproduce sexually. Unlike parasitic copepods, however, female fish lice leave the host to lay their eggs on submerged plants or rocks. After hatching, the larvae pass through several stages before becoming adults. All fish lice in Connecticut belong to the genus *Argulus*.

Fish Kills

Fish kills are common in Connecticut lakes and ponds. The vast majority of kills result from natural causes and usually occur at times of high environmental stress (for example, during spawning or at times of high water temperature or low oxygen). These types of fish kills are, for the most part, unpreventable and are a natural mechanism whereby weaker individuals are "weeded out" of a population. However, some fish kills are caused by environmental degradation resulting from human influence. If you suspect that a kill may be due to unnatural causes, please report it to the DEP Fisheries Division (860-424-3474).

Be aware that a fish kill is not generally of great concern unless it involves large numbers of fish. This is because fish populations in Connecticut lakes typically number in the tens of thousands, so even several hundred dead fish would not be enough to significantly impact a fishery.

Unless a kill is severe, cleanup or removal of dead fish is also not an important issue. The dead fish will be consumed by wildlife or decompose on the lake bottom, and will not harm the lake.

Common Causes of Natural Fish Kills

Summer Kills. Summer kills are usually caused by a combination of low dissolved oxygen and very warm water temperatures. Summer kills often take place in shallow, vegetation-choked and nutrient-enriched lakes just before sunrise, when dissolved oxygen levels are at their lowest. Oxygen depletion occurs when more oxygen is being consumed by animals and decomposition than is being produced by aeration and photosynthesis. There are several common summer-kill scenarios. Most common is the development of an algal bloom that prevents sunlight from reaching deeper portions of a lake, thereby inhibiting photosynthesis. When this occurs, oxygen is consumed but not produced, resulting in oxygen deficiency. In addition, a sudden die-off of either abundant macrophytes or algae can result in decreased dissolved-oxygen levels because of bacterial decay of the dead plant material.

Winter Kills. Winter kills occur under the cover of ice, and are usually not discovered until the ice melts. Winter kills occur most frequently in very shallow, nutrient-enriched lakes that are subject to abundant growth of aquatic vegetation or algae. Conditions conducive to a winter kill arise when heavy snow cover on the ice inhibits sunlight penetration and plant photosynthesis. This, coupled with decay of dead vegetation, causes dissolved oxygen to drop below levels necessary for survival of fish and other aquatic organisms. The largest and oldest fish are usually the first to succumb to low oxygen conditions. As a result, ponds that experience frequent winter kills are typically dominated by small fish.

Natural fish kills are common and occur at times of high environmental stress.

Toxic Algae Blooms. Although a rare occurrence, some species of algae (typically blue-green algae, dinoflagellates and haptophytes), at times of very high abundance, can cause fish kills through the release of toxic substances. Toxic algae blooms usually occur in the summer or fall. Blue-green algal blooms can be a concern because drinking water that contains toxins can cause illness or sometimes death to pets, waterfowl and other animals, including humans. A blue-green algae bloom often looks like green paint floating on the water. If you notice a bloom, avoid prolonged contact with the water (such as swimming), and keep pets and live-stock away from the water.

Fish Diseases. Fish are most susceptible to disease-related mortality in the late spring when water temperatures rise, the fish are spawning and environmental conditions favor the production of disease organisms. These stresses can combine to weaken the immune system of fish and predispose them to diseases, particularly bacterial infections. Common fish kills due to bacterial infections involve bass and sunfish after spawning (typically June). This type of fish kill occurs gradually over two to four weeks. As with other animal populations, outbreaks of disease occasionally occur in fish populations to the extent that they will cause a noticeable kill. These are unfortunate but natural occurrences from which fish populations typically rebound quickly. In general, fish kills resulting from disease will affect only a few species, whereas those due to other causes, such as pollution, usually kill a greater variety of species.

Contaminants in Fish

Fish from Connecticut's lakes and ponds are generally a healthy, low-cost, good-tasting source of protein. Unfortunately, Connecticut freshwater fish occasionally contain chemical contaminants, such as mercury or polychlorinated biphenyls (PCBs), which in high concentrations are potentially hazardous to human health. These chemicals enter the water from industrial spills and air pollution. Some chemicals, such as mercury, travel long distances in the air before being deposited on the landscape and being washed into lakes and streams. Much of the mercury found in our waters comes from pollution sources far outside Connecticut. Because it is airborne, low concentrations of mercury can be found in any Connecticut lake or pond.

Contaminants such as PCBs are passed up the food chain and tend to build up in fish to levels many times higher than in the surrounding environment. This process, called bioaccumulation, happens because the chemicals cannot be digested, so they build up in the tissue of fish and other animals. Invertebrates such as aquatic insects pick up minute levels of chemicals from the small plants and animals they eat. Each time a small fish eats one of these invertebrates, its contaminant level rises. In this manner, small fish accumulate higher levels of contaminants than are present in any of their individual prey. Contaminant levels become higher still in larger fish as they accumulate chemicals from the small fish they eat. This is why the largest and oldest fish tend to have the highest levels of contaminants.

The Connecticut DEP and Department of Public Health collaborate to ensure that appropriate fish-consumption guidelines are provided to anglers. The DEP routinely collects fish from lakes, ponds, rivers and streams throughout the state. Fish tissues are tested for a variety of possible contaminants, including mercury, PCBs, heavy metals and pesticides. The Department of Public Health then issues fish-consumption advice based on nationally accepted risk-assessment guidelines.

The fish-consumption advisory is updated annually and is included in the Connecticut Anglers' Guide. However, the most up-to-date information is available in a pamphlet titled "If I Catch It, Can I Eat It," published each spring by the Department of Public Health. The advisory lets you know how often you can safely eat fish from Connecticut waters. It includes a general advisory that applies to most freshwater fish in the state and specific advice for waters with higher contaminant levels. Separate advice is given for people in "High Risk" and "Low Risk" groups. The High Risk Group includes pregnant women, women planning to become pregnant within a year, and children under age 6. All others are considered to be in the Low Risk Group. Anglers are encouraged to read the updated fish-consumption advisory each year and to adhere to the guidelines.

Some contaminants, such as PCBs, are concentrated in the fatty portions of the fish. Exposure to these contaminants can be greatly reduced by removing the skin and other fatty parts and by cooking the fish in a manner (such as on a rack) that the fat can drip away. Unfortunately, mercury is found in the muscle tissue (the edible portion) of fish and levels cannot be lowered by cooking or cleaning methods. It is useful to remember that large fish tend to have the highest levels of contaminants, including mercury and PCBs; therefore, exposure can be lessened by eating smaller fish of any given species.

Recently stocked trout are safe to eat, but large, holdover trout may have some level of accumulated contaminants in their bodies.

LAKE AND POND FISHERIES MANAGEMENT

History of Fisheries Management in Connecticut

During the first half of the 20th century, most fisheries-management efforts in Connecticut centered around the stocking and introduction of non-native fish species. The State Board of Fisheries and Game attempted to introduce almost every fish species conceivable, into every lake or pond possible, in an effort to see "what would take." Most of these introductions were apparently done with little consideration for their potential impact on lake ecosystems, including the native fish species. Some introductions, like that of largemouth bass, were very successful and beneficial. Others, in hindsight, were doomed to failure by habitat limitations (for example, landlocked salmon). Some, such as white perch and carp, are thought to have negatively affected other fish populations.

The earliest management regulations — primarily minimum length limits, creel limits and closed spawning seasons — were imposed to protect newly introduced fish. The philosophies behind these were to prevent overharvest (creel limits), to protect fish during spawning (closed seasons) and to allow fish to grow large enough to spawn at least once (minimum length limits). Later (from the 1960s to the early '80s), minimum length limits were tailored to maximize the weight of fish harvested by anglers. During the same period, however, many anglers were becoming more interested in the quality of sport fishing (average size and numbers of larger fish caught) than with harvest. New management strategies were required to address this need.

Despite advances in fisheries management, biologists were discovering that similar management strategies did not necessarily have the same effect in every lake. For example, changes in length limit regulations usually resulted in improved bass fishing. In other lakes, however, the same measures caused bass growth rates, and subsequently the quality of fishing, to decline. It became apparent that different inherent characteristics of lakes, such as lake productivity or fish-species composition, were affecting the outcome of attempts to improve

fishing. It was also apparent that optimum angling quality could be best addressed on a lake-by-lake basis. Moreover, the single-species approach to management was too simplistic because of the complex interactions that exist among resident fish species. Successful management could be achieved only through an understanding of these interactions in the context of lake and pond ecosystems. Taking all of these factors under consideration, Connecticut now manages lakes and ponds to 1) maximize fishing quality, 2) create a diversity of angling opportunities and 3) achieve desirable balance in fish populations.

Early management in Connecticut centered on introductions of non-native fish species. Some, like the largemouth bass, were highly successful and beneficial. Others were either doomed to failure due to habitat restrictions or did harm to existing fish populations.

Coldwater Fisheries Management

Coldwater fishes are those that require cool water temperatures and high oxygen levels to grow and survive (see Table 2). The only true coldwater fishes in Connecticut lakes and ponds are the trout (brook, brown and rainbow), smelt and the kokanee salmon. Unfortunately, most of the state's lakes and ponds lack suitable spawning habitat for these species, and few have temperature and dissolved-oxygen levels suitable for trout survival through the summer months. Due to these habitat limitations, stocking is necessary to support coldwater fisheries in Connecticut lakes and ponds.

Trout Management

Trout Stocking. The DEP stocks approximately 300,000 catchable-size (9- to 12-inch) trout into 80 to 90 lakes and ponds each year. Most of these lakes are managed as "put-and-take" fisheries, where adult trout are stocked for immediate taking by anglers. Fishing pressure is generally high in these lakes, and anglers harvest a large percentage of the trout soon after they are stocked. The number of trout stocked in any given water depends on several factors. First and foremost, a lake must have public access to justify stocking by the state. In addition, the type of boat launch (trailer ramp vs. car-top), parking capacity, amount of shore access, proximity to population centers, boating restrictions, fishing pressure, facilities (picnic areas, campgrounds), lake size, and habitat quality all contribute in determining the numbers of trout to be stocked.

All lakes and ponds are stocked before Opening Day (the third Saturday in April) to provide trout for the spring fishery. The more popular lakes are also stocked one or more times after Opening Day to maintain good fishing quality throughout the spring. A number of lakes are stocked in October to support fall and winter trout fisheries. Connecticut's put-and-take trout fisheries are managed with statewide regulations that include a five-fish daily creel limit and no minimum length limit. The open season typically runs from Opening Day through the last day of February in the following year (see Connecticut Anglers' Guide for exceptions).

Approximately 300,000 catchable-size trout are stocked annually into Connecticut lakes and ponds.

Lakes and ponds are stocked primarily with brown and rainbow trout. Brook trout are stocked in some smaller ponds and lakes with low pH levels, where they survive better than other species. The ratio of brown to rainbow trout that are stocked often depends on the amount of available shore access. Rainbow trout are easier for shore anglers to catch because they spend more time in shallow water than do either brooks or browns, whereas boat anglers readily catch both rainbow and brown trout.

Holdover Trout. Connecticut has about 20 lakes with sufficient water quality or thermal refuges (near springs and/or tributary streams) for brown trout to survive through the summer. For the most part, neither brook trout nor rainbows will hold over well in Connecticut lakes.

Several lakes with good year-round trout habitat are managed as holdover brown trout fisheries. Some of the best holdover waters in Connecticut are Beach Pond, Crystal Lake in Ellington, Candlewood Lake, East Twin Lake, Highland Lake, West Branch (Hogsback) Reservoir, Saugatuck Reservoir, and Wononscopomuc Lake. Beyond water quality adequate for trout survival, these lakes support abundant populations of open-water forage fish — either landlocked alewives or smelt. These lakes are designated as Trophy Trout Lakes and are managed with conservative length and creel limits to allow brown trout to reach larger, more desirable sizes before they can be harvested (see Connecticut Anglers' Guide for details).

Harvest restrictions are necessary in managing trophy-trout fisheries because newly stocked trout are highly vulnerable to angling. Connecticut angler survey data indicate that more than 60 percent of stocked trout are typically removed from lakes within a few months after stocking. High minimum length limits, slot length limits and closed seasons have all been successfully used to increase the abundance of holdover trout in Connecticut lakes. In general, the more restrictive the harvest regulations (for example, a 14- to 24-inch slot length limit with a short open season), the more holdover trout survive and are caught by anglers.

Trout Strain Evaluation. The DEP Fisheries Division is attempting to enhance coldwater fishing by selectively stocking and evaluating different strains of brown trout. Strains are genetically distinct groups of plants or animals within the same species that exhibit different traits. Many wild and hatchery strains of brown trout are available that differ in growth rate, longevity, vulnerability to angling and/or habitat requirements. The Seeforellen strain, originating from Germany, has exciting possibilities. Seeforellens grow faster and live longer than other available strains and can reach weights of 20 pounds or more. Seeforellen brown trout were first stocked during the 1990s in several Connecticut lakes, including Crystal Lake, East Twin Lake, Highland Lake, Quonnipaug Lake and Saugatuck Reservoir, and results have been encouraging.

Other Coldwater Species

Smelt are important forage for brown trout and a popular sport fish in a few Connecticut lakes. Smelt were stocked into many lakes in the early to mid-1900s, with populations becoming established at Crystal Lake, Shenipsit Lake, West Hill Pond, Colebrook Reservoir and West Branch Reservoir. The ice fishery at Crystal Lake was quite popular in the 1950s, with smelt being the most commonly caught species. However, this fishery disappeared in the 1960s, several years after alewives became established. West Hill Pond supported a smelt fishery into the 1970s and early '80s, but the smelt have since been largely displaced by kokanee salmon (both feed on zooplankton). Although not as good forage for brown trout as alewives, smelt are not known to affect water clarity and they provide interesting sport for ice anglers. At time of publication, West Branch Reservoir supported the most significant ice fishery for smelt. Smelt are regulated in Connecticut with a 50-fish possession limit.

Seeforellen strain brown trout grow faster and live longer than many other types and can reach weights of 20 pounds or more.

Kokanee are a landlocked form of the anadromous Pacific sockeye salmon. The first introduction of kokanee in Connecticut was into East Twin Lake in the mid-1930s. The source of this introduction is unclear. For a time, East Twin supported a very popular kokanee fishery. However, natural reproduction was limited and angler harvest heavy, causing the fishery to collapse by the late 1940s. Kokanee were reintroduced to East Twin Lake in the late 1950s, but special management was required to assure that the population would continue to support a fishery. Eggs were taken from broodstock collected in the fall and were incubated at the Burlington Fish

Close-up displaying the hooked jaw or "kype" of a spawning male kokanee salmon.

Hatchery. The kokanee were then stocked as 1-inch fry the following spring. After three summers in the lake, the fish reached maturity and full size (generally 12 to 16 inches). Because this management was so successful, kokanee were introduced into a number of other Connecticut lakes in the 1960s. Several lakes supported good kokanee fishing through the late 1980s, but West Hill Pond is now the only significant fishery in the state. Competition for zooplankton with landlocked alewives led to the demise of kokanee in the other lakes. Regulations on kokanee include an eight-fish possession limit, no length limit and a closed season from March 1 until the third Saturday in April.

Lake Trout were stocked in many Connecticut lakes beginning in the early 1900s. Only Lake Wononscopomuc supported a significant population, but this fishery succumbed to declines in water quality during the 1960s. Today, none of our public lakes contain the very cold, well-oxygenated water that lake trout need to survive. The only remaining potential for lake trout management in Connecticut is in a few large water supply reservoirs that are closed to public fishing.

Warmwater Fisheries Management

All of the more than 180 Connecticut lakes and ponds with public access contain warmwater fisheries. Warmwater fishes are those that can thrive at higher water temperature and lower dissolved-oxygen levels than coldwater species (see Table 2). Most fish species in Connecticut fall under this category. Two gamefish species, northern pike and walleye, are sometimes referred to as "coolwater" species because their temperature/oxygen requirements are somewhere in between.

The biggest difference between management of Connecticut's coldwater and warmwater fisheries is that most warmwater fish are capable of sustaining naturally reproducing populations, even under moderate to heavy fishing pressure. For this reason, management of warmwater fish typically does not revolve around stocking. The key to improving angling quality in warmwater fish populations is to employ management tools that will achieve desirable fish community balance and are cost-effective on a statewide scale (see discussion under The Concept of Balance in Lake and Pond Fisheries).

Some Important Findings of the Statewide Lake and Pond Electrofishing Survey:

The Statewide Lake and Pond Electrofishing Survey (1988-95) revealed that many of the state's lakes and ponds are in a healthy state of balance. Other lakes were identified where angling quality was not optimal and might be improved through alternative management. Four problems/conditions were discovered to exist in many Connecticut lakes and ponds:

> **1) High Bass Mortality.** Among Connecticut lakes and ponds, annual bass mortality rates were found to be high (greater than 50 percent) in 27 percent of largemouth bass populations and 74 percent of smallmouth populations. Most of this mortality is from angler harvest because, in typical populations, only 15 to 20 percent of adult bass die of natural causes each year. Excessive harvest results in low densities of larger bass, adversely affecting angling quality. Under these conditions, the statewide 12-inch minimum length limit does not provide enough protection to maintain angling quality.

> **2) Bass Stockpiling.** Angling quality suffers in many (39 percent of) Connecticut lakes and ponds due to an overabundance of either largemouth or smallmouth bass smaller than the 12-inch minimum length limit. Stockpiling occurs when bass recruitment (the number of young fish that are spawned and survive) greatly exceeds predation (the number eaten by predators). A high density of small bass causes increased competition for limited food supplies and, subsequently, growth rates decline. Under these circumstances, bass do not grow fast enough to replenish the legal-size fish (12 inches or greater) that are harvested by anglers. This results in poor angling quality because the fishery is dominated by 8-to-12-inch fish with few larger ones present. Angling quality could be improved in stockpiled populations by employing management practices, such as slot length limits, that increase the mortality of smaller fish while protecting the larger ones.

> **3) Panfish Stockpiling.** Fifty-three percent of Connecticut lakes exhibit moderate to severe stockpiling of panfish below catchable size, with slow panfish growth rates.

This causes angling quality for these species to suffer. Panfish become stockpiled for the same reasons as bass (excessive numbers of young fish produced in conjunction with inadequate predation). In some severe cases, panfish become so overabundant that stunting occurs, meaning that the fish die of old age before becoming large enough to interest anglers. Management practices that protect resident predators and/or introduce new ones can result in improved panfish populations because increased predation thins out the small panfish, leading to improved panfish growth rates.

4) Surplus Forage. Many lakes and ponds (59 percent) contain surplus forage fish populations (alewives, shiners, killifish, etc.). This is not a problem in itself, but indicates an opportunity for fishery enhancement because these lakes have the capacity to support more predatory gamefish.

Removal of too many large bass results in poor fishing quality and can have indirect, negative effects on panfish populations.

Lake-Specific Management. One of the most important conclusions of the electrofishing survey was that statewide regulations do not provide adequate protection to afford quality angling in all instances. Conditions among the state's freshwater fisheries vary widely, and, in many cases, optimal angling quality can be accomplished only through lake-specific management strategies.

Potential Management Tools for Warmwater Fisheries

Numerous techniques and strategies have been attempted nationwide in efforts to protect warmwater-fish stocks and/or improve angling quality. Management strategies generally fall into two categories: 1) physical, or intensive, management and 2) management through fishing regulations. Physical management involves direct physical, chemical or biological manipulation of fish or fish habitat. Management by regulation typically involves protecting fish or certain size classes of fish from harvest. Regulations may be lake-specific or more general (as in statewide regulations). Typically, physical management techniques have less statewide application because of the expense and manpower involved.

Physical Management Tools

Maintenance Stocking of Resident Warmwater Fish

Stocking warmwater fish species that are already present in a lake and are capable of reproducing on their own (such as largemouth bass or chain pickerel) is generally an ineffective management technique. A "more is better" philosophy frequently backfires because growth rates decline as densities of young fish increase. In the Southern and Western United States, stocking of fingerling bass has been successfully employed in some large reservoirs where the spawning success and survival of young fish is extremely limited by lack of spawning and nursery habitat. Connecticut survey data indicate that there generally are plenty of young warmwater fish in our lakes and ponds. In fact, excessive numbers of young fish and subsequent stockpiling of small bass and panfish is a common problem among our warmwater fisheries. In these cases, stocking more fish would only make the situation worse.

Stocking warmwater fish of catchable size temporarily improves fishing in direct proportion to the numbers stocked. Unlike trout, however, warmwater fish are extremely expensive to raise to adult size in hatcheries. They do not tolerate crowding, generally have slower and more variable growth rates than domestic hatchery trout, are cannibalistic and usually require live food (for example, shiners). Moreover, there is always a danger of altering the genetics and, therefore, reducing the survival rates of resident fish populations when hatchery fish are introduced. For these reasons, it is wisest to stock warmwater fish only to re-establish populations in waters where they have been extirpated.

Introduction of New Predators

Introductions of large predatory gamefish can create exciting new fisheries and increase the diversity of fishing opportunities. Two such species, the walleye and northern pike, have the best potential for management in Connecticut lakes. Although neither species is native to Connecticut, their natural distributions extend into neighboring parts of the Northeast, and healthy populations of both species have existed in the Connecticut River for more than 100 years. They have only recently been introduced into Connecticut lakes.

Introduction of walleye and pike into suitable Connecticut lakes provides two very important benefits. First, both species are highly prized gamefish. Walleye often grow to 8 pounds or larger and are reputed to be one of the best tasting of all fish. Pike also are good table fare and grow even larger than walleye, with some individuals reaching 20 pounds or more. The second benefit of introducing walleye and pike is their predatory control of overabundant forage fish and panfish, which results in improved growth rates and average sizes of those species.

Partly because of its recent glaciation, Connecticut has relatively few native fish species. In fact, the only large predator native to our lakes is the chain pickerel. Pickerel and the two introduced bass species (largemouth and smallmouth) are primarily inshore predators, and therefore are not efficient at feeding on open-water prey, such as the non-native alewife and white perch. Alewives and white perch often become overabundant because they lack natural predators. Walleye and northern pike are capable of exploiting prey species such as these that other gamefish cannot.

The first experimental stocking of northern pike in a Connecticut lake took place at Bantam Lake in 1971. Before pike introduction, Bantam Lake had a serious overabundance of stunted yellow and white perch. Over time, a healthy pike population was established that successfully reduced perch numbers and created a very popular recreational fishery. After this success, pike stocking was initiated in Mansfield Hollow Reservoir in 1992. The population expanded rapidly, and a popular fishery was established by the late 1990s. Two more introductions were made in 1999 in Pachaug Pond and Quaddick Reservoir, and both show signs of success.

Walleye were first introduced in Connecticut to Candlewood Lake in 1931. Stocking continued in this and several other lakes during the 1930s. Although fishable populations were established in a few lakes, the program was discontinued due to lack of natural reproduction.

Introduced predators like the walleye are capable of exploiting prey species that other gamefish cannot.

Since then, establishing walleye fisheries through annual stocking of fingerlings has become more cost-effective because of advances in culture techniques. In 1993, annual stocking of 5-inch walleye fingerlings began in several Connecticut lakes. Within a few years, successful fisheries were developed at Gardner Lake, Squantz Pond and Lake Saltonstall. Based on these successful fisheries, another walleye stocking program was initiated at Saugatuck Reservoir in 1998.

One of the drawbacks to walleye and pike management is that, due to very specific spawning requirements, they typically will not reproduce in most Connecticut lakes. For this reason, annual stocking of fingerlings is necessary to maintain fishable populations. Pike fingerlings are produced at specially managed spawning marshes at Bantam Lake, Mansfield Hollow Reservoir and at Haddam Meadows State Park along the Connecticut River. Walleye fingerlings are purchased from commercial suppliers in the Midwest. The Statewide Lake and Pond Electrofishing Survey has identified additional waters that hold promise for pike or walleye management.

Introductions of Forage Fish

Although forage-fish introductions have occasionally produced desirable results with salmon and trout fisheries (for example, alewives supporting salmon in the Great Lakes), they are generally ineffective management tools for warmwater fisheries. New forage fish usually have difficulty surviving in environments where every ecological niche is already filled. Also, if new forage fish become established, the effects on warmwater fish populations are often difficult to predict. For example, bass spawning success typically decreases when planktivores such as alewives or threadfin shad are introduced into lakes because these fish compete with young bass for food. In addition, many popular forage fish species are pelagic (living in open waters away from shore) and are thus underused by warmwater predators that tend to stay in shallow water close to shore.

Northern pike can reach weights in excess of 20 pounds.

The amount of available forage in a warmwater lake or pond is generally governed by the lake's fertility. Most Connecticut lakes and ponds are classified as eutrophic or meso-eutrophic, meaning they are highly fertile. Thus, quantity of forage is typically not a problem among the state's water bodies. Forage fish introductions in Connecticut would probably be ineffective in improving warmwater fisheries and should only be used to restore extirpated populations.

Removal of Overabundant Fish

Physical removal of rough fish (e.g., suckers and carp) or small panfish can help to improve the quality of bass angling in small ponds. Dense panfish populations compete for food with young gamefish such as bass and can inhibit their reproduction. In larger lakes, however, it would be highly impractical to remove the numbers of fish necessary to make an impact on angling quality. Research has indicated that 40 to 50 percent of undesirable fish may have to be removed from a lake to noticeably improve gamefish growth rates or densities. To capture this many fish using traditional gear such as electrofishing or nets would require tremendous manpower. Anglers could help by harvesting small panfish and (where legal) small bass, but most of the target fish are too small to be caught by angling.

Habitat Management

Artificial Structure can be created by submerging a variety of natural or man-made objects. Such structures provide attachment points for many aquatic organisms, as well as cover for game and forage fish. Artificial structure serves to concentrate gamefish, and angler catches can be improved. Natural materials such as brush piles and trees have been found to be more effective than man-made items (tires, for example). In a small pond devoid of cover, it may be possible to alter the habitat enough to increase the number of gamefish. However, there is no evidence that artificial structure can increase fish productivity in larger lakes and ponds. Rather, artificial structure serves only to make it easier for anglers to catch fish by concentrating them in known areas.

Water Level Manipulation can be an effective warmwater management tool where feasible. The flooding of terrestrial vegetation in spring and early summer can result in greater survival of young bass because it provides them with additional food and cover. Also, late summer water drawdowns may result in improved bass growth rates because they concentrate predators and forage fish into a smaller area. Controlled early spring flooding has been used at Mansfield Hollow Reservoir to create optimal spawning conditions for northern pike.

It is possible to manipulate water levels in many Connecticut lakes with control valves in dams. There are potential pitfalls that would preclude drawdown management in most public lakes, however. Most important, lakeshore property owners probably would not want their land flooded in the spring and/or their docks and boat launches to be high and dry in late summer. Also, it may be impossible to draw down many lakes enough to have noticeable effects on the fish populations. Moreover, drawdowns do not always result in the desired effects on fish populations.

The timing of drawdowns is critical to prevent harm to fish populations and to aquatic ecosystems in general. For example, a substantial drawdown during May or June, when most warmwater fish spawn, can destroy fish nests and/or nursery habitat and result in spawning failure. Winter drawdowns are commonly requested by lakeshore residents to prevent ice damage to shorelines and structures, and to facilitate dock and shoreline maintenance. Although they can be an effective method of controlling some types of aquatic vegetation, winter drawdowns can also harm a lake ecosystem in several ways. In very shallow lakes, winter drawdowns expose fish to a possible winter kill caused by the supercooling of bottom waters and/or oxygen depletion. Lakefront property owners often request winter drawdowns to eliminate nearshore vegetation. This vegetation, however, is critical spawning and nursery habitat for many fish species. Species such as yellow perch and chain pickerel that spawn in the early spring on shallow-water vegetation can experience spawning failure in the wake of a winter drawdown. Winter drawdowns may result in substantial mortality of juvenile fish that need nearshore vegetation to feed in and hide from predators. Also, exposed lake-bottom sediment may flush deeper into the lake and create water quality problems such as low dissolved oxygen and reduced clarity. For these reasons, winter drawdowns should generally be avoided. If determined to be absolutely necessary, winter drawdowns should be conducted on a biennial or, preferably, less frequent basis.

Control of Aquatic Vegetation. Aquatic vegetation can have both positive and negative effects on warmwater fisheries. Excessive plant growth can become a "nutrient sink" in lakes and ponds. Energy that might otherwise ascend the food chain (and be used by fish and other animals) is monopolized by the overabundant plants. At high densities, aquatic plants also reduce the ability of fish predators to find and capture forage species. This often results in overcrowding and stunting of panfish species as well as reduced growth rates of predatory gamefish.

On the positive side, aquatic plants provide habitat and food for invertebrates, which are eaten by fish. In addition, vegetation provides escape cover for the young of most warmwater fish species and spawning habitat for many, including pickerel, yellow perch and golden shiners.

Lake drawdown can be an effective fish management tool, but usually does more harm than good due to indiscriminate destruction of nearshore vegetation.

Research indicates that up to a certain point, there is a positive relationship between plant abundance and warmwater fish production. For example, according to published reports, the best largemouth bass production occurs when 20 to 36 percent of a lake bottom is vegetated. (Smallmouths, however, prefer lakes with lower plant densities.) Based on this, it is recommended that the abundance of aquatic plants be limited to moderate levels (20 to 40 percent of a lake's surface area) when feasible. This will serve to maximize both production and catchability of sportfish. Eradicating submerged vegetation to below 20 percent should be discouraged due to possible harm to fish production.

Potential methods of controlling overabundant aquatic vegetation include:

• **Drawdowns.** As previously discussed (see Water Level Manipulation), drawdowns can be effective in controlling some types of overabundant aquatic plants. Other plant species, however, typically are unaffected or may actually increase in abundance. Drawdowns can have serious drawbacks and consequently have limited value as a fish management tool in Connecticut. When a winter drawdown is considered for vegetation control, the DEP recommends that supporting information be collected to document the need, possible negative impacts and expected level of vegetation control. The potential negative effects underscore the need for thorough investigation before choosing this method.

• **Aquatic Herbicides.** Application of chemical herbicides can be a very efficient method of eliminating or reducing aquatic plants. However, most "whole-lake" chemical treatments should be avoided for a number of reasons. First, whole-lake treatments typically reduce vegetation to below the recommended 20 to 40 percent coverage. In addition, many aquatic herbicides are indiscriminate, destroying valuable native plants along with exotic nuisance species. Destroying large areas of aquatic vegetation can cause a rapid release of nutrients into the water, which can lead to undesirable algal blooms. Some herbicides can adversely impact lake and pond food chains, and improper dosages can kill fish (for example, zooplankton and trout are especially sensitive to copper sulfate, a common algicide). Also, using herbicides for long-term vegetation control typically requires frequent retreatment and can therefore be prohibitively expensive. In light of the many drawbacks, the use of aquatic herbicides and algicides is most practical for small private ponds with severe vegetative growth. In larger lakes, use of chemicals should be limited to those with a documented ability to either "spot treat" selected areas or to selectively kill invasive exotic species.

Excessive aquatic vegetation can reduce the ability of fish predators to find and capture forage species.

Important Notice: The use of aquatic herbicides and algicides is restricted in Connecticut. Anyone considering the use of aquatic herbicides and algicides in any waters, private or public, must first obtain a permit from the Pesticide Management Unit of the DEP Bureau of Waste Management (call 860-424-3369 for information).

• **Mechanical Harvesting.** Mechanical harvesting is a generally effective and environmentally benign method of reducing areas of dense aquatic vegetation. Physical removal of plant material avoids the quick release of nutrients caused by decaying plants, which can trigger algal blooms. Perhaps the greatest advantage of mechanical harvesting is that it controls where and when plants are removed from a lake. For example, selective plant removal can increase the amount of weedbed edge, thereby optimizing fish habitat. A drawback to this method is the possible inadvertent transfer of invasive plants or animals (for example, zebra mussels) from lake to lake on the harvesting equipment. This concern can be minimized by carefully observing the precautions listed earlier to prevent spreading invasive species (see conclusion of Introduced Animals and Plants section). Unfortunately, mechanical harvesting can be both expensive and labor-intensive, thereby limiting its utility for fisheries management.

• **Grass Carp.** The grass carp is an exotic fish species native to Asia. It is a relative of the common carp, but is atypical because it feeds entirely on vegetation. Grass carp are fast-growing and reach weights in excess of 40 pounds. Various states have experimented

Mechanical harvesting is an environmentally benign method of local vegetation control, but is expensive and labor-intensive.

with introducing triploid (sterile) grass carp into lakes to control nuisance aquatic plants. In many instances, these fish have been extremely effective in reducing plant abundance. One advantage to grass carp is that they are a "natural," or biological, control as opposed to measures such as chemical treatment. Another advantage is that waters need not be treated annually because one stocking can remain effective for as long as the carp survive. Also, because these fish cannot reproduce, grass carp introductions are reversible.

Although grass carp are a promising method of controlling aquatic plants, there are several concerns about the introduction of this species. Among them are: 1) The magnitude of plant control can be difficult to predict. Stocking small numbers of carp has resulted in little impact on plants, whereas higher stocking levels have completely denuded some lakes. 2) Grass carp prefer some plant species to others, and thus may eliminate desirable native plants instead of unwanted nuisance species. 3) Removal of too many macrophytic plants can result in undesirable algal blooms. 4) Grass carp could escape to other waters, where they could produce undesirable effects. 5) Either the grass carp themselves, the removal of too many aquatic plants, or the removal of the wrong species of aquatic plants may have negative effects on other fish species and/or lake ecosystems in general.

The use of triploid grass carp has been legal in Connecticut, on a restricted basis, since 1988. Most stockings have been in small, privately owned ponds. The effects of these introductions have not been completely assessed. Because of the expense (10- to 12-inch fish can cost more than $10 each), grass carp will probably never be a widespread method of controlling aquatic vegetation. The first experimental stocking of sterile grass carp into a large, public pond in Connecticut (Ball Pond, 82 acres) occurred in the fall of 1997. The effects of this introduction on water quality, aquatic vegetation and resident fish populations had not been assessed by the time of publication. The use of triploid grass carp in other public lakes will be reviewed case by case after the conclusion of the Ball Pond experiment. It is expected that introducing grass carp will be deemed inappropriate for many lakes due to; 1) inability to prevent offsite emigration, 2) opposition by lakefront property owners to the introduction of an exotic species, 3) incompatibility with habitat-management objectives, and 4) potential negative effects on endangered or threatened species.

Grass carp are a promising method of vegetation control, but also have their drawbacks.

Fishing Regulations

Closed Seasons

It is a popular belief among many anglers that fish such as bass should be protected during the nesting season in order to ensure spawning success. Very few states, however, have closed seasons for bass or other warmwater fish species. Removing the male bass from a nest usually does result in mortality of the eggs or fry. However, the number of young produced annually in a lake appears to be more affected by abiotic conditions, such as water-level fluctuations and temperature changes at the time of spawning, than by the number of successful nests. Apparently, survival of young warmwater fish is highly compensatory, meaning that a higher percentage survive whenever fewer are produced. No relationship has been established between the number of spawning bass and subsequent number of young produced. In addition, studies have indicated that no more young are produced as a result of closed seasons than during more liberalized seasons. Closed seasons around spawning time may be justified in certain geographic areas where some species have limited spawning success (such as smallmouth bass in northern Canadian lakes). In Connecticut lakes and ponds, however, spawning success of warmwater fish species (including smallmouth bass) is more often excessive than inadequate. Thus, a closed season to protect spawning fish does not appear necessary.

Creel Limits

It is generally accepted that creel limits have little effect on harvest rates of most warmwater fish species. This is primarily because a very small percentage of anglers catch their limits. For example, angler survey data from a number of Connecticut lakes reveal that more than 80 percent of the bass harvested were taken one or two at a time and that fewer than 1 percent of anglers who kept bass took their legal limit of six fish. Furthermore, the most highly skilled anglers in Connecticut (such as bass tournament anglers) release most or all of the fish they catch.

In 2001, Connecticut had 6-fish limits on bass and pickerel and no creel limit on panfish in lakes and ponds. In other states, panfish creel limits as low as 10 to 15 fish have had no effect on reducing harvest. Limits of one or two fish are typically necessary to significantly reduce harvest of most gamefish species. Restrictive creel limits may be warranted in selected lakes that are being managed for trophy fisheries or that contain highly vulnerable fish populations, such as newly opened reservoirs. Although Connecticut's statewide creel limits may not directly reduce harvest of gamefish, they do serve to reinforce a conservation ethic and should be retained for that purpose.

Length Limits

Manipulation of fish population structure through lake-specific length limit regulations has proved the most cost-effective method of managing warmwater gamefish nationwide. The earliest length limits in Connecticut (early 1900s) were implemented to protect newly introduced bass and allow them to spawn at least once before they could be harvested. Most length limit experiments during the 1970s were designed to maximize the weight of fish harvested by anglers. Results from these experiments were quite variable, however. While some researchers claimed that length limits improved yields of both gamefish and panfish, others reported increases in gamefish abundance below legal size (stockpiling) that resulted in reduced growth rates due to increased competition for forage. It became apparent that the optimal length limit strategy was lake-specific, because fish population growth and possibly natural mortality are density-dependent and individual lakes vary in their capacities to produce prey and predator biomass.

More recent length limit applications have acknowledged the importance of angling quality (i.e. improved catch rates of larger fish and average size of catch) and panfish population control

Conservative length limit regulations can result in impressive increases in numbers of large bass.

rather than attaining maximum yield of harvested fish. This new approach was adopted because increasing numbers of anglers said they thought it more important to be able to hook and fight a "quality-size" fish than to catch their creel limit. Moreover, preventing overharvest of larger predators can result in increased predation on panfish, leading to improved panfish growth rates and a more balanced fishery. This new approach to length limit management involves protecting the larger, quality-size fish through either higher minimum length limits or slot length limits.

Minimum Length Limits protect smaller fish until they reach a desirable size, and are typically used when spawning success is low to moderate. Statewide minimum length limits are liberal regulations that serve their original purpose of protecting fish until they can spawn at least once and of providing optimal catch and harvest in the majority of waters.

When harvest rates are high, more conservative lake-specific length limits can result in improved fishing quality. Minimum length limits of 15 inches or more have been successful in many lakes nationwide in improving bass population structure and angler catch rates of large bass. In Connecticut, increasing the minimum length limit from 12 to 15 inches in Moodus Reservoir resulted in a 74 percent increase in population densities and a 61 percent increase in angler catch rates of larger bass. In other states, lake-specific minimum length limits have also successfully been used to improve fishing for various panfish species, such as black crappie.

Slot length limits are usually applied when small gamefish, most notably bass, are overabundant (due to high spawning success), resulting in slow growth rates. Slot limits protect fish in a discrete size range to provide quality catch-and-release angling as well as increased predation on panfish. In the case of a 12-to-16-inch slot limit, smaller (less than 12 inches) as well as larger (greater than 16 inches) fish may be harvested. Thinning out overabundant small fish can improve growth rates and prevent stockpiling of fish below quality size. Slot length limits have an added appeal in that they can please anglers who wish to take fish to eat as well as those who are more concerned with fighting and releasing quality-size fish.

Slot length limits have been widely used on bass throughout the country and have resulted in dramatic improvements in population structure and sometimes growth rates. Slot length limits of 12 to 15 inches and 12 to 16 inches resulted in 60 to 100 percent increases in the densities of bass 12 inches or larger in three Connecticut lakes (Chamberlain, Maltby and Pickerel).

It is important to realize that a slot limit is not necessarily a failure when anglers do not harvest enough small fish to positively affect growth rates. A slot limit provides anglers the opportunity to harvest fish of sizes that are in surplus (the smaller fish), yet protects the larger ones. Harvesting smaller in preference to larger fish is also referred to as "selective harvest." Another advantage to slot limits is that they actually increase the opportunity for anglers to take fish home to eat because small fish are both more abundant and easier to catch than larger fish. An angler has a greater chance of harvesting a legal limit of bass under a 12-to-16-inch slot limit than under a 12-inch minimum length limit.

Slot length limits allow anglers to harvest surplus small fish while protecting larger ones.

LIFE HISTORIES OF COMMON LAKE AND POND FISHES

Gamefish

The term gamefish refers to fishes that typically reach a large size and fight hard when caught on rod and reel. They are aggressive fish with strong swimming abilities. For these reasons, they are usually the fish most sought after by anglers. For the same reasons, gamefish are the apex predators in Connecticut lakes and ponds. Apex predators are those that prey on smaller animals and have few natural enemies because of their large size; thus they are at the top of the food web. Apex predators serve an important role in aquatic ecosystems by controlling the populations of smaller fish species. Thus, in most natural systems, a balance is achieved between predators and prey species such that neither becomes so abundant that they overrun their food supply.

Largemouth and Smallmouth Bass

The two "black bass" species are collectively the most sought-after gamefish in most Connecticut lakes and ponds. Angler surveys conducted on three Connecticut lakes that were not stocked with trout found that 45 to 60 percent of the anglers were fishing for bass. Many bass anglers practice catch-and-release, with more than half releasing all of the legal size (12 inches or greater) fish caught. Competitive catch-and-release bass tournaments have also become very popular in Connecticut, with the number of registered events increasing from 124 in 1986 to nearly 700 in 2001.

Statewide regulations on bass in lakes and ponds are a 12-inch minimum length limit and a 6-fish (both bass species in aggregate) creel limit. A number of lakes have been designated as "Bass Management Lakes" and have special length and creel limits. Additional Bass Management Lakes are scheduled for 2002 (see current Connecticut Anglers' Guide).

© Joseph Tomelleri

Largemouth bass

Largemouth bass (*Micropterus salmoides*) are the largest members of the sunfish family (Centrarchidae). Although not native to the state, the largemouth is our most widely distributed fish species and can be found in almost all Connecticut lakes and ponds. It is also the dominant predator in most of our warmwater fish populations. It can thrive in a wide range of habitats, but prefers lakes that have at least a moderate amount of submerged vegetation. Largemouth

Smallmouth bass put up a tremendous fight on rod and reel.

bass eat a variety of food items, including fish, crayfish and insects. Bass are generalists in their feeding strategies, sometimes lying near cover and using ambush tactics and sometimes actively foraging for prey. They spawn between mid-May and June in Connecticut. The males build saucer-shaped nests in shallow water (2 to 8 feet) then guard the eggs and later the fry for several weeks after spawning. In Connecticut, it takes largemouth bass 3.6 years on average to reach 12 inches; they can live for 15 years or more. Largemouths commonly grow to 4 or 5 pounds and 18 to 20 inches in length (state record: 12 pounds, 15 ounces).

Largemouth bass are usually dark olive-green on their backs fading to a brassy green on their sides. A dark horizontal band extends from the gill cover to the base of the tail. As the name implies, they have exceptionally large mouths, with the end of the jaw extending to or beyond the back of the eye.

Smallmouth bass (*Micropterus dolomieu*), also an introduced member of the sunfish (Centrarchidae) family, are more habitat-limited than largemouths, preferring clearer, deeper lakes with rocky shoal areas and less vegetative cover. Because of this, smallmouths occur in only half of Connecticut's lakes. They also are less tolerant of high water temperatures than are largemouths (see Table 2) and are most often found in the deeper, cooler waters when temperatures rise in summer. Smallmouth bass feed on a similar variety of food items as largemouths; however, they are more likely to forage out in the open and are rarely associated with dense vegetative cover. Smallmouth spawning habits are similar to those of largemouths. The male builds a nest in shallow water during late spring (mid-May to June) and guards it for several weeks after the eggs hatch. Smallmouth bass are slower-growing than largemouths, averaging 4.4 years to reach 12 inches (state record: 7 pounds, 12 ounces).

Smallmouths are brownish, usually with dark splotches that may form vertical bands on their sides. The jaw extends only to the middle of the eye.

© Joseph Tomelleri

Smallmouth bass

Walleye

The **walleye** (*Stizostedion vitreum*) is a very popular gamefish species throughout much of North America. Although called "pike-perch" and "walleyed-pike" in some parts of the country, they are not related to northern pike but are the largest North American member of the perch family (Percidae). Although not native to Connecticut, a self-sustaining population exists in the Connecticut River, with spawning areas located in Massachusetts. Walleye populations have been successfully established through annual fingerling stocking in four Connecticut lakes: Gardner Lake, Lake Saltonstall, Squantz Pond and Saugatuck Reservoir. The addition of walleye has doubled the number of large gamefish available to anglers in these lakes.

Walleye

Walleyes are a coolwater fish and prefer lakes with low to moderate amounts of submerged vegetation. They can exist in shallow, turbid lakes, but in clear lakes require deep-water sanctuary because of their large, extremely light-sensitive eyes. Adult walleyes will eat almost any species of fish, as well as some invertebrates. Their ability to see in low light conditions make them very effective night predators, but they are most active just after dusk and just before dawn. The walleye is both a pelagic and shallow-water predator and fills a unique predatory niche, one that is particularly valuable in lakes with limited trout habitat. Most walleyes migrate up sizable river tributaries in the early spring to spawn. Some populations are also capable of spawning in lakes on clean, wave-washed gravel. Because neither of these habitats is common among Connecticut lakes, supplemental fingerling stocking is required to sustain walleye populations in most of the state's waters. Walleye grow quickly in Connecticut, with many fish reaching the statewide 15-inch minimum length limit by age 3. Walleyes have low natural mortality rates (fewer than 10 percent of adults die of natural causes annually) and can reach ages of 15 years or more. They can also grow to large sizes, with 2- to 6-pound fish being common and weights over 10 pounds occasionally attained (state record: 14 pounds, 8 ounces).

Successful walleye angling often requires special techniques, and because of their relatively recent introduction, walleyes present challenging sportfishing for Connecticut anglers. Walleyes are reputedly the best-tasting freshwater fish and have the added attractiveness of being catchable year-round, both during times of open water as well as through the ice. Statewide regulations for walleye are a 15-inch minimum length limit and a 5-fish creel limit.

Walleyes are generally a dark brown on their backs fading to a brassy yellow or light brown color on their flanks. The young often

Walleyes are stocked annually as 5-inch fingerlings into several Connecticut lakes.

have dark irregular blotches on their sides. There is a large black spot at the rear edge of the first dorsal fin. In addition, there is a white spot on the lower lobe of the tail fin. Large, sharp teeth distinguish the walleye from its cousin, the yellow perch. The walleye's most unique feature is its large eyes, which appear to glow when reflecting light.

Pike and Pickerel

Northern pike (*Esox lucius,* family Esocidae*)* are widely distributed throughout northern regions of Europe, Asia and North America and are the largest predatory freshwater fish in Connecticut. Although not native to the state, a naturally reproducing population has existed in the Connecticut River since the late 1800s. Pike populations have also been established in four lakes in the state (Bantam Lake, Mansfield Hollow Reservoir, Pachaug Pond and Quaddick Reservoir) through annual stockings of fingerlings that are produced from managed spawning marshes. Pike prefer lakes with at least moderate amounts of submerged vegetation, which provides protective cover for juveniles as well as ambush and foraging sites for adults.

© Joseph Tomelleri

Northern pike

Adult pike are voracious predators that feed almost exclusively on fish. Because of their size, they can eat much larger prey than most other freshwater predators. Pike spawn just after ice-out in very shallow water, usually over flooded terrestrial vegetation. No parental care is provided to the young. Potential for natural reproduction of pike is extremely limited in most Connecticut lakes due to these stringent requirements. Consequently, supplemental fingerling stocking is typically required to maintain a fishable population. In Connecticut, pike are fast growing and short-lived, usually reaching 26 inches by age 3 with a maximum life span of about 8 years. In more northern latitudes where water is cooler, pike grow more slowly and live longer (up to 25 years). Pike commonly reach lengths exceeding 30 inches and weights of 6 to 10 pounds and can get much larger (state record: 29 pounds).

Pike are especially popular with ice anglers because, like pickerel, they are very active in winter. During the open-water period, pike are often caught incidentally by bass anglers. Statewide regulations on northern pike are a 26-inch minimum length limit and a 2-fish creel limit. Special regulations apply in Bantam Lake (36-inch minimum length, 1-fish creel limit during December-February) and the Connecticut River (24-inch minimum length limit).

Side by side of a northern pike (top) and chain pickerel.

Northern pike are long and somewhat cylindrical. The snout is flat and elongate. The body is generally dark blue-gray or olive-green with light spots covering the back and sides. Unlike pickerel, the lower half of the gill cover is scaleless.

Chain pickerel (*Esox niger,* family Esocidae) are present in almost all lakes and ponds in Connecticut. Historically, the chain pickerel was probably THE apex predator in most lakes and ponds, being the only native warmwater species that can reach weights exceeding 5 pounds. They can exist in a variety of habitats but, similar to bass, thrive best in waters with at least some submerged vegetation.

Chain pickerel feed primarily on fish and sometimes crayfish and, similar to pike, can eat large prey. Chain pickerel are typically ambush feeders, meaning that they remain motionless most of the time and rely on great bursts of speed to intercept prey. Consequently, they are usually associated with some kind of structure (vegetation, stumps, etc.). Pickerel spawn in early spring (usually March to early April in Connecticut). Their eggs are deposited over vegetation in very shallow water, thus egg survival is particularly dependent on stable water levels. No parental care is afforded the young. Chain pickerel are relatively fast-growing, short-lived fish. They reach 15 inches in 2.8 years on average and have a maximum life span of around 8 years. Pickerel commonly grow to sizes of more than 24 inches and 4 pounds in unfished water supply reservoirs, but such size is uncommon in waters where fishing occurs (state record: 7 pounds, 14 ounces).

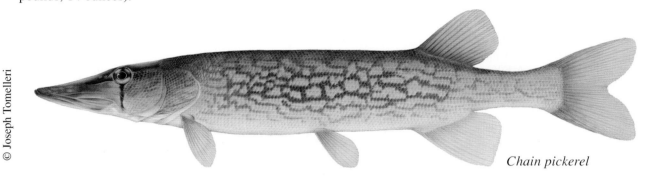

Chain pickerel

Anglers in Connecticut do not often target chain pickerel; however, many enjoy catching and releasing them. Because pickerel are active during winter, most are harvested through the ice. Angler survey data from Connecticut lakes show that more than 40 percent of chain pickerel caught through the ice are harvested, whereas fewer than 6 percent are harvested during the open-water season. Statewide pickerel regulations for lakes and ponds are a 15-inch minimum length limit and a 6-fish creel limit.

Pickerel are similar in general appearance to northern pike. Chain pickerel are dark olive-green to brown on their backs, with yellowish sides that have dark chain-like markings. Pickerel also have a dark vertical bar extending down from the middle of the eye. Unlike pike, pickerel have scales over the entire cheek and gill cover.

Another member of the pike family, the **redfin pickerel** (*Esox americanus*) is present in some Connecticut lakes and ponds; however, it is not as widespread as chain pickerel and prefers small-stream habitats. Feeding and spawning habits are similar to chain pickerel. They do not grow as large as the chain pickerel (maximum length 10 to 12 inches) and, therefore, are not sought by anglers. Characteristics that distinguish the redfin from the chain pickerel are a shorter snout, no chain-like pattern on their sides, and occasionally bright orange or red fins.

Redfin pickerel

LIFE HISTORIES OF COMMON LAKE AND POND FISHES   37

Trout and Salmon

Members of the family Salmonidae (trout, salmon and charr) are extremely popular game-fish in Connecticut. They are coldwater species that require cool, well-oxygenated water to survive (see Table 2). Most Connecticut lakes are shallow and eutrophic; therefore, a limited number contain good trout habitat. Trout also require cool, clean tributary streams to spawn. For these reasons, and because angler harvest rates are high, stocking must be conducted to sustain viable trout fisheries. Statewide trout regulations are a 5-fish creel limit and a closed season from the last day of February to the third Saturday in April.

Brown trout (*Salmo trutta*) are native to Europe and western Asia and were first introduced into Connecticut in the 1860s. They have since established naturally reproducing populations in many streams. However, natural spawning does not produce significant numbers of brown trout in Connecticut lakes. Brown trout spawn in the fall, migrating from the lake to the head-waters of tributary streams. The female creates a nest (or "redd") by clearing a depression in the gravel. Once the eggs are laid and fertilized, they are covered with gravel and receive no further parental care.

Adult trout, depending on their size, will eat a variety of prey, ranging from invertebrates to small fish. They are predominantly pelagic (open-water) predators and can play a significant role in the control of species such as alewives. As temperatures rise in the summer, brown

© Joseph Tomelleri

Brown trout

trout retreat to the deep, cool waters of lakes. Where deep-water oxygen levels are sufficient for brown trout survival, they can grow to over 16 inches in their first year. Holdover brown trout (those that have survived at least one year) commonly reach weights of 2 to 5 pounds (state record: 16 pounds, 14 ounces). Connecticut lakes that have the most potential for holdovers are managed as Trophy Trout Lakes, with special length, creel and season limits (see current Connecticut Anglers' Guide for details).

Brown trout are light brown to silver on their sides with small dark spots on their back, sides, head, and the dorsal and adipose fins. Unlike the rainbow, there are very few or no spots on the tail. In addition, there may be red spots surrounded by a lighter colored halo on their sides. Wild brown trout may have a white leading edge on their anal and pelvic fins similar to those on brook trout.

Rainbow trout (*Oncorhynchus mykiss*) are native to western North America and are actually more closely related to Pacific salmon than to the "true" trouts (members of the genus *Salmo*). Rainbows were first introduced to Connecticut in the 1870s. Rainbows eat a variety of prey, ranging from invertebrates to small fish. Unlike brown and brook trout, rainbows are capable of reaching large size by feeding exclusively on zooplankton. Most rainbows spawn in the spring; however, Connecticut uses a fall-spawning rainbow strain to better coordinate hatchery production with that of the other two trout species (brooks and browns). In the wild, rainbow trout migrate into the headwaters of tributary streams, where the female creates a nest by clearing a depression in the gravel. Once the eggs are fertilized, they are covered with gravel and no further parental care is rendered. There is little natural reproduction of rainbows in Connecticut; therefore, lake fisheries must be sustained through regular stocking of adult fish.

© Joseph Tomelleri

Rainbow trout

An advantage to rainbow trout is that they are more accessible to shore anglers than brown trout, because they spend relatively more time in shallow water. As water temperatures rise in the summer, rainbow trout seek deep, cool water to survive. Rainbows cannot tolerate warm water or low oxygen as well as brown trout (see Table 2), and so holdovers are rare in Connecticut lakes. Larger rainbows caught by Connecticut anglers are almost always hatchery-reared, surplus broodstock (state record: 14 pounds, 10 ounces).

Rainbow trout are brownish to greenish on their backs fading to silver on their sides. There are many small black spots on their heads, backs and sides. Unlike brown trout, most of the tail fin is spotted. A pink horizontal band running from the cheek to the tail is usually present on their sides.

Brook trout (*Salvelinus fontinalis*) and other members of their genus (e.g., lake trout) are also called "charr." Brook trout are native to Connecticut and are found in small to moderate-size streams throughout the state. They are rare in Connecticut lakes and ponds due to their sensitivity to high temperatures and low oxygen levels (see Table 2). Brook trout migrate to the headwaters of tributary streams in the fall to spawn. The female clears a depression in the gravel to lay her eggs. Once the eggs are fertilized, they are covered with gravel and no further parental care is rendered. Adult brook trout eat a variety of prey, ranging from invertebrates to small fish.

Like most charr species, brook trout are distinguished from the other trouts by having light markings on a darker background. They are dark olive-green to brown on their backs and have light spots on their sides. There are light worm-like markings on their backs and dorsal fins. They may also have small red spots surrounded by a light-blue halo on their sides. The leading edge of the pectoral, pelvic and anal fins is white.

Kokanee salmon (*Oncorhynchus nerka*) are a landlocked form of the sockeye salmon that are native to the Pacific Northwest. Kokanee were first introduced in Connecticut during the early 1900s, and successful fisheries were later established in a few northwestern Connecticut lakes. Kokanee spawn over gravel shoals during late fall. As with all Pacific salmon, kokanee die after spawning. In Connecticut, natural kokanee reproduction is not adequate to keep up with angler harvest; therefore, supplemental fry and fingerling stocking is necessary to support significant fisheries. Kokanee are pelagic (open-water) fish that feed solely on plankton.

Brook trout

They mature in 2 to 4 years and may reach lengths of 12 to 14 inches in Connecticut (state record: 2 pounds, 12 ounces). In recent years, kokanee populations have collapsed in both East Twin and Wononscopomuc lakes due to competition with alewives (another pelagic plankti-vore). West Hill Pond now supports the only viable kokanee fishery in Connecticut.

Kokanee are steel blue to green-blue along the head and back, blending to silvery on the side. There are no outstanding spots or markings; however, the appearance of both sexes changes before spawning. The females become dark reddish-gray in color, while the males turn bright red and their jaws transform into prominent hooks or "kypes."

Atlantic salmon (*Salmo salar*) are not currently stocked into Connecticut lakes, but Massachusetts has occasionally stocked surplus broodstock into Congamond Lake on the state border. Atlantic salmon can be distinguished from trout by a slightly forked tail and a smaller mouth (the jaw extends only to the rear edge of the eye). The base of the tail fin is relatively narrow compared with that of a trout, allowing a salmon to be lifted by its tail (a maneuver that would be very difficult with a trout).

Panfish

The term panfish is applied to almost any fish species that is good to eat and typically will "fit in the pan." These intermediate-size fish species play transitional roles in lake and pond food webs. When small, they feed primarily on zooplankton and insects and are themselves important food items for larger predators such as bass and pickerel. As adults, the larger pan-fish can become significant predators in their own right, helping to keep the numbers of often overabundant small fishes in check. Panfish (especially sunfish) are usually much more abun-dant than gamefish and make up the bulk of the biomass in most warmwater lakes. Although their individual spawning habits vary, all are capable of producing extremely high numbers of young when conditions are optimal. Because of their tremendous reproductive potential, pop-ulations can easily become stunted when the densities of young fish are too high.

Larger Panfish (black crappie, yellow perch and white perch)

The larger panfish species are very important components of Connecticut's warmwater fisheries. According to angler surveys on typical warmwater lakes and ponds, as many as 40 to 50 percent of anglers fish for "anything." These anglers often prefer to catch one of these large panfish species, because all three are good to eat, are often abundant and grow large enough (10 inches or more) to be worth keeping. There are currently no creel or size limits on panfish in Connecticut.

Black crappie (*Pomoxis nigromaculatus*), also called "calico bass," are introduced members of the sunfish family (Centrarchidae) that are found in 74 percent of Connecticut lakes. Crappies spend most of their time in shallow water and are usually associated with some kind of structure, such as beds of vegetation or sunken trees. Crappie spawn earlier than other members of the sunfish family (April in Connecticut). As with other sunfish, the male builds a nest by clearing a small depression in sand or gravel, often in very shallow water (10 to 24 inches). The male protects the eggs and subsequently the fry for a few days until they leave the nest. Young crappie eat primarily zooplankton, switching to aquatic insects and finally to fish as they

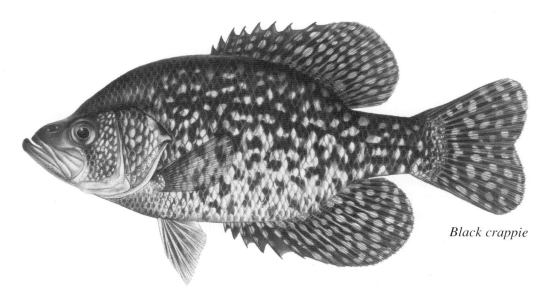

© Joseph Tomelleri

Black crappie

grow. Black crappie can grow very quickly, averaging 10 inches in 3 to 4 years. Adults are commonly 10 to 12 inches in length and can exceed 16 inches (state record: 4 pounds). Although they are not particularly strong fighters on rod and reel, crappie are nonetheless popular with anglers because they are easy to catch, reach reasonable size and are good to eat.

Crappie are laterally compressed and have a relatively large mouth. Black crappie are an iridescent green to silver in color, mottled with black spots. They can be distinguished from other sunfish by the position of the dorsal fin directly above the anal fin and by having five to seven anal spines instead of three. The distance from the eye to the base of the first dorsal spine is equal to the length of the dorsal fin base.

A population of closely related **white crappie** (*Pomoxis annularis*) exists in the Connecticut River. They are usually, but not always, lighter in color than black crappie. The dark spots on the sides of white crappie form a series of 5 to 10 irregular black vertical bands. The distance from the eye to the base of the first dorsal spine is longer than the length of the dorsal fin base.

Yellow perch (*Perca flavescens*, family Percidae) are the most common of the three larger panfish species and can be found in almost all (97 percent) of Connecticut lakes and ponds. Yellow perch can exist in almost any freshwater habitat, from slow-moving streams and small farm ponds to large reservoirs. In larger lakes, they are semipelagic, forming large schools that seek out deeper, cooler water in the summer. In Connecticut, yellow perch spawn from late March to early April. Their eggs are draped in gelatinous, ribbon-like masses over vegetation in shallow water. For this reason, yellow perch are dependent on stable water levels during the early spring. The adults do not

Kids love yellow perch because they're typically abundant and eager to bite.

Yellow perch

protect the eggs or newly hatched fry. Yellow perch are omnivorous, feeding on many small animals including crayfish, aquatic insects, mollusks and fish. Growth rates can be extremely variable. Healthy perch populations grow quickly to about 10 inches in 4 to 5 years and very slowly thereafter. They can live as long as 13 years and reach sizes up to 16 inches (state record: 2 pounds, 13 ounces). Yellow perch are good-tasting and very active in the winter. For this reason, they are extremely popular with ice anglers and are perhaps the state's most commonly caught fish during the winter.

Yellow perch are most easily recognized by their distinctive pattern of dark vertical stripes on a yellowish background. The pelvic and pectoral fins are often a bright reddish-orange. Unlike their walleye cousin, they have no sharp teeth.

White perch (*Morone americana*) are members of the sea bass family (Serranidae) and are native to the coastal fresh and brackish waters of Connecticut. They were later introduced to inland lakes and ponds where landlocked populations developed; they now exist in 30 percent of the state's lakes and ponds. They are semi-pelagic and seem to do best in larger, deeper lakes. Spawning takes place in early spring, with eggs being broadcast over gravel or vegetation in 2 to 20 feet of water. No parental protection is provided to the eggs or fry. White perch eat a variety of food items, including aquatic insects, small crustaceans and fish. They forage in large schools and usually seek deeper water during the summer. Normally, white perch will

White perch

reach 10 inches in 4 to 5 years and can reach sizes up to 16 inches and ages exceeding 12 years (state record: 2 pounds, 15 ounces). Because they are extremely prolific spawners, landlocked white perch tend to become overcrowded and subsequently stunted. Their abundance is their main appeal to anglers, because large numbers can often be caught in a short time.

White perch are laterally compressed. They are gray to olive colored on their backs, blending to silver on the sides with no conspicuous markings. Similar to many sunfish species, they have three anal spines; however, in white perch the second spine is as long as the third.

Sunfish

Only the smaller members of the sunfish family (Centrarchidae) are typically called "sunfish." Sunfish are the most widespread and often the most numerous fish in Connecticut lakes and ponds. There are six sunfish species in Connecticut, and at least one species can be found in each of the state's lakes and ponds. Sunfish spend most of their time in shallow water and prefer lakes with at least moderate levels of aquatic vegetation. Even as adults, sunfish have relatively small mouths, thus their diet consists of mostly smaller food items such as aquatic insects, fish eggs and fish larvae. They spawn in colonies by building and guarding nests in shallow water between mid-May and July. Sunfish are often the primary food source for large predators such as bass, hence they produce vast numbers of young to ensure their survival. In lakes with too few predators, sunfish can easily become overabundant. This may lead to stunting, where the maximum size may only be 5 inches, too small for most anglers to consider worth catching. Because they are typically many times more numerous than gamefish, far more sunfish (especially bluegill) are caught by lake and pond anglers than any other type of fish. Their availability, willingness to bite and great numbers make them ideal for children or anglers who cannot afford a boat or expensive tackle, because they can be caught from shore on very simple gear.

© Joseph Tomelleri

Bluegill

Bluegills (*Lepomis macrochirus*) are our most widespread sunfish species, occurring in 97 percent of Connecticut lakes. Although an introduced species, bluegills have out-competed and are now more abundant than the native pumpkinseed in most lakes. They are one of the largest sunfish in Connecticut, commonly reaching 8 to 9 inches in lakes where growth rates are good and fishing pressure is light. On average, bluegills reach 7 inches in 4 to 5 years (state record: 2 pounds, 4 ounces). Bluegills are dark green to brown on their backs, blending to yellow or orange on their breasts. There may be faint vertical bars on their sides. The gill flap is entirely black; their pectoral fins are long and pointed; and there is a dark spot at the rear edge of the soft dorsal fin. Only mature males exhibit the namesake blue on their jaws and lower gill flaps.

Pumpkinseed

Pumpkinseeds (*Lepomis gibbosus*), or "common sunfish," are our most common native sunfish species, occurring in 97 percent of Connecticut lakes. They typically grow more slowly than bluegills, reaching 7 inches in 6 to 7 years (state record: 1 pound, 3 ounces). Pumpkinseeds are dark brown to green on their backs and yellowish to orange on their bellies. Their head and cheeks often have iridescent, wavy, greenish-blue lines, and their sides are dotted with irregular olive, orange and red spots. Their pectoral fins are long and pointed. Pumpkinseeds can be distinguished from bluegills by a red spot on the tip of their black gill flap and the absence of a dark spot on the base of their soft dorsal fin.

Redbreast sunfish (*Lepomis auritus*) are native, but less widespread than either the bluegill or pumpkinseed, occurring in only 39 percent of Connecticut lakes. They are most abundant in rivers and riverine impoundments. They grow more slowly in Connecticut than either bluegills or pumpkinseeds, reaching 6 inches in 7 to 8 years. Redbreasts are brown to olive on their backs

Redbreast sunfish

with reddish spots on their sides and irregular wavy blue streaks on their head and cheeks. The breast is often a bright red-orange. Unlike bluegill and pumpkinseed, the pectoral fins are rounded. The redbreast's most distinguishing characteristic is an elongated black gill flap.

Green sunfish (*Lepomis cyanellus*) is an introduced species that occurs in only 4 percent of Connecticut lakes. They typically reach 5 inches in 4 to 5 years and have a maximum size of about 7 inches. Green sunfish are brown to olive on their backs, blending to yellow-green on their sides. They have emerald spots and/or wavy emerald lines on their heads. Their mouths are larger than bluegills or pumpkinseeds, and they have rounded pectoral fins. The gill flap is black with a yellow, pink or orange edge.

© Joseph Tomelleri

Green sunfish

Rock bass (*Ambloplites rupestris*) is an introduced species that occurs in 38 percent of Connecticut lakes, mostly west of the Connecticut River. Populations of rock bass exist in the Thames River drainage area, and their distribution may be slowly expanding in the eastern part of the state. Rock bass prefer clear lakes with sparse vegetation and gravel or rock bottoms. Their diet is similar to other sunfish; however, their larger mouths allow them to also prey on small fish and crayfish. They typically grow to 8 inches in 4 to 5 years and can reach lengths to 12 inches or greater (state record: 1 pound, 3 ounces). Rock bass are usually brown on their backs, blending to a brassy color on their sides. There are eight to 10 horizontal rows of spots below the lateral line, each scale having one spot. Rock bass have red eyes and five to seven anal spines instead of three like most other sunfish.

Banded sunfish (*Enneacanthus obesus*) is a native species but relatively rare in Connecticut, occurring in only 1 percent of lakes and ponds. They are most common in coastal freshwater ponds in the eastern part of the state, and prefer shallow, vegetated habitats. Banded sunfish are the smallest of the sunfish species in Connecticut, reaching a maximum length of only 3 to 4 inches. For this reason, they are rarely observed by anglers. They can be distinguished from the other sunfish species by a rounded tail fin, five to eight dark vertical bands on a light background and numerous light spots on the dorsal, caudal and anal fins.

Catfish

Members of the catfish family (Ictaluridae) can be distinguished by their lack of scales and by the familiar barbels, or "whiskers," extending from their chins and corners of their mouths. These barbels are extremely sensitive organs that allow catfish to both feel and taste their sur-

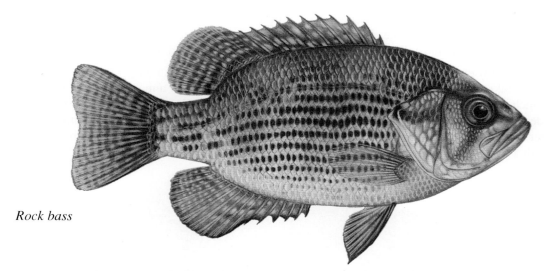

Rock bass

roundings. This makes them very effective at scavenging in little or no light. For this reason, most catfish are nocturnal and are most readily caught at night. All Connecticut catfish build nests, spawn in spring or early summer, and guard their young (usually both parents) for a few weeks after hatching. Catfishing is extremely popular in many parts of the country and is moderately so in Connecticut, especially in the Connecticut River. Bullheads, although good to eat, are underused in many lakes and ponds, probably because most anglers are unwilling to fish at night when these fish are most vulnerable. There are no creel or length limits on catfish in Connecticut.

Channel catfish (*Ictalurus punctatus*) have been widely introduced throughout Connecticut. They occur in low numbers in a few lakes. The only abundant population occurs in the Connecticut River. Throughout their range, channel catfish populations seem to do best in larger impoundments with significant river tributaries.

Channel cats are opportunistic feeders, eating such items as insects, crayfish, snails, clams, worms and fish. They are more active predators than other Connecticut catfish species and can be caught on artificial lures as well as on live bait. Spawning takes place in late spring or early summer, when a nest is typically built under a log or an undercut bank. Because they prefer spawning in rivers, supplemental stocking of fingerlings is necessary to sustain channel catfish populations in most lakes and ponds. Channel cats are long-lived, slow-growing fish. They typically reach 10 to 12 inches by their third or fourth year and may live as long as 25 years. Channel cats are the largest catfish species in Connecticut and commonly reach 2 to 6 pounds (state record: 23 pounds). They are extremely popular in other areas of the country

Channel catfish

(nationally, catfish are the third most sought after type of fish) and are probably the best tasting of the Connecticut catfish species.

Channel cats are gray on their backs fading to light gray on the sides. There may be a few black spots on their sides (more common in juveniles). They have four darkly colored chin barbels, a deeply forked tail and 25 to 29 anal fin rays.

White catfish

© Joseph Tomelleri

White catfish (*Ameiurus catus*) have been widely introduced throughout the state and are found in 15 percent of Connecticut lakes. They are salt-tolerant and are common in the brackish waters of the lower Connecticut, Thames and Housatonic rivers. Though these fish prefer riverine systems, they can also live in lakes with moderate amounts of vegetation. White cats are opportunistic feeders, eating a variety of prey ranging from aquatic insects to fish. White catfish typically reach 12 inches by their fifth year. In Connecticut, they commonly reach 15 to 18 inches and can be greater than 22 inches (state record: 12 pounds, 4 ounces).

The white catfish is gray on its back, blending to creamy white on the underbelly. There are no prominent spots. It can be distinguished from the channel cat by having four white chin barbels, 18 to 25 anal rays and a proportionally wider head and mouth.

The **brown bullhead** (*Ameiurus nebulosus*) is our only native catfish species and can be found in almost all Connecticut lakes and ponds. They can be very abundant, making it certain that they play significant roles in lake ecosystems. However, they have been much less studied than other, more popular sport fishes, thus these roles are poorly understood. Bullheads prefer shallow lakes with at least moderate amounts of submerged vegetation. They eat a variety of foods, including insects, crayfish, snails and fish. Bullheads typically reach 10 inches in 3 to 5 years. They commonly attain lengths of 12 to 14 inches, with maximum size exceeding 15 inches (state record: 3 pounds).

Brown bullheads are dark brown on their backs, with slightly lighter sides that are sometimes mottled with dark blotches. The underbody is pale yellow to white. The chin barbels are dark brown to black, often with a yellow or white base. The tail is square or slightly rounded, and the anal fin has fewer than 24 rays. The underside of the pectoral fin spine has distinct barbs.

Two other species of bullheads have been introduced into Connecticut lakes and ponds. Both are very similar in appearance to the brown bullhead. The **yellow bullhead** (*Ameiurus natalis*) has been observed in every major drainage basin. It is typically lighter in color than the brown bullhead with no dark mottling on the sides. Its belly

Yellow (left) vs. brown bullhead (right) showing their light vs. dark chin barbels.

Brown bullhead

ranges from white to bright yellow. It has four white chin barbels and more than 24 anal fin rays. The **black bullhead** (*Ameiurus melas*) has been observed in only a few sites, the most recent being Candlewood Lake in 1999. It can be distinguished from the brown bullhead by a pale vertical bar at the base of the tail and pectoral spines that are smooth or only slightly serrated.

Forage Fishes

Forage fishes are typically not targeted by anglers (usually due to their small size), but are nonetheless extremely important to lake and pond fisheries because they are the preferred food sources for many predatory fish species. All Connecticut fish species in this category lack the rigid spines that many fish use as defense against predation. These fishes are also generally cylindrical in shape, making them easy for predatory fish to swallow. Forage species make up for this lack of defense by being extremely prolific spawners, ensuring their continued existence through sheer strength of numbers. The most abundant and important forage fish species in Connecticut lakes and ponds are alewives, golden shiners and (in riverine systems) spottail shiners.

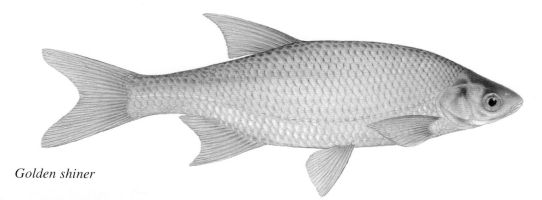

Golden shiner

Golden shiners (*Notemigonus chrysoleucas*, minnow family, Cyprinidae) are native minnows that are present in almost all Connecticut lakes and ponds. They are the preferred food species of resident predators such as bass and pickerel, and seem to be most numerous in lakes with significant submerged vegetation. Predator growth rates are usually good in waters with dense golden shiner populations. Golden shiners feed primarily on small insects, mollusks, large zooplankters and to some extent algae. They scatter their eggs over submerged vegetation during late spring or early summer and provide no parental care to their offspring. Golden shiners average about 7 inches in 3 years in Connecticut, with a maximum size of 10 to 11 inches. Golden shiners are laterally compressed and have a sharply forked tail. Adults are distinctly golden in color, whereas juveniles are silver. The key identifying characteristics are a sharply curved lateral line and the presence of a scaleless fleshy keel on the midline of the abdomen between the pelvic and anal fins.

Tench (*Tinca tinca*) are common European minnows (Cyprinidae) that have recently become established in Bantam Lake. Tench can reach fairly large size (12 to 20 inches). They are greenish brown on their backs, silvery on their sides and may have bright orange fins. They have much smaller scales than golden shiners, a small barbel at the back edge of the mouth, no fleshy keel on the underside, and have a single small dorsal fin spine.

Spottail shiners (*Notropis hudsonius*, minnow family, Cyprinidae) are found in almost all of Connecticut's larger rivers and riverine impoundments and can be extremely abundant. In riverine systems, they often far outnumber any other fish species present. They are typically absent from lakes with no significant river tributaries. Their diet is similar to that of golden shiners. Spottail shiners spawn in fast-moving streams during spring. Their maximum size is typically about 5 inches. Spottails are cylindrical in shape and have a sharply forked tail. They are silver and usually have a faint, dusky lateral band extending at the midline from the gill to the tail. There is usually a spot at the base of the tail that is more prominent in juveniles than adults. They have relatively large eyes and scales, a triangular head and a pronounced snout that overhangs the mouth.

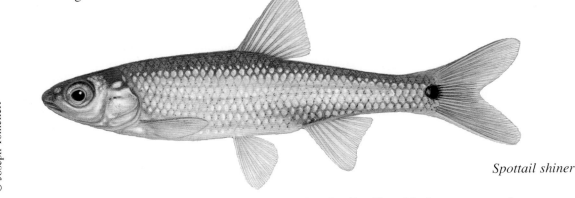

© Joseph Tomelleri

Spottail shiner

Landlocked alewives (*Alosa pseudoharengus*, herring family, Clupeidae) are a non-native, landlocked form of a normally anadromous species. Instead of spending most of their lives in saltwater and ascending rivers to spawn, they complete their entire life cycle in freshwater lakes. They were first introduced to Connecticut in the 1950s and were subsequently stocked throughout the state to provide forage for trout. Landlocked alewives can now be found in 36 percent of Connecticut lakes and ponds.

Alewives spawn by scattering their eggs over lake bottoms during late May or early June. They feed almost entirely on zooplankton and fish larvae. When overabundant, alewives are significant competitors with other fish species, because almost all freshwater fishes eat zooplankton during their larval stages. Large zooplankters, which most larval fishes prefer to eat, are often nearly nonexistent in lakes that contain alewives. Their predation on fish larvae can also be significant enough to affect recruitment (the number of fish that survive to adulthood) of other fish species. Alewives are pelagic (open-water) fish that swim in large schools. They are an especially good food source for predators because of their high body-fat content. Pelagic predators such as trout and walleye feed heavily on them, whereas predators such as bass and pickerel that stick closer to shore opportunistically encounter them.

Alewives are short-lived and rarely survive past age 4. Their growth is extremely density-dependent (dense populations grow more slowly), thus both growth rate and maximum size vary considerably among lakes. On average, alewives reach 5 inches in about 2 years. Their maximum length is around 11 inches, but they are usually much smaller. Alewives are a very silvery fish with a single dark spot behind the head at eye level. They have large eyes, are laterally compressed and have a strongly forked tail. They have a saw-like ridge of scutes (sharp, pointed scales) along the midline of the belly, for which they are called "sawbellies" in some areas.

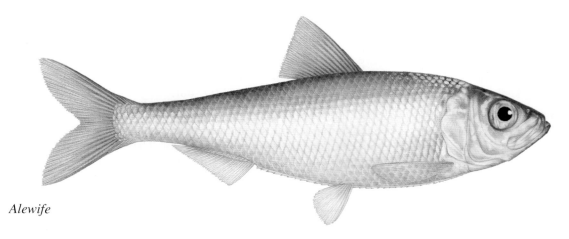

Alewife

Rainbow smelt (*Osmerus mordax*, smelt family, Osmeridae) are native to Connecticut only as an anadromous species. They were widely introduced, but landlocked populations now occur in only a few Connecticut lakes. Smelt feed predominantly on invertebrates and small fish and are themselves important forage for open-water predators such as trout and walleye. Spawning takes place during late winter and early spring in tributary streams or along the shallow shoal areas of lakes. Eggs are broadcast over gravel substrate, to which they adhere. No parental care is given. Landlocked smelt typically reach 5 to 7 inches. Where abundant, large numbers can be caught by angling, and they are especially popular with ice anglers. The smelt is a slender fish that is laterally compressed, with a large mouth and well-developed teeth. They are pale green on their backs and silvery on their sides. They have an adipose fin and a sharply forked tail.

Other Fish Species

Common carp (*Cyprinus carpio*) are native to Asia and Europe and are among the world's largest members of the minnow family (Cyprinidae). They have been widely introduced throughout the world and were first reported in Connecticut in 1844. Carp exist in 26 percent of Connecticut lakes and can be found in all of the major drainage basins. Although they can do well in lakes, the largest populations are found in the Connecticut River and in riverine impoundments. Carp are omnivorous and are mostly bottom feeders. They typically suck up a mouthful of bottom material, spit it out, and then select the food items to eat. Spawning takes place in late spring to early summer, when the fish move into shallow, vegetated areas and broadcast their eggs over aquatic vegetation. No parental care is provided. Connecticut carp typically grow to over 18 inches in 3 years and can reach lengths in excess of 35 inches (state

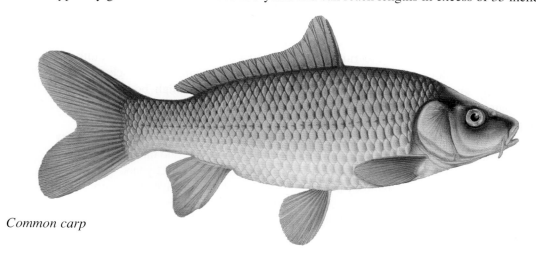

Common carp

record: 38 pounds, 8 ounces). Carp are underused in Connecticut, although they put up a strong fight on rod and reel and are a highly prized game and food fish throughout their native range. There are no creel or length limit restrictions on this species.

Carp are robust, somewhat laterally compressed fish with large scales and a triangular head. They have a long dorsal fin with a single stout spine. There are two pairs of barbels on the upper lip, the most conspicuous of which are at the corners of their down-turned mouth. They are typically brown on their backs, fading to bronze on their sides.

Grass carp (*Ctenopharyngodon idella*, minnow family, Cyprinidae) are native to eastern Asia. They are widely used to control aquatic plants because of their preference for eating such vegetation. In the late 1980s, Connecticut began permitting the importation of sterile grass carp for aquatic-vegetation control in private ponds. Grass carp are large fish that commonly reach sizes in excess of 30 inches and 20 pounds, with a maximum weight of 100 pounds. They are silver and are not as laterally compressed as the common carp. Unlike common carp, the dorsal fin is short (fewer than 12 dorsal rays), the mouth is not down-turned, and it has no barbels.

Wild goldfish (bottom) can be very similar in appearance to the common carp (top).

Goldfish (*Carassius auratus*, minnow family, Cyprinidae) are native to Asia and were first reported in Connecticut in 1844. Goldfish have become established in 6 percent of Connecticut lakes, primarily the result of pet and bait releases. Goldfish are omnivorous feeders, primarily eating a variety of aquatic insects, worms and mollusks. They spawn in the spring by broadcasting their eggs over aquatic vegetation to which the eggs adhere. They commonly reach lengths of 10 to 12 inches. Similar to carp, goldfish have a long dorsal fin that has a single stout spine. Unlike carp, they do not have barbels on the ends of their mouths. They may be brown, gold, orange, white or multicolored.

American eels (*Anguilla rostrata*, freshwater eel family, Anguillidae) are found in 68 percent of the state's lakes and ponds, being most common in lakes near the shoreline or major rivers. They are primarily nocturnal and prefer lakes with some kind of cover (vegetation) to hide in during the day. American eels are opportunistic feeders that will eat almost any animal food items they can find. They are active predators of smaller fish, but can also be scavengers, feeding off the carcasses of larger dead fish. It is unclear to what extent eels are preyed on by other fishes in freshwater lakes and ponds.

Eels have a unique and complex life cycle. It is believed that all eels spawn in the same general area of the central North Atlantic known as the Sargasso Sea. Similar to Pacific salmon, the adults die after spawning. After hatching, the larval eels drift north with the Gulf Stream. Once they reach a developmental stage where they can actively swim (at which time they are called elvers), they migrate inshore and swim up rivers and streams along the Atlantic Coast. The females may migrate far inland and spend most of their adult lives in freshwater lakes and streams. The males usually stay closer to saltwater, in estuaries and coastal streams. When they are sexually mature (males at 4 to 6 years, females at 7 to 9 years in Connecticut), they migrate back to the Sargasso Sea to spawn and complete their life cycle. Most eels caught on rod and reel are between 12 and 24 inches, with a maximum size of more than 3 feet (state record: 10 pounds, 3 ounces). Although they are a highly esteemed food fish in Europe and Asia, they are underused by anglers in Connecticut. Their nocturnal habits and an ability to produce large quantities of slime can make them difficult and unpleasant to handle and unhook. Statewide regulations are a 6-inch minimum length limit and a 50-fish creel limit.

The American eel has a snake-like body, an elongate head with a well-developed jaw and teeth, no pelvic fins and one continuous dorsal, caudal and anal fin. Their coloration changes through their life cycle. They are called glass eels when they first transform from the larval stage and are nearly transparent. Adults are dark green or olive-brown on their backs and yellowish green on their sides. When they mature and begin migrating back to the sea, their backs become metallic bronze or black and their sides silvery.

© Joseph Tomelleri

White sucker

The **white sucker** (*Catostomus commersoni*, sucker family, Catostomidae) is a native species found in 61 percent of Connecticut lakes. While young, they provide forage for some of the state's more common predatory fish, such as bass and pickerel. White suckers grow quickly, reaching 10 to 13 inches in 2 to 3 years and commonly reaching lengths of 20 inches or more. They are bottom feeders with a diet consisting mostly of aquatic invertebrates. Adult suckers migrate up tributary streams in the spring to spawn, where they broadcast their eggs over gravel. No parental care is given, and the adults move back to lakes or deeper stream stretches after spawning. White suckers are a robust, torpedo-shaped fish. They have a blunt, rounded snout with a down-turned, sucker-like mouth. Their lips are thick, fleshy and covered with small papillae. They are typically brown on their backs and bronze on their sides. During spawning, males develop a wide rose-colored lateral band and nuptial tubercles (raised bumps) on the anal fin and tail.

Another native sucker species, the **creek chubsucker** (*Erimyzon oblongus*) is found in 12 percent of Connecticut lakes. Although they reach sizes of 12 to 14 inches, chubsuckers are rarely caught by anglers. Creek chubsuckers are robust fish with a deep body and an arched back. The snout is blunt, with a small down-turned mouth. They are bronze in color with no prominent markings, except for a dark lateral band in juveniles.

Descriptions and Maps of Lakes and Ponds

Field Methods

Electrofishing

Electrofishing is the most effective technique for sampling most lake and pond fish species. Electrofishing is a sampling method in which an electric current is passed through the water, immobilizing fish so they can be collected by biologists. Connecticut's electrofishing boats are 17 to 19-foot aluminum jon boats with 40-horsepower outboard engines. Each boat is equipped with a 6,000-watt gasoline generator that supplies power to the shocking control unit and work lights. Four floodlights — two above water, two below — illuminate the fish-capture area ahead of the boat. An array of six cables hang down about 5 feet into the water from two long booms that extend off the front of the boat. A pulsed DC current (80 pulses per second) of up to 200 volts and 8 amps is passed through the water between the cables (which are the positive electrodes, or "anodes") and the boat hull (the negative electrode, or "cathode").

Fish muscles, like those of all animals, are controlled by electrical impulses generated within their bodies. A pulsed DC current in the water interferes with their muscle function and, therefore, ability to swim. At first, the current forces the fish to swim involuntarily toward the positive electrodes (the dropper cables at the front of the boat). When the fish get closer to the electrodes, they become immobilized and can be netted from the water. Once the electric current is removed, fish typically recover in a few minutes. It requires such a strong current to immobilize fish because cold-blooded animals like fish are only slightly more conductive than water, so each fish receives only a tiny fraction of the total amperage that the boat puts out.

A typical electrofishing crew consists of a boat driver, two fish netters and two data processors. The boat slowly advances, usually near shore in 2 to 8 feet of water, with the current alternately being turned on and off. Immobilized fish are captured by two people with long-handled nets who stand behind a safety rail on the bow of the boat. After the fish are netted, they are placed in the boat's livewell. Biologists then identify and measure the fish and record the data. A small patch of scales is removed from some fish to determine their age. (Fish have annual rings on their scales, much like the rings in a tree trunk, which can be counted when magnified.) After each fish is processed, it is released back into the lake unharmed.

Electrofishing is usually conducted at night when fish are less active.

Electrofishing is conducted at night during spring (late April through early June) or fall (October through early November). During these times a variety of fish species can be found sleeping (yes, fish do sleep) in shallow water, causing them to be especially vulnerable to electrofishing. During daylight hours, when fish are more active, they can readily avoid the electrofishing boat by simply swimming out of the way.

Electrofishing is an excellent sampling method for a number of reasons:

- It does little or no harm to the fish.
- It efficiently samples a variety of fish species. Hundreds of fish can be caught and released in a typical night of electrofishing.
- Biologists can selectively capture species for which data is needed.
- Unlike nets, electrofishing gear is logistically simple to use — it does not have to be set and hauled or left overnight, and it does not require extensive cleaning or repair after use.

The Statewide Lake and Pond Electrofishing Survey

More than 100 sites were electrofished, many several times, during the course of the Statewide Lake and Pond Electrofishing Survey (1988-95). Sites included all of the state's important public lakes and ponds, some smaller ponds, a number of water supply reservoirs (in which no fishing is allowed) and a number of cove and mainstem sites on the Connecticut River. The survey was initiated to gather baseline data on all of the state's important warmwater fish populations and to identify those waters that may be in need of alternative or more intensive management. The unfished water supply reservoirs were sampled to give biologists an idea of what Connecticut fish populations are like in a "natural" state of balance and hence provide insight into the fisheries potential of our public lakes. The fish information in this publication is based primarily on data from this survey, but also incorporates more recent electrofishing data as well as data from other standard sampling methods (creel survey, nets, etc).

Lake Mapping

Bathymetry (water depth) data were collected by two methods. From 1985 to 1998, a chart-recording sonar unit mounted on a boat was used to record depths. Numerous transects were run at a uniform speed between known reference points to provide paper records of lake cross-sections. Back at the office, the latest aerial photography was used as a base map, and each depth cross-section was scaled to fit and plotted on the base map. Equal depth contour lines were then hand-drawn to create the final maps.

In 1999, new equipment was purchased that provided more accurate and timely surveys.

An electrofishing boat temporarily immobilizes fish, which can then be captured with long-handled nets.

This equipment included a sonar device that interfaced with a Global Positioning System (GPS) and a computer data recorder. Numerous transects of each lake were run with accurate position/depth information now being automatically recorded every five seconds. These data were later uploaded into a computer for processing.

Maps were created using Geographical Information System (GIS) software (Arc View and Arc/Info). Base maps were generated from U.S. Geological Survey and state computer databases that contain roads, waterways, property boundaries, etc. Before 1999, hand-drawn depth contours were digitized and fit to base maps to produce the final map. After 1999, equal depth contours were automatically calculated from the data by using specially designed computer software (Arc View Spatial Analyst & 3-D Analyst).

Aquatic Plant Survey

Aquatic plant information in this publication comes from an ongoing statewide aquatic plant survey conducted by the State Geological and Natural History Survey of Connecticut. Most of the plant surveying was done immediately after bathymetric data were collected. Detailed depth information made it possible to focus on the areas that provided the best habitat for plant growth. The perimeter of the water body was surveyed by boat, and plant species, locations and densities were recorded. Specimens were collected for all but the most common plants. These were later identified and stored for future reference at the University of Connecticut's Torrey Herbarium. Typically, each lake or pond was surveyed once between late May and early November.

There are limitations to any plant survey based on only one visit. For example, late-season surveys can overlook curly-leaved pondweed *(Potamogeton crispus),* which appears early in the year but drops off by the end of summer. Early-season surveys will probably miss water-nymph *(Najas)* species, however, because they are primarily annual plants that appear later in the growing season. Early-season surveys will not describe fully developed coverages and densities, because aquatic plants are most abundant during July through September. Therefore, this publication provides only a general description of aquatic plant densities and species assemblages for each lake. Furthermore, plant assemblages and densities can change over time in response to water levels, temperature fluctuations, nutrient inputs and modifications to adjacent land use.

Pickerelweed and yellow pond-lily.

Aerial view of Lake Chamberlain, Bethany.

How to Use This Section

Text Descriptions of Individual Lakes and Ponds

Description: Contains a general description for each lake, its watershed and its shoreline.

Depth: Maximum depth is the deepest point measured during our survey. Maximum depths based on pre-1999 data are approximate (usually within 2 ft.). Mean depth was calculated as lake volume divided by surface area.

Transparency (or water clarity): These are late summer secchi disk readings. A secchi disk is a black and white disk of standard size that is lowered from the side of a boat. The depth just before the disk goes out of sight is the measured transparency. Most data are from DEP Fisheries; some are from other sources. Water transparency can vary considerably over a season, being influenced by such things as algal blooms and turbidity caused by rain.

Productivity: The most recent published trophic classifications available were used. A range is given where published classifications varied. See section on Lake Productivity and Classification for explanation of the trophic classification system.

Stratification: Most descriptions are based on oxygen-temperature data taken at 1-meter intervals during late summer by DEP Fisheries. Published data was used where no recent information was available. See section on The Lake Environment for discussion on lake thermal stratification.

Vegetation: A description of the extent of aquatic vegetation during summer. Most data is from the statewide Aquatic Plant Survey conducted by the State Geological and Natural History Survey of DEP. See section on Field Methods for discussion on the survey.

Access: All established state-owned boat and shore access areas are described. Included also are major, well-established town or private access sites that are open to the public. Directions are provided for boat access areas only. Other private boat or shore access may be available at some sites. Check with local towns for details.

Fish: This section describes the relative abundance (or density) of all fish species known to inhabit the waterbody. Relative abundance is based on recent fish sampling by DEP Fisheries. "Average" refers to the average abundance of that particular species among all Connecticut public lakes. A text box is provided for a quick reference of what species are present and whether they are relatively abundant, common, uncommon or rare. Be aware that fish population numbers naturally fluctuate to some extent within lakes. Population levels reported in this book are the average of those found during our sampling. Changes in factors such as fishing pressure, water level management or aquatic vegetation can also cause shifts in fish population abundance and/or average size. See Appendix 1 for explanation of fish growth rates.

Fishing: Predictions of how good fishing should be for major species based on sizes and abundance found during DEP Fisheries sampling. See Appendix 5 for which lakes should have the best fishing for selected common fish species.

Management: Describes any special fish management regulations present. Please refer to the current Connecticut Anglers' Guide for specifics.

Boating: Describes the most important boating restrictions that might affect anglers. For full details on specific waters, please refer to the current Connecticut Boater's Guide.

Comments: Other interesting details about the specific waterbody.

Maps of Individual Lakes and Ponds

Maps were created using the State of Connecticut DEP Geographic Information System (GIS) database (see section on "Methods" for more discussion). Although this database is updated regularly, some features such as road positions and names, and locations of state properties may have changed. We have gone to a lot of effort to ensure that the maps are as accurate as possible, but make no guarantees to that effect. Please check local signage before assuming that you are on public land and secure permission from the landowner before crossing any private land.

Lake depth contour lines in the maps are graphic simplifications of actual lake bottom features. The maps should give you a good "feel" for the shape of the bottom and where the deep vs. shallow areas are. Smaller features, such as rockpiles, can be totally omitted through this type of presentation, however. **Please do not use these maps for navigational purposes.** Use caution and judgement whenever navigating shallow waters. Also, realize that some lakes experience wide depth variations (for example, flood control impoundments or those with hydropower facilities). In all cases, maps show lake depths at full pool elevation. Hence, if water levels are down, all areas will be shallower than indicated on the maps. Please also realize that riverine systems – especially the Connecticut River – are subject to depth changes as sandbars and shoals shift often with changes in flow (such as after large storms).

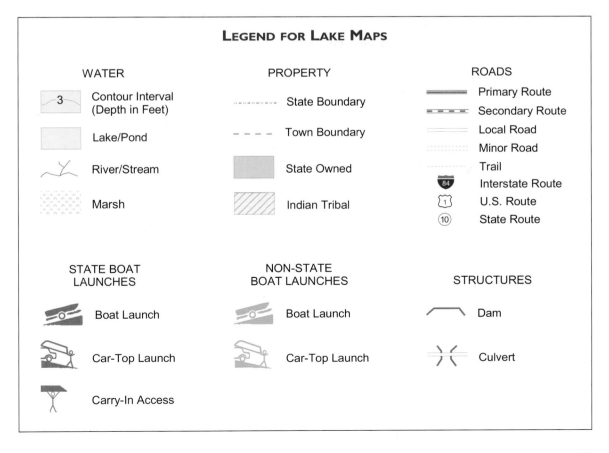

LEGEND FOR LAKE MAPS

WATER

3   Contour Interval (Depth in Feet)

Lake/Pond

River/Stream

Marsh

PROPERTY

State Boundary

Town Boundary

State Owned

Indian Tribal

ROADS

Primary Route

Secondary Route

Local Road

Minor Road

Trail

84   Interstate Route

U.S. Route

10   State Route

STATE BOAT LAUNCHES

Boat Launch

Car-Top Launch

Carry-In Access

NON-STATE BOAT LAUNCHES

Boat Launch

Car-Top Launch

STRUCTURES

Dam

Culvert

Alexander Lake

Town(s): Killingly   **215 acres**

Description: Alexander Lake is a natural lake within the Thames River Drainage Basin. The water level was raised slightly by a small dam on the outlet. The lake consists of two deep basins separated by an area of shallow water (less than 6 ft.) with an island in the middle. *Watershed:* 568 acres. There is some industrial development to the north and east of the lake. The remainder of the watershed includes moderate residential development and some undeveloped woodland and agricultural land. The lake is fed by groundwater and surface runoff and drains southward into a small wetland stream that flows into the Quinebaug River. *Shoreline:* Residences have been built along the entire shoreline. There is a private beach on the eastern shoreline. *Depth:* Max 51 ft., Mean 25 ft. *Transparency:* Very clear, 18 ft. in late summer. *Productivity:* Moderate (early mesotrophic–mesotrophic). *Bottom type:* Mostly sand, gravel, coarse rubble and boulders. *Stratification:* Occurs with a thermocline forming between 23 and 36 ft. Late summer oxygen levels remain high (greater than 6 ppm) to a depth of 33 ft., creating a wide band of suitable trout habitat. Oxygen then declines to less than 2 ppm in deeper water. *Vegetation:* Not surveyed by the State. Generally sparse. There are patchy growths of pipewort, stonewort, spike-rush, rush and arrowhead in shallow open water and dense beds of white water-lily, spatterdock, bladderwort and water-shield in the coves.

Access: There is no public access; however, small boats can launch via a private right-of-way on the southeastern shoreline of the northern basin. The sand and gravel launch is shallow and narrow. *Shore:* No public shore access.

Fish: Alexander Lake is stocked each spring with 1,800 catchable size **brown** and **rainbow trout**. There is sufficient dissolved oxygen in deeper water to allow some trout to holdover. Largemouth and smallmouth bass populations are both stockpiled — small (8-13") **largemouth bass** are very abundant with densities of larger fish less than average and little **smallmouth bass** are at above average densities with larger fish being relatively rare. **Chain pickerel**, **black crappie**, and **yellow perch** are all present at low densities. **White Perch** are rare at smaller sizes, but very common in the 9-12" range. Similarly, there are low densities of smaller **sunfish** (mostly bluegill, occasional pumpkinseed), but large fish (7-9") are abundant. Both **brown** and **yellow bullhead** are present at low densities. Banded killifish are very abundant, but the forage base is otherwise poor. The only other fish species present at low density is the American eel.

Fishing: This is an excellent lake for exceptionally large bluegills. Fishing should be good for bass, with action especially fast for 10-13" fish. Expect fair to good trout fishing during April and May and again during the fall with some chance of a holdover brown or rainbow. Fishing should also be good for large white perch, but poor for other species.

Management: Statewide regulations apply for all species (see current *Connecticut Anglers' Guide*).

Boating: Motors limited to 12 cu. in. (Approximately 10 hp) (see current *Connecticut Boater's Guide*).

Comments: Boating traffic is light on this lake because of motor and access restrictions.

Alexander Lake Fish Species and Abundance	ALL SIZES	BIG FISH	GROWTH
Gamefish			
Largemouth bass	A	C	Slow
Smallmouth bass	C	U	Slow
Brown trout	U	U	Avg
Rainbow trout	C		
Chain pickerel	U	U	< Avg
Panfish			
Black crappie	U	U	< Avg
White perch	R	C	> Avg
Yellow perch	U	U	Avg
Brown bullhead	R	R	
Yellow bullhead	U	U	
Sunfish			
Bluegill	U	C	> Avg
Pumpkinseed	U	U	> Avg
Other			
Banded killifish	A		
American eel	R		
A=Abundant, C=Common, U=Uncommon, R=Rare			

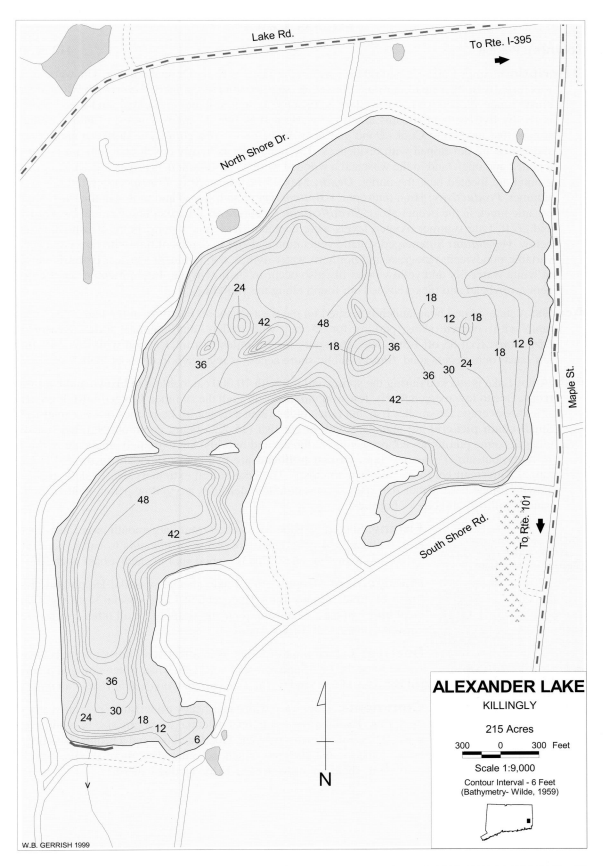

Lake Rd.

To Rte. I-395

North Shore Dr.

24

42   48   18
                              12   18
36   18   36
                              18
                      36   30   24
                                    18   12   6
              42

Maple St.

48

42

South Shore Rd.

To Rte. 101

36

24   30   18   12

6

N

ALEXANDER LAKE

KILLINGLY

215 Acres

300   0   300 Feet

Scale 1:9,000

Contour Interval - 6 Feet
(Bathymetry- Wilde, 1959)

W.B. GERRISH 1999

Amos Lake

Town(s): Preston   **113 acres**

Description: Amos Lake is a natural lake within the Thames River Drainage Basin. The water level was raised 2 ft. by a small masonry dam at the southern end of the lake. **Watershed:** 920 acres of mostly undeveloped woods or wetland with some agricultural and residential land use. The lake is fed by five wetland streams along the western shoreline. It drains southward into a wetland stream that feeds into Cooks Pond and then Avery Pond. **Shoreline:** The northern and eastern shorelines are developed with residences. The remainder is lightly developed with a mixture of wooded and open land to the west and a wooded wetland to the south. A private beach and campground are located near the outlet. **Depth:** Max 45 ft., Mean 20 ft. **Transparency:** Fair; 7 ft. in summer. **Productivity:** High (eutrophic). **Bottom type:** Sand, gravel and rubble in the shoal areas; organic muck in the deeper areas. **Stratification:** Occurs with a thermocline forming between 13 and 26 ft. Late summer oxygen levels were depleted (less than 1 ppm) in the thermocline and below. **Vegetation:** Submerged aquatic vegetation is dense to depths of 6 ft. with fern pondweed, variable pondweed, tapegrass and northern water-nymph the dominant species. Extensive areas of white water-lily and yellow pond-lily also occur in shallow water. Intermittent areas of emergent arrowhead and pickerelweed are found along the shoreline.

Access: A state-owned boat launch is located on the western shore. Facilities at the launch include a ramp with concrete slabs, parking for 25 cars with trailers, and chemical toilets (seasonal). **Directions:** Exit 85 off I-395, Rte. 164 south for 1.5 miles past intersection with Rte. 165, turn left (east) onto access road. **Shore:** Public shore access is restricted to the boat launch area.

Fish: Amos Lake is stocked during the spring and fall with 10,000 catchable size **brown** and **rainbow trout**. Due to low oxygen levels, few trout holdover through the summer. **Largemouth bass** densities are average for smaller fish, but much higher than average for large ones (greater than 15"). Small **chain pickerel** are abundant with larger fish (15-22") being common. **Sunfish** (mostly bluegill, some pumpkinseed, occasional redbreast and hybrids) are extremely abundant in the 5-7" range but larger ones are rare. **Brown bullhead** are extremely abundant in the 8-12" size range. **American eel** to 25" are also abundant. The lake has an extremely dense, slow-growing alewife forage base. Other fish species present at low densities are yellow perch, golden shiner, banded killifish and creek chubsucker.

Fishing: Should be good for stocked trout, largemouth bass, chain pickerel, bullhead and eels. There are plenty of bluegills to catch, but don't expect too many big ones. This is a good spot to catch a bass over 20".

Management: Trophy Trout Lake; special seasonal length and creel limits on trout. Trophy Bass Management Lake; special slot length and creel limits on bass. Statewide regulations apply for all other species (see current *Connecticut Anglers' Guide*).

Boating: A speed limit of 8 mph is in effect at all times except between June 15 and the first Sunday after Labor Day when water-skiing is permitted between 11 a.m. and 6 p.m. (see current *Connecticut Boater's Guide*).

Comments: Amos Lake withstands heavy trout fishing pressure early in the spring. The lake has exceptional potential for trophy size bass and averages 10 bass tournaments per year. Good facilities and a healthy bass population indicate that the lake could accommodate more events. Special regulations should improve fishing by protecting larger bass.

Amos Lake
Fish Species and Abundance

	ALL SIZES	BIG FISH	GROWTH
Gamefish			
Largemouth bass	A	C	< Avg
Brown trout	C	U	Avg
Rainbow trout	A		
Chain pickerel	A	C	Avg
Panfish			
Yellow perch	U	U	> Avg
Brown bullhead	A	C	
Sunfish			
Bluegill	A	U	Slow
Pumpkinseed	C	R	Slow
Redbreast	R	R	
Other			
Golden Shiner	U		
Banded killifish	U		
Alewife	A		
Creek chubsucker	U		
American eel	A		

A=Abundant, C=Common, U=Uncommon, R=Rare

AMOS LAKE

PRESTON

113 Acres

300   0   300   Feet

Scale 1:8,000

Contour Interval - 6 Feet
(Bathymetry - Hunter, 1995)

164

42
36
30
24
18
12
6

N

Hollowell Rd.

W.B. GERRISH 1999

Anderson Pond (Blue Lake)

Town(s): North Stonington   **56.6 acres**

Description: Anderson Pond is a small artificial impoundment of Ashwillet Brook and is located in the Thames River Drainage Basin. *Watershed*: 982 acres of mostly undeveloped woods and wetland with some residential development. The pond is fed by and drains into Ashwillet Brook which runs north into Billings Brook, a tributary of Pachaug Pond. A small wetland stream also feeds the pond from the northwest. *Shoreline*: The eastern shore is entirely developed with residences. The western shore is wooded with a few homes set back from the water's edge. *Depth*: Max 7.5 ft., Mean 5.4 ft. *Transparency*: Turbid; 5 ft. in summer, tea-colored. *Productivity*: Moderate (mesotrophic). *Bottom type*: Mud and organic ooze. *Stratification*: Does not occur due to limited depth. *Vegetation*: Submergent Eurasian water-milfoil and bladderworts are extremely dense throughout the lake. Floating mats of white water-lily, yellow pond-lily, floating-heart, floating-leaved pondweeds and water-shield fringe many areas of the shoreline.

Access: A state-owned boat launch is located on the southern shore. Facilities at the launch include a gravel ramp and parking for 8 cars. The launch is shallow and steep with a narrow approach. *Directions*: Exit 85 off I-395, Rte. 138 east, right (south) on Rte. 201 for 3.5 miles past the intersection with Rte. 165, right on Lakeside Dr. (a gravel road), launch is on right. *Shore*: Restricted to the boat launch area.

Fish: Not sampled during the lake and pond electrofishing survey.

Fishing: Is reportedly fair for largemouth bass, chain pickerel, black crappie, yellow perch, sunfish and bullhead.

Management: Statewide regulations apply for all species (see current *Connecticut Anglers' Guide*).

Boating: No special regulations (see current *Connecticut Boater's Guide*).

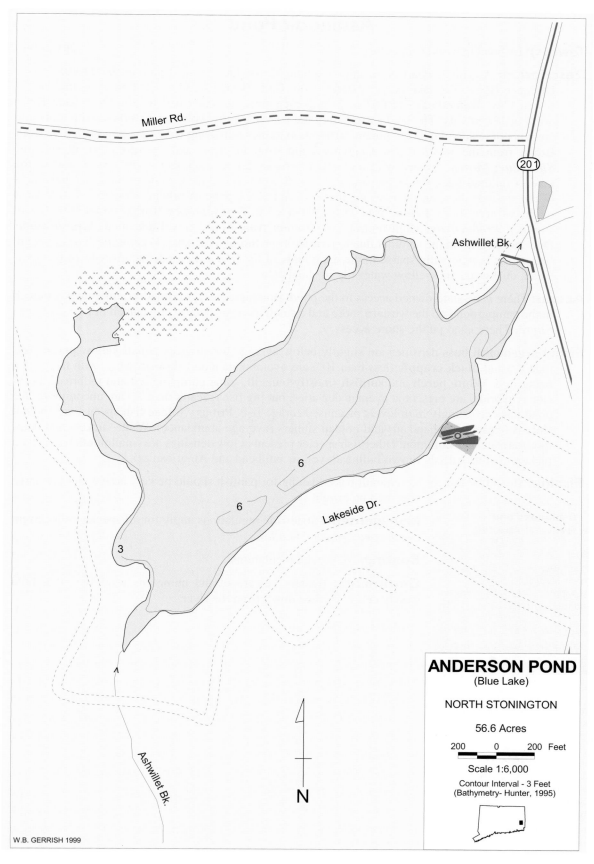

Miller Rd.

201

Ashwillet Bk.

6

6

3

Lakeside Dr.

Ashwillet Bk.

ANDERSON POND
(Blue Lake)

NORTH STONINGTON

56.6 Acres

200   0   200 Feet

Scale 1:6,000

Contour Interval - 3 Feet
(Bathymetry- Hunter, 1995)

N

W.B. GERRISH 1999

Aspinook Pond

Town(s): Lisbon/Griswold/Canterbury

301 acres

Description: Aspinook Pond is an impoundment of the Quinebaug River in the Thames River Drainage Basin. The lake proper extends from Butts Bridge Road in Canterbury to the dam at Jewett City. *Watershed*: 415,667 acres encompassing the watershed for the Quinebaug River north of Jewett City. The land surrounding the lake is mostly woods and wetland with moderate amounts of residential development. In addition to the Quinebaug River, the pond is fed by Cory Brook from the west, nearby Clayville Pond from the east, and by several small streams. *Shoreline*: Mostly wooded with a cluster of residential development in the central part of the lake. A railroad track flanks the southeastern shore for 0.75 miles. Another track parallels most of the western shore and crosses the northern end of the pond. A private campground is located on the western shore. *Depth*: Max 25 ft., Mean 8.7 ft. *Transparency*: Turbid; reduced to 3 ft. in summer. *Productivity*: High (eutrophic). *Bottom type*: Sand, gravel and mud. *Stratification*: Does not stratify in the summer due to riverine flow through the lake. *Vegetation*: Not surveyed. Vegetation is reportedly sparse in the main body of the lake with moderate growths of pickerel-weed, duckweed and yellow water-lily in shoal areas.

Access: There is no state-owned access to the pond. Boating access is limited to a private pay launch in the campground on the western shore and a small town-owned car-top launch in Bennett Cove. *Shore*: There is no public shore access.

Fish: **Largemouth bass** densities are slightly below average for all sizes. Small **yellow perch** (less than 8") and **black crappie** (less than 10") are overabundant and slow-growing, with larger fish being rare. **White perch** and **sunfish** (mostly bluegill, some pumpkinseed and redbreast, occasional hybrids) are present at average densities, but big fish (greater than 7") are uncommon. The pond has exceedingly high levels of unused forage fish. Primary forage fish species are spottail shiners (extremely abundant) and golden shiners (average abundance). White suckers and common carp are also common. Other fish species present at low densities are smallmouth bass, chain pickerel, white catfish, brown bullhead, yellow bullhead and American eel.

Fishing: Should be fair for largemouth bass. Fishing for panfish should be very active, but few large ones will be caught.

Management: Statewide regulations apply for all species (see current *Connecticut Anglers' Guide*).

Boating: No special regulations.

Comments: Boaters beware of the numerous sand flats that hold woody debris washed down from the river.

Aspinook Pond
Fish Species and Abundance

	ALL SIZES	BIG FISH	GROWTH
Gamefish			
Largemouth bass	C	C	> Avg
Smallmouth bass	R	R	
Chain pickerel	U	U	Avg
White catfish	R	R	
Panfish			
Black crappie	A	U	< Avg
White perch	C	U	Avg
Yellow perch	A	R	Slow
Brown bullhead	U	R	
Yellow bullhead	U	R	
Sunfish			
Bluegill	C	U	> Avg
Pumpkinseed	C	U	Avg
Redbreast	C	U	
Other			
Common carp	C		
Golden shiner	C		
Spottail shiner	A		
White sucker	A		
American eel	U		

A=Abundant, C=Common, U=Uncommon, R=Rare

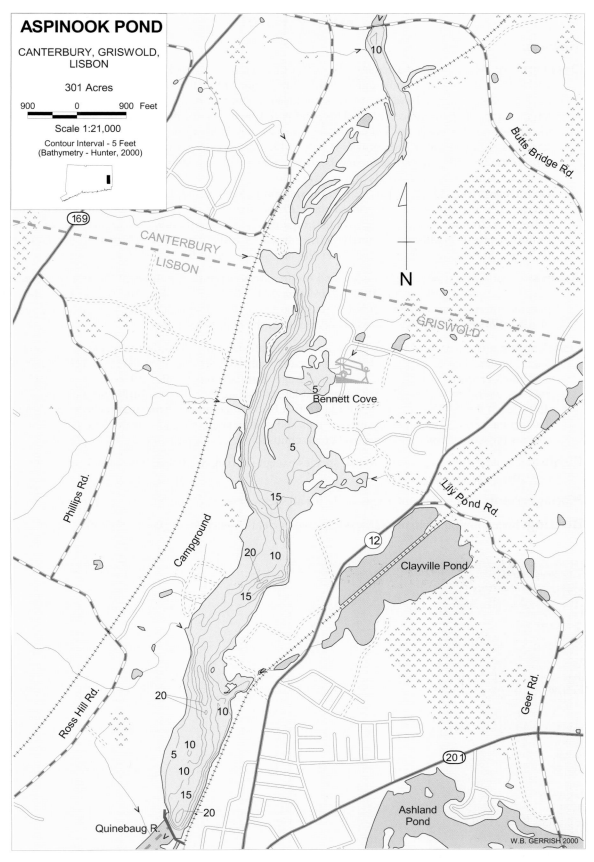

ASPINOOK POND

CANTERBURY, GRISWOLD,
LISBON

301 Acres

900   0   900   Feet

Scale 1:21,000

Contour Interval - 5 Feet
(Bathymetry - Hunter, 2000)

169

CANTERBURY

LISBON

GRISWOLD

Butts Bridge Rd.

10

N

5
Bennett Cove

5

15

Phillips Rd.

Campground

20   10

15

Lily Pond Rd.

12   Clayville Pond

Geer Rd.

20

10

Ross Hill Rd.

10

5

10

15

20

201

Ashland
Pond

Quinebaug R.

W.B. GERRISH 2000

Avery Pond

Town(s): Preston

35.7 acres

Description: Avery Pond is a natural lake within the Thames River Drainage Basin. *Watershed*: 2,015 acres of mostly woods and wetland with minor amounts of agricultural and residential development. There is, however, increasing development within the watershed associated with a large casino and conference center. The pond is fed by a marsh from the north, which is fed by the outlet stream from Amos Lake. It also receives water from bottom springs and surface runoff. It drains southeast into Indiantown Brook, which eventually flows into Poquetanuck Cove. *Shoreline*: Only the western shore has been developed with residences. To the north and east, the shoreline is undeveloped woods and marshes; to the south is extensive agricultural and marshland. *Depth*: Max 11 ft., Mean 8.2 ft. *Transparency*: Very turbid; reduced to 2.5 ft. in summer due to algal blooms and a tea-colored stain. *Productivity*: High to very high (eutrophic-highly eutrophic). *Bottom type*: Sand, gravel and organic muck. *Stratification*: Does not occur due to limited depth. *Vegetation*: Extremely dense carpets of Robbin's pondweed grow to depths of 8 ft. Scattered floating mats of white water-lily and yellow pond-lily occur along the shoreline.

Access: A state-owned boat launch is located on the northern shore. Facilities at the launch include a paved ramp and parking for 10 cars. *Directions*: Exit 85 off I-395, Rte. 164 south for 2.5 miles past the intersection with Rte. 165, left (east) on Lynn Dr., becomes a gravel road, launch at end of road. *Shore*: Public shore access is restricted to the boat launch area.

Fish: **Largemouth bass** densities are below average for all sizes. Small **chain pickerel** are very abundant, but densities of catchable size fish (greater than 13") are less than average. **Yellow perch** and **black crappie** densities are less than average. **Sunfish** (mostly bluegill, some pumpkinseed) are very abundant in the 5-7" size range, but larger fish are rare. **Brown bullhead** are at average densities in the 9-11" size range, with large fish being uncommon. **American eels** are common. The primary forage fish species are alewives and golden shiners (moderate densities). Other fish species present are spottail shiner and creek chubsucker.

Fishing: Should be fair to poor for all fish species except sunfish. Sunfish action should be fast; however, there are few large ones.

Management: Statewide regulations apply for all species (see current *Connecticut Anglers' Guide*).

Boating: Speed limit 8 mph, no water-skiing (see current *Connecticut Boater's Guide*).

Avery Pond Fish Species and Abundance	ALL SIZES	BIG FISH	GROWTH
Gamefish			
Largemouth bass	C	U	Avg
Chain pickerel	A	C	< Avg
Panfish			
Black crappie	U	U	Slow
Yellow perch	C	C	Avg
Brown bullhead	C	U	
Sunfish			
Bluegill	A	U	< Avg
Pumpkinseed	C	U	< Avg
Other			
Golden shiner	C		
Spottail shiner	U		
Alewife	C		
Creek chubsucker	C		
American eel	C		

A=Abundant, C=Common, U=Uncommon, R=Rare

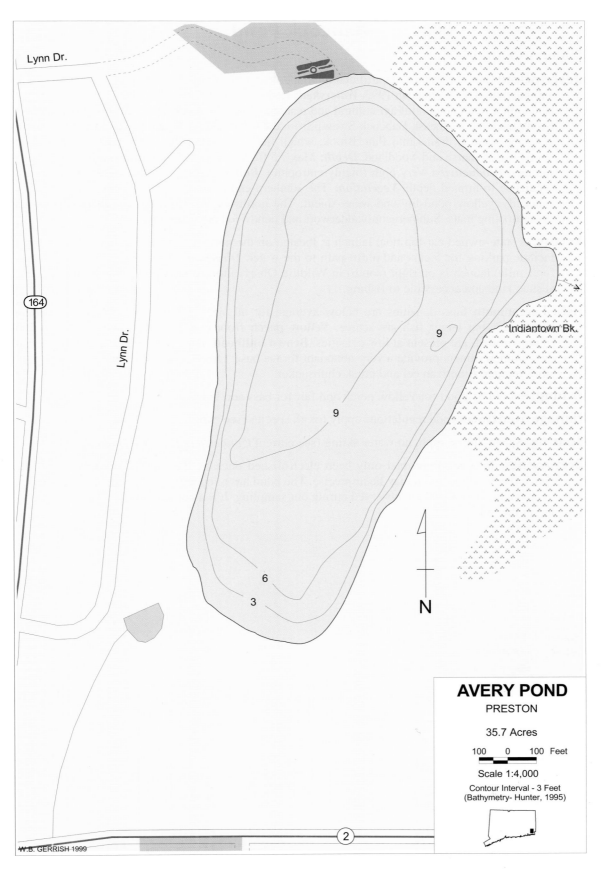

Lynn Dr.

164

Lynn Dr.

9

9

Indiantown Bk.

6

3

N

AVERY POND

PRESTON

35.7 Acres

100   0   100 Feet

Scale 1:4,000

Contour Interval - 3 Feet
(Bathymetry- Hunter, 1995)

2

W.B. GERRISH 1999

Babcock Pond

Town(s): Colchester   **119 acres**

Description: Babcock Pond is an artificial impoundment in the Connecticut River Drainage Basin. It was purchased by the State in 1993. *Watershed:* 1,839 acres of mostly undeveloped woods and wetland with a small amount of agricultural and residential development. The pond is fed by Standish Brook from the southeast, Babcock Swamp from the south and two small streams from the northwest and west. It drains into Pine Brook, which flows north into the Jeremy River. *Shoreline:* Undeveloped marsh and woodland. *Depth:* Max 7.5 ft., Mean 3.9 ft. *Transparency:* Turbid; 4 ft. in summer. *Productivity:* Very high (highly eutrophic). *Bottom type:* Mud. *Stratification:* Does not occur due to limited depth. *Vegetation:* The southern end is choked with floating mats of white water-lily, yellow pond-lily and water-shield. The northwest cove has narrow channels through dense floating mats. Submergent bladderwort and pondweed are common.

Access: A state-owned car-top boat launch is located on the northern shore. Facilities at the launch include parking for 5 cars and a dirt path to the water. *Directions:* From Rte. 149, Rte. 16 east for 1 mile, launch is on right (south) in Wildlife Observation Area. *Shore:* The entire shoreline is state land and accessible to fishing.

Fish: **Largemouth bass** densities are below average for all sizes. **Chain pickerel** very abundant below 12", but larger fish are scarce. **Yellow perch** from 6-10" are very abundant. **Sunfish** (pumpkinseed) are present at low densities. **Brown bullhead** range from 8-12" at average densities. Golden shiners provide a very abundant forage base. Other fish species present at low densities include American eel and creek chubsucker.

Fishing: Should be good for yellow perch and fair for bass and bullheads.

Management: Statewide regulations apply for all species (see current *Connecticut Anglers' Guide*).

Boating: Speed limit 8 mph, no water-skiing (see current *Connecticut Boater's Guide*).

Comments: Babcock Pond had only been electrofished once by the time of printing. Thus, the above fishery description may be imprecise. The pond has a reputation for containing trophy size bass, but no large fish were observed during our sampling. It is a popular area for waterfowl hunting in the fall.

Babcock Pond Fish Species and Abundance	ALL SIZES	BIG FISH	GROWTH
Gamefish			
Largemouth bass	C	U	> Avg
Chain pickerel	A	U	Slow
Panfish			
Yellow perch	A	C	Avg
Brown bullhead	C	C	
Sunfish			
Pumpkinseed	C	C	Fast
Other			
Golden shiner	A		
Creek chubsucker	C		
American eel	C		
A=Abundant, C=Common, U=Uncommon, R=Rare			

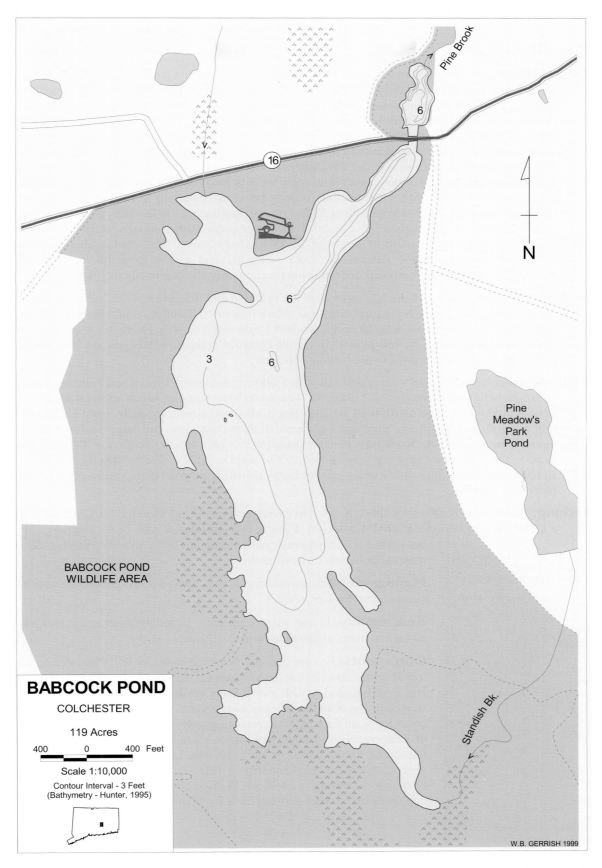

BABCOCK POND

COLCHESTER

119 Acres

400   0   400 Feet

Scale 1:10,000

Contour Interval - 3 Feet
(Bathymetry - Hunter, 1995)

BABCOCK POND
WILDLIFE AREA

Pine
Meadow's
Park
Pond

Pine Brook

Standish Bk.

16

6

6

3

6

6

N

W.B. GERRISH 1999

Ball Pond

Town(s): New Fairfield

82.5 acres

Description: Ball Pond is a natural kettle lake within the Housatonic River Drainage Basin. It is located in a region of limestone deposits known as the Marble Valley. *Watershed*: 246 acres of mostly developed residential land. It is fed entirely by bottom springs and surface runoff and drains east into Ball Pond Brook, a tributary of Candlewood Lake. *Shoreline*: Much of the shoreline is heavily developed with residences, many of which have retaining walls at the water's edge. Rte. 39 runs along the northern and eastern shores for 1 mile. *Depth*: Max 51 ft., Mean 24 ft. *Transparency*: Fair; 7 ft. in summer. *Productivity*: Moderate to high (late mesotrophic–eutrophic). *Bottom type*: Mostly organic muck with some areas of mixed gravel and sand along the shore. *Stratification*: Occurs with a thermocline forming between 16 and 30 ft. Late summer oxygen levels are marginal (5 ppm) to a depth of 20 ft. Oxygen then declines to less than 2 ppm in deeper water. *Vegetation*: Extremely dense beds of submergent coontail, Eurasian water-milfoil and southern water-nymph extend to depths of 12-15 ft. Curly-leaved pondweed is also abundant until early summer. Some patches of white water-lily and yellow pond-lily are present. Filamentous green algae and marl deposits coat much of the submergent aquatic plants.

Access: A state-owned boat launch is located on the southern end. Facilities at the launch include a gravel ramp, parking for 8 cars and chemical toilets (seasonal). Launch conditions are shallow. *Directions*: Exit 5 off I-84, Rte. 39 north, proceed 1 mile north of New Fairfield town line, right (east) on Gillotti Rd., bear left at fork onto Ball Pond Rd., launch is 100 yds. on left. *Shore*: Public shore access is limited to the boat launch area.

Fish: Ball Pond is stocked each spring and fall with 8,000 catchable size **brown** and **rainbow trout**. A narrow band of cool, oxygenated water persists through late summer which allows some brown trout to holdover. **Largemouth bass** are abundant in all size classes, especially in the 15-20" size range. **Sunfish** (bluegill and pumpkinseed) are extremely abundant, but large sunfish (greater than 7") are uncommon. **Rock bass** are abundant, but fish over 8" are uncommon. **Brown bullhead** in the 9-12" size range are very abundant. The pond has a low-density alewife and golden shiner forage base. Other fish species present at low densities are grass carp, yellow perch, white perch and goldfish.

Fishing: Should be excellent for bullheads, good to excellent for bass and good for stocked trout with a chance for an occasional holdover brown. Fishing for sunfish and rock bass should be very active, but few large ones will be caught. Heavy submergent vegetation may make fishing difficult at times.

Management: Statewide regulations apply for all species (see current *Connecticut Anglers' Guide*).

Boating: Vessels with motors attached, including electric, are prohibited (see current *Connecticut Boater's Guide*).

Comments: Fishing pressure is probably low in Ball Pond due to the motor restriction. It has good potential for trophy bass management. However, bass and sunfish growth rates are slow and rock bass appear to be stunted. It is possible that heavy submergent vegetation provides excessive cover for small fish, thereby preventing bass from finding them. Reduction of submergent vegetation may improve angling quality. Grass carp were introduced into the pond in 1997 and may have an effect on submergent vegetation, water quality and fishing. Effects of grass carp introduction will be monitored through various studies (see discussion on grass carp in section on Potential Management Tools for Warmwater Fisheries).

Ball Pond
Fish Species and Abundance

	ALL SIZES	BIG FISH	GROWTH
Gamefish			
Largemouth bass	A	A	Slow
Brown trout	A	U	
Rainbow trout	C		
Panfish			
White perch	R	R	> Avg
Yellow perch	R	R	Fast
Brown bullhead	A	A	
Sunfish			
Bluegill	A	U	Slow
Pumpkinseed	A	U	< Avg
Rock bass	A	U	< Slow
Other			
Golden shiner	U		< Avg
Goldfish	C		
Grass carp	U		
Alewife	C		Avg

A=Abundant, C=Common, U=Uncommon, R=Rare

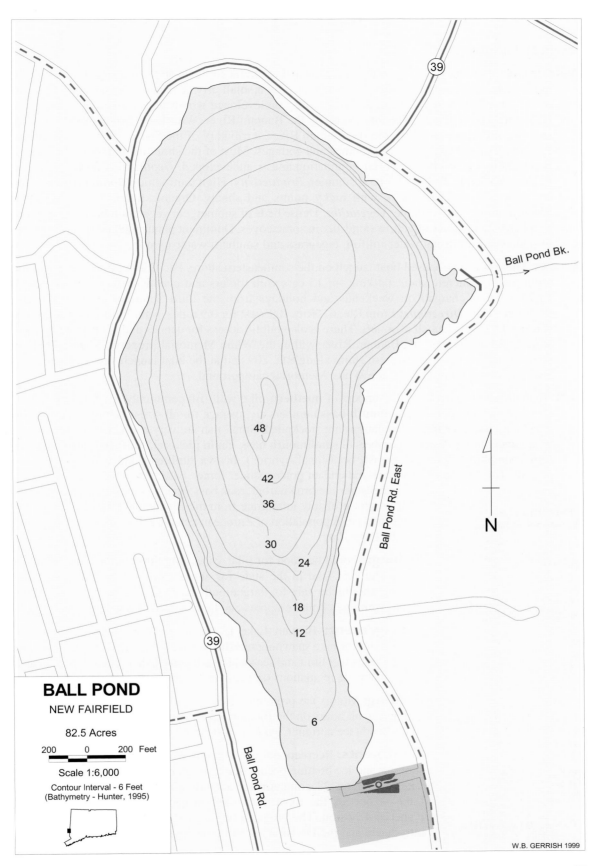

48

42

36

30

24

18

12

6

Ball Pond Bk.

Ball Pond Rd. East

Ball Pond Rd.

39

39

N

BALL POND

NEW FAIRFIELD

82.5 Acres

200   0   200 Feet

Scale 1:6,000

Contour Interval - 6 Feet
(Bathymetry - Hunter, 1995)

W.B. GERRISH 1999

Bantam Lake

Town(s): Litchfield/Morris

947 acres

Description: Bantam Lake is in the Housatonic River Drainage Basin and is the largest natural lake in the state. The original water level was raised by a small private dam on the northwestern end of the lake. *Watershed*: 20,962 acres of mostly undeveloped woods and wetland with moderate residential development. The lake is fed by the Bantam River, Whittlesey Brook, and two small streams. It drains northwest into the Bantam River, a tributary of the Shepaug River. *Shoreline*: Partially wooded with numerous homes and cottages. Most of the shoreline to the north and east is owned by the White Memorial Foundation and is undeveloped. *Depth*: Max 26 ft., Mean 16 ft. *Transparency*: Turbid; 2-3 ft. in summer. *Productivity*: High (eutrophic). *Bottom type*: A variety of sand, gravel or muck with rocky points and shoals. Organic muck in deeper water. *Stratification*: Not available. *Vegetation*: Dense beds of submergent vegetation occur throughout shoal areas with areas of yellow pond-lily in some coves. Dominant plants include several species of pondweed, Eurasian water-milfoil, tapegrass and southern water-nymph.

Access: There is a state-leased boat launch on the southeastern shore. Facilities at the launch include a ramp with concrete slabs, parking for 15 cars with trailers and chemical toilets (seasonal). A parking fee is charged on weekends and holidays from the third Saturday in April through Columbus Day. *Directions*: From Rte. 61, Rte. 109 west for 0.9 miles, right (north) on East Shore Rd. for 0.5 miles, launch is on left. There is also public access for canoes and small car-top boats at several locations on the Bantam River within the White Memorial property. *Shore*: There is some access on the southwestern shore along Rte. 209 and at the boat launch site. Campers may also fish off of Point Folly at the White Memorial campground.

Fish: Bantam Lake contains good numbers of **northern pike** with fish commonly reaching weights of 10-15 pounds or more. **Largemouth bass** numbers are average for all sizes. **Yellow perch**, **white perch** and **black crappie** populations are stockpiled. Small fish are very abundant, but those over 9" are uncommon. Average numbers of **smallmouth bass**, **chain pickerel**, **sunfish** (mostly bluegill, some pumpkinseed and redbreast, occasional hybrids), **brown bullhead** and white suckers are present. The lake has a moderately abundant golden shiner forage base. Other fish species present at low densities are brown trout, rock bass, banded killifish. The few brown trout present probably immigrate from the Bantam River because the lake is not stocked. A population of European tench has become established and may be expanding.

Fishing: Should be good for pike, especially through the ice. Currently, this is the best lake in the state for anglers to catch a really big pike. Fishing should be fair for largemouth bass. Good numbers of yellow perch, white perch and crappies can be caught, but few large ones.

Management: Bantam Lake is managed for northern pike through maintenance of pike spawning marshes on the Bantam River and by special length limit, creel limit and seasonal restrictions. Other species are managed under statewide regulations (see current *Connecticut Anglers' Guide*).

Boating: Motors are prohibited from 11 p.m. to 5 a.m. on Bantam Lake and during all hours on the Bantam River between the lake and the inlet to Little Pond (see current *Connecticut Boater's Guide*).

Comments: Recreational use is high. Water skiing is popular during summer and ice boating occurs during winter. A popular bass tournament lake, averaging 22 competitions annually. The pike fishery in Bantam Lake is one of the most successful projects ever undertaken by the Fisheries Division. The program began in 1971 when the first pike were introduced and the Division began to manage one small, experimental ▼

Bantam Lake
Fish Species and Abundance

	ALL SIZES	BIG FISH	GROWTH
Gamefish			
Largemouth bass	C	C	Avg
Smallmouth bass	C	U	< Slow
Brown trout	R	R	
Northern pike	C	C	Fast
Chain pickerel	C	C	Avg
Panfish			
Black crappie	A	U	< Avg
White perch	A	U	Stunted
Yellow perch	A	U	< Avg
Brown bullhead	C	C	
Sunfish			
Bluegill	C	U	Avg
Pumpkinseed	C	U	> Avg
Redbreast	U	U	Avg
Rock bass	R	R	Avg
Other			
Golden shiner	A		Avg
Banded killifish	U		
White sucker	C		
Tench	U		

A=Abundant, C=Common, U=Uncommon, R=Rare

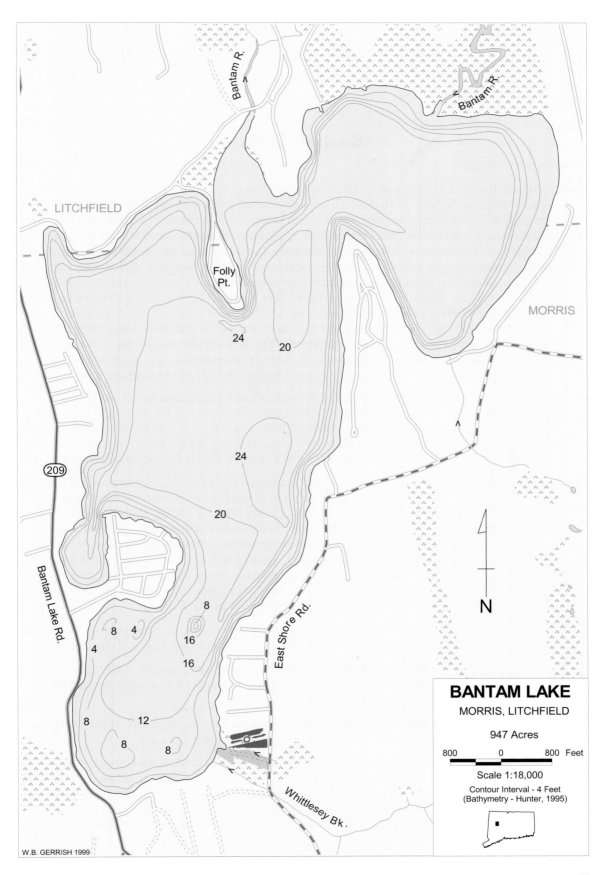

LITCHFIELD

Bantam R.

Bantam R.

Folly
Pt.

MORRIS

24

20

24

20

8

8   4

16

4

16

8

12

8

8

Bantam Lake Rd.

209

East Shore Rd.

Whittlesey Bk.

N

BANTAM LAKE

MORRIS, LITCHFIELD

947 Acres

800   0   800 Feet

Scale 1:18,000

Contour Interval - 4 Feet
(Bathymetry - Hunter, 1995)

W.B. GERRISH 1999

spawning marsh. In the mid-1980s this marsh was expanded and a second marsh was added. By the early 1990s, an impressive pike fishery had developed in Bantam. Ten pound pike are now commonly caught and some over 20 pounds have been taken (lake record 28.5 lb.). Currently, anglers spend over 10,000 hours fishing for pike and catch more than 2,000 pike during a typical ice fishing season alone.

Bashan Lake

Town(s): East Haddam

273 acres

Description: Bashan Lake is a natural lake within the Connecticut River Drainage Basin. Water levels have been raised by a 25 ft. dam. Historically, the lake was controlled by the Moodus Water Company and underwent moderate water level fluctuations. The State of Connecticut now owns the controlling rights to the lake. *Watershed*: 1,257 acres of mostly wooded land with moderate to light levels of residential development and agricultural land. The lake is fed by five small tributary streams, surface runoff and bottom springs. It drains northeast directly into Moodus Reservoir. *Shoreline*: Most of the shoreline is developed with cottages and permanent residences. *Depth*: Max 47 ft., Mean 17 ft. *Transparency*: Very clear, 19 ft. in summer. *Productivity*: Low (oligotrophic). *Bottom type*: Sand, gravel, coarse rubble and boulders. Muck in deeper water. *Stratification*: Occurs with a thermocline forming between 26 and 36 ft. Late-summer oxygen levels remain marginal (4-5 ppm) to a depth of 33 ft. then decline to less than 1 ppm in deeper water. *Vegetation*: Submerged vegetation is sparse throughout the lake except in the shallow cove areas where waterweed, water-milfoil (low and variable-leaved) and bladderworts are common.

Access: A state-owned boat launch is located at the southern end. Facilities at the launch include a gravel ramp, parking for 10 cars and chemical toilets (seasonal). Access to the lake is through a narrow rocky channel. *Directions*: Take Rte. 149 south from Rte. 16 for 2.5 miles, left (south) on Falls Bashan Rd. for 1 mile, left (east) on Haddam-Colchester Tnpk. for 0.3 miles, right on Bashan Rd. for 1 mile, right on Lakeside Dr., launch is 0.9 miles on right. *Shore*: Restricted to boat launch area.

Fish: Bashan Lake is stocked during the spring and fall with 4,000 catchable size **brown** and **rainbow trout**. Holdover trout are rare due to a limited area of suitable deep-water habitat. **Largemouth bass** are common with densities of larger fish (greater than 12") being slightly above average. **Smallmouth bass** densities are higher than average for small fish (less than 12") and average for larger ones. **Chain pickerel** densities are average for all sizes. **Yellow perch** up to 11" are common. Large **sunfish** (8-9", mostly bluegill, occasional pumpkinseed and redbreast) are particularly abundant in the lake. Forage fish species (golden shiner and banded killifish) abundance is low. Other species present at low densities are black crappie and brown bullhead.

Fishing: Should be excellent for large bluegills; good for trout, largemouth bass and yellow perch; and fair for smallmouth bass and chain pickerel.

Management: Bass Management Lake; special slot length and creel limits on bass. Statewide regulations apply for all other species (see current *Connecticut Anglers' Guide*).

Boating: Speed limit 35 mph during the day, 8 mph from 9:00 p.m. to 8:00 a.m. (see current *Connecticut Boater's Guide*).

Comments: Bashan Lake contains excellent smallmouth bass habitat. However, the smallmouth population is stockpiled below 12" with fish growing too slowly to adequately replenish the fish that are harvested by angling. Special regulations should improve fishing by protecting larger bass and allowing anglers to harvest overabundant small bass.

Bashan Lake
Fish Species and Abundance

	ALL SIZES	BIG FISH	GROWTH
Gamefish			
Largemouth bass	C	C	> Avg
Smallmouth bass	C	C	Slow
Brown trout	C	R	
Rainbow trout	A		
Chain pickerel	C	C	Avg
Panfish			
Black crappie	U	U	Fast
Yellow perch	C	C	< Avg
Brown bullhead	U	U	
Sunfish			
Bluegill	A	A	> Avg
Pumpkinseed	C	C	> Avg
Redbreast	U	U	< Avg
Other			
Golden shiner	U		
Banded killifish	U		

A=Abundant, C=Common, U=Uncommon, R=Rare

BASHAN LAKE
EAST HADDAM

273 Acres

Scale 1:13,000

400   0   400 Feet

Contour Interval - 3 Feet
(Bathymetry - DEP & USGS 1987)

Upper Moodus Reservoir

Bashan Rd.

Lakeside Dr.

Smith Rd.

Alger Rd.

To Rte. 151

Haddam Colchester Tnpk.

W.B. GERRISH 1999

N

Batterson Park Pond

Town(s): Farmington/New Britain

Description: Batterson Park Pond is an artificial impoundment within the Connecticut River Drainage Basin. It was constructed in the late 1800s and is located within Batterson Park. The park and pond are owned by the City of Hartford. *Watershed:* 2,652 acres of mostly urbanized and industrial land with some undeveloped wetland and woods to the south. The pond is fed by Bass Brook and two other small streams. It drains northeast into Bass Brook, which feeds into Piper Brook, a tributary of the South Branch Park River. *Shoreline:* The western shore is low brush and marsh with a beach on the northern end. The eastern shoreline is wooded between the water and the railroad tracks. There is no residential development. *Depth:* Max 20 ft., Mean 14 ft. *Transparency:* Turbid; 2.5 ft. in summer. Algal blooms color the water green. *Productivity:* High to very high (eutrophic-highly eutrophic). *Bottom type:* Rock, gravel and mud. *Stratification:* Partially stratifies with a temperature gradient forming between 6 and 9 ft. Late summer oxygen levels are reduced to less than 4 ppm at 9 ft. and deeper. *Vegetation:* Submergent vegetation is generally sparse with a few small areas of moderately dense coverage that extend to depths of 8 ft. Pondweed, Eurasian water-milfoil and water-nymph are the dominant species.

Access: A state-leased boat launch is located on the southern shore. Facilities at the launch include a paved ramp, and parking for 25 cars with trailers. *Directions:* Exit 37 off I-84, south on Finneman Rd. for 0.4 miles, left (east) on Alexander Rd., launch is 0.2 miles on left. *Shore:* Most of the shoreline is accessible to public fishing.

Fish: **Largemouth bass** are common with densities of 14-19" fish being higher than average. **Yellow perch**, **black crappie** and **white perch** are abundant, but stockpiled below 9" with larger fish being uncommon. Densities of small **sunfish** (mostly bluegill, some pumpkinseed) are average, but larger (greater than 7") sunfish are uncommon. **Rock bass** and **brown bullhead** are present at less than average densities. **American eels** are common. The pond has low forage fish densities that include golden shiner, goldfish and banded killifish. Other fish species present are chain pickerel, white sucker, tessellated darter and common carp.

Fishing: Should be fair to good for largemouth bass and fair to poor for other species. Panfish are plentiful, but don't expect big ones.

Management: Annual walleye stocking began here in 2001. Statewide regulations apply for all species (see current *Connecticut Anglers' Guide*).

Boating: Gas motors prohibited (see current *Connecticut Boater's Guide*).

Comments: Few bass tournaments are held here. A fairly healthy bass population and good facilities indicate that the lake could accommodate more of these events.

Batterson Park Pond
Fish Species and Abundance

	ALL SIZES	BIG FISH	GROWTH
Gamefish			
Largemouth bass	C	C	Fast
Chain pickerel	R	R	
Panfish			
Black crappie	A	C	Slow
White perch	A	C	< Avg
Yellow perch	A	U	< Slow
Brown bullhead	C	U	
Sunfish			
Bluegill	C	U	Fast
Pumpkinseed	C	U	> Avg
Rock bass	C	C	> Avg
Other			
Tessellated darter	U		
Common carp	U		
Golden shiner	U		< Avg
Goldfish	U		
Banded killifish	U		
White sucker	C		
American eel	C		

A=Abundant, C=Common, U=Uncommon, R=Rare

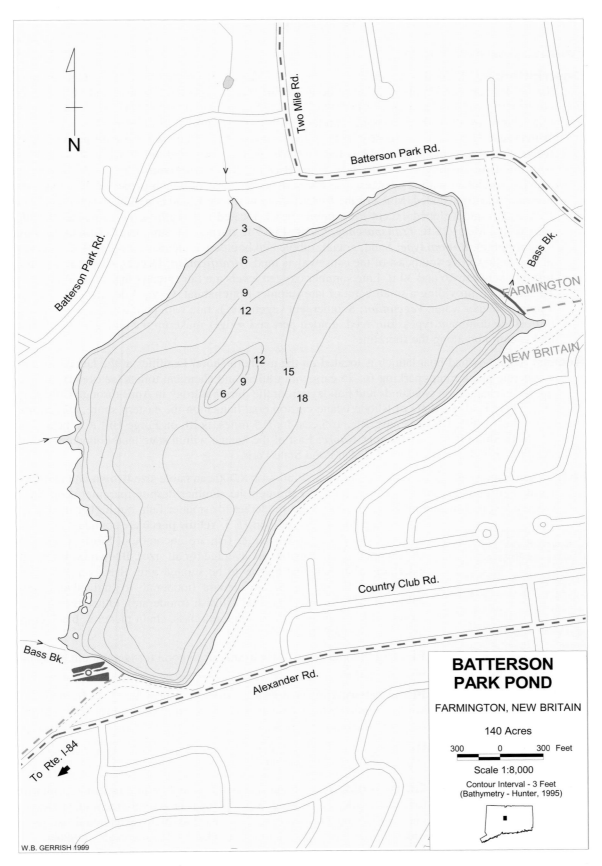

3
6
9
12

12
9
6

15
18

Two Mile Rd.

Batterson Park Rd.

Bass Bk.

FARMINGTON

NEW BRITAIN

Batterson Park Rd.

Country Club Rd.

Bass Bk.

Alexander Rd.

To Rte. I-84

W.B. GERRISH 1999

BATTERSON PARK POND

FARMINGTON, NEW BRITAIN

140 Acres

300   0   300 Feet

Scale 1:8,000

Contour Interval - 3 Feet
(Bathymetry - Hunter, 1995)

Beach Pond

Town(s): Voluntown/Exeter (RI)   **372 acres**

Description: Beach Pond is a natural lake within the Thames River Drainage Basin that straddles the border between Connecticut and Rhode Island. Water levels have been raised 10 ft. by the construction of a concrete dam. A causeway (Rte 165) separates a shallow eastern cove from the main body of the lake. Clearance under the bridge is insufficient for boats to navigate. *Watershed*: 3,002 acres of mostly undeveloped woods and wetland with a small percentage of residential development. The lake is fed by three small streams and drains west via a spillway over the dam, creating the headwaters of the Pachaug River. *Shoreline*: The southern shore is heavily developed with residences. The northern shore, some of which is part of Pachaug State Forest, is mostly wooded. Much of the eastern shore in Rhode Island is part of Beach Pond State Park and is undeveloped except for a public beach located just north of the causeway. *Depth*: Max 63 ft., Mean 25 ft. *Transparency*: Clear; 13-15 ft. during late summer. *Productivity*: Low (oligotrophic). *Bottom type*: Sand, gravel, rubble and boulders in the deeper areas. The substrate in the shallow cove southeast of the causeway is mud. *Stratification*: Occurs with a thermocline forming between 16 and 30 ft. Late summer oxygen levels are fair (greater than 6 ppm) between 16 and 23 ft., providing a small band of late summer trout habitat. Oxygen declines to less than 1 ppm in deeper water. *Vegetation*: Submergent vegetation is rare with pondweed and low water-milfoil the dominant types. Bur-reed, golden pert and sedges make up the emergent vegetation that is common along the shoreline.

Access: A state-owned boat launch is located on the northern shore. Facilities at the launch include a concrete plank ramp, parking for 25 cars with trailers and chemical toilets (seasonal). A parking fee is charged on weekends and holidays from the third Saturday in April through Columbus Day. There is also a State of Rhode Island car-top boat launch on the eastern shore. *Directions*: Exit 85 off I-395, Rte. 138 east, Rte. 165 east for 0.5 miles, north on Forge Hill Rd., bear right on North Shore Rd. to access area. *Shore*: East of the launch within state land boundaries, from the dam or within Rhode Island Beach Pond State Park.

Fish: Beach Pond is stocked during the spring and fall with 8,000 catchable size **brown** and **rainbow trout**. Fair numbers of brown trout holdover through the summer despite marginal deep-water oxygen levels. **Largemouth bass** densities are moderate for smaller fish, but higher than average for large ones (greater than 15"). **Yellow perch** are abundant in smaller sizes (less than 8"), but larger fish are uncommon. **Sunfish** (bluegill and pumpkinseed) densities are average for all sizes. **Brown bullhead** are extremely abundant, but appear to be stunted with fish over 10" being uncommon. Forage fishes are alewife (moderate to high abundance), golden shiner (low) and banded killifish (moderate). Other fish species present at low densities are smallmouth bass, chain pickerel, black crappie and white catfish.

Fishing: Should be good for trout, fair to good for largemouth bass, and fair for sunfish.

Management: Annual walleye stocking began here in 2001. This is a border pond. Some Rhode Island regulations apply (see current *Connecticut Anglers' Guide*).

Boating: No water skiing is allowed near the dam (see current *Connecticut Boater's Guide*).

Comments: Beach Pond withstands heavy fishing pressure, primarily for trout, in the early spring. It is a popular bass tournament lake, averaging 12 tournaments per year. The lake has high recreational use (e.g., water skiing) during the summer months. Ice fishing is also popular.

Beach Pond
Fish Species and Abundance

	ALL SIZES	BIG FISH	GROWTH
Gamefish			
Largemouth bass	C	C	Avg
Smallmouth bass	R	R	
Brook trout	U		Slow
Brown trout	C	U	Avg
Rainbow trout	C		Slow
Chain pickerel	U	U	Fast
White catfish	U	U	
Panfish			
Black crappie	R	R	< Avg
Yellow perch	C	U	Avg
Brown bullhead	A	U	
Sunfish			
Bluegill	C	C	Avg
Pumpkinseed	C	C	< Avg
Other			
Golden shiner	U		
Banded killifish	C		
Alewife	C		Slow

A=Abundant, C=Common, U=Uncommon, R=Rare

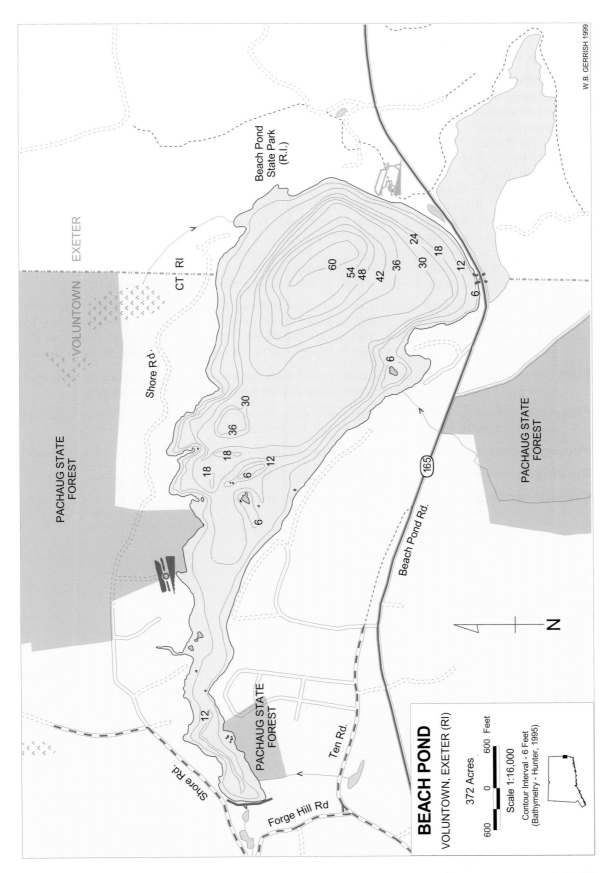

BEACH POND

VOLUNTOWN, EXETER (RI)

372 Acres

Scale 1:16,000

Contour Interval - 6 Feet
(Bathymetry - Hunter, 1995)

600   0   600   Feet

N

W.B. GERRISH 1999

Beach Pond State Park
(R.I.)

EXETER

VOLUNTOWN

CT   RI

Shore Rd.

PACHAUG STATE
FOREST

PACHAUG STATE
FOREST

PACHAUG STATE
FOREST

Beach Pond Rd.

165

Ten Rd.

Forge Hill Rd

Shore Rd.

60
54
48
42
36
30
24
18
12
6

6

30
36
18
12
18
6
6

12

12

Beachdale Pond

Town(s): Voluntown   **45.9 acres**

Description: Beachdale Pond is an impoundment on the Pachaug River in the Thames River
Drainage Basin. *Watershed:* 17,991 acres. The surrounding land is almost entirely undeveloped
woods and wetland. In addition to the Pachaug River, the pond is fed by Denison Brook from the
southeast and Mount Misery Brook from the north. It drains to the southwest into Sawmill Pond
via the Pachaug River. *Shoreline:* Most of the shoreline north of the dam is within the Pachaug
State Forest. There are a few homes south of the dam. The western shore is forested, whereas the
eastern shore is a combination of forest and marshland. *Depth:* Max 10.5 ft., Mean 3.5 ft.
Transparency: Turbid; reduced to 3.7 ft. in summer by a tea-colored stain. *Productivity:* High
(eutrophic). *Bottom type:* Mostly gravel and rubble with organic muck in the channel.
Stratification: Does not occur due to limited depth. *Vegetation:* Extremely dense during summer.
A narrow channel that follows the old riverbed cuts through dense floating, submergent and
emergent vegetation providing access from the boat launch to the dam at the southern end of the
pond. Submergent species include pondweeds, bladderworts, waterweed, water-marigold and
coontail. Floating mats of white water-lily and yellow pond-lily are also present.

Access: A state-owned boat launch is located on the Pachaug River where it enters the pond on the
eastern shore. Facilities at the launch include a gravel ramp, disabled-access area for fishing, and
parking for 20 cars with trailers. *Directions:* Exit 85 off I-395, Rte. 138 east, left (north) on Rte.
49, launch is 1 mile on right. *Shore:* Pachaug State Forest borders most of the northern shore.

Fish: Not sampled during the lake and pond electrofishing survey. Although not directly stocked, **trout**
move into Beachdale Pond during the spring and fall from Pachaug River stockings.

Fishing: Is reportedly fair for trout, largemouth bass, yellow perch and bullheads. Fishing is difficult
during summer months due to dense aquatic vegetation.

Management: Statewide regulations apply for all species (see current *Connecticut Anglers' Guide*).

Boating: Speed limit 8 mph, no water-skiing (see current *Connecticut Boater's Guide*).

Comments: Boaters should beware of boulders in the river channels on the northern and eastern inlets.

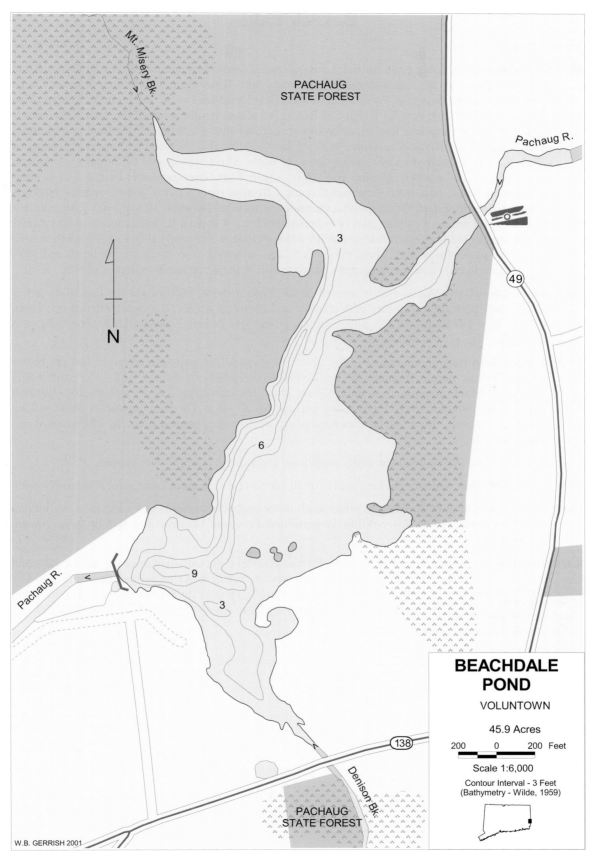

BEACHDALE POND

VOLUNTOWN

45.9 Acres

200　　0　　200　Feet

Scale 1:6,000

Contour Interval - 3 Feet
(Bathymetry - Wilde, 1959)

W.B. GERRISH 2001

PACHAUG
STATE FOREST

PACHAUG R.

Pachaug R.

Mt. Misery Bk.

Denison Bk.

PACHAUG
STATE FOREST

N

49

138

3

6

9

3

Beseck Lake

Town(s): Middlefield   **116 acres**

Description: Beseck Lake is an artificial impoundment in the Connecticut River Drainage Basin that was created by the construction of a masonry dam. **Watershed:** 1,311 acres of mostly agricultural land to the east, and wooded but densely developed land to the west (on the eastern slope of Beseck Mountain). Powder Ridge Ski Resort is located 1 mile south of the pond. The lake is fed by bottom springs and five small brooks and drains east into Ellen Doyle Brook, a tributary of the Coginchaug River. **Shoreline:** Most of the shoreline is dominated by residences, many of which have permanent docks extending into the water. The southern end of the lake is undeveloped and partially wooded. **Depth:** Max 26 ft., Mean 12 ft. **Transparency:** Fair; 6.5 ft. in summer. **Productivity:** Moderate (late mesotrophic). **Bottom type:** Coarse gravel, rubble, boulders and mud. **Stratification:** Occurs with a thermocline forming between 10 and 16 ft. Late summer oxygen levels are poor to marginal (4-6 ppm) between 10 and 12 ft. and reduced to less than 1 ppm in deeper water. **Vegetation:** Eurasian water-milfoil is extremely dense at the southern end of the lake to depths of 9 ft. Some pondweeds and stonewort also occur. At the north end, submergent pondweeds and water-nymphs are common in localized areas to depths of 9 ft.

Access: A state-owned boat launch is located on the eastern shore. Facilities at the launch include a paved ramp, parking for 20 cars with trailers, and chemical toilets (seasonal). **Directions:** From Rte. 66, Rte. 147 south for 1.5 miles, launch is on right (west). **Shore:** Public shore access is restricted to the boat launch area.

Fish: Largemouth bass are abundant in the 12-15" size range, but densities of larger fish are below average. **Yellow perch** (less than 8") are severely stockpiled and stunted with large perch being rare. Small **black crappie** (less than 9") are abundant, but large fish are uncommon. **Sunfish** (bluegill and pumpkinseed) densities are average for all sizes. The lake contains a dense golden shiner forage base. Other fish species present are white perch, banded killifish, white sucker and American eel.

Fishing: Should be fair to good for largemouth bass and sunfish, and fair for crappie.

Management: Statewide regulations apply for all species (see current *Connecticut Anglers' Guide*).

Boating: A speed limit of 8 mph is in effect at all times except between June 15 and the first Sunday after Labor day when water-skiing is permitted between 11 a.m. and 6 p.m. (see current *Connecticut Boater's Guide*).

Comments: Crowded on weekends. Beseck Lake was only electrofished once during the lake and pond survey. Thus, the above fishery description may be imprecise. The lake has undergone severe (6 ft.) winter drawdowns for weed control and dock maintenance that may have adversely affected fish and other aquatic animals.

Beseck Lake Fish Species and Abundance	ALL SIZES	BIG FISH	GROWTH
Gamefish			
Largemouth bass	A	U	Avg
Panfish			
Black crappie	A	U	Avg
White perch	R	R	
Yellow perch	A	R	< Slow
Sunfish			
Bluegill	C	C	> Avg
Pumpkinseed	C	C	Avg
Other			
Golden shiner	A		
Banded killifish	U		
White sucker	U		
American eel	U		
A=Abundant, C=Common, U=Uncommon, R=Rare			

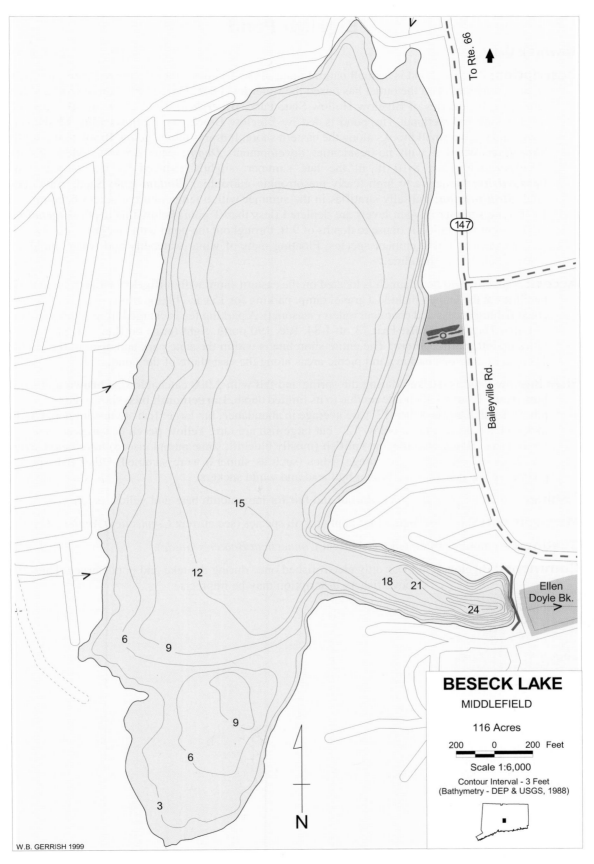

To Rte. 66

147

Baileyville Rd.

Ellen
Doyle Bk.

15

12

18   21

24

6
9

9

6

3

BESECK LAKE

MIDDLEFIELD

116 Acres

200   0   200 Feet

Scale 1:6,000

Contour Interval - 3 Feet
(Bathymetry - DEP & USGS, 1988)

N

W.B. GERRISH 1999

Bigelow Pond

Town(s): Union   **24.5 acres**

Description: Bigelow Pond is a small natural pond in the Thames River Drainage Basin. An earthen dam constructed on the outlet has raised the water level 8 ft. The pond is state-owned and lies within the boundaries of Bigelow Hollow State Park. *Watershed*: 3,815 acres; mostly undeveloped woods and wetland. The pond is fed by Bigelow Brook, which flows from Mashapaug Lake, and by two small brooks along the eastern shore. It drains into Bigelow Brook to the south. *Shoreline*: Wooded with no residential development. *Depth*: Max 15.4 ft., Mean 7.5 ft. *Transparency*: Fair; 8-10 ft. in the late summer; slightly reduced by tea-colored stain. *Productivity*: Moderate to high (early mesotrophic–eutrophic). *Bottom type*: Sand, gravel and mud. *Stratification*: Partially stratifies in the summer with a temperature gradient beginning at 10 ft. Late summer oxygen levels are depleted (less than 1 ppm) below this depth. *Vegetation*: Submergent vegetation is dense to depths of 9 ft. throughout the pond with tapegrass, pondweeds and bladderworts as dominant species. Floating mats of white water-lily and water-shield are scattered along the shoreline.

Access: A state-owned boat launch is located on the eastern shore within Bigelow Hollow State Park. Facilities at the launch include a gravel ramp, parking for 15 cars, hiking trails, picnic tables, disabled fishing access and chemical toilets (seasonal). A parking fee is charged from Memorial Day to Labor Day. *Directions*: Exit 73 off I-84, Rte. 190 north, right (east) on Rte. 171, park is 1.3 miles on left (north). *Shore*: The entire shoreline is within the state park and open to the public. There are numerous parking and picnic areas along the east shore of the pond.

Fish: Bigelow Pond is stocked during the spring and fall with 2,000 catchable size **brown** and **rainbow trout**. Trout do not holdover due to its limited depth. **Largemouth bass** show signs of stockpiling. Small bass (less than 12") are average in abundance, but larger fish are uncommon. **Chain pickerel** are also common below 12", but large fish are rare. **Yellow perch** densities are average for all sizes. **Black crappie** and **sunfish** (mostly bluegill, some pumpkinseed) have below average densities. No soft-rayed forage fishes (such as shiners) were sampled. Other fish species present at low densities are brown bullhead and white suckers.

Fishing: Should be good for stocked trout and fair for largemouth bass and yellow perch.

Management: Statewide regulations apply for all species (see current *Connecticut Anglers' Guide*).

Boating: Gas motors prohibited (see current *Connecticut Boater's Guide*).

Comments: Bigelow Pond was only electrofished once during the lake and pond survey. Thus, the above fishery description may be imprecise.

Bigelow Pond Fish Species and Abundance			
	ALL SIZES	BIG FISH	GROWTH
Gamefish			
Largemouth bass	C	C	< Avg
Brown trout	C		
Rainbow trout	A		
Chain pickerel	C	R	
Panfish			
Black crappie	U	U	
Yellow perch	C	C	> Avg
Brown bullhead	U	U	
Sunfish			
Bluegill	C	C	Avg
Pumpkinseed	C	U	
Other			
White sucker	U		
A=Abundant, C=Common, U=Uncommon, R=Rare			

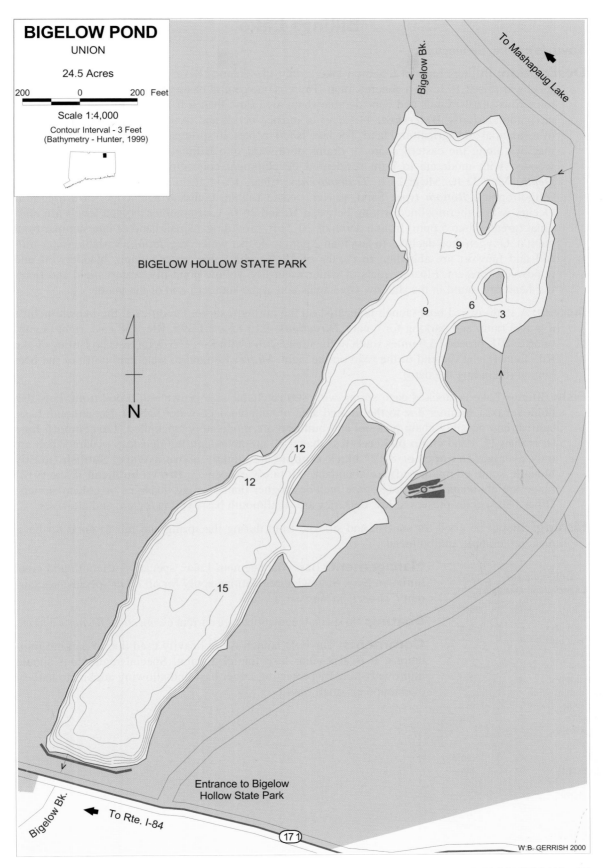

BIGELOW POND

UNION

24.5 Acres

200   0   200   Feet

Scale 1:4,000

Contour Interval - 3 Feet
(Bathymetry - Hunter, 1999)

BIGELOW HOLLOW STATE PARK

Bigelow Bk.

To Mashapaug Lake

9

9   6   3

12

12

15

N

Entrance to Bigelow
Hollow State Park

Bigelow Bk.

To Rte. I-84

171

W.B. GERRISH 2000

Billings Lake

Town(s): North Stonington

97.4 acres

Description: Billings Lake is a natural lake within the Thames River Drainage Basin. The water level was raised 10 ft. by a concrete dam. There is one central basin of deep water surrounded by numerous small islands and considerable shoal area (less than 6 ft.) which include some rocky navigation hazards. *Watershed:* 448 acres of mostly woods and wetland with a small percentage of residential and agricultural land. The lake is fed by bottom springs and surface runoff from two marshes along the eastern shore. It drains northward into Billings Brook. *Shoreline:* Mostly wooded with moderate to light residential development concentrated on the western shore. *Depth:* Max 33 ft., Mean 14 ft. *Transparency:* Clear; 12-15 ft. in summer. *Productivity:* Low (oligotrophic). *Bottom type:* Sand, gravel, coarse rubble, boulders and ledge. *Stratification:* Occurs with a thermocline forming between 16 and 26 ft. Late summer oxygen levels are marginal (greater than 5 ppm) from a depth of 20-23 ft. providing a small band of late summer trout habitat. Oxygen then declines to less than 2 ppm in deeper water. *Vegetation:* Variable water-milfoil and fanwort are abundant to depths of 12 ft. with some water-nymph, bladderwort and pondweeds present. Floating mats of white water-lily, yellow pond-lily, water-shield and floating-heart are found in the shallow cove areas and at the southern end of the pond.

Access: A state-owned boat launch is located on the northern shore. Facilities at the launch include a gravel ramp and parking for 6 cars. *Directions:* Exit 85 off I-395, Rte. 138 east, right (south) on Rte. 201, proceed 3.5 miles south of the intersection with Rte. 165, left (east) on Billings Lake Rd., launch is at the end of the road on the right. *Shore:* Limited to state land north of the boat launch (including the dam).

Fish: Billings Lake is stocked each spring with 800 catchable size brown and brook trout. Few fish holdover past summer due to the limited area of suitable deep-water habitat. Largemouth bass, sunfish and possibly chain pickerel and bullhead are moderately stockpiled. **Largemouth bass** (less than 12") and **chain pickerel** (less than 15") are abundant, but densities of larger fish are only average. Densities of 8-12" **black crappie** are slightly above average. **Sunfish** (mostly bluegill, some pumpkinseed) are abundant, but rarely exceed 7". **Brown bullhead** in the 9-12" range are abundant. The forage base includes higher than average densities of golden shiners. Other fish species present at low densities are smallmouth bass, yellow perch, and alewives.

Fishing: Should be good for sunfish and stocked trout during the spring and fair to good for bass, pickerel, crappie and bullhead.

Billings Lake Fish Species and Abundance			
Gamefish	ALL SIZES	BIG FISH	GROWTH
Largemouth bass	A	C	< Avg
Smallmouth bass	R	R	
Brook trout	C		
Brown trout	C	R	
Chain pickerel	A	C	< Avg
Panfish			
Black crappie	C	C	Avg
Yellow perch	U	U	Avg
Brown bullhead	A	A	
Sunfish			
Bluegill	A	C	Slow
Pumpkinseed	C	C	Slow
Other			
Golden shiner	A		
Alewife	R		

A=Abundant, C=Common, U=Uncommon, R=Rare

Management: Bass Management Lake; special slot length and creel limits on bass. Statewide regulations apply for all other species (see current *Connecticut Anglers' Guide*).

Boating: No special regulations (see current *Connecticut Boater's Guide*).

Comments: The boat launch is not heavily used due to parking limitations. It is a popular lake for ice fishing. Special regulations should improve fishing by protecting larger bass and allowing anglers to harvest overabundant small bass.

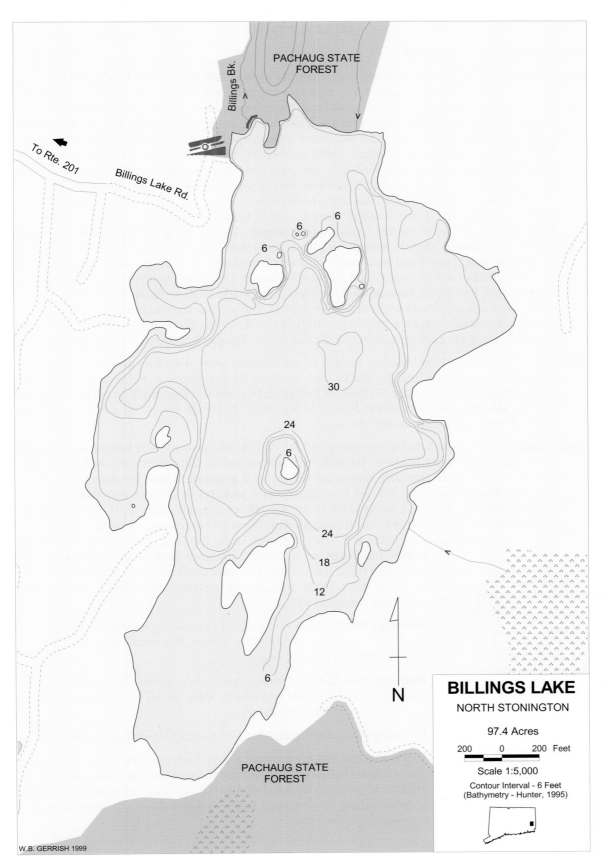

PACHAUG STATE
FOREST

Billings Bk.

To Rte. 201

Billings Lake Rd.

6

6

6

0

30

24

6

24

18

12

6

N

PACHAUG STATE
FOREST

BILLINGS LAKE

NORTH STONINGTON

97.4 Acres

200   0   200 Feet

Scale 1:5,000

Contour Interval - 6 Feet
(Bathymetry - Hunter, 1995)

W.B. GERRISH 1999

Black Pond

Town(s): Meriden/Middlefield

76.0 acres

Description: Black Pond is a natural lake within the South Central Coastal (Quinnipiac) Drainage Basin. The water level was raised 5 ft. by a concrete and earthen dam. The pond is divided into two basins separated by a narrow spit of land. There is an area of shallow water and flooded vegetation in the center of the pond with a narrow channel connecting the two basins. *Watershed*: 752 acres that is mostly residential with some undeveloped woodland and agricultural land. The lake is fed by two streams, surface runoff and bottom springs. It drains northwest into Spoon Shop Brook, which eventually feeds into the Quinnipiac River. *Shoreline*: Mostly undeveloped state-owned land. The eastern and western shores are part of Black Pond Wildlife Area. The eastern shore is a cliff face with a talus slope to the water's edge. The western and southern shores are wooded marshland. The northern shore is part of Cockaponset State Forest and is wooded. There is a private beach located near the outlet. *Depth*: Max 22 ft., Mean 8.6 ft. *Transparency*: Fair; 9 ft. in summer, slightly reduced by a tea-colored stain. *Productivity*: Moderate (mesotrophic). *Bottom type*: Gravel and rock in the shoal areas; mud and silt in deeper areas. *Stratification*: Partially stratifies with a temperature gradient forming at 13 ft. Oxygen levels decline to less than 2 ppm below this depth. *Vegetation*: Extremely dense in the shallow areas. Submergent vegetation is predominantly pondweeds and water-milfoil. The western and southern shores of the main basin have extensive areas of yellow pond-lily, white water-lily and water-shield. No vegetation is present along the eastern shore below the talus slope, but the rocks provide good cover for fish.

Access: A state-owned boat launch is located on the northern shore. Facilities at the launch include a shallow gravel ramp, parking for 10 cars, disabled fishing access and chemical toilets (seasonal). *Directions*: East Main St. Exit off I-91 (Exit 16 north or 17 south), East Main St. east for 2 miles, launch is on right. *Shore*: Fishing is permitted off Thorpe Rd. on the western shore and off the hiking trail on the eastern shore.

Fish: Black Pond is stocked during the spring and fall with 4,700 catchable size **brown and rainbow trout**. Few or no trout holdover through the summer due to lack of oxygen in deeper water. Almost all the popular sport fish species are stockpiled. **Largemouth bass** less than 13" are abundant, but densities of larger fish are low. Small **chain pickerel** (8-12") are extremely abundant with densities of larger fish being close to average. **Black crappie** in the 6-9" range are abundant, but larger fish are almost nonexistent. **Sunfish** (mostly bluegill, some pumpkinseed) densities are higher than average in the 6-7" size range with larger fish being uncommon. **Brown** and **yellow bullheads** are extremely abundant in the 6-10" size range with larger fish being uncommon. The pond contains an abundant golden shiner forage base. Other fish species present at low densities are yellow perch and American eel.

Fishing: Should be good to excellent seasonally for stocked trout; fair to good for sunfish and fair for other species. In general, there are plenty of fish to catch, but few big ones.

Management: Bass Management Lake; special slot length and creel limits on bass. Statewide regulations apply for all other species (see current *Connecticut Anglers' Guide*).

Boating: Gas motors prohibited (see current *Connecticut Boater's Guide*).

Comments: Fishing pressure is very high in Black Pond. High densities of unused forage (golden shiners) indicate that the pond could support more large predators than it currently contains. Special regulations should improve fishing by protecting larger bass and allowing anglers to harvest overabundant small bass.

Black Pond
Fish Species and Abundance

	ALL SIZES	BIG FISH	GROWTH
Gamefish			
Largemouth bass	A	U	Slow
Brown trout	C		
Rainbow trout	C		
Chain pickerel	A	C	< Avg
Panfish			
Black crappie	A	R	Slow
Yellow perch	U	U	Fast
Brown bullhead	A	U	
Yellow bullhead	A	U	
Sunfish			
Bluegill	A	U	Slow
Pumpkinseed	C	U	Avg
Other			
Golden shiner	A		
American eel	U		

A=Abundant, C=Common, U=Uncommon, R=Rare

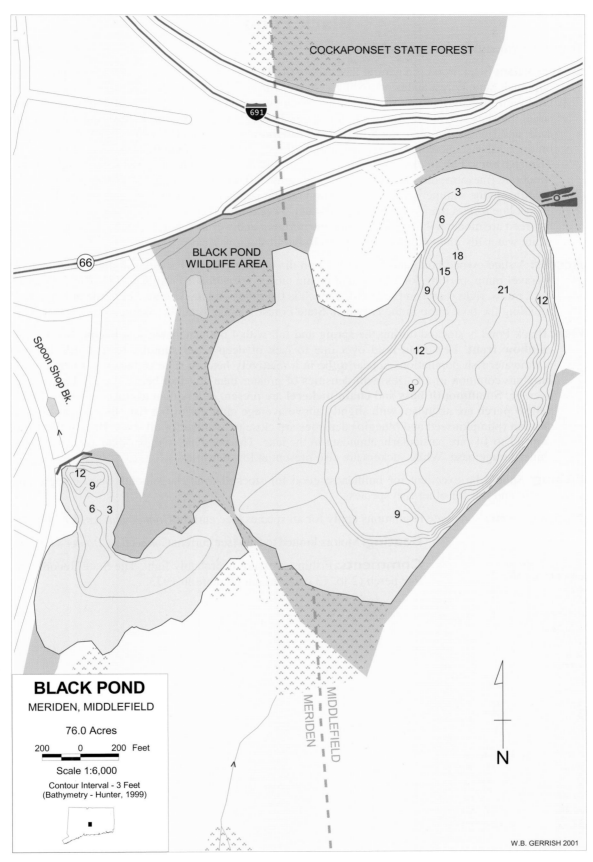

COCKAPONSET STATE FOREST

691

66

BLACK POND
WILDLIFE AREA

Spoon Shop Bk.

3
6
18
15
9
21
12
12
9

12

9

9

12
9
6 3

MIDDLEFIELD
MERIDEN

N

BLACK POND

MERIDEN, MIDDLEFIELD

76.0 Acres

200   0   200 Feet

Scale 1:6,000

Contour Interval - 3 Feet
(Bathymetry - Hunter, 1999)

W.B. GERRISH 2001

Black Pond

Town(s): Woodstock   **73.4 acres**

Description: Black Pond is a natural lake within the Thames River Drainage Basin. It is adjacent to Nipmuck State Forest and is relatively secluded. *Watershed*: 319 acres of mostly woods and wetland with little agricultural or residential development. The pond is fed by bottom springs, two small marshes and surface runoff. It drains into Black Pond Brook, which flows south to Bungee Lake and Bungee Brook to the Still River. *Shoreline*: Mostly wooded with only a few residences on the northeast shore and a private camp on the western shore. *Depth*: Max 23 ft., Mean 14 ft. *Transparency*: Fair to clear; 9-14 ft. in summer with a moderate tea-colored stain. *Productivity*: Moderate (mesotrophic). *Bottom type*: Sand, gravel, boulders and mud. *Stratification*: Partially stratifies in the summer with a temperature gradient beginning at 16 ft. Late summer oxygen levels decline to less than 1 ppm in deeper water. *Vegetation*: Pickerelweed, pipewort, bulrush and bur-reed are moderately abundant along the northern and western shores. Patches of water-shield, white water-lily and yellow pond-lily are found in shallow areas.

Access: A state-owned boat launch is located on the southern shore. Facilities at the launch include a gravel ramp, parking for 10 cars and picnic tables. *Directions*: From Rte. 171, Rte. 198 north for 2 miles, right (east) on Camp Rd., launch is 0.5 miles on left. *Shore*: 750 ft. of shoreline surrounding the boat ramp in the Nipmuck State Forest is open to public fishing.

Fish: Black Pond is stocked during the spring and fall with 1,600 catchable size **brook**, **brown** and **rainbow trout**. Few trout hold over due to lack of deep-water summer habitat. Black Pond warmwater fish populations appear to be in a relatively healthy state of balance. **Largemouth bass** are common in all sizes with densities of greater than 12" fish being slightly higher than average. **Smallmouth bass** and **chain pickerel** are present at less than average densities. Small **yellow perch** are abundant with slightly above average numbers of big fish. **Black crappie** and **sunfish** (pumpkinseed and bluegill) densities are close to average for all sizes. **Brown bullhead** from 11 to 14" are particularly abundant in the lake. The pond has a higher than average golden shiner forage base. White suckers are also present at low densities.

Fishing: Should be excellent for bullheads; good for stocked trout, largemouth bass, crappie and perch; and fair for other fish species.

Management: Statewide regulations apply for all species (see current *Connecticut Anglers' Guide*)

Boating: Motors limited to 5 hp (see current *Connecticut Boater's Guide*).

Comments: Fishing pressure is probably light. The State Record yellow perch (2 lb. 13 oz.) was caught here in 1973.

Black Pond
Fish Species and Abundance

	ALL SIZES	BIG FISH	GROWTH
Gamefish			
Largemouth bass	C	C	Avg
Smallmouth bass	U	U	Avg
Brook trout	C		
Brown trout	C	R	
Rainbow trout	C		
Chain pickerel	U	U	Slow
Panfish			
Black crappie	C	C	Avg
Yellow perch	A	C	Avg
Brown bullhead	A	A	
Sunfish			
Bluegill	C	C	Avg
Pumpkinseed	C	C	Avg
Other			
Golden shiner	A		
White sucker	U		

A=Abundant, C=Common, U=Uncommon, R=Rare

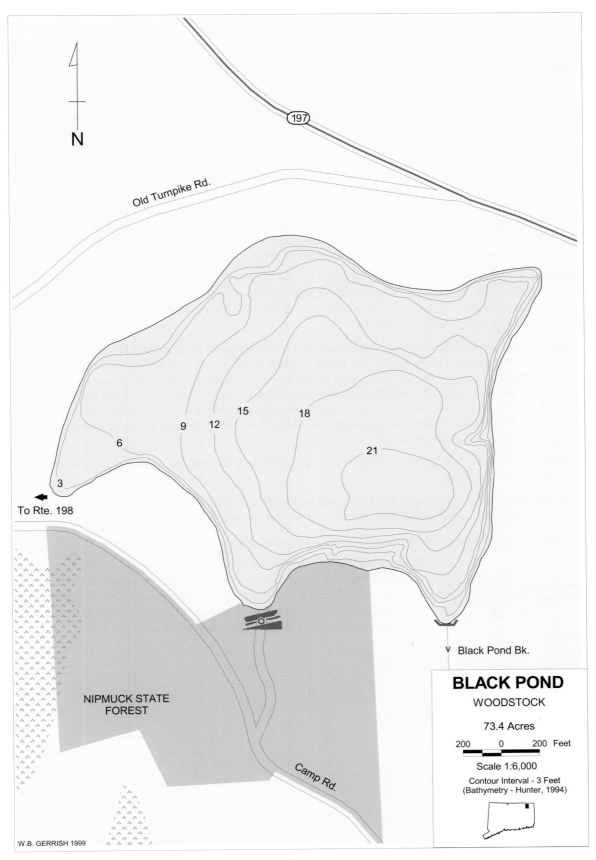

N

197

Old Turnpike Rd.

15

18

9 12

6

21

3

To Rte. 198

Black Pond Bk.

NIPMUCK STATE
FOREST

Camp Rd.

BLACK POND

WOODSTOCK

73.4 Acres

200   0   200 Feet

Scale 1:6,000

Contour Interval - 3 Feet
(Bathymetry - Hunter, 1994)

W.B. GERRISH 1999

Bolton Lake, Lower

Town(s): Bolton/Vernon   **175 acres**

Description: Lower Bolton Lake is a natural lake within the Thames River Drainage Basin. Its water level was raised by an earthen dam with a concrete spillway that was rebuilt in 1994. *Watershed*: 2,379 acres of mostly woods and wetland with moderate levels of residential and agricultural development dispersed throughout. The lake is fed by Middle Bolton Lake and surface runoff. It drains into Bolton Pond Brook to the southeast. *Shoreline*: Heavily developed with residences. A town beach is located on the southeastern shore. *Depth*: Max 20 ft., Mean 11 ft. *Transparency*: Fair; 6 ft. in late summer. *Productivity*: Moderate (mesotrophic). *Bottom type*: Sand, gravel, coarse rubble and boulders in the shallows; mud and organic muck in the deeper areas. *Stratification*: Partially stratifies in the summer with a temperature gradient beginning at 13 ft. Late summer oxygen levels decline to less than 1 ppm below this depth. *Vegetation*: Generally scarce; however, there are localized areas of emergent cat-tail, arrowhead, pickerelweed and bul-rush along the shoreline. Submergent waterweed, pondweed, and variable-leaved water-milfoil occur in moderate densities throughout shallow areas.

Access: A state-owned boat launch is located on the southern shore. Facilities at the launch include a paved ramp, parking for 30 cars and chemical toilets (seasonal). *Directions*: From Rte. 6 & I-384, Rte. 44 east for 1 mile, launch is on the left (north). *Shore*: Public shore access is restricted to the dam and boat launch areas.

Fish: Lower Bolton Lake contains higher than average densities of **largemouth bass** to 14", but larg-er fish are scarce. **Yellow perch** and **black crappie** densities are average for all sizes with 10-11" fish being common. Densities of small **sunfish** (mostly bluegill, some pumpkinseed, occasional green and hybrids) are average with the abundance of larger fish (7-8") being above average. Major forage fish species are golden shiner (average densities) and banded killifish (very abun-dant). White suckers are also very common. Other fish species present at low densities are small-mouth bass and chain pickerel.

Fishing: Should be fair to good for bass, perch, crappie and sunfish. Bass fishing is reportedly best during early spring.

Management: Bass Management Lake; special slot length and creel limits on bass. Statewide reg-ulations apply for all other species (see current *Connecticut Anglers' Guide*).

Boating: Motors limited to 6 hp (see current *Connecticut Boater's Guide*).

Comments: The lake had only been electrofished once by the time of printing. Thus, the above fishery description may be imprecise. Special reg-ulations should improve fishing by protecting larger bass and allowing anglers to harvest overabundant small bass. Fishing pressure is moderate in this lake. Many canoes, kayaks and small sailboats in summer.

Bolton Lake, Lower
Fish Species and Abundance

	ALL SIZES	BIG FISH	GROWTH
Gamefish			
Largemouth bass	A	U	Avg
Smallmouth bass	U	R	Avg
Chain pickerel	U	U	> Avg
Panfish			
Black crappie	C	C	> Avg
Yellow perch	C	C	< Avg
Sunfish			
Bluegill	A	A	> Avg
Pumpkinseed	C	C	< Avg
Green	C	R	
Other			
Golden shiner	C		
Banded killifish	A		
White sucker	C		

A=Abundant, C=Common, U=Uncommon, R=Rare

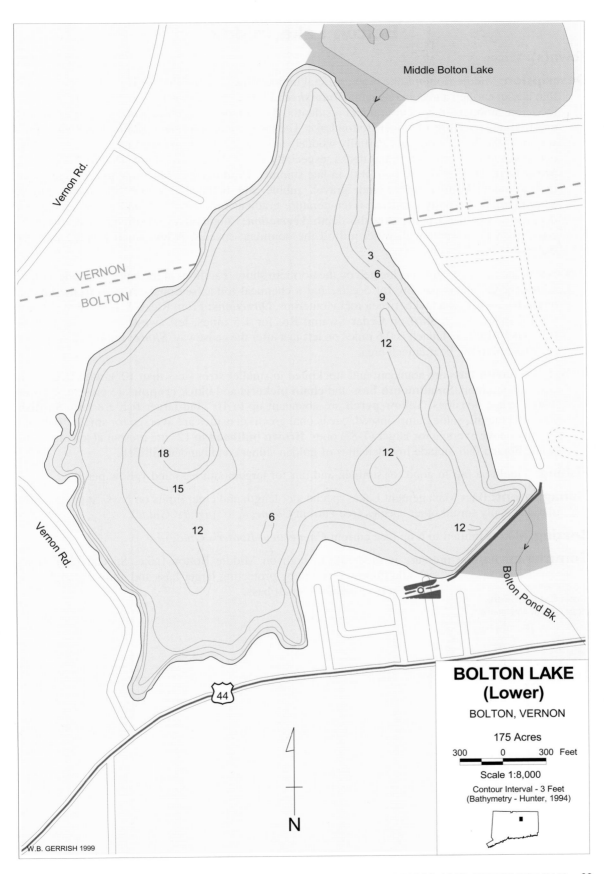

Middle Bolton Lake

Vernon Rd.

VERNON

BOLTON

3
6
9

12

12

18

15

12

6

12

12

Vernon Rd.

Bolton Pond Bk.

44

**BOLTON LAKE
(Lower)**

BOLTON, VERNON

175 Acres

300   0   300   Feet

Scale 1:8,000

Contour Interval - 3 Feet
(Bathymetry - Hunter, 1994)

N

W.B. GERRISH 1999

Bolton Lake, Middle

Town(s): Vernon

121 acres

Description: Middle Bolton Lake is an artificial impoundment in the Thames River Drainage Basin that has an earthen and concrete dam. *Watershed:* 1,946 acres of mostly woods and wetland with moderate amounts of agricultural and residential development. The lake is fed by surface runoff and from the overflow of Upper Bolton Lake. The lake drains into Lower Bolton Lake via a spillway over the dam. *Shoreline:* Partially wooded and heavily developed with residences lining the entire shoreline. There are many docks, especially along the eastern shore. *Depth:* Max 20 ft., Mean 12 ft. *Transparency:* Fair; 8 ft. in late summer. *Productivity:* Moderate (mesotrophic-late mesotrophic). *Bottom type:* Sand, gravel, rubble and boulders covered by organic muck. *Stratification:* Partially stratifies; a temperature gradient forms at 13 ft. and dissolved oxygen declines to less than 1 ppm below this depth. *Vegetation:* Submerged vegetation is sparse to moderate in shallow water with water-milfoil the dominant species. A few small floating mats of water-shield are also present.

Access: A state-owned launch is located on the northern shore. Facilities at the launch include a ramp with concrete slabs, parking for 5 cars, and a chemical toilet (seasonal). Access to the lake is through a narrow channel between rocky outcrops. *Directions:* From Rte. 6 & I-384, Rte. 44 east for 1.8 miles, left (north) on Cedar Swamp Rd. for 1.5 miles, left (west) on Vernon Branch Rd./Hatch Hill Rd., launch is 0.6 miles on left just after the causeway. *Shore:* Public shore access is restricted to the boat launch area.

Fish: Largemouth bass are abundant and stockpiled in smaller sizes (less than 12"), with larger fish being uncommon. **Smallmouth bass** and **chain pickerel** and **black crappie** are present at lower than average densities. **Yellow perch** are abundant up to 10", but larger fish are rare. **Sunfish** (mostly bluegill, some pumpkinseed, occasional green) densities are average for smaller fish and slightly above average for larger (7-8") ones. **Brown bullhead** to 12" are present at average densities. Forage fish include low densities of golden shiners and banded killifish.

Fishing: Should be fair to good for sunfish; and fair for largemouth bass and yellow perch.

Management: Bass Management Lake; special slot length and creel limits on bass. Statewide regulations apply for all other species (see current *Connecticut Anglers' Guide*).

Boating: Motors limited to 6 hp (see current *Connecticut Boater's Guide*).

Comments: Fishing pressure is moderate to high on Middle Bolton Lake. Special regulations should improve fishing by protecting larger bass and allowing anglers to harvest overabundant small bass.

Bolton Lake, Middle
Fish Species and Abundance

	ALL SIZES	BIG FISH	GROWTH
Gamefish			
Largemouth bass	A	U	< Avg
Smallmouth bass	C	U	Slow
Chain pickerel	U	U	> Avg
Panfish			
Black crappie	U	U	> Avg
Yellow perch	A	U	Avg
Brown bullhead	C	C	
Sunfish			
Bluegill	C	C	Avg
Pumpkinseed	C	C	> Avg
Green	U	R	
Other			
Golden shiner	U		
Banded killifish	U		

A=Abundant, C=Common, U=Uncommon, R=Rare

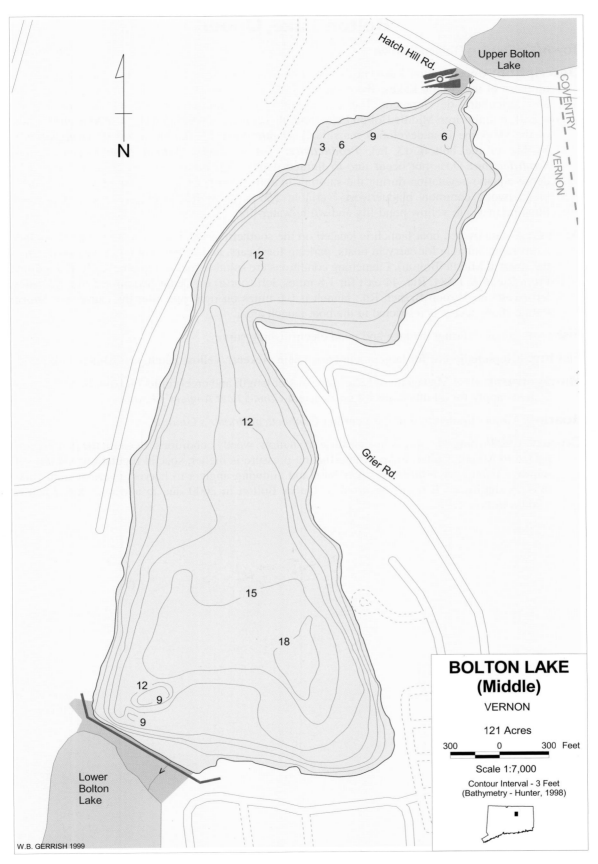

N

Hatch Hill Rd.

Upper Bolton
Lake

COVENTRY
VERNON

3 6   9   6

12

12

Grier Rd.

15

18

12
9

9

Lower
Bolton
Lake

**BOLTON LAKE
(Middle)**

VERNON

121 Acres

300   0   300   Feet

Scale 1:7,000

Contour Interval - 3 Feet
(Bathymetry - Hunter, 1998)

W.B. GERRISH 1999

Bolton Lake, Upper

Town(s): Coventry/Tolland/Vernon   **50.3 acres**

Description: Upper Bolton Lake, in the Thames River Drainage Basin, is the smallest and most northern of the Bolton Lakes. *Watershed*: 1,293 acres of mostly wetland with some residential and agricultural development. The lake is fed from the north by a wetland and from surface runoff. It drains into Middle Bolton Lake through a culvert under Hatch Hill Rd. *Shoreline*: Most of the shoreline is undeveloped marshland. *Depth*: Max 7.5 ft., Mean 3.0 ft. *Transparency*: Visible to the bottom (3 ft.). *Productivity*: Not available. *Bottom type*: Organic muck. *Stratification*: Does not occur due to limited depth. *Vegetation*: Almost entirely covered by dense aquatic vegetation during the summer months. Dominant submergent species are purple bladderwort, common bladderwort, variable leaf water-milfoil and thread-leaf pondweed. Floating mats are yellow pond-lily and white water-lily.

Access: A state-owned boat launch is located on the southern shore. Facilities at the launch include a dirt ramp suitable for carry-in boats, parking for 2 cars, and a chemical toilet (seasonal across the street at Middle Bolton). Launching conditions are suitable for car-top boats only. *Directions*: From Rte. 6 & I-384, Rte. 44 east for 1.8 miles, left (north) on Cedar Swamp Rd. for 1.5 miles, left (west) on Vernon Branch Rd., launch is 0.6 miles on right just after the causeway. *Shore*: Public shore access is restricted to the boat launch area.

Fish: Not sampled during the lake and pond electrofishing survey.

Fishing: Is reportedly fair for largemouth bass, chain pickerel, yellow perch, sunfish and bullheads.

Management: Bass Management Lake; special slot length and creel limits on bass. Statewide regulations apply for all other species (see current *Connecticut Anglers' Guide*).

Boating: Motors limited to 6 hp (see current *Connecticut Boater's Guide*).

Comments: Fishing pressure is low because of shallow, weedy conditions. Because the pond is connected to Middle Bolton Lake, where fishing pressure is higher, special regulations should still improve fishing by protecting larger bass and allowing anglers to harvest overabundant small bass. A significant fish kill occurred in Upper Bolton in 2000 due to a winter drawdown of Middle Bolton Lake.

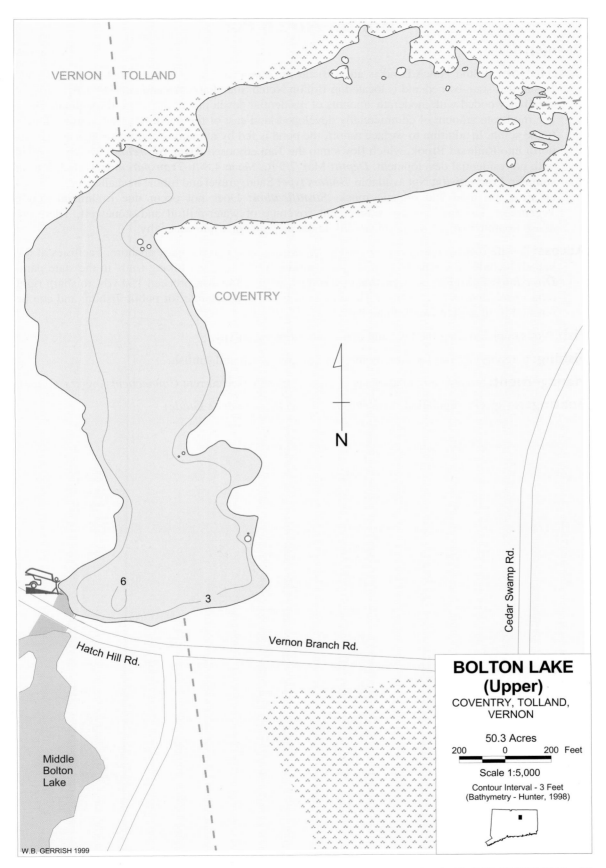

VERNON TOLLAND

COVENTRY

N

Cedar Swamp Rd.

6

3

Vernon Branch Rd.

Hatch Hill Rd.

Middle
Bolton
Lake

**BOLTON LAKE
(Upper)**

COVENTRY, TOLLAND,
VERNON

50.3 Acres

200   0   200 Feet

Scale 1:5,000

Contour Interval - 3 Feet
(Bathymetry - Hunter, 1998)

W.B. GERRISH 1999

Bolton Notch Pond

Town(s): Bolton   **16.6 acres**

Description: Bolton Notch Pond is an artificial impoundment in the Connecticut River Drainage Basin. It is state-owned and is located in Bolton Notch State Park. **Watershed:** 344 acres, most of which is wooded with moderate amounts of residential development dispersed throughout. There is a moderate amount of commercially developed land east of the pond. Rte. 384 is immediately to the south. In addition to surface runoff, the pond is fed by numerous bottom springs and drains north into Railroad Brook, which flows into the Tankerhoosen River. **Shoreline:** Mostly wooded with no residential development. **Depth:** Max 7.5 ft., Mean 4.8 ft. **Transparency:** Turbid; 5 ft. in summer. **Productivity:** Not available. **Bottom type:** Sand, gravel and rubble in shallow areas; deeper areas are mud and organic muck. **Stratification:** Does not occur due to limited depth. **Vegetation:** Extremely dense submergent coverage of water-milfoil and stonewort. There are dense floating mats of water-shield with lesser amounts of white water-lily.

Access: A state-owned, undeveloped car-top access is located on the eastern shore. Facilities at the launch include an unimproved dirt ramp, parking for 5 cars and hiking trails in the state park. **Directions:** From Rte. 44 westbound, continue onto I-384 west, proceed 150 yds. to sharp right onto gravel access road. **Shore:** The entire shoreline is accessible for public fishing and can be reached from Bolton Notch State Park.

Fish: Not sampled during the lake and pond electrofishing survey.

Fishing: Is reportedly fair for largemouth bass, yellow perch and sunfish.

Management: Statewide regulations apply for all species (see current *Connecticut Anglers' Guide*).

Boating: No special regulations (see current *Connecticut Boater's Guide*).

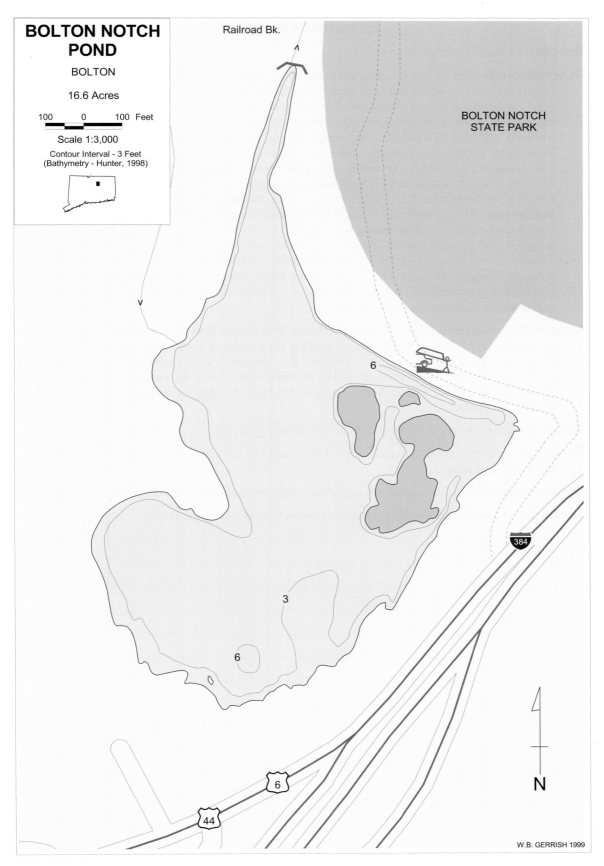

BOLTON NOTCH
POND

BOLTON

16.6 Acres

100   0   100 Feet

Scale 1:3,000

Contour Interval - 3 Feet
(Bathymetry - Hunter, 1998)

Railroad Bk.

BOLTON NOTCH
STATE PARK

6

3

6

384

6

44

N

W.B. GERRISH 1999

Breakneck Pond

Town(s): Union/Sturbridge (MA)   **91.7 acres**

Description: Breakneck Pond is a natural lake in the Thames River Drainage Basin. Most of this long (1.5 miles), narrow pond is located within the Nipmuck State Forest. The northern tip of the pond crosses the state line into Massachusetts. There are two large submerged cedar stands along the western shore in the southern half of the lake. Two relatively large islands are located at the southern end and two smaller ones are near the western shore in the middle of the lake. *Watershed*: 1,050 acres of mostly undeveloped woods. The pond is fed by several small streams and groundwater springs. It drains into Breakneck Brook, which flows northward to the Quinebaug River. *Shoreline*: Entirely wooded. *Depth*: Max 14 ft., Mean 6.7 ft. *Transparency*: Fair; 8 ft. in summer; reduced by tea-colored stain. *Productivity*: Moderate (early mesotrophic). *Bottom type*: Mostly mud and organic muck. *Stratification*: Partially stratifies in the summer, with a temperature gradient forming at a depth of 6 ft. Late summer oxygen levels are poor to marginal (3-5 ppm) below this depth. *Vegetation*: Submergent vegetation, predominantly bladderwort, is very dense to depths of 6 ft., particularly in the southern and western areas of the lake. Floating mats of white water-lily, yellow pond-lily, water-shield and floating-leaved pondweed are dense in the southern end and common in the northern end. Several inundated white cedar stands are located on the western shore.

Access: There is no boat launch. Access is through Bigelow Hollow State Park and boats or canoes must be carried 1.3 miles to the water. A parking fee is charged from Memorial Day to Labor Day. *Directions*: To state park — Exit 73 off I-84, Rte. 190 north, right (east) on Rte. 171, park is 1.3 miles on left (north). Beginning of trail to Breakneck Pond is at the parking area near the north end of Bigelow Pond. *Shore*: All of the shoreline located within Connecticut is state land and is open to the public.

Fish: Not sampled during the lake and pond electrofishing survey.

Fishing: Is reportedly good to excellent for crappie and fair for largemouth bass, chain pickerel, yellow perch and sunfish.

Management: Statewide regulations apply for all species (see current *Connecticut Anglers' Guide*).

Boating: Gas motors prohibited (see current *Connecticut Boater's Guide*).

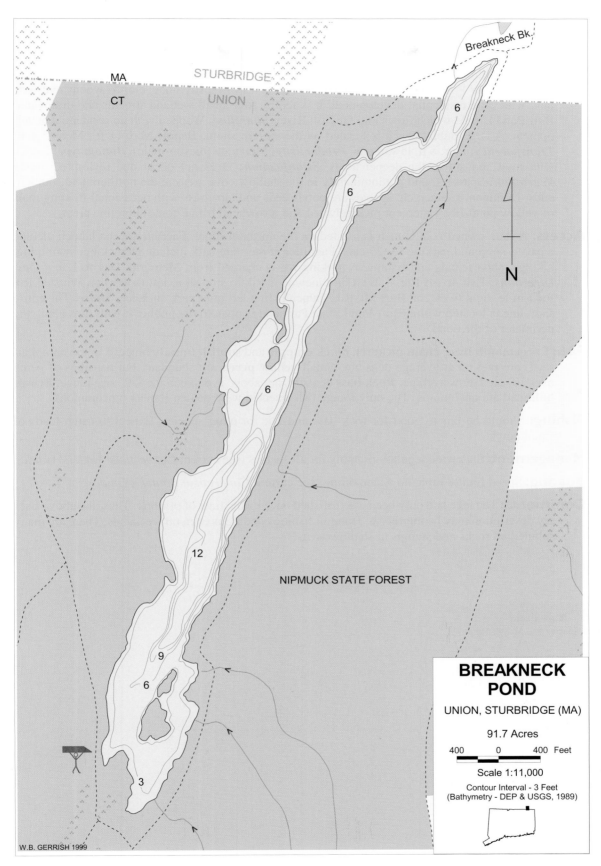

Breakneck Bk.

STURBRIDGE

MA

CT

UNION

6

6

N

6

12

NIPMUCK STATE FOREST

9

6

3

W.B. GERRISH 1999

BREAKNECK POND

UNION, STURBRIDGE (MA)

91.7 Acres

400   0   400   Feet

Scale 1:11,000

Contour Interval - 3 Feet
(Bathymetry - DEP & USGS, 1989)

Burr Pond

Town(s): Torrington
                                                                      85.1 acres

Description: Burr Pond is an artificial impoundment in the Connecticut River Drainage Basin located within Burr Pond State Park. *Watershed:* 864 acres of mostly undeveloped woods and wetland with little residential development. It is fed by four small wetland streams and drains into Burr Pond Brook, which flows into the Still River. *Shoreline:* Wooded with no residential development. A large public beach is located on the eastern shore. *Depth:* Max 11 ft., Mean 5.1 ft. *Transparency:* Fair; 8 ft. in summer. *Productivity:* Moderate (mesotrophic). *Bottom type:* Rocky with mud and silt in the deeper areas. *Stratification:* Does not occur due to limited depth. *Vegetation:* Sparse, found predominantly in the shallow cove areas at the northern and southern ends. Dominant submergent species are pondweeds and tapegrass with occasional floating mats of yellow pond-lily. Emergent pickerelweed and arrowhead fringe some shoreline areas.

Access: A state-owned boat launch is located on the northern shore. Facilities at the launch include a paved ramp and parking for 25 cars. Facilities at the state park include picnicking, swimming, hiking, canoe rentals and fishing. A parking fee is charged from Memorial Day to Labor Day. *Directions:* Exit 46 off Rte. 8, west on Pinewoods Rd. to stop sign, left (south) on Winsted Rd. for 1 mile, right (west) on Burr Mt. Rd., launch is first left after park entrance. *Shore:* The entire shoreline is located within Burr Pond State Park and is open to the public. A path runs along the perimeter of the pond.

Fish: Largemouth bass, **chain pickerel**, **black crappie** and **sunfish** (mostly bluegill, some pumpkinseed) are present at average densities. Small **yellow perch** are abundant, but densities of perch over 10" are below average. **Rock bass** densities are above average in the 8-9" size range. **Brown bullhead** are uncommon. The only forage fish detected were golden shiners (uncommon).

Fishing: Should be fair to good for rock bass and fair for other species. Expect to catch loads of small perch.

Management: Statewide regulations apply for all species (see current *Connecticut Anglers' Guide*).

Boating: Speed limit 8 mph, no water-skiing (see current *Connecticut Boater's Guide*).

Comments: The lake had only been electrofished once by the time of printing. Thus, the above fishery description may be imprecise. Tranquil fishing conditions even on weekends. There are many submerged rocks and stumps in shallow areas.

Burr Pond
Fish Species and Abundance

	ALL SIZES	BIG FISH	GROWTH
Gamefish			
Largemouth bass	C	C	Fast
Chain pickerel	C	C	Avg
Panfish			
Yellow perch	A	U	Slow
Black crappie	C	C	> Avg
Brown bullhead	U	U	
Sunfish			
Bluegill	C	C	Fast
Pumpkinseed	C	U	> Avg
Rock bass	C	C	> Avg
Other			
Golden shiner	U		Avg

A=Abundant, C=Common, U=Uncommon, R=Rare

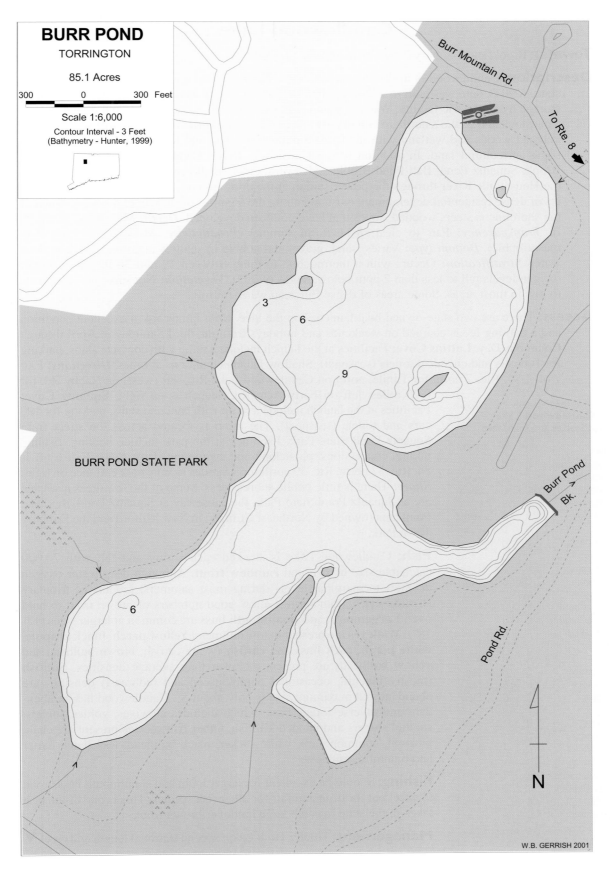

BURR POND

TORRINGTON

85.1 Acres

300   0   300 Feet

Scale 1:6,000

Contour Interval - 3 Feet
(Bathymetry - Hunter, 1999)

Burr Mountain Rd.

To Rte. 8

BURR POND STATE PARK

3

6

9

Burr Pond

Bk.

6

Pond Rd.

N

W.B. GERRISH 2001

Candlewood Lake

Town(s): Brookfield/Danbury/New Fairfield/New Milford/Sherman   **5,064 acres**

Description: Candlewood is in the Housatonic River Drainage Basin and is the largest lake in the state. A 90 ft. dam was built in 1923, flooding the former Rocky River Basin, to create a pumped storage hydroelectric facility. Water is pumped in from the Housatonic River and drawn out via a penstock at the lake's northern end to generate power. *Watershed:* 25,907 acres of mostly undeveloped woods and wetland with moderate amounts of urban and residential development and some agricultural land. In addition to the Housatonic River, Candlewood is fed by Sawmill Brook, Squantz Pond, Ball Pond Brook, and several other small brooks. The only outflow is to the Housatonic River through the power station at the northern end. *Shoreline:* There are pockets of dense residential development clustered along the 65 miles of shoreline; however, much of the shoreline is steep, wooded slopes that have not been developed. *Depth:* Max 89 ft., Mean 33 ft. *Transparency:* Fair to clear; 8-11 ft. in summer. *Productivity:* Moderate to high (late mesotrophic). *Bottom type:* Varies; sand, gravel and cobble in shallow areas and muck in deep water. *Stratification:* Occurs with a thermocline forming between 19 and 36 ft. Late summer oxygen levels fall to less than 2 ppm below depths of 22 ft. *Vegetation:* Not surveyed. Moderate to low in most areas. Some areas of dense Eurasian water-milfoil.

Access: There are two state-owned boat launches on the lake. Both ramps are in excellent condition and a parking fee is charged on weekends and holidays from the third Saturday in April through Columbus Day. **Lattins Cove:** Facilities at the launch include a ramp with concrete slabs, parking for 100 cars and chemical toilets (seasonal). Shallow launch conditions at times. *Directions:* Exit 7 off I-84, Rte. 7 north for 1 mile, north on Candlewood Lake Rd., left (west) on Nabby Rd. for 0.75 miles, left on Forty Acre Rd., launch is on right. **Squantz Cove:** Facilities at the launch include a ramp with concrete slabs, parking for 100 cars and toilets (seasonal). The ramp is located across the street from Squantz Pond State Park. Facilities at the park include boating, fishing, hiking, concessions, picnicking and swimming. *Directions:* Exit 6 off I-84, Rte. 37 north, Rte. 39 north for 3.8 miles to state park entrance on right. *Shore:* There is little public shore access. Some of the few areas available are at Squantz Pond State Park, the causeway at Squantz Pond, the Dike Point area (owned by Northeast Utilities) in New Milford and the Danbury Town Park.

Fish: Candlewood Lake is stocked each spring and fall with 24,000 catchable size **brown** and **rainbow trout**. Although deep-water oxygen declines to marginal levels during most summers, mouths of tributary streams and bottom springs allow good numbers of brown trout to hold over. **Largemouth** and **smallmouth bass** are common at larger sizes (12-18"). **Walleyes** are present in low numbers. **Yellow perch**, **black crappie**, **white perch**, **rock bass** and **catfish** (white catfish, brown bullhead and yellow bullhead) are present at lower than average densities. **Sunfish** (mostly bluegill, occasional pumpkinseed and redbreast) densities are abundant, but maximum size is only about 8". Candlewood has an abundant and diverse forage base, which includes alewives, golden shiners, spottail shiners and banded killifish. Other fish species present are chain pickerel, common carp, white sucker, black bullhead, tessellated darter and bluntnose minnow.

Fishing: Should be excellent for largemouth and smallmouth bass, good to excellent for trout and fair for other fish species. This is one of the best lakes in the state to catch large holdover brown trout.

Management: Trophy Trout Lake; special seasonal length and creel ▼

Candlewood Lake
Fish Species and Abundance

	ALL SIZES	BIG FISH	GROWTH
Gamefish			
Largemouth bass	C	C	Avg
Smallmouth bass	C	C	Avg
Brown trout	C	C	Slow
Rainbow trout	C		
Chain pickerel	R	R	> Avg
Walleye	U	U	Fast
White catfish	U	U	
Panfish			
Black crappie	U	U	Fast
White perch	U	U	Avg
Yellow perch	U	U	Fast
Brown bullhead	U	U	
Yellow bullhead	U	U	
Black bullhead	R	R	
Sunfish			
Bluegill	A	U	< Avg
Pumpkinseed	C	R	< Avg
Redbreast	C	R	< Avg
Rock bass	C	C	Slow
Other			
Tessellated darter	U		
Common carp	C		
Golden shiner	C		Avg
Spottail shiner	U		
Bluntnose minnow	R		
Banded killifish	C		
Alewife	A		Avg
White sucker	U		

A=Abundant, C=Common, U=Uncommon, R=Rare

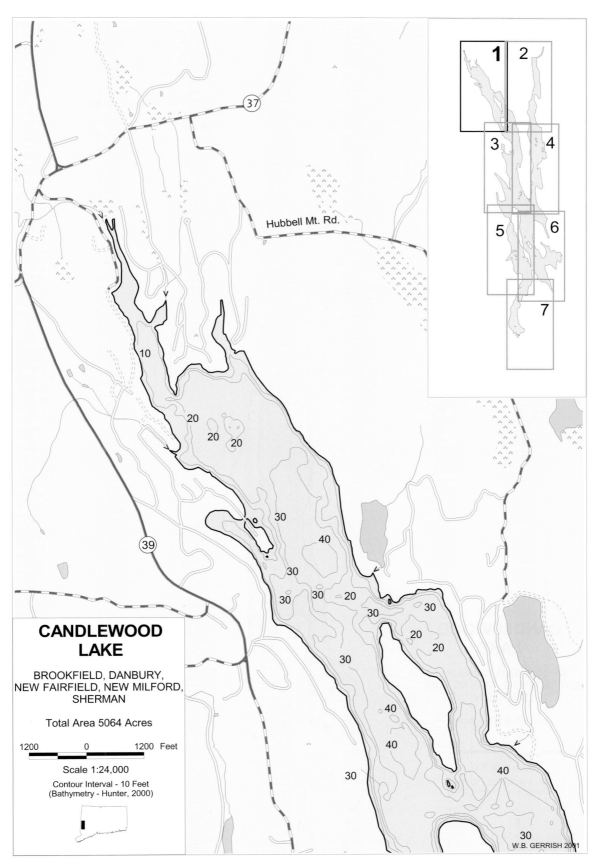

CANDLEWOOD
LAKE

BROOKFIELD, DANBURY,
NEW FAIRFIELD, NEW MILFORD,
SHERMAN

Total Area 5064 Acres

1200   0   1200   Feet

Scale 1:24,000

Contour Interval - 10 Feet
(Bathymetry - Hunter, 2000)

Hubbell Mt. Rd.

W.B. GERRISH 2001

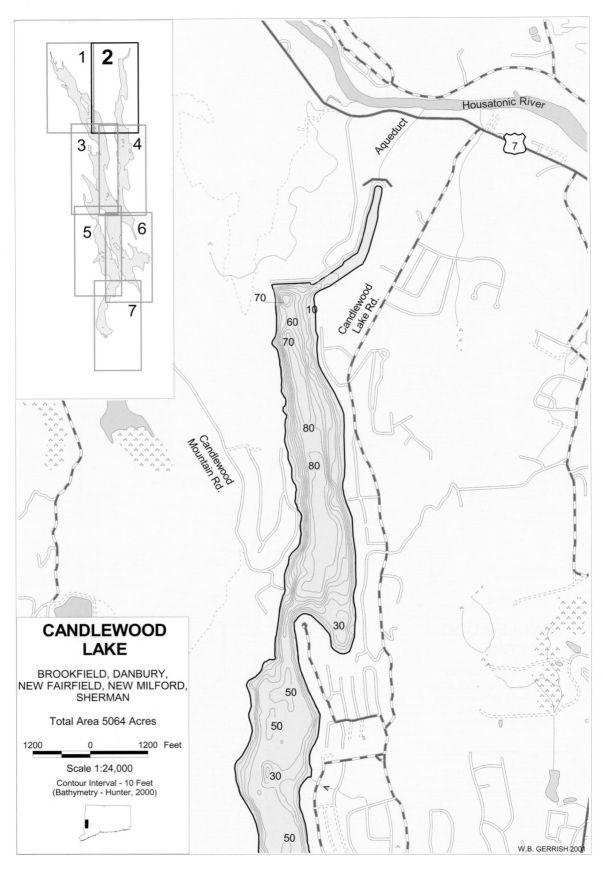

CANDLEWOOD LAKE

BROOKFIELD, DANBURY,
NEW FAIRFIELD, NEW MILFORD,
SHERMAN

Total Area 5064 Acres

1200   0   1200 Feet

Scale 1:24,000

Contour Interval - 10 Feet
(Bathymetry - Hunter, 2000)

W.B. GERRISH 2001

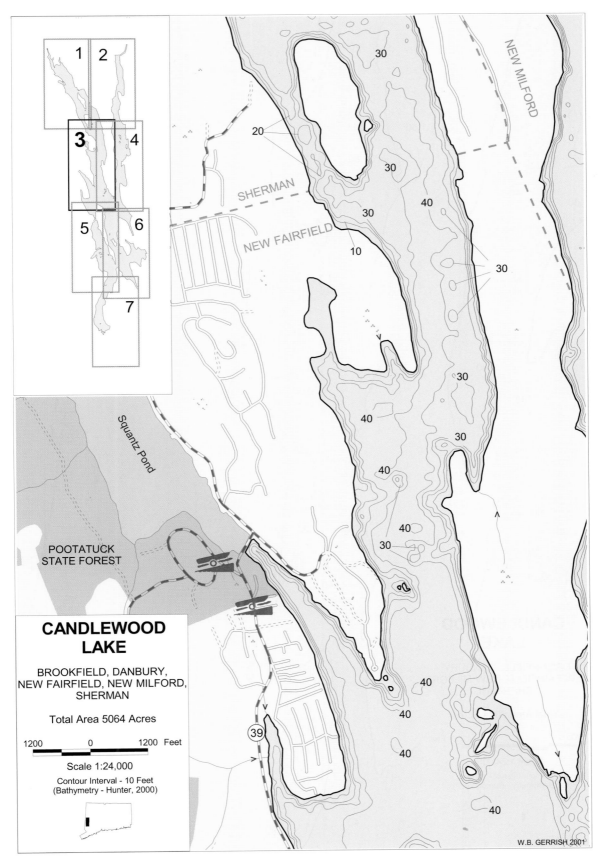

1 2

3 4

5 6

7

30

NEW MILFORD

20

30

SHERMAN

30

40

NEW FAIRFIELD

30

10

30

30

30

40

30

Squantz Pond

40

40

POOTATUCK
STATE FOREST

40

30

CANDLEWOOD LAKE

BROOKFIELD, DANBURY,
NEW FAIRFIELD, NEW MILFORD,
SHERMAN

Total Area 5064 Acres

1200   0   1200 Feet

Scale 1:24,000

Contour Interval - 10 Feet
(Bathymetry - Hunter, 2000)

40

40

39

40

40

40

W.B. GERRISH 2001

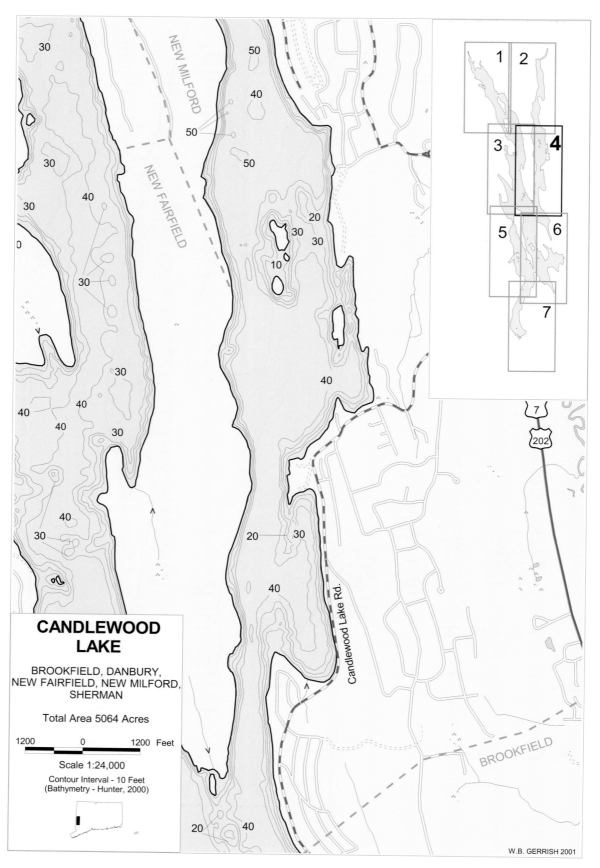

30

50

NEW MILFORD

40

50

NEW FAIRFIELD

50

30

40

50

30

20

30

30

0

10

30

40

30

40

30

40

40

40

40

30

40

20

30

30

Candlewood Lake Rd.

40

7

202

BROOKFIELD

20

40

1   2

3   **4**

5   6

7

CANDLEWOOD LAKE

BROOKFIELD, DANBURY, NEW FAIRFIELD, NEW MILFORD, SHERMAN

Total Area 5064 Acres

1200   0   1200   Feet

Scale 1:24,000

Contour Interval - 10 Feet
(Bathymetry - Hunter, 2000)

W.B. GERRISH 2001

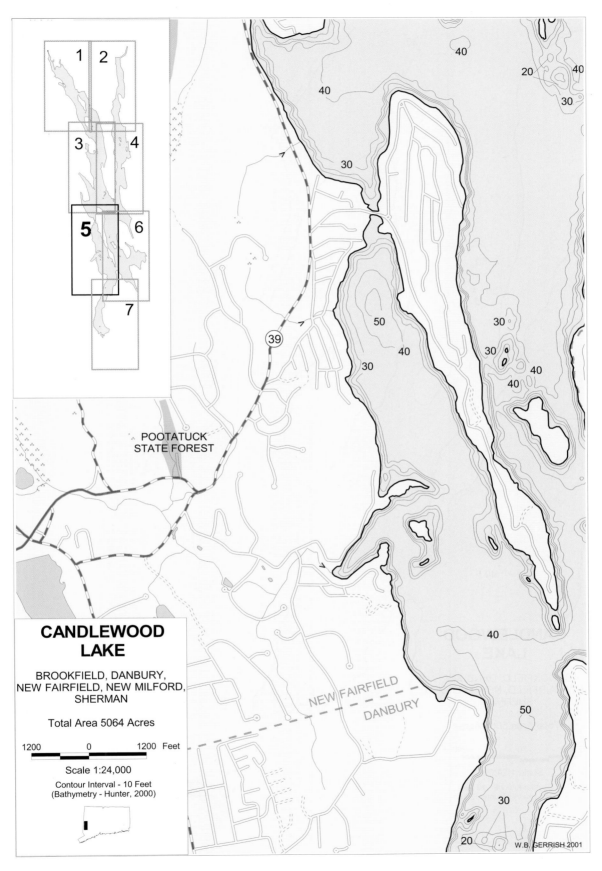

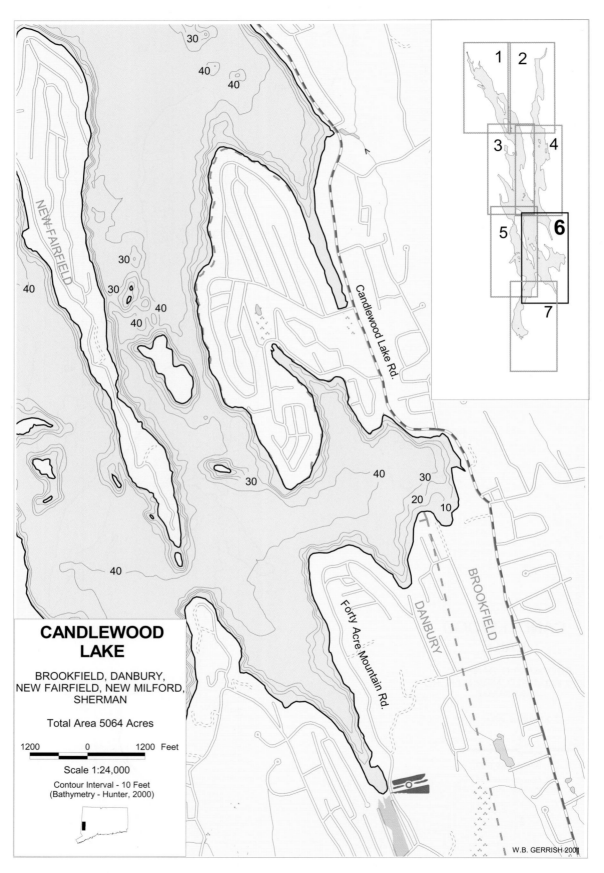

CANDLEWOOD LAKE

BROOKFIELD, DANBURY,
NEW FAIRFIELD, NEW MILFORD,
SHERMAN

Total Area 5064 Acres

1200   0   1200 Feet

Scale 1:24,000

Contour Interval - 10 Feet
(Bathymetry - Hunter, 2000)

W.B. GERRISH 2001

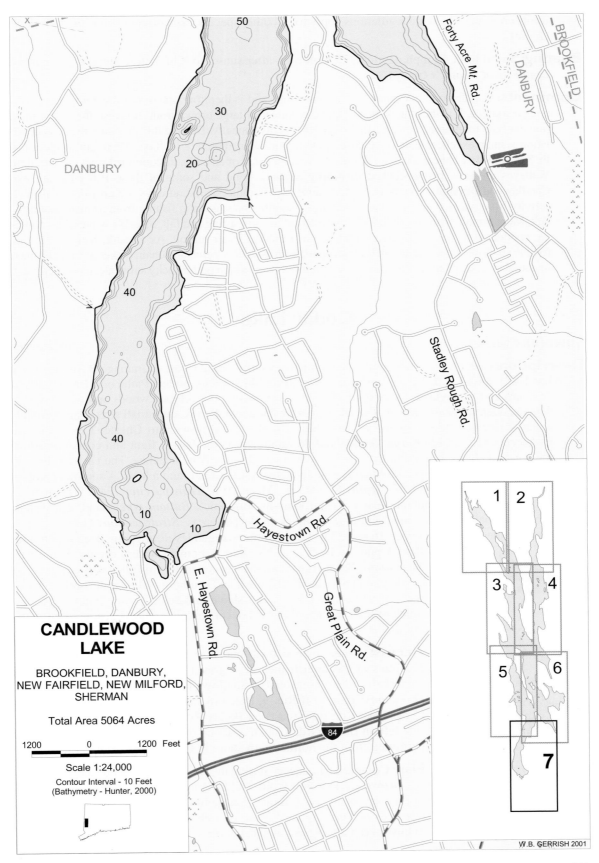

CANDLEWOOD LAKE

BROOKFIELD, DANBURY,
NEW FAIRFIELD, NEW MILFORD,
SHERMAN

Total Area 5064 Acres

1200   0   1200 Feet

Scale 1:24,000

Contour Interval - 10 Feet
(Bathymetry - Hunter, 2000)

DANBURY

BROOKFIELD

Forty Acre Mt. Rd.

Stadley Rough Rd.

Hayestown Rd.

E. Hayestown Rd.

Great Plain Rd.

84

W.B. GERRISH 2001

limits on trout. Statewide regulations apply for all other species (see current *Connecticut Anglers' Guide*).

Boating: Speed limit 45 mph daytime, 25 mph ½ hr. after sunset to ½ hr. before sunrise (see current *Connecticut Boater's Guide*).

Comments: Candlewood is Connecticut's largest lake and is therefore one of our most important fisheries resources. It is the state's most reliable producer of large brown trout. It is also the state's most popular bass tournament site, hosting over 100 events annually. Despite this pressure, the bass population is in an excellent state of balance. State Record white perch (2 lb. 8 oz., 1996) and walleye (14 lb. 8 oz., 1941) were caught here. The walleye was a result of an early, discontinued stocking program. Walleyes are now being stocked in nearby Squantz Pond and some of these fish emigrate into Candlewood through culverts under the causeway. Summer weekend days are crowded with high activity from water skiers, jet skiers and large pleasure boats, making fishing from a small boat difficult. More tranquil fishing conditions can be found in early spring and fall. Sizeable winter drawdowns are conducted to control an overabundance of Eurasian water-milfoil. As a result, fish species that require shallow water vegetation for spawning, such as yellow perch and chain pickerel, have declined in abundance. Conversely, numbers of smallmouth bass, which prefer rocky substrate, have increased.

Cedar Lake

Town(s): Chester   **69.3 acres**

Description: Cedar Lake is a natural lake within the South Central Coastal Drainage Basin. Its water level was raised 2 ft. by the construction of Rte. 148 over its outlet (Pattaconk Brook) at the southern end of the lake. *Watershed*: 294 acres of mostly undeveloped woods and wetland with some residential development. The lake is fed by Pattaconk Brook, one small stream and groundwater springs. It drains southward into Burr Brook, which flows into Chester Creek and the Connecticut River. *Shoreline*: Residential development on the lake is light and concentrated on the western shore. It is partially wooded with a couple of private beaches. The eastern shore is mostly wooded. Cockaponset State Forest abuts the northern half and a YMCA summer camp is located on the southern half. *Depth*: Max 43 ft., Mean 20 ft. *Transparency*: Fair; 9 ft. in summer. *Productivity*: Moderate (early mesotrophic-mesotrophic). *Bottom type*: Sand, gravel and rubble in shallow areas; mud and organic muck in deeper areas. *Stratification*: Occurs with a thermocline forming between 16 and 23 ft. Late summer oxygen levels are poor, declining to less than 3 ppm at 16 ft. and less than 1 ppm in waters deeper than 19 ft. *Vegetation*: Submergent variable-leaved water-milfoil is very dense at the northern end near the boat launch and southern end near the outlet. Dense mats of white water-lily, water-shield and some yellow pond-lily fringe much of the shoreline. Fanwort occurs in low numbers scattered throughout the lake.

Access: A state-owned boat launch is located on the northern shore. Facilities at the launch include a gravel ramp, parking for 6 cars and chemical toilets (seasonal). Shallow launching conditions prevail. *Directions*: Exit 6 off Rte. 9, Rte. 148 west for 2 miles, right (north) on Cedar Lake Rd., right (east) on Bailey Rd., first right on Brookside Rd., first left on Bishop Rd., launch is at end of road. *Shore*: Public fishing is permitted from the northeastern shore in Cockaponset State Forest.

Fish: Cedar Lake is stocked during the spring and fall with 6,600 catchable size **brown** and **rainbow trout**. Holdover trout are rare due to low dissolved oxygen levels in the summer. **Largemouth bass** are abundant to 18". Densities of larger (greater than 15") **chain pickerel** are above average. **Yellow perch** are present at average densities. **Sunfish** (mostly bluegill,▼

Cedar Lake Fish Species and Abundance			
	ALL SIZES	BIG FISH	GROWTH
Gamefish			
Largemouth bass	A	C	Avg
Brown trout	A	R	
Rainbow trout	A		
Chain pickerel	C	C	> Avg
Panfish			
Yellow perch	C	C	< Slow
Brown bullhead	C	C	
Sunfish			
Bluegill	A	A	< Avg
Pumpkinseed	C	C	Avg
Other			
Golden shiner	A		Avg
Banded killifish	C		
Alewife	C		Slow
American eel	U		

A=Abundant, C=Common, U=Uncommon, R=Rare

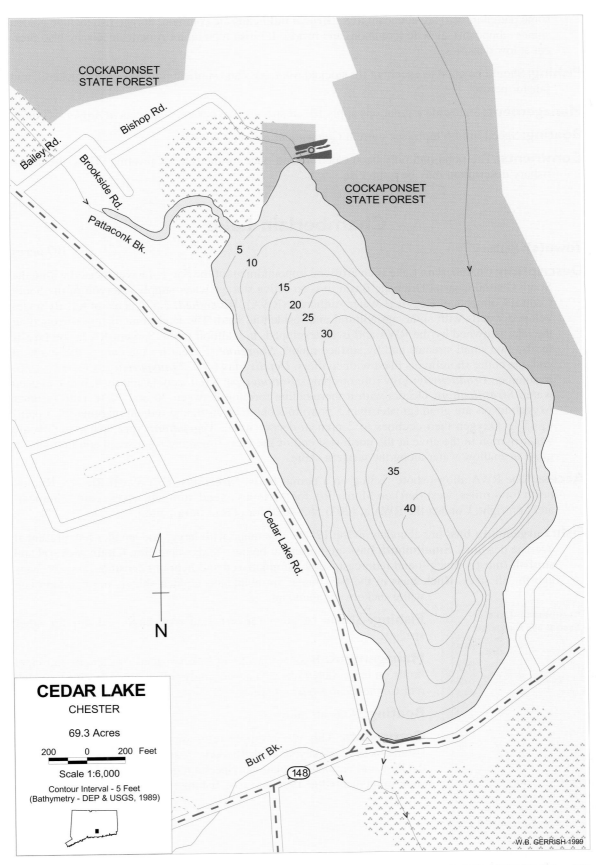

COCKAPONSET
STATE FOREST

Bishop Rd.

Bailey Rd.

Brookside Rd.

Pattaconk Bk.

COCKAPONSET
STATE FOREST

5
10
15
20
25
30

35
40

Cedar Lake Rd.

N

Burr Bk.

148

CEDAR LAKE

CHESTER

69.3 Acres

200   0   200 Feet

Scale 1:6,000

Contour Interval - 5 Feet
(Bathymetry - DEP & USGS, 1989)

W.B. GERRISH 1999

some pumpkinseed) are abundant to 8". **Brown bullheads** are common. Forage fish include golden shiner (abundant), alewife (common) and banded killifish (common). American eels are also present at low densities.

Fishing: Should be good to excellent for stocked trout, bass and sunfish; fair to good for pickerel; and fair for perch.

Management: Statewide regulations apply for all species (see current *Connecticut Anglers' Guide*).

Boating: Speed limit 6 mph (see current *Connecticut Boater's Guide*).

Comments: The pond had only been electrofished once by the time of printing. Thus, the above fishery description may be imprecise.

Chamberlain Lake

Town(s): Bethany   **107 acres**

Description: Chamberlain Lake is an artificial impoundment of the Sargent River located within the South Central Coastal Drainage Basin. It is an active storage water supply reservoir of the South Central Connecticut Regional Water Authority (RWA). *Watershed*: 2,572 acres of mostly undeveloped woods with some agricultural and residential land. The land immediately surrounding the lake is owned by the RWA and is undeveloped. In addition to the Sargent River, the lake is fed by two small streams and by surface runoff. *Shoreline*: Except for the dam at the southern end, the entire shoreline is lined with conifers. *Depth*: Max 65 ft. *Transparency*: Clear; 11-15 ft. in summer. *Productivity*: Low (oligotrophic). *Bottom type*: Sand, cobble and rock, muck in deep water. *Stratification*: Occurs with a thermocline forming between 20 and 32 ft. Late summer oxygen levels are good (greater than 5 ppm) to a depth of 26 ft. and remain marginal (4-5 ppm) to 45 ft. Oxygen then declines to 2 ppm in deeper water. *Vegetation*: Very sparse with some water-nymph in the cove at the northwest end of the lake. Emergent smartweed and buttonbush grow in shallow water along the western shore.

Access: The RWA allows shore fishing on a permit basis. *Directions*: Exit 59 off Rte. 15, Rte. 69 north for 4 miles, west (left) on Morris Rd. for 0.6 miles to end, turn left, access gate is immediately on right. Contact the RWA at (203) 562-4020 for permit information.

Fish: **Largemouth bass** are abundant in the 12-15" size range with larger and smaller fish present at average densities. **Smallmouth bass** are present at below average densities. **Chain pickerel** and **sunfish** (mostly bluegill and redbreast, some pumpkinseed and hybrids) densities are near average for all sizes. **Rock bass** in the 6-8" range are abundant. Golden shiners are common and white suckers are abundant.

Chamberlain Lake Fish Species and Abundance			
	ALL SIZES	BIG FISH	GROWTH
Gamefish			
Largemouth bass	A	C	Avg
Smallmouth bass	U	R	Avg
Chain pickerel	C	C	Avg
Sunfish			
Bluegill	C	C	Avg
Pumpkinseed	C	C	Avg
Redbreast	C	U	Avg
Rock bass	A	C	> Avg
Other			
Golden shiner	A		Slow
White sucker	A		
American eel	U		
A=Abundant, C=Common, U=Uncommon, R=Rare			

Fishing: Should be good for bass and rock bass; and fair for other species.

Management: Bass Management Lake; special slot length and creel limits on bass. Statewide regulations apply for all other species (see current *Connecticut Anglers' Guide*).

Boating: No boats allowed.

Comments: This water supply reservoir was first opened to public fishing in 1992. First year angler harvests resulted in drastic reductions in the bass and panfish populations. Special regulations on largemouth bass were implemented in 1996 and bass fishing should continue to improve.

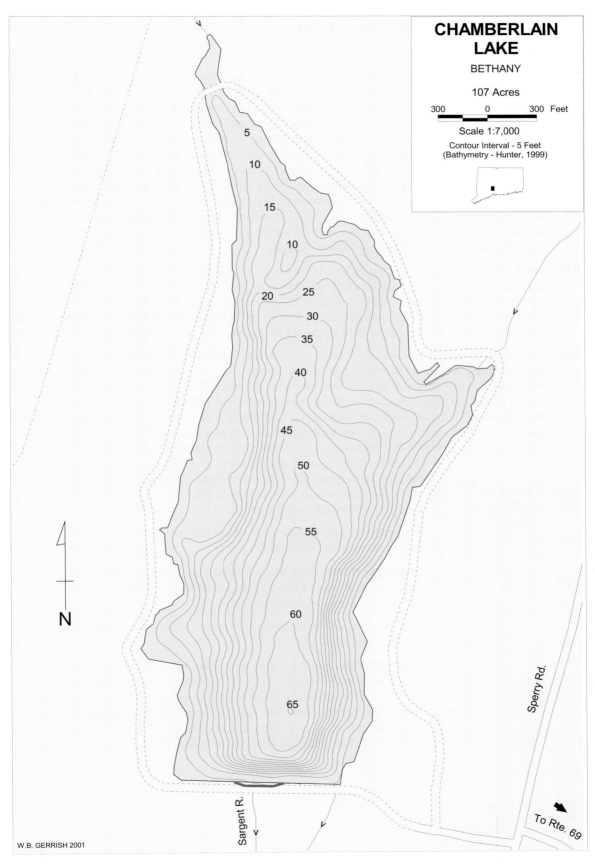

CHAMBERLAIN
LAKE

BETHANY

107 Acres

300   0   300 Feet

Scale 1:7,000

Contour Interval - 5 Feet
(Bathymetry - Hunter, 1999)

5
10
15
10
20   25
30
35
40
45
50
55
60
65

N

Sperry Rd.

Sargent R.

To Rte. 69

W.B. GERRISH 2001

Colebrook River Reservoir

Town(s): Colebrook/Sandisfield/Tolland (MA)   **826 acres**

Description: Colebrook is an artificial impoundment on the West Branch Farmington River in the Connecticut River Drainage Basin. It was created with a 1,300 ft. long dam by the U.S. Army Corps of Engineers who maintain it as a flood-control impoundment. When filled to capacity, this lake can cover as many as 1,185 acres. The Metropolitan District Commission (MDC) operates a hydroelectric facility at the dam. *Watershed*: 65,882 acres encompassing the Farmington River watershed. The surrounding land is undeveloped forest with some wetland to the east. In addition to the river, the reservoir is fed by seven small streams. *Shoreline*: Most of the shoreline is exposed gravel and boulders bordered by coniferous forest. There is no residential development. *Depth*: Max 136 ft., Mean 53 ft. *Transparency*: Very clear; 15 ft. in late summer. *Productivity*: Low (oligotrophic). *Bottom type*: Rock, sand, gravel and cobble. *Stratification*: Occurs with a thermocline forming at 29 ft. Late summer dissolved oxygen levels are marginal (4-5 ppm) to 43 ft. *Vegetation*: Not surveyed. Vegetation is sparse.

Access: A public boat launch owned by the Army Corps is located on the western shore. Facilities at the launch include a ramp with concrete slabs, parking for 50 cars and chemical toilets (seasonal). The launch may be unusable at times of extreme low or high water. *Directions*: From Rte. 44, Rte. 8 north for 7 miles, access is on right (east) side of road. *Shore*: The entire shore is owned by the Army Corps and is open to public fishing, except for a 100 ft. area immediately adjacent to the dam.

Fish: Colebrook Reservoir is stocked by the State each spring with 2,700 catchable size **brown** and **rainbow trout**. A similar number of fish are stocked annually into the reservoir by the MDC. The bottom release of water through the dam depletes potential trout habitat during most summers causing holdovers to be uncommon. **Smallmouth bass** and **yellow perch** are stockpiled. Small bass (less than 12") and perch (less than 9") are abundant, but larger fish are uncommon. **Rock bass** are common at all sizes. **Brown bullheads** are common, but small (usually less than 11"). White suckers are extremely abundant. Colebrook has an abundant and diverse forage base, which includes spottail shiners (very abundant), common shiners, golden shiners, fallfish and rainbow smelt. Other fish species present at low densities are largemouth bass, northern pike, chain pickerel, white catfish, bluegill and pumpkinseed sunfish.

Colebrook Reservoir Fish Species and Abundance	ALL SIZES	BIG FISH	GROWTH
Gamefish			
Largemouth bass	U	U	Avg
Smallmouth bass	A	U	Slow
Brown trout	C	U	
Rainbow trout	C		
Northern pike	R		
Chain pickerel	R	R	
White catfish	R	R	
Panfish			
Yellow perch	A	U	< Avg
Brown bullhead	C	R	
Sunfish			
Bluegill	U	R	> Avg
Pumpkinseed	R	R	Avg
Rock bass	C	C	Slow
Other			
Tessellated darter	R		
Common shiner	R		
Fallfish	R		
Golden shiner	U		
Spottail shiner	A		
Rainbow smelt	C		
White sucker	A		

A=Abundant, C=Common, U=Uncommon, R=Rare

Fishing: Should be fair to good for rock bass and fair for stocked trout (in the spring) and smallmouth bass.

Management: Bass Management Lake; special slot length and creel limits on bass. Statewide regulations apply for all other species (see current *Connecticut Anglers' Guide*).

Boating: Speed limit 20 mph. No water skiing (see current *Connecticut Boater's Guide*).

Comments: Special regulations should improve fishing by protecting larger bass and allowing anglers to harvest overabundant small bass. However, Colebrook is a flood-control reservoir that experiences extreme water level fluctuations. This results in unstable fish populations and may cause the effects of any special management efforts to be unpredictable and inconsistent. The State Record rock bass (1 lb. 3 oz.) was caught here in 1989.

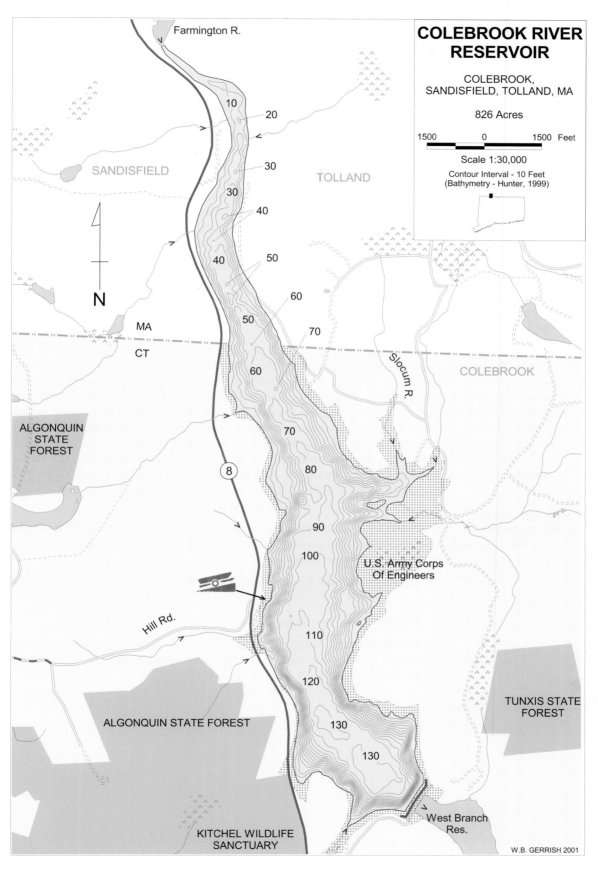

COLEBROOK RIVER RESERVOIR

COLEBROOK, SANDISFIELD, TOLLAND, MA

826 Acres

1500   0   1500 Feet

Scale 1:30,000

Contour Interval - 10 Feet
(Bathymetry - Hunter, 1999)

Farmington R.

SANDISFIELD

TOLLAND

10

20

30

30

40

40

50

60

50

70

60

MA

CT

70

ALGONQUIN
STATE
FOREST

8

80

90

100

Slocum R.

COLEBROOK

U.S. Army Corps
Of Engineers

Hill Rd.

110

120

130

130

ALGONQUIN STATE FOREST

TUNXIS STATE
FOREST

KITCHEL WILDLIFE
SANCTUARY

West Branch
Res.

W.B. GERRISH 2001

Congamond Lake (South, Middle, North Ponds)

Town(s): Suffield/Southwick (MA)   **465 acres**

Description: Congamond Lake is a natural lake within the Connecticut River Drainage Basin. It is located primarily in Massachusetts with only a small length of shoreline in Connecticut. The lake is separated into three distinct basins; North Pond (46 acres), Middle Pond (277 acres) and South Pond (142 acres). Small boats can pass through the culverts that connect the three basins. *Watershed*: The surrounding land is mostly agricultural with a moderate level of residential development. There is very little undeveloped woods or wetland. The lake is fed by Mountain Brook, bottom springs and surface runoff and drains into Great Brook. *Shoreline*: Almost entirely developed with homes. There is a large town beach (Babbs Beach) on the eastern shore. *Depth*: Max 40 ft., Mean 18 ft. *Transparency*: Fair; 7 ft. in summer. *Productivity*: High (eutrophic). *Bottom type*: Not available. *Stratification*: Occurs with a thermocline forming between 16 and 26 ft. Late summer oxygen levels decline to less than 4 ppm by a depth of 16 ft. and remain near zero in waters below 23 ft. *Vegetation*: Not surveyed. Eurasian water-milfoil is present.

Access: A boat launch operated by the town of Southwick is located on the western shore of Middle Pond. Facilities at the launch include a ramp with concrete slabs, parking for 20 cars, and chemical toilets (seasonal). *Directions*: Exit 40 off I-91, Rte. 20 west, Rte. 187 north, Rte. 168 west for 5 miles, first right after the causeway over the lake, launch is on the right. *Shore*: Limited to the launch area.

Fish: Congamond Lake is stocked by Connecticut and Massachusetts each spring with 6,100 catchable size **brown** and **rainbow trout**. In addition, 150-200 Atlantic salmon broodstock are stocked annually by Massachusetts when available. Few holdover trout are reported despite the presence of an extremely abundant alewife forage base. The bass population is in a good state of balance. **Largemouth bass** densities are average for smaller fish, but large fish (14-19") are abundant. **Chain pickerel** and **rock bass** are present at less than average densities. Small **sunfish** (mostly bluegill, some pumpkinseed, occasional hybrids) are extremely abundant and severely stockpiled with fish over 6" being rare. **Brown bullhead** are very abundant in the 8-12" size range. **American eels** are abundant and reach lengths to 3 ft. White suckers are common. Other fish species present at low densities are smallmouth bass, yellow perch, black crappie, tessellated darter and banded killifish.

Fishing: Should be good to excellent for largemouth bass, bullheads and eels and good seasonally for stocked trout. You can catch loads of sunfish, but most will be small.

Management: Border lake; some Massachusetts regulations apply (see current *Connecticut Anglers' Guide*).

Boating: No special regulations.

Comments: Anglers wishing to hold fishing tournaments here should contact Massachusetts Division of Fisheries and Wildlife at (413) 323-7632.

Congamond Lake
Fish Species and Abundance

	ALL SIZES	BIG FISH	GROWTH
Gamefish			
Largemouth bass	A	A	Avg
Smallmouth bass	R	R	Fast
Atlantic salmon	U	U	
Brown trout	C	R	
Rainbow trout	C		
Chain pickerel	U	U	Fast
Panfish			
Black crappie	R	R	< Avg
Yellow perch	R	R	> Avg
Brown bullhead	A	C	
Sunfish			
Bluegill	A	U	Slow
Pumpkinseed	A	R	Slow
Rock bass	U	U	> Avg
Other			
Tessellated darter	U		
Banded killifish	U		
Alewife	A		
White sucker	C		
American eel	A		

A=Abundant, C=Common, U=Uncommon, R=Rare

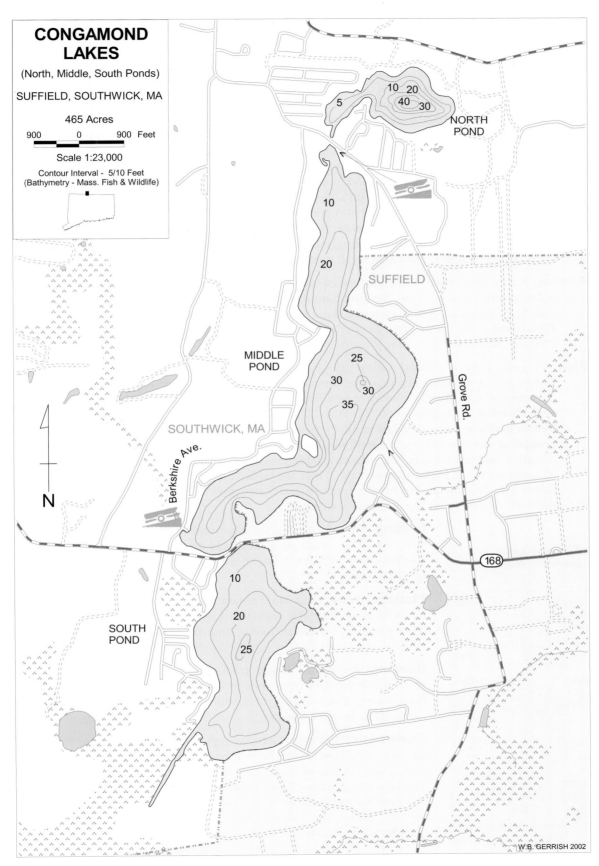

CONGAMOND LAKES

(North, Middle, South Ponds)

SUFFIELD, SOUTHWICK, MA

465 Acres

900   0   900   Feet

Scale 1:23,000

Contour Interval - 5/10 Feet
(Bathymetry - Mass. Fish & Wildlife)

NORTH POND

SUFFIELD

MIDDLE POND

Grove Rd.

SOUTHWICK, MA

Berkshire Ave.

168

SOUTH POND

W.B. GERRISH 2002

Coventry Lake (Wangumbaug Lake)

Town(s): Coventry

373 acres

Description: Coventry Lake is a natural lake within the Thames River Drainage Basin. The water level was raised several feet by a small masonry dam. *Watershed:* 1,896 acres of mostly residential land with moderate amounts of undeveloped woods and wetland and some agricultural land. The lake is fed mainly by bottom springs and surface runoff channeled through several small brooks. It drains southeast into Mill Brook, which flows into the Willimantic River. *Shoreline:* Heavily developed with cottages and permanent homes. *Depth:* Max 39 ft., Mean 21 ft. *Transparency:* Fair to clear; reduced to 10 ft. in late summer by algal blooms. *Productivity:* High (eutrophic). *Bottom type:* Sand, gravel, rubble and boulders in the shallows; mud in deeper water. *Stratification:* Occurs with a thermocline forming between 19 and 29 ft. Late summer oxygen levels are poor to marginal (4-5 ppm) between 16 and 20 ft. Oxygen then declines to less than 2 ppm in deeper water. *Vegetation:* Relatively sparse to moderately abundant with tapegrass the dominant submergent species. Eurasian water-milfoil and pondweeds are common in some areas. Water-nymph is present in small numbers.

Access: A state-owned boat launch is located on the southeastern shore. A parking fee is charged on holidays and weekends from the third Saturday in April through Columbus Day. Facilities at the launch include a ramp with concrete slabs, parking for 26 cars and chemical toilets (seasonal). *Directions:* From Rte. 44, Rte. 31 south for 4 miles, right (south) on Lake St., launch is 0.4 miles on right. *Shore:* Public access is restricted to launch area.

Fish: Coventry Lake is stocked during the spring and fall with 3,700 **brown** and **rainbow trout**. Holdover fish are limited by marginal summer oxygen levels in deeper water. **Largemouth bass** are common with slightly above average densities of greater than 12" fish. **Smallmouth bass** are very abundant in smaller sizes (less than 12"), but densities of legal size fish are only average. **Yellow perch** are very abundant in the 7-10" size range, with larger fish being uncommon. **Black crappie** numbers are average. **Chain pickerel** and **brown bullhead** are present at below average densities. **Sunfish** (mostly bluegill, some pumpkinseed, occasional redbreast) densities in the 7-9" range are much higher than average. There are higher than average densities of large (greater than 8") golden shiners, but smaller forage fish are uncommon. Other fish species present at low densities are common carp and American eel.

Fishing: Should be good for large sunfish; and fair to good for trout, bass and yellow perch. Anglers should catch good numbers of perch, but few large ones. Holdover brown trout are occasionally taken. A popular ice fishing spot.

Management: Bass Management Lake; special slot length and creel limits on bass. Statewide regulations apply for all other species (see current *Connecticut Anglers' Guide*). Annual walleye stocking began here in 2001.

Boating: Speed limit 6 mph from sunset to one hour after sunrise all days and on Sundays from noon to 4 p.m., May 15 to September 15 and from noon to 2 p.m. on July 4. Limit 40 mph at other times (see current *Connecticut Boater's Guide*).

Comments: Coventry Lake has high fishing pressure during the spring and summer and very high general recreational use (especially water skiing). It is a popular bass tournament lake, averaging 15 events annually. The lake has good smallmouth bass potential, but this species is stockpiled and harvest rates are high. Special regulations should improve fishing by protecting larger bass and allowing anglers to harvest overabundant small bass.

Coventry Lake Fish Species and Abundance

	ALL SIZES	BIG FISH	GROWTH
Gamefish			
Largemouth bass	C	C	Avg
Smallmouth bass	A	U	Slow
Brown trout	C	R	
Rainbow trout	C		
Chain pickerel	U	U	Avg
Panfish			
Black crappie	C	C	> Avg
Yellow perch	A	U	Avg
Brown bullhead	U	U	
Sunfish			
Bluegill	A	A	Fast
Pumpkinseed	C	C	Fast
Redbreast	R	R	
Other			
Golden shiner	C		
Common carp	U		
American eel	U		

A=Abundant, C=Common, U=Uncommon, R=Rare

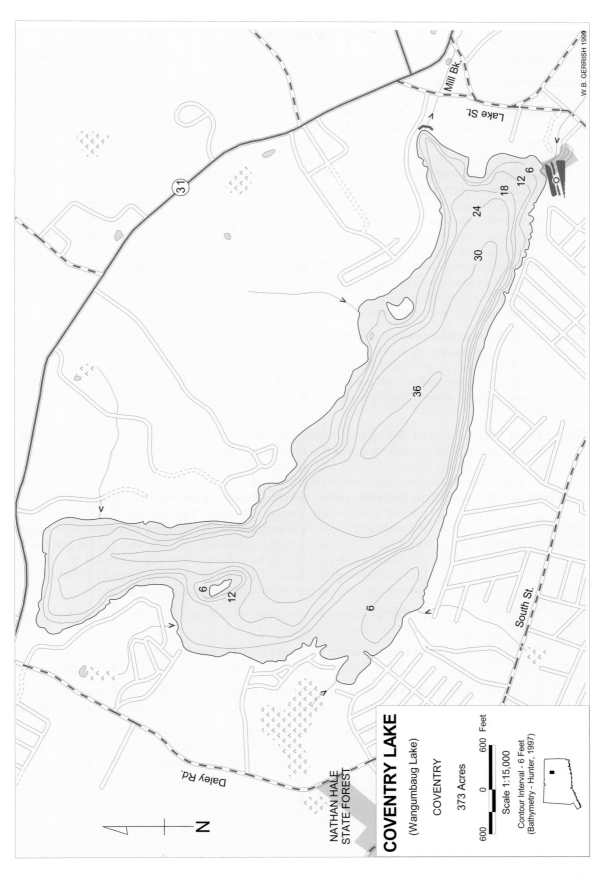

N

COVENTRY LAKE

(Wangumbaug Lake)

COVENTRY

373 Acres

Scale 1:15,000

600   0   600 Feet

Contour Interval - 6 Feet
(Bathymetry - Hunter, 1997)

NATHAN HALE
STATE FOREST

Daley Rd.

South St.

Lake St.

Mill Bk.

6
12
18
24
30
36
6
12
6

W.B. GERRISH 1999

Crystal Lake

Town(s): Ellington/Stafford

183 acres

Description: Crystal Lake is a natural lake within the Thames River Drainage Basin. The water level was raised 6 ft. by the construction of a stone and masonry dam with a concrete spillway. *Watershed*: 1,805 acres of mostly undeveloped woods and wetland interspersed with some residential development. The lake is fed by Aborn Brook, two other small brooks and by bottom springs. It drains north into Crystal Lake Brook, which flows into the Middle River and the Willimantic River. *Shoreline*: Dominated by private residences. The only areas without residences are: a town beach on the southern shore, a marshy cove on the southeastern shore and a small stretch of shrubs and trees on the northwestern shore where Rte. 30 borders the lake. *Depth*: Max 45 ft., Mean 25 ft. *Transparency*: Clear; 13-14 ft. in summer. *Productivity*: Moderate (mesotrophic). *Bottom type*: Sand, gravel and boulders in shoal areas; mud in deeper water. *Stratification*: Occurs with a thermocline forming between 20 and 30 ft. Late summer oxygen levels remain fair to good (5-7 ppm) between 20 and 26 ft. providing a zone of late summer trout habitat. Oxygen then declines to less than 3 ppm in deeper water. *Vegetation*: Relatively sparse along most areas of the shoreline and moderately abundant in the coves. Submergent vegetation is a mix of coontail, tapegrass, pondweeds, bladderwort and variable water-milfoil. Floating mats of white water-lily and water-shield are also in the coves.

Access: A state-owned boat launch is located on the western shore. Facilities at the launch include a paved ramp with concrete slabs, parking for 7 cars (across the road), and chemical toilets (seasonal). *Directions*: Exit 67 off I-84, north on Rte. 31 for 0.3 miles, right (north) on Rte. 30, proceed 0.5 miles north of Rte. 140 intersection, right on West Shore Rd., launch is on right. *Shore*: The most popular shore fishing spots are off Rte. 30 on the northwestern shore and near the town beach.

Fish: Crystal Lake is stocked during the spring and fall with 16,000 **brown** and **rainbow trout**. Holdover brown trout are very common due to good summer oxygen levels in deeper water. The lake retains a healthy bass population because most of the fishing pressure is directed toward trout. **Largemouth bass** are abundant in the 10-16" size range, but larger fish are less common. **Smallmouth bass, chain pickerel, yellow perch, black crappie** and **brown bullhead** are all present at less than average densities. **Sunfish** (mostly bluegill, some pumpkinseed, occasional redbreast and hybrids) are common with densities of 6-7" fish being higher than average. The lake has an extremely abundant, slow-growing alewife forage base supplemented by slightly less than average densities of golden shiners and banded killifish. Other fish species present are tessellated darter and white sucker.

Fishing: Should be excellent for both stocked and holdover trout; and good for bass and sunfish.

Management: Managed as a Trophy Trout Lake with special length and creel limits in place (see current *Connecticut Anglers' Guide*).

Boating: Speed limit 6 mph sunset to 9 a.m. and on Sundays from noon to 3 p.m., 45 mph at other times (see current *Connecticut Boater's Guide*).

Comments: Crystal Lake is one of Connecticut's best trout lakes. Holdovers commonly reach weights up to 2-5 pounds. The lake withstands extremely heavy fishing pressure, especially during the spring.

Crystal Lake
Fish Species and Abundance

	ALL SIZES	BIG FISH	GROWTH
Gamefish			
Largemouth bass	A	C	Avg
Smallmouth bass	U	U	Avg
Brown trout	A	C	
Rainbow trout	A		
Chain pickerel	U	U	Avg
Panfish			
Black crappie	R	R	Avg
Yellow perch	U	U	Avg
Brown bullhead	U	U	
Sunfish			
Bluegill	A	A	< Avg
Pumpkinseed	C	C	< Avg
Redbreast	U	R	
Other			
Tessellated darter	U		
Golden shiner	C		Slow
Banded killifish	C		
Alewife	A		Slow
White sucker	C		

A=Abundant, C=Common, U=Uncommon, R=Rare

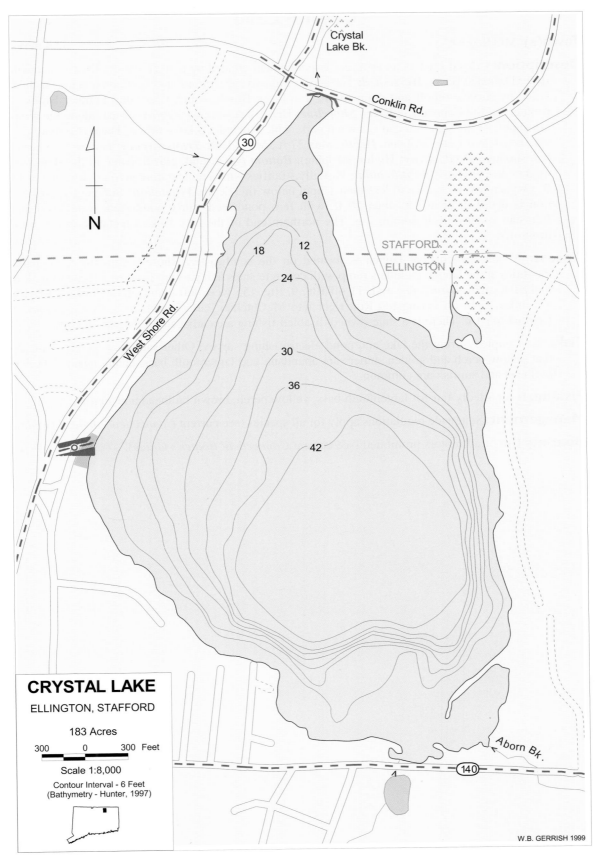

Crystal
Lake Bk.

Conklin Rd.

30

6

18   12

STAFFORD

ELLINGTON

24

30

36

42

West Shore Rd.

N

CRYSTAL LAKE

ELLINGTON, STAFFORD

183 Acres

300   0   300 Feet

Scale 1:8,000

Contour Interval - 6 Feet
(Bathymetry - Hunter, 1997)

Aborn Bk.

140

W.B. GERRISH 1999

Crystal Lake

Town(s): Middletown

Description: Crystal Lake is an artificial impoundment created by a 30 ft. dam in the Connecticut River Drainage Basin. **Watershed:** 176 acres of mostly agricultural and residential land. The lake is fed by surface runoff and drains north into Prout Brook, which flows into Sumner Brook, a tributary of the Connecticut River. **Shoreline:** Heavily developed with residences along the western shore. At the southern end is a town park, which includes a large beach. There is a small private beach at the northern end. **Depth:** Max 27 ft., Mean 10 ft. **Transparency:** Fair, 6-7 ft. during late summer. **Productivity:** High (eutrophic). **Bottom type:** Sand, gravel, ledge in the shallows; mud in deeper water. **Stratification:** Partially stratifies with a temperature gradient forming at 13 ft. Oxygen levels decline to less than 1 ppm below this depth. **Vegetation:** Submergent vegetation is dense in areas less than 10 ft. with fern pondweed, curly pondweed, waterweed and Eurasian water-milfoil dominating. The northern end of the lake lacks vegetation along steep drop-offs.

Access: A state-owned boat launch is located on the southeastern shore within the town park. Facilities at the launch include a ramp with concrete slabs and parking for 9 cars. Gate to park is locked at night. **Directions:** Exit 11 off Rte. 9, Rte. 155 west, left (south) on Millbrook Rd. for 1.5 miles, right on Livingston Rd., right into McCutchen Park, launch is in the park. **Shore:** Limited to park. There is a state-owned disabled fishing area adjacent to the parking lot.

Fish: Not sampled during the lake and pond electrofishing survey. Other sampling records indicate that yellow perch and golden shiners are abundant, and largemouth bass, chain pickerel, brown bullhead and sunfish are common.

Fishing: Is reportedly fair for largemouth bass, yellow perch, brown bullhead and sunfish.

Management: Statewide regulations apply for all species (see current *Connecticut Anglers' Guide*).

Boating: Use of all motors prohibited (see current *Connecticut Boater's Guide*).

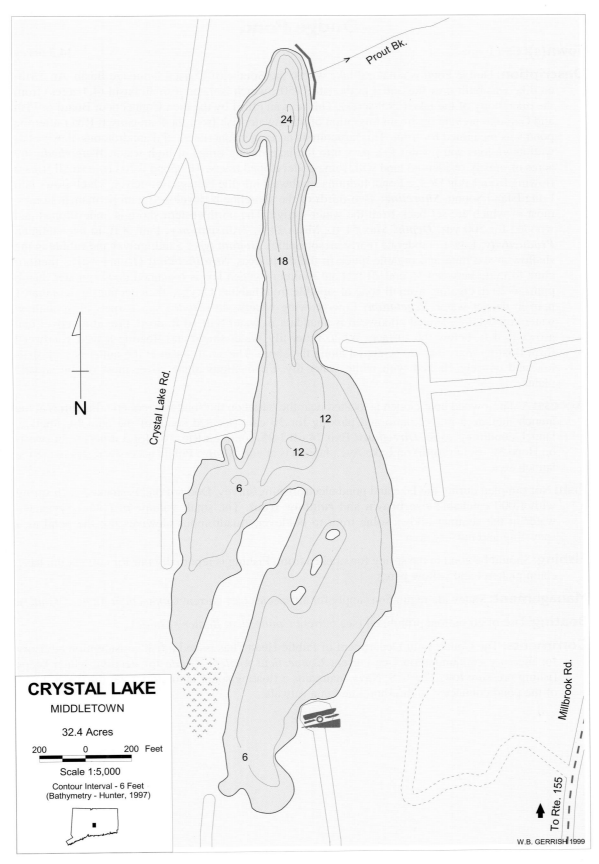

Prout Bk.

24

18

Crystal Lake Rd.

12

12

6

CRYSTAL LAKE

MIDDLETOWN

32.4 Acres

200   0   200   Feet

Scale 1:5,000

Contour Interval - 6 Feet
(Bathymetry - Hunter, 1997)

6

Millbrook Rd.

To Rte. 155

N

W.B. GERRISH 1999

Dodge Pond

Town(s): East Lyme

Description: Dodge Pond is a natural lake within the Southeast Coastal Drainage Basin. An earthen dike was built near the outlet in the late 1950s, which isolated a small basin (4.4 acres) from the main body of the lake (29.9 acres). This was an effort by the then Connecticut Board of Fish and Game to prevent upstream migration of warmwater fish from the Pattagansett River after the pond was reclaimed for trout. This structure is no longer functional, and anadromous alewives as well as various warmwater fish pass into the lake during times of high water. *Watershed*: 369 acres of mostly residential land with some undeveloped tracts. The pond is fed by a small stream flowing from Little Dodge Pond. It drains southwest into the Pattagansett River, which flows into Long Island Sound. *Shoreline*: Two-thirds of the shoreline is developed with permanent homes, most of which are set back from the water's edge. The northwestern shore is undeveloped and wooded for 500 yds. *Depth*: Max 51 ft., Mean 24 ft. *Transparency*: Fair; 8 ft. in late summer. *Productivity*: Low to moderate (early mesotrophic). *Bottom type*: Sand, gravel and rubble in the shallow areas; mud and organic muck in the deep areas. *Stratification*: Occurs with a thermocline forming between 16 and 23 ft. Late summer oxygen levels remained good (greater than 6 ppm) to 20 ft. creating a small zone of suitable trout habitat. Oxygen then declines to less than 1 ppm in deeper water. *Vegetation*: Low-growing waterweed (*Elodea* sp.) carpets most shallow water areas. Large-leaved pondweed is abundant in water 8 to 10 ft. deep, providing cover that grows to 4 ft. below the surface. White water-lily, water-shield and floating-leaved pondweed form floating mats that are scattered along the shore. The small basin at the outlet is very shallow and entirely choked with white water-lily. Filamentous algae cover most of the aquatic plants.

Access: A state-owned boat launch is located near the outlet on the southwestern end. Facilities at the launch include a gravel ramp and parking for 30 cars (located south of the launch). Shallow launch conditions exist. *Directions*: Exit 74 off I-95, south on Rte. 161 for 3 miles, right (west) on Hope St., right (north) on Lake Ave., launch is at end. *Shore*: Public access is restricted to the launch area.

Fish: Not sampled during the lake and pond electrofishing survey. Dodge Pond is stocked each spring with 1,000 catchable size **brown** and **rainbow trout**. The small volume of cold, oxygenated water in the summer allows some trout to holdover. Anadromous alewives use the pond as a spawning and nursery area.

Fishing: Should be good in the spring for stocked trout. Fishing is reportedly fair for largemouth bass, chain pickerel and yellow perch.

Management: Statewide regulations apply for all species (see current *Connecticut Anglers' Guide*).

Boating: Use of all motors prohibited (see current *Connecticut Boater's Guide*).

Comments: The Connecticut Department of Public Health has issued a fish consumption advisory for mercury contamination (see current *Connecticut Anglers' Guide* for details), which keeps fishing pressure low. The U.S. Navy maintains a floating sonar laboratory over the deepest part of the pond connected to the shoreline via a catwalk.

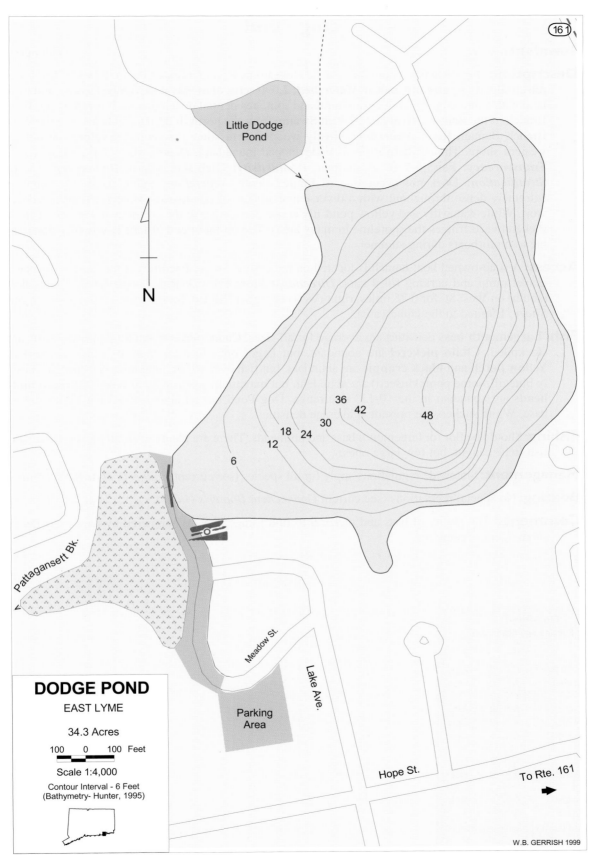

Little Dodge
Pond

N

36
42
48
30
18 24
12
6

Pattagansett Bk.

Meadow St.

Lake Ave.

Parking
Area

DODGE POND

EAST LYME

34.3 Acres

100   0   100 Feet

Scale 1:4,000

Contour Interval - 6 Feet
(Bathymetry- Hunter, 1995)

Hope St.

To Rte. 161

W.B. GERRISH 1999

Dog Pond

Town(s): Goshen   **65.8 acres**

Description: Dog Pond is a natural lake in the Housatonic River Drainage Basin. Its water level was raised slightly by an earthen dam. *Watershed*: 2,090 acres of mostly undeveloped woods and wetland with a moderate level of agricultural and some residential development. It is fed by the West Branch of the Bantam River and by Peat Swamp from the north. It drains southeast into the West Branch Bantam River. *Shoreline*: Mostly wooded with some residential development on the western shore. The northern shore is undeveloped marshland. *Depth*: Max 11 ft., Mean 4.7 ft. *Transparency*: Fair; 6-7 ft. in summer. *Productivity*: High (eutrophic). *Bottom type*: Mud. *Stratification*: Does not occur due to limited depth. *Vegetation*: Submergent vegetation is extremely dense throughout with a diverse assemblage of pondweeds, waterweed and bladderwort. White water-lily and yellow pond-lily create dense mats at the northern and southern ends. Pickerelweed fringes the shoreline in many areas. The northern end of lake is virtually impassable to motorboats during summer.

Access: A state-owned boat launch is located on the eastern shore. Facilities at the launch include a gravel ramp and parking for 4 cars. *Directions*: From Rte. 63, Rte. 4 west for 0.7 miles, left (south) on West St. for 0.75 miles, right (west) on Town Hill Rd. for 0.6 miles, launch is on right. *Shore*: Limited to the launch area.

Fish: **Largemouth bass** densities are average for all sizes. Chain pickerel and all panfish species are stockpiled. **Chain pickerel** are abundant, but larger ones (greater than 16") are uncommon. **Yellow perch** and **black crappie** are abundant, but fish over 10" are uncommon. **Sunfish** (mostly bluegill, some pumpkinseed) are abundant, but maximum size is only around 7". **Brown bullheads** are abundant in the 10-12" size range. Dog Pond has an abundant golden shiner forage base. White suckers are present at average densities.

Fishing: Should be fair for largemouth bass and bullheads. There are plenty of small pickerel and panfish to be caught, but few large ones.

Management: Statewide regulations apply for all species (see current *Connecticut Anglers' Guide*).

Boating: No special regulations (see current *Connecticut Boater's Guide*).

Comments: The ability of bass and pickerel to find forage may be hampered by the overly dense submergent vegetation.

Dog Pond Fish Species and Abundance	ALL SIZES	BIG FISH	GROWTH
Gamefish			
Largemouth bass	C	C	Avg
Chain pickerel	A	U	< Slow
Panfish			
Black crappie	A	R	< Avg
Yellow perch	A	U	< Slow
Brown bullhead	A	C	
Sunfish			
Bluegill	A	R	Avg
Pumpkinseed	A	R	Slow
Other			
Golden shiner	A		< Slow
White sucker	C		

A=Abundant, C=Common, U=Uncommon, R=Rare

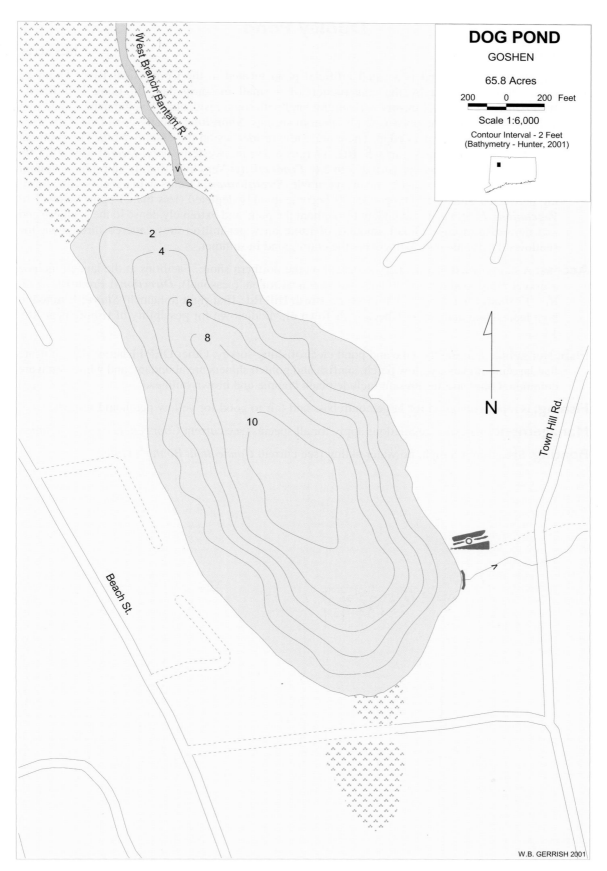

DOG POND

GOSHEN

65.8 Acres

200   0   200   Feet

Scale 1:6,000

Contour Interval - 2 Feet
(Bathymetry - Hunter, 2001)

West Branch Bantam R.

2

4

6

8

10

N

Town Hill Rd.

Beach St.

W.B. GERRISH 2001

Dooley Pond

Town(s): Middletown   **18.5 acres**

Description: Dooley Pond is a small artificial pond located in the Connecticut River Drainage Basin. It was created by the construction of a small masonry dam on Long Hill Brook. *Watershed:* 495 acres of mostly agricultural land with some residential development. In addition to Long Hill Brook, the pond is fed by bottom springs. *Shoreline:* Mostly open land with grass and small shrubs to waters edge. There are a few residences on the eastern shore. The southern end of the pond becomes a marsh. Rte. 17 runs along the western shore. *Depth:* Max 16.5 ft., Mean 7.2 ft. *Transparency:* Turbid; 3 to 5 ft. *Productivity:* Very high (highly eutrophic). *Bottom type:* Mostly mud; some sand, gravel and rubble. *Stratification:* Occurs with a thermocline forming between 7 and 13 ft. Oxygen levels become quickly depleted (less than 1 ppm) below 7 ft. *Vegetation:* Waterweed is abundant throughout the pond and extremely dense in the southern end and northeastern cove. Small amounts of Eurasian water-milfoil are scattered throughout the shallows. Dense algal growth covers the entire pond in summer.

Access: A state-owned boat launch is located on the northern shore. Facilities at the launch include a gravel ramp, parking for 20 cars and chemical toilets (seasonal). *Directions:* From Rte. 155, Rte. 17 south for 1.2 miles, left (east) on Brush Hill Rd., first right to launch. *Shore:* Limited to boat launch and dam areas. Check with Town of Middletown for possibility of fishing near Rte. 17.

Fish: Not sampled during the lake and pond electrofishing survey. Other DEP Fisheries data indicate that largemouth bass, yellow perch, sunfish and golden shiners are abundant, and white perch are common. Other species present include black crappie and brown bullhead.

Fishing: Is reportedly good for largemouth bass and fair to good for yellow perch and sunfish.

Management: Statewide regulations apply for all species (see current *Connecticut Anglers' Guide*).

Boating: Speed limit 8 mph, no water-skiing (see current *Connecticut Boater's Guide*).

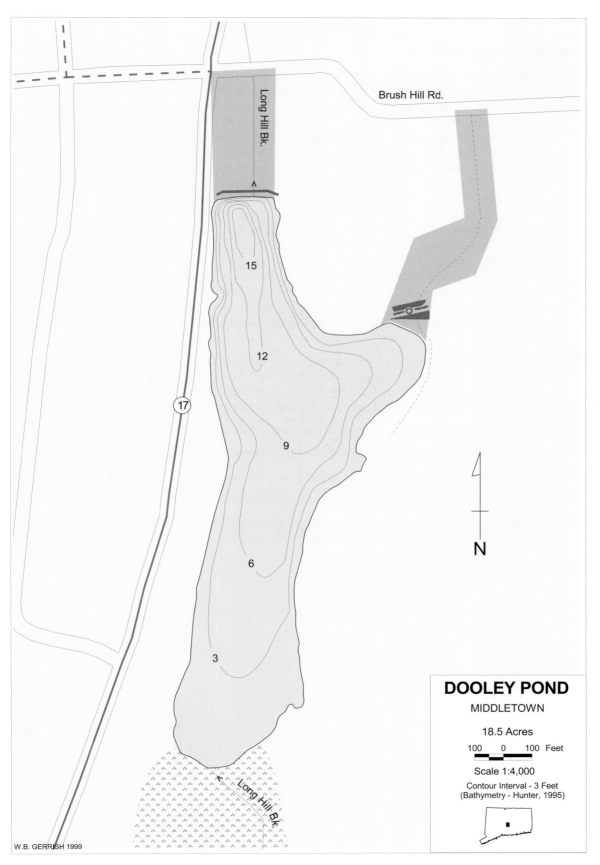

Brush Hill Rd.

Long Hill Bk.

15

12

17

9

6

3

N

Long Hill Bk.

DOOLEY POND

MIDDLETOWN

18.5 Acres

100   0   100 Feet

Scale 1:4,000

Contour Interval - 3 Feet
(Bathymetry - Hunter, 1995)

W.B. GERRISH 1999

Eagleville Lake

Town(s): Coventry/Mansfield

76.9 acres

Description: Eagleville Lake is an old millpond impoundment on the Willimantic River in the Thames River Drainage Basin. The 18 ft. dam was restored in 1994. There are a number of low, brushy islands in the northern end of the lake with numerous channels winding between them. *Watershed*: 68,984 acres encompassing the Willimantic River watershed. The land surrounding the lake is mostly agricultural with moderate levels of residential development. In addition to the Willimantic River, the pond is fed by Cedar Swamp Brook, Eagleville Brook and several small brooks. Outlet water spills over the dam and continues onward as the Willimantic River. *Shoreline*: The western shore is mostly wooded with some cottages and a small town beach. The eastern shoreline, primarily open farmland, is flanked by a railroad track. *Depth*: Max 9 ft., Mean less than 3 ft. *Transparency*: Turbid; 5 ft. in late summer. *Productivity*: High (eutrophic). *Bottom type*: Sand, gravel, rubble and organic muck. *Stratification*: Does not occur due to limited depth. Although the waters are usually mixed, oxygen levels in deeper water can be reduced to less than 2 ppm during periods of low flow. *Vegetation*: Submergent vegetation is common in most areas to depths of 5 ft. with ribbonleaf pondweed the dominant species. The southwestern shoreline lacks vegetation. Islands of water willow, an emergent shrubby species, are scattered along the shoreline and are frequently fringed by floating mats of yellow pond-lily and water-shield. Water willow islands are abundant in the north end of the lake where numerous channels wind through them.

Access: A state-owned car-top access is located on the southern shore at the dam on the west side of the river. There is a gravel parking area with room for 10 cars. *Directions*: From Rte. 32, Rte. 275 west, first right (north) on Pine Lake Shores Rd. after bridge and waterfall, access is immediately on the right. *Shore*: Public shore access is limited to state property on either side of the dam.

Fish: Not sampled during the lake and pond electrofishing survey.

Fishing: Is reportedly fair for largemouth bass, chain pickerel, yellow perch, sunfish and bullheads.

Management: Statewide regulations apply for all species (see current *Connecticut Anglers' Guide*).

Boating: Speed limit 8 mph, no water-skiing (see current *Connecticut Boater's Guide*).

Comments: The access area is heavily used in the spring by a combination of pond anglers, canoeists and anglers fishing the Willimantic River below the dam.

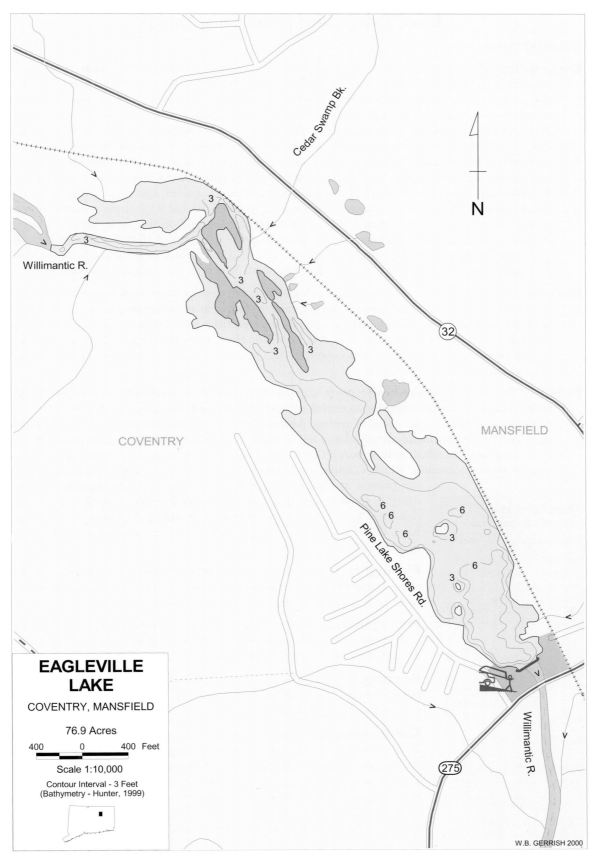

Cedar Swamp Bk.

N

Willimantic R.

32

3

3

3

3

3

COVENTRY

MANSFIELD

Pine Lake Shores Rd.

6
6
6
6
6
3
6
3

EAGLEVILLE LAKE

COVENTRY, MANSFIELD

76.9 Acres

400   0   400 Feet

Scale 1:10,000

Contour Interval - 3 Feet
(Bathymetry - Hunter, 1999)

Willimantic R.

275

W.B. GERRISH 2000

East Twin Lake (Washining Lake)

Town(s): Salisbury   **569 acres**

Description: East Twin Lake is a natural lake in the Housatonic River Drainage Basin. The lake is connected to West Twin Lake by a culvert with about 3 ft. of clearance. A large, narrow island in the middle of the lake is joined to the shore via a causeway. *Watershed*: 2,639 acres of mostly undeveloped woods and wetland. The lake is fed by three wetland streams and by bottom springs. It drains into West Twin Lake. *Shoreline*: There is moderate residential development along the eastern and southern shores. Much of the northern shore is wetland and owned by the State. There is farmland and several private residences on the western shore. The island is privately owned and mostly wooded. *Depth*: Max 81 ft., Mean 32 ft. *Transparency*: Clear; 13-15 ft. in summer. *Productivity*: Moderate (mesotrophic). *Bottom type*: Sand, gravel and rock in the shallows. *Stratification*: Occurs with a thermocline forming between 19 and 33 ft. Late summer oxygen levels remain good (greater than 5 ppm) to a depth of 30 ft. and decline to less than 2 ppm in deeper water. *Vegetation*: Submergent vegetation is dense to depths of 15 ft. Eurasian water-milfoil is the dominant species, with tapegrass and a diverse assemblage of pondweeds. Some shallow areas (less than 4 ft.) are carpeted with stonewort. Waterweed and coontail are common.

Access: A state-owned car-top launch area is located on the eastern shore with parking for 4 cars. There is also a private marina located on the eastern shore that rents motorboats and allows public launching for a fee. *Directions*: To state access area from Rte. 7, Rte. 44 west, right (north) on Twin Lakes Rd. (0.3 miles after Rte. 44 crosses the Housatonic River) for 0.75 miles, bear left at fork onto Twin Lakes Rd., access is on left, 0.25 miles past O'Hara's Marina. *Shore*: Limited to state land at car-top launch area.

Fish: East Twin Lake is stocked each spring with 16,000 catchable size **brown** and **rainbow trout**. Many brown trout hold over due to excellent water quality and special regulations (see below). Smaller **largemouth bass** occur at average densities, but 13-19" fish are abundant. **Smallmouth bass** and **brown bullhead** are present at less than average densities. Large **chain pickerel** (15-22") are abundant. Small **yellow perch** (less than 8") are very abundant with larger ones occurring at average densities. **Black crappie** are common in the 8-13" size range. **Rock bass** to 9" are present at slightly higher than average densities. **Sunfish** (mostly bluegill, some pumpkinseed, occasional redbreast) are present at average densities. East Twin has an abundant alewife and golden shiner forage base. Other fish species present at low densities are white perch, white suckers and bridled shiners.

Fishing: Should be excellent for stocked trout, large holdover brown trout, largemouth bass and chain pickerel; fair to good for crappie and rock bass; and fair for yellow perch and sunfish.

Management: Trophy Trout Lake; special length and creel limits on trout. Statewide regulations apply for all other species with restrictions on the use of live bait (see current *Connecticut Anglers' Guide*).

Boating: Daytime speed limit 35 mph, 6 mph ½ hr. after sunset to ½ hr. before sunrise. Use of radios prohibited from 11:00 p.m. to 6:00 a.m. (see current *Connecticut Boater's Guide*).

Comments: The illegal introduction of alewives (circa 1990) into East Twin Lake destroyed Connecticut's best kokanee fishery. However, a now thriving alewife population and special trout regulations have caused East Twin to become one of the best lakes in the state for large, holdover brown trout. The lake could easily support another pelagic gamefish such as walleye; however, its best potential lies in management for trophy brown trout. Zebra mussels were discovered in the lake in 1998. The ▼

East Twin Lake
Fish Species and Abundance

	ALL SIZES	BIG FISH	GROWTH
Gamefish			
Largemouth bass	A	A	Ave
Smallmouth bass	U	U	Avg
Brown trout	A	C	
Rainbow trout	A		
Kokanee	R		
Chain pickerel	A	A	Avg
Panfish			
Black crappie	C	C	Avg
Yellow perch	A	C	< Avg
Brown bullhead	C	C	
Sunfish			
Bluegill	C	C	< Avg
Pumpkinseed	C	U	< Avg
Redbreast	U	R	Slow
Rock bass	C	C	Slow
Other			
Bridled shiner	R		
Golden shiner	C		Avg
Alewife	A		< Avg
Creek chubsucker	C		

A=Abundant, C=Common, U=Uncommon, R=Rare

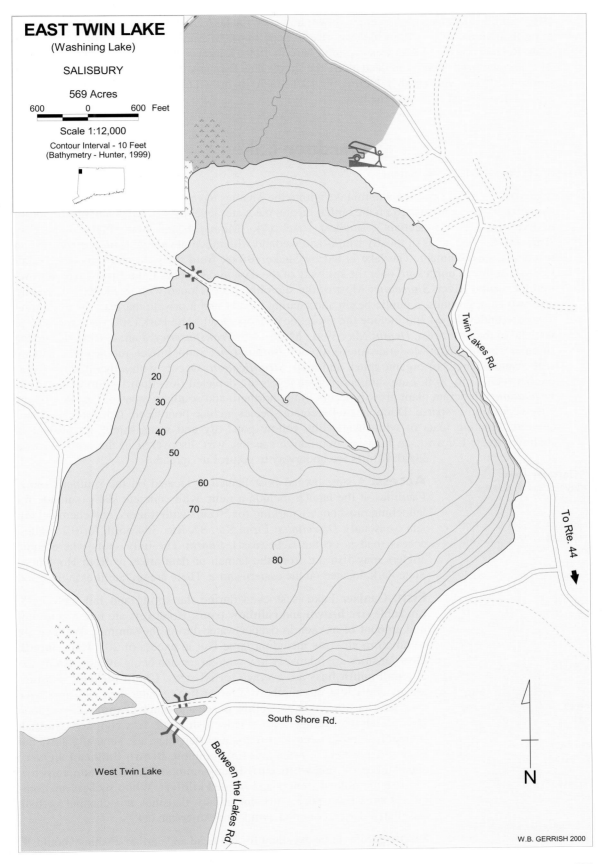

EAST TWIN LAKE

(Washining Lake)

SALISBURY

569 Acres

600   0   600 Feet

Scale 1:12,000

Contour Interval - 10 Feet
(Bathymetry - Hunter, 1999)

10

20

30

40

50

60

70

80

Twin Lakes Rd.

To Rte. 44

South Shore Rd.

Between the Lakes Rd.

West Twin Lake

N

W.B. GERRISH 2000

effects of this introduction are yet unknown; however, the lake will be closely monitored to determine their impact. East Twin has historically been home to some very large brown trout. The State Record (16 lb. 14 oz.) was captured here in 1986. Larger fish have also been observed. A 21 lb. brown trout was found dead along the shore. This fish was 10 inches in length when it was stocked only two years earlier. During the 1970s, a 30 lb. brown trout was captured by DEP biologists and released back into the lake.

Gardner Lake

Town(s): Bozrah/Montville/Salem

529 acres

Description: Gardner Lake is a natural lake within the Thames River Drainage Basin. A 168 ft. long earthen dam was constructed on the outlet, raising the water level by 4 ft. An island off the southeastern shore is Connecticut's smallest state park (Minnie Island State Park, 0.4 acres). *Watershed*: 3,537 acres of mostly woods and wetland with moderate amounts of agricultural and residential development. The lake is fed by Sucker Brook from the west and four other small streams. It drains northward over the spillway of the dam into Gardner Lake Brook, which flows into the Yantic River. *Shoreline*: Most of the shoreline is developed with residences. There are also two campgrounds, a public beach and boating facility and a private marina. The remaining areas are undeveloped and include the shoreline of Hopemead State Park (300 yds.) and a large wetland to the northwest. *Depth*: Max 39 ft., Mean 14 ft. *Transparency*: Fair; 8-10 ft. during the summer. *Productivity*: Moderate (mesotrophic). *Bottom type*: Sand, gravel, rubble and boulders, with scattered areas of organic muck and mud. *Stratification*: Occurs with a thermocline forming between 23 to 30 ft. Late summer oxygen levels are depleted (less than 1 ppm) below 23 ft. *Vegetation*: Moderate plant growth occurs in the northern and southern areas of the lake, otherwise vegetation is sparse. Dominant submergent species include pondweed, tapegrass and bladderwort. Floating mats of white water-lily, yellow pond-lily and water-shield are present in shallow coves. Fanwort, an invasive non-native species, was discovered in the north cove in 2000. Efforts are underway to control its spread.

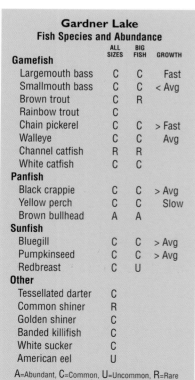

Gardner Lake
Fish Species and Abundance

Gamefish	ALL SIZES	BIG FISH	GROWTH
Largemouth bass	C	C	Fast
Smallmouth bass	C	C	< Avg
Brown trout	C	R	
Rainbow trout	C		
Chain pickerel	C	C	> Fast
Walleye	C	C	Avg
Channel catfish	R	R	
White catfish	C	C	
Panfish			
Black crappie	C	C	> Avg
Yellow perch	C	C	Slow
Brown bullhead	A	A	
Sunfish			
Bluegill	C	C	> Avg
Pumpkinseed	C	C	> Avg
Redbreast	C	U	
Other			
Tessellated darter	C		
Common shiner	R		
Golden shiner	C		
Banded killifish	C		
White sucker	C		
American eel	U		

A=Abundant, C=Common, U=Uncommon, R=Rare

Access: A state-owned boat launch is located on the southern shore. Facilities at the launch include a ramp with concrete slabs (suitable for launching most boats), parking for 50 cars with trailers, and chemical toilets (seasonal). *Directions*: From Rte. 82, Rte. 354 north for 0.25 miles, access road is on the right (east). *Shore*: The only spots where shore anglers may fish are from the launch or dam areas or from Hopemead State Park, located on the eastern shore. There are no facilities at the park.

Fish: Gardner Lake is stocked during the spring and fall with 7,000 catchable size **brown** and **rainbow trout**. Holdovers are rare due to limited amount of oxygen in deeper water during the summer. **Walleye** are common in all sizes including large fish in excess of 20". **Largemouth bass** densities are relatively low with larger fish being average. Densities of **smallmouth bass** are average for all sizes. **Chain pickerel** densities are generally low, but numbers of larger fish (greater than 18") are above average. Densities of larger **yellow perch** and **black crappie** (greater than 10") are above average with smaller fish being less common. **Sunfish** (bluegill, pumpkinseed and redbreast) densities are generally low, but large (greater than 7") bluegills are common. **Brown bullhead** are very abundant to 13" and **white catfish** are common. The most numerous forage fish are golden shiners and banded killifish. White suckers are common. Other fish species present at low densities are channel catfish, tessellated darter, common shiner and American eel.

Fishing: Should be excellent for bullhead and catfish. Fishing should ▼

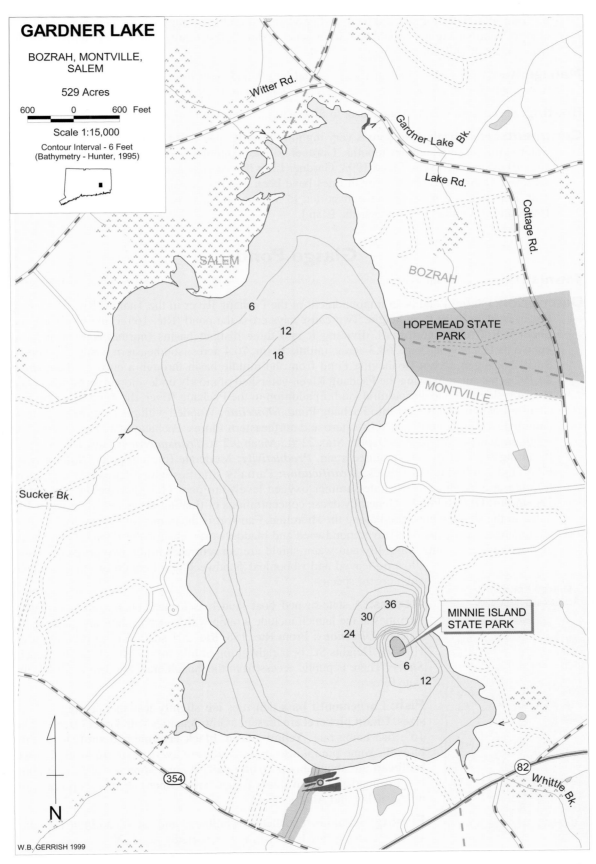

GARDNER LAKE

BOZRAH, MONTVILLE, SALEM

529 Acres

600   0   600   Feet

Scale 1:15,000

Contour Interval - 6 Feet
(Bathymetry - Hunter, 1995)

Witter Rd.

Gardner Lake Bk.

Lake Rd.

Cottage Rd.

SALEM

6

12

18

BOZRAH

HOPEMEAD STATE
PARK

MONTVILLE

Sucker Bk.

36

30

24

MINNIE ISLAND
STATE PARK

6

12

N

354

82

Whittle Bk.

W.B. GERRISH 1999

be good seasonally for stocked trout and good year-round for walleye, bass, pickerel, perch and crappie. Sunfish angling should be fair. In general, don't expect large numbers of panfish, but the fish you catch will probably be good sized.

Management: Bass Management Lake; special length and creel limits on bass. Statewide regulations apply for all other species (see current *Connecticut Anglers' Guide*).

Boating: Speed limit 6 mph from sunset to 8:00 a.m. (see current *Connecticut Boater's Guide*).

Comments: Trout fishing pressure is very high in the early spring. Heavy recreational boating and water skiing during summer months. Gardner is also a popular bass tournament lake and averages 10 events each year. Since 1993, Gardner Lake has been stocked annually with 7,500, 4-5" walleyes. Both survival and growth rates have been good with fish reaching 16" by their third year. Reportedly, a house being transported to Minnie Island went through the ice in the early 1900s and lies on the bottom near the island.

Glasgo Pond

Town(s): Griswold/Voluntown

168 acres

Description: Glasgo Pond is an impoundment of the Pachaug River in the Thames River Drainage Basin. Its dam is 20 ft. in height. Two causeways cross the pond (Rte. 165 to the southeast and Sheldon Rd. to the northeast), dividing it into three distinct basins (northeastern basin, also known as Doaneville Pond, 68.3 acres; middle basin, 76.4 acres; southeastern basin 23.0 acres). Small boats can access Doaneville Pond from the middle basin through a culvert. *Watershed*: 24,192 acres encompassing the Pachaug River watershed of mostly undeveloped forest with clusters of residential and agricultural land. In addition to the Pachaug River, the pond is fed by five small brooks. It drains west into Pachaug Pond. *Shoreline*: Wooded with concentrations of residential development on the southwestern and northeastern shores. Pachaug State Forest abuts the southern and eastern shores. *Depth*: Max 21 ft., Mean 9.2 ft. *Transparency*: Fair; reduced to 5 ft. during summer by a tea-colored stain. *Productivity*: Moderate (mesotrophic). *Bottom type*: Fine sand, silt and organic muck. *Stratification*: Partially stratifies with a temperature gradient forming at a depth of 16 ft. Late summer oxygen levels are poor (1.3 ppm) below this depth. *Vegetation*: Glasgo Pond – Generally dense concentrations of floating-heart and white water-lily occur in the shallow coves and along the shoreline. Fanwort is the dominant submergent species with some areas of floating-leaved pondweed and bladderworts. Doaneville Pond – Dense mats of floating-heart, white water-lily and water-shield are concentrated in the two northern coves. Floating-leaved and ribbonleaf pondweed and fanwort are the dominant submergent species.

Access: A state-owned boat launch is located on the northern shore. Facilities at the launch include a ramp with concrete slabs and parking for 20 cars. *Directions*: From Rte. 138, Rte. 201 south for 1.5 miles, east on Hillview Heights St., bear right at top of hill, follow gravel road to launch. *Shore*: There is public access from the launch area, the dam and from the state forest.

Fish: Largemouth bass densities are slightly less than average for all sizes. **Chain pickerel** are present at low densities with larger (greater than 16") fish being rare. **Yellow perch**, **black crappie** and **sunfish** (mostly bluegill, some pumpkinseed) densities are average for all sizes. **Brown bullhead** are abundant and **white catfish** are common to 13". The pond has an abundant golden shiner forage base. Other fish species present are white sucker and American eel.

Fishing: Should be excellent for bullhead and catfish and fair for other species. Early spring bass fishing is reportedly good. ▼

Glasgo Pond Fish Species and Abundance			
	ALL SIZES	BIG FISH	GROWTH
Gamefish			
Largemouth bass	C	C	> Avg
Chain pickerel	C	U	Slow
White catfish	C	C	
Panfish			
Black crappie	C	C	Avg
Yellow perch	C	C	Avg
Brown bullhead	A	A	
Sunfish			
Bluegill	C	C	> Avg
Pumpkinseed	C	C	Avg
Other			
Golden shiner	A		
White sucker	C		
American eel	R		

A=Abundant, C=Common, U=Uncommon, R=Rare

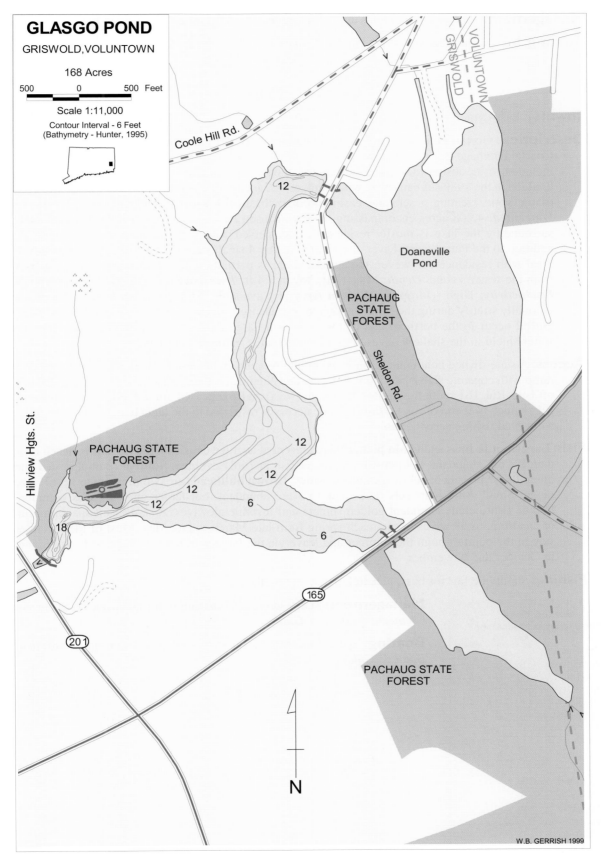

GLASGO POND

GRISWOLD, VOLUNTOWN

168 Acres

500   0   500   Feet

Scale 1:11,000

Contour Interval - 6 Feet
(Bathymetry - Hunter, 1995)

Coole Hill Rd.

VOLUNTOWN
GRISWOLD

Doaneville
Pond

PACHAUG
STATE
FOREST

Sheldon Rd.

Hillview Hgts. St.

PACHAUG STATE
FOREST

12

12

12

12

6

12

12

6

18

165

201

PACHAUG STATE
FOREST

N

W.B. GERRISH 1999

Management: Statewide regulations apply for all species (see current *Connecticut Anglers' Guide*).

Boating: No special regulations (see current *Connecticut Boater's Guide*).

Gorton Pond

Town(s): East Lyme   **52.4 acres**

Description: Gorton Pond is an artificial impoundment of the Pattagansett River in the Southeast Coastal Drainage Basin. When the dam was rebuilt in the late 1980s, a permanent fish ladder was included in its design to allow anadromous alewives to migrate into the pond. The pond was dredged in the 1980s. A causeway with a culvert (22 inches of clearance) crosses the northern end of the pond creating a separate basin (northern basin 5.1 acres, southern basin 47.3 acres). *Watershed*: 4,208 acres encompassing the Pattagansett River watershed. The land immediately surrounding the lake is mostly residential, interspersed with some industrial development. In addition to the Pattagansett River, the pond is fed by 4 small streams. *Shoreline*: Entirely developed with residences; however, the eastern shore is partially wooded with the homes set back from the water's edge. *Depth*: Max 11 ft., Mean 7.4 ft. *Transparency*: Turbid; 4 ft. in summer. *Productivity*: High (eutrophic). *Bottom type*: Not available. *Stratification*: The lake does not thermally stratify during the summer. *Vegetation*: Dense concentrations of variable-leaved water-milfoil occur in the northern end of the pond with large floating mats of white water-lily and water-shield in the shallow coves. Vegetation is scarce in the southern end.

Access: A state-owned boat launch is located on the western shore. Facilities at the launch include a ramp with concrete slabs, parking for 15 cars and chemical toilets (seasonal). *Directions*: Exit 74 off I-95, Rte. 161 south for 2 miles, turn right (west) on Roxbury Rd. for 0.2 miles, right on Kevin Rd., launch is at end of road. *Shore*: Public access is restricted to the launch area, which includes a disabled fishing access area.

Fish: **Largemouth bass** and **chain pickerel** are present at average densities. Small **yellow perch** (less than 8") are abundant, but densities of larger fish are only average. **Sunfish** (pumpkinseed and bluegill) are present at below average densities. **Brown bullheads** are common in the 12-13" size range. Small **American eels** (less than 15") are abundant, but larger ones are less common. Forage fish include abundant golden shiners and juvenile alewives. A significant spawning run of anadromous alewives occurs each spring from late March to late May. Most of the juveniles stay in the pond through the summer and leave via the Pattagansett River to Long Island Sound in October and November.

Fishing: Should be fair for bass, pickerel, perch and bullheads.

Management: Statewide regulations apply for all species (see current *Connecticut Anglers' Guide*).

Boating: Speed limit 8 mph, no water-skiing (see current *Connecticut Boater's Guide*).

Gorton Pond
Fish Species and Abundance

	ALL SIZES	BIG FISH	GROWTH
Gamefish			
Largemouth bass	C	C	Fast
Chain pickerel	C	C	< Avg
Panfish			
Yellow perch	A	C	Avg
Brown bullhead	C	C	
Sunfish			
Bluegill	C	C	Fast
Pumpkinseed	C	C	Fast
Other			
Golden shiner	A		
Alewife	A		
American eel	A		

A=Abundant, C=Common, U=Uncommon, R=Rare

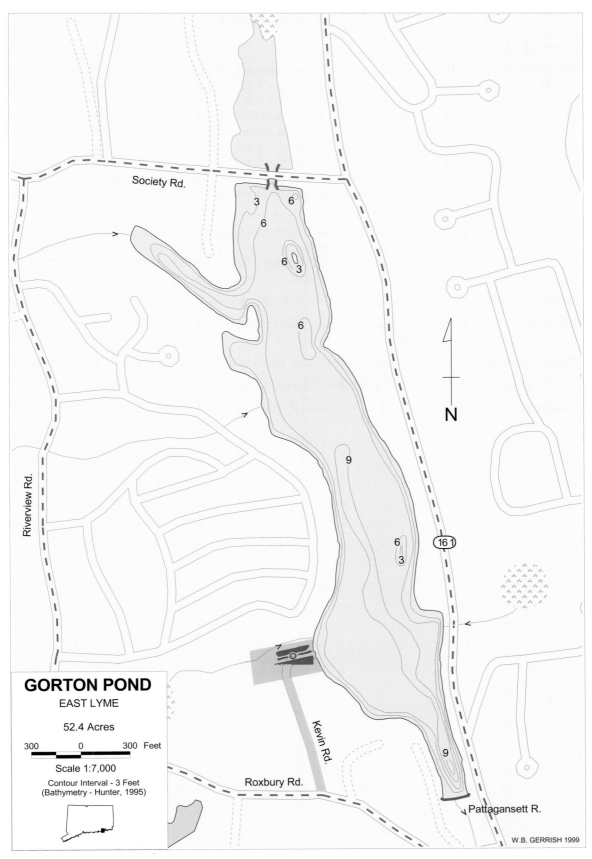

GORTON POND

EAST LYME

52.4 Acres

300 0 300 Feet

Scale 1:7,000

Contour Interval - 3 Feet
(Bathymetry - Hunter, 1995)

Society Rd.

Riverview Rd.

Kevin Rd.

Roxbury Rd.

Pattagansett R.

N

16 1

W.B. GERRISH 1999

Great Hill Pond

Town(s): Portland   **76.1 acres**

Description: Great Hill Pond is an artificial impoundment in the Connecticut River Drainage Basin. It was created by the construction of a 10 ft. earthen dike on Great Hill Pond Brook. *Watershed*: 768 acres of mostly undeveloped woods with little residential and agricultural development. The lake is fed by Rattlesnake Brook and a small stream from the north. *Shoreline*: The southern half of the lake is heavily developed with residences; however, the northern shore is mostly wooded. *Depth*: Max 8 ft., Mean 5.5 ft. *Transparency*: Fair; 5-6 ft. in late summer. *Productivity*: Moderate (early mesotrophic). *Bottom type*: Sand, rubble and mud. *Stratification*: Does not occur due to limited depth. *Vegetation*: Common in summer with fanwort, pondweeds, tapegrass, coontail and bladderworts present. Floating mats of water-shield and yellow pond-lily are also scattered along the shoreline.

Access: Car-top anglers may access the pond at state-owned property on the eastern shore. There is a dirt pull-off on Great Hill Pond Rd. with parking for 2 cars. *Directions*: From Rtes. 66 and 151 in Colbalt, Depot Hill Rd. north for 1 mile, continue straight on Great Hill Pond Rd. for 100 yds., access is on left. *Shore*: Limited to state land.

Fish: Not sampled during the lake and pond electrofishing survey.

Fishing: Is reportedly fair for largemouth bass, chain pickerel, yellow perch, black crappie, sunfish, bullheads and white catfish.

Management: Statewide regulations apply for all species (see current *Connecticut Anglers' Guide*).

Boating: Motors limited to 6 hp, speed limit 12 mph (see current *Connecticut Boater's Guide*).

Comments: Fishing pressure is low on this pond. The State Record white catfish (12 lb. 4 oz.) was caught here in 1986.

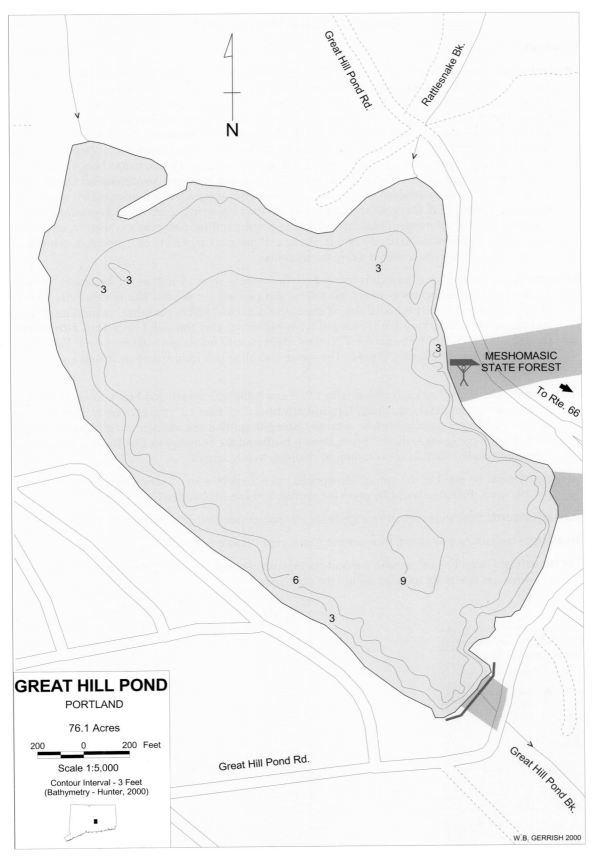

GREAT HILL POND

PORTLAND

76.1 Acres

200   0   200 Feet

Scale 1:5,000

Contour Interval - 3 Feet
(Bathymetry - Hunter, 2000)

Great Hill Pond Rd.

Great Hill Pond Rd.

Great Hill Pond Bk.

Rattlesnake Bk.

MESHOMASIC
STATE FOREST

To Rte. 66

N

3

3

3

3

6

9

3

W.B. GERRISH 2000

Green Falls Reservoir

Town(s): Voluntown

48.2 acres

Description: Green Falls Reservoir is a small artificial impoundment in the Pawcatuck River Drainage Basin. It is located entirely within Pachaug State Forest. The 30 ft. dam, located on the southern shore, was repaired in 1992. **Watershed:** 1,224 acres, the majority of which is undeveloped state forest. The lake is fed by Green Falls River from the east and by two smaller streams from the north. It drains southward into the Green Falls River via a spillway. **Shoreline:** No residential development and well wooded with the exception of a small beach on the northern shore. **Depth:** Max 26 ft., Mean 12 ft. **Transparency:** Very clear; 19 ft. during summer. **Productivity:** Low to moderate (oligotrophic-mesotrophic). **Bottom type:** Gravel, rubble and boulders. **Stratification:** Occurs with a thermocline forming between 10 and 16 ft. Late summer oxygen levels remain high (greater than 6 ppm) to a depth 13 ft. Oxygen then declines to less than 2 ppm in deeper water. **Vegetation:** Dense concentrations of submergent bladderwort and low water-milfoil dominate the shallow coves and areas along the shoreline to depths of 9 ft. Pockets of bur-reed, pickerelweed, pipewort, arrowhead and meadow beauty are scattered along the shoreline.

Access: A state-owned boat launch is located on the western shore. Facilities at the launch include a gravel ramp (car-top boats only), pit toilets and parking for 6 cars. The Green Falls section of Pachaug State Forest borders almost the entire pond and offers camping, swimming, hiking and picnicking. A parking fee is charged from Memorial Day through Labor Day. **Directions:** Exit 85 off I-395, Rte. 138 east for 7.5 miles, right (south) on access road for Green Falls State Park, follow signs to launch. **Shore:** The entire shoreline is within state forest land and is open to the public.

Fish: Green Falls is stocked each spring with 1,200 catchable size brown and brook trout. Holdovers are rare due to limited depth. Small **largemouth bass** (less than 12") are extremely abundant, but densities of larger bass are below average. **Bluegill sunfish** are abundant with above average numbers of large (greater than 7") fish. **Brown bullhead** are common to 13". Banded killifish are common. Banded sunfish are common in shallow, weedy areas.

Fishing: Should be good in the spring for stocked trout. Expect a lot of action from small bass, but few big ones. Fishing should be good for sunfish and fair for bullhead.

Management: Statewide regulations apply for all species (see current *Connecticut Anglers' Guide*).

Boating: Gas motors prohibited (see current *Connecticut Boater's Guide*).

Comments: Green Falls Reservoir supports heavy recreational use during the summer by boaters and swimmers due to its location within the state park.

Green Falls Reservoir Fish Species and Abundance	ALL SIZES	BIG FISH	GROWTH
Gamefish			
Largemouth bass	A	U	< Slow
Brook trout	C		
Brown trout	C	R	
Panfish			
Brown bullhead	C	C	
Sunfish			
Bluegill	A	A	Avg
Banded	C		
Other			
Banded killifish	C		
A=Abundant, C=Common, U=Uncommon, R=Rare			

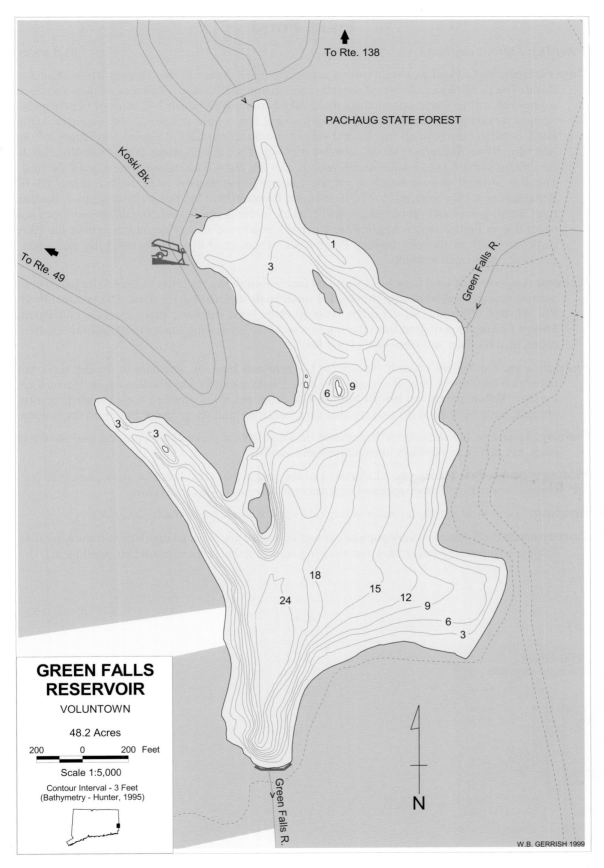

To Rte. 138

PACHAUG STATE FOREST

Koski Bk.

To Rte. 49

Green Falls R.

1

3

6 9

3

3

18

24

15

12

9

6

3

GREEN FALLS RESERVOIR

VOLUNTOWN

48.2 Acres

200   0   200 Feet

Scale 1:5,000

Contour Interval - 3 Feet
(Bathymetry - Hunter, 1995)

Green Falls R.

N

W.B. GERRISH 1999

Halls Pond

Town(s): Ashford/Eastford   **81.5 acres**

Description: Halls Pond is a state-owned artificial impoundment in the Thames River Drainage
Basin. The pond has a convoluted shoreline and many small islands. Remains of numerous tree
stumps can still be found scattered about the lake bottom. *Watershed:* 742 acres of mostly unde-
veloped woods and wetland with some agricultural and a little residential development. Halls
Pond is fed by three small brooks and drains northeast into Slovik Brook, a tributary of the
Natchaug River. *Shoreline:* Mostly wooded with very little development. Halls Pond Road abuts
the eastern shore for 0.25 miles and several homes are located on the opposite side of the road.
There is a small private beach is on the eastern shore. *Depth:* Max 14 ft., Mean 8.5 ft.
Transparency: Fair, reduced to 7 ft. in summer. *Productivity:* Moderate (mesotrophic). *Bottom
type:* Sand, gravel and rubble with organic muck in the deeper areas. *Stratification:* Does not
occur due to limited depth. *Vegetation:* Robbin's pondweed is very dense throughout the lake,
carpeting much of the lake bottom. Pondweeds, white water-lily, yellow pond-lily and water-
shield occur in small amounts.

Access: A state-owned boat launch is located on the eastern shore. Facilities at the site include a very
narrow, unimproved boat ramp suitable for small boats and parking for 5 cars. *Directions:* From
Rte. 44, Rte. 198 south for 4.5 miles, west on Halls Pond Rd. for 1 mile, access is on the left.
Shore: Fishing is permitted from the state-owned land (Natchaug State Forest) off the southern
shore, near the dam and from Halls Pond Rd.

Fish: Bass and sunfish are severely stockpiled. **Largemouth bass** are abundant in smaller sizes, but
larger fish are present only at average densities. **Chain pickerel** and **black crappie** densities are
average. **Yellow perch** and **brown bullhead** densities are below average. Small **sunfish** (mostly
bluegill, some pumpkinseed) are very abundant, but larger sunfish (greater than 6") are uncommon.

Fishing: Should be fair to good for largemouth bass and fair for pickerel, crappie and sunfish. Good
place to catch large numbers of small bass and sunfish.

Management: Bass Management Lake; special slot length and creel limits on bass. Statewide regulations apply for all other species (see current *Connecticut Anglers' Guide*).

Boating: Speed limit 8 mph, no water-skiing (see current *Connecticut Boater's Guide*).

Comments: Halls Pond is a very popular car-top and canoe site. Special regulations should improve
fishing by protecting larger bass and allowing anglers to harvest overabundant small bass.

Halls Pond
Fish Species and Abundance

Gamefish	ALL SIZES	BIG FISH	GROWTH
Largemouth bass	A	C	Slow
Chain pickerel	C	U	Slow
Panfish			
Black crappie	C	U	Slow
Yellow perch	C	C	Avg
Brown bullhead			
Sunfish			
Bluegill	A	U	< Slow
Pumpkinseed	C	U	Slow

A=Abundant, C=Common, U=Uncommon, R=Rare

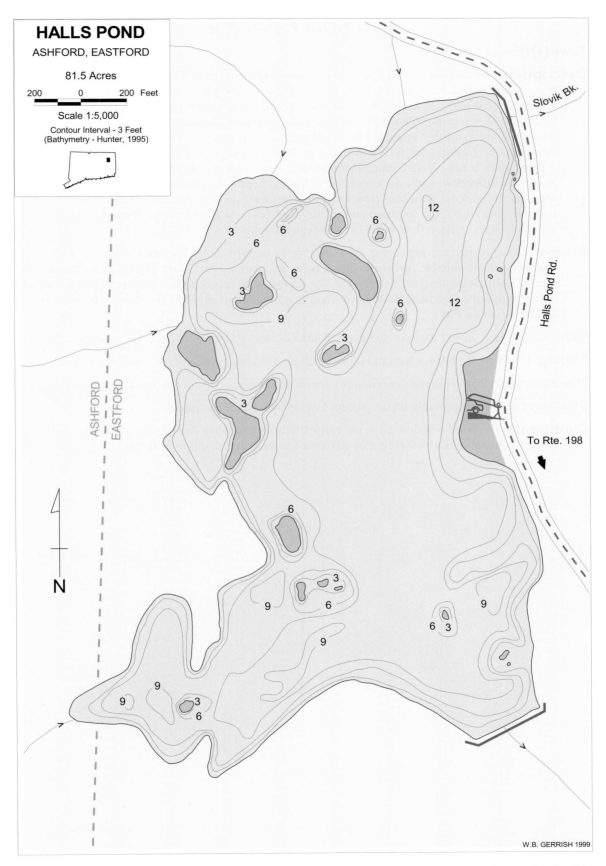

HALLS POND

ASHFORD, EASTFORD

81.5 Acres

200   0   200   Feet

Scale 1:5,000

Contour Interval - 3 Feet
(Bathymetry - Hunter, 1995)

Slovik Bk.

Halls Pond Rd.

To Rte. 198

ASHFORD

EASTFORD

N

W.B. GERRISH 1999

Hampton Reservoir

Town(s): Eastford/Hampton   **88.3 acres**

Description: Hampton Reservoir is an artificial impoundment in the Thames River Drainage Basin. It is entirely within the Natchaug State Forest. There are numerous islands of water willow found throughout the pond. *Watershed:* 557 acres of mostly undeveloped woods and wetland. It is fed by a marsh from the north and four small streams. The pond drains to the southeast into the Little River, a tributary of the Shetucket River. *Shoreline:* The shoreline is wooded with no residential development. *Depth:* Max 8.0 ft., Mean 3 ft. *Transparency:* Turbid; transparency is reduced to 3 ft. by dark a tea-colored stain. *Productivity:* Not available. *Bottom type:* Mud and organic muck. *Stratification:* Does not occur due to limited depth. *Vegetation:* Submergent vegetation is abundant throughout with bladderwort as the dominant species. Pondweeds are also present. In late summer, all but the southern end of the pond is covered with dense floating mats of white water-lily with some yellow pond-lily and water-shield.

Access: A state-owned car-top access is located on the eastern shore. Facilities at the site include an unimproved site suitable for small car-top boats and parking for 3 cars. *Directions:* From Rte. 6, Rte. 97 north, left (west) on Kenyon Rd. for 1.5 miles, access is on left. *Shore:* The entire shoreline is within the Natchaug State Forest and is accessible to anglers. The dam is the most popular shore fishing site.

Fish: Not sampled during the lake and pond electrofishing survey.

Fishing: Is reportedly fair for largemouth bass, chain pickerel, yellow perch, sunfish and bullheads.

Management: Statewide regulations apply for all species (see current *Connecticut Anglers' Guide*).

Boating: Gas motors prohibited (see current *Connecticut Boater's Guide*).

Comments: The pond was drained in the early 1990s for extensive dam repairs and fish populations are in the process of recovering. Popular area for waterfowl hunting in the fall.

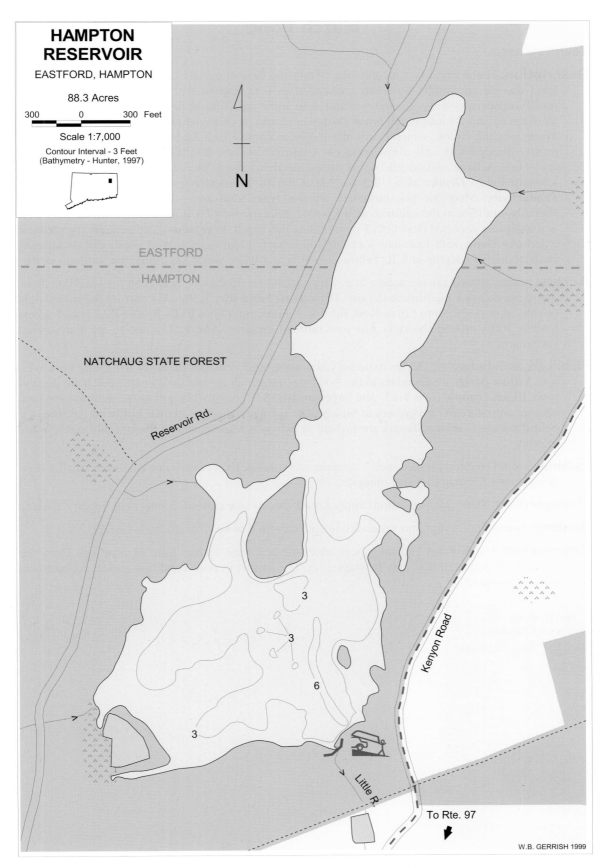

HAMPTON RESERVOIR

EASTFORD, HAMPTON

88.3 Acres

300   0   300   Feet

Scale 1:7,000

Contour Interval - 3 Feet
(Bathymetry - Hunter, 1997)

N

EASTFORD

HAMPTON

NATCHAUG STATE FOREST

Reservoir Rd.

Kenyon Road

3

3

6

3

Little R.

To Rte. 97

W.B. GERRISH 1999

Hatch Pond

Town(s): Kent

Description: Hatch Pond is a natural lake within the Housatonic River Drainage Basin. Its water level was raised slightly by a low concrete dam with flashboards. *Watershed*: 2,324 acres of mostly undeveloped woods and wetland with some agricultural development. The lake is fed from the north by a marshland brook (Womenshenuk). It drains southward into a continuation of Womenshenuk Brook, which flows into the Housatonic River. *Shoreline*: The western shore is mostly wooded with only a few cottages. A railroad bed and South Kent Road parallel the eastern shore. A large marshland begins on the northern shore and continues for a mile north to Leonard Pond. *Depth*: Max 18.5 ft., Mean 8.6 ft. *Transparency*: Turbid, 2 ft. in summer. *Productivity*: Moderate (mesotrophic). *Bottom type*: Mud and organic muck. *Stratification*: Partially stratifies in the summer with a temperature gradient forming at 7 ft. Late summer oxygen levels are depleted (less than 1 ppm) below this depth. *Vegetation*: Submergent vegetation is extremely dense with Eurasian water-milfoil, coontail and curly-leaved pondweed dominating shallow areas to depths of 8 ft. Yellow pond-lily and white water-lily fringe the southern shore.

Access: A state-owned car-top access area with parking for 15 cars is located on the southern shore. There are no other facilities at the site. *Directions*: From Rte. 7, Rte. 341 east for 0.7 miles, right (south) at stop sign onto South Kent Rd. for 2 miles, right onto Bulls Bridge Rd., gravel access road is 100 yards on the right just past railroad crossing. *Shore*: Limited to the state-owned access area.

Fish: **Largemouth bass** to 13" are extremely abundant, with densities of larger fish being near average. **Yellow perch** are abundant in the 9-11" size range; larger and smaller size perch are uncommon. **Black crappie** from 9-12" and large **sunfish** (8-9", mostly bluegill, some pumpkinseed and occasional redbreast) are present at higher than average densities. **Brown bullhead** densities are below average. Golden shiners are present at below average densities. Redfin pickerel are also present.

Fishing: Should be good for bass, perch, crappie and sunfish. Expect very fast action for smaller bass. A good spot for bragging size bluegills.

Management: Statewide regulations apply for all species (see current *Connecticut Anglers' Guide*).

Boating: Speed limit 8 mph, no water-skiing (see current *Connecticut Boater's Guide*).

Comments: Hatch Pond had only been electrofished once by the time of printing. Thus, the above fishery description may be imprecise. The dam is in poor condition and its replacement is being planned.

Hatch Pond
Fish Species and Abundance

	ALL SIZES	BIG FISH	GROWTH
Gamefish			
Largemouth bass	A	C	< Avg
Panfish			
Black crappie	C	C	Fast
Yellow perch	A	A	> Avg
Brown bullhead	U	U	
Sunfish			
Bluegill	C	C	Fast
Pumpkinseed	C	C	> Avg
Redbreast	C	U	Avg
Other			
Golden shiner	C		Fast
Redfin pickerel	U		

A=Abundant, C=Common, U=Uncommon, R=Rare

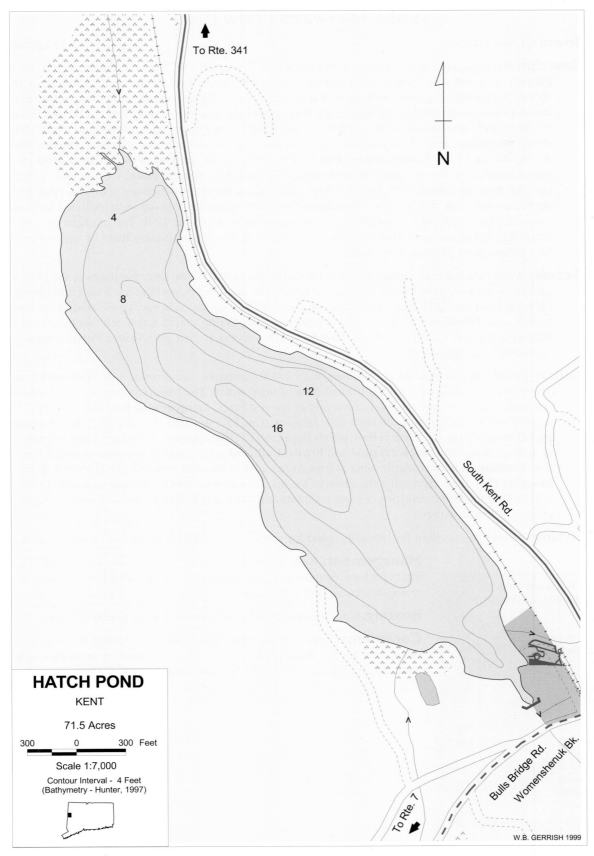

HATCH POND

KENT

71.5 Acres

300   0   300 Feet

Scale 1:7,000

Contour Interval - 4 Feet
(Bathymetry - Hunter, 1997)

To Rte. 341

N

South Kent Rd.

Bulls Bridge Rd.

Womenshenuk Bk.

To Rte. 7

4

8

12

16

W.B. GERRISH 1999

Lake Hayward (Shaw Lake)

Town(s): East Haddam

174 acres

Description: Hayward Lake is a natural lake within the Thames River Drainage Basin. A 55 ft. long earthen dam was constructed on the outlet to raise the water level. *Watershed*: 1,489 acres of mostly undeveloped woods, wetland and agricultural land. There is moderately dense residential development immediately surrounding the lake, especially near the western shore. The lake is fed by five small streams and drains southward into Lake Hayward Brook, a tributary of Eight Mile River. *Shoreline*: Heavily developed with seasonal cottages and permanent homes. *Depth*: Max 35 ft., Mean 11 ft. *Transparency*: Fair-Clear; 10-12 ft. in summer. *Productivity*: Moderate (mesotrophic-late mesotrophic). *Bottom type*: Not available. *Stratification*: Occurs with a thermocline forming between 16 and 29 ft. Oxygen levels in the thermocline are poor (2-4 ppm) and decline to near zero below 23 ft. *Vegetation*: Generally sparse throughout with localized areas of fanwort, pondweeds, tapegrass and pipewort occurring to depths of 12 ft. The northern cove has extremely dense concentrations of submerged fanwort and dense floating mats of white water-lily, yellow pond-lily and water-shield.

Access: A state-owned boat launch is located at the northern end of the lake. Facilities at the launch include a shallow, paved ramp suitable for launching small boats, parking for 5 cars and chemical toilets (seasonal). During mid to late summer, aquatic vegetation is very dense around the boat launch area. *Directions*: Exit 6 off Rte. 11, west at end of ramp for 0.5 miles, left (south) on Lake Hayward Rd. for 1.5 miles, left on East Shore Dr., access is on right. *Shore*: Public access is restricted to the launch area.

Fish: Hayward Lake is stocked each spring with 1,000 catchable size **brown** and **rainbow trout**. Trout rarely holdover due to the limited area of deep water. The bass population is moderately stockpiled and sustains relatively high angler harvest rates. **Largemouth bass** are abundant in smaller sizes, but densities of large fish (greater than 15") are less than average. Small **chain pickerel** (less than 15") and **yellow perch** (less than 8") are abundant with larger fish occurring at average densities. **Black crappie** and **brown bullhead** are present at less than average densities. **Sunfish** (mostly bluegill, some pumpkinseed, and occasional hybrids) are abundant. **Large bluegills** (7-9") are especially abundant in the lake. **American eels** to 20" are common. Forage fish include moderate densities of golden shiners and banded killifish. Tessellated darters are also present at low densities.

Fishing: Should be excellent for bluegills; good for stocked trout and eels; and fair for other species

Management: Bass Management Lake; special slot length and creel limits on bass. Statewide regulations apply for all other species (see current *Connecticut Anglers' Guide*).

Boating: Gas motors prohibited (see current *Connecticut Boater's Guide*).

Comments: Special regulations should improve fishing by protecting larger bass and allowing anglers to harvest overabundant small bass. The State Record brown bullhead (3 lb.) was caught here in 1969.

Hayward Lake
Fish Species and Abundance

	ALL SIZES	BIG FISH	GROWTH
Gamefish			
Largemouth bass	A	U	> Avg
Chain pickerel	A	C	< Avg
Panfish			
Black crappie	C	U	> Avg
Yellow perch	A	C	< Avg
Brown bullhead	U	U	
Sunfish			
Bluegill	A	A	Fast
Pumpkinseed	C	C	Fast
Other			
Tessellated darter	U		
Golden shiner	C		
Banded killifish	C		
American eel	C		

A=Abundant, C=Common, U=Uncommon, R=Rare

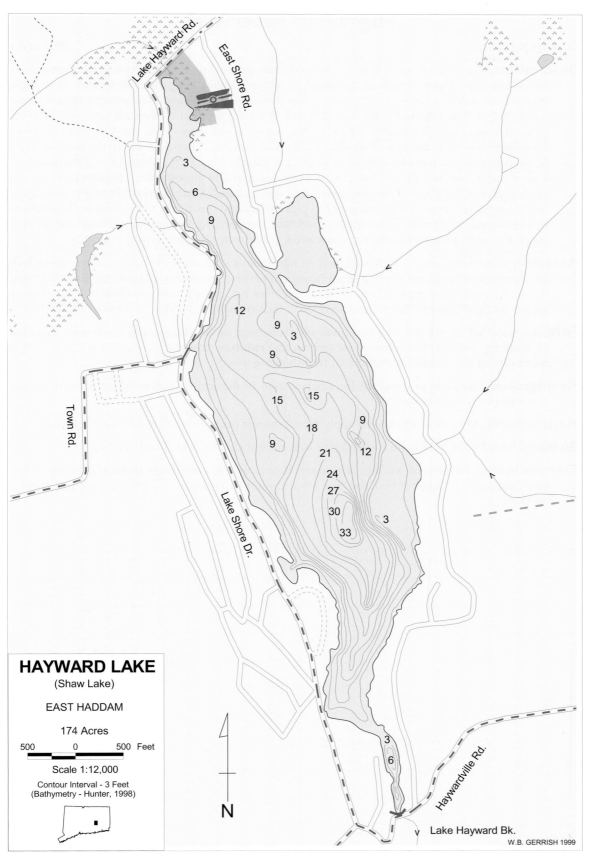

HAYWARD LAKE

(Shaw Lake)

EAST HADDAM

174 Acres

500   0   500 Feet

Scale 1:12,000

Contour Interval - 3 Feet
(Bathymetry - Hunter, 1998)

W.B. GERRISH 1999

Higganum Reservoir

Town(s): Haddam

30.8 acres

Description: Higganum Reservoir is an artificial impoundment on Ponset Brook in the Connecticut River Drainage Basin. Much of the pond is located within Higganum Reservoir State Park. *Watershed*: 4,264 acres of mostly undeveloped woods with a moderate amount of residential development. The lake is fed by Ponset Brook from the south and two small streams from the west. It drains into Higganum Creek to the north, which flows into the Connecticut River. *Shoreline*: Mostly wooded with a moderate level of residential development to the north and east of the reservoir just outside of the park boundary. *Depth*: Max 33 ft., Mean 13 ft. *Transparency*: Fair; 8 feet in summer. *Productivity*: Low to moderate (early mesotrophic). *Bottom type*: Mostly sand, gravel and boulders with mud and silt in deeper areas. *Stratification*: Partially stratifies in the summer; however, a late summer oxygen-temperature profile is not available. *Vegetation*: Not surveyed. Vegetation is reportedly moderate and concentrated in the southern and western areas. Plants include pickerelweed, waterweed, white water-lily and yellow pond-lily.

Access: A state-owned access area is located on the southwestern shore. Facilities at the site include an unimproved ramp suitable for small boats and parking for 4 cars. *Directions*: Exit 9 off Rte. 9, Rte. 81 north for 0.6 miles, left (west) on Skinner Rd., right (north) on Dish Mill Rd., launch area is on right. *Shore*: The entire shoreline is state-owned land and accessible to anglers.

Fish: Not sampled during the lake and pond electrofishing survey. Higganum Reservoir is stocked each spring with 1,600 catchable size **brown** and **rainbow trout**. Poor oxygen levels in deeper water during the summer prevent trout from holding over.

Fishing: Should be good to excellent for stocked trout in the spring. Before being drained, fishing was reportedly fair for sunfish.

Management: Statewide regulations apply for all species (see current *Connecticut Anglers' Guide*).

Boating: Speed limit 8 mph, no water-skiing (see current *Connecticut Boater's Guide*).

Comments: At the time of writing, Higganum Reservoir was completely drained awaiting extensive dam repairs. Once refilled, the lake's warmwater fish populations will take several years to recover.

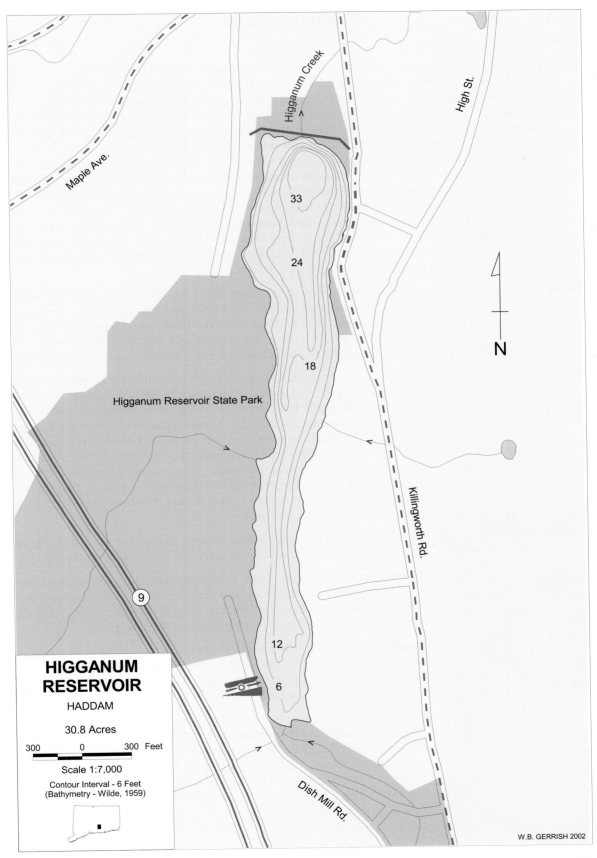

Higganum Creek

Maple Ave.

High St.

33

24

18

Higganum Reservoir State Park

N

Killingworth Rd.

9

12

6

HIGGANUM RESERVOIR

HADDAM

30.8 Acres

300   0   300   Feet

Scale 1:7,000

Contour Interval - 6 Feet
(Bathymetry - Wilde, 1959)

Dish Mill Rd.

W.B. GERRISH 2002

Highland Lake

Town(s): Winchester

445 acres

Description: Highland Lake is a natural lake within the Connecticut River Drainage Basin. Its water level was raised 10 ft. by a dam at its northern end. The lake consists of three contiguous basins. The southern basin is the largest, but the deepest area of the lake is found in the middle basin. *Watershed:* 4,481 acres of mostly undeveloped woods with moderate levels of residential development. The lake is fed by Taylor and Sucker Brooks and bottom springs. It drains northward into the Mad River, a tributary of the Still River. *Shoreline:* Dominated by residences, many of which have extensive docks and retaining walls. *Depth:* Max 63 ft., Mean 24 ft. *Transparency:* Good; 13-14 ft. in summer. *Productivity:* Low to moderate (oligotrophic-early mesotrophic). *Bottom type:* Boulders, rocks, sand and gravel. *Stratification:* Occurs with a thermocline forming between 16 and 33 ft. Late summer oxygen levels remain good (greater than 5 ppm) to a depth of 23 ft., but decline to less than 2 ppm in deeper water. *Vegetation:* Moderate to dense submergent vegetation extends to depths of 15 ft. Species include Eurasian water-milfoil, waterweed, tapegrass, large-leaved pondweed, variable pondweed, perfoliate pondweed, eutrophic water-nymph and stonewort. Vegetation is especially dense in the northern cove.

Access: A state-owned boat launch is located on the northern shore. Facilities at the launch include a ramp with concrete slabs, concrete bulkhead, parking for 40 cars and chemical toilets (seasonal). A parking fee is charged on weekends and holidays from the third Saturday in April through Columbus Day. *Directions:* From Rte. 44, Rte. 263 west (Boyd St.) for 0.2 miles, left on Woodland Rd. to end, right on West Lake St., launch is on the left. *Shore:* Limited to launch area.

Fish: Highland Lake is stocked during the spring and fall with 15,800 catchable size **brown** and **rainbow trout**. A moderate amount of deep, oxygenated water extends through summer to allow some brown trout to holdover. **Largemouth bass** from 11-16" are above average in abundance. **Smallmouth bass** densities are near average for all sizes. **Chain pickerel** densities are average for all sizes. Large (greater than 12") **black crappie** are above average. **Yellow perch** and **rock bass** are stockpiled. Small (less than 6") yellow perch and rock bass (less than 7") are abundant, but larger fish are uncommon. **Sunfish** (mostly bluegill, some pumpkinseed, occasional redbreast and hybrids) are abundant in the 6-8" range. **Brown bullhead** densities are average. Forage fish include abundant alewives and golden shiners. Other fish species present are white catfish and white sucker.

Fishing: Should be good for bass, crappie, sunfish and trout, with a good chance for a holdover trout; fair for other species. Popular ice fishing spot.

Management: Trophy Trout Lake managed with special length and creel limits and an alternative season closure schedule. Bass Management Lake; special length and creel limits on bass. Statewide regulations apply for all other species (see current *Connecticut Anglers' Guide*).

Boating: Speed limit 6 mph ½ hr. after sunset to ½ hr. before sunrise from Sunday before Memorial Day to Sunday preceding Labor Day. Speed limit 45 mph during the day on Saturdays, Sundays and holidays (see current *Connecticut Boater's Guide*).

Comments: The lake is located in a populated area and angling pressure and boating use are high during the spring and summer months. This is one of the better lakes for holdover brown trout, with 2 to 5 pounders being fairly common. Highland is a popular bass tournament lake with an average of 25 competitions held annually. Special bass regulations should improve fishing for larger bass. The State Record kokanee (2 lb. 12 oz.) was caught here in 1976. Kokanee are no longer present due to introduction of alewives, which out-competed them for the zooplankton forage base.

Highland Lake
Fish Species and Abundance

	ALL SIZES	BIG FISH	GROWTH
Gamefish			
Largemouth bass	C	C	< Avg
Smallmouth bass	C	C	Avg
Brown trout	A	U	Avg
Rainbow trout	A		
Chain pickerel	C	C	Avg
White catfish	R	R	
Panfish			
Black crappie	C	C	Avg
Yellow perch	A	U	Slow
Brown bullhead	C	U	
Sunfish			
Bluegill	A	C	Avg
Pumpkinseed	C	U	< Avg
Redbreast	U	R	Slow
Rock bass	A	C	Slow
Other			
Golden shiner	C		Avg
Alewife	A		Avg
White sucker	C		

A=Abundant, C=Common, U=Uncommon, R=Rare

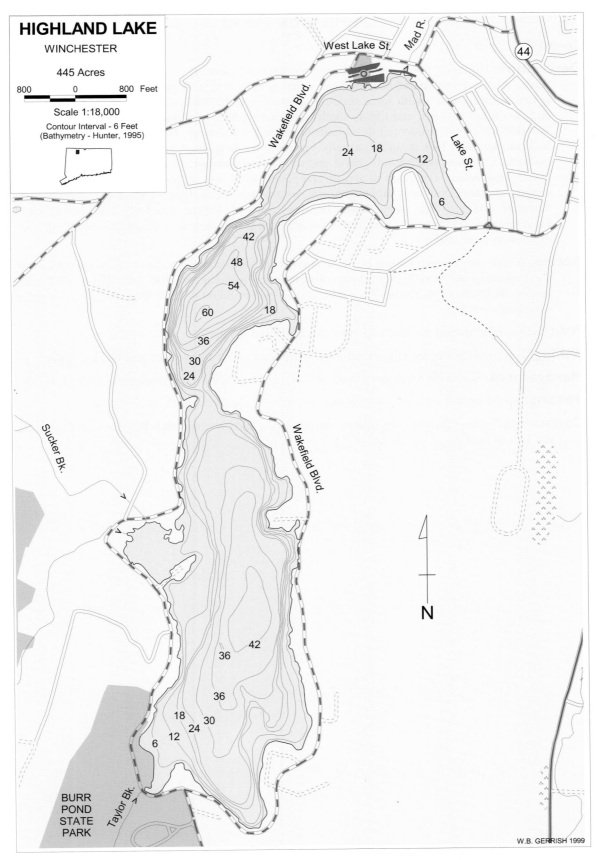

HIGHLAND LAKE

WINCHESTER

445 Acres

800   0   800 Feet

Scale 1:18,000

Contour Interval - 6 Feet
(Bathymetry - Hunter, 1995)

West Lake St.

Mad R.

44

Wakefield Blvd.

Lake St.

24   18   12

6

42

48

54

60   18

36

30

24

Sucker Bk.

Wakefield Blvd.

42

36

36

18   30

24

6   12

N

BURR
POND
STATE
PARK

Taylor Bk.

W.B. GERRISH 1999

Holbrook Pond

Town(s): Hebron

83.3 acres

Description: Holbrook Pond is a small artificial impoundment in the Connecticut River Drainage Basin. It is state-owned and is in the Salmon River State Forest. *Watershed*: 1,196 acres of mostly undeveloped woods with some agricultural and residential land. The pond is fed by marshland and two small streams, and drains southward into a tributary of the Jeremy River. *Shoreline*: Wooded with some residential development set back from shore. *Depth*: Max 7.5 ft., Mean 4.9 ft. *Transparency*: Fair to turbid; usually visible to the bottom. *Productivity*: Very high (highly eutrophic). *Bottom type*: Sand, gravel and mud. *Stratification*: Does not occur due to limited depth. *Vegetation*: The pond is almost completely choked with aquatic vegetation during the summer months. Dominant submergent species are pondweeds, bladderworts and tapegrass. The northern end also has very dense floating mats of yellow pond-lily and water-shield. Pickerelweed and bur-reed grow in shallow water near the shore in many places. Small numbers of fanwort were also noted.

Access: A state-owned boat launch is located on the southern shore. Facilities at the launch include a gravel ramp and parking for 50 cars. *Directions*: From Rte. 66, Rte. 85 north for 0.7 miles, access road is on right. *Shore*: The entire pond is within Salmon River State Forest and is accessible to the public.

Fish: Not sampled during the lake and pond electrofishing survey.

Fishing: Is reportedly fair for largemouth bass, chain pickerel, yellow perch and black crappie.

Management: Statewide regulations apply for all species (see current *Connecticut Anglers' Guide*).

Boating: Speed limit 8 mph, no water-skiing (see current *Connecticut Boater's Guide*).

Comments: Fishing pressure is moderate during spring and low thereafter. Popular waterfowl hunting area in the fall.

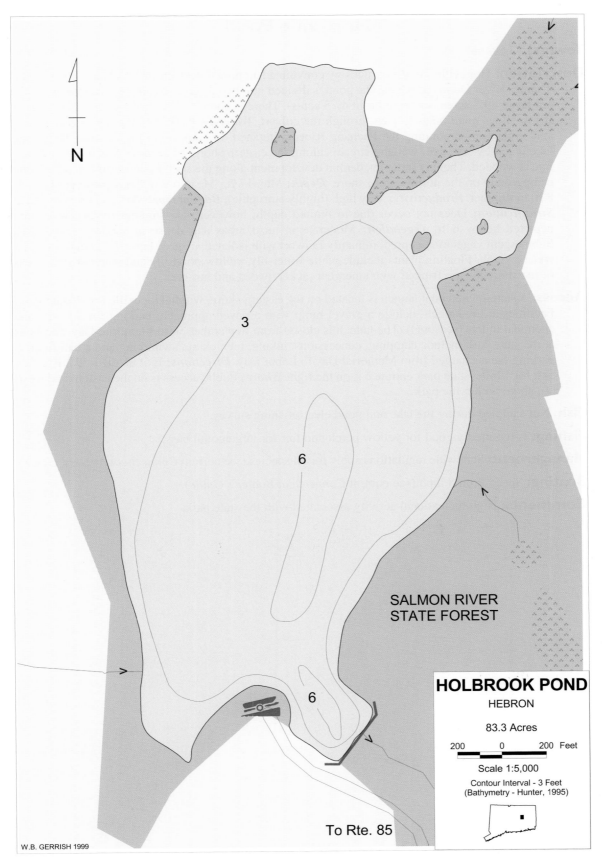

HOLBROOK POND

HEBRON

83.3 Acres

200 0 200 Feet

Scale 1:5,000

Contour Interval - 3 Feet
(Bathymetry - Hunter, 1995)

3

6

6

SALMON RIVER
STATE FOREST

N

To Rte. 85

W.B. GERRISH 1999

Hopeville Pond

Town(s): Griswold   **137 acres**

Description: Hopeville Pond is a narrow, convoluted impoundment on the Pachaug River in the Thames River Drainage Basin. The pond is divided into two discrete basins by a causeway (nothern basin 89.5 acres, southern basin 47.5 acres). There is enough clearance (3.5 ft.) and depth (5 ft.) to allow small boats to pass through the culvert. *Watershed:* 37,821 acres of mostly woods and wetland incorporating the Pachaug River watershed. In addition to the Pachaug River, the lake is fed by six small wetland streams along the eastern shore. *Shoreline:* Much of the shoreline is wooded. There is some residential development along the southeastern shore and a private campground on the northwestern shore. *Depth:* Max 17 ft., Mean 6.7 ft. *Transparency:* Fair; 7-8 ft. in summer. *Productivity:* Very high (highly eutrophic). *Bottom type:* Mud and organic muck. *Stratification:* Does not occur due to limited depth; however, late summer oxygen levels are depleted below 6 ft. *Vegetation:* Moderate in most areas and dense in shallow cove areas. Submergent vegetation is predominantly fanwort with isolated areas of tapegrass, pondweed and water-nymph. Floating plants include white water-lily, yellow pond-lily and water-shield. Areas of the shoreline are fringed with emergent pickerelweed and bur-reed.

Access: A state-owned boat launch is located on the eastern shore, within Hopeville Pond State Park. Facilities at the launch include a gravel ramp with a paved approach, parking for 20 cars, and chemical toilets (seasonal). The launch is closed from September 30 to Memorial Day. Facilities at the state park include camping, concessions, hiking, picnicking, swimming and a ball field. A parking fee is charged from Memorial Day to Labor Day. *Directions:* Exit 86 off I-395, Rte. 201 east for 1 mile, state park entrance is on the right. *Shore:* Public access is on the eastern and western shore within the park.

Fish: Not sampled during the lake and pond electrofishing survey.

Fishing: Is reportedly good for yellow perch and fair for largemouth bass.

Management: Statewide regulations apply for all species (see current *Connecticut Anglers' Guide*).

Boating: Speed limit 8 mph (see current *Connecticut Boater's Guide*).

Comments: High recreational activity associated with the state park.

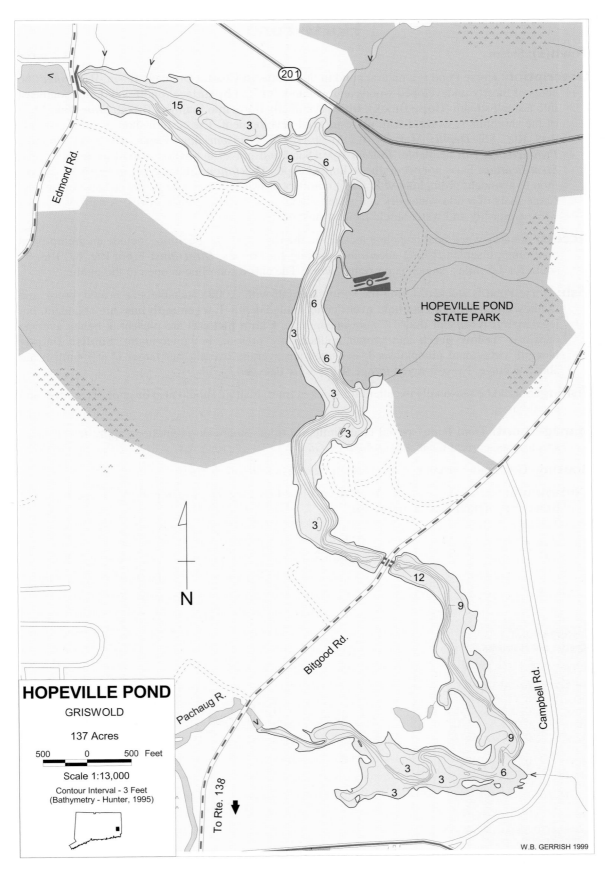

HOPEVILLE POND

GRISWOLD

137 Acres

500   0   500 Feet

Scale 1:13,000

Contour Interval - 3 Feet
(Bathymetry - Hunter, 1995)

201

HOPEVILLE POND
STATE PARK

Edmond Rd.

Bitgood Rd.

Campbell Rd.

Pachaug R.

To Rte. 138

N

15 6 3
9 6
6
3
6
3
3
3
12
9
9
3 6
3 3
3

W.B. GERRISH 1999

Horse Pond

Town(s): Salem

Description: Horse Pond is a natural pond in the Southeast Coastal Drainage Basin. *Watershed:* 66 acres of mostly undeveloped woods and wetland. It is fed by surface runoff and drains southeast into a small stream (Horse Brook), which eventually flows into Latimers Brook. *Shoreline:* Most of the shoreline is wooded with no residential development. The eastern shore is open and borders Rte. 85. *Depth:* Max 17 ft., Mean 12 ft. *Transparency:* Clear; 12 ft. in summer. *Productivity:* Not available. *Bottom type:* Sand and gravel in shallows, mud in deeper water. *Stratification:* Does not occur due to limited depth. *Vegetation:* Submerged bladderwort is common to abundant throughout with small numbers of water-nymph and pondweed also occurring. Large mats of white water-lily and water-shield occur in the shallow coves. A narrow band of white water-lily and water-shield fringes most of the shoreline.

Access: A state-owned boat launch is located on the eastern shore. Facilities include an unimproved boat ramp, disabled fishing access and parking for 10 cars. *Directions:* From Rte. 82, Rte. 85 south for 1.5 miles, launch is on right. *Shore:* The entire shoreline is open to the public.

Fish: Horse Pond is stocked during the spring and fall with 2,000 catchable size brown, brook and rainbow trout. Trout do not hold over due to limited depth. **Largemouth bass** are abundant, but legal size fish (greater than 12") are uncommon. **Chain pickerel** are present at below average densities. **Yellow perch** and brown bullhead are present, but uncommon. **Sunfish** (mostly bluegill, occasional pumpkinseed) densities are average overall, but larger (7-9") sunfish are above average. No soft-rayed forage fishes were detected.

Fishing: Should be seasonally excellent for stocked trout. Fishing should also be good for sunfish and small bass.

Management: Trout Park; special creel limits on trout. Statewide regulations apply for all other species (see current *Connecticut Anglers' Guide*).

Boating: Gas motors prohibited (see current *Connecticut Boater's Guide*).

Comments: Horse Pond had only been electrofished once by the time of printing. Thus, the above fishery description may be imprecise.

Horse Pond
Fish Species and Abundance

	ALL SIZES	BIG FISH	GROWTH
Gamefish			
Largemouth bass	A	U	< Avg
Brown trout	C	R	
Rainbow trout	C	R	
Brook trout	C	R	
Chain pickerel	C	C	< Avg
Panfish			
Yellow perch	U	U	
Brown bullhead	U	U	
Sunfish			
Bluegill	C	C	< Avg
Pumpkinseed	U	U	

A=Abundant, C=Common, U=Uncommon, R=Rare

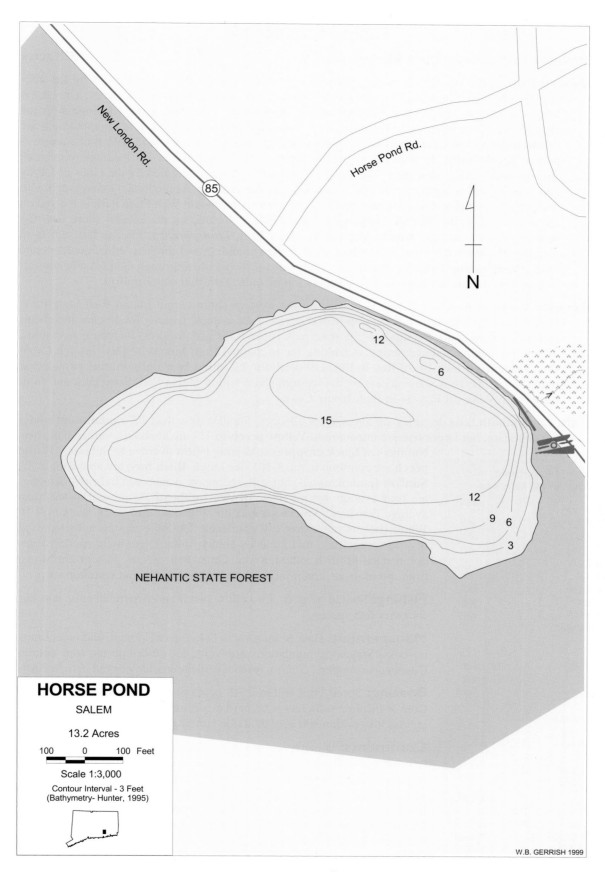

New London Rd.

85

Horse Pond Rd.

N

12

6

15

12

9   6

3

NEHANTIC STATE FOREST

HORSE POND

SALEM

13.2 Acres

100   0   100 Feet

Scale 1:3,000

Contour Interval - 3 Feet
(Bathymetry- Hunter, 1995)

W.B. GERRISH 1999

Lake Housatonic

Town(s): Derby/Monroe/Oxford/Seymour/Shelton   **328 acres**

Description: Lake Housatonic is an impoundment of the Housatonic River formed by the construction of a 20 ft. high hydroelectric dam between the cities of Shelton and Derby. The lake is long and narrow, retaining a riverine nature. **Watershed:** 1,007,400 acres encompassing the Housatonic River watershed. The downstream areas of land surrounding this impoundment are urban, whereas upstream areas are a combination of woods and open land with moderate residential development. In addition to the Housatonic River, the lake is fed by numerous small streams and brooks. **Shoreline:** The lower section of the lake is bordered by the cities of Derby and Shelton and is highly developed. Further north, the shoreline is moderately developed with residences. A railroad line runs parallel to the western shore. Indian Well State Park is located on the western shore in Shelton. Osbornedale State Park is located on the eastern shore near the southern end of the lake. **Depth:** Max 26 ft., Mean 10 ft. **Transparency:** Poor to fair; 5-6 ft. in summer. **Productivity:** High (eutrophic). **Bottom type:** Sand, gravel, broken ledge, boulders and mud. **Stratification:** Does not thermally stratify due to riverine flow through the lake. **Vegetation:** Not surveyed. Can be dense in coves. Vegetation includes Eurasian water-milfoil.

Access: A state-owned boat launch is located on the western shore within Indian Well State Park. Facilities at the launch include a ramp with concrete slabs, a dock, parking for 45 cars and chemical toilets (seasonal). Facilities at the state park (open 8:00 a.m. to dusk) include concessions, hiking, picnicking and swimming. A parking fee is charged from Memorial Day through Labor Day. **Directions:** Exit 14 off Rte. 8, Rte. 110 north for 2.2 miles, bear right on state park access road. **Shore:** There is shore access on the western shore within Indian Well State Park and from the eastern shore off Rte. 34 in Pink House Cove.

Fish: **Largemouth bass** densities are average for all sizes. Smaller (less than 12") **smallmouth bass** are abundant, but larger fish are uncommon. **Yellow perch** to 11" are at above average densities. Numbers of **black crappie** are slightly below average for all sizes. **White perch** are common in the 8-10" size range. **Rock bass** are abundant to 8". **Sunfish** (pumpkinseed, bluegill, redbreast, occasional hybrids) densities are near average for all sizes. **Brown bullhead** are present at less than average densities. **American eels** are abundant and reach sizes to 2 ft. White suckers are extremely abundant. The lake has an abundant and diverse forage base that includes golden shiners, goldfish, spottail shiners, banded killifish and alewives. Other fish species present are brown trout, brook trout, chain pickerel, tessellated darter and common carp.

Fishing: Should be good for yellow perch and American eels; and fair for other fish species.

Management: Bass Management Lake; special length and creel limits on bass. Statewide regulations apply for all other species (see current *Connecticut Anglers' Guide*). Annual walleye stocking began here in 2001.

Boating: Speed limit within 25 ft. of shore is 45 mph daytime, 25 mph from ½ hr after sunset to ½ hr before sunrise. Boats are prohibited from approaching within 300 ft. of dam (see current *Connecticut Boater's Guide*).

Comments: Water levels are subject to changes due to hydroelectricity production. The lake has a considerable amount of surplus forage fish. Few bass tournaments are held here, although it has the bass population and facilities to accommodate more. Special regulations should improve fishing by protecting larger bass. The Connecticut Department of Public Health has issued a fish consumption advisory for PCBs on some fish species in the lake (see current *Connecticut Anglers' Guide* for details).

Lake Housatonic
Fish Species and Abundance

	ALL SIZES	BIG FISH	GROWTH
Gamefish			
Largemouth bass	C	C	Avg
Smallmouth bass	A	U	Slow
Brook trout	R		
Brown trout	R		
Panfish			
Black crappie	C	C	Avg
White perch	C	U	Avg
Yellow perch	C	C	Fast
Brown bullhead	U	U	
Sunfish			
Bluegill	C	C	Fast
Pumpkinseed	C	C	Fast
Redbreast	C	U	> Avg
Rock bass	A	C	Fast
Other			
Tessellated darter	U		
Common carp	U		
Golden shiner	A		> Avg
Goldfish	R		
Spottail shiner	C		
Banded killifish	U		
Alewife	R		> Fast
White sucker	A		
American eel	A		

A=Abundant, C=Common, U=Uncommon, R=Rare

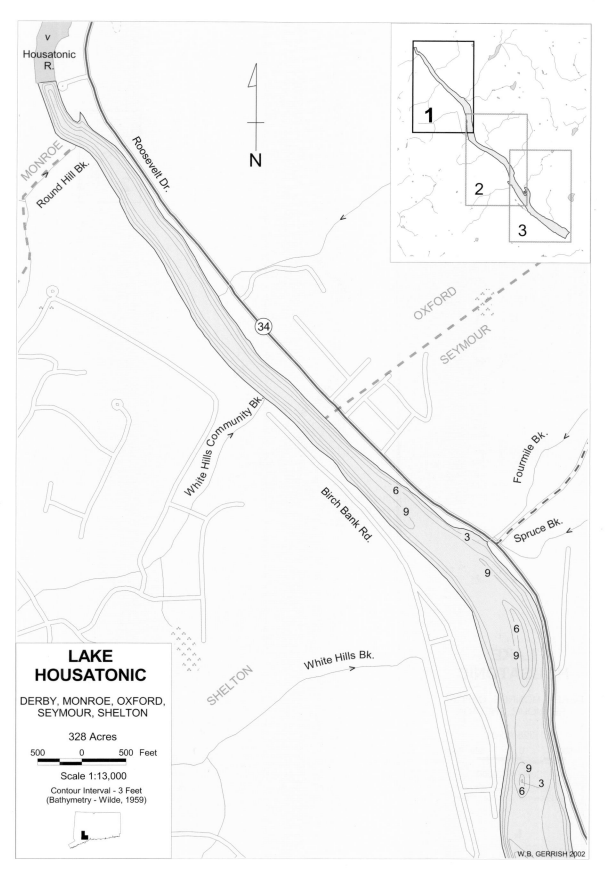

**LAKE
HOUSATONIC**

DERBY, MONROE, OXFORD,
SEYMOUR, SHELTON

328 Acres

500   0   500   Feet

Scale 1:13,000

Contour Interval - 3 Feet
(Bathymetry - Wilde, 1959)

Housatonic
R.

MONROE

Round Hill Bk.

Roosevelt Dr.

(34)

White Hills Community Bk.

Birch Bank Rd.

SHELTON

White Hills Bk.

OXFORD

SEYMOUR

Fourmile Bk.

Spruce Bk.

W.B. GERRISH 2002

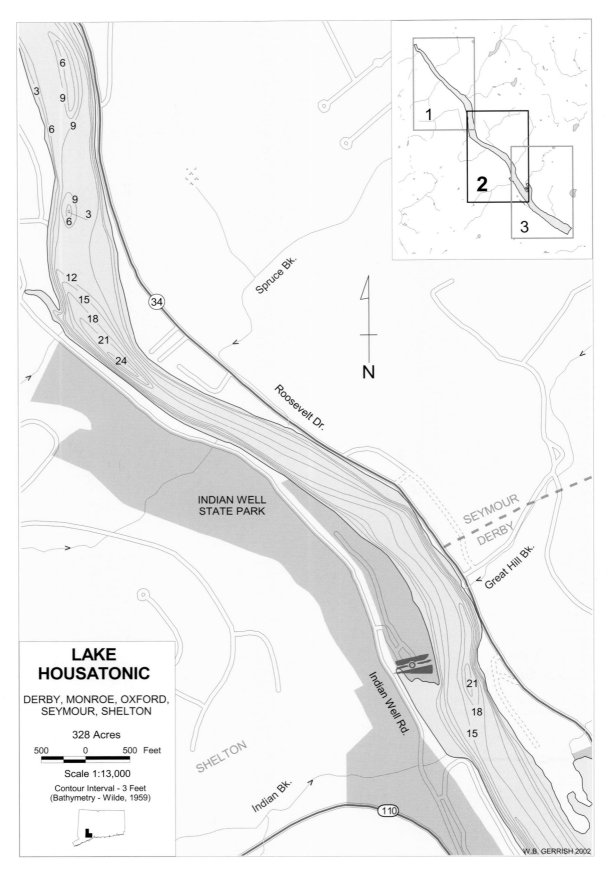

**LAKE
HOUSATONIC**

DERBY, MONROE, OXFORD,
SEYMOUR, SHELTON

328 Acres

500   0   500 Feet

Scale 1:13,000

Contour Interval - 3 Feet
(Bathymetry - Wilde, 1959)

W.B. GERRISH 2002

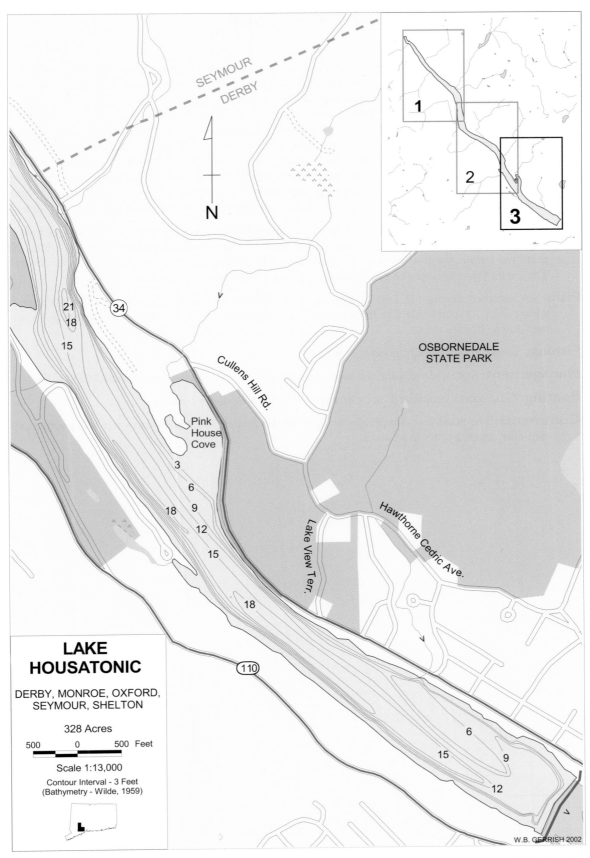

SEYMOUR
DERBY

N

1

2

3

21
18
15

34

OSBORNEDALE
STATE PARK

Cullens Hill Rd.

Pink
House
Cove

3

6

9

18

12

15

Lake View Terr.

Hawthorne Cedric Ave.

18

110

6

15

9

12

**LAKE
HOUSATONIC**

DERBY, MONROE, OXFORD,
SEYMOUR, SHELTON

328 Acres

500   0   500   Feet

Scale 1:13,000

Contour Interval - 3 Feet
(Bathymetry - Wilde, 1959)

W.B. GERRISH 2002

Howells Pond

Town(s): Hartland

14.3 acres

Description: Howells Pond is an artificial impoundment located within Tunxis State Forest in the Connecticut River Drainage Basin. *Watershed:* 1,009 acres of mostly undeveloped woods and wetland. It is fed by two small streams from the north and west and drains south into Howells Brook, a tributary of the West Branch Farmington River. *Shoreline:* Wooded with no residential development. *Depth:* Max 8.1 ft., Mean 6.4 ft. *Transparency:* Poor; 3.5 ft. in summer. *Productivity:* High (eutrophic). *Bottom type:* Gravel, rock and mud. *Stratification:* Does not occur due to limited depth. *Vegetation:* Submergent vegetation is common in water less than 4 ft. deep with a diverse assemblage of pondweeds and bladderworts as dominant species. Floating mats of water-shield and yellow pond-lily are sparse to occasional in cove areas. Emergent bur-reed, arrowhead and sedges grow along much of the shoreline and in water less than 1 ft. deep.

Access: A state-owned boat launch is located on the southern shore. Facilities at this site include a paved ramp, disabled fishing pier and parking for 10 cars. *Directions:* From Rte. 181, Rte. 20 north for 1 mile, west on West St. for 1.5 miles, left on Dish Mill Rd., access is on right. *Shore:* The entire shore borders Tunxis State Forest and is available to the public.

Fish: Not sampled during the lake and pond electrofishing survey. Howells Pond is stocked each spring with 700 catchable size **brown**, **brook** and **rainbow trout**. No trout survive through summer due to limited depth.

Fishing: Should be seasonally good for stocked trout.

Management: Statewide regulations apply for all species (see current *Connecticut Anglers' Guide*).

Boating: Gas motors prohibited (see current *Connecticut Boater's Guide*).

Comments: The pond was completely drained for dam repair in 1999. Warmwater fish populations will take several years to recover.

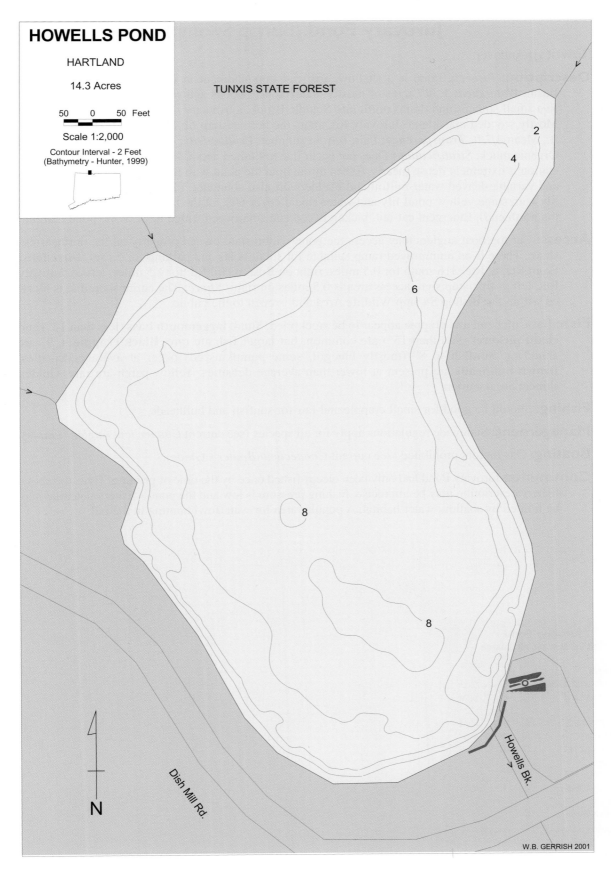

HOWELLS POND

HARTLAND

14.3 Acres

50   0   50 Feet

Scale 1:2,000

Contour Interval - 2 Feet
(Bathymetry - Hunter, 1999)

TUNXIS STATE FOREST

2

4

6

8

8

Dish Mill Rd.

Howells Bk.

N

W.B. GERRISH 2001

Jurovaty Pond (Bishop Swamp)

Town(s): Andover **52.5 acres**

Description: Jurovaty Pond is a shallow, artificial impoundment in the Thames River Drainage Basin. *Watershed*: 1,395 acres of mostly undeveloped woods and wetlands. The pond is fed by five small streams and drains north into Staddle Brook, a tributary of the Hop River. *Shoreline*: Mostly wooded marshland. Jurovaty Rd. abuts the northeastern tip of the pond. *Depth*: Max 11 ft., Mean 4.7 ft. *Transparency*: Fair; 6 ft. in summer. *Productivity*: Not available. *Bottom type*: Organic muck. *Stratification*: Does not occur due to limited depth. *Vegetation*: Submergent vegetation is extremely dense (nearly 100%) throughout the pond with fanwort the dominant species and variable-leaved water-milfoil and bladderwort also abundant. Floating mats of white water-lily with some yellow pond-lily and water-shield cover 60% of the lake surface (nearly 100% in the north end). Emergent cat-tail, pickerelweed and smartweed fringe most of the pond margin.

Access: Car-top boat anglers may access the pond within state-owned property on the northeastern shore. There is an unimproved ramp suitable for small boats and parking for 5 cars. *Directions*: From Rte. 6, Rte. 316 south for 0.5 miles, right on Boston Hill Rd. for 1.5 miles, left on Jurovaty Rd., left at first stop sign, access area is 0.5 miles on right. *Shore*: The entire shoreline is located within the Bishop Swamp Wildlife Area and is open to the public.

Fish: Bass, pickerel and crappie appear to be stockpiled. Small **largemouth bass** (less than 12") and **chain pickerel** (less than 15") are common, but larger fish are rare. **Black crappie** to 9" are abundant. **Sunfish** to 8" (mostly bluegill, some pumpkinseed) occur at average densities. **Brown bullheads** are present at lower than average densities. Yellow perch are rare. Golden shiners are common.

Fishing: Should be good for small crappie and fair for sunfish and bullheads.

Management: Statewide regulations apply for all species (see current *Connecticut Anglers' Guide*).

Boating: Gas motors prohibited (see current *Connecticut Boater's Guide*).

Comments: Jurovaty Pond had only been electrofished once by the time of printing. Thus, the above fishery description may be imprecise. Fishing pressure is low and the pond's fishery potential may be limited by shallow-water habitat. A popular area for waterfowl hunting in the fall.

Jurovaty Pond
Fish Species and Abundance

	ALL SIZES	BIG FISH	GROWTH
Gamefish			
Largemouth bass	C	R	< Slow
Chain pickerel	C	R	Slow
Panfish			
Black crappie	A	R	Slow
Yellow perch	R	R	Avg
Brown bullhead	C	C	
Sunfish			
Bluegill	C	C	Avg
Pumpkinseed	C	C	Avg
Other			
Golden shiner	C		

A=Abundant, C=Common, U=Uncommon, R=Rare

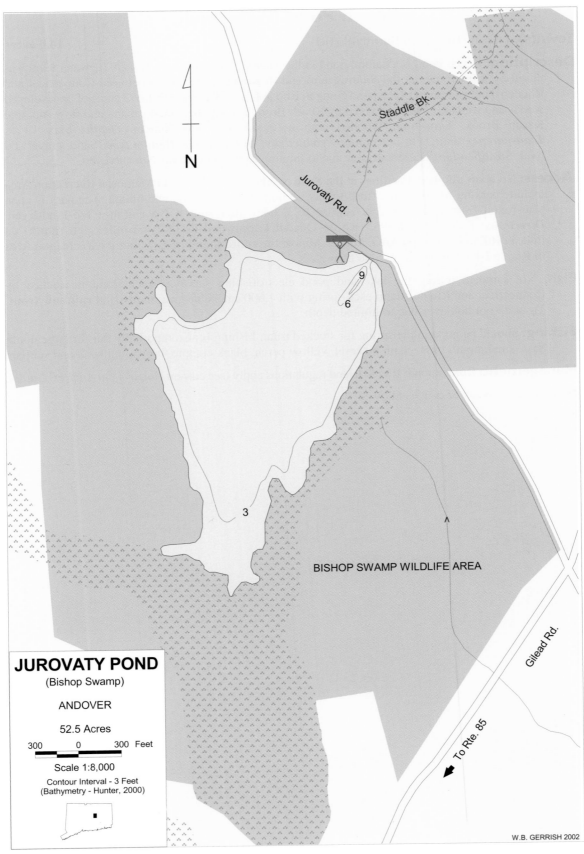

Staddle Bk.

Jurovaty Rd.

9

6

3

BISHOP SWAMP WILDLIFE AREA

Gilead Rd.

To Rte. 85

JUROVATY POND

(Bishop Swamp)

ANDOVER

52.5 Acres

300   0   300   Feet

Scale 1:8,000

Contour Interval - 3 Feet
(Bathymetry - Hunter, 2000)

W.B. GERRISH 2002

Keach Pond (Peck Pond)

Town(s): Putnam/Thompson/Burrillville (RI)   **14.0 acres**

Description: Keach Pond is a natural pond in the Thames River Drainage Basin. Its water level was raised by a stone dam at the southwestern end. It straddles the border between Connecticut and Rhode Island with most of the pond being in Rhode Island. *Watershed:* 1,673 acres of undeveloped woods and wetland. The pond is fed by Keach Brook and another small stream, and flows out into Keach Brook. *Shoreline:* Wooded with no residential development. *Depth:* Max 13 ft. *Transparency:* Fair; 9 ft. in summer. *Productivity:* Not available. *Bottom type:* Sand, gravel and mud. *Stratification:* Does not occur due to limited depth. *Vegetation:* Not surveyed.

Access: No boats allowed. Facilities at the State of Rhode Island Pulaski Memorial Recreation Area include parking for 100 cars, flush toilets, swimming, picnicking, and hiking. The park is open year-round from ½ hour before sunrise to ½ hour after sunset. No entrance fee is charged. *Directions:* Exit 99 off I-395, east on Quaddick/Elmwood Rd. for 4.3 miles, left (north) on Pulaski Rd. to Recreation Area. *Shore:* Almost the entire shoreline is within the Recreation Area in Rhode Island and is accessible to anglers.

Fish: Not sampled during the lake and pond electrofishing survey. Keach Pond is stocked by Connecticut and Rhode Island each spring with 1,600 catchable size **brown** and **rainbow trout**. Trout do not holdover due to limited depth.

Fishing: Should be good in the spring for stocked trout. Fishing is also reportedly fair for largemouth bass, smallmouth bass, chain pickerel, yellow perch, black crappie, brown bullhead and sunfish.

Management: Border pond; Rhode Island regulations apply (see current *Connecticut Anglers' Guide*).

Boating: No boats or canoes allowed.

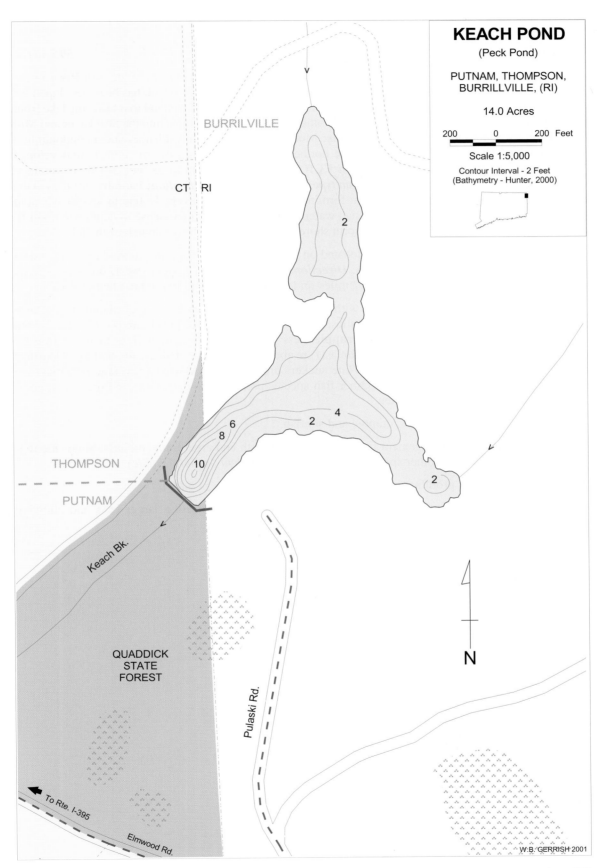

KEACH POND

(Peck Pond)

PUTNAM, THOMPSON,
BURRILLVILLE, (RI)

14.0 Acres

200   0   200 Feet

Scale 1:5,000

Contour Interval - 2 Feet
(Bathymetry - Hunter, 2000)

BURRILVILLE

CT   RI

THOMPSON

PUTNAM

Keach Bk.

QUADDICK
STATE
FOREST

Pulaski Rd.

To Rte. I-395

Elmwood Rd.

N

W.B. GERRISH 2001

Lake Kenosia

Town(s): Danbury   **59.5 acres**

Description: Lake Kenosia is an artificial impoundment on the headwaters of the Still River in the Housatonic River Drainage Basin. *Watershed:* 3,224 acres, most of which has been developed for either industrial or residential use. The Still River begins as a small wetland that feeds the lake from the northwest. The lake is also fed by two other small streams. It drains into the Still River and Mill Plain Swamp to the southeast. *Shoreline:* Mostly developed with residences and a condominium complex. There is a town park on the northern shore. The northwestern shore is undeveloped marshland. *Depth:* Max 18 ft., Mean 13 ft. *Transparency:* Turbid to fair; 3-6 ft. in summer. *Productivity:* High (eutrophic). *Bottom type:* Not available. *Stratification:* Partially stratifies in the summer with a temperature gradient forming at 10 ft. Oxygen levels decline to less than 1 ppm below this depth. *Vegetation:* Eurasian water-milfoil and coontail are dense to depths of 12-14 ft. with pondweeds present along the north shore. White water-lily fringes much of the lake.

Access: A state-owned boat launch is located on the eastern shore. Facilities at the launch include a gravel ramp and parking for 6 cars. *Directions:* Exit 3 off Rte. 7, right (west) on Backus Ave., right on Kenosia Ave., launch is 0.7 miles on left. *Shore:* Limited to the boat launch area.

Fish: **Largemouth bass** are stockpiled with small (less than 13") bass being very abundant and larger fish present only at average densities. **Yellow perch** and **white perch** are present at less than average densities. Smaller **black crappie** (less than 10") and **sunfish** (less than 7") (mostly bluegill, some pumpkinseed and redbreast) are abundant, but larger fish are uncommon. Densities of **brown bullhead** are average. White suckers are abundant. Alewives (average densities) are the primary forage fish species. Other fish species present at low densities are rock bass, common carp and tessellated darter.

Fishing: Should be fair for bass, crappie and sunfish.

Management: Bass Management Lake; special slot length and creel limits on bass. Statewide regulations apply for all other species (see current *Connecticut Anglers' Guide*).

Boating: Gas motors prohibited (see current *Connecticut Boater's Guide*).

Comments: Special regulations should improve fishing by protecting larger bass and allowing anglers to harvest overabundant small bass.

Lake Kenosia
Fish Species and Abundance

	ALL SIZES	BIG FISH	GROWTH
Gamefish			
Largemouth bass	A	C	Slow
Panfish			
Black crappie	A	U	Avg
White perch	U	U	Avg
Yellow perch	C	U	Avg
Brown bullhead	C	U	
Sunfish			
Bluegill	A	U	< Avg
Pumpkinseed	C	U	Slow
Redbreast	C	R	< Slow
Other			
Tessellated darter	U		
Common carp	U		
Alewife	C		
White sucker	A		

A=Abundant, C=Common, U=Uncommon, R=Rare

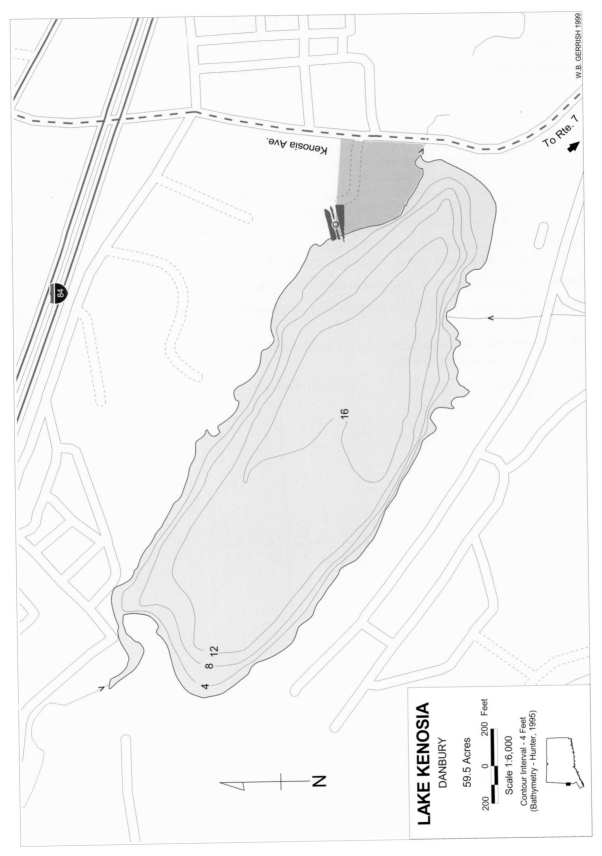

LAKE KENOSIA

DANBURY

59.5 Acres

Scale 1:6,000

Contour Interval - 4 Feet
(Bathymetry - Hunter, 1995)

Kenosia Ave.

To Rte. 7

W.B. GERRISH 1999

84

16

12
8
4

N

Killingly Pond

Town(s): Killingly/Glocester (RI)   **122 acres**

Description: Killingly Pond is an artificial impoundment in the Thames River Drainage Basin. It straddles the border between Connecticut and Rhode Island. *Watershed:* 847 acres of mostly undeveloped wetland and woods. The pond is fed by a wetland from the northeast (Mowry Meadow) and drains southeast into Middle Reservoir, whose outflow eventually feeds into the Fivemile and Quinebaug Rivers. *Shoreline:* Mostly wooded with a few residences on the southern and northern shores. Much of the southwestern end of the pond is within Killingly Pond State Park, an undeveloped park. *Depth:* Max 22 ft., Mean 15 ft. *Transparency:* Very clear; visible to the bottom (18-20 ft.). *Productivity:* Low to moderate (early mesotrophic). *Bottom type:* Mostly sand, gravel, rubble, boulders and ledge. *Stratification:* Does not occur due to limited depth. *Vegetation:* Sparse and confined to depths of 2 ft. or less along the shore. Dominant submergent species are low water-milfoil and bladderwort. Some yellow pond-lily is present.

Access: A state-owned boat launch is planned to be located on the southwestern shore. *Shore:* The southern and western shores are within an undeveloped state park, but parking is limited.

Fish: Not sampled during the lake and pond electrofishing survey.

Fishing: Is reportedly fair for largemouth bass, smallmouth bass, chain pickerel, yellow perch and sunfish.

Management: Connecticut-Rhode Island border pond. Rhode Island regulations apply. (see current *Connecticut Anglers' Guide*).

Boating: Motors are limited to 12 cu. in. (approximately 10 hp) (see current *Connecticut Boater's Guide*).

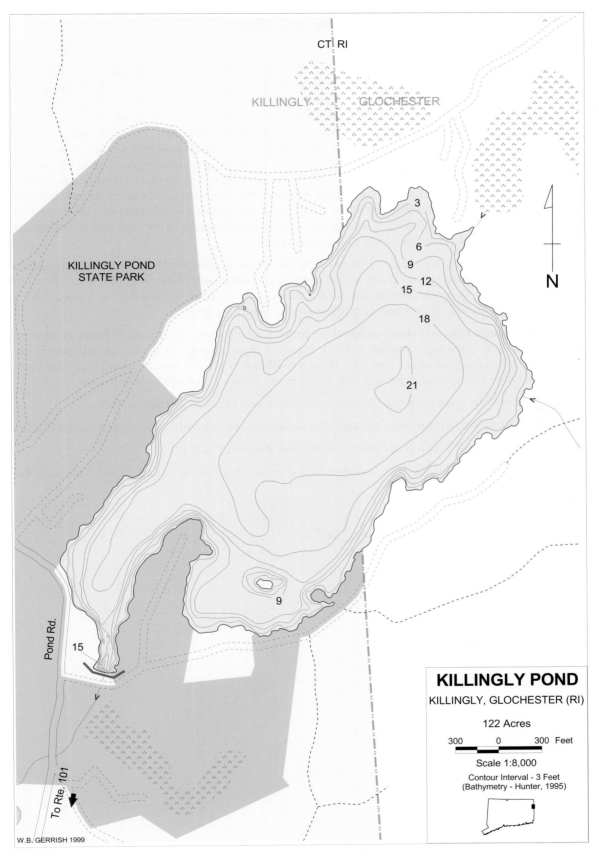

CT RI

KILLINGLY GLOCHESTER

KILLINGLY POND
STATE PARK

3

6

9

12

15

18

21

N

9

Pond Rd.

15

To Rte. 101

W.B. GERRISH 1999

KILLINGLY POND

KILLINGLY, GLOCHESTER (RI)

122 Acres

300   0   300   Feet

Scale 1:8,000

Contour Interval - 3 Feet
(Bathymetry - Hunter, 1995)

Lake of Isles

Town(s): North Stonington   **88.7 acres**

Description: Lake of Isles is a small natural lake within the Thames River Drainage Basin. A small dam on the outlet has raised the water level slightly. *Watershed*: 323 acres of predominantly undeveloped woods and wetland. The lake is fed by five small wetland streams, as well as by surface runoff and bottom springs. It drains into Lake of Isles Brook to the northwest, which feeds into tributaries of Poquetanuck Cove on the Thames River. *Shoreline*: Wooded with very little residential development. *Depth*: Max 11 ft., Mean 5.8 ft. *Transparency*: Relatively clear; transparent to the bottom. *Productivity*: Moderate to very high (early mesotrophic-highly eutrophic). *Bottom type*: Gravel and broken ledge overlain in places with organic muck. *Stratification*: Does not occur due to limited depth. *Vegetation*: Submergent vegetation is very dense throughout with variable-leaved water-milfoil the dominant species. Pondweeds and bladderworts are present in small numbers. Large floating mats of white water-lily cover much of the lake with less abundant water-shield and yellow pond-lily also being present.

Access: A state-owned boat launch is located on the northern shore. Facilities at the launch include a gravel ramp, parking for 10 cars and pit-type toilets. *Directions*: From Rte. 164, Rte. 2 east, left at first intersection onto Watson Rd. for 0.5 miles, right on Lake of Isles Rd. for 1 mile, launch is on left. *Shore*: Public access is restricted to the launching area.

Fish: **Largemouth bass** and **chain pickerel** are present at below average densities. **Black crappie** to 11" are very abundant. **Sunfish** (mostly bluegill, some pumpkinseed, occasional hybrid) are abundant, but sunfish over 7" are rare. **Brown bullhead** to 13" and **American eel** to 24" are common. Other fish species present at low densities are yellow perch and golden shiners.

Fishing: Should be good for pickerel, crappie, bullhead and eels; and fair for sunfish.

Management: Statewide regulations apply for all species (see current *Connecticut Anglers' Guide*).

Boating: Speed limit 8 mph (see current *Connecticut Boater's Guide*).

Comments: Except for the boat launch area, the entire shoreline is owned by the Mashantucket Pequot Tribal Nation.

Lake of Isles
Fish Species and Abundance

	ALL SIZES	BIG FISH	GROWTH
Gamefish			
Largemouth bass	C	U	Avg
Chain pickerel	C	C	< Avg
Panfish			
Black crappie	A	A	< Slow
Yellow perch	U	U	> Avg
Brown bullhead	C	C	
Sunfish			
Bluegill	A	R	< Avg
Pumpkinseed	A	R	< Avg
Other			
Golden shiner	U		
American eel	C		

A=Abundant, C=Common, U=Uncommon, R=Rare

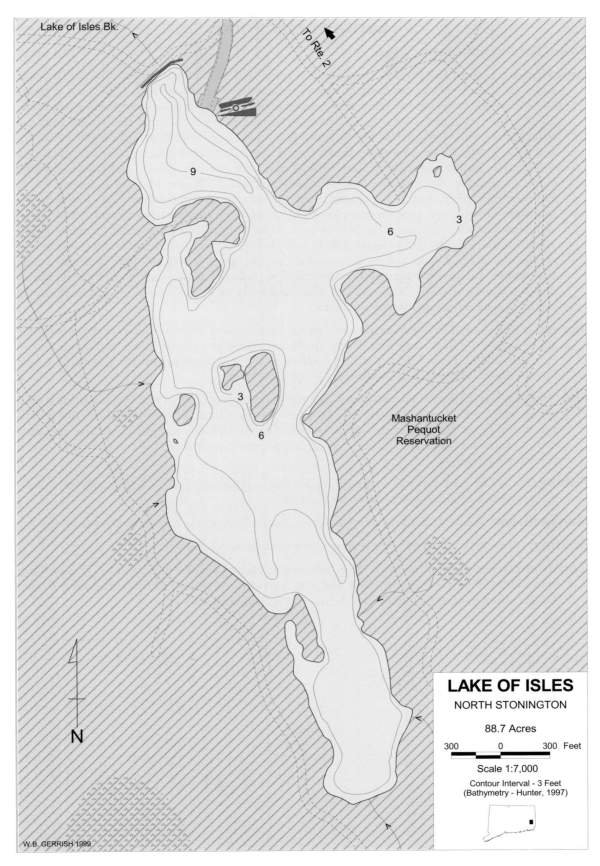

Lake of Isles Bk.

To Rte. 2

9

6

3

3

6

Mashantucket
Pequot
Reservation

N

W.B. GERRISH 1999

LAKE OF ISLES

NORTH STONINGTON

88.7 Acres

300   0   300 Feet

Scale 1:7,000

Contour Interval - 3 Feet
(Bathymetry - Hunter, 1997)

Lantern Hill Pond

Town(s): Ledyard/North Stonington   **23.1 acres**

Description: Lantern Hill Pond is a small glacial kettle lake within the Southeast Coastal Drainage Basin. Its water level was raised slightly by a small earthen dam. *Watershed*: 1,306 acres of mostly undeveloped woods and wetland; however, there is increasing development due to a large casino and resort complex within the watershed. The lake is fed by Lantern Hill Brook from the north. It drains into Lantern Hill Brook, which feeds into Long Pond, Whitford's Brook and eventually the Mystic River. *Shoreline*: Undeveloped woods and marshland with the exception of a silica quarry on the southeastern shore. The northeastern shore is wooded and flanked by high cliffs. In contrast, the western shore is mostly marshland. *Depth*: Max 33 ft., Mean 14 ft. *Transparency*: Fair; 8-9 ft. in summer; slightly reduced by tea-colored stain. *Productivity*: Moderate to very high (late mesotrophic-highly eutrophic). *Bottom type*: Gravel, rubble, mud and organic muck. Portions of the bottom are covered with silica residue from the mine runoff. *Stratification*: Occurs with a thermocline forming between 7 and 20 ft. Late summer oxygen levels are reduced to 3-4 ppm in the thermocline then decline to less than 2 ppm in deeper water. *Vegetation*: Submergent vegetation, dominated by fanwort, pondweeds and bladderworts, is dense to depths of 10 ft. Dense mats of white water-lily and yellow pond-lily are found in the shallow coves and along the shoreline areas.

Access: A state-owned boat launch is located on the southwestern shore. Facilities at the site include an unimproved gravel ramp with a very small turnaround and a steep slope, and parking for 6 cars. *Directions*: From Rte. 2, Rte. 214 south, bear left onto Lantern Hill Rd. Launch is 1 mile on left. *Shore*: Public access is restricted to the launch area.

Fish: Not sampled during the lake and pond electrofishing survey. Lantern Hill Pond is stocked each spring with 1,300 catchable size brown, brook and rainbow trout. Few trout holdover due to limited depth. Other sampling records indicate that bluegill, alewives and golden shiners are abundant; largemouth bass, chain pickerel, black crappie and pumpkinseed are common; and yellow perch are uncommon.

Fishing: Should be good for trout in the spring. Fishing is reportedly fair for largemouth bass, chain pickerel, black crappie, yellow perch and sunfish.

Management: Statewide regulations apply for all species (see current *Connecticut Anglers' Guide*).

Boating: No special regulations (see current *Connecticut Boater's Guide*).

Comments: Runoff from the silica mine historically leached directly into the lake. This problem was addressed by DEP in the 1980s and was corrected. At present, the Mashantucket Pequot Tribal Nation owns the property and the mine is no longer operating.

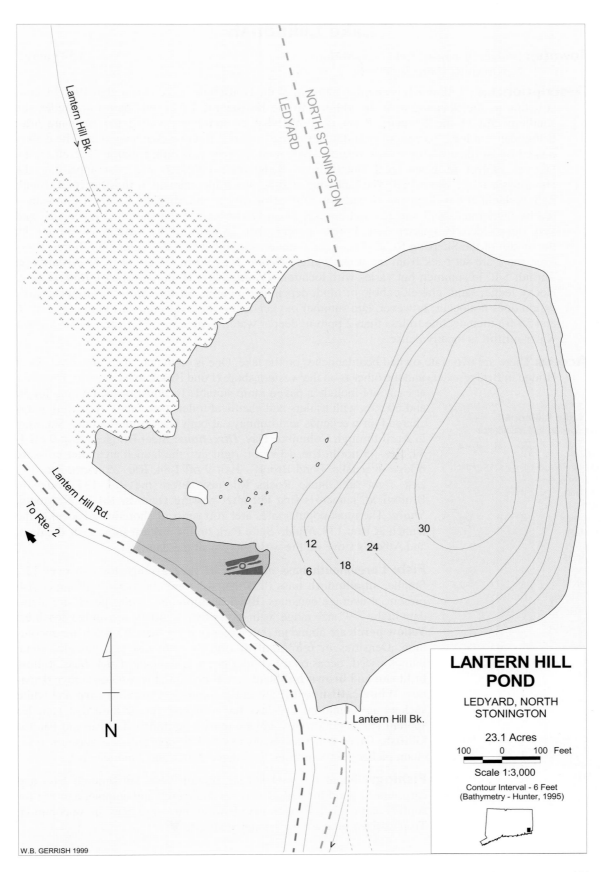

Lantern Hill Bk.

NORTH STONINGTON
LEDYARD

Lantern Hill Rd.

To Rte. 2

12
6
18
24
30

Lantern Hill Bk.

N

LANTERN HILL POND

LEDYARD, NORTH STONINGTON

23.1 Acres

100   0   100 Feet

Scale 1:3,000

Contour Interval - 6 Feet
(Bathymetry - Hunter, 1995)

W.B. GERRISH 1999

Lake Lillinonah

Town(s): Bridgewater/Brookfield/New Milford/ Newtown/Roxbury/Southbury

1,547 acres

Description: Lake Lillinonah is an impoundment of the Housatonic River, created in 1955 by construction of the Shepaug dam. In addition to the Housatonic River, this dam impounded the southern end of the Shepaug River creating what is commonly called the Shepaug arm. Lillinonah is a long, narrow impoundment that has retained riverine characteristics. The dam is owned by Northeast Utilities and operated as a hydroelectric generating station. Therefore, the lake is subject to water-level fluctuations. **Watershed:** 890,433 acres encompassing the Housatonic River watershed. The land surrounding this impoundment is mostly wooded with light residential development. In addition to the Housatonic and Shepaug Rivers, Lillinonah is fed by numerous small streams and brooks. **Shoreline:** Much of the shoreline is wooded and very steep-sided. Paugussett State Forest encompasses 2.8 miles of the western shore opposite the mouth of the Shepaug River. There are a moderate number of homes along its shores; however, most are set back from the water's edge. **Depth:** Max 90 ft., Mean 44 ft. **Transparency:** Turbid; 5 ft. in summer, but varies with location. **Productivity:** High (eutrophic). **Bottom type:** Rocky ledge, sand, gravel, cobble or mud, depending on area. **Stratification:** Thermal stratification does not occur; however, late summer oxygen levels are reduced to 3-4 ppm between 26 and 55 ft., then decline to less than 2 ppm in deeper water. **Vegetation:** Not surveyed. Eurasian water-milfoil is locally dense.

Access: There are two state-owned boat launches on the lake. One is on the northeastern shore (Steel Bridge in Bridgewater) and the other is on the western shore (Pond Brook in Newtown). Facilities at each site include a paved ramp suitable for most boats, parking for 50 and 60 cars with trailers and chemical toilets (seasonal). A parking fee is charged on weekends and holidays at both sites from the third Saturday in April through Columbus Day. **Directions:** Steel Bridge – Exit 9 off I-84, Rte. 25 north, Rte. 133 east, right into the launch area after crossing bridge over lake. Pond Brook – Exit 9 off I-84, Rte. 25 north, Rte. 133 east, right on Obtuse Rocks Rd. just before the Rte. 133 bridge in Brookfield, launch is first left after passing Hanover Rd. in Newtown. **Shore:** The most popular sites are; 200 yards of shoreline adjacent to the launch at Rte. 133, Waldo State Park on the eastern shore near the dam, and Albert's Cove on the west shore near the dam.

Fish: Largemouth bass densities are near average for fish over 12". Smaller **smallmouth bass** (less than 12") are abundant, with larger fish present at average densities. **Black crappie** and **white perch** are abundant in the 7-9" size range, with larger fish occurring at average densities. **Yellow perch** are abundant, but larger (greater than 9") perch are uncommon. Densities of 6-8" **sunfish** (mostly redbreast and bluegill, some pumpkinseed, occasional hybrids) are near average. **Rock bass, yellow bullhead** and **brown bullhead** are all present at less than average densities. **White catfish** to 16" are fairly common. **Common carp** and white suckers are common. The lake has a diverse forage base that includes spottail shiners, alewives, golden shiners, goldfish, fallfish and banded killifish. Other fish species present at low densities are northern pike, chain pickerel, brown trout, tessellated darter and American eel.

Fishing: Should be good for largemouth bass, smallmouth bass and carp; fair to good for yellow perch, white perch and crappie; and fair for sunfish and catfish. Panfish are plentiful, but large ones are uncommon. Trophy-sized pike are occasionally caught. ▼

Lake Lillinonah Fish Species and Abundance	ALL SIZES	BIG FISH	GROWTH
Gamefish			
Largemouth bass	C	C	Fast
Smallmouth bass	A	C	Avg
Brown trout	R		
Northern pike	R	R	
Chain pickerel	R	R	Avg
White catfish	C	C	
Panfish			
Black crappie	A	C	Avg
White perch	A	U	Slow
Yellow perch	A	U	Avg
Brown bullhead	C	U	
Yellow bullhead	U	R	
Sunfish			
Bluegill	C	C	Fast
Pumpkinseed	C	U	Fast
Redbreast	C	U	> Avg
Rock bass	U	U	Fast
Other			
Tessellated darter	R		
Common carp	C		
Fall fish	R		
Golden shiner	C		> Avg
Gold fish	R		
Spottail shiner	C		
Banded killifish	R		
Alewife	U		Fast
White sucker	C		
American eel	R		

A=Abundant, C=Common, U=Uncommon, R=Rare

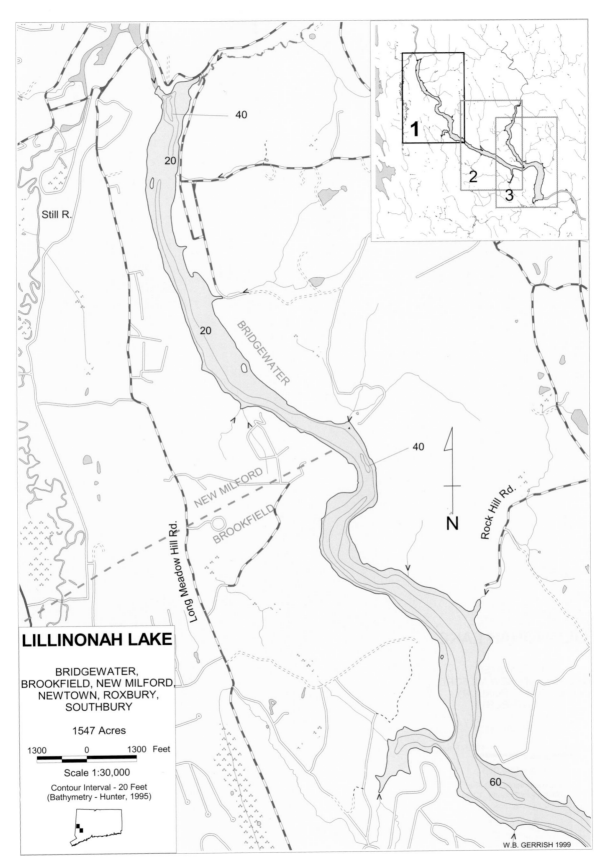

LILLINONAH LAKE

BRIDGEWATER,
BROOKFIELD, NEW MILFORD,
NEWTOWN, ROXBURY,
SOUTHBURY

1547 Acres

1300   0   1300 Feet

Scale 1:30,000

Contour Interval - 20 Feet
(Bathymetry - Hunter, 1995)

Still R.

40

20

20

BRIDGEWATER

40

N

NEW MILFORD

BROOKFIELD

Long Meadow Hill Rd.

Rock Hill Rd.

60

1

2

3

W.B. GERRISH 1999

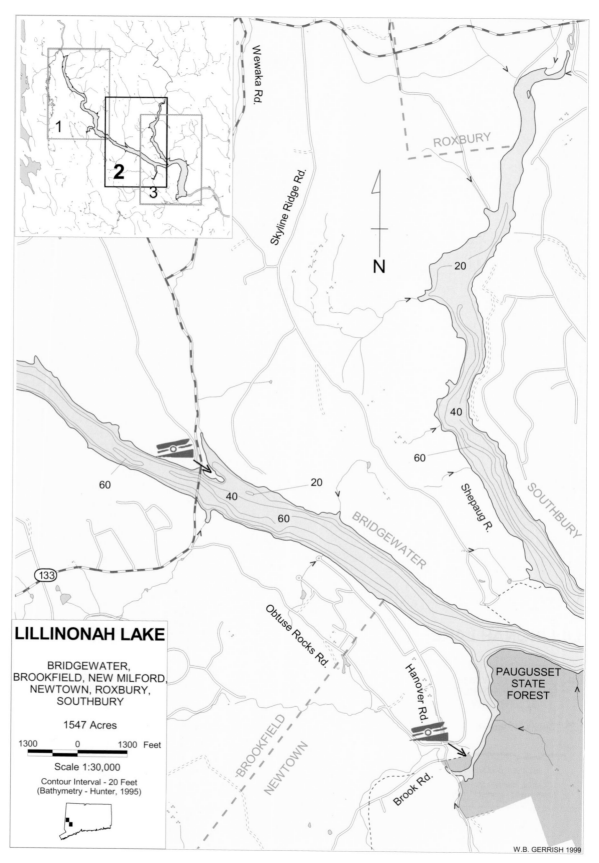

LILLINONAH LAKE

BRIDGEWATER,
BROOKFIELD, NEW MILFORD,
NEWTOWN, ROXBURY,
SOUTHBURY

1547 Acres

1300   0   1300 Feet

Scale 1:30,000

Contour Interval - 20 Feet
(Bathymetry - Hunter, 1995)

W.B. GERRISH 1999

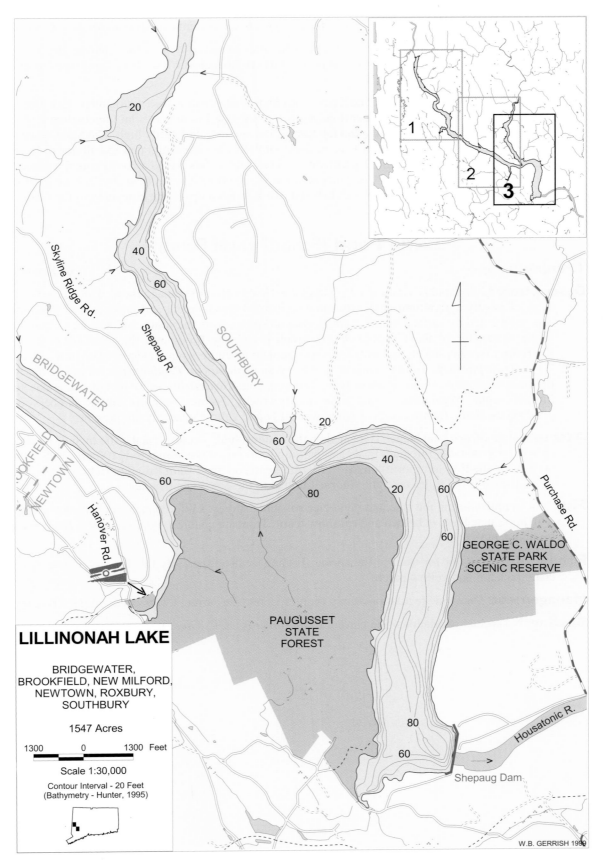

LILLINONAH LAKE

BRIDGEWATER,
BROOKFIELD, NEW MILFORD,
NEWTOWN, ROXBURY,
SOUTHBURY

1547 Acres

1300   0   1300   Feet

Scale 1:30,000

Contour Interval - 20 Feet
(Bathymetry - Hunter, 1995)

Skyline Ridge Rd.

Shepaug R.

BRIDGEWATER

SOUTHBURY

BROOKFIELD

NEWTOWN

Hanover Rd.

PAUGUSSET
STATE
FOREST

GEORGE C. WALDO
STATE PARK
SCENIC RESERVE

Purchase Rd.

Housatonic R.

Shepaug Dam

20

40

60

60

20

60

40

20

60

80

60

80

60

1

2

3

W.B. GERRISH 1999

Management: Statewide regulations apply for all species (see current *Connecticut Anglers' Guide*).

Boating: Daytime speed limit 45 mph, 25 mph ½ hr. after sunset to ½ hr. before sunrise. Boats are prohibited from approaching within 300 ft. of either the Shepaug or Bleachery dams (see current *Connecticut Boater's Guide*).

Comments: Lake Lillinonah is Connecticut's second most popular bass tournament lake (after Candlewood), averaging 50 competitions annually. Because Lillinonah is an impoundment of a major river, both fish productivity and the forage base are extraordinarily high. The State Record northern pike (29 lb.) was caught here in 1980, probably having emigrated to Lillinonah from Bantam Lake. The Connecticut Department of Public Health has issued a consumption advisory on some fish species due to PCB contamination (see current *Connecticut Anglers' Guide* for details). Boaters should be cautious of logs that wash in from upstream, especially in the spring.

Little Pond (Schoolhouse Pond)

Town(s): Thompson   **64.8 acres**

Description: Little Pond is a natural lake within the Thames River Drainage Basin. *Watershed:* 477 acres of mostly agricultural land with some residential development and undeveloped wetland. The pond is fed by surface runoff, a small wetland stream from the south, and bottom springs. It is the headwater of the Fivemile River, which eventually flows into the Quinebaug River. *Shoreline:* Heavily developed with residences around its entire length. *Depth:* Max 14 ft., Mean 7.1 ft. *Transparency:* Turbid; reduced to 3 ft. by an algal bloom. *Productivity:* Moderate (early mesotrophic-mesotrophic). *Bottom type:* Not available. *Stratification:* Does not occur due to limited depth. *Vegetation:* Sparse; the sandy, rocky bottom supports small numbers of pondweeds. Some floating mats of white water-lily and yellow pond-lily are present.

Access: A state-owned boat launch is located on the eastern shore. Facilities at the site include a gravel boat ramp suitable for small boats and parking for 6 cars. *Directions:* Exit 100 off I-395, east on Wilsonville Rd., left (north) on Rte. 193, right (east) on Sand Dam Rd., first right on Jezierski Lane, launch is 0.7 miles on right. *Shore:* Limited to the boat launch area.

Fish: Not sampled during the lake and pond electrofishing survey. Little Pond is stocked each spring with 800 catchable size **brown** and **rainbow trout**. Trout are unable to holdover due to the pond's limited depth.

Fishing: Should be fair for trout in the spring. Fishing is also reportedly fair for largemouth bass, chain pickerel and yellow perch.

Management: Statewide regulations apply for all species (see current *Connecticut Anglers' Guide*).

Boating: No special regulations (see current *Connecticut Boater's Guide*).

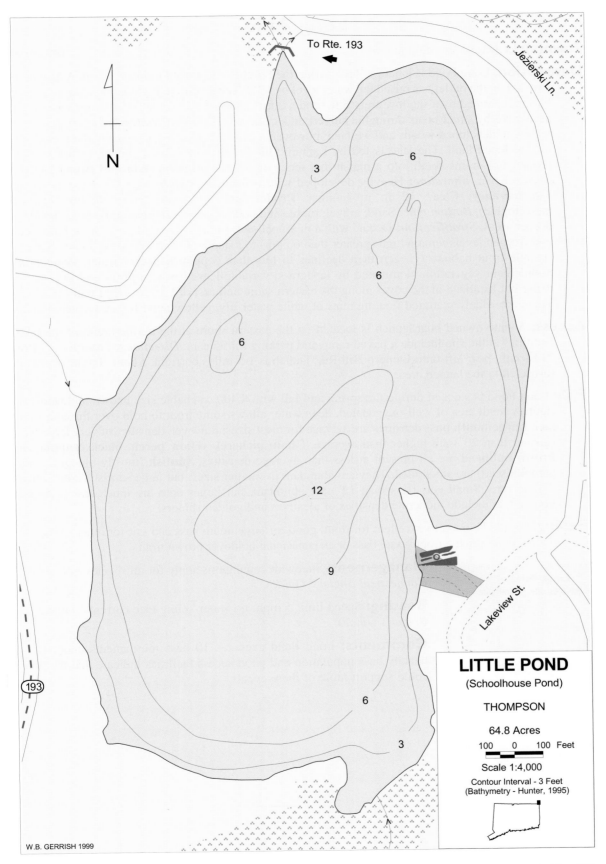

To Rte. 193

Jezierski Ln.

N

3

6

6

6

12

9

6

3

Lakeview St.

193

LITTLE POND
(Schoolhouse Pond)

THOMPSON

64.8 Acres

100   0   100 Feet

Scale 1:4,000

Contour Interval - 3 Feet
(Bathymetry - Hunter, 1995)

W.B. GERRISH 1999

Long Pond

Town(s): Ledyard/North Stonington

Description: Long Pond is a natural lake within the Southeast Coastal Drainage Basin. A dam constructed on the outlet has raised the water level by 12 ft. The resulting impoundment has two deep basins separated by a shallow area (6 ft.) and a third shallow basin (23.0 acres) to the east that is accessible by small boats through a culvert under Lantern Hill Road. *Watershed:* 2,918 acres of mostly undeveloped woods and wetland; however, a casino complex is increasing the proportion of developed land. The lake is fed by Lantern Hill Brook, Silex Brook and three other small brooks and drains south into a marsh that feeds into Whitford Pond, Whitford Brook and the Mystic River. *Shoreline:* Heavily developed with residences. *Depth:* Max 69 ft., Mean 18 ft. *Transparency:* Clear; 12 ft. in summer. *Productivity:* Moderate (early mesotrophic-late mesotrophic). *Bottom type:* Sand, gravel, rubble and boulders in shoal areas and organic muck in deeper areas. *Stratification:* Occurs with a thermocline forming between 13 and 30 ft. Late summer oxygen levels remain high (greater than 6 ppm) to a depth of 30 ft., creating a wide band of suitable trout habitat. Oxygen then declines to less than 3 ppm in deeper water. *Vegetation:* Submergent vegetation, dominated by tapegrass, variable-leaved water-milfoil and fanwort, is dense but localized in the coves along the eastern shore and east of Lantern Hill Road causeway. There are widely scattered floating mats of white water-lily, yellow pond-lily and water-shield.

Access: A state-owned boat launch is located on the eastern shore at the northern end of the lake. Facilities at the site include a paved ramp and parking for 35 cars. *Directions:* From Rte. 2, Rte. 214 south, bear left onto Lantern Hill Rd., launch is 1.5 miles on right. *Shore:* Public access is restricted to the launch area.

Fish: Long Pond is stocked during the spring and fall with 8,400 catchable size **brown** and **rainbow** trout. A small area of well-oxygenated, deep water allows some trout to hold over through summer. **Largemouth bass** densities are average for most sizes; however, densities of very large bass (greater than 20") are higher than average. **Chain pickerel**, **yellow perch**, **black crappie** and **brown bullhead** are all present at less than average densities. **Sunfish** (mostly bluegill, some pumpkinseed) are stockpiled. They are abundant in smaller sizes, but large sunfish (greater than 7") are rare. Small eels (less than 12") are abundant, but larger ones are much less common. Forage fish include moderate densities of alewives and golden shiners.

Fishing: Should be good to excellent for trout, good for largemouth bass and fair for other species. A good spot to catch a trophy-size bass or an occasional holdover brown trout.

Long Pond
Fish Species and Abundance

	ALL SIZES	BIG FISH	GROWTH
Gamefish			
Largemouth bass	C	C	Avg
Brown trout	A	U	
Rainbow trout	A		
Chain pickerel	C	C	Avg
Panfish			
Black crappie	C	C	< Avg
Yellow perch	C	C	< Avg
Brown bullhead	U	U	
Sunfish			
Bluegill	A	U	< Slow
Pumpkinseed	C	U	Slow
Other			
Golden shiner	C		
Alewife	C		
American eel	A		

A=Abundant, C=Common, U=Uncommon, R=Rare

Management: Statewide regulations apply for all species (see current *Connecticut Anglers' Guide*).

Boating: Speed limit 5 mph, no water-skiing (see current *Connecticut Boater's Guide*).

Comments: Long Pond averages 10 bass tournaments annually. A healthy bass population and good access facilities indicate that the pond could support more of these events.

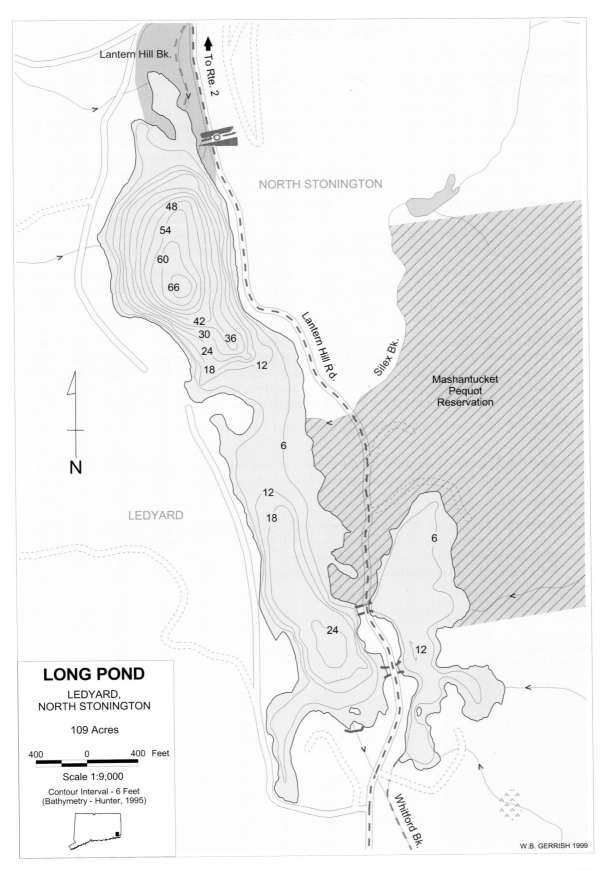

Lantern Hill Bk.

To Rte. 2

NORTH STONINGTON

48

54

60

66

42
30   36
24
18   12

Lantern Hill Rd.

Silex Bk.

Mashantucket
Pequot
Reservation

6

12

18

6

N

LEDYARD

24

12

LONG POND

LEDYARD,
NORTH STONINGTON

109 Acres

400   0   400   Feet

Scale 1:9,000

Contour Interval - 6 Feet
(Bathymetry - Hunter, 1995)

Whitford Bk.

W.B. GERRISH 1999

Maltby Lakes (1, 2 & 3)

Town(s): Orange/West Haven   **19, 23, & 25.3 acres**

Description: The Maltby Lakes are three small artificial impoundments in the South Central Coastal Drainage Basin. They are active distribution reservoirs owned by South Central Connecticut Regional Water Authority (RWA). *Watershed*: 755 acres of mostly undeveloped woods with a moderate proportion of residential land and a golf course. The lakes are fed by three small streams from the north. Water flows over the spillways of Maltby Lakes #2 and #3 into Lake #1, which drains eastward into the West River. There is a conduit connecting Maltby #2 and 3 that allows water to pass between the two reservoirs. *Shoreline*: Lined by conifers. There is no residential development; however, Rte. 34 abuts the southern shores of Maltby #1 and #3. *Depth*: Max #1: 21 ft., #2: 32 ft., #3: 26 ft. *Transparency*: Not available. *Productivity*: Low (oligotrophic). *Bottom type*: Sand, gravel and cobble in shallows. *Stratification*: Not available. *Vegetation*: Variable pondweed is common to dense in all three lakes. Large-leaved pondweed, slender pondweed and eutrophic water-nymph are present in small numbers in Maltby #2.

Access: No boats allowed. Angling restricted to shore fishing on a permit-only basis. *Directions*: From Rte. 122, Rte. 34 west for 0.75 miles, right (north) through gated entrance to RWA property. *Shore*: The entire shorelines of all 3 lakes are open to permitted fishing. Contact the RWA at (203) 562-4020 for permit information.

Fish: The Maltby Lakes are stocked during the spring by the RWA with 1,800 **rainbow trout**. **Largemouth bass** and **yellow perch** less than 10" are abundant with densities of larger fish being above average. **Chain pickerel** are present at less than average densities. Small **sunfish** (mostly bluegill, some pumpkinseed and hybrids) are abundant, but numbers of larger sunfish are below average. Other fish species present at low densities are brown bullhead and American eel.

Fishing: Should be good in the spring for trout, good for perch; fair to good for bass; and fair for sunfish.

Management: Bass Management Lakes; special slot length and creel limits on bass. Statewide regulations apply for all other species (see current *Connecticut Anglers' Guide*).

Boating: No boats allowed.

Comments: Only Maltby #2 & #3 were electrofished. The Maltby Lakes are water supply reservoirs that were first opened to public fishing in 1994. First year angler harvests resulted in drastic reductions in the bass and panfish populations. Special regulations on largemouth bass were implemented in 1996, thus bass fishing should continue to improve.

Maltby Lakes 2 & 3
Fish Species and Abundance

	ALL SIZES	BIG FISH	GROWTH
Gamefish			
Largemouth bass	A	C	Ave
Rainbow trout	C		
Panfish			
Yellow perch	A	C	Fast
Brown bullhead	U	U	
Sunfish			
Bluegill	A	U	Fast
Pumpkinseed	C	U	Slow
Other			
American eel	U		

A=Abundant, C=Common, U=Uncommon, R=Rare

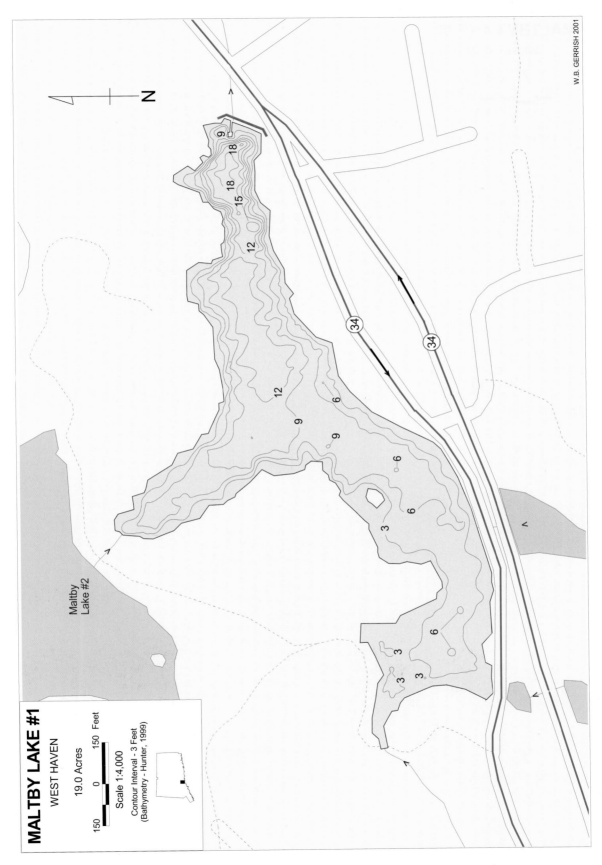

MALTBY LAKE #1

WEST HAVEN

19.0 Acres

150   0   150   Feet

Scale 1:4,000

Contour Interval - 3 Feet
(Bathymetry - Hunter, 1999)

N

Maltby
Lake #2

34

34

9
18
18
15
12

12

9

6

9

6

6

3

6

3
3

3
3

W.B. GERRISH 2001

MALTBY LAKE #2

WEST HAVEN

23.0 Acres

100 0 100 Feet

Scale 1:3,000

Contour Interval - 5 Feet
(Bathymetry - Hunter, 1999)

N

10

5

15

30

30

25

20

15

10

5

Maltby Lake #1

W.B. GERRISH 2001

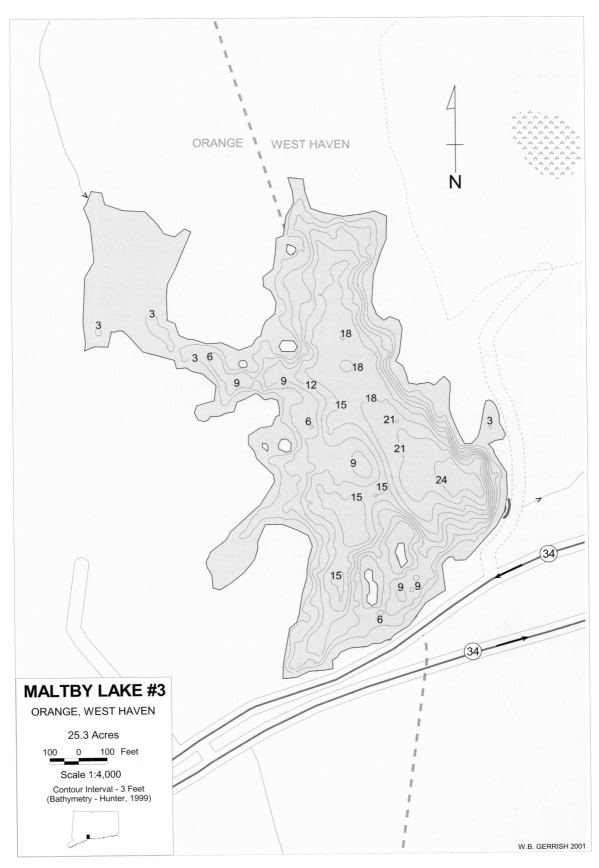

ORANGE   WEST HAVEN

N

3
3
3
3   6
9   9   12
15
6
18
18
18
21
21
9
24
15
15
3
34
34
15
9   9
6

MALTBY LAKE #3

ORANGE, WEST HAVEN

25.3 Acres

100   0   100 Feet

Scale 1:4,000

Contour Interval - 3 Feet
(Bathymetry - Hunter, 1999)

W.B. GERRISH 2001

Mamanasco Lake

Town(s): Ridgefield

89.2 acres

Description: Mamanasco Lake is a natural lake within the Hudson River Drainage Basin. The water level was raised slightly by an earthen dam. *Watershed*: 901 acres of mostly residentially developed and some agricultural land. It is fed by the outlet stream of Turtle Pond and by surface runoff. The lake drains northward through a marsh into the Titicus River, which eventually feeds into the Croton River in New York State. *Shoreline*: The southwestern shore is dominated by residential development with some homes right at the water's edge. The northeastern shore is mostly wooded with some steep cliff areas and a moderate number of homes set back from the water. *Depth*: Max 11 ft., Mean 7.5 ft. *Transparency*: Very turbid; 2.5 ft. in summer. *Productivity*: Moderate (late mesotrophic). *Bottom type*: Ledge, broken ledge and organic muck. *Stratification*: Does not occur due to limited depth. *Vegetation*: Submergent vegetation is very dense to depths of 6-7 ft. Eurasian water-milfoil, curly pondweed and southern water-nymph are the dominant species. Small, scattered floating mats of white water-lily and yellow pond-lily are present. Pickerelweed fringes the lake margins.

Access: A state-owned boat launch is located on the southern shore. Facilities at the launch include a paved boat ramp and parking for 10 cars. *Directions*: Exit 3 off I-84, Rte. 7 south, Rte. 35 south, Rte. 116 west for 3.4 miles, left (south) on Mamanasco Rd., launch is 1 mile on left. *Shore*: Limited to the boat launch area.

Fish: **Largemouth bass** are extremely abundant to 14", but densities of larger fish are only average. **Yellow perch** are present at low densities. Small **black crappie** (6-8") are extremely abundant, with larger fish being common. **Sunfish** (mostly bluegill, some pumpkinseed, and occasional hybrids) are extremely abundant to 8". **Brown bullheads** are abundant in the 9-13" size range. Mamanasco has an abundant golden shiner forage base. Chain pickerel are rare.

Fishing: Should be good to excellent for bass (especially during spring), crappie, sunfish and bullheads. Heavy submergent vegetation makes fishing difficult in the summer, however.

Management: Bass Management Lake; special slot length and creel limits on bass. Statewide regulations apply for all other species (see current *Connecticut Anglers' Guide*).

Boating: Gas motors prohibited (see current *Connecticut Boater's Guide*).

Comments: Mamanasco Lake is one of the most fertile ponds sampled during the lake and pond electrofishing survey. This high fertility causes its fish population to be very abundant, but also results in heavy submergent vegetation and dense algal blooms. Despite its productivity, the bass population is stockpiled and angler harvest is apparently high. Special regulations should improve fishing by protecting larger bass and allowing anglers to harvest overabundant small bass.

Mamanasco Lake
Fish Species and Abundance

	ALL SIZES	BIG FISH	GROWTH
Gamefish			
Largemouth bass	A	C	< Avg
Chain pickerel	R	R	
Panfish			
Black crappie	A	C	Avg
Yellow perch	U	U	> Avg
Brown bullhead	A	C	
Sunfish			
Bluegill	A	A	< Avg
Pumpkinseed	A	C	Avg
Other			
Golden shiner	A		Fast

A=Abundant, C=Common, U=Uncommon, R=Rare

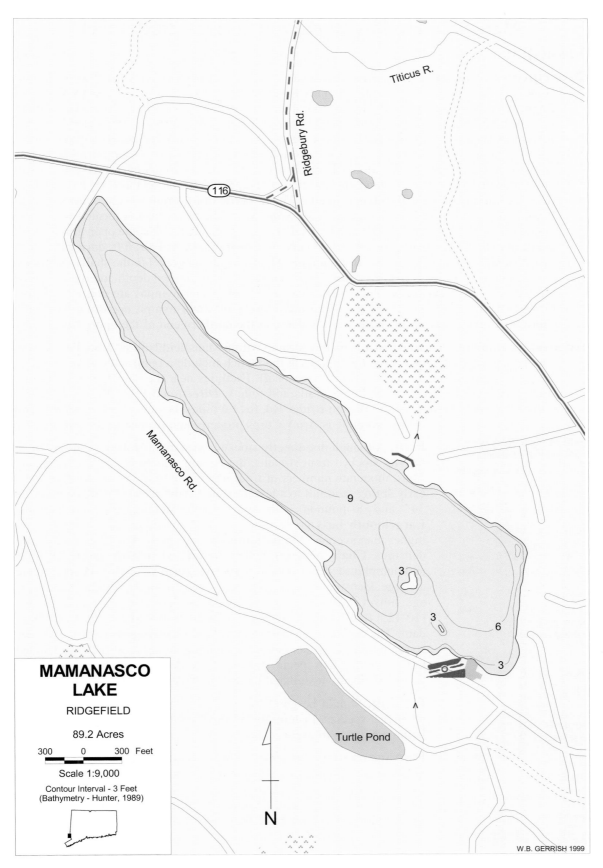

**MAMANASCO
LAKE**

RIDGEFIELD

89.2 Acres

300   0   300 Feet

Scale 1:9,000

Contour Interval - 3 Feet
(Bathymetry - Hunter, 1989)

Titicus R.

Ridgebury Rd.

116

Mamanasco Rd.

9

3

3

6

3

Turtle Pond

N

W.B. GERRISH 1999

Mansfield Hollow Reservoir (Naubesatuck Lake)

Town(s): Mansfield/Windham
460 acres

Description: Mansfield Hollow Reservoir is an artificial impoundment of the Fenton, Mount Hope and Natchaug Rivers in the Thames River Drainage Basin. The U.S. Army Corps of Engineers constructed it as a flood control impoundment in the early 1950s. The impoundment is comprised of two basins (upper basin 211 acres, lower basin 249 acres) separated by a culvert under Bassett Bridge Rd., which is navigable by small boats. Water levels vary considerably due to its flood control function. *Watershed*: 104,742 acres incorporating the watersheds of the Natchaug, Fenton and Mount Hope Rivers. The land surrounding the lake is mostly undeveloped woods and wetland. In addition to being fed by these three rivers, the lake receives water from 3 small wetland streams. The reservoir drains southwest into the Natchaug River, which feeds into the Shetucket River. *Shoreline*: The entire lake is located within the boundaries of Mansfield Hollow State Park and is mostly wooded with some open grassy areas adjacent to the dam. *Depth*: Max 23 ft., Mean 6.5 ft. *Transparency*: Fair; 6 ft. during the summer. *Productivity*: Not available. *Bottom type*: Mostly sand and gravel in the shallows, organic muck in deeper areas. *Stratification*: Does not occur due to limited depth and riverine flow through the lake. *Vegetation*: Waterweed, pondweeds and water-nymphs are generally sparse throughout the reservoir. There are some dense areas of water-nymph occurring along the shoreline in the lower basin. Waterweed is dense at the northern end of the upper basin.

Access: An Army Corps-owned boat launch is located within Mansfield Hollow State Park on the southern shore of the upper basin. Facilities at the launch include a ramp with concrete slabs, parking for 50 cars and chemical toilets (seasonal). Facilities near the launch and within the state park include picnic areas, hiking trails and toilets. *Directions*: From Rte. 6, Rte. 195 north for 2 miles, right (east) on Bassett Bridge Rd. for 1.5 miles, launch is on left. *Shore*: The entire shoreline is Army Corps property and is open to the public.

Mansfield Hollow Reservoir
Fish Species and Abundance

	ALL SIZES	BIG FISH	GROWTH
Gamefish			
Largemouth bass	C	C	> Avg
Smallmouth bass	U	U	Avg
Brook trout	U		
Brown trout	U	R	
Rainbow trout	U	R	
Northern Pike	C	C	Avg
Chain pickerel	C	C	Avg
Panfish			
Black crappie	C	C	> Avg
Yellow perch	C	C	< Avg
Brown bullhead	U	U	
Yellow bullhead	U	U	
Sunfish			
Bluegill	C	C	> Ave
Pumpkinseed	C	C	Avg
Redbreast	U	R	
Green	U	R	
Other			
Tessellated darter	U		
Common shiner	U		
Fallfish	U		
Golden shiner	A		
Spottail shiner	A		
Banded killifish	C		
White sucker	A		
American eel	U		

A=Abundant, C=Common, U=Uncommon, R=Rare

Fish: Although not directly stocked, Mansfield Hollow is fed by three heavily stocked trout streams; the Fenton, Mount Hope and Natchaug. Thus, moderate numbers of trout immigrate to the reservoir during the early spring (and fall to a lesser extent). **Northern pike** are common to 34" and 8 pounds with some fish reaching over 15 pounds. **Largemouth bass** are common with densities of 10-14" bass being higher than average. **Smallmouth bass** are present at less than average densities. **Chain pickerel**, **yellow perch** and **sunfish** (mostly bluegill and pumpkinseed, occasional redbreast, green and hybrid) densities are average. Densities of larger sunfish (7-8") are slightly higher than average, however. **Black crappie** densities are less than average, but larger (10-12") fish are above average in abundance. White suckers are abundant. The lake has an abundant and diverse forage base that includes spottail shiners, golden shiners, common shiners, fallfish and banded killifish. Other fish species present at low densities are brown bullhead, yellow bullhead, tessellated darter and American eel.

Fishing: Should be good for bass and sunfish; and fair to good for other fish species. Fishing for northern pike is improving as the population continues to expand.

Management: Mansfield Hollow is stocked annually with 2,700 northern pike fingerlings to supplement natural recruitment in the lake. Northern pike were first introduced into the lake in 1992 and the fishery was still expanding at the time of writing. Bass Management Lake; special slot length and creel limits on bass. Statewide regulations ▼

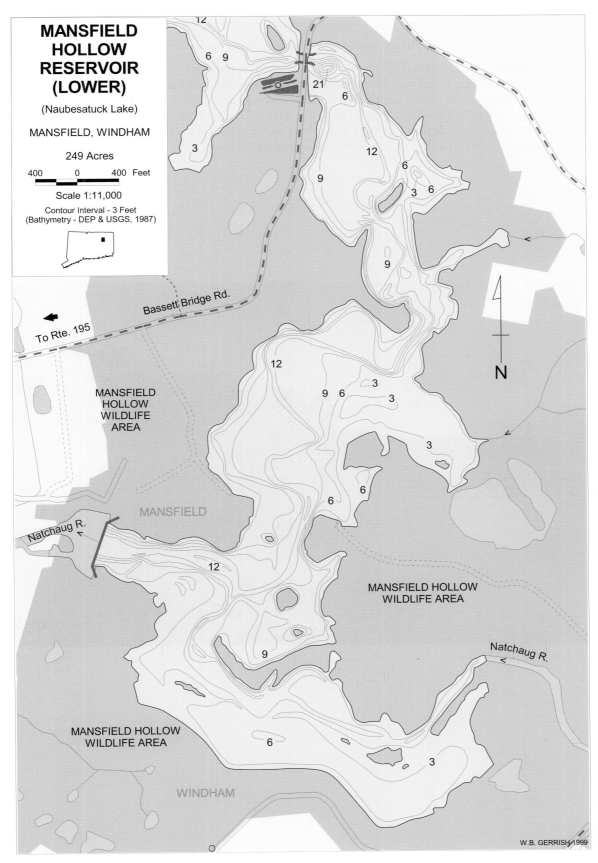

MANSFIELD HOLLOW RESERVOIR (LOWER)

(Naubesatuck Lake)

MANSFIELD, WINDHAM

249 Acres

400   0   400   Feet

Scale 1:11,000

Contour Interval - 3 Feet
(Bathymetry - DEP & USGS, 1987)

Bassett Bridge Rd.

To Rte. 195

MANSFIELD HOLLOW WILDLIFE AREA

MANSFIELD

Natchaug R.

MANSFIELD HOLLOW WILDLIFE AREA

MANSFIELD HOLLOW WILDLIFE AREA

Natchaug R.

WINDHAM

N

W.B. GERRISH 1999

apply for all other species (see current *Connecticut Anglers' Guide*).

Boating: Speed limit 8 mph (see current *Connecticut Boater's Guide*).

Comments: Special bass regulations should improve fishing by protecting larger bass and allowing anglers to harvest overabundant small bass. Mansfield is a popular bass tournament lake, averaging 22 events annually. The State Record rainbow trout (14 lb. 10 oz.) was caught here in 1998. Fluctuating water levels and currents can result in hazardous ice conditions for winter anglers. Waterfowl hunting is popular in the fall. No water contact activities, such as swimming, sailboarding or personal watercraft, are allowed.

Mansfield Hollow Reservoir

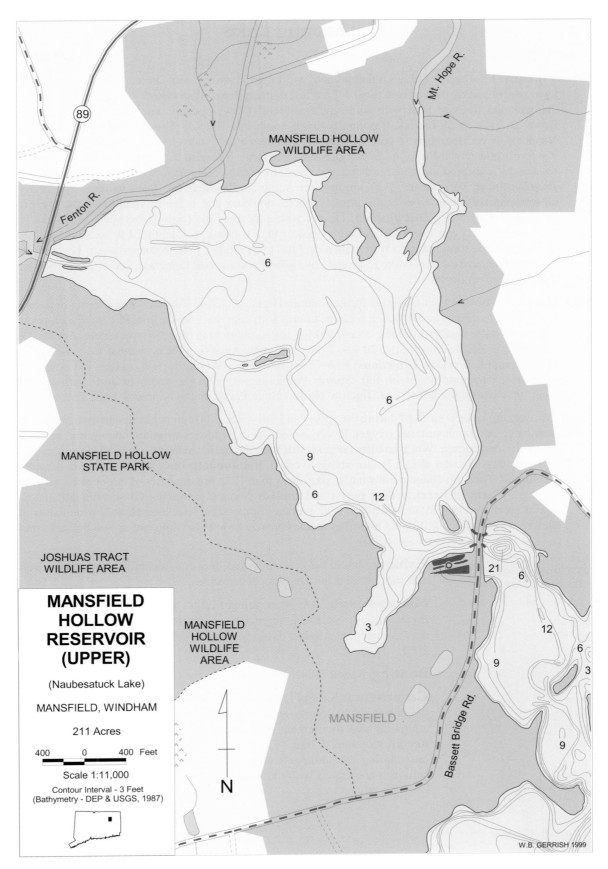

MANSFIELD HOLLOW
WILDLIFE AREA

Mt. Hope R.

Fenton R.

89

6

6

9

12

6

MANSFIELD HOLLOW
STATE PARK

JOSHUAS TRACT
WILDLIFE AREA

MANSFIELD
HOLLOW
WILDLIFE
AREA

21

6

12

6

3

3

9

9

Bassett Bridge Rd.

MANSFIELD

**MANSFIELD
HOLLOW
RESERVOIR
(UPPER)**

(Naubesatuck Lake)

MANSFIELD, WINDHAM

211 Acres

400   0   400   Feet

Scale 1:11,000

Contour Interval - 3 Feet
(Bathymetry - DEP & USGS, 1987)

N

W.B. GERRISH 1999

Mashapaug Lake

Town(s): Union

287 acres

Description: Mashapaug Lake is a natural lake within the Thames River Drainage Basin. The water level was raised by the construction of three low earthen dams. **Watershed:** 2,932 acres of mostly undeveloped forested land with some light residential development. The lake is fed by Wells Brook and two small brooks. It normally drains south into Bigelow Brook, which feeds into the Natchaug River. However, a control structure can also allow water to flow north into Hamilton Reservoir and onward into the upper Quinebaug system. **Shoreline:** Mostly wooded with some residences clustered on the northern and western shores. **Depth:** Max 38 ft., Mean 19 ft. **Transparency:** Very clear; 28 ft. during late summer. **Productivity:** Low to moderate (early mesotrophic). **Bottom type:** Sand, gravel, rubble, boulders and ledge in shallow areas; organic muck in deeper areas. **Stratification:** Occurs with a thermocline forming between 23 and 33 ft. Late summer oxygen levels remain high (greater than 6 ppm) to a depth 29 ft., creating a wide zone of suitable trout habitat. Oxygen then declines to less than 2 ppm in deeper water. **Vegetation:** Is virtually absent except for the southeast cove where pondweeds, tapegrass, spike-rush, pipewort and bladderwort occur.

Access: A state-owned boat launch is located within Bigelow Hollow State Park at the southern end of the lake. Facilities at the launch include a ramp with concrete slabs, a concrete bulkhead, parking for 15 cars, disabled fishing access, hiking trails, picnicking and pit-type toilets. Additional parking is available in the park 500 yds. from the launch. A parking fee is charged from Memorial Day through Labor Day. **Directions:** Exit 73 off I-84, Rte. 190 north, right on Rte. 171 south for 1.3 miles, Park entrance is on left. **Shore:** Public access is on the southern and southwestern shorelines within the borders of Bigelow Hollow State Park and the Nipmuck State Forest.

Fish: Mashapaug Lake is stocked during the spring and fall with 8,500 catchable size **brown** and **rainbow** trout. Although summer oxygen levels are sufficient, holdover trout are uncommon because of insufficient forage. While smaller **largemouth bass** are below average in abundance, densities of larger bass (greater than 13") are above average. **Smallmouth bass** appear to be moderately stockpiled. They are abundant in smaller sizes (less than 12"), but densities of larger ones are only average. **Chain pickerel**, **yellow perch** and **sunfish** (mostly pumpkinseed and bluegill, occasional green and hybrid) densities are near average. Forage fish species include low densities of alewives and banded killifish. Other fish species present at low densities are brown bullhead and white sucker.

Fishing: Should be seasonally excellent for stocked trout; good for bass and sunfish; and fair for other fish species.

Management: Bass Management Lake; special slot length and creel limits on bass. Statewide regulations apply for all other species (see current Connecticut Anglers' Guide). Annual walleye stocking began here in 2001.

Boating: Speed limit 10 mph (see current *Connecticut Boater's Guide*).

Comments: Special regulations should improve fishing by protecting larger bass and allowing anglers to harvest overabundant small bass. It is a popular bass tournament lake, averaging 12 events annually. The State Record largemouth bass (12 lb. 14 oz.) was caught here in 1961. Very busy during the summer with boating, swimming, picnicking and other activities associated with the state park.

Mashapaug Lake
Fish Species and Abundance

	ALL SIZES	BIG FISH	GROWTH
Gamefish			
Largemouth bass	C	C	> Avg
Smallmouth bass	C	C	Slow
Brown trout	C	U	
Rainbow trout	C		
Chain pickerel	U	U	Avg
Panfish			
Yellow perch	A	C	Avg
Brown bullhead	U	U	
Sunfish			
Bluegill	C	C	> Avg
Pumpkinseed	C	C	Avg
Green	U	R	
Other			
Banded killifish	C		
Alewife	U		
White sucker	U		

A=Abundant, C=Common, U=Uncommon, R=Rare

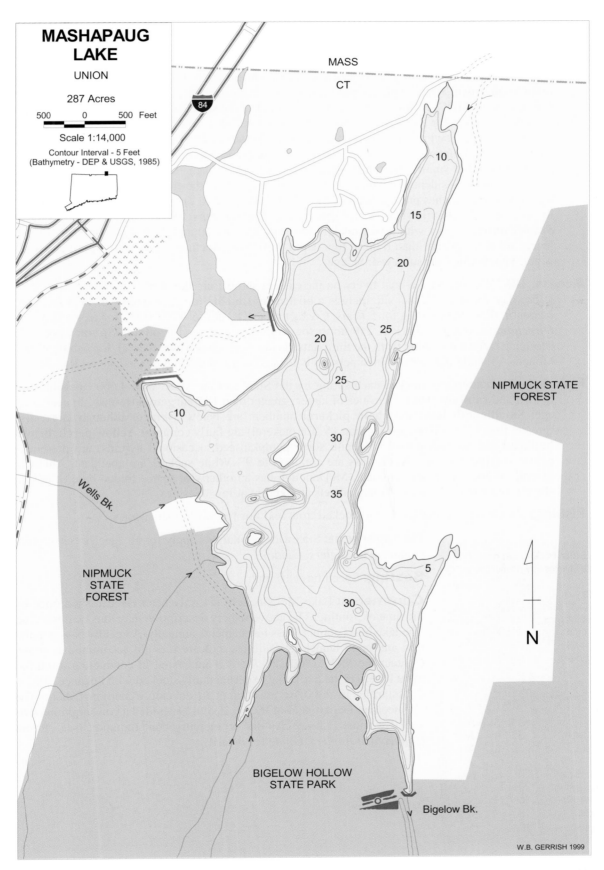

MASHAPAUG LAKE

UNION

287 Acres

500   0   500 Feet

Scale 1:14,000

Contour Interval - 5 Feet
(Bathymetry - DEP & USGS, 1985)

MASS

CT

I-84

10

15

20

25

20

25

30

35

10

5

30

NIPMUCK STATE FOREST

Wells Bk.

NIPMUCK STATE FOREST

N

BIGELOW HOLLOW STATE PARK

Bigelow Bk.

W.B. GERRISH 1999

Lake McDonough (Compensating Reservoir)

Town(s): Barkhamsted   **391 acres**

Description: Lake McDonough is an artificial impoundment of the East Branch Farmington River in the Connecticut River Drainage Basin. It is owned and managed by the Metropolitan District Commission (MDC). This reservoir was originally constructed to augment flows in the Farmington River for hydropower production; however, it is now maintained as a recreational facility providing swimming, boating and fishing. *Watershed*: 39,837 acres of mostly forested land. It is fed by intermittent releases of water from Barkhamsted Reservoir, by Beaver Brook and by two other small streams. It drains into the East Branch Farmington River. *Shoreline*: Wooded with no residential development. Rte. 219 runs along the entire eastern shoreline. There are four public beaches present. *Depth*: Max 53 ft., Mean 22 ft. *Transparency*: Very clear; 30 ft. in summer. *Productivity*: Low (oligotrophic). *Bottom type*: Sand, gravel and boulders. *Stratification*: Occurs with a thermocline forming between 20 and 23 ft. Late summer oxygen levels are high (greater than 6 ppm) to a depth 36 ft., then decline to less than 4 ppm in deeper water. *Vegetation*: Not surveyed. Scarce.

Access: The MDC operates a boat livery on the eastern shore from the third Saturday in April until Labor day. Facilities at this site include a boat ramp suitable for most boats, rowboat and paddleboat rentals and parking for 50 cars. Contact the MDC at (860) 379-0916 for fees and hours. *Directions*: From Rte. 44, Rte. 219 north for 3 miles, access road is on left. *Shore*: The entire shoreline is open to fishing from the third Saturday in April until November 30. Ice fishing is prohibited. A fishing pier for disabled persons is located at the south end of the lake on Rte. 219.

Fish: Lake McDonough is stocked each spring by the State and the MDC with 4,600 catchable size **brown** and **rainbow trout**. Densities of larger (greater than 12") **largemouth bass** are near average. **Smallmouth bass** and **chain pickerel** numbers are below average, although larger fish (greater than 12" for bass, greater than 15" for pickerel) are fairly common. **Yellow perch, brown bullhead** and **sunfish** (mostly bluegill, some pumpkinseed, occasional hybrids) are present at below average densities. **Rock bass** are common to 9". White suckers are abundant. Although juvenile yellow perch are abundant, McDonough has an otherwise sparse forage base of golden shiners and banded killifish. American eels are present at low densities.

Fishing: Should be seasonally fair for stocked trout and fair for most other species.

Management: Statewide regulations apply for all species (see current *Connecticut Anglers' Guide*).

Boating: Speed limit 10 mph.

Comments: Lake McDonough had only been electrofished once by the time of printing. The above fishery description may thus be imprecise. The lake hosts about 9 bass tournaments annually. A healthy bass population and good launching facilities indicate it could accommodate more. Contact the MDC (860-278-7850) if interested in conducting a tournament here. The lake is being experimentally stocked with kokanee salmon fry (starting in 2000) in an attempt to develop a salmon fishery. The Connecticut Department of Public Health has issued a consumption advisory for some fish species due to mercury contamination (see current *Connecticut Anglers' Guide* for details).

Lake McDonough
Fish Species and Abundance

	ALL SIZES	BIG FISH	GROWTH
Gamefish			
Largemouth bass	C	C	> Fast
Smallmouth bass	C	C	Fast
Brown trout	C	R	
Rainbow trout	C		
Chain pickerel	C	C	> Avg
Panfish			
Yellow perch	C	C	Avg
Brown bullhead	C	C	
Sunfish			
Bluegill	U	U	> Avg
Pumpkinseed	U	R	Avg
Rock bass	C	C	Avg
Other			
Golden shiner	U		Avg
Banded killifish	C		
White sucker	A		
American eel	R		

A=Abundant, C=Common, U=Uncommon, R=Rare

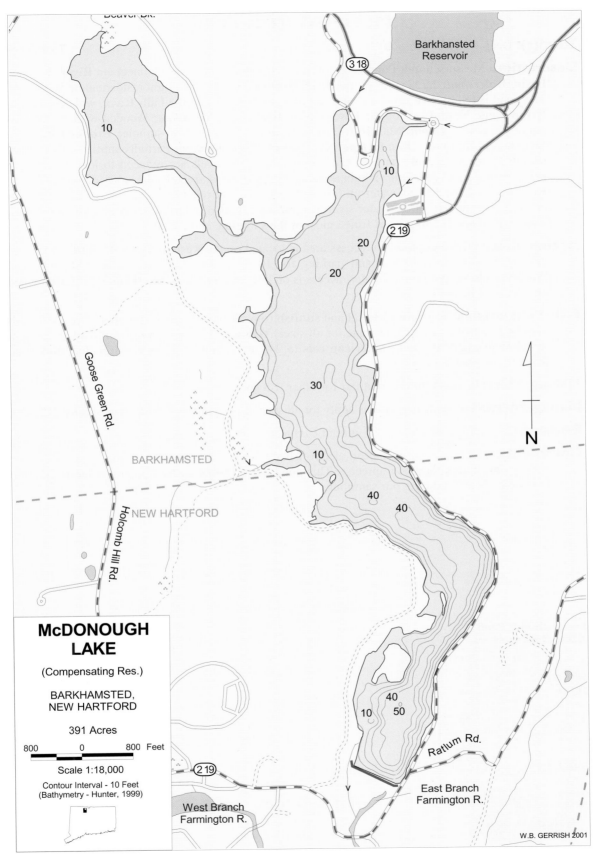

McDONOUGH LAKE

(Compensating Res.)

BARKHAMSTED,
NEW HARTFORD

391 Acres

800   0   800 Feet

Scale 1:18,000

Contour Interval - 10 Feet
(Bathymetry - Hunter, 1999)

Barkhansted
Reservoir

Goose Green Rd.

BARKHAMSTED

NEW HARTFORD

Holcomb Hill Rd.

Rattlum Rd.

East Branch
Farmington R.

West Branch
Farmington R.

N

10

10

20

20

20

30

10

40

40

40

50

10

10

W.B. GERRISH 2001

Messerschmidt Pond

Town(s): Deep River/Westbrook   **73.0 acres**

Description: Messerschmidt Pond is an artificial impoundment in the Connecticut River Drainage Basin. *Watershed*: 2,722 acres of mostly undeveloped woods with light residential development. The pond is fed by five small streams and drains southeast into the Falls River, which eventually flows into North Cove on the lower Connecticut River. *Shoreline*: Wooded with no residential development. *Depth*: Max 16 ft. *Transparency*: Turbid; 5 ft. in summer. *Productivity*: Very high (highly eutrophic). *Bottom type*: Not available. *Stratification*: Partially stratifies with a temperature gradient forming at 7 ft. Late summer oxygen levels are reduced to less than 1 ppm below this depth. *Vegetation*: Submergent vegetation is extremely dense to depths of 10 ft. Fanwort, variable leaved water-milfoil and bladderworts are the dominant species. Fanwort grows to within 1 ft. of the water's surface. Floating mats of white water-lily, yellow pond-lily, water-shield and floating-heart fringe most of the shoreline and islands.

Access: A state-owned car-top boat access area is located on the western shore. Facilities at the site include an unimproved ramp and parking for 10 cars. *Directions*: From Rte. 80, Rte. 145 (Stevenson Rd.) south for 1.5 miles, access is on left. *Shore*: The entire shoreline is state-owned and open to the public.

Fish: Largemouth bass, **chain pickerel** and **sunfish** (mostly bluegill, some pumpkinseed, occasional hybrid) densities are near average for all sizes. **Yellow perch** and **brown bullhead** are present at below average densities. **American eels** to 24" are abundant. Forage fish include moderate densities of golden shiners.

Fishing: Should be good for eels and fair for other fish species.

Management: Statewide regulations apply for all species (see current *Connecticut Anglers' Guide*).

Boating: Gas motors prohibited (see current *Connecticut Boater's Guide*).

Comments: The pond had only been electrofished once by the time of printing. Thus the above fishery description may be imprecise. This pond has a reputation for containing large bass, but few were observed during our sampling.

Messerschmidt Pond
Fish Species and Abundance

	ALL SIZES	BIG FISH	GROWTH
Gamefish			
Largemouth bass	C	C	Avg
Chain pickerel	C	C	Fast
Panfish			
Yellow perch	C	U	< Avg
Brown bullhead	U	U	
Sunfish			
Bluegill	C	C	Avg
Pumpkinseed	C	U	Avg
Other			
Golden shiner	C		
American eel	A		

A=Abundant, C=Common, U=Uncommon, R=Rare

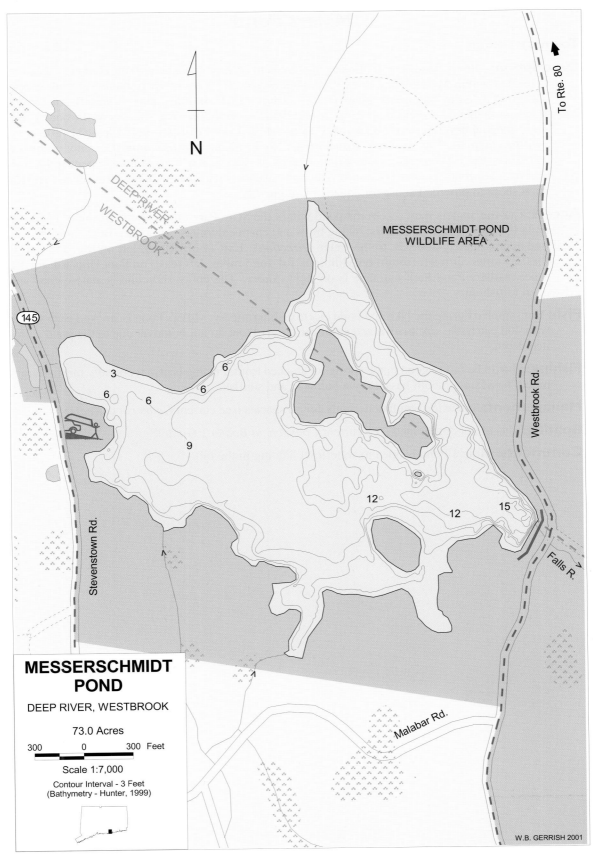

N

To Rte. 80

DEEP RIVER
WESTBROOK

MESSERSCHMIDT POND
WILDLIFE AREA

145

3

6

6

6

6

6

9

12

12

15

Westbrook Rd.

Falls R.

Stevenstown Rd.

Malabar Rd.

MESSERSCHMIDT POND

DEEP RIVER, WESTBROOK

73.0 Acres

300   0   300 Feet

Scale 1:7,000

Contour Interval - 3 Feet
(Bathymetry - Hunter, 1999)

W.B. GERRISH 2001

Millers Pond

Town(s): Durham   **32.6 acres**

Description: Millers Pond is an artificial impoundment in the Connecticut River Drainage Basin. It is located within Millers Pond State Park. *Watershed*: 203 acres of mostly undeveloped woods. The pond is fed by one small stream and by surface runoff. It drains into Sumner Brook, which flows north into the Connecticut River at Middletown. *Shoreline*: The shore is well wooded with no residential development. *Depth*: Max 18 ft., Mean 11 ft. *Transparency*: Clear; 11 ft. in summer. *Productivity*: Not available. *Bottom type*: Not available. *Stratification*: Does not occur due to limited depth. *Vegetation*: Low-growing blankets (less than 6" tall) of golden pert, spike-rush and rush are found on the bottom in scattered, shallow areas. Many areas drop off too steeply from shore to provide habitat for aquatic plant growth.

Access: Car-top anglers may access the pond within the State Park on the northern shore. Facilities include a parking lot for 15 cars, hiking trails and chemical toilets (seasonal). Boats must be carried approximately 200 yds. to the water. *Directions*: Exit 11 off Rte. 9, left on Rte. 155 (west) for 0.75 miles, turn left (south) on Millbrook Rd. for 5 miles, left (east) on Foot Hills Rd. for 1.2 miles, Millers Pond Park entrance is on right. *Shore*: The entire shoreline is state-owned and open to fishing.

Fish: Not sampled during the lake and pond electrofishing survey. Millers Pond is stocked each spring with 400 catchable size **brown** and **rainbow trout**. Trout do not holdover due to the pond's limited depth.

Fishing: Should be fair to good in the spring for stocked trout. Fishing is also reportedly fair for largemouth bass, smallmouth bass, brown bullhead and sunfish.

Management: Statewide regulations apply for all species (see current *Connecticut Anglers' Guide*).

Boating: Gas motors prohibited (see current *Connecticut Boater's Guide*).

Comments: Millers Pond is open to waterfowl hunting in the fall.

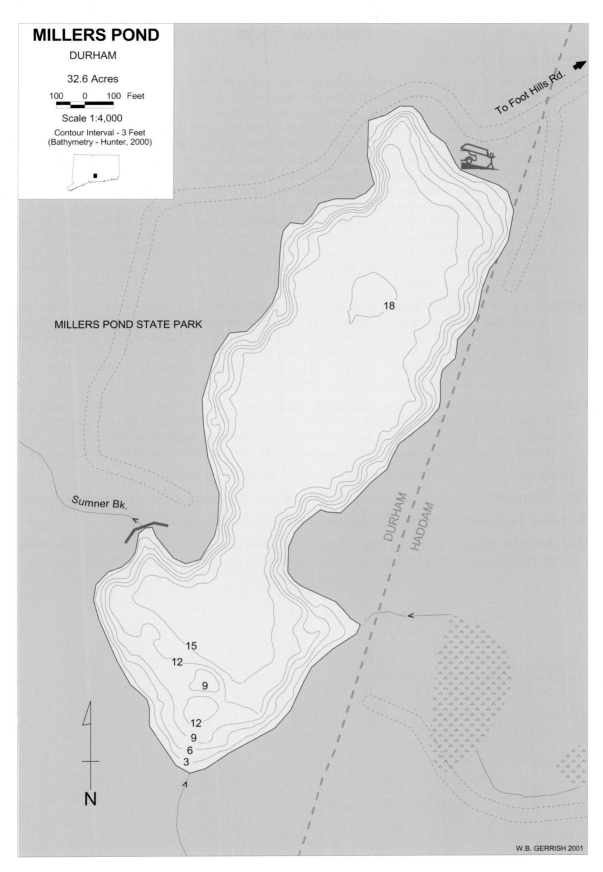

MILLERS POND

DURHAM

32.6 Acres

100   0   100 Feet

Scale 1:4,000

Contour Interval - 3 Feet
(Bathymetry - Hunter, 2000)

MILLERS POND STATE PARK

To Foot Hills Rd.

Sumner Bk.

DURHAM
HADDAM

18

15

12

9

12

9

6

3

N

W.B. GERRISH 2001

Mohawk Pond

Town(s): Cornwall/Goshen   **16.2 acres**

Description: Mohawk Pond is a natural kettle pond within the Housatonic River Drainage Basin. Except for a YMCA summer camp on the northern shore, it is located entirely within the Mohawk State Forest. *Watershed*: 122 acres of undeveloped woods. It is fed by runoff and bottom springs. It drains into a marsh on the western shore that feeds into the East Branch Shepaug River. *Shoreline*: Mostly wooded with no residential development. The western shore is a marshland. The eastern shore is mostly wooded. *Depth*: Max 26 ft., Mean 15 ft. *Transparency*: Very clear; 14-20 ft. in summer. *Productivity*: Moderate (early mesotrophic). *Bottom type*: Coarse rubble, boulders and mud. *Stratification*: Occurs with a thermocline forming between 16 and 22 ft. Late summer oxygen levels remain good (greater than 5 ppm) to a depth of 18 ft., but decline to less than 2 ppm in deeper water. *Vegetation*: Dense growths of submergent aquatic vegetation grow along the western and southern shores with pondweed and bladderwort the dominant species. Dense growths of white water-lily, yellow pond-lily and water-shield are also found in these areas. Intermittent patches of emergent pickerelweed and arrowhead are found along most of the shoreline.

Access: A state-owned boat launch is located on the southern shore. Facilities at the launch include a gravel ramp, parking for 8 cars, and pit-type toilets. *Directions*: From the intersection of Rtes. 4, 43 and 128, Rte. 4 west for 0.16 miles, left (south) on Great Hollow Rd. for 2.3 miles, left (east) on Great Hill Rd. for 1.3 miles, left (north) on Camp Rd., launch is on right. *Shore*: The entire shoreline, except for the camp, is within the state forest and open to the public. However, many areas are inaccessible due to thick vegetation and wetland habitat.

Fish: Mohawk Pond is stocked during the spring and fall with 3,400 catchable size **brown, brook** and **rainbow trout**. Holdover trout are rare due to limited summer habitat and high fishing pressure. **Largemouth bass** densities are average for all sizes. **Bluegill sunfish** are present at less than average densities. White suckers are abundant. Creek chubsuckers are present at low densities.

Fishing: Should be excellent seasonally for stocked trout and fair for bass.

Management: Statewide regulations apply for all species (see current *Connecticut Anglers' Guide*).

Boating: No motors of any kind (see current *Connecticut Boater's Guide*).

Comments: Mohawk Pond had only been electrofished once by the time of printing. The above fishery description may thus be imprecise. Fish species diversity in this pond is very low.

Mohawk Pond
Fish Species and Abundance

	ALL SIZES	BIG FISH	GROWTH
Gamefish			
Largemouth bass	C	C	< Slow
Brook trout	C		
Brown trout	A		
Rainbow trout	C		
Sunfish			
Bluegill	C	U	< Avg
Other			
Creek chubsucker	U		
White sucker	A		

A=Abundant, C=Common, U=Uncommon, R=Rare

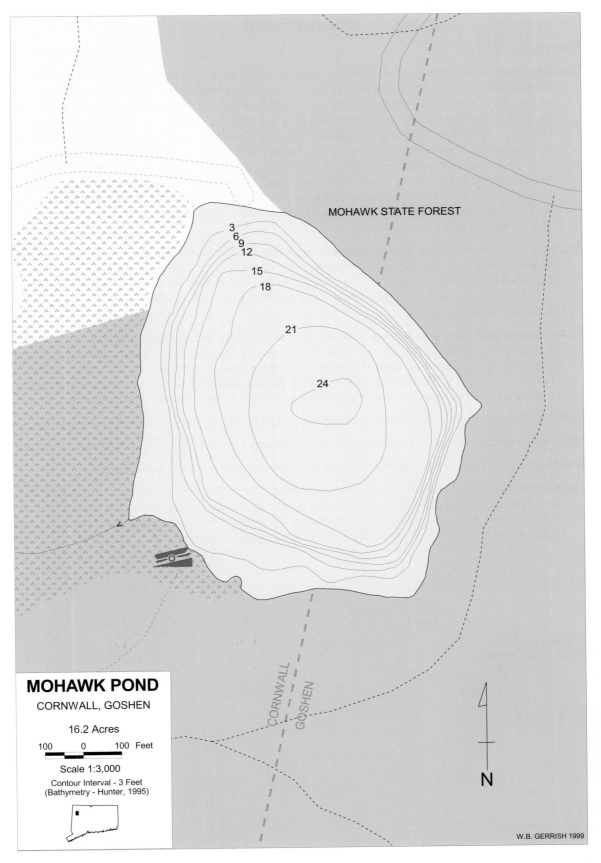

MOHAWK STATE FOREST

3
6
9
12

15

18

21

24

MOHAWK POND

CORNWALL, GOSHEN

16.2 Acres

100   0   100 Feet

Scale 1:3,000

Contour Interval - 3 Feet
(Bathymetry - Hunter, 1995)

CORNWALL
GOSHEN

N

W.B. GERRISH 1999

Mono Pond

Town(s): Columbia

113 acres

Description: Mono Pond is an artificial impoundment in the Thames River Drainage Basin. *Watershed*: 770 acres of mostly undeveloped woods and wetland. It is fed by two small streams and drains in two directions; southward into a marsh, which feeds into Williams Pond and eventually into the Yantic River, and northward over the spillway of the dam into Giffords Brook, a tributary of the Ten Mile and Willimantic Rivers. *Shoreline*: Wooded with some residential development set back from the water's edge. *Depth*: Max 11 ft., Mean 3.3 ft. *Transparency*: Fair; 7 ft. in summer. *Productivity*: Very high (highly eutrophic). *Bottom type*: Organic muck. *Stratification*: Does not occur due to limited depth. *Vegetation*: Water-shield, white water-lily and yellow pond-lily are extremely dense in areas less than 6 ft. Pondweed, bladderwort and water-milfoil (low and variable-leaved) are also abundant. The area south of the island is impassable by boat in mid to late summer.

Access: A state-owned boat launch is located near the dam on the northern shore. Facilities at the launch include a ramp with concrete slabs, parking for 14 cars and chemical toilets (seasonal). *Directions*: From Rte. 87, Rte. 66 west for 0.9 miles, left on Pine St. for 1.0 mile, right on Hunt Rd., launch is 0.2 miles on left. *Shore*: The eastern shore and the dam are state property and accessible to the public.

Fish: **Largemouth bass** densities are relatively low for all sizes. Small **chain pickerel** are abundant with densities of larger fish (greater than 15") being just above average. **Yellow perch** to 10" are at above average densities. **Sunfish** (bluegill and pumpkinseed) densities are well below average, but larger sunfish to 9" are relatively common. **Brown bullhead** to 10" are extremely abundant with larger fish being present at average densities. Golden shiners provide an abundant forage base.

Fishing: Should be good for pickerel and bullheads; fair to good for perch; and fair for bass.

Management: Statewide regulations apply for all species (see current *Connecticut Anglers' Guide*).

Boating: Speed limit 8 mph, no water-skiing (see current *Connecticut Boater's Guide*).

Comments: Mono Pond had only been electrofished once by the time of printing. The above fishery description may thus be imprecise. The pond has a historical reputation for good bass fishing, but few large bass were sampled during our survey. Fishing pressure is reportedly low. Occasional winter kills occur during years of prolonged ice cover.

Mono Pond
Fish Species and Abundance

	ALL SIZES	BIG FISH	GROWTH
Gamefish			
Largemouth bass	U	U	> Ave
Chain pickerel	A	C	< Ave
Panfish			
Yellow perch	C	C	Ave
Brown bullhead	A	C	
Sunfish			
Bluegill	C	C	Fast
Pumpkinseed	C	C	> Ave
Other			
Golden shiner	A		< Ave

A=Abundant, C=Common, U=Uncommon, R=Rare

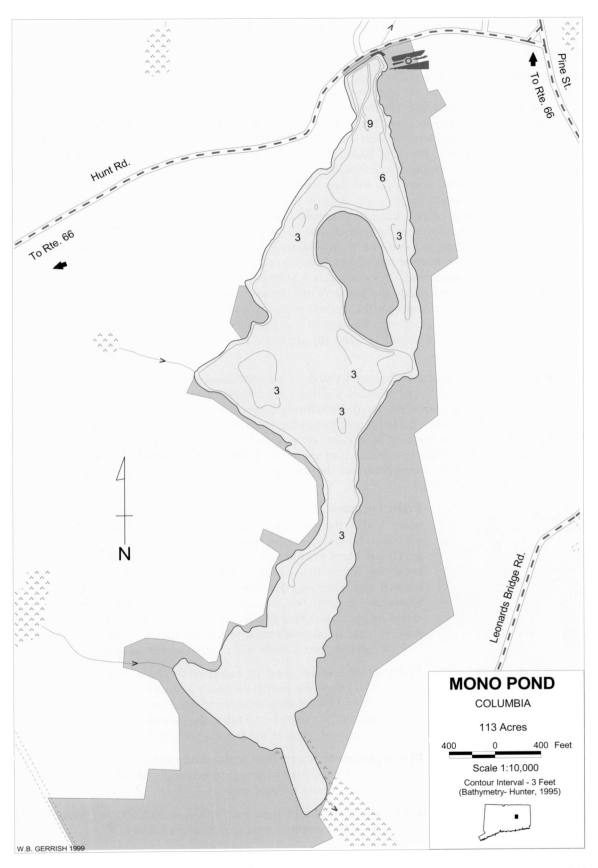

To Rte. 66

Hunt Rd.

To Rte. 66

Pine St.

To Rte. 66

9

6

3

3

3

3

3

3

3

Leonards Bridge Rd.

N

MONO POND

COLUMBIA

113 Acres

400   0   400 Feet

Scale 1:10,000

Contour Interval - 3 Feet
(Bathymetry- Hunter, 1995)

W.B. GERRISH 1999

Moodus Reservoir

Town(s): East Haddam

486 acres

Description: Moodus is a shallow, artificial impoundment in the Connecticut River Drainage Basin. A causeway separates the lake into two discrete basins: Upper Moodus (361 acres; the southeastern basin) and Lower Moodus (125 acres; the northwest basin). The eastern cove of Upper Moodus is very shallow (less than 3 ft.) with many submerged stumps. *Watershed:* 6,720 acres of mostly woods and wetland with some agricultural and residential land use. Moodus is fed from the north by Molley, Pine and Pickerel Lake Brooks and by a number of other small streams. Upper Moodus intermittently receives water from nearby Bashan Lake via a culvert in the western cove. The outlet flows over the dam spillway at the western end of Lower Moodus into the Moodus River, which empties into Salmon Cove on the Connecticut River. *Shoreline:* Lower Moodus is almost entirely lined by cottages. Upper Moodus is surrounded by woods, farmland and swamp with most housing restricted to its western shore. *Depth:* Max 14 ft., Mean 6.2 ft. *Transparency:* Fair; reduced to 6 ft. in summer by a tea-colored stain. *Productivity:* Moderate (late mesotrophic). *Bottom type:* Sand, mud and detritus. *Stratification:* Does not occur due to limited depth. *Vegetation:* Upper Moodus – Submergent fanwort is very dense throughout and intermixed with pondweeds and bladderworts. Extensive areas on the western side are covered with floating mats of water-shield. Yellow pond-lily and white water-lily are common. Lower Moodus – Fanwort is common throughout and intermixed with bladderwort. Areas of yellow pond-lily, water-shield and white water-lily are found along the shore with dense coverage in the shallow coves.

Access: State-owned boat launches are located on the northeastern shore of Lower Moodus and on the western shore of Upper Moodus. Facilities at each site include paved ramps, parking for 10 cars and chemical toilets (seasonal). *Directions:* Lower Moodus – From Rte. 16, Rte. 149 south 2.3 miles, left (south) on Mott Lane (just before causeway), launch is 50 yds. on right. Upper Moodus – Continue south on Mott Lane, right at end of road, left on Launching Area Rd. (second left past the causeway), launch is at end of road. *Shore:* Shore fishing access is very limited. The most popular access points are the causeway that separates the two basins and the launch area on Lower Moodus.

Moodus Reservoir
Fish Species and Abundance

	ALL SIZES	BIG FISH	GROWTH
Gamefish			
Largemouth bass	A	C	Fast
Smallmouth bass	R		
Chain pickerel	A	C	< Avg
Panfish			
Black crappie	C	C	> Avg
Yellow perch	C	C	< Avg
Brown bullhead	U	U	
Sunfish			
Bluegill	C	C	< Avg
Pumpkinseed	C	U	< Avg
Redbreast	U	R	
Other			
Tessellated darter	U		
Bridled shiner	U		
Golden shiner	A		
Banded killifish	U		
Alewife	U		
Creek chubsucker	U		
White sucker	U		
American eel	U		

A=Abundant, C=Common, U=Uncommon, R=Rare

Fish: **Largemouth bass** are abundant to 15" with larger bass numbers being higher than average. **Chain pickerel** below 15" are extremely abundant; however, densities of larger pickerel are only average. **Yellow perch** and **black crappie** are common with densities of 8-12" fish being somewhat higher than average. **Sunfish** (primarily bluegill, also pumpkinseed and redbreast) densities are average for all sizes. **Brown bullheads** are present, but uncommon. Moodus has an abundant golden shiner forage base. Other fish species present at low densities in Moodus Reservoir are smallmouth bass, tessellated darter, bridled shiner, banded killifish, alewife, creek chubsucker, white sucker and American eel.

Fishing: Should be good to excellent for bass, especially for those anglers who know how to fish the heavy vegetation. A good spot to catch a trophy bass. Fishing should be fair to good for yellow perch and black crappie and fair for sunfish. Additionally, pickerel should provide plenty of action, although most of the fish caught will be small.

Management: Trophy Bass Management Lake; special slot length and creel limits on bass. Statewide regulations apply for all other species (see current *Connecticut Anglers' Guide*).

Boating: Speed limit 8 mph from 9:00 p.m. to 8:00 a.m., 35 mph at all other times (see current *Connecticut Boater's Guide*). ▼

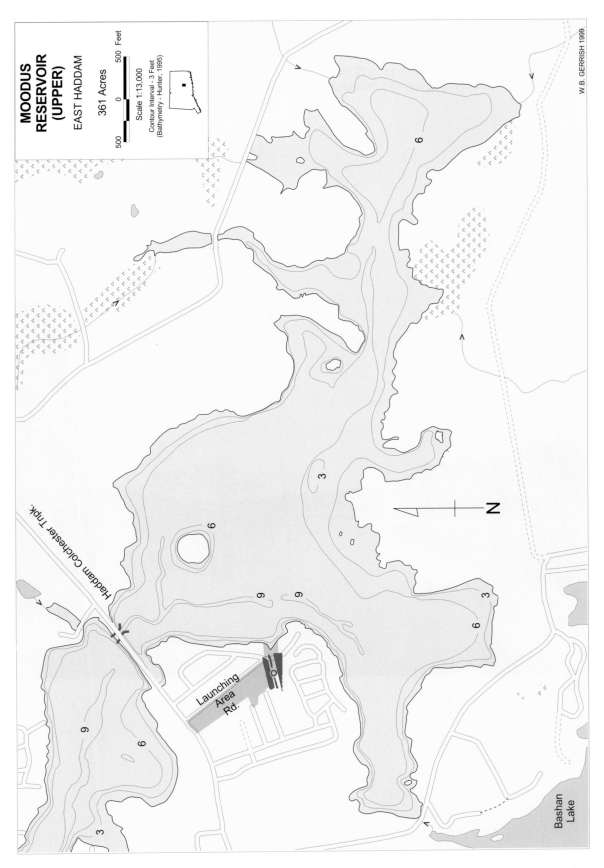

MOODUS RESERVOIR (UPPER)

EAST HADDAM

361 Acres

Scale 1:13,000
Contour Interval - 3 Feet
(Bathymetry - Hunter, 1995)

500   0   500   Feet

W.B. GERRISH 1999.

N

Haddam Colchester Tnpk.

Launching
Area
Rd.

Bashan
Lake

6

3

3

6

9

9

6

6

9

9

6

3

3

Comments: Moodus Reservoir is one of the top trophy bass waters in the state. Angling quality improved in the 1990s due to special bass regulations and should improve further with its designation as a Trophy Bass Management Lake. Moodus currently hosts about 9 bass tournaments annually and could support greater numbers of small tournaments. During the fall, the eastern coves are hunted for waterfowl. Moodus is a popular ice fishing spot when conditions permit.

Moodus Reservoir

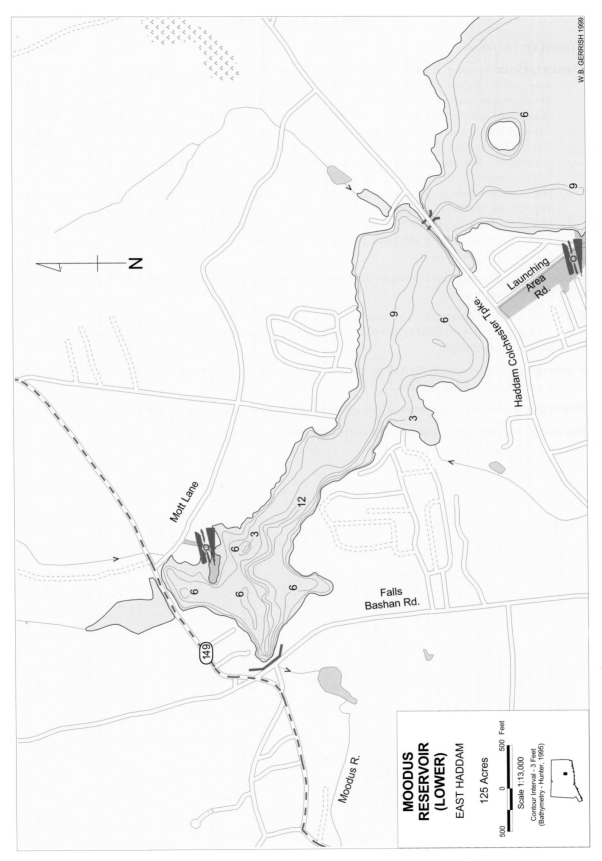

W.B. GERRISH 1999

N

6

9

6

9

Launching
Area
Rd.

Haddam Colchester Tpke.

9

6

3

Mott Lane

12

3

6

6

6

6

Falls
Bashan Rd.

149

Moodus R.

**MOODUS
RESERVOIR
(LOWER)**

EAST HADDAM

125 Acres

Scale 1:13,000

Contour Interval - 3 Feet
(Bathymetry - Hunter, 1995)

500   0   500 F Feet

Moosup Pond

Town(s): Plainfield   **95.8 acres**

Description: Moosup Pond is a natural pond in the Thames River Drainage Basin. Its water level was raised slightly by a small dam. *Watershed*: 726 acres of undeveloped woods, residential development and some agricultural land. The pond is fed by Tyler Brook from the north and drains east into Snake Meadow Brook, a tributary of the Moosup River. *Shoreline*: Partially wooded with residential development around much of the pond. A town beach is on the southern shore. *Depth*: Max 23 ft., Mean 9 ft. *Transparency*: Clear; 11 ft. in summer. *Productivity*: High (eutrophic). *Bottom type*: Sand, gravel, coarse rubble and mud. *Stratification*: Partially stratifies in the summer with a temperature gradient forming at 10 ft. Late summer oxygen levels remain high (greater than 6 ppm) to a depth of 16 ft. but decline to less than 2 ppm in deeper water. *Vegetation*: Robbin's pondweed grows on the bottom of most of the pond creating a thin carpet of vegetation to depths of 12 ft. Isolated stands of ribbon-leaf pondweed are in some shore areas. In the northern area of the pond, white water-lily and water-shield completely cover the water surface to depths of 4 ft.

Access: Anglers may carry in boats next to the town beach off of Moosup Pond Rd. *Shore*: Limited to boat launch area.

Fish: Not sampled during the lake and pond electrofishing survey. Moosup Pond is stocked during the spring and fall with 2,700 catchable size **brown** and **rainbow trout**. No trout holdover due to the pond's limited depth.

Fishing: Should be seasonally fair to good for trout. Fishing is also reportedly fair for yellow perch, brown bullhead and sunfish.

Management: Statewide regulations apply for all species (see current *Connecticut Anglers' Guide*).

Boating: No special regulations (see current *Connecticut Boater's Guide*).

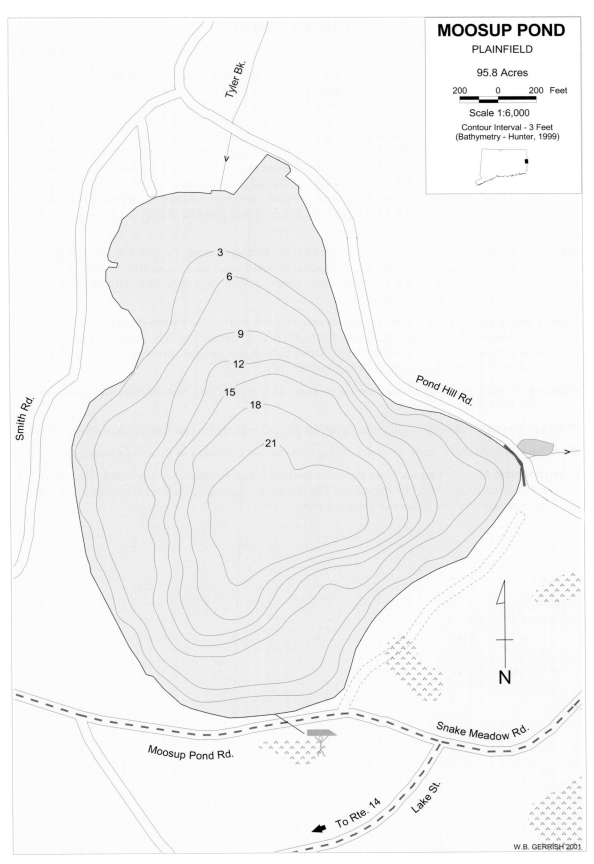

MOOSUP POND

PLAINFIELD

95.8 Acres

200   0   200   Feet

Scale 1:6,000

Contour Interval - 3 Feet
(Bathymetry - Hunter, 1999)

Tyler Bk.

3

6

9

12

15

18

21

Smith Rd.

Pond Hill Rd.

N

Snake Meadow Rd.

Moosup Pond Rd.

To Rte. 14

Lake St.

W.B. GERRISH 2001

Morey Pond

Town(s): Ashford/Union   **44.8 acres**

Description: Morey Pond is state-owned artificial impoundment in the Thames River Drainage Basin. I-84 traverses the pond, dividing it into two discrete basins (northern basin 16.3 acres, southern basin 28.5 acres). The culvert dividing the two basins is navigable with 4 ft. of clearance. *Watershed:* 419 acres of mostly undeveloped woods and wetland with light residential and agricultural development. It is fed by three small streams and drains southward into the Mount Hope River. *Shoreline:* Wooded with no residential development. *Depth:* Max 11 ft., Mean 6.7 ft. *Transparency:* Clear; 11 ft. in summer. *Productivity:* Moderate (mesotrophic). *Bottom type:* Not available. *Stratification:* Does not occur due to limited depth. *Vegetation:* Low water-milfoil and bladderwort provide dense, low-growing coverage on most of the pond bottom (especially areas to the east of I-84). Tapegrass, bur-reed and pondweed provide some vertical cover for fish.

Access: A state-owned boat launch is located on the northern shore. Facilities at the launch include a paved ramp, parking for 10 cars, and picnic tables. *Directions:* From Rte. 89, Rte. 190 east for 0.5 miles, right (south) into Nipmuck State Forest, follow road to launch. *Shore:* From the state forest property on the northern basin.

Fish: **Largemouth bass** are near average in abundance for all sizes. **Chain pickerel** are abundant to 22". **Yellow perch** are very abundant, but perch over 8" are uncommon. **Sunfish** (mostly bluegill, some pumpkinseed) are abundant to 9". Other fish species present at low densities are black crappie, brown bullhead, golden shiner and white sucker.

Fishing: Should be good to excellent for pickerel and sunfish; and fair for bass and perch. Popular ice fishing pond.

Management: Statewide regulations apply for all species (see current *Connecticut Anglers' Guide*).

Boating: Speed limit 8 mph, no water-skiing (see current *Connecticut Boater's Guide*).

Comments: Morey Pond had only been electrofished once by the time of printing. The above fishery description may thus be imprecise. The pond was drained in 1997 for dam repairs. It will take several years for the fishery to fully recover.

Morey Pond
Fish Species and Abundance

	ALL SIZES	BIG FISH	GROWTH
Gamefish			
Largemouth bass	C	C	< Avg
Chain pickerel	A	A	Avg
Panfish			
Black crappie	U	U	-
Yellow perch	A	U	< Avg
Brown bullhead	U	U	
Sunfish			
Bluegill	A	A	Fast
Pumpkinseed	C	C	> Avg
Other			
Golden shiner	U		-
White sucker	U		
American eel	U		

A=Abundant, C=Common, U=Uncommon, R=Rare

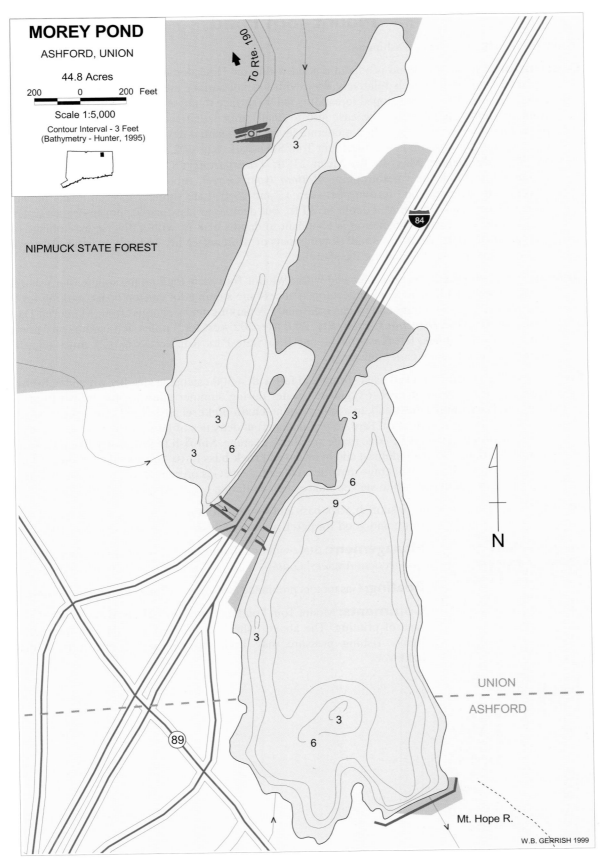

MOREY POND

ASHFORD, UNION

44.8 Acres

200   0   200 Feet

Scale 1:5,000

Contour Interval - 3 Feet
(Bathymetry - Hunter, 1995)

To Rte. 190

NIPMUCK STATE FOREST

84

3

3

3

6

3

3

6

9

6

3

3

6

N

UNION

ASHFORD

89

Mt. Hope R.

W.B. GERRISH 1999

Mount Tom Pond

Town(s): Litchfield/Morris/Washington

56.3 acres

Description: Mount Tom Pond is a natural pond within the Housatonic River Drainage Basin. It is a glacial kettle pond that is relatively deep with a small surface area. *Watershed:* 701 acres of agricultural land and undeveloped forest. It is fed by surface runoff and by a small wetland stream from the north. It drains to the east into a small stream that feeds into the Bantam River. *Shoreline:* Mostly wooded with a moderate level of residential development. A 350 yd. stretch of the southeastern shore is within Mount Tom State Park. Rte. 202 abuts the northwestern shore for 500 yds. *Depth:* Max 46 ft., Mean 21 ft. *Transparency:* Clear; 13-15 ft. in summer. *Productivity:* Moderate (mesotrophic). *Bottom type:* Gravel, rubble and mud. *Stratification:* Occurs with a thermocline forming between 13 and 23 ft. Late summer oxygen levels remain good (greater than 5 ppm) to a depth of 20 ft., but decline to less than 1 ppm in deeper water. *Vegetation:* Submergent vegetation is abundant to depths of 8 ft. with a diverse assemblage of pondweeds dominating. A few small floating mats of white water-lily and yellow pond-lily are at the north end and scattered along the shoreline.

Access: A state-owned access site is located within Mount Tom State Park on the southeastern shore. Facilities at the Park include an undeveloped access site suitable for car-top boats, parking for 9 cars, picnicking, swimming and toilets (seasonal). A parking fee is charged from Memorial Day through Labor Day. *Directions:* From Rte. 209, Rte. 202 west for 3 miles, left (south) on Mount Tom Rd. for 0.2 miles, left (east) on Mount Tom State Park Rd., access is 0.25 miles on left. *Shore:* Limited to state park boundaries.

Fish: Mount Tom Pond is stocked each spring and fall with 4,500 catchable size **brown** and **rainbow trout**. A narrow band of cool, oxygenated water during summer allows some brown trout to holdover. **Largemouth bass** and, to a lesser extent, **chain pickerel** are severely stockpiled. Small bass and pickerel (less than 13") are very abundant, but densities of larger fish are low. Numbers of **yellow perch** in the 10-12" size range are above average. **Sunfish** to 9" (mostly bluegill, some pumpkinseed, occasional redbreast and hybrids) and **rock bass** to 10" are abundant. Golden shiners are present at less than average densities. Other fish species present at low densities are black crappie, brown bullhead, white sucker and tessellated darter.

Fishing: Should be excellent for sunfish, rock bass and stocked trout with some chance for a holdover trout; and good for perch and small bass.

Management: Statewide regulations apply for all species (see current *Connecticut Anglers' Guide*).

Boating: Gas motors prohibited (see current *Connecticut Boater's Guide*).

Comments: Mount Tom Pond had only been electrofished once by the time of printing. The above fishery description may thus be imprecise. Heavy fishing pressure may limit the number of brown trout that holdover.

Mount Tom Pond Fish Species and Abundance	ALL SIZES	BIG FISH	GROWTH
Gamefish			
Largemouth bass	A	U	Slow
Brown trout	C	U	
Rainbow trout	A		
Chain pickerel	A	U	Slow
Panfish			
Black crappie	U	U	
Yellow perch	C	C	Avg
Brown bullhead	U	U	
Sunfish			
Bluegill	A	A	Avg
Pumpkinseed	C	C	> Avg
Redbreast	U	R	
Rock bass	A	A	> Avg
Other			
Tessellated darter	U		
Golden shiner	C		
White sucker	U		

A=Abundant, C=Common, U=Uncommon, R=Rare

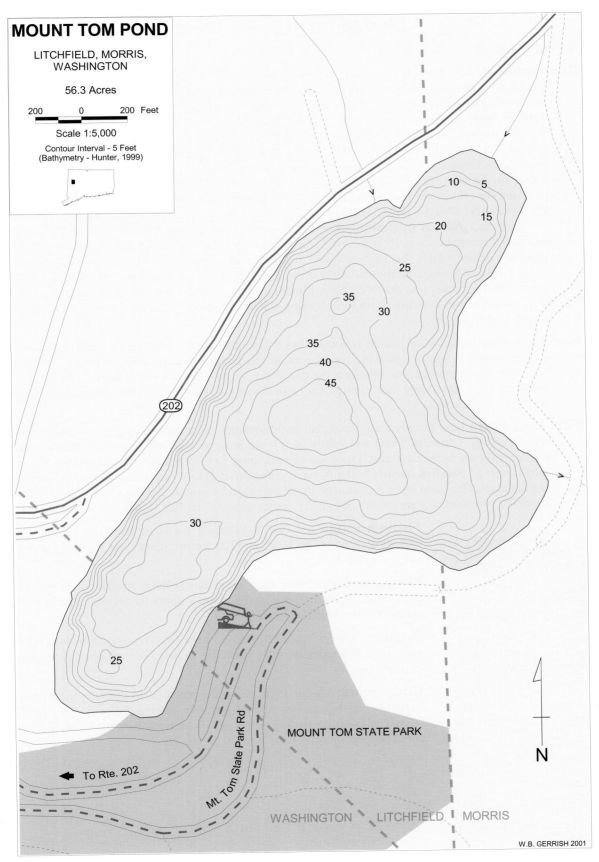

MOUNT TOM POND

LITCHFIELD, MORRIS, WASHINGTON

56.3 Acres

200   0   200   Feet

Scale 1:5,000

Contour Interval - 5 Feet
(Bathymetry - Hunter, 1999)

10   5

15

20

25

35

30

35

40

45

30

25

(202)

30

25

Mt. Tom State Park Rd

◄ To Rte. 202

MOUNT TOM STATE PARK

WASHINGTON   LITCHFIELD   MORRIS

N

W.B. GERRISH 2001

Mudge Pond (Silver Lake)

Town(s): Sharon

207 acres

Description: Mudge Pond is a natural pond within the Housatonic River Drainage Basin. The water level was raised slightly by an earthen dam. *Watershed:* 7,361 acres of undeveloped woods and agricultural land with some light residential development. The pond is fed by a wetland from the north formed by the convergence of Spring Brook and the outflow of Wononpakook Lake, by two wetland streams from the east, and by a small stream from the north. The pond drains southward into Mudge Pond Brook, which flows into Webatuck Creek, a tributary of the Ten Mile River. *Shoreline:* The eastern shore is mostly wooded with only light residential development. Indian Mountain Rd. abuts much of the western shore. There are scattered trees and bushes between this road and the shoreline. The northern shore is open marshland. *Depth:* Max 34 ft., Mean 18 ft. *Transparency:* Fair to good; ranging between 9-13 ft. in summer. *Productivity:* Moderate (mesotrophic). *Bottom type:* Mostly mud and organic muck. *Stratification:* Occurs with a thermocline forming between 10 and 20 ft. Late summer oxygen levels remain good (greater than 5 ppm) to a depth of 16 ft., but decline to less than 1 ppm in deeper water. *Vegetation:* Aquatic vegetation is dense throughout the shallower areas. Coontail, Eurasian water-milfoil and pondweeds are common in water less than 8 ft. deep. Floating mats of white water-lily and yellow pond-lily fringe much of the shoreline, with well-developed mats in the south and north ends. Some watershield is also present.

Access: A state-owned boat launch is located on the southeastern shore. Facilities at the launch include a gravel ramp and parking for 14 cars. In the summer, boaters must navigate a channel through extensive vegetation to access the main body of the lake. *Directions:* From Rte. 4, Rte. 361 north for 1 mile, right (north) on Silver Lake Shore Rd., launch is on left. *Shore:* Limited to the boat launch area.

Fish: Largemouth bass are generally abundant with densities of greater than 15" bass being well above average. **Chain pickerel** and **yellow perch** are present at average densities. **Black crappie** densities are below average. Densities of **rock bass** to 9" and **brown bullhead** to 13" are above average. **Sunfish** (mostly bluegill, some pumpkinseed) to 9" are abundant. White suckers are abundant. The pond has a moderately abundant golden shiner forage base. Other fish species present at low densities are creek chubsucker, redfin pickerel, bridled shiner and American eel.

Fishing: Should be good to excellent for bass, bullhead, sunfish and rock bass; good for pickerel; and fair for perch and crappie. Good spot to catch a lunker bass.

Management: Trophy Bass Management Lake; special slot length and creel limits on bass. Statewide regulations apply for all other species (see current *Connecticut Anglers' Guide*).

Boating: Motors limited to 7.5 hp, speed limit 6 mph. Motorboat operation is prohibited ½ hr. after sunset to sunrise (see current *Connecticut Boater's Guide*).

Comments: Mudge Pond has good potential to produce trophy size bass. Special regulations should improve fishing by protecting larger bass. The pond hosts only a few small bass tournaments annually and could support more of these events.

Mudge Pond
Fish Species and Abundance

	ALL SIZES	BIG FISH	GROWTH
Gamefish			
Largemouth bass	A	C	Avg
Chain pickerel	C	C	Avg
Panfish			
Black crappie	C	C	Avg
Yellow perch	C	C	< Avg
Brown bullhead			
Sunfish			
Bluegill	A	A	Slow
Pumpkinseed	C	C	Avg
Rock bass	C	U	Avg
Other			
Redfin pickerel	C		
Bridled shiner	R		
Golden shiner	C		Avg
Creek chubsucker	C		
White sucker	A		
American eel	U		

A=Abundant, C=Common, U=Uncommon, R=Rare

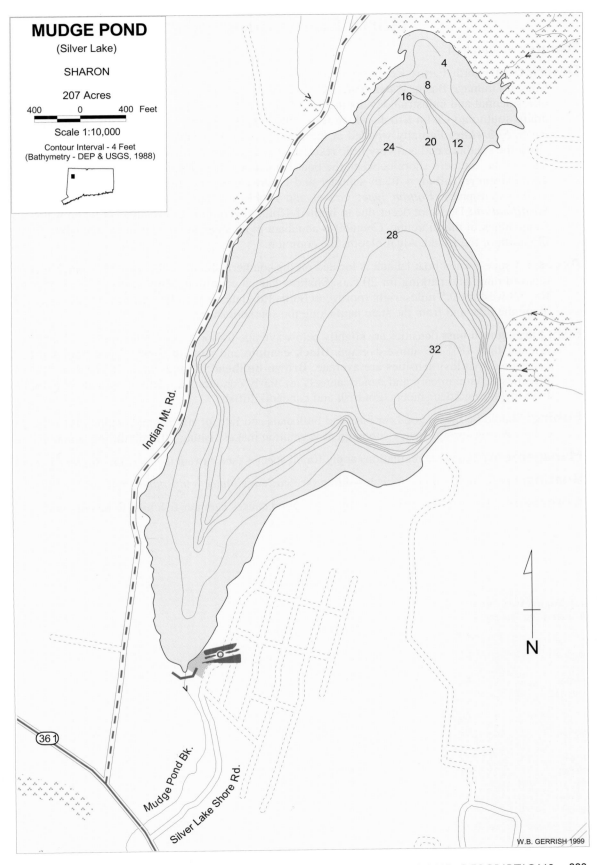

MUDGE POND

(Silver Lake)

SHARON

207 Acres

400   0   400   Feet

Scale 1:10,000

Contour Interval - 4 Feet
(Bathymetry - DEP & USGS, 1988)

4

8

16

24   20   12

28

32

Indian Mt. Rd.

Mudge Pond Bk.

Silver Lake Shore Rd.

36 1

N

W.B. GERRISH 1999

North Farms Reservoir

Town(s): Wallingford

64.4 acres

Description: North Farms Reservoir is a state-owned, artificial pond within the South Central Coastal Drainage Basin. *Watershed:* 488 acres of mostly agricultural land with moderate levels of residential and industrial development. The pond is fed by a small stream from the north and drains south into Catlin Brook, which flows into Wharton Brook and eventually the Quinnipiac River. *Shoreline:* Partially wooded at the northern end with mostly low shrubs and grassland along the southern end and very little residential development. There is a section of state-owned land on the southern shore between the boat launch and dam. *Depth:* Max 7.5 ft., Mean 4.5 ft. *Transparency:* Turbid; 4 ft. in summer and colored green by algae. *Productivity:* Very high (highly eutrophic). *Bottom type:* Gravel and rubble overlain with organic muck and mud. *Stratification:* Does not occur due to limited depth. *Vegetation:* Dense areas of white water-lily fringe much of the shoreline. Coontail is abundant in the open areas adjacent to the white water-lily north of the island. Algal blooms are common.

Access: A state-owned boat launch is located on the southern shore. Facilities at the launch include a paved ramp and parking for 20 cars. Shallow launch conditions. *Directions:* Exit 15 off I-91, Rte. 68 west for 0.5 miles, right (north) on Barns Rd., launch is on left. *Shore:* Anglers may fish along the dike and from the state land along the southern shore.

Fish: Largemouth bass densities are slightly below average for most sizes, but numbers of large fish (greater than 18") are above average. **Black crappie** and **sunfish** (bluegill and pumpkinseed, occasional hybrids) densities are average. **Brown bullhead** are present at higher than average densities. Common carp and American eels are fairly common. A relatively low-density forage base includes golden shiners, goldfish and banded killifish.

Fishing: Should be fair to good for bass and bullheads and fair for sunfish and crappie. Bass fishing is best during spring. Heavy submergent vegetation makes fishing difficult during summer.

Management: Statewide regulations apply for all species (see current *Connecticut Anglers' Guide*).

Boating: Speed limit 8 mph, no water-skiing (see current *Connecticut Boater's Guide*).

Comments: The shallow, weedy nature of this pond causes summer fish kills to be common.

North Farms Reservoir
Fish Species and Abundance

	ALL SIZES	BIG FISH	GROWTH
Gamefish			
Largemouth bass	C	C	Avg
Panfish			
Black crappie	C	C	Avg
Brown bullhead	C	C	
Sunfish			
Bluegill	C	C	< Avg
Pumpkinseed	C	R	< Avg
Other			
Common carp	C		
Golden shiner	U		Fast
Gold fish	R		
Banded killifish	U		
American eel	C		

A=Abundant, C=Common, U=Uncommon, R=Rare

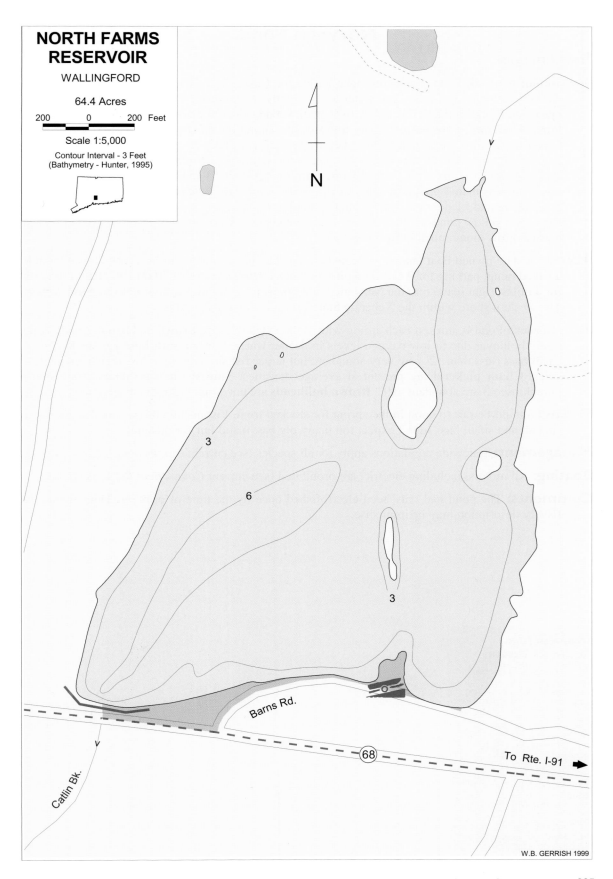

NORTH FARMS
RESERVOIR

WALLINGFORD

64.4 Acres

200   0   200 Feet

Scale 1:5,000

Contour Interval - 3 Feet
(Bathymetry - Hunter, 1995)

N

0

0

0

3

6

3

Barns Rd.

68   To Rte. I-91

Catlin Bk.

W.B. GERRISH 1999

Norwich Pond

Town(s): Lyme   **30.1 acres**

Description: Norwich Pond is a natural lake within the Connecticut River Drainage Basin. A small dam on the outlet has raised the water level slightly. *Watershed*: 309 acres of mostly undeveloped woods and wetland. It is fed by two small wetland streams and drains southwest into Uncas Pond. *Shoreline*: Forested with only a few homes along the eastern shore. The Nehantic State Forest borders the western shoreline. *Depth*: Max 33 ft., Mean 22 ft. *Transparency*: Fair; 9-10 ft. in early summer. *Productivity*: Moderate (mesotrophic). *Bottom type*: Gravel and mud. *Stratification*: Occurs with a thermocline forming between 10 and 16 ft. Late summer oxygen levels are less than 4 ppm in the thermocline and below. *Vegetation*: Dense beds of submergent pondweeds and bladderworts grow under floating mats of white water-lily, with some water-shield and yellow pond-lily to depths of 6 ft. Emergent stands of pipewort, yellow-eyed grass and nutrush grow along much of the shoreline.

Access: A state-owned boat launch is located on the southern shore. Facilities at the launch include a paved ramp, parking for 9 cars, and pit-type toilets. *Directions*: Exit 70 off I-95, Rte. 156 north for 4 miles, right (east) into the Nehantic State Forest for 2.5 miles, follow signs to pond. *Shore*: The western shore within the Nehantic State Forest is open to the public.

Fish: Norwich Pond is stocked each spring with 1,400 catchable size **brown** and **brook trout**. Trout rarely holdover due to low oxygen levels in deeper water. **Largemouth bass** are stockpiled — small bass (less than 12") are very abundant, but larger fish are present at less than average densities. **Chain pickerel** are present at average densities. **Sunfish** (mostly bluegill, occasional pumpkinseed) are abundant to 9". **Brown bullheads** are uncommon. American eels are common.

Fishing: Should be fair to good in the spring for stocked trout. Fishing should be excellent for large sunfish and small bass (don't expect too many big bass); and fair for pickerel.

Management: Statewide regulations apply for all species (see current *Connecticut Anglers' Guide*).

Boating: All motors, including electric, are prohibited (see current *Connecticut Boater's Guide*).

Comments: The pond had only been electrofished once by the time of printing. Thus, the above fishery description may be imprecise.

Norwich Pond
Fish Species and Abundance

	ALL SIZES	BIG FISH	GROWTH
Gamefish			
Largemouth bass	A	C	< Avg
Brown trout	C	R	
Brook trout	C		
Chain pickerel	C	C	Avg
Panfish			
Brown bullhead	U	U	
Sunfish			
Bluegill	A	A	Avg
Pumpkinseed	U	U	Avg
Other			
American eel	C		

A=Abundant, C=Common, U=Uncommon, R=Rare

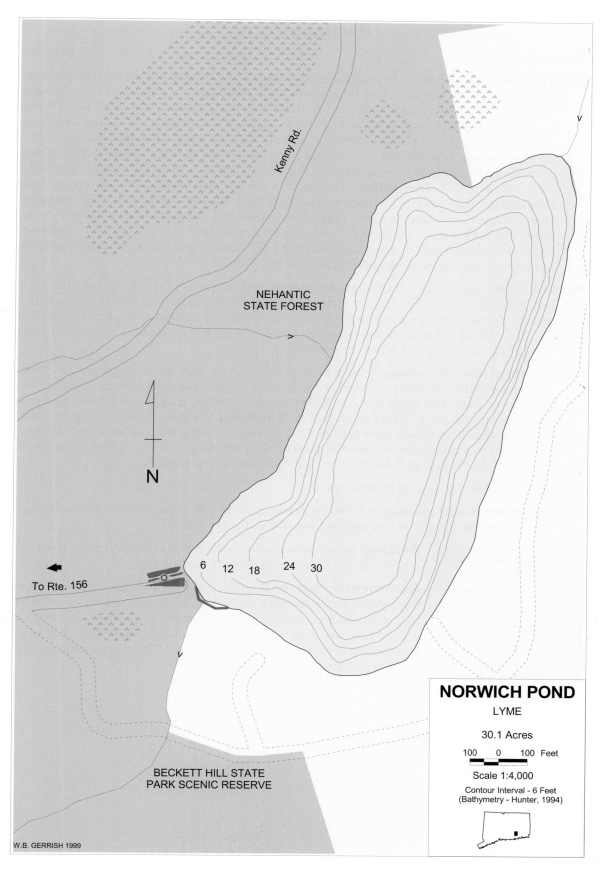

NEHANTIC
STATE FOREST

Kenny Rd.

N

To Rte. 156

6 12 18 24 30

BECKETT HILL STATE
PARK SCENIC RESERVE

W.B. GERRISH 1999

NORWICH POND

LYME

30.1 Acres

100   0   100 Feet

Scale 1:4,000

Contour Interval - 6 Feet
(Bathymetry - Hunter, 1994)

Pachaug Pond

Town(s): Griswold

841 acres

Description: Pachaug Pond is an artificial impoundment in the Thames River Drainage Basin and is the state's largest lake east of the Connecticut River. **Watershed:** 33,408 acres of mostly woods or wetland with some agricultural and very little urban development. The pond is fed by the Pachaug River from Glasgo Pond, and by Burton Brook, Billings Brook and several small intermittent streams. The lake drains northward into the Pachaug River. **Shoreline:** Wooded with a moderate amount of residential development along most of the shoreline. Approximately 1 mile of the northeast shoreline is within Pachaug State Forest and is undeveloped woods. **Depth:** Max 17 ft., Mean 6.6 ft. **Transparency:** Turbid; 5 ft. in summer; reduced by tea-colored stain. **Productivity:** High (eutrophic). **Bottom type:** Fine sand, silt and organic muck. **Stratification:** Does not occur due to limited depth. **Vegetation:** Submergent vegetation is abundant in localized areas. Dominant species are fanwort, a submergent form of bur-reed (that resembles tapegrass) and well-developed beds of tapegrass. Patches of white water-lily, water-shield, yellow pond-lily and floating-heart grow along scattered areas of the shoreline.

Access: A state-owned boat launch is located near the dam on the northern shore. Facilities at the launch include a ramp with concrete slabs, parking for 40 cars and chemical toilets (seasonal). A marked channel provides access to the lake from the launch area. **Directions:** Exit 85 off I-395, Rte. 138 east for 2.5 miles, access is on right (south). **Shore:** Public access is restricted to the areas of Pachaug State Forest and the launch site.

Fish: **Northern pike** were present at the time of writing and the population is expected to expand. **Largemouth bass** densities are average for all sizes. Small **chain pickerel** are abundant with densities of larger fish being average. **Yellow perch** and **black crappie** are present at slightly above average densities. **White perch** to 9" and **sunfish** to 8" (mostly bluegill, some pumpkinseed) are abundant. **Brown bullheads** to 13" are common and **white catfish** to 16" are occasionally taken. Pachaug has an abundant golden shiner forage base. White suckers are common. Other fish species present at low densities are American eel and banded killifish.

Fishing: Should be fair to good for most species.

Management: Annual stockings of 6,700 fingerling northern pike began in 1999. Statewide regulations apply for all species (see current *Connecticut Anglers' Guide*).

Boating: No special regulations. Some areas are off-limits to water-skiing (see current *Connecticut Boater's Guide*).

Comments: Pachaug Pond is the largest public lake in eastern Connecticut and recreational use is high. It is a very popular bass fishing lake, and hosts an average of 20 bass tournaments each year. Pachaug has a reputation and good potential for producing trophy bass. Pike were introduced into Pachaug to provide additional fishing opportunities and to better exploit the abundant forage base.

Pachaug Pond
Fish Species and Abundance

	ALL SIZES	BIG FISH	GROWTH
Gamefish			
Largemouth bass	C	C	Fast
Northern Pike	C		
Chain pickerel	C	C	< Avg
White catfish	U	U	
Panfish			
Black crappie	C	C	Avg
White perch	A	C	Slow
Yellow perch	C	C	Slow
Brown bullhead	C	C	
Sunfish			
Bluegill	A	C	Avg
Pumpkinseed	C	C	> Avg
Other			
Golden shiner	A		
Banded killifish	U		
White sucker	C		
American eel	U		

A=Abundant, C=Common, U=Uncommon, R=Rare

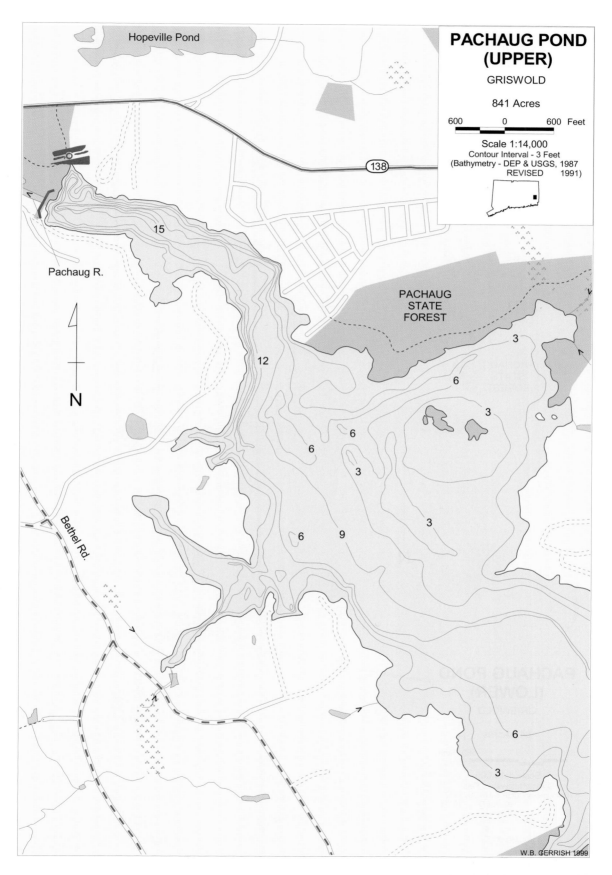

Hopeville Pond

138

Pachaug R.

15

12

N

6

3

6

3

6

3

9

3

6

3

Bethel Rd.

1

PACHAUG POND (UPPER)

GRISWOLD

841 Acres

600   0   600 Feet

Scale 1:14,000
Contour Interval - 3 Feet
(Bathymetry - DEP & USGS, 1987
REVISED   1991)

PACHAUG
STATE
FOREST

W.B. GERRISH 1999

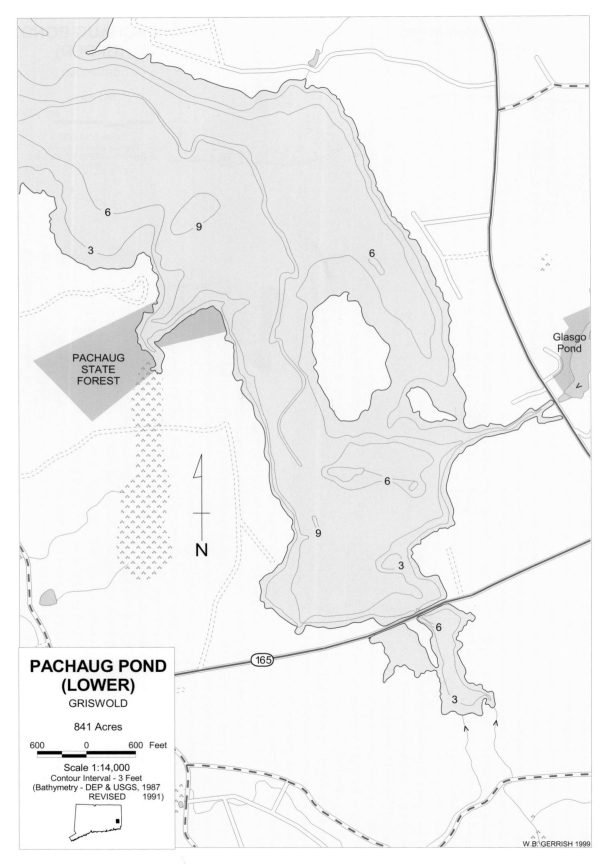

PACHAUG
STATE
FOREST

6
9
3
6
6
9
6
3

Glasgo
Pond

6

N

165

6

3

**PACHAUG POND
(LOWER)**

GRISWOLD

841 Acres

600   0   600   Feet

Scale 1:14,000
Contour Interval - 3 Feet
(Bathymetry - DEP & USGS, 1987
REVISED   1991)

W.B. GERRISH 1999

Pachaug Pond

Park Pond

Town(s): Winchester   **82.0 acres**

Description: Park Pond is an artificial impoundment located in the Housatonic River Drainage Basin. The dam, originally created for industrial use, was rebuilt in the 1980s and is now owned by the State. *Watershed*: 299 acres of mostly undeveloped woods and wetland with some agricultural and residential development. It is fed from the northwest by a wetland stream and drains southeast into the East Branch Naugatuck River. *Shoreline*: Mostly wooded with a moderate number of homes clustered on the northwestern shore near the boat ramp. Two summer camps and a beach are located on the southern shore. *Depth*: Max 17 ft., Mean 12 ft. *Transparency*: Clear to bottom in summer. *Productivity*: Moderate (mesotrophic). *Bottom type*: Rock, sand, gravel and organic muck. *Stratification*: Does not occur due to limited depth. *Vegetation*: Submergent aquatic plants are dense in the northern end of the pond and in the shallow cove areas to depths of 6 ft. Dominant species are tapegrass, pondweed and Eurasian water-milfoil, with waterweed scattered along the western shore.

Access: A state-owned boat launch is located on the northern end. Facilities include a paved ramp, parking for 12 cars and chemical toilets (seasonal). *Directions*: From Rte. 44, Rte. 263 west for 6.5 miles, left on Blue St, launch is on left. *Shore*: Limited to boat launch area.

Fish: Abundance of **largemouth bass** is average for all sizes. Small **chain pickerel** densities are average, but larger fish (greater than 15") are uncommon. **Yellow perch** in the 6-9" size range are abundant with larger perch occurring at average densities. **Black crappie** and **brown bullhead** are present at less than average densities. **Sunfish** (mostly bluegill, some pumpkinseed) and **rock bass** are common to 8". Golden shiners and white suckers are present at less than average densities. White perch are present, but rare.

Fishing: Should be fair to good for bass, yellow perch, sunfish and rock bass and fair to poor for other species.

Management: Statewide regulations apply for all species (see current *Connecticut Anglers' Guide*).

Boating: Speed limit 8 mph (see current *Connecticut Boater's Guide*).

Park Pond Fish Species and Abundance	ALL SIZES	BIG FISH	GROWTH
Gamefish			
Largemouth bass	C	C	Avg
Chain pickerel	C	U	Avg
Panfish			
Black crappie	C	C	> Avg
White perch	R	R	Fast
Yellow perch	A	C	Avg
Brown bullhead	C	C	
Sunfish			
Bluegill	C	C	> Avg
Pumpkinseed	C	C	> Avg
Rock bass	C	R	Avg
Other			
Golden shiner	C		> Avg
White sucker	C		

A=Abundant, C=Common, U=Uncommon, R=Rare

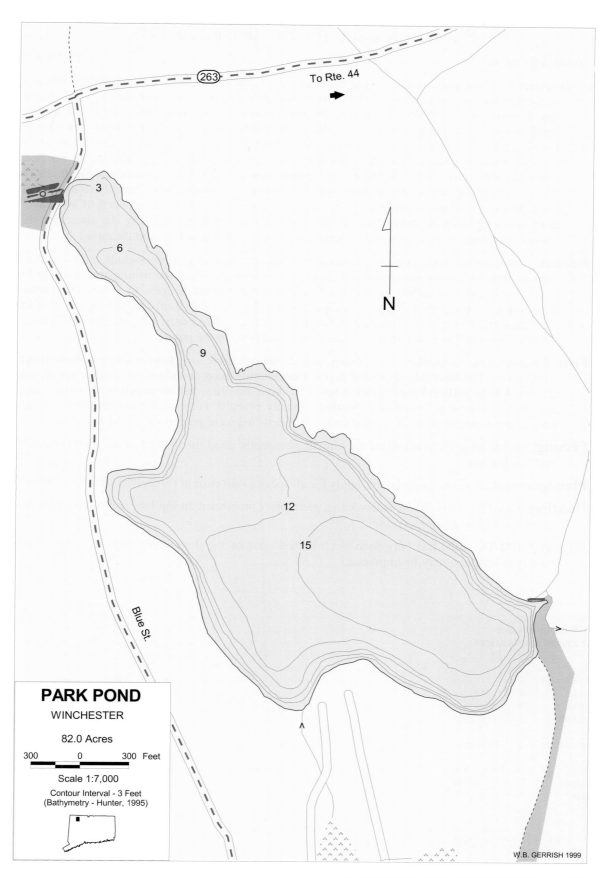

263

To Rte. 44

3

6

9

12

15

N

Blue St.

PARK POND

WINCHESTER

82.0 Acres

300   0   300   Feet

Scale 1:7,000

Contour Interval - 3 Feet
(Bathymetry - Hunter, 1995)

W.B. GERRISH 1999

Pataconk Lake (Russell Jennings Pond)

Town(s): Chester   **56.1 acres**

Description: Pataconk Lake is an artificial impoundment in the Connecticut River Drainage Basin. It is located within Cockaponset State Forest. *Watershed*: 1,195 acres of mostly undeveloped woods with some agricultural and very little residential development. The lake is fed by four small streams and drains southeast into Pataconk Brook, which eventually flows into Chester Creek, a tributary of the Connecticut River. *Shoreline*: Mostly wooded with no residential development. There is a small beach near the outlet and a youth group campground on the northern shore. *Depth*: Max 17 ft., Mean 9.3 ft. *Transparency*: Fair; 8 ft. in summer. *Productivity*: Moderate (early mesotrophic). *Bottom type*: Not available. *Stratification*: Partially stratifies with a temperature gradient forming at 10 ft. Late summer oxygen levels are reduced to less than 1 ppm below this depth. *Vegetation*: White water-lily and water-shield ring the shoreline and almost completely cover the northwestern cove. Pondweed is also found in the coves.

Access: A state-owned access area is located on the southern shore. Facilities include an unimproved area suitable for car-top boats, parking in the recreation area, a disabled fishing area, parking for 5 cars and chemical toilets (seasonal). Boats must be carried 50 yds. to water. *Directions*: Pataconk Lake Recreation Area in Cockaponset State Forest – Exit 6 off Rte. 9, Rte. 148 west for 1.5 miles, right (north) on Cedar Lake Rd., left (west) on State Forest Rd., access is 0.25 miles on right. *Shore*: The entire shore is state-owned and open to the public.

Fish: Pataconk Lake is stocked each spring with 2,700 catchable size **brown** and **rainbow trout**. Trout do not holdover due to limited depth. **Largemouth bass** abundance is average for all size classes. **Chain pickerel** are present at below average densities. **Yellow perch** in the 9-12" range are above average in abundance. **Sunfish** (mostly bluegill, occasional pumpkinseed and red-breast) are abundant to 9". The only forage fish detected were golden shiners at low densities.

Fishing: Should be good to excellent for sunfish; seasonally good for stocked trout; good for perch; and fair for bass.

Management: Statewide regulations apply for all species (see current *Connecticut Anglers' Guide*).

Boating: Speed limit 8 mph; no water-skiing; gas motors prohibited during July and August (see current *Connecticut Boater's Guide*).

Comments: The pond had only been electrofished once by the time of printing. Thus, the above fishery description may be imprecise.

Pataconk Lake
Fish Species and Abundance

	ALL SIZES	BIG FISH	GROWTH
Gamefish			
Largemouth bass	C	C	< Avg
Brown trout	C		
Rainbow trout	C		
Chain pickerel	C	C	Fast
Panfish			
Yellow perch	C	C	Avg
Sunfish			
Bluegill	A	A	< Avg
Pumpkinseed	U	U	< Avg
Redbreast	R	R	
Other			
Golden shiner	U		

A=Abundant, C=Common, U=Uncommon, R=Rare

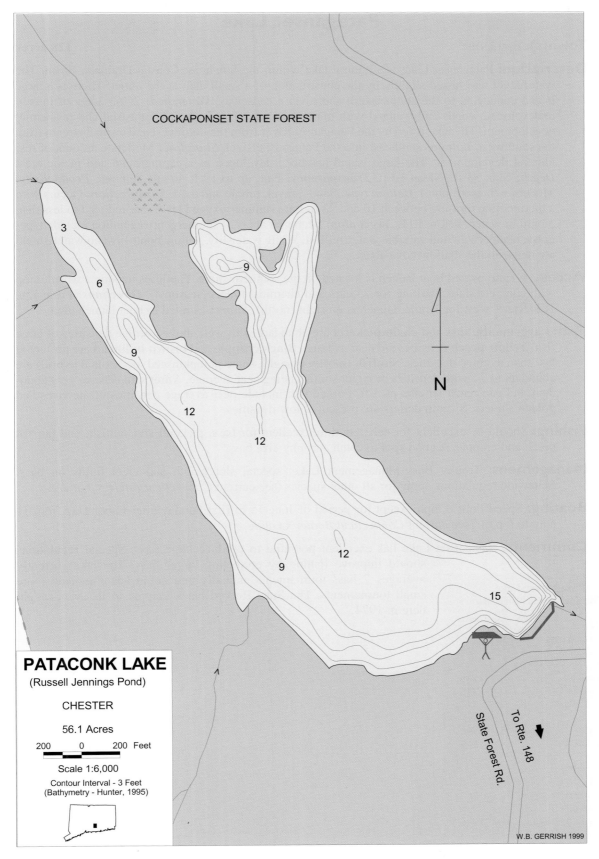

COCKAPONSET STATE FOREST

3

6

9

9

12

12

12

12

9

15

N

PATACONK LAKE
(Russell Jennings Pond)

CHESTER

56.1 Acres

200 0 200 Feet

Scale 1:6,000

Contour Interval - 3 Feet
(Bathymetry - Hunter, 1995)

State Forest Rd.

To Rte. 148

W.B. GERRISH 1999

Pataganset Lake

Town(s): East Lyme

128 acres

Description: Pataganset Lake is a natural lake within the Southeast Coastal Drainage Basin. The water level was raised slightly by the construction of a small dam at the outlet. There is a large island connected to the southeastern shore via a causeway. *Watershed:* 2,463 acres of mostly undeveloped woods and wetland with minor amounts of agricultural, industrial and residential development. The lake is fed by the Pataganset River from the northwest and a small stream from the southwest. It drains southeast into the Pataganset River. *Shoreline:* Moderate amount of residential development. The large island has been developed as a campground and picnic area. *Depth:* Max 33 ft., Mean 14 ft. *Transparency:* Fair, up to 10 ft. in late summer. *Productivity:* Moderate (mesotrophic). *Bottom type:* Sand, gravel, rubble and mud. *Stratification:* Occurs with a thermocline forming between 10 and 23 ft. Late summer oxygen levels are reduced to less than 3 ppm in waters below 10 ft. *Vegetation:* Scattered areas of submergent vegetation include tapegrass, bladderwort and variable water-milfoil. White water-lily, yellow pond-lily and water-shield are dense in the shallow cove areas.

Access: A state-owned boat launch is located on the southern shore. Facilities include a paved ramp with concrete slabs, parking for 15 cars and chemical toilets (seasonal). *Directions:* From Rte. 161, Rte. 1 west for 1 mile, launch is on right (north). *Shore:* Limited to boat launch area.

Fish: Largemouth bass and **chain pickerel** are abundant with well above average densities of large fish. **Yellow perch** densities are near average. **Black crappie** and **brown bullhead** are present at less than average densities. **Sunfish** (mostly bluegill, some pumpkinseed, occasional hybrid) are abundant to 7", with densities of larger sunfish being near average. **American eels** are very abundant and can reach lengths of 3 ft. Forage fish include near average densities of alewives and golden shiners. Swamp darters are present at low densities.

Fishing: Should be excellent for eels; good to excellent for bass, pickerel and sunfish; and fair for perch and crappie. A good spot to catch a trophy-size bass.

Management: Trophy Bass Management Lake; special slot length and creel limits on bass. Statewide regulations apply for all other species (see current *Connecticut Anglers' Guide*).

Boating: Speed limit 8 mph except for period of June 15 to first Sunday after Labor Day from 11 a.m. to 6 p.m. (see current *Connecticut Boater's Guide*).

Comments: Pataganset Lake has excellent potential to produce large bass. Special regulations should improve fishing by protecting larger bass. The lake currently averages 7 bass tournaments annually and could accommodate more small tournaments. The State Record black crappie (4 lb.) was caught here in 1974.

Pataganset Lake Fish Species and Abundance	ALL SIZES	BIG FISH	GROWTH
Gamefish			
Largemouth bass	A	C	Avg
Chain pickerel	A	C	Avg
Panfish			
Black crappie	U	U	< Avg
Yellow perch	C	C	< Avg
Brown bullhead	U	U	
Sunfish			
Bluegill	A	C	Avg
Pumpkinseed	C	C	Avg
Other			
Golden shiner	C		
Alewife	C		
American eel	A		
Swamp darter	U		

A=Abundant, C=Common, U=Uncommon, R=Rare

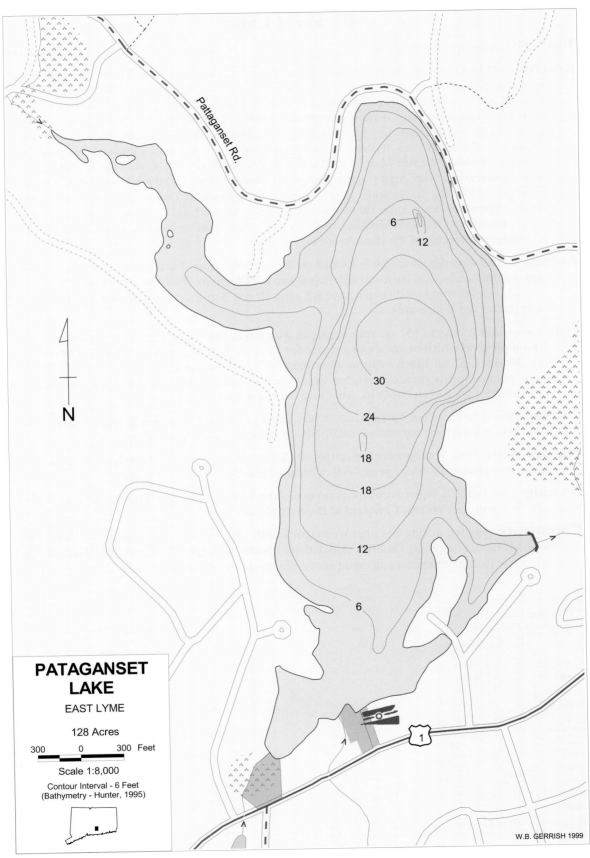

PATTAGANSET LAKE

EAST LYME

128 Acres

300   0   300 Feet

Scale 1:8,000

Contour Interval - 6 Feet
(Bathymetry - Hunter, 1995)

Pattaganset Rd.

6
12

30
24
18
18
12
6

1

W.B. GERRISH 1999

Pickerel Lake

Town(s): Colchester/East Haddam

82.2 acres

Description: Pickerel Lake is an artificial impoundment in the Connecticut River Drainage Basin. It was originally created for industrial use; the dam is now owned by the State. *Watershed*: 801 acres of mostly woods and wetland with low-density residential development. The lake is fed by two small wetland brooks, bottom springs and surface runoff. It drains southward into Pickerel Lake Brook, which feeds into Moodus Reservoir. *Shoreline*: The eastern shore is completely developed with residences, whereas the western shore is wooded with a few residences set back from the shoreline. *Depth*: Max 10 ft., Mean 6 ft. *Transparency*: Relatively clear; visible to bottom. *Productivity*: Very high (highly eutrophic). *Bottom type*: Mostly organic muck with scattered areas of sand, gravel and coarse boulders. *Stratification*: Does not occur due to limited depth. *Vegetation*: Very dense submergent coverage of fanwort and variable-leaved water-milfoil occurs throughout the lake. Floating mats of water-shield with some white water-lily and yellow pond-lily cover much of the shallow coves.

Access: A state-owned boat launch is located on the northern shore. Facilities include a paved ramp, parking for 10 cars, and chemical toilets (seasonal). *Directions*: From Rte. 16, Rte. 149 south for 200 yds., right (west) on Pickerel Lake Rd., launch is 1.5 miles on left. *Shore*: Public access is restricted to the launch area.

Fish: **Largemouth bass** to 15" are very abundant with larger bass being present at average densities. **Chain pickerel** densities are above average for all sizes. **Yellow perch** are present at below average densities. Small **black crappie** (less than 10") and **sunfish** (less than 7", mostly bluegill, some pumpkinseed) are abundant, but larger ones are uncommon. Other fish species present at low densities are brown bullhead, American eel and golden shiner.

Fishing: Should be excellent for largemouth bass and fair to good for pickerel, crappie and sunfish. Extensive submergent vegetation makes fishing difficult during the summer.

Management: Bass Management Lake; special slot length and creel limits on bass. Statewide regulations apply for all other species (see current *Connecticut Anglers' Guide*).

Boating: Speed limit 8 mph except for periods of June 15 to first Sunday after Labor Day from 11 a.m. to 6 p.m. (see current *Connecticut Boater's Guide*).

Comments: Angling quality has improved significantly since special bass regulations were implemented. Bass, crappie and sunfish populations remain stockpiled, however. The lake currently hosts few bass tournaments and could accommodate more of these events.

Pickerel Lake
Fish Species and Abundance

	ALL SIZES	BIG FISH	GROWTH
Gamefish			
Largemouth bass	A	C	Slow
Chain pickerel	C	C	> Avg
Panfish			
Black crappie	A	U	< Slow
Yellow perch	C	U	< Avg
Brown bullhead	U	U	
Sunfish			
Bluegill	A	U	Slow
Pumpkinseed	C	U	Slow
Other			
Golden shiner	U		
American eel	R		

A=Abundant, C=Common, U=Uncommon, R=Rare

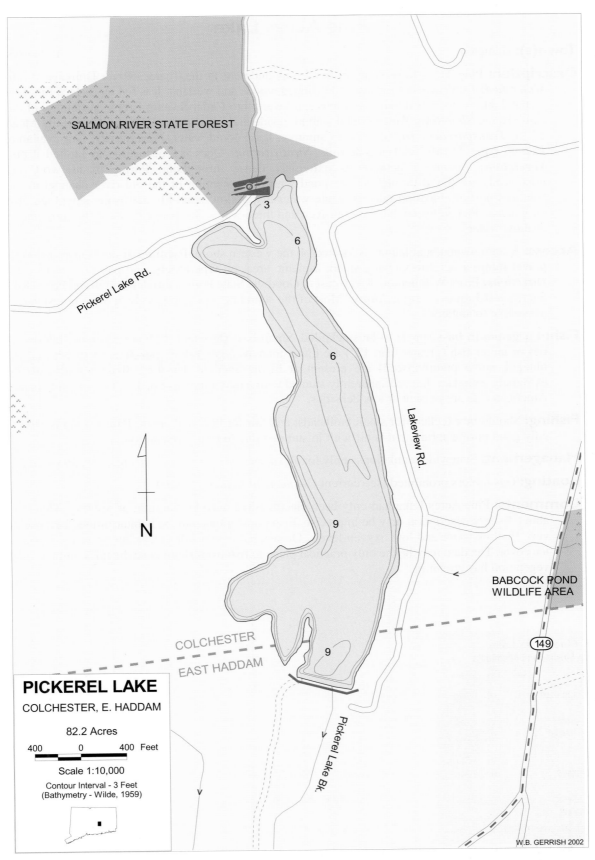

SALMON RIVER STATE FOREST

3

6

6

9

9

Pickerel Lake Rd.

Lakeview Rd.

COLCHESTER

EAST HADDAM

Pickerel Lake Bk.

BABCOCK POND
WILDLIFE AREA

149

PICKEREL LAKE

COLCHESTER, E. HADDAM

82.2 Acres

400   0   400 Feet

Scale 1:10,000

Contour Interval - 3 Feet
(Bathymetry - Wilde, 1959)

W.B. GERRISH 2002

Pine Acres Lake

Town(s): Hampton

190 acres

Description: Pine Acres Lake is an artificial impoundment in the Thames River Drainage Basin. *Watershed*: 1,055 acres of mostly undeveloped woods and wetland. It is fed by surface runoff, a wetland and two small streams. It drains southward into Cedar Swamp Brook, a tributary of the Little River. *Shoreline*: Well wooded with no residential development. *Depth*: Max 10 ft., Mean 3.7 ft. *Transparency*: Turbid; 3 ft. in summer, tea-colored water. *Productivity*: Not available. *Bottom type*: Mostly mud and detritus. *Stratification*: Does not occur due to limited depth. *Vegetation*: Aquatic vegetation is extremely dense throughout. Purple bladderwort and pondweeds are found throughout the pond with the exception of the old river channel in the southern portion. Floating mats of white water-lily, yellow pond-lily and water-shield are also very dense. Pickerelweed, bulrush, bur-reed and three-way sedge fringe much of the shoreline in shallow water.

Access: A state-owned boat launch is located on the western shore. Facilities at the launch include a gravel ramp, a wildlife viewing stand, a picnic area, pit-type toilets, and parking for 15 cars. *Directions*: From Willimantic, Rte. 6 east to Goodwin State Forest, turn left (north) on Potter Rd., launch is 0.5 miles on right. *Shore*: Most of the shoreline is within Goodwin State Forest and is accessible to anglers.

Fish: Largemouth bass appear to be stockpiled. Small bass (less than 12") are common, but densities of larger fish (greater than 12") are lower than average. **Yellow perch** and **sunfish** (mostly bluegill, some pumpkinseed) are present at below average densities. **Brown bullhead** are extremely abundant, but are apparently stunted with a maximum size of 10". Golden shiners and American eels are present at low densities.

Fishing: Should be excellent for small bullheads; and fair for bass and perch. Bass fishing is reportedly good during spring, but is difficult in summer due to heavy vegetation.

Management: Statewide regulations apply for all species (see current *Connecticut Anglers' Guide*).

Boating: Gas motors prohibited (see current *Connecticut Boater's Guide*).

Comments: Pine Acres Lake had only been electrofished once by the time of printing. Thus, the above fishery description may be imprecise. Fish populations may be habitat-limited because of very shallow water and low oxygen levels. Occasional winter kills occur during years of heavy ice cover. The dam may be the only practical place to fish from shore once the thick summertime vegetation has grown in.

Pine Acres Lake
Fish Species and Abundance

	ALL SIZES	BIG FISH	GROWTH
Gamefish			
Largemouth bass	C	U	< Avg
Panfish			
Yellow perch	C	C	Avg
Brown bullhead	A	U	
Sunfish			
Bluegill	C	U	Slow
Pumpkinseed	C	U	Avg
Other			
Golden shiner	U		
American eel	U		

A=Abundant, C=Common, U=Uncommon, R=Rare

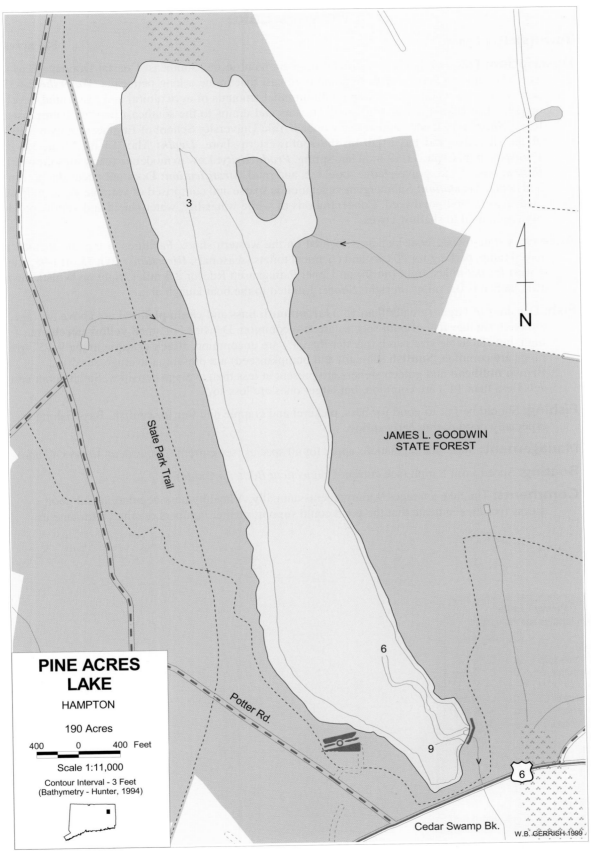

PINE ACRES LAKE

HAMPTON

190 Acres

400   0   400 Feet

Scale 1:11,000

Contour Interval - 3 Feet
(Bathymetry - Hunter, 1994)

JAMES L. GOODWIN
STATE FOREST

State Park Trail

Potter Rd.

Cedar Swamp Bk.

W.B. GERRISH 1999

N

3

6

9

6

Powers Lake

Town(s): East Lyme

144 acres

Description: Powers Lake is an artificial impoundment in the Southeast Coastal Drainage Basin. The lake has two narrow arms trending northeast that frame a long peninsula. *Watershed:* 637 acres of mostly woods and wetland with minimal amounts of agricultural and residential development. The lake is fed by four small streams and drains to the southeast into the Pattagansett River. *Shoreline:* Undeveloped and wooded. Yale University School of Engineering owns most of the shoreline and has a lab on the southwestern shore. *Depth:* Max 14 ft., Mean 7.0 ft. *Transparency:* Clear; 11-12 ft. in late spring. *Productivity:* Low to moderate (early mesotrophic). *Bottom type:* Sand, gravel, ledge, boulders and mud. *Stratification:* Does not occur due to limited depth. *Vegetation:* Submergent vegetation is sparse and comprised of variable water-milfoil, bladderworts and pondweed. Concentrations of white water-lily, water-shield and yellow pond-lily are limited to shallow coves.

Access: A state-owned boat launch is located on the western shore. Facilities at the site include a paved ramp, parking for 20 cars and chemical toilets (seasonal). *Directions:* Exit 75 off I-95, Rte. 1 west for 0.9 miles, right (north) on Upper Pattagansett Rd. for 2.5 miles, right on Whistletown Rd., launch is 0.6 miles on right. *Shore:* Limited to the boat launch area.

Fish: Densities of larger (greater than 15") **largemouth bass** and **chain pickerel** are above average, although smaller fish of both species are less common. Densities of small **yellow perch** are high, but catchable size perch (greater than 9") are uncommon. **Black crappie** in the 9-13" size range are common. **Sunfish** (bluegill and pumpkinseed) are present at average densities. **Brown bullhead** and golden shiners are present at less than average densities. Small American eels (less than 14") are common, but larger ones are less so.

Fishing: Should be fair to good for bass, pickerel and crappie and fair for sunfish. Bass fishing is especially good during early spring.

Management: Statewide regulations apply for all species (see current *Connecticut Anglers' Guide*).

Boating: Speed limit 8 mph (see current *Connecticut Boater's Guide*).

Comments: The lake averages 9 tournaments annually. A healthy bass population and good access facilities indicate that the pond could support greater numbers of small tournaments.

Powers Lake
Fish Species and Abundance

	ALL SIZES	BIG FISH	GROWTH
Gamefish			
Largemouth bass	C	C	Fast
Chain pickerel	C	C	> Avg
Panfish			
Black crappie	C	C	> Avg
Yellow perch	U	U	< Avg
Brown bullhead	C	C	
Sunfish			
Bluegill	C	C	Avg
Pumpkinseed	C	C	> Avg
Other			
Golden shiner	U		
American eel	C		

A=Abundant, C=Common, U=Uncommon, R=Rare

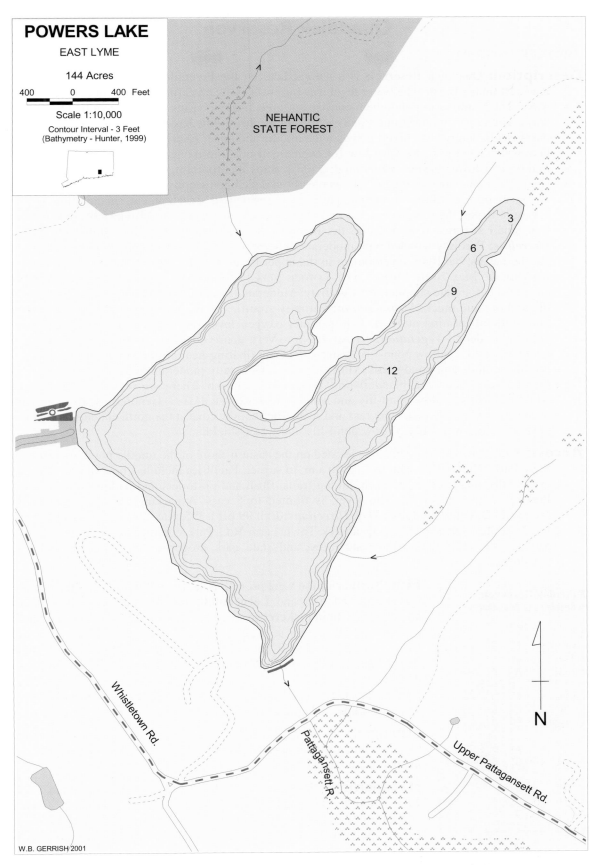

POWERS LAKE

EAST LYME

144 Acres

400　　0　　400　Feet

Scale 1:10,000

Contour Interval - 3 Feet
(Bathymetry - Hunter, 1999)

NEHANTIC
STATE FOREST

3

6

9

12

Whistletown Rd.

Pattagansett R.

Upper Pattagansett Rd.

N

W.B. GERRISH 2001

Quaddick Reservoir

Town(s): Thompson

408 acres

Description: Quaddick Reservoir is a natural lake on the Fivemile River within the Thames River Drainage Basin. The water level was raised 11 ft. by an earthen dam with concrete spillways. The resulting impoundment consists of three discrete basins that are separated by causeways. The upper basin (Stump Pond) is 80.7 acres, the middle basin is 203 acres and the lower basin is 124 acres. The culvert between the middle and upper basins is navigable; however, the lake water level must be very low for even small boats to navigate the culvert between the middle and lower basins. *Watershed*: 15,561 acres incorporating the Fivemile River watershed. The land surrounding the lake is mostly undeveloped woods and wetland with a moderate level of agricultural land and patches of residential development. In addition to the Fivemile River, the reservoir is fed by Jason, Robins, Blackmore and Brandy Brooks, and by four small streams. It drains into the Fivemile River, a tributary of the Quinebaug River. *Shoreline*: Partially wooded with moderate to heavy residential development in the lower and middle basins, but light development in the upper basin. *Depth*: UPPER: Max 11 ft., Mean 4.9 ft., MIDDLE: Max 20 ft., Mean 7.6 ft., LOWER: Max 17 ft., Mean 7.3 ft. *Transparency*: Fair to clear; 8-11 ft. in late summer. *Productivity*: Moderate (mesotrophic). *Bottom type*: Sand, rubble and organic muck. *Stratification*: Partially stratifies in the middle basin with a temperature gradient forming at 13 ft. Late summer oxygen levels are reduced to less than 4 ppm below this depth. *Vegetation*: STUMP POND – Very dense coverage with a channel through white water-lily, yellow pond-lily, water-shield and floating-heart. Submergent plants are tapegrass, coontails and pondweeds. MIDDLE BASIN – Generally moderate to dense coverage, with dense areas of fanwort, bladderworts, pondweed and rush. There are scattered locations of white water-lily, yellow pond-lily and water-shield. LOWER BASIN – Generally sparse, but with dense areas of pondweed, tapegrass and rush. The shallow cove at the north end has dense coverage of white water-lily, yellow pond-lily and water-shield.

Access: A state-owned boat launch is located on the eastern shore of the middle pond in Quaddick State Park. The park is open from 8:00 a.m. to sunset. Facilities include a boat ramp with concrete slabs, picnic areas, a beach, hiking trails, flush and pit toilets and parking for 100 cars. Parking at the launch site, however, is limited to 5 cars. A parking fee is charged from Memorial Day through Labor Day. *Directions*: Exit 99 off I-395, Rte. 200 east (Quaddick Rd.) for 2.8 miles, left (north) on Quaddick Town Farm Rd., Park entrance is 1.5 miles on left. *Shore*: The areas within the state forest and state park properties on Upper and Middle Quaddick.

Quaddick Reservoir Fish Species and Abundance	ALL SIZES	BIG FISH	GROWTH
Gamefish			
Largemouth bass	C	C	Avg
Northern Pike	C		
Chain pickerel	A	C	< Avg
Panfish			
Black crappie	C	C	< Avg
Yellow perch	C	C	Slow
Brown bullhead	C	C	
Sunfish			
Bluegill	A	A	Avg
Pumpkinseed	C	C	Avg
Other			
Golden shiner	C		
White sucker	U		
American eel	U		
A=Abundant, C=Common, U=Uncommon, R=Rare			

Fish: **Northern pike** were present at the time of writing and the population is expected to expand. **Largemouth bass** densities are average for all size classes. **Chain pickerel** are abundant to 15". **Yellow perch** and **black crappie** are all present at slightly less than average densities, although larger fish (greater than 9") are common. **Sunfish** (mostly bluegill, some pumpkinseed, occasional hybrid) are abundant to 9". **Brown bullhead** densities are average for all sizes. Quaddick contains slightly less than average densities of golden shiners. Other fish species present at low densities are white sucker and American eel.

Fishing: Should be excellent for pickerel and sunfish, fair to good for bass and fair for other species. Northern pike fishing should improve as the population expands.

Management: The reservoir is stocked annually (beginning in 1999) with 3,800 northern pike fingerlings to provide additional fishing opportunities and to help control overabundant panfish. Statewide regulations apply for all species (see current *Connecticut Anglers' Guide*).▼

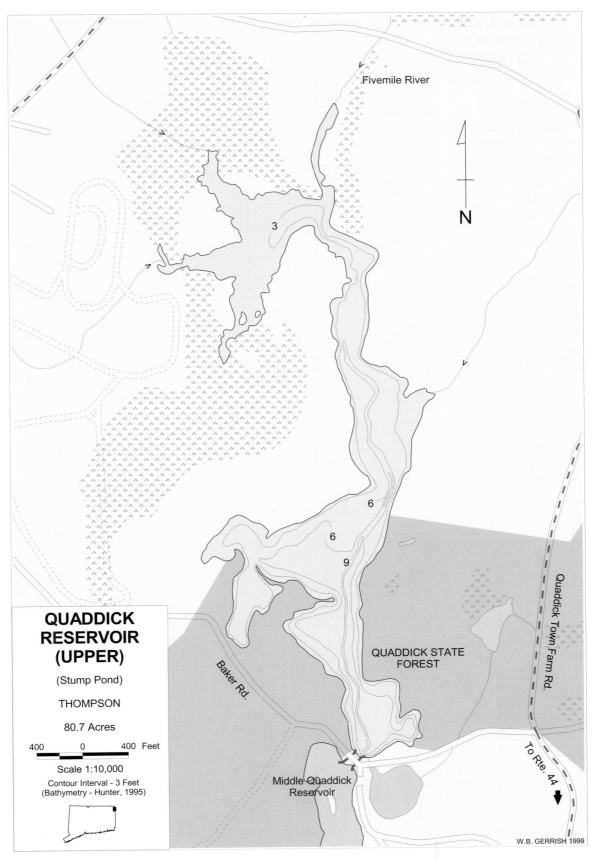

QUADDICK
RESERVOIR
(UPPER)

(Stump Pond)

THOMPSON

80.7 Acres

400   0   400 Feet

Scale 1:10,000

Contour Interval - 3 Feet
(Bathymetry - Hunter, 1995)

Fivemile River

N

3

6

6

9

QUADDICK STATE
FOREST

Baker Rd.

Quaddick Town Farm Rd.

To Rte. 44

Middle Quaddick
Reservoir

W.B. GERRISH 1999

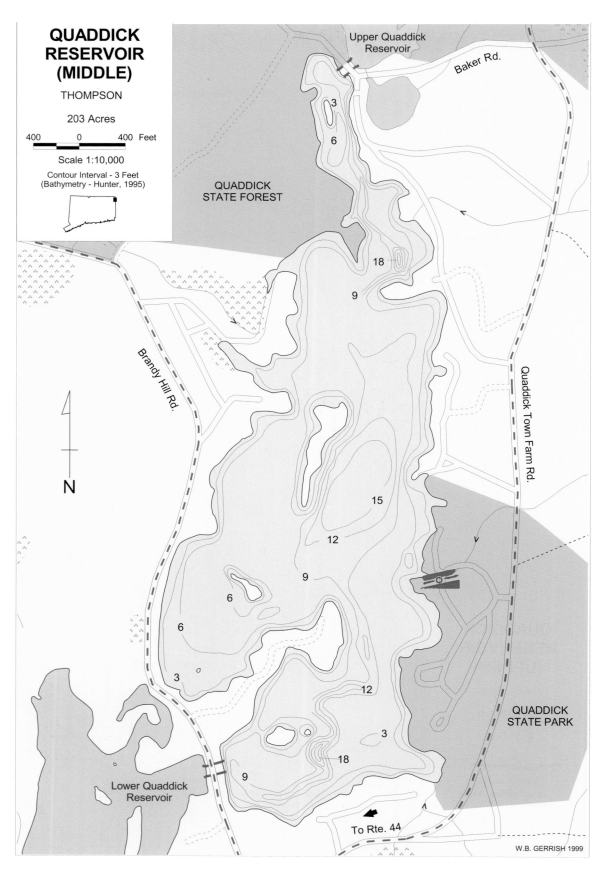

QUADDICK RESERVOIR (MIDDLE)

THOMPSON

203 Acres

400   0   400   Feet

Scale 1:10,000

Contour Interval - 3 Feet
(Bathymetry - Hunter, 1995)

Upper Quaddick
Reservoir

Baker Rd.

QUADDICK
STATE FOREST

Brandy Hill Rd.

N

Quaddick Town Farm Rd.

QUADDICK
STATE PARK

Lower Quaddick
Reservoir

To Rte. 44

W.B. GERRISH 1999

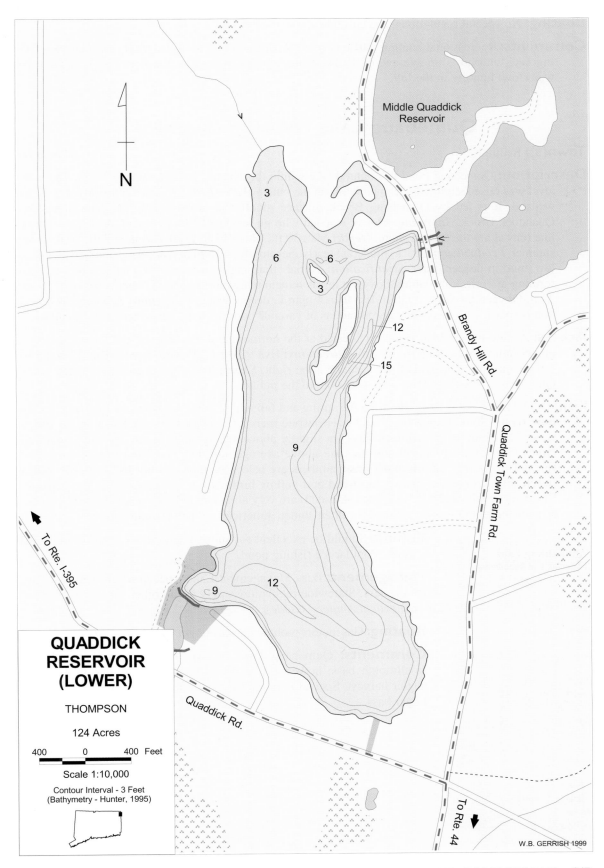

Middle Quaddick
Reservoir

3

6   6

3

12

15

9

Brandy Hill Rd.

Quaddick Town Farm Rd.

To Rte. I-395

9   12

N

**QUADDICK
RESERVOIR
(LOWER)**

THOMPSON

124 Acres

400   0   400   Feet

Scale 1:10,000

Contour Interval - 3 Feet
(Bathymetry - Hunter, 1995)

Quaddick Rd.

To Rte. 44

W.B. GERRISH 1999

Boating: No special regulations (see current *Connecticut Boater's Guide*).

Comments: Recreational boating traffic is heavy during summer. It is also a very popular bass fishing lake, and hosts an average of 19 bass tournaments each year. Northern end is popular for waterfowl hunting in the fall.

Quinebaug Lake (Wauregan Reservoir)

Town(s): Killingly   **87.6 acres**

Description: Quinebaug Pond is a natural lake within the Thames River Drainage Basin. The water level was raised slightly by a small berm on the outlet. *Watershed:* 623 acres of mostly woods and wetland. It is fed by Quinebaug Brook, surface runoff and groundwater. The lake drains into Quandock Brook. *Shoreline:* Mostly wooded with no residential development. An active railroad line runs along the eastern shore. *Depth:* Max 30 ft., Mean 15 ft. *Transparency:* Fair; 10 ft. in late summer. *Productivity:* Low to moderate (early mesotrophic). *Bottom type:* Sand and gravel in shallow, mud in deeper water. *Stratification:* Partial stratification occurs with a temperature gradient forming at 16 ft. Late summer oxygen levels remain marginal to good (5-7 ppm) between 16 and 23 ft. Oxygen levels then fall to less than 4 ppm in deeper water. *Vegetation:* Submergent vegetation is sparse with localized concentrations of variable pondweed, tapegrass and water-nymph.

Access: A state-owned boat launch is located at the northern end. Facilities at the launch include a gravel ramp and parking for 12 cars. *Directions:* Exit 92 off I-395, Rte. 6 west, Rte. 12 south for 1 mile, east on Shepard Hill Rd., launch is on right. *Shore:* The pond is entirely located within Quinebaug Lake State Park and accessible to the public.

Fish: Quinebaug Lake is stocked during the spring and fall with 2,500 catchable size **brown and rainbow trout**. Some brown trout hold over despite marginal summer oxygen levels in the deeper water. Densities of **largemouth bass** are slightly above average for 10-15" fish and average for larger fish. **Chain pickerel** densities are above average and they commonly reach large sizes (greater than 20"). **Smallmouth bass** numbers are below average and big fish are rare. **Yellow perch**, **black crappie**, **brown bullhead** and **yellow bullhead** are present at average densities. **Sunfish** (mostly bluegill, some pumpkinseed) are very abundant in larger sizes (6-8"). Other fish species present at low densities are golden shiner, American eel and swamp darter.

Quinebaug Lake Fish Species and Abundance			
	ALL SIZES	BIG FISH	GROWTH
Gamefish			
Largemouth bass	C	C	Avg
Smallmouth bass	U	U	Avg
Brown trout	C	U	
Rainbow trout	C		
Chain pickerel	C	C	Avg
Panfish			
Black crappie	C	C	Avg
Yellow perch	C	C	Avg
Brown bullhead	C	C	
Yellow bullhead	C	C	
Sunfish			
Bluegill	A	A	Avg
Pumpkinseed	C	C	> Avg
Other			
Golden shiner	U		
Swamp darter	R		
American eel	U		
A=Abundant, C=Common, U=Uncommon, R=Rare			

Fishing: Should be excellent for sunfish and fair to good for other fish species. Popular ice fishing pond.

Management: Bass Management Lake; special length and creel limits on bass. Statewide regulations apply for all other species (see current *Connecticut Anglers' Guide*).

Boating: Gas motors prohibited (see current *Connecticut Boater's Guide*).

Comments: Quinebaug Lake appears to have good potential for smallmouth bass; however, population levels are low due to excessive angler harvest. Special regulations should improve fishing by protecting larger bass.

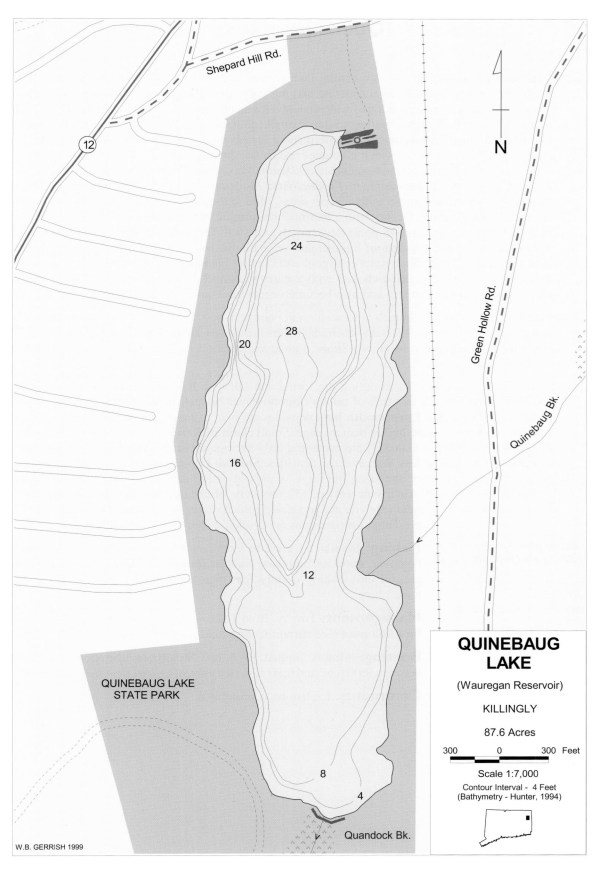

Shepard Hill Rd.

12

24

28

20

16

12

8

4

Green Hollow Rd.

Quinebaug Bk.

N

QUINEBAUG LAKE
STATE PARK

Quandock Bk.

W.B. GERRISH 1999

**QUINEBAUG
LAKE**

(Wauregan Reservoir)

KILLINGLY

87.6 Acres

300   0   300   Feet

Scale 1:7,000

Contour Interval - 4 Feet
(Bathymetry - Hunter, 1994)

Quonnipaug Lake

Town(s): Guilford

98.7 acres

Description: Quonnipaug Lake is a natural lake within the Central Coastal Drainage Basin. The water level was raised 4 ft. by a concrete and masonry dam. *Watershed:* 1,700 acres of mostly woods and wetland with moderate residential development. The lake is fed by Sucker Brook and two small streams. It drains southward into a small tributary of the West River, which flows into Long Island Sound. *Shoreline:* The eastern shore is heavily developed with residences. Rte. 77 parallels the western shore, which precludes residential development along this side of the lake. A town beach is located on the western shore. *Depth:* Max 45 ft., Mean 18 ft. *Transparency:* Fair to clear; 10-13 ft. in late summer. *Productivity:* Moderate (early mesotrophic-mesotrophic). *Bottom type:* Sand and gravel in the deeper areas. Mud in the shallows at the northern and southern ends. *Stratification:* Occurs with a thermocline forming between 16 and 26 ft. Late summer oxygen levels are marginal (5 ppm) between 16 and 19 ft. Oxygen then declines to less than 2 ppm in deeper water. *Vegetation:* Submergent vegetation is a solid carpet of Robbins pondweed with Eurasian water-milfoil, water-marigold and fanwort interspersed. The boat launch area and the north cove are vegetation-choked with a narrow channel leading to the main water body. Shallow areas in the southern end also become vegetation-choked during summer.

Access: A state-owned boat launch is located on the northern end. Facilities at the launch include a paved ramp, parking for 8 cars and chemical toilets (seasonal). *Directions:* From Rte. 17, Rte. 77 south for 5 miles, launch is on left. *Shore:* Public shore access is on the western shore adjacent to Rte. 77 and the launch area.

Fish: Quonnipaug Lake is stocked during the spring and fall with 8,300 catchable size **brown** and **rainbow trout**. Decent numbers of brown trout holdover because of favorable summer oxygen levels in deeper water. **Largemouth bass** densities are near average, but numbers of very large fish (greater than 18") are higher than average. Small **chain pickerel** are extremely abundant, but larger pickerel (greater than 12") are present at only average densities. **Yellow perch** and **black crappie** are present at less than average densities. **Sunfish** (mostly bluegill and pumpkinseed, some redbreast) are very abundant, but large sunfish (greater than 7") are uncommon. **Brown bullhead** to 12" and **American eel** to 15" are very abundant, but larger sizes are rare. Quonnipaug has an abundant alewife and moderate golden shiner forage base. Other fish species present at low densities are bridled shiner and white sucker.

Quonnipaug Lake Fish Species and Abundance	ALL SIZES	BIG FISH	GROWTH
Gamefish			
Largemouth bass	C	C	Slow
Brown trout	A	U	< Avg
Rainbow trout	C		
Chain pickerel	A	C	Slow
Panfish			
Black crappie	C	U	> Avg
Yellow perch	C	U	> Avg
Brown bullhead	A	C	
Sunfish			
Bluegill	A	C	Slow
Pumpkinseed	A	C	Slow
Redbreast	U	R	
Other			
Bridled shiner	R		
Golden shiner	C		
Alewife	A		
White sucker	U		
American eel	A		
A=Abundant, C=Common, U=Uncommon, R=Rare			

Fishing: Should be good to excellent for trout with a chance for a holdover; good for bullhead; and fair for pickerel and sunfish. Although general bass fishing is only fair, there's potential for tying into a real lunker here.

Management: Trophy Trout Lake; special seasonal length and creel limits on trout (see current *Connecticut Anglers' Guide*).

Boating: Motors limited to 6 hp. Motorboat operation prohibited between 9:00 p.m. and 6:00 a.m. (see current *Connecticut Boater's Guide*).

Comments: Ice fishing is prohibited.

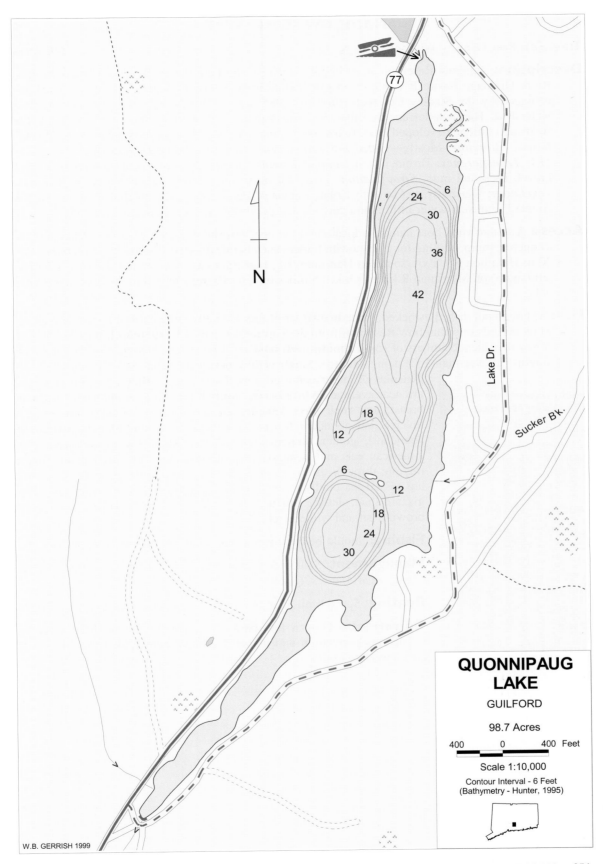

**QUONNIPAUG
LAKE**

GUILFORD

98.7 Acres

400   0   400   Feet

Scale 1:10,000

Contour Interval - 6 Feet
(Bathymetry - Hunter, 1995)

W.B. GERRISH 1999

Rainbow Reservoir

Town(s): East Granby/Windsor   **240 acres**

Description: Rainbow Reservoir is an impoundment of the Farmington River in the Connecticut River Drainage Basin. It was created to generate hydroelectricity and is currently owned and managed by the Stanley Co. *Watershed:* 375,985 acres encompassing the Farmington River watershed. The area surrounding the reservoir is mostly residential with some active tobacco fields and little undeveloped land. In addition to the Farmington River, it is fed by several small brooks. *Shoreline:* Mostly wooded with little residential development. *Depth:* Max 38 ft., Mean 11 ft. *Transparency:* Turbid; 6 ft. in summer. *Productivity:* High (eutrophic). *Bottom type:* Sand, gravel, rock and mud. *Stratification:* Does not occur due to riverine flow through the lake. *Vegetation:* Generally sparse with isolated areas of dense vegetation in shallow coves where coontail, Eurasian water-milfoil and curly-leafed pondweed are the dominant species.

Access: A state-owned boat launch is located on the northern shore. Facilities at the launch include a concrete ramp, parking for 20 cars with trailers and chemical toilets (seasonal). *Directions:* Rte. 20 to Hamilton Rd. Exit, south on Hamilton Rd., first right (west) on Rainbow Rd. for 1 mile, left (south) on Merriman Rd., launch is 0.5 miles on left. *Shore:* Limited to the boat launch area only.

Fish: Although not directly stocked, some **brown trout** (occasionally large ones) migrate during cool water periods into Rainbow Reservoir from the Farmington River. **Largemouth bass** are present at low densities. Numbers of small **smallmouth bass** are higher than average with larger small- mouths (greater than 13") being average. Small **yellow perch** (less than 6") are abundant, but densities of larger perch are less than average. **Black crappie** densities are near average. **White perch**, **sunfish** (bluegill, pumpkinseed and red- breast) and **rock bass** densities are less than average for all sizes. A diverse and abundant forage base includes spottail shiners (extremely abundant), golden shiners and fallfish. White suckers are abundant. American eels and common carp are common. Atlantic salmon smolts migrate through the reservoir seasonally. Anadromous fish species that are passed seasonally through the fishway at the dam are American shad, gizzard shad, alewife, blueback herring, sea lamprey, striped bass, sea-run brown trout and white perch.

Fishing: Should be fair for bass and fair to poor for other species.

Management: Statewide regulations apply for all species (see current *Connecticut Anglers' Guide*).

Boating: Speed limit 35 mph (see current *Connecticut Boater's Guide*).

Comments: Only a few bass tournaments are held here annually. Good bass population and launch facilities indicate that the lake could accommodate more.

Rainbow Reservoir
Fish Species and Abundance

	ALL SIZES	BIG FISH	GROWTH
Gamefish			
Largemouth bass	U	U	> Avg
Smallmouth bass	C	C	Avg
Atlantic salmon	U		
Brown trout	U	U	
Panfish			
Black crappie	C	C	Avg
White perch	C	C	Avg
Yellow perch	A	U	Avg
Sunfish			
Bluegill	C	C	> Avg
Pumpkinseed	U	U	> Avg
Redbreast	U	R	> Avg
Rock bass	C	U	Avg
Other			
Common carp	C		
Fall fish	U		
Golden shiner	C		Avg
Spottail shiner	A		
Sea lamprey	U		
White sucker	A		
American eel	C		
Anadromous			
American shad	C		
Gizzard shad	R		
Alewife	R		
Blueback herring	U		
Sea lamprey	C		
Striped bass	R		
Brown trout	R		

A=Abundant, C=Common, U=Uncommon, R=Rare

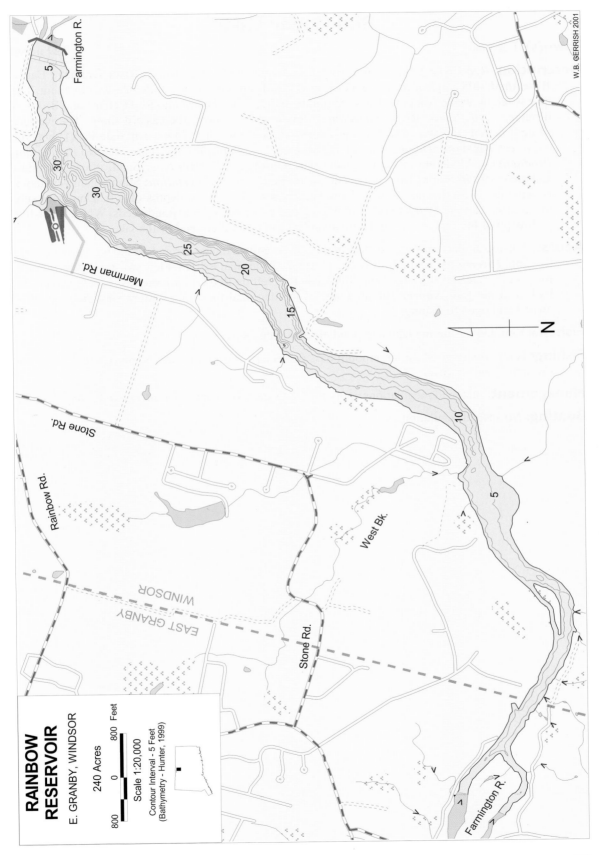

RAINBOW RESERVOIR

E. GRANBY, WINDSOR

240 Acres

800   0   800 Feet

Scale 1:20,000

Contour Interval - 5 Feet
(Bathymetry - Hunter, 1999)

Farmington R.

Merriman Rd.

Stone Rd.

Rainbow Rd.

West Bk.

EAST GRANBY

WINDSOR

Stone Rd.

Farmington R.

N

W.B. GERRISH 2001

Red Cedar Lake

Town(s): Lebanon

127 acres

Description: Red Cedar Lake is an artificial impoundment in the Thames River Drainage Basin. *Watershed:* 408 acres of mostly undeveloped woodland with some residential development. The lake is fed by groundwater and surface runoff. It drains northward into Red Cedar Lake Brook, a tributary of the Yantic River. *Shoreline:* Mostly wooded along the eastern shore. The western shore is heavily developed with homes. Undeveloped state land (Mooween State Park) abuts the entire eastern shore. *Depth:* Max 11 ft., Mean 6.2 ft. *Transparency:* Fair; clear to the bottom. *Productivity:* Moderate to high (mesotrophic–eutrophic). *Bottom type:* Sand, gravel, boulders and mud. *Stratification:* Does not occur due to limited depth. *Vegetation:* Submergent vegetation is generally dense in the coves and southern area of the lake to depths of 4 ft. Dominant submergent species are bladderwort, variable-leaved water-milfoil and pondweeds. White water-lily, yellow pond-lily and water-shield are abundant in the southern end of the lake.

Access: Car-top anglers may access the pond from state-owned land located on the northern end near the dam. *Directions:* Exit 22 off Rte. 2, north on Waterman Rd., first left (west) on Norwich Rd. for 1.4 miles, left (south) on Camp Mooween Rd., left on Red Cedar Lake Rd., access is on right. Park near the gate. *Shore:* The area around the dam and the entire eastern shoreline are state-owned and open to fishing.

Fish: Not sampled during the lake and pond electrofishing survey.

Fishing: Is reportedly good for largemouth bass (especially during the early spring), and fair for yellow perch and sunfish.

Management: Statewide regulations apply for all species (see current *Connecticut Anglers' Guide*).

Boating: No special regulations.

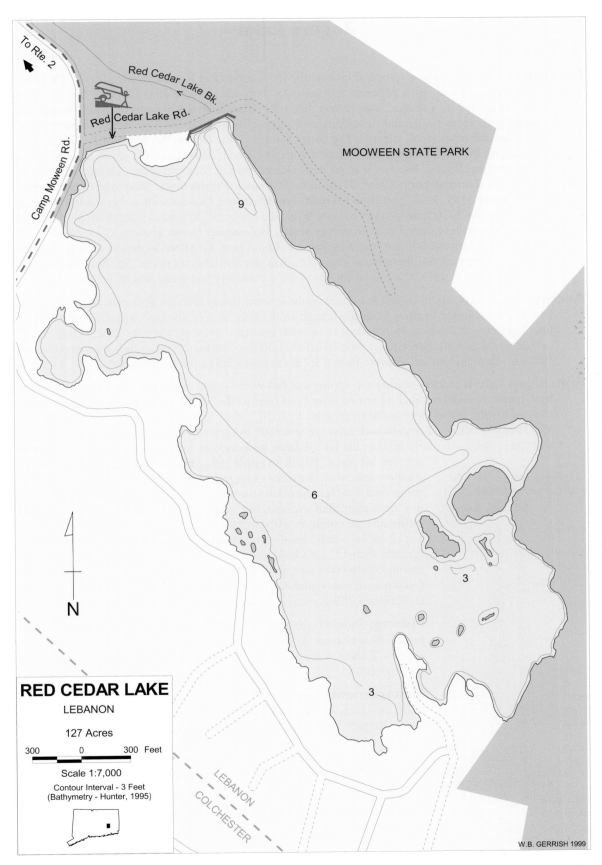

To Rte. 2

Red Cedar Lake Bk.

Red Cedar Lake Rd.

Camp Moween Rd.

MOOWEEN STATE PARK

9

6

3

3

N

RED CEDAR LAKE

LEBANON

127 Acres

300　　　0　　　300　Feet

Scale 1:7,000

Contour Interval - 3 Feet
(Bathymetry - Hunter, 1995)

LEBANON

COLCHESTER

W.B. GERRISH 1999

Rogers Lake

Town(s): Lyme/Old Lyme

260 acres

Description: Rogers Lake is a natural lake within the Connecticut River Drainage Basin. The water level was raised 4 ft. by a concrete and masonry dam across the outlet. The lake has two deep basins connected by a shallow area of less than 6 ft. *Watershed:* 4,819 acres of mostly woods and wetland with some residential development. Rogers is fed by Grassy Hill Brook from the north and by several other small streams. The outlet is through the dam at the southern end of the lake. It flows into Mill Brook, a tributary of the Lieutenant River. *Shoreline:* The shore is lined almost entirely by residences. There is a town park located on the southern shore. *Depth:* Max 63 ft., Mean 19 ft. *Transparency:* Clear; 11 ft. in late summer. *Productivity:* Moderate (mesotrophic). *Bottom type:* Mud, sand, gravel and rubble. *Stratification:* Occurs with a thermocline forming between 16 and 30 ft. Late summer oxygen levels are marginal (5 ppm) to a depth of 20 ft. Oxygen then declines to less than 3 ppm in deeper water. *Vegetation:* Dense growths of tapegrass, variable-leaved water-milfoil, and water-nymph are found near the shore to depths of 6 ft. in many areas of both basins. Southern naiad is present. Bladderwort also occurs in the shallower midsection of the lake. Patches of white water-lily, yellow pond-lily and water-shield are present.

Access: A state-owned boat launch is located on the eastern shore, 100 yds. upstream into Grassy Hill Brook. The channel leading from the launch to the lake is very shallow when the lake level is low. Facilities at the launch include a ramp with concrete slabs, parking for 20 cars and chemical toilets (seasonal). *Directions:* Exit 70 off I-95, Rte. 1 east for 2.5 miles, left (north) on Grassy Hill Rd., launch is on left. *Shore:* Public access is restricted to the launch area.

Fish: Rogers Lake is stocked during the spring and fall with 10,200 catchable size **brown** and **rainbow trout**. A small number of brown trout hold over to the following year despite low summer oxygen levels. Some large **walleye** (greater than 20") were still present at time of writing (see Management below). **Largemouth bass** are abundant in all sizes. Densities of bass in the 12-19" size range are particularly high in the lake. **Chain pickerel** densities are slightly less than average for all sizes. **Black crappie** and **yellow perch** are uncommon at smaller sizes, with densities of larger crappie and perch (greater than 10") being near average. **Sunfish** (mostly bluegill, some pumpkinseed) densities are higher than average, but sunfish greater than 8" are rare. **Brown bullheads** are common with slightly higher than average numbers of larger (12 to 14") fish. Small **American eels** are abundant, but larger eels (greater than 15") are less common. Forage fish include abundant populations of alewives and golden shiners. Other fish species present at low densities are tessellated darter, bridled shiner, common carp, spottail shiner, banded killifish, fourspine stickleback and creek chubsucker.

Fishing: Should be excellent for largemouth bass, good to excellent for trout with a chance for a holdover; good for bullheads, and fair for other species. Expect walleye fishing to be slow, but fish caught will be large (to 8 pounds).

Management: Trophy Trout Lake; special seasonal length and creel limits on trout (see current *Connecticut Anglers' Guide*). From 1993 to 1998, Rogers Lake was stocked annually in the fall with fingerling walleyes. Although growth rates were good, survival of stocked walleyes was poor. Because of this and the proximity of other successful walleye lakes (Gardner and Saltonstall), stocking was discontinued in 1999.

Boating: Speed limit 6 mph sunset to 10:00 a.m. except 12 mph sunset to 10:00 a.m. November 1 to May 14. Motors limited to 135 hp (see current *Connecticut Boater's Guide*). ▼

Rogers Lake
Fish Species and Abundance

	ALL SIZES	BIG FISH	GROWTH
Gamefish			
Largemouth bass	A	A	Avg
Brown trout	C	U	Avg
Rainbow trout	C		
Chain pickerel	C	C	Avg
Walleye	U	U	> Avg
Panfish			
Black crappie	C	C	> Avg
Yellow perch	C	C	Avg
Brown bullhead	C	C	
Sunfish			
Bluegill	C	U	< Avg
Pumpkinseed	C	U	< Avg
Other			
Tessellated darter	U		
Bridled shiner	U		
Common carp	R		
Golden shiner	A		
Spottail shiner	U		
Banded killifish	U		
Fourspine stickleback	U		
Alewife	A		
Creek chubsucker	R		
American eel	A		

A=Abundant, C=Common, U=Uncommon, R=Rare

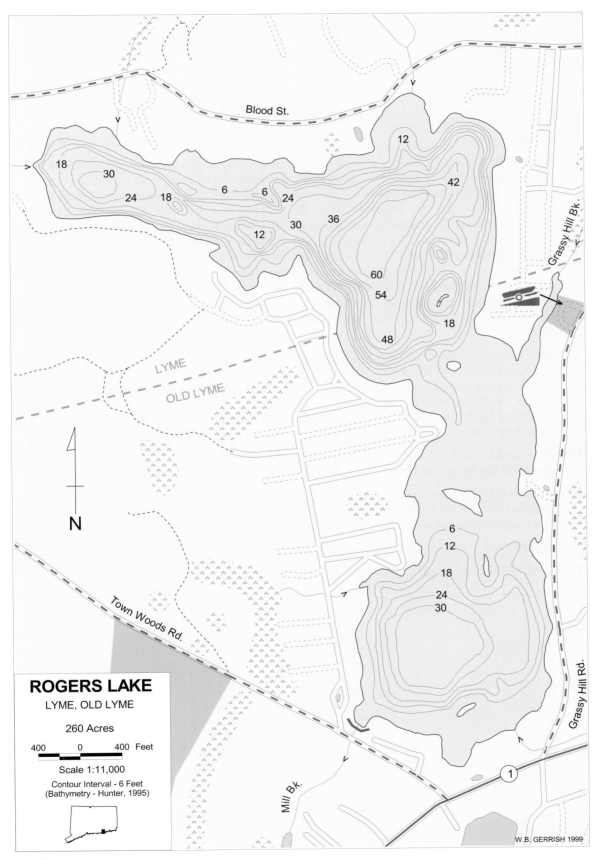

ROGERS LAKE

LYME, OLD LYME

260 Acres

400   0   400 Feet

Scale 1:11,000

Contour Interval - 6 Feet
(Bathymetry - Hunter, 1995)

Blood St.

Grassy Hill Bk.

LYME

OLD LYME

Grassy Hill Rd.

Town Woods Rd.

Mill Bk.

1

N

12

18   30
24   18   6   6   24
12   30   36   42
60
54
48
18

6
12
18
24
30

W.B. GERRISH 1999

Comments: Recreational use on Rogers lake is very high. It withstands heavy fishing pressure, primarily for trout, in the early spring. It is a very popular bass fishing lake, and hosts an average of 18 bass tournaments each year. There is considerable recreational boating activity (such as water-skiing) during the summer months.

Roseland Lake

Town(s): Woodstock   **96.1 acres**

Description: Roseland Lake is a natural lake within the Thames River Drainage Basin. **Watershed:** 19,393 acres of mostly agricultural land with some undeveloped woods and wetland and some residential development. The lake is fed by Muddy Brook from the north and by two small streams. It drains southward into Shepards Pond, which flows into the Little River, a tributary of the Quinebaug River. **Shoreline:** Mostly wooded with a few residential dwellings. The western shoreline adjoining Roseland Park is flanked by dense stands of *Phragmites*. **Depth:** Max 19 ft., Mean 9 ft. **Transparency:** Turbid; 2 ft. in late summer. **Productivity:** Very high (highly eutrophic). **Bottom type:** Not available. **Stratification:** Occurs; however, a late summer temperature-oxygen profile was not available. **Vegetation:** A late season survey indicated that submergent waterweed and smartweed is sparse to occasional in waters less than 3 ft. deep. Much of the lake is fringed with emergent pickerelweed and bur-reed and floating mats of white water-lily and yellow pond-lily.

Access: A town-owned boat launch is located on the western side of the lake in Roseland Park. Facilities at the park include an unimproved dirt boat ramp suitable for launching small boats, a picnic area, a playground and flush-type toilets. The park is open year-round from 7:00 a.m. to sunset. No fee is charged. **Directions:** From Putnam, Rte. 171 west for 2.5 miles, right (north) on Roseland Park Rd., park is on right. **Shore:** Anglers may fish from anywhere within the park boundaries; however, stands of tall reeds make access difficult along most of this area.

Fish: Not sampled during the lake and pond electrofishing survey. Roseland Lake is stocked each spring with 900 catchable size **brown** and **rainbow trout**. Trout do not hold over due to limited depth.

Fishing: Should be seasonally fair to good for stocked trout. Fishing is also reportedly good for black crappie; and fair for largemouth bass, chain pickerel, yellow perch, brown bullhead and sunfish. Very popular ice fishing spot for panfish.

Management: Statewide regulations apply for all species (see current *Connecticut Anglers' Guide*).

Boating: No special regulations (see current *Connecticut Boater's Guide*).

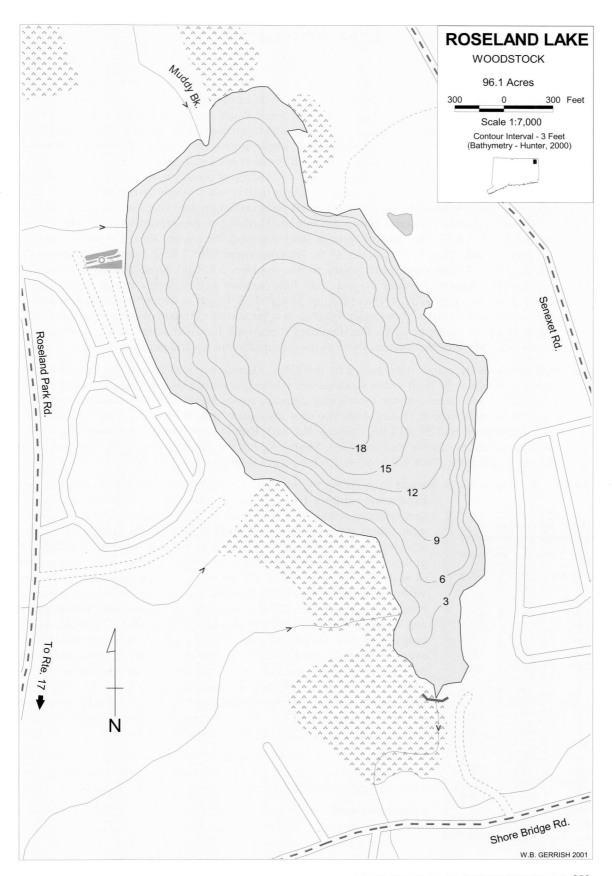

ROSELAND LAKE

WOODSTOCK

96.1 Acres

300   0   300 Feet

Scale 1:7,000

Contour Interval - 3 Feet
(Bathymetry - Hunter, 2000)

Muddy Bk.

Senexet Rd.

Roseland Park Rd.

To Rte. 17

N

18

15

12

9

6

3

Shore Bridge Rd.

W.B. GERRISH 2001

Lake Saltonstall

Town(s): Branford/East Haven

422 acres

Description: Lake Saltonstall is a natural lake within the South Central Coastal Drainage Basin. The water level was raised 20 ft. by the construction of an earthen dam at its southern end. The lake is owned by the South Central Connecticut Regional Water Authority (RWA) and is a primary water supply for the New Haven area. The lake was formed along a fault line which caused it to be long (nearly 3 miles), narrow (less than half a mile at its widest) and deep. Although the lake is less than 2 miles from Long Island Sound, its bottom is 84 ft. below sea level, making it the lowest (inland) spot in the state. *Watershed*: 2,522 acres of mostly agricultural and residential land. The land immediately surrounding the lake is undeveloped woods owned by the RWA. The lake is fed from the north by the Farm River via an aqueduct, by two small streams from the east and by surface runoff. It drains southward into the Farm River. *Shoreline*: Wooded with no residential development. The western shore is steeply sloped; the eastern shore has a more moderate slope. *Depth*: Max 113 ft., Mean 41 ft. *Transparency*: Fair; 7 ft. in summer. *Productivity*: Not available. *Bottom type*: Sand, gravel, rubble, boulders and mud. *Stratification*: Occurs with a thermocline forming between 16 and 32 ft. Late summer oxygen levels remain good (greater than 5 ppm) to a depth of 19 ft. and decline to less than 3 ppm in deeper water. *Vegetation*: A moderate to dense ring of submergent vegetation is present along much of the northern and eastern shore up to depths of 12 ft. The dominant species are Eurasian water-milfoil, coontail and pondweeds. Much of the western shore drops off rapidly and aquatic plants are scarce.

Access: Access is by permit only, issued by the RWA. There is a paved launch, but only rowboats rented on-site may be used. Other facilities at the launch area include a fishing pier with disabled access, boat and electric motor rentals and chemical toilets (seasonal). There are three parking areas on the west side of Hosley Ave., two near the launch and one near the northern end of the lake. *Directions*: Exit 51 off I-95, Frontage Rd. east (Rte. 1) for 1.5 miles, left (north) on Hosley Ave. for 1.5 miles, access road is on left. *Shore*: All but the southern end of the lake is open to fishing. Contact the RWA (203-562-4020) for permit information.

Fish: Lake Saltonstall is stocked each spring by the State and the RWA with 3,000 catchable size **brown** and **rainbow trout**. Holdover brown trout production is inconsistent because of marginal trout habitat. Some years holdovers are common; others almost nonexistent. **Walleye:** Annual fingerling (5") walleye stockings were initiated by the RWA in the fall of 1995. The fish are growing and surviving well and the population was still expanding at time of writing. Walleye in the 16-22" size range were common at the time of writing. Overall, **largemouth bass** densities are relatively low, but numbers of bass greater than 18" may be the highest in the state. **Yellow perch** and **white perch** densities are average to sizes of 11". Smaller **black crappie** are uncommon, but catchable size (greater than 9") crappies are average. **Sunfish** (mostly bluegill, some pumpkinseed, rarely redbreast) densities are average, but fish over 7" are uncommon. **American eels** are abundant to 18". Common carp and white suckers are common. An abundant alewife forage base is supplemented by lower densities of golden shiners and banded killifish. Other fish species present at low densities are brown bullhead, redfin pickerel and fathead minnows.

Fishing: Should be good for trophy bass; fair to good seasonally for stocked trout with a chance for a holdover; fair to good for walleye; and fair for other fish species.

Management: Trophy Bass Management Lake; special length and creel limits on bass. Statewide regulations apply for all other species (see current *Connecticut Anglers' Guide*). ▼

Lake Saltonstall
Fish Species and Abundance

	ALL SIZES	BIG FISH	GROWTH
Gamefish			
Largemouth bass	C	C	> Avg
Brown trout	C	U	
Rainbow trout	C		
Walleye	C	C	> Avg
Panfish			
Black crappie	C	C	Fast
White perch	C	U	< Slow
Yellow perch	C	U	< Avg
Sunfish			
Bluegill	C	U	Avg
Pumpkinseed	U	R	
Redbreast	R	R	Slow
Other			
Redfin pickerel	R		
Common carp	C		
Golden shiner	C		Avg
Banded killifish	U		
Alewife	A		Avg
White sucker	C		
American eel	A		

A=Abundant, C=Common, U=Uncommon, R=Rare

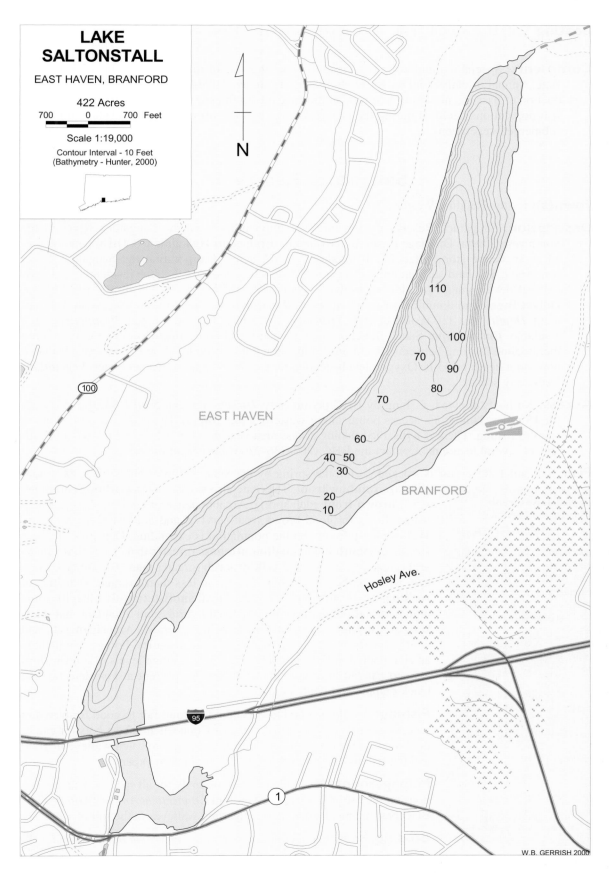

LAKE
SALTONSTALL

EAST HAVEN, BRANFORD

422 Acres

700   0   700   Feet

Scale 1:19,000

Contour Interval - 10 Feet
(Bathymetry - Hunter, 2000)

N

100

EAST HAVEN

110

100

70

90

80

70

60

40 50

30

20

10

BRANFORD

Hosley Ave.

95

1

W.B. GERRISH 2000

Boating: Only boats rented on-site allowed. Gas motors prohibited (see current *Connecticut Boater's Guide*).

Comments: Special regulations have helped to make this one of the best trophy bass lakes in the state. Annual or daily (sold on-site) fishing permits are available from the RWA. Year-class production of bass has always been erratic in this lake due to fluctuating water levels. Bass and sunfish populations declined during the late 1990s due to a die-off of the once substantial beds of submerged vegetation.

Saugatuck Reservoir

Town(s): Easton/Redding/Weston   **827 acres**

Description: Saugatuck Reservoir is an artificial impoundment on the Saugatuck River in the Southwest Coastal Drainage Basin. It is owned by Bridgeport Hydraulic Co. (BHC) and operated as an active storage facility. *Watershed:* 22,076 acres incorporating the Saugatuck River watershed. The land surrounding the reservoir is mostly wooded with some residential and agricultural development. In addition to the Saugatuck River, the lake is fed by the Little River, Gilbert Brook and a number of small streams. *Shoreline:* Wooded with no residential development. *Depth:* Max 110 ft., Mean 45 ft. *Transparency:* Clear; 12 ft. in summer. *Productivity:* Not available. *Bottom type:* Sand, gravel, cobble, boulders and mud. *Stratification:* Occurs with a thermocline forming between 19 and 36 ft. Late summer oxygen levels are good (greater than 6 ppm) to a depth of 33 ft. Oxygen levels decline to less than 4 ppm in deeper water. *Vegetation:* Extremely scarce.

Access: No boats allowed. Fishing by BHC permit only. *Directions:* Exit 5 off I-84, Rte. 53 south for 15 miles. Numerous access points along western shore. *Shore:* The entire western shore is open to fishing. There is a disabled fishing access area near the dam. Chemical toilets are available at several locations. Contact the BHC (203-336-7763) for permit information.

Fish: Saugatuck Reservoir is stocked during the spring by the State and the BHC with 3,000 catchable size **rainbow trout**. The State also stocks 7,000 yearling Seeforellen strain **brown trout** each spring. An abundance of cool, well-oxygenated water allows for good brown trout survival and holdovers are common. **Walleye** are present and the population is expanding. Densities of larger size **largemouth bass**, **smallmouth bass** (greater than 12"), **chain pickerel** (greater than 15") and **yellow perch** (greater than 10") are near average, with numbers of smaller fish being less than average. Densities of **rock bass** to 9" are above average. Small **sunfish** (mostly bluegill, some redbreast and pumpkinseed, occasional hybrids) are abundant, but numbers of catchable size sunfish are below average. **American eels** and white suckers are present at below average densities. Forage fish include an abundant alewife population and below average levels of golden shiners and banded killifish. Other fish species present at low densities are black crappie and white perch.

Saugatuck Reservoir Fish Species and Abundance	ALL SIZES	BIG FISH	GROWTH
Gamefish			
Largemouth bass	C	C	Avg
Smallmouth bass	C	C	Avg
Brown trout	C	C	Fast
Rainbow trout	C	R	
Chain pickerel	C	C	> Avg
Walleye	(see Management)		
Panfish			
Black crappie	U	U	Fast
White perch	U	U	> Avg
Yellow perch	C	C	> Avg
Sunfish			
Bluegill	A	C	< Avg
Pumpkinseed	C	U	> Avg
Redbreast	A	U	Slow
Rock bass	A	C	Avg
Other			
Golden shiner	U		Slow
Banded killifish	U		
Alewife	A		Slow
White sucker	C		
American eel	U		

A=Abundant, C=Common, U=Uncommon, R=Rare

Fishing: Should be good to excellent for trout; fair to good for bass and rock bass; and fair for sunfish. One of Connecticut's best bets for catching holdover brown trout. Anglers should begin to catch walleye in 2000 and the fishing should improve as the population expands.

Management: Statewide regulations apply for all species, with restrictions on the use of live bait (see current *Connecticut Anglers' Guide*). The BHC began annual stocking of fingerling walleyes in the fall of 1998.

Boating: Boats are prohibited (see current *Connecticut Boater's Guide*). ▼

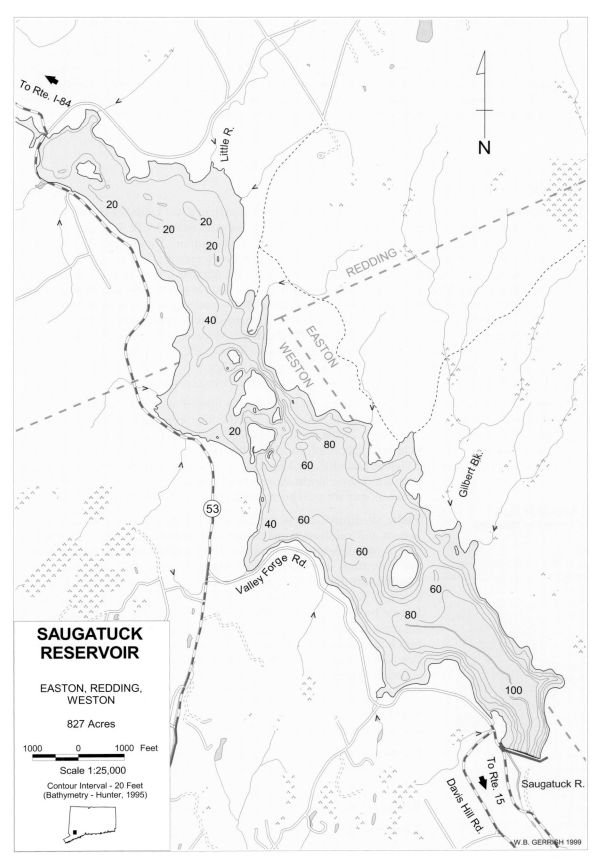

To Rte. I-84

Little R.

20

20 20

20

20

40

REDDING

EASTON
WESTON

20

80

60

40 60

60

Gilbert Bk.

60

80 60

53

Valley Forge Rd.

100

To Rte. 15

Davis Hill Rd.

Saugatuck R.

N

SAUGATUCK
RESERVOIR

EASTON, REDDING,
WESTON

827 Acres

1000   0   1000 Feet

Scale 1:25,000

Contour Interval - 20 Feet
(Bathymetry - Hunter, 1995)

W.B. GERRISH 1999

Comments: Saugatuck Reservoir once had a rare and thriving holdover rainbow trout population, which was virtually eliminated after illegally introduced alewives (circa 1990) became established. Bass recruitment has also declined since the alewife introduction. One of the best holdover brown trout (which feed heavily on alewives) fisheries in the state has now taken place of the rainbows. Saugatuck Reservoir has an excellent potential of developing a quality walleye fishery. Although anglers are restricted to shore fishing, the steeply sloping shoreline provides ready access to deeper water and the trout and walleye that reside there.

Shenipsit Lake

Town(s): Ellington/Tolland/Vernon   **532 acres**

Description: Shenipsit Lake is a natural lake within the Connecticut River Drainage Basin. A dam was built on the outlet to supply water for drinking and to run the mills of Rockville. It is currently owned by the Connecticut Water Co. and is a primary distribution reservoir. *Watershed*: 10,441 acres of mostly woods interspersed with low-density residential development and a moderate amount of agricultural land. The lake is fed by Charter Brook from the northeast, West Brook from the southeast, Sucker Brook from the east and three small brooks. It drains southwest into Papermill Pond and is the source of the Hockanum River. *Shoreline*: Mostly undeveloped woodland owned by the water company. There are a few homes along the northern shore. *Depth*: Max 68 ft., Mean 30 ft. *Transparency*: Clear; 11-13 ft. in summer. *Productivity*: Moderate (mesotrophic). *Bottom type*: Sand, gravel, boulders, ledge and mud. *Stratification*: Occurs with a thermocline forming between 16 and 36 ft. Late summer oxygen levels are marginal (5 ppm) to a depth of 18 ft. Oxygen then declines to less than 3 ppm in deeper water. *Vegetation*: Extremely scarce.

Access: There is no state-owned access to the lake; however, a limited number of rowboats are available to the public from the Connecticut Water Co., and the Shenipsit Lake Association operates a boat storage facility for members on the northern shore. Contact the Lake Association (P.O. Box 1475, Vernon, CT) for additional access information. *Directions*: From Rte. 74, Rte. 83 north for 2.3 miles, right (east) on Snipsic Lake Rd. for 1.6 miles, access is on right. *Shore*: Fishing is permitted along the north shore from Ellington Rd./Snipsic Lake Rd. These access points are well posted and permits are not required.

Fish: Shenipsit Lake is stocked each spring with 1,000 catchable size **brown** and **rainbow trout**. Some trout holdover despite marginal summer oxygen levels in deeper water. **Largemouth bass** are present at average densities, but larger bass (greater than 16") are uncommon. **Smallmouth bass** are apparently stockpiled. They are abundant in smaller sizes, but are uncommon over 14". **Chain pickerel**, **yellow perch**, **brown bullhead** and **sunfish** (mostly bluegill, occasional pumpkinseed) are present at less than average densities. Small **black crappie** and **white perch** are uncommon, but 9-11" fish occur at higher than average densities. **Rock bass** are present at average densities. White suckers are very abundant. Other fish species present at low densities are golden shiner, spottail shiner, banded killifish and American eel.

Fishing: Should be fair to good for crappie and white perch; and fair for trout (with a chance for a holdover), bass and rock bass.

Management: Taking smelt from tributary streams is prohibited. Statewide regulations apply for all other species. (see current *Connecticut Anglers' Guide*).

Boating: Water company regulations apply.

Comments: Open fishing season is determined by a recreational ▼

Shenipsit Lake
Fish Species and Abundance

	ALL SIZES	BIG FISH	GROWTH
Gamefish			
Largemouth bass	A	U	Avg
Smallmouth bass	A	U	Slow
Brown trout	C	U	
Rainbow trout	C		
Chain pickerel	U	U	> Avg
Panfish			
Black crappie	C	C	Avg
White perch	C	C	Avg
Yellow perch	U	U	Avg
Brown bullhead	U	U	
Sunfish			
Bluegill	C	U	Avg
Pumpkinseed	U	R	> Avg
Rock bass	C	U	Avg
Other			
Golden shiner	C		
Spottail shiner	U		
Banded killifish	U		
White sucker	A		
American eel	U		

A=Abundant, C=Common, U=Uncommon, R=Rare

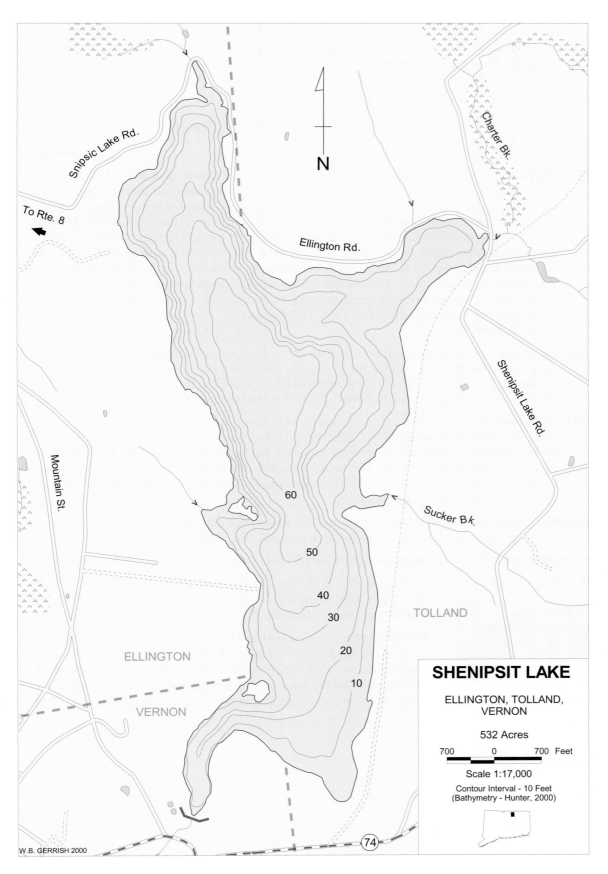

SHENIPSIT LAKE

ELLINGTON, TOLLAND,
VERNON

532 Acres

700   0   700   Feet

Scale 1:17,000

Contour Interval - 10 Feet
(Bathymetry - Hunter, 2000)

W.B. GERRISH 2000

permit issued to the Connecticut Water Co. by the Connecticut Department of Public Health. Season is sunrise to sunset from opening day until October 31. Shenipsit used to contain smelt. Although the population declined, some may still be present. State Record smallmouth bass (7 lb. 12 oz., 1980) and rock bass (1 lb. 3 oz., 1995) were caught here.

Silver Lake (Peat Works Pond)

Town(s): Berlin/Meriden   **146 acres**

Description: Silver Lake is an artificial impoundment in the Connecticut River Drainage Basin. *Watershed*: 1,279 acres of mostly undeveloped woods and wetland to the west and predominantly industrial and residential land to the east. The lake is fed by Beaver Pond and a small stream. It drains north into Belcher Brook, a tributary of the Mattabesset River. *Shoreline*: Partially wooded with residential development clustered on the northern and southern shores. An active railroad line abuts the western shore and there is an industrial park located on the southern shore. *Depth*: Max 16 ft., Mean 5 ft. *Transparency*: Turbid; 3-5 ft. in summer. *Productivity*: Very high (highly eutrophic). *Bottom type*: Not available. *Stratification*: Does not occur due to limited depth. *Vegetation*: Very dense submergent coverage of coontail, Eurasian water-milfoil and waterweed extends to depths of 12 ft. Yellow pond-lily is common in the coves and along some shoreline areas.

Access: A state-owned boat launch is located on the western shore. Facilities at the launch include a ramp with concrete slabs, parking for 15 cars and chemical toilets (seasonal). *Directions*: Exit 21 off Rte. 9, Rte. 15 south for 3 miles, right (west) on Toll Gate Rd., first left (west) on Norton Lane, access is 0.5 miles on left. *Shore*: Limited to the boat launch area.

Fish: Largemouth bass densities are less than average for all sizes. **Black crappie** and **sunfish** are badly stockpiled and stunted. Small black crappie (less than 8") and sunfish (less than 6", mostly bluegill, some pumpkinseed) are very abundant, but larger fish are rare. **Brown bullhead** are present at below average levels. The forage base includes moderate densities of golden shiners and low densities of banded killifish. Other fish species present at low densities are chain pickerel, yellow perch and American eel.

Fishing: Should be generally fair for bass and fair to poor for other fish species. Early spring bass fishing is reportedly good. Dense vegetation makes fishing difficult during summer.

Management: Statewide regulations apply for all species (see current *Connecticut Anglers' Guide*).

Boating: A speed limit of 8 mph is in effect at all times except between June 15 and the first Sunday after Labor Day when water-skiing is permitted between 11 a.m. and 6 p.m. (see current *Connecticut Boater's Guide*).

Comments: The Connecticut Department of Public Health has issued a consumption advisory for some fish species due to mercury contamination (see current *Connecticut Anglers' Guide* for details). At the time of writing, parts of the lake were being dredged to increase water depth. Hence, some areas may be deeper than indicated on the map.

Silver Lake
Fish Species and Abundance

	ALL SIZES	BIG FISH	GROWTH
Gamefish			
Largemouth bass	C	U	< Avg
Chain pickerel	U	R	Avg
Panfish			
Black crappie	A	R	Slow
Yellow perch	U	R	Avg
Brown bullhead	C	C	
Sunfish			
Bluegill	A	R	< Slow
Pumpkinseed	C	R	
Other			
Golden shiner	C		Avg
Banded killifish	R		
American eel	U		

A=Abundant, C=Common, U=Uncommon, R=Rare

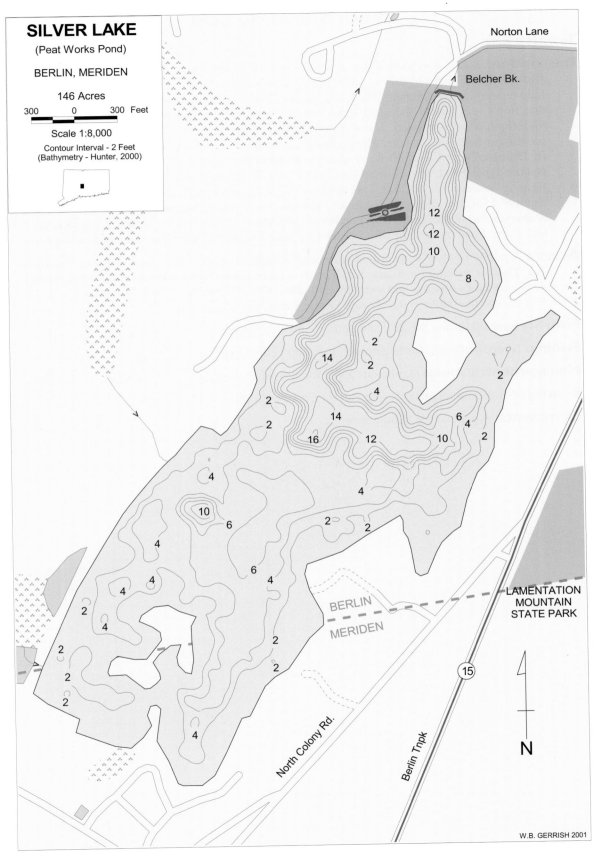

SILVER LAKE

(Peat Works Pond)

BERLIN, MERIDEN

146 Acres

300   0   300 Feet

Scale 1:8,000

Contour Interval - 2 Feet
(Bathymetry - Hunter, 2000)

Norton Lane

Belcher Bk.

12
12
10
8

2
14
2
2
4
6
2
2
14
2
4
2
16
12
10
2
4
4
2
2
4
10
6
4
6
4
4
4
2
4
2
2
2
2
4

BERLIN

MERIDEN

LAMENTATION
MOUNTAIN
STATE PARK

15

N

North Colony Rd.

Berlin Tnpk.

W.B. GERRISH 2001

South Spectacle Lake

Town(s): Kent

85.4 acres

Description: South Spectacle Lake is a natural lake in the Housatonic River Drainage Basin. *Watershed*: 349 acres of mostly undeveloped woods and wetland with some agricultural and very little residential development. The lake is mainly spring-fed and drains north into a wetland stream that flows into North Spectacle Lake, which eventually flows into the West Aspetuck River. *Shoreline*: Mostly wooded. There are only a few residences, a summer camp (Camp Kent) and some farm fields on the lake. The northwestern shore is marshland. *Depth*: Max 41 ft., Mean 19 ft. *Transparency*: Clear; 13 ft. in summer. *Productivity*: Low to moderate (early mesotrophic). *Bottom type*: Sand, gravel, mud and organic muck. *Stratification*: Occurs with a thermocline forming between 10 and 26 ft. Late summer oxygen levels remain good (greater than 5 ppm) to a depth of 13 ft. and decline to less than 1 ppm in deeper water. *Vegetation*: Eurasian water-milfoil is abundant to depths of 8-10 ft. Pondweeds, bladderwort and water-nymph are common in shallow water. Floating mats of white water-lily, yellow pond-lily and water-shield are also present.

Access: A public right-of-way, provided through an easement on private land, is located along Rte. 341. There is parking for 6 cars. Small boats must be carried over 400 yds. from the parking area on a sometimes obscure and swampy trail. *Directions*: From Rte. 7 and 341, take Rte. 341 east 3.8 miles to the public right-of-way. *Shore*: Limited to access area.

Fish: Not sampled during the lake and pond electrofishing survey.

Fishing: Is reportedly fair for largemouth bass and yellow perch.

Management: Statewide regulations apply for all species (see current *Connecticut Anglers' Guide*).

Boating: No special regulations (see current *Connecticut Boater's Guide*).

Comments: A popular ice fishing spot.

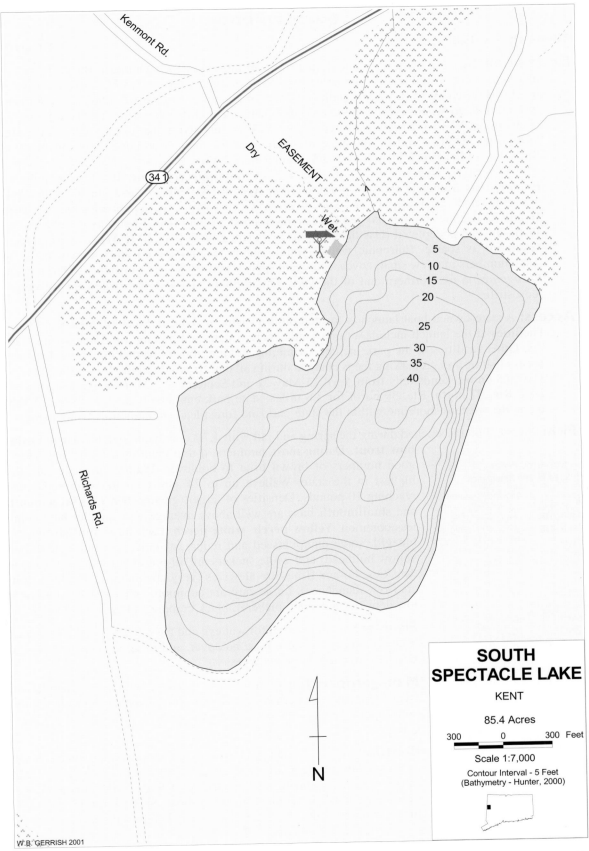

Kenmont Rd.

Dry

EASEMENT

34 1

Wet

5
10
15
20

25

30
35
40

Richards Rd.

N

**SOUTH
SPECTACLE LAKE**

KENT

85.4 Acres

300   0   300   Feet

Scale 1:7,000

Contour Interval - 5 Feet
(Bathymetry - Hunter, 2000)

W.B. GERRISH 2001

Squantz Pond

Town(s): New Fairfield/Sherman

270 acres

Description: Squantz Pond is a natural lake in the Housatonic River Drainage Basin. It is connected to Candlewood Lake by underwater culverts through a causeway (Rte. 39) and its water level was raised by 15 ft. when Candlewood was impounded. *Watershed:* 3,662 acres of mostly undeveloped woods with a moderate level of residential development. The lake is fed by Glen Brook, Worden Brook and three other small streams and drains into Candlewood Lake. *Shoreline:* Mostly wooded. The majority of the western shore is within either Squantz Pond State Park or Pootatuck State Forest and is undeveloped; the eastern shore is heavily developed with residences. *Depth:* Max 45 ft., Mean 27 ft. *Transparency:* Fair; 10-11 ft. in summer. *Productivity:* Moderate (mesotrophic). *Bottom type:* Rock, ledge, coarse gravel in the shallows, mud and silt in deep waters. *Stratification:* Occurs with a thermocline forming between 16 and 32 ft. Late summer oxygen levels remain good (greater than 5 ppm) to a depth of only 13 ft. Oxygen is depleted (less than 3 ppm) in waters greater than 20 ft. *Vegetation:* Aquatic vegetation is sparse. Eutrophic water-nymph, ribbon-leaf pondweed and coontail occur in small numbers in a few small coves. Emergent species consist of several patches of cat-tail and *Phragmites* at the northern end of the lake. The northern end also has large areas of purple loosestrife.

Access: A state-owned boat launch is located on the southern shore in Squantz Pond State Park. Facilities at the launch include a ramp with concrete slabs and parking for 25 cars with trailers. Other facilities at the park include swimming, hiking, toilets, picnicking and a disabled-access fishing area. A parking fee is charged during all days from Memorial Day through Labor Day and on weekends only from April 15-May 21 and September 9-24. *Directions:* Exit 6 off I-84, Rte. 37 north, Rte. 39 north for 3.8 miles, state park entrance is on left. *Shore:* A trail along the western shoreline within the state park and forest leads to numerous fishing spots.

Fish: Squantz Pond is stocked during the spring and fall with 4,700 catchable size **brown and rainbow trout**. During most summers, a thin band of trout habitat allows good numbers of brown trout to holdover. **Walleye** densities are the highest in the state. Walleye up to 24" are common with some fish reaching 10 pounds. Densities of larger (greater than 12") **largemouth** and **smallmouth bass** are well above average with smaller bass being less common. **Yellow perch**, **white perch**, **rock bass**, **sunfish** (mostly bluegill, some pumpkinseed and redbreast) **catfish** (white catfish and yellow bullhead) and white suckers are all present at less than average densities. Forage fishes are alewives (very abundant) and golden shiners (low abundance). Large carp are common. Other species present at low densities are chain pickerel, black crappie and brown bullhead.

Fishing: Should be good for walleye and bass, fair to good for stocked trout with a good chance for a holdover, and fair for other fish species. Best lake to catch large walleyes.

Management: Trophy Trout Lake managed with special length and creel limits and an alternate-season closure schedule. Statewide regulations apply for all other species (see current *Connecticut Anglers' Guide*).

Boating: Motors greater than 7½ hp prohibited at state launch. Note: At most lakes, tilting a larger engine up and/or removing the prop could satisfy this requirement. At Squantz Pond State Park, engines larger than 7½ hp must be removed from the boat. Speed limit 45 mph daytime, 25 mph ½ hr. after sunset to ½ hr. before sunrise (see current *Connecticut Boater's Guide*).▼

Squantz Pond
Fish Species and Abundance

	ALL SIZES	BIG FISH	GROWTH
Gamefish			
Largemouth bass	C	C	Avg
Smallmouth bass	C	C	Avg
Brown trout	C	U	
Rainbow trout	C		
Chain pickerel	U	U	
Walleye	C	C	Fast
White catfish	U	U	
Panfish			
White perch	C	C	< Avg
Yellow perch	C	U	< Slow
Brown bullhead	R	R	
Yellow bullhead	U	R	
Sunfish			
Bluegill	C	U	Slow
Pumpkinseed	C	U	Slow
Redbreast	U	R	Slow
Rock bass	C	U	Slow
Other			
Tessellated darter	R		
Common carp	C		
Golden shiner	U		Avg
Alewife	A		< Avg
White sucker	C		

A=Abundant, C=Common, U=Uncommon, R=Rare

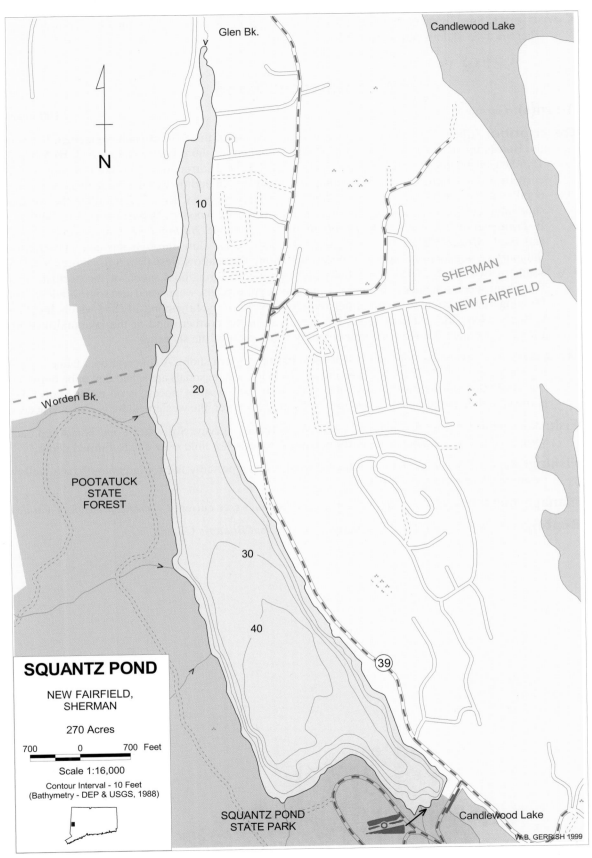

Glen Bk.

Candlewood Lake

10

SHERMAN

NEW FAIRFIELD

Worden Bk.

20

POOTATUCK
STATE
FOREST

30

40

39

SQUANTZ POND

NEW FAIRFIELD,
SHERMAN

270 Acres

700   0   700   Feet

Scale 1:16,000

Contour Interval - 10 Feet
(Bathymetry - DEP & USGS, 1988)

SQUANTZ POND
STATE PARK

Candlewood Lake

W.B. GERRISH 1999

Comments: Small boaters should be aware that lake residents may use unlimited-horsepower boats. There is a ski slalom course on the lake.

Stillwater Pond

Town(s): Torrington

100 acres

Description: Stillwater Pond is an artificial impoundment of the West Branch Naugatuck River in the Housatonic River Drainage Basin. The pond and entire shoreline is state-owned. *Watershed:* 15,608 acres encompassing the Naugatuck River. The land surrounding the lake is mostly wooded with some agricultural and residential development. In addition to the Naugatuck River, the pond is fed by two small streams. *Shoreline:* Mostly wooded. Rte. 272 parallels the western shore and the land between the lake and the road is mostly wooded. *Depth:* Max 27 ft., Mean 13 ft. *Transparency:* Not available. *Productivity:* Not available. *Bottom type:* Gravel, rubble, rocks and mud. *Stratification:* Does not occur due to riverine flow through the lake. *Vegetation:* Submergent vegetation is sparse to occasional along the shallow (less than 6 ft.) shoreline in the southern two thirds of the water body and very dense throughout much of the northern end. Dominant species include a diverse assemblage of pondweeds, waterweed and some bladderwort. Floating mats of white water-lily (including the pink form), yellow pond-lily and water-shield are scattered along the southern shore, but are dense in the northern end of the lake and near the islands. Emergent bur-reed is common along some areas of the shoreline.

Access: A state-owned car-top launch is located on the western shore. A concrete boat launch, parking for 8 cars, a disabled fishing pier and chemical toilets (seasonal) are scheduled to be built during 2002. *Directions:* From Rte. 4, Rte. 272 north for 1.3 miles, access is on right. *Shore:* The entire shoreline is state-owned and open to fishing; however, the western shore is easier to access.

Fish: Not sampled during the lake and pond electrofishing survey. Stillwater Pond is stocked each spring with 500 catchable size **rainbow trout**. Trout do not hold over due to limited depth.

Fishing: Should be fair seasonally for stocked trout and is reportedly fair for largemouth bass, yellow perch, black crappie and sunfish.

Management: Statewide regulations apply for all species (see current *Connecticut Anglers' Guide*).

Boating: Gas motors prohibited (see current *Connecticut Boater's Guide*).

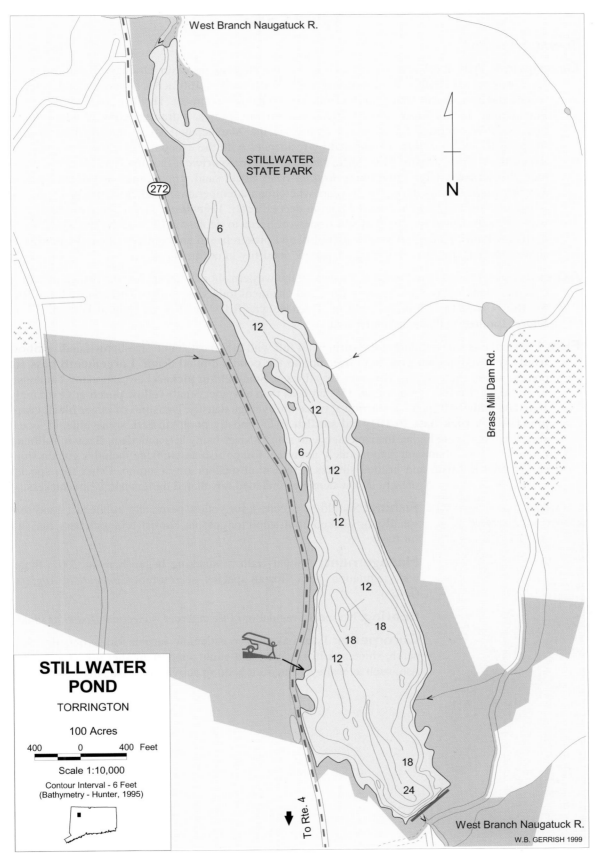

West Branch Naugatuck R.

STILLWATER
STATE PARK

272

6

12

12

6

12

12

12

18

18

12

18

24

N

Brass Mill Dam Rd.

West Branch Naugatuck R.

W.B. GERRISH 1999

To Rte. 4

STILLWATER POND

TORRINGTON

100 Acres

400   0   400 Feet

Scale 1:10,000

Contour Interval - 6 Feet
(Bathymetry - Hunter, 1995)

Tyler Lake

Town(s): Goshen

187 acres

Description: Tyler Lake is a natural lake within the Housatonic River Drainage Basin. Its water level was raised slightly by a masonry dam. *Watershed*: 4,166 acres of mostly undeveloped woods and agricultural land with moderate residential development. The lake is fed by West Side Pond Brook, Sucker Brook, a small stream and bottom springs. It drains southward into a stream that feeds Woodbridge Lake, which drains via the Marshepaug River into the East Branch Shepaug River. *Shoreline*: Dominated by residences with the exception of a wooded marsh on the northern shore. *Depth*: Max 23 ft., Mean 13 ft. *Transparency*: Fair to clear; 7-11 ft. in summer. *Productivity*: High (eutrophic). *Bottom type*: Rock, sand, gravel, mud and organic muck. *Stratification*: Occurs during some years whereupon a temperature gradient forms at 13 ft. and oxygen levels decline to less than 2 ppm in deeper water. *Vegetation*: Dense areas of pondweed, water-nymph, tapegrass, coontail and stonewort occur to depths of 12 ft. along the western and northern shores. Patches of yellow pond-lily and pickerelweed are common along the northwest shore and there are extensive areas of yellow pond-lily in northern coves.

Access: A state-owned boat launch is located on the western shore. Facilities at the launch include a concrete plank ramp, parking for 5 cars, and chemical toilets (seasonal). *Directions*: From Rte. 63, Rte. 4 west for 1.5 miles, right on Tyler Heights Rd., launch is on right at bottom of hill. *Shore*: Limited to the boat launch area.

Fish: Tyler Lake is stocked during the spring and fall with 5,500 catchable size **brown and rainbow trout**. Very few brown trout hold over due to the pond's limited depth. **Largemouth bass** are present at less than average densities for all sizes. Small **chain pickerel** are abundant, but densities of legal size fish (greater than 15") are less than average. Small **yellow perch** are extremely abundant with 9-10" perch occurring at twice the average density. Densities of larger **black crappie** (10-13"), **rock bass** (6-10") and **sunfish** (6-7", mostly pumpkinseed, some bluegill, occasional redbreast) are higher than average with smaller sizes being less abundant. **Brown bullhead** from 11-13" are abundant. A moderately abundant forage fish assemblage includes golden shiners, banded killifish, and bridled shiners. Creek chubsuckers are common. Other fish species present at low densities included tessellated darters and white suckers.

Tyler Lake
Fish Species and Abundance

	ALL SIZES	BIG FISH	GROWTH
Gamefish			
Largemouth bass	C	C	Avg
Brown trout	C	R	
Rainbow trout	C		
Chain pickerel	A	C	< Slow
Panfish			
Black crappie	C	C	> Avg
Yellow perch	A	A	Avg
Brown bullhead	A	A	
Sunfish			
Bluegill	C	U	Fast
Pumpkinseed	C	C	> Avg
Redbreast	U	R	Avg
Rock bass	C	C	> Avg
Other			
Tessellated darter	R		
Bridled shiner	C		
Golden shiner	C		> Avg
Banded killifish	R		
Creek chubsucker	C		
White sucker	R		

A=Abundant, C=Common, U=Uncommon, R=Rare

Fishing: Should be excellent for yellow perch and bullheads, good seasonally for stocked trout; good for crappie, sunfish and rock bass; and fair for bass.

Management: Annual walleye stocking began here in 2001. Statewide regulations apply for all species (see current *Connecticut Anglers' Guide*).

Boating: No special regulations (see current *Connecticut Boater's Guide*).

Comments: Tyler Lake has considerable surplus forage (small yellow perch, shiners, killifish, etc.) and could support another predatory gamefish, such as walleye. Pleasure boating activity is seasonally heavy.

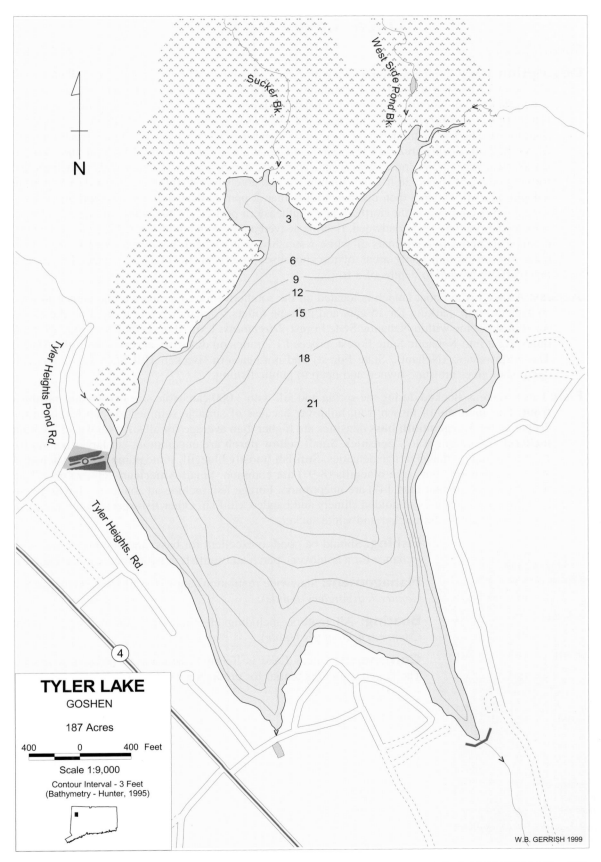

West Side Pond Bk.

Sucker Bk.

3

6

9

12

15

18

21

Tyler Heights Pond Rd.

Tyler Heights. Rd.

4

TYLER LAKE

GOSHEN

187 Acres

400   0   400 Feet

Scale 1:9,000

Contour Interval - 3 Feet
(Bathymetry - Hunter, 1995)

W.B. GERRISH 1999

N

Uncas Lake (Hog Pond)

Town(s): Lyme

68.9 acres

Description: Uncas Pond is a natural lake within the Connecticut River Drainage Basin. **Watershed:** 977 acres of mostly undeveloped woodland. The pond is fed by several small brooks, one of which flows from Norwich Pond, and a marsh. It drains west into Falls Brook, which flows into Hamburg Cove. **Shoreline:** The northern and northeastern shorelines are wooded, undeveloped state forest. There are a moderate number of residences along the southern shore. **Depth:** Max 39 ft., Mean 24 ft. **Transparency:** Clear; 13 ft. in late summer. **Productivity:** Moderate (mesotrophic). **Bottom type:** Sand, mud, gravel and boulders. **Stratification:** Occurs with a thermocline forming between 16 and 26 ft. Late summer oxygen levels remain marginal to good (5-8 ppm) to a depth of 19 ft. Oxygen then declines to less than 2 ppm in deeper water. **Vegetation:** Aquatic vegetation is common in the northern and southeastern portions of the pond. Dominant submergent species include fern pondweed, floating-leaved pondweed, common bladderwort and water-nymph. Scattered floating mats of white water-lily, water-shield, pondweeds and some yellow pond-lily are present along areas of the shoreline. Emergent pickerelweed, water lobelia and pipewort are present to depths of 3 ft.

Access: A state-owned boat launch is located on the southern shore. Facilities at the launch include an asphalt ramp, parking for 15 cars and pit-type toilets. A picnic area is located on the northwestern shoreline within Nehantic State Forest. **Directions:** Exit 70 off I-95, Rte. 156 north for 4 miles, right into Nehantic State Forest, proceed 1.2 miles on dirt road, access is on right. **Shore:** The northwestern (Nehantic State Forest) and northeastern (Beckett Hill State Park, undeveloped) shorelines are state-owned and open to public fishing.

Fish: Uncas Lake is stocked during the spring and fall with 3,000 catchable size **brown** and **rainbow trout**. Fair numbers of brown trout holdover because of suitable summer oxygen levels in the deeper water. **Largemouth bass** densities are higher than average for all sizes above 12". **Chain pickerel** are present at low densities. Small **yellow perch** are uncommon, but larger perch (10-12") are at higher than average densities. **Sunfish** (mostly bluegill, some pumpkinseed) densities are below average, but large bluegills (8-9") are common. Small **American eels** are abundant, but larger eels (greater than 14") are uncommon. Forage fish include an abundant alewife population and low densities of golden shiners and banded killifish. Other fish species present at low densities are creek chubsucker and white sucker.

Fishing: Should be good to excellent for bass; and good for trout (with a chance for a holdover), perch and sunfish. A good spot to catch big bass.

Management: Statewide regulations apply for all species (see current *Connecticut Anglers' Guide*).

Boating: All motors, including electric, are prohibited (see current *Connecticut Boater's Guide*).

Comments: Uncas Lake is lightly fished due to motor restrictions. The lake has good potential for producing trophy bass.

Uncas Lake Fish Species and Abundance	ALL SIZES	BIG FISH	GROWTH
Gamefish			
Largemouth bass	C	C	Avg
Brown trout	C	U	
Rainbow trout	C		
Chain pickerel	U	U	Avg
Panfish			
Yellow perch	C	C	> Fast
Sunfish			
Bluegill	C	C	Avg
Pumpkinseed	C	C	Avg
Other			
Golden shiner	U		
Banded killifish	U		
Alewife	A		
Creek chubsucker	U		
White sucker	U		
American eel	A		

A=Abundant, C=Common, U=Uncommon, R=Rare

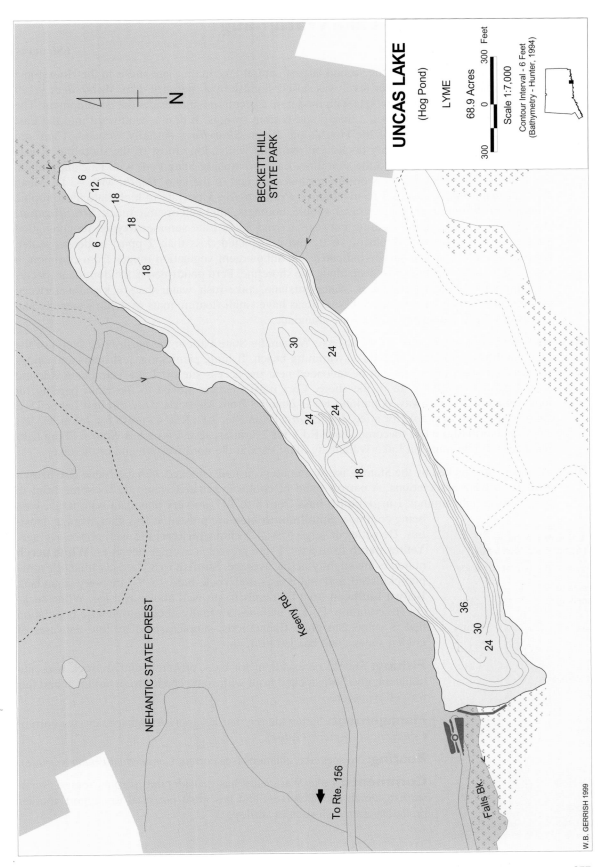

UNCAS LAKE
(Hog Pond)

LYME

68.9 Acres

Scale 1:7,000
Contour Interval - 6 Feet
(Bathymetry - Hunter, 1994)

300   0   300   Feet

N

BECKETT HILL
STATE PARK

NEHANTIC STATE FOREST

Keeny Rd.

To Rte. 156

Falls Bk.

W.B. GERRISH 1999

Lake Waramaug

Town(s): Kent/Warren/Washington

656 acres

Description: Lake Waramaug is the second largest natural lake in the state and is in the Housatonic River Drainage Basin. Its water level was raised slightly by a masonry dam. *Watershed:* 9,199 acres of mostly undeveloped woods with moderate agricultural and residential development. The lake is fed by five small brooks, a marsh and bottom springs. It drains southward into the East Aspetuck River, a tributary of the Housatonic River. *Shoreline:* Partially wooded. There are numerous residences with many docks and retaining walls along most of the shoreline. Roads encircle the entire lake close to the shoreline. Lake Waramaug State Park with its campground, beach and car-top boat access is on the northwestern end of the lake. *Depth:* Max 43 ft., Mean 25 ft. *Transparency:* Fair; 6-7 ft. in summer. *Productivity:* Moderate to high (late mesotrophic –eutrophic). *Bottom type:* Sand, gravel, rubble, boulders, mud and organic muck. *Stratification:* Occurs with a thermocline forming between 13 and 33 ft. Late summer oxygen remains good (greater than 5 ppm) to a depth of 16 ft. and is depleted (less than 2 ppm) in deeper water. *Vegetation:* A late season survey indicated that submergent vegetation ranges from common to abundant in areas less than 6 ft. deep along the shoreline. Fern pondweed is the dominant species carpeting most shallow water areas. Water-purslane, spike-rush, water shamrock and waterweed are present in low numbers. Several cove areas have small floating mats of white water-lily and yellow pond-lily. Filamentous algae are abundant.

Access: There is a car-top access area at Lake Waramaug State Park at the northwestern end of the lake. Facilities at the park include a swimming beach, fishing, picnicking, restrooms and camping. Car-top boats or canoes can be unloaded near the access site off Lake Waramaug Rd. and carried approximately 75 ft. to the shore. Cars must then be moved to the main parking lot approximately 200 ft. away. A parking fee is charged from Memorial Day through Labor Day. Canoe rentals are available for a fee. *Directions:* From Rte. 202, Rte. 45 north for 2.0 miles, left (west) on North Shore Rd. (becomes Lake Rd.), for 2.3 miles, access is on left. *Shore:* Shore fishing access can be found in Lake Waramaug State Park at the northwestern end of the lake.

Fish: Although not stocked by the State, Lake Waramaug is usually stocked with catchable size **brown trout** by private associations. A narrow band of cool, oxygenated water allows some trout to holdover through summer. **Largemouth bass** from 8 to 14" are very abundant with larger bass being common. **Smallmouth bass** are present at less than average densities. Densities of large (15-24") **chain pickerel** are well above average. **Yellow perch** from 8 to 11" are present at average densities. **White perch** numbers are slightly below average. **Sunfish** to 8" (mostly bluegill, some pumpkinseed and redbreast) and **rock bass** to 9" are very abundant. **Brown bullhead** (to 14") numbers are well above average. White suckers are common. Forage includes a usually abundant alewife population that is subject to great fluctuations, supplemented by low densities of golden shiners and banded killifish.

Fishing: Should be excellent for bass, pickerel, sunfish, rock bass and bullhead; good for stocked trout with some chance for a holdover and fair for yellow perch.

Management: Statewide regulations apply for all species (see current *Connecticut Anglers' Guide*).

Boating: No special regulations (see current *Connecticut Boater's Guide*).

Comments: Lake Waramaug has considerable surplus forage (small sunfish, perch and alewives) and has great potential to support another predatory gamefish such as walleye.

Lake Waramaug
Fish Species and Abundance

	ALL SIZES	BIG FISH	GROWTH
Gamefish			
Largemouth bass	A	C	Avg
Smallmouth bass	C	C	< Avg
Brown trout	C	U	
Chain pickerel	C	C	> Avg
Panfish			
White perch	U	U	< Avg
Yellow perch	C	C	< Slow
Brown bullhead	C	C	
Sunfish			
Bluegill	A	A	< Avg
Pumpkinseed	A	C	> Avg
Redbreast	C	C	< Avg
Rock bass	A	C	Avg
Other			
Golden shiner	U		Avg
Banded killifish	R		
Alewife	A		Avg
White sucker	C		

A=Abundant, C=Common, U=Uncommon, R=Rare

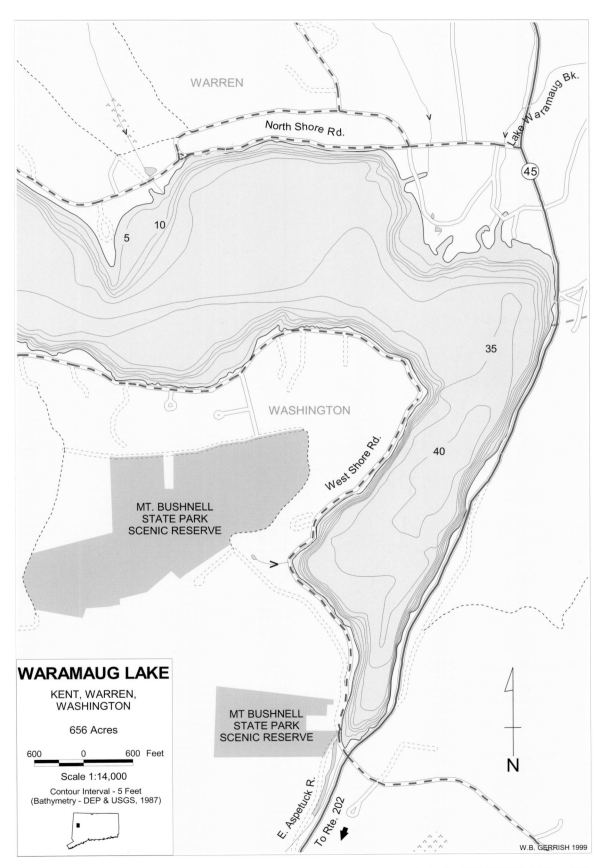

WARREN

North Shore Rd.

Lake Waramaug Bk.

45

10

5

35

WASHINGTON

40

West Shore Rd.

MT. BUSHNELL
STATE PARK
SCENIC RESERVE

MT BUSHNELL
STATE PARK
SCENIC RESERVE

WARAMAUG LAKE

KENT, WARREN,
WASHINGTON

656 Acres

600   0   600   Feet

Scale 1:14,000

Contour Interval - 5 Feet
(Bathymetry - DEP & USGS, 1987)

E. Aspetuck R.

To Rte. 202

N

W.B. GERRISH 1999

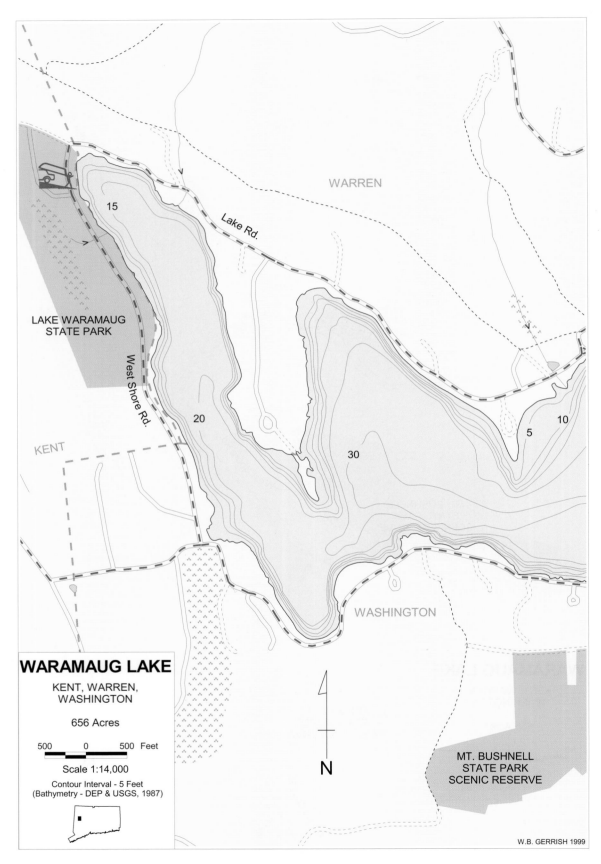

WARREN

Lake Rd.

LAKE WARAMAUG
STATE PARK

West Shore Rd.

15

20

KENT

5

10

30

WASHINGTON

WARAMAUG LAKE

KENT, WARREN,
WASHINGTON

656 Acres

500   0   500 Feet

Scale 1:14,000

Contour Interval - 5 Feet
(Bathymetry - DEP & USGS, 1987)

N

MT. BUSHNELL
STATE PARK
SCENIC RESERVE

W.B. GERRISH 1999

Lake Waramaug

West Branch Reservoir (Hogsback Reservoir)

Town(s): Colebrook/Hartland

201 acres

Description: West Branch Reservoir is an artificial impoundment of the West Branch Farmington River in the Connecticut River Drainage Basin. It is owned by the Metropolitan District Commission (MDC) and is primarily used as a flood-control impoundment. The MDC began operating a small hydroelectric facility at the dam during the early 1990s. *Watershed:* 65,882 acres encompassing the Farmington River drainage. The land surrounding this reservoir is mostly forested with little residential development. West Branch is fed by releases from Colebrook Reservoir and one small brook. *Shoreline:* Most of the shoreline is exposed gravel and boulders bordered by woods with no residential development. *Depth:* Max 95 ft., Mean 45 ft. *Transparency:* Clear; 12 ft. in summer. *Productivity:* Not available. *Bottom type:* Not available. *Stratification:* Usually does not thermally stratify in summer due to the deepwater drawdowns. *Vegetation:* Submergent vegetation is sparse with scattered growths of water-starwort and spike-rush in shallow water.

Access: An MDC car-top access area is located on the southwestern shore. Facilities at the launch include a gravel ramp, parking for 30 cars, and a chemical toilet. Gate to area is closed at night and fishing is prohibited. *Directions:* From Rte. 8, Rte. 20 east for 2.9 miles, left on Hogsback Rd. for 1.4 miles, left on Durst Rd. for 350 yds., access is on right. *Shore:* Anglers can fish from MDC property at the car-top access area and along the entire western shore. MDC maintains a hiking trail for disabled persons along the western shore.

Fish: The State and the MDC stock 5,000 catchable size **brown trout** annually in the spring. Holdover brown trout are common during years when water levels are relatively stable. **Smallmouth bass** are present at average densities. Small **yellow perch** are very abundant, but perch over 8" are uncommon. **Rock bass** are extremely abundant to 6" with larger fish at average densities. White suckers are abundant. Forage fish include abundant rainbow smelt and low densities of golden shiners. Brown bullheads, sunfish (mostly bluegills, rarely pumpkinseed) and tessellated darters are present at low densities.

Fishing: Should be good for rock bass and stocked trout; and fair for smallmouth bass. Fishing should be good during some years for holdover brown trout. Ice fishing for smelt can be good.

Management: Statewide regulations apply for all species. The possession or use as bait of live alewives or other herring species is prohibited (see current *Connecticut Anglers' Guide*). West Branch is being experimentally stocked with kokanee fry (starting in 2000) in an attempt to develop a salmon fishery.

Boating: No special regulations (see current *Connecticut Boater's Guide*).

Comments: Fishing pressure is generally light. West Branch is a flood control reservoir that has experienced great water level fluctuations (as much as 40 ft.). This uncertain environment caused fish populations to be unstable. Water levels have been more stable since the hydropower facility was installed so conditions may improve. Winter anglers should be wary of uncertain ice conditions due to fluctuating water levels.

West Branch Reservoir
Fish Species and Abundance

	ALL SIZES	BIG FISH	GROWTH
Gamefish			
Smallmouth bass	C	C	Avg
Brook trout	U		
Brown trout	C	C	< Avg
Rainbow trout	U		
Panfish			
Yellow perch	A	U	Slow
Brown bullhead	U	R	
Sunfish			
Bluegill	U	R	
Pumpkinseed	R	R	
Rock bass	A	C	Slow
Other			
Tessellated darter	R		
Golden shiner	U		Avg
Rainbow smelt	C		
White sucker	A		

A=Abundant, C=Common, U=Uncommon, R=Rare

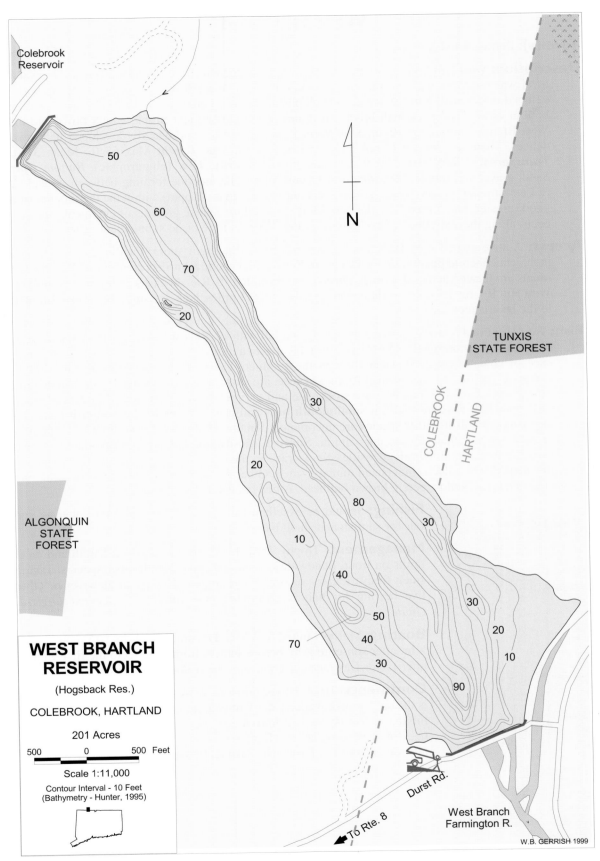

Colebrook
Reservoir

50

60

70

20

30

20

80

30

10

40

50

70

40

30

90

30

20

10

N

TUNXIS
STATE FOREST

COLEBROOK

HARTLAND

ALGONQUIN
STATE
FOREST

**WEST BRANCH
RESERVOIR**

(Hogsback Res.)

COLEBROOK, HARTLAND

201 Acres

500   0   500 Feet

Scale 1:11,000

Contour Interval - 10 Feet
(Bathymetry - Hunter, 1995)

Durst Rd.

To Rte. 8

West Branch
Farmington R.

W.B. GERRISH 1999

West Hill Pond

Town(s): Barkhamsted/New Hartford

261 acres

Description: West Hill Pond is a natural lake in the Connecticut River Drainage Basin. The water level was raised by the construction of a masonry dam. *Watershed*: 790 acres of mostly undeveloped woods with some residential development concentrated near the pond. The lake is fed by bottom springs and two small brooks. It drains north into Morgan Brook, which flows into the West Branch Farmington River. *Shoreline*: Partially wooded and heavily developed with residences. There are several camps and town beaches present. *Depth*: Max 63 ft., Mean 34 ft. *Transparency*: Very clear; 20 ft. in summer. *Productivity*: Low (oligotrophic). *Bottom type*: Sand, gravel and rubble. *Stratification*: Occurs with a thermocline forming between 20 and 32 ft. Late summer oxygen levels remain excellent (greater than 10 ppm) within the thermocline and good (greater than 5 ppm) to a depth of 49 ft. *Vegetation*: Sparse growths of emergent pipewort occur along the shoreline in very shallow water. There is little or no submergent vegetation.

Access: A state-owned boat launch is located on the northeastern shore. Facilities at the launch include a concrete plank ramp, parking for 20 cars, and chemical toilets (seasonal). Parking and toilets are located across the street. *Directions*: From Rte. 8, Rte. 44 east 1 mile, right (south) on West Hill Rd. for 1.5 miles, right on Perkings Rd. for 0.1 miles, launch is on right. *Shore*: Limited to the boat launch area.

Fish: West Hill Pond is stocked during the spring and fall with 17,500 catchable size **brown** and **rainbow trout**. Few brown trout hold over, possibly due to a limited forage base and despite the presence of cold, oxygenated water through the summer. The pond is also stocked with 50,000 **kokanee** fry during the spring. Adult kokanee are common and average 12-14" in length. Smallmouth bass and rock bass are stockpiled and the rock bass are stunted. Densities of small (less than 12") bass are high for **smallmouth bass** and near average for **largemouth bass**, but larger individuals of either species are uncommon. Small **rock bass** are very abundant, but larger ones (greater than 7") are uncommon. **Sunfish** (mostly bluegill, some pumpkinseed, occasional redbreast and hybrids) densities are average in the 6-8" size range. Forage fishes include low densities of golden shiners and rainbow smelt. Other fish species present at low densities are chain pickerel, yellow perch, brown bullhead, American eel and white sucker.

Fishing: Should be excellent for stocked trout; good for kokanee; and fair for sunfish and small bass.

Management: Trophy Trout Lake; special seasonal length and creel limits on trout. Statewide regulations apply for all other species. Taking smelt from tributary streams is prohibited. The use of alewives or other live herring for bait is prohibited (see current *Connecticut Anglers' Guide*).

Boating: Motors limited to 7.5 hp. Daytime speed limit 15 mph; 6 mph ½ hr. after sunset to ½ hr. before sunrise from June 15 to the first Sunday after Labor Day (see current *Connecticut Boater's Guide*).

Comments: Trout fishing pressure in West Hill Pond is very heavy. It is the only good kokanee fishery remaining in the state. Alewives are prohibited as bait because, if introduced, they would out-compete the kokanee for their zooplankton food source and destroy the fishery, as has already occurred in East Twin Lake and Lake Wononscopomuc.

West Hill Pond
Fish Species and Abundance

	ALL SIZES	BIG FISH	GROWTH
Gamefish			
Largemouth bass	C	U	Fast
Smallmouth bass	A	U	Slow
Brown trout	A	R	
Kokanee	C		
Rainbow trout	A		
Chain pickerel	U	U	Slow
Panfish			
Yellow perch	U	U	Avg
Brown bullhead	U	U	
Sunfish			
Bluegill	C	C	> Avg
Pumpkinseed	C	C	< Avg
Redbreast	U	R	Avg
Rock bass	A	U	< Slow
Other			
Golden shiner	R		
Rainbow smelt	R		
White sucker	U		
American eel	U		

A=Abundant, C=Common, U=Uncommon, R=Rare

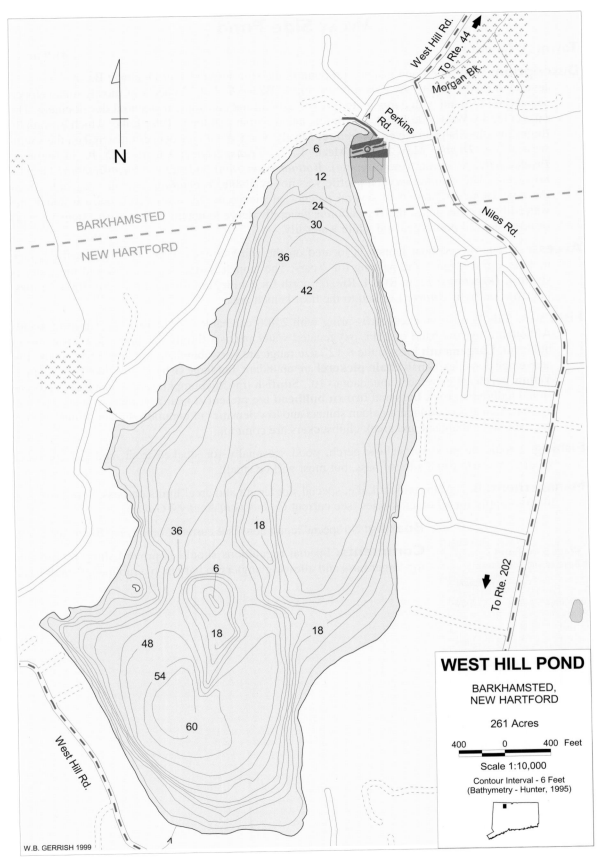

6

12

24

30

36

42

BARKHAMSTED

NEW HARTFORD

West Hill Rd.

To Rte. 44

Morgan Bk.

Perkins Rd.

Niles Rd.

To Rte. 202

36

18

6

18

18

48

54

60

West Hill Rd.

W.B. GERRISH 1999

N

WEST HILL POND

BARKHAMSTED,
NEW HARTFORD

261 Acres

400   0   400 Feet

Scale 1:10,000

Contour Interval - 6 Feet
(Bathymetry - Hunter, 1995)

West Side Pond

Town(s): Goshen

41.9 acres

Description: West Side Pond is a natural pond in the Housatonic River Drainage Basin. The water level was raised slightly by a dam on its outlet. *Watershed*: 2,273 acres of mostly undeveloped woods and wetland with a moderate level of agricultural and some residential development. The lake is fed by West Side Brook and drains into a marsh that feeds Tyler Lake, which eventually drains into the Shepaug River. *Shoreline*: Mostly wooded with residences clustered on the southwest shore. *Depth*: Max 32 ft., Mean 15 ft. *Transparency*: Clear; 8-15 ft. in summer. *Productivity*: Moderate (mesotrophic). *Bottom type*: Mud and gravel. *Stratification*: Occurs; however, a late summer oxygen profile was not available. *Vegetation*: Aquatic vegetation near the boat launch is limited to several patches of pickerelweed, arrowhead, bulrush and white water-lily. In other areas, the vegetation is generally dense to depths of 9 ft. with extensive areas of broad-leaved pondweed and white water-lily.

Access: A state-owned boat launch is located on the southwestern shore. Facilities at the launch include a gravel ramp and parking for 3 cars. The launch is steep and narrow and the water is shallow. *Directions*: From Rte. 4, Rte. 63 north for 1 mile, left on West Side Rd. for 1.5 miles, launch is on right. *Shore*: Limited to the boat launch area.

Fish: West Side Pond is stocked each spring with 2,400 catchable size **brown** and **rainbow trout**. Although a narrow band of cold, oxygenated water persists through summer, few brown trout holdover. **Largemouth bass** in the 8-12" size range are very abundant, but larger fish occur only at average densities. Small **chain pickerel** are abundant, but large fish (greater than 15") are rare. **Yellow perch** are extremely abundant to 10". **Sunfish** (mostly pumpkinseed, some bluegill, occasional redbreast), **rock bass** and **brown bullhead** are present at near average densities. The forage base consists of abundant golden shiners and low densities of common shiners. White suckers are extremely abundant and creek chubsuckers are common.

Fishing: Should be good for yellow perch, good seasonally for stocked trout, and fair for other species. You can catch a lot of bass, but most will be small.

Management: Bass Management Lake; special slot length and creel limits on bass. Statewide regulations apply for all other species (see current *Connecticut Anglers' Guide*).

Boating: No special regulations (see current *Connecticut Boater's Guide*).

Comments: Special regulations should improve fishing by protecting larger bass and allowing anglers to harvest overabundant small bass.

West Side Pond Fish Species and Abundance	ALL SIZES	BIG FISH	GROWTH
Gamefish			
Largemouth bass	A	C	Slow
Brown trout	C	R	
Rainbow trout	C		
Chain pickerel	A	R	< Slow
Panfish			
Yellow perch	A	C	< Slow
Brown bullhead	C	C	
Sunfish			
Bluegill	C	C	> Avg
Pumpkinseed	C	U	< Avg
Redbreast	U	R	
Rock bass	C	C	> Avg
Other			
Common shiner	U		
Golden shiner	A		Slow
Creek chubsucker	C		
White sucker	A		

A=Abundant, C=Common, U=Uncommon, R=Rare

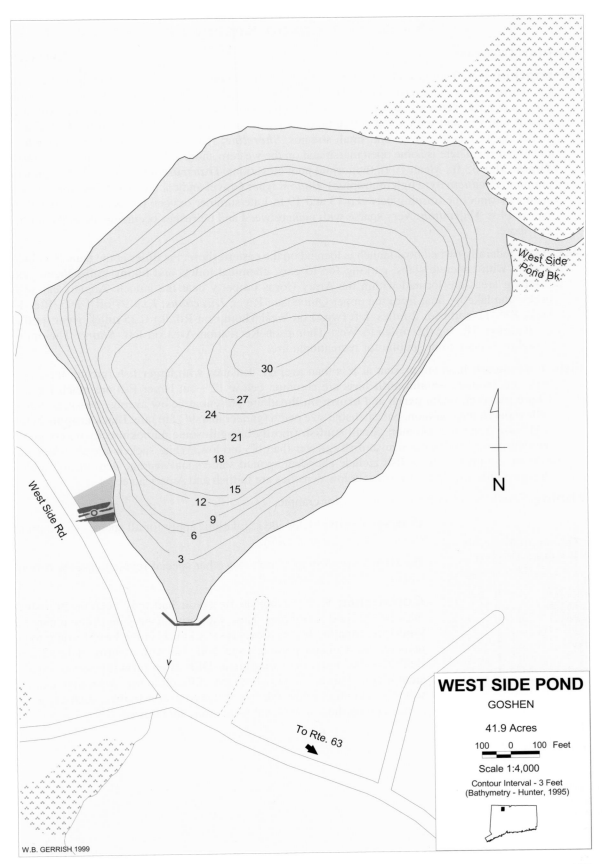

West Side
Pond Bk.

30

27

24

21

18

15

12

9

6

3

West Side Rd.

To Rte. 63

N

WEST SIDE POND

GOSHEN

41.9 Acres

100   0   100 Feet

Scale 1:4,000

Contour Interval - 3 Feet
(Bathymetry - Hunter, 1995)

W.B. GERRISH 1999

West Thompson Reservoir

Town(s): Thompson

239 acres

Description: West Thompson Reservoir is a flood-control impoundment on the Quinebaug River in the Thames River Drainage Basin. The U.S. Army Corps of Engineers owns and manages the lake and 1,700 acres of surrounding land. *Watershed:* 107,329 acres of mostly undeveloped woods and wetland with some agricultural and residential areas. In addition to the Quinebaug River, the lake is fed by several small streams. *Shoreline:* Partially wooded with no residential development. There is some open marshland on the western shore at the southern end of the lake. *Depth:* Max 33 ft., Mean 10 ft. (at normal pool elevation). *Transparency:* Fair; up to 6 ft. in late summer. *Productivity:* High (eutrophic). *Bottom type:* Gravel and cobble. *Stratification:* Occurs with a thermocline forming between 13 and 19 ft. Late summer oxygen levels are zero in waters below 14 ft. *Vegetation:* Very sparse with pickerelweed and bulrushes occurring along the northern shore.

Access: A federally owned boat launch is located on the eastern shore. Facilities at the launch include a ramp with concrete slabs, parking for 15 cars, chemical toilets and hiking trails. Picnic and camping areas are located within the Army Corps property near the launch. Anglers can also access the lake by boat from the upper Quinebaug River. *Directions:* Exit 97 off I-395, Rte. 44 west, Rte. 12 north for 2 miles, left (west) on West Thompson Rd. for 0.25 miles, right (north) on Reardon Rd. for 0.5 miles to West Thompson Recreation Area on left. *Shore:* The entire shoreline is open to the public for recreational use.

Fish: **Largemouth bass** are present at less than average densities with larger fish (greater than 16") being uncommon. **Smallmouth bass** are common below 12", but larger fish are much less so. **Chain pickerel**, **white perch** and **brown bullhead** are present at below average densities. Small **yellow perch** are common, but catchable size perch (greater than 9") are rare. **Black crappie** in the 8-11" size range are common. Small **sunfish** (mostly bluegill, some pumpkinseed) are common, but densities of catchable size sunfish (greater than 6") are low. White suckers are abundant and carp are common. Forage fish include abundant spottail shiners and average densities of golden shiners. Other fish species present at low densities are fallfish and American eel.

Fishing: Should be good for bass and fair for crappie.

Management: Statewide regulations apply for all species (see current *Connecticut Anglers' Guide*).

Boating: Speed limit 5 mph. No other special regulations (see current *Connecticut Boater's Guide*).

Comments: West Thompson Reservoir had only been electrofished once by the time of printing. Thus, the above fishery description may be imprecise. Smallmouth bass may be stockpiled in the lake. Fishing tournaments must obtain permits from both the Army Corps of Engineers (860-923-2982) and the Connecticut DEP. High turbidity makes shoals, stumps and other navigational hazards difficult to see. A popular area for waterfowl hunting in the fall. No water contact activities, such as swimming, sailboarding or personal watercraft, are allowed.

West Thompson Reservoir
Fish Species and Abundance

	ALL SIZES	BIG FISH	GROWTH
Gamefish			
Largemouth bass	C	U	> Avg
Smallmouth bass	C	U	< Avg
Chain pickerel	U	U	> Avg
Panfish			
Black crappie	C	C	Avg
White perch	U	U	> Avg
Yellow perch	C	R	Slow
Brown bullhead	U	U	
Sunfish			
Bluegill	C	U	> Avg
Pumpkinseed	C	R	Avg
Other			
Common carp	C		
Fallfish	U		
Golden shiner	C		
Spottail shiner	A		
White sucker	A		
American eel	U		

A=Abundant, C=Common, U=Uncommon, R=Rare

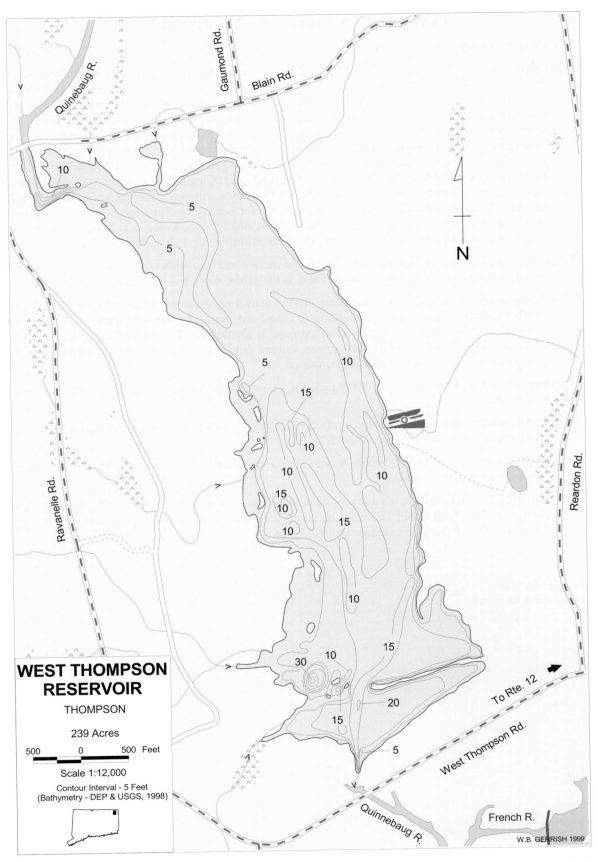

**WEST THOMPSON
RESERVOIR**

THOMPSON

239 Acres

500   0   500   Feet

Scale 1:12,000

Contour Interval - 5 Feet
(Bathymetry - DEP & USGS, 1998)

W.B. GERRISH 1999

West Twin Lake (Washinee Lake)

Town(s): Salisbury

Description: West Twin Lake is a natural lake in the Housatonic River Drainage Basin. The water level has been slightly raised by a small earthen dam. The lake is connected to East Twin Lake by a culvert with about 3 ft. of clearance. *Watershed:* 4,575 acres of mostly woods and wetland with some residential development. It is fed by bottom springs, two marshes, a small brook and water from East Twin Lake. It drains northward into Schenob Brook, a tributary of the Housatonic River. *Shoreline:* Mostly wooded with some residences concentrated on the northern shore. A large open marsh is located on the western shore and an abandoned railroad bed crosses the lake. *Depth:* Max 22 ft., Mean 8.7 ft. *Transparency:* Clear; 10 ft. in summer. *Productivity:* Not available. *Bottom type:* The bottom varies from rock, rubble, sand and gravel to mud and organic muck. *Stratification:* Does not occur; however, summer oxygen levels are depleted (less than 1 ppm) in waters below 18 ft. *Vegetation:* Not surveyed; however, it is reported to be very weedy with significant growths of Eurasian water-milfoil and pondweed.

Access: There is no public boat launching area, but canoes and smaller boats can pass under the road crossing from East Twin Lake. *Shore:* There is no public shore fishing access.

Fish: Largemouth bass and **yellow perch** are present at average densities. **Chain pickerel** to 20" and **sunfish** (mostly bluegill, some pumpkinseed) to 8" are abundant. **Black crappie** and **rock bass** in the 8-11" size range are higher than average in abundance. **Brown bullhead** densities are below average. Forage fish include golden shiners (abundant) and alewives (common). Creek chubsuckers are also present at low abundance.

Fishing: Should be good to excellent for pickerel, crappie, rock bass and sunfish; and fair for bass and perch.

Management: Statewide regulations apply for all species with restrictions on the use of live bait (see current *Connecticut Anglers' Guide*).

Boating: Daytime speed limit 35 mph; 6 mph ½ hr. after sunset to ½ hr. before sunrise (see current *Connecticut Boater's Guide*).

Comments: Fishing pressure is relatively light. Zebra mussels may gain a foothold in this lake from connected East Twin Lake. The pond had only been electrofished once by the time of printing. Thus the above fishery description may be imprecise.

West Twin Lake
Fish Species and Abundance

	ALL SIZES	BIG FISH	GROWTH
Gamefish			
Largemouth bass	C	C	Avg
Chain pickerel	A	A	Avg
Panfish			
Black crappie	C	C	> Avg
Yellow perch	C	C	< Avg
Brown bullhead	C	C	
Sunfish			
Bluegill	A	A	Slow
Pumpkinseed	C	U	Slow
Rock bass	C	C	Avg
Other			
Golden shiner	A		Slow
Alewife	C		
Creek chubsucker	U		

A=Abundant, C=Common, U=Uncommon, R=Rare

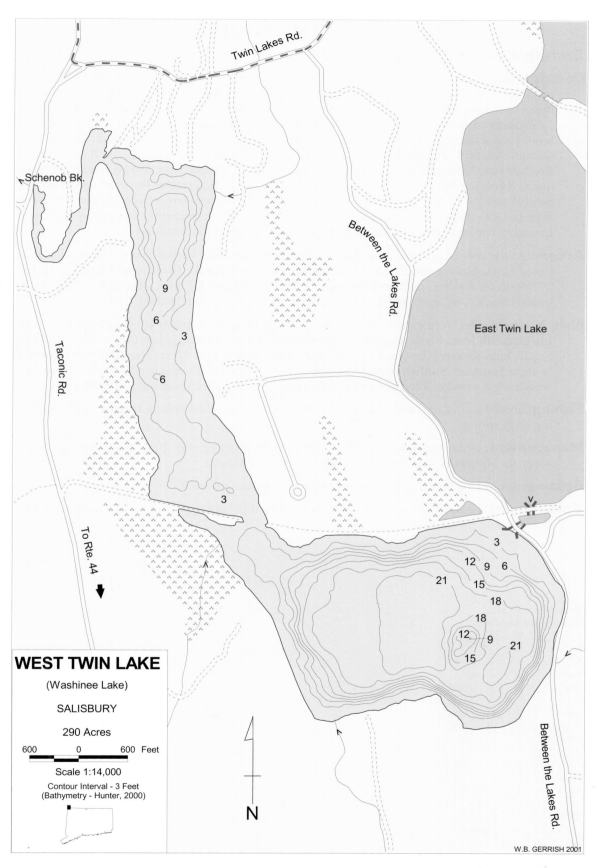

Twin Lakes Rd.

Schenob Bk.

Between the Lakes Rd.

East Twin Lake

Taconic Rd.

9

6

3

6

3

3

12 9 6

21

15

18

18

12 9

15 21

To Rte. 44

WEST TWIN LAKE

(Washinee Lake)

SALISBURY

290 Acres

600   0   600   Feet

Scale 1:14,000

Contour Interval - 3 Feet
(Bathymetry - Hunter, 2000)

N

Between the Lakes Rd.

W.B. GERRISH 2001

Winchester Lake

Town(s): Winchester

246 acres

Description: Winchester Lake is an artificial lake in the Housatonic River Drainage Basin. The trees and shrubs were cut at ice level during the winter following flooding of the lake. This resulted in many tree stumps just under the surface of the water causing boating to be difficult. *Watershed:* 1,449 acres of mostly woods with little residential development. The lake is fed by five small brooks and drains into the East Branch Naugatuck River. *Shoreline:* Wooded with little residential development. *Depth:* Max 17 ft., Mean 9.1 ft. *Transparency:* Fair; 10 ft. in summer. *Productivity:* Moderate (early mesotrophic-mesotrophic). *Bottom type:* Mostly mud and organic muck. *Stratification:* Does not occur due to limited depth. *Vegetation:* Bur-reed, tapegrass, ribbonleaf pondweed and filamentous algae are the dominant submergent species and form large mats in some shallow water areas. Rocky areas near the shore frequently support no vegetation. Emergent bur-reed, pickerelweed and sedges fringe much of the shoreline.

Access: A state-owned boat launch is located on the southern end. Facilities at the launch include a paved ramp, parking for 25 cars and chemical toilets (seasonal). *Directions:* From Rte. 4, Rte. 272 north for 6 miles, right on Winchester Rd. (Rte. 263) for 1.7 miles, left on West Rd. for 0.5 miles, launch is on right. *Shore:* Limited to boat launch area and the dam.

Fish: **Northern pike** were present at the time of writing and the population is expected to expand. **Largemouth bass**, **black crappie** and **brown bullhead** are present at less than average densities. Small **chain pickerel** (less than 12") and **yellow perch** (less than 9") are abundant with larger fish being uncommon. **Sunfish** (mostly bluegill, some pumpkinseed) are abundant to 8". **Rock bass** densities are average. The only forage fish sampled were golden shiners at low densities.

Fishing: Should be fair for rock bass and smaller yellow perch. Bass fishing is reportedly good during early spring.

Management: Annual stockings of fingerling northern pike began in 2001. Statewide regulations apply for all species (see current *Connecticut Anglers' Guide*).

Boating: Speed limit 8 mph (see current *Connecticut Boater's Guide*).

Comments: Pike were introduced to provide additional fishing opportunities and to better exploit the abundant forage base.

Winchester Lake
Fish Species and Abundance

	ALL SIZES	BIG FISH	GROWTH
Gamefish			
Largemouth bass	C	C	Avg
Northern pike	C		
Chain pickerel	A	U	Stunted
Panfish			
Black crappie	C	U	Avg
Yellow perch	A	U	< Avg
Brown bullhead	U	U	
Sunfish			
Bluegill	A	A	Avg
Pumpkinseed	C	U	> Avg
Rock bass	C	C	> Avg
Other			
Golden shiner	U		< Avg

A=Abundant, C=Common, U=Uncommon, R=Rare

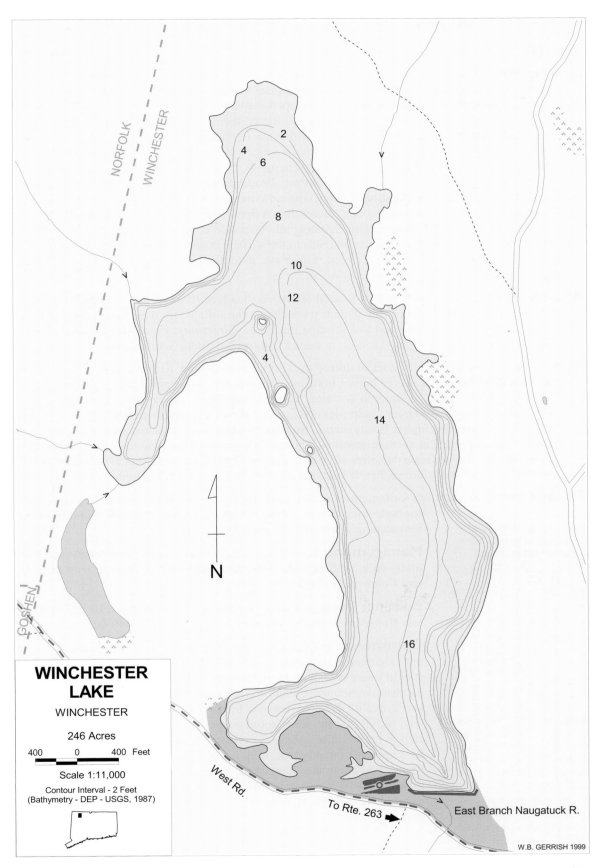

WINCHESTER
LAKE

WINCHESTER

246 Acres

400   0   400 Feet

Scale 1:11,000

Contour Interval - 2 Feet
(Bathymetry - DEP - USGS, 1987)

2

4

6

8

10

12

4

14

16

NORFOLK

WINCHESTER

GOSHEN

West Rd.

To Rte. 263

East Branch Naugatuck R.

N

W.B. GERRISH 1999

Wononscopomuc Lake (Lakeville Lake)

Town(s): Salisbury

348 acres

Description: Wononscopomuc Lake is a natural lake in the Housatonic River Drainage Basin. The water level was raised slightly by flashboards placed at the outlet. *Watershed*: 1,621 acres of mostly residential land with a small undeveloped wetland to the southeast. It is fed by Sucker Brook and one other small stream. It drains to the northeast into Factory Brook, a tributary of Salmon Creek. *Shoreline*: Mostly wooded with homes set back from the shore. Many of the larger homes on the western shore have lawns to the water's edge. The eastern shore is mostly wooded. There is a town beach is on the northern shore. *Depth*: Max 102 ft., Mean 36 ft. *Transparency*: Very clear; 16-17 ft. in summer. *Productivity*: Moderate (mesotrophic). *Bottom type*: Not available. *Stratification*: Occurs with a thermocline forming between 19 and 32 ft. Late summer oxygen levels remain good (greater than 6 ppm) to a depth of 26 ft. and decline to less than 1 ppm below 36 ft. *Vegetation*: Submergent vegetation is very dense and diverse. Eurasian water-milfoil, the dominant species, extends to the surface in waters from 2 to 15 ft. deep. Other submergent species include waterweed, tapegrass, mud-plantain, southern water-nymph, fanwort, stonewort and a variety of pondweeds.

Access: A town-owned boat launch is located on the northeastern shore. A fee is charged to nonresidents. Facilities at the access site include a concrete ramp suitable for most boats, parking for 20 cars, toilets, a concession stand and vending machines. *Directions*: From Rte. 44, Rte. 41 south for 0.1 miles, right on Ethan Allen St. to launch. *Shore*: No public shore access.

Fish: Wononscopomuc Lake is stocked during the spring and fall with 10,000 catchable size **brown** and **rainbow trout**. Holdover brown trout are common due to plentiful forage (alewives) and habitat (cold, oxygenated water in summer). **Largemouth bass** are very abundant in the 11-15" size range. Densities of larger **chain pickerel** (greater than 15"), **yellow perch** (9-13"), and **rock bass** (8-10") are also higher than average. **Sunfish** (mostly bluegill, some pumpkinseed, a few redbreast) are present at average densities. The lake has an abundant alewife and banded killifish forage base with moderate densities of golden shiners. Other species present at low densities are brown bullhead and white sucker. If kokanee are still present, they are extremely rare.

Fishing: Should be excellent for largemouth bass, chain pickerel, yellow perch and rock bass; good for both stocked and holdover trout; and fair for sunfish. Good prospects for catching a brown trout over 20".

Management: Bass Management Lake; special slot length and creel limits on bass. Statewide regulations apply for all other species (see current *Connecticut Anglers' Guide*).

Boating: Motors limited to 12 cu. in. (approximately 10 hp) (see current *Connecticut Boater's Guide*).

Comments: Fishing season is open from the third Saturday in April until October 31. No night or ice fishing allowed. Special bass regulations should improve fishing by protecting larger bass and allowing anglers to harvest overabundant small bass. As recently as 1995, Wononscopomuc had a quality kokanee fishery. Illegal introductions of alewives, which feed heavily on the same zooplankton food source that kokanee require, caused the kokanee fishery to collapse. Wononscopomuc has a reputation for producing large brown trout. In 1969, a 26 lb. 12 oz. brown trout was found dead along the shore of the lake. The trout was stocked in 1963 at a length of 10 inches. The State Record lake trout (29 lb. 13 oz.) was caught here in 1918. Dissolved oxygen levels are now insufficient to support lake trout.

Wononscopomuc Lake
Fish Species and Abundance

	ALL SIZES	BIG FISH	GROWTH
Gamefish			
Largemouth bass	A	A	Slow
Kokanee	R		
Brown trout	C	C	
Rainbow trout	C		
Chain pickerel	C	C	> Avg
Panfish			
Yellow perch	A	A	Avg
Brown bullhead	U	U	
Sunfish			
Bluegill	C	C	< Slow
Pumpkinseed	C	U	< Avg
Redbreast	U	R	Avg
Rock bass	C	C	Avg
Other			
Golden shiner	C		Avg
Banded killifish	A		
Alewife	A		Avg
White sucker	U		

A=Abundant, C=Common, U=Uncommon, R=Rare

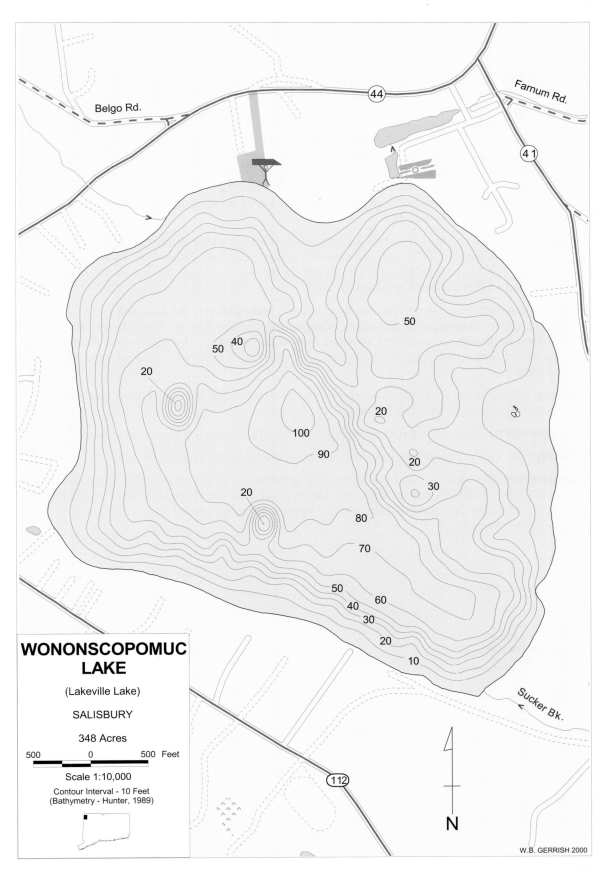

WONONSCOPOMUC LAKE

(Lakeville Lake)

SALISBURY

348 Acres

500   0   500 Feet

Scale 1:10,000

Contour Interval - 10 Feet
(Bathymetry - Hunter, 1989)

Belgo Rd.

Farnum Rd.

44

41

Sucker Bk.

112

N

W.B. GERRISH 2000

Wood Creek Pond

Town(s): Norfolk   **145 acres**

Description: Wood Creek Pond is a state-owned artificial pond in the Housatonic River Drainage Basin. *Watershed*: 1,206 acres of mostly undeveloped woods and wetland. It is fed by Holleran Swamp from the north and drains southward into Wood Creek, a tributary of the Blackberry River. *Shoreline*: Wooded with little residential development. *Depth*: Max 9 ft., Mean 4 ft. *Transparency*: Fair; 5 ft. in summer. *Productivity*: Very high (highly eutrophic). *Bottom type*: Rock, mud and organic muck. *Stratification*: Does not occur due to limited depth. *Vegetation*: Submergent vegetation is very dense throughout the pond. Dominant submergent vegetation is bladderwort, Robbin's pondweed and large-leaved pondweed. Floating vegetation composed of white water-lily, yellow pond-lily, water-shield, floating leaved pondweeds and bur-reed covers 50% of the surface by late June.

Access: A state-owned boat launch is located on the southern end. Facilities at the launch include a paved ramp, parking for 12 cars and chemical toilets (seasonal). *Directions*: From Rte. 44, north on Rte. 272 for 12.5 miles, right on Ashpohtag Rd. for 0.3 miles, left on access road. *Shore*: Limited to the boat launch area and the dam.

Fish: **Largemouth bass** are present, but uncommon. **Chain pickerel** are abundant to 15", but larger fish are rare. **Yellow perch** and **black crappie** densities are average, but fish over 10" are rare. **Brown bullheads** are extremely abundant, but rarely exceed 9". The pond has an abundant golden shiner forage base. Other fish species present at low densities are pumpkinseed and bridled shiners.

Fishing: Should be fair for chain pickerel, perch and crappie, but don't expect many large ones. Good place to catch loads of small bullheads.

Management: Statewide regulations apply for all species (see current *Connecticut Anglers' Guide*).

Boating: No special regulations (see current *Connecticut Boater's Guide*).

Comments: This shallow pond has historically suffered severe winter kills. The pond was drained in the early 1990s for dam repairs. Navigation is difficult due to shallow water conditions with dense vegetation and the existence of many stumps. There are several large stumps located directly in the channel.

Wood Creek Pond
Fish Species and Abundance

	ALL SIZES	BIG FISH	GROWTH
Gamefish			
Largemouth bass	U	R	Fast
Chain pickerel	A	R	Slow
Panfish			
Black crappie	C	R	> Ave
Yellow perch	C	R	Slow
Brown bullhead	A	R	
Sunfish			
Pumpkinseed	R	R	
Other			
Bridled shiner	R		
Golden shiner	A		Slow

A=Abundant, C=Common, U=Uncommon, R=Rare

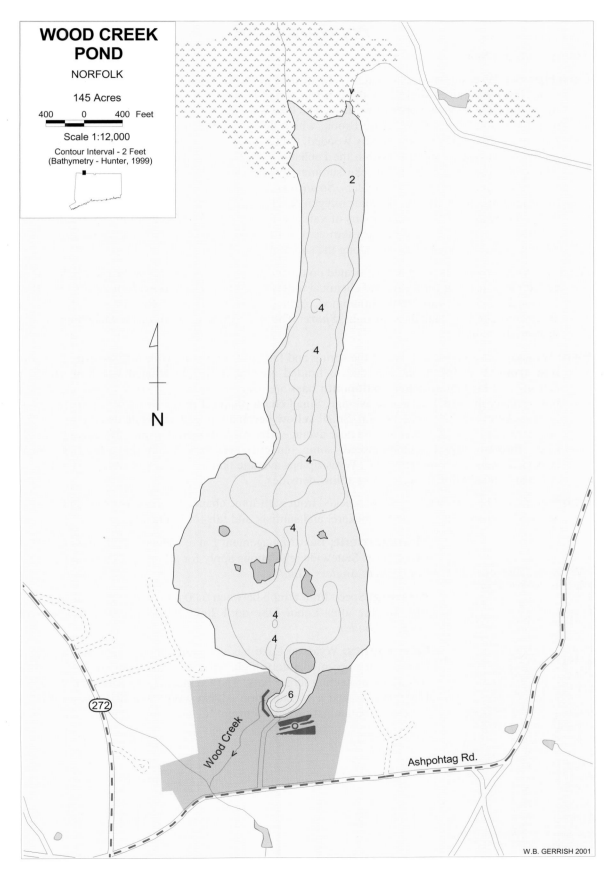

WOOD CREEK POND

NORFOLK

145 Acres

400   0   400   Feet

Scale 1:12,000

Contour Interval - 2 Feet
(Bathymetry - Hunter, 1999)

N

2

4

4

4

4

4

4

4

6

(272)

Wood Creek

Ashpohtag Rd.

W.B. GERRISH 2001

Wyassup Lake

Town(s): North Stonington

101 acres

Description: Wyassup is a small natural lake located in the Pawcatuck River Drainage Basin. The water level was raised slightly by the construction of a dam on the outlet. *Watershed*: 518 acres of mostly undeveloped woods or wetland. The lake is fed by two wetland streams from the north and drains southeast into Wyassup Brook, which flows into the Green Falls River and then the Pawcatuck River. *Shoreline*: Mostly wooded, with a moderate number of homes. About 300 yds. on the southwestern shore is within the Pachaug State Forest. *Depth*: Max 27 ft., Mean 10 ft. *Transparency*: Fair; 8-10 ft. in lake summer. *Productivity*: Moderate (mesotrophic). *Bottom type*: Sand, gravel, rubble and boulders. *Stratification*: Partially stratifies with a temperature gradient forming at 13 ft. Late summer oxygen levels are reduced to less than 4 ppm below this depth. *Vegetation*: Dense populations of variable-leaved water-milfoil and fanwort occur in the shallow cove located in the northeastern area of the lake. Tapegrass, pipewort, golden pert and cat-tail grow in scattered patches along the shoreline.

Access: A state-owned boat launch is located on the western shore. Facilities at the launch include a paved ramp, parking for 8 cars and chemical toilets (seasonal). *Directions*: Exit 92 off I-95, Rte. 2 west for 2.5 miles to North Stonington, right (north) on Wyassup Rd. for 3 miles, left on Wyassup Lake Rd., launch is on right. *Shore*: The state property south of the launching area is open to the public.

Fish: Wyassup Lake is stocked during the spring and fall with 3,800 catchable size **brown and rainbow trout**. Few fish hold over due to limited area of deep, oxygenated water in summer. Densities of **largemouth and smallmouth bass** are near average for all sizes, except that larger bass (greater than 16") are above average. Small **chain pickerel** densities are below average, but large pickerel (15-22") are common. Small **yellow perch** are abundant, while densities of catchable size perch (greater than 8") are near average. **Brown bullhead** densities are average for all sizes. **Sunfish** (mostly pumpkinseed, some bluegill) are common in the 6-8" size range. **American eels** are common to 24". Wyassup has average numbers of golden shiners. White catfish and banded killifish are present at low densities.

Fishing: Should be seasonally good for stocked trout with some chance for a holdover; good for bass, eels and sunfish; fair to good for pickerel and sunfish; and fair for bullheads.

Wyassup Lake
Fish Species and Abundance

	ALL SIZES	BIG FISH	GROWTH
Gamefish			
Largemouth bass	C	C	> Avg
Smallmouth bass	C	C	Avg
Brown trout	C	R	
Rainbow trout	C		
Chain pickerel	C	C	> Avg
White catfish	U	U	
Panfish			
Yellow perch	A	C	< Avg
Brown bullhead	C	C	
Sunfish			
Bluegill	C	C	> Avg
Pumpkinseed	C	C	> Avg
Other			
Golden shiner	C		
Banded killifish	U		
American eel	C		

A=Abundant, C=Common, U=Uncommon, R=Rare

Management: Bass Management Lake; special length and creel limits on bass. Statewide regulations apply for all other species (see current *Connecticut Anglers' Guide*).

Boating: Speed limit 8 mph between 6:00 p.m. and 11:00 a.m and from first Sunday after Labor Day until June 15 (see current *Connecticut Boater's Guide*).

Comments: Wyassup Lake has good smallmouth bass potential, but harvest rates are moderately high. Special regulations should improve fishing by protecting larger bass. The Connecticut Department of Public Health has issued a consumption advisory on some fish species due to mercury contamination (see current *Connecticut Anglers' Guide* for details).

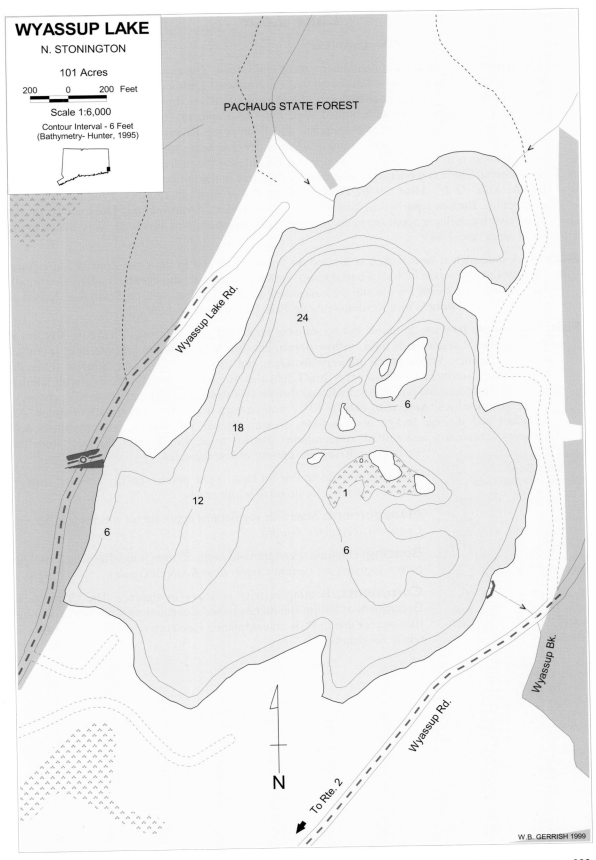

Lake Zoar

Town(s): Monroe/Newtown/Oxford/Southbury

909 acres

Description: Lake Zoar is an impoundment of the Housatonic River created by the Stevenson Dam in Monroe. The dam is owned and operated by Northeast Utilities as a hydroelectric facility. *Watershed*: 986,420 acres encompassing the Housatonic River drainage. The land surrounding the lake is mostly wooded with limited residential development. In addition to the Housatonic River, Lake Zoar is fed by the Pootatauck and Pomperaug Rivers and several small streams. *Shoreline*: Mostly wooded with some residential development. Approximately 2.5 miles of the western shore is in Paugussett State Forest and 1.5 miles of the eastern shore is within Kettletown State Forest. There is moderate residential development in the northern part of the impoundment. *Depth*: Max 72 ft., Mean 29 ft. *Transparency*: Fair; 7-8 ft. in summer. *Productivity*: High (eutrophic). *Bottom type*: Rock, broken ledge and boulders. *Stratification*: Does not occur due to its riverine influence and periodic drawdowns. *Vegetation*: Not surveyed. Very dense in the shoal areas near I-84.

Access: A state-owned boat launch is located on the northern end in the Lake Zoar Wildlife Area. Facilities at the launch include a paved ramp, parking for 60 cars and chemical toilets (seasonal). *Directions*: Exit 14 off I-84, south on Lakeside Rd. for 1.5 miles, right on Scout Rd., launch is at end of road. *Shore*: From Kettletown State Park on the eastern shore.

Fish: Smallmouth bass are common, but densities of larger fish (greater than 12") are slightly lower than average. **Largemouth bass**, **yellow perch**, and **black crappie** are all present at less than average densities. **White perch** are very abundant, but fish over 9" are rare. **Sunfish** (bluegill, pumpkinseed, redbreast, occasional hybrid) densities are slightly below average with sunfish over 7" being rare. Chain pickerel, rock bass, brown bullhead and white catfish (to 16") are present at low densities. **American eels** to 30", common carp and white suckers are common. An abundant and diverse forage base includes spottail shiners (abundant), golden shiners and alewives (common), and fallfish (uncommon). Brown trout, which enter the lake from the Pomperaug River, are present at low densities.

Fishing: Should be fair for bass, white perch, sunfish, eels and catfish. Expect to catch a lot of small white perch.

Management: Statewide regulations apply for all species (see current *Connecticut Anglers' Guide*).

Boating: Daytime speed limit 45 mph; 25 mph ½ hr. after sunset to ½ hr. before sunrise (see current *Connecticut Boater's Guide*).

Comments: Boating activity is heavy in summer. The Connecticut Department of Public Health has issued a consumption advisory for some fish species due to PCB contamination (see current *Connecticut Anglers' Guide* for details).

Lake Zoar Fish Species and Abundance	ALL SIZES	BIG FISH	GROWTH
Gamefish			
Largemouth bass	C	C	Avg
Smallmouth bass	C	U	Avg
Brown trout	R		
Chain pickerel	R	R	
White catfish	U	U	
Panfish			
Black crappie	C	U	Avg
White perch	C	R	Slow
Yellow perch	C	U	> Avg
Brown bullhead	U	U	
Sunfish			
Bluegill	C	U	> Avg
Pumpkinseed	C	U	> Avg
Redbreast	C	U	> Avg
Rock bass	U	R	> Avg
Other			
Common carp	C		
Fallfish	U		
Golden shiner	C		> Fast
Spottail shiner	A		
Alewife	C		
White sucker	C		
American eel	C		

A=Abundant, C=Common, U=Uncommon, R=Rare

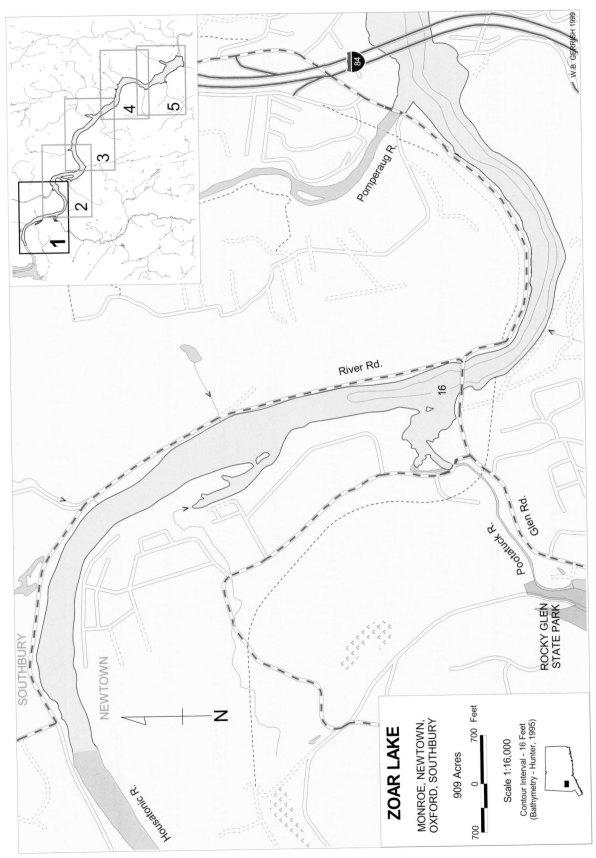

ZOAR LAKE

MONROE, NEWTOWN,
OXFORD, SOUTHBURY

909 Acres

Scale 1:16,000

Contour Interval - 16 Feet
(Bathymetry - Hunter, 1995)

700   0   700 Feet

N

SOUTHBURY

NEWTOWN

Housatonic R.

River Rd.

Pomperaug R.

16

Pootatuck R.

Glen Rd.

ROCKY GLEN
STATE PARK

84

W. B. GERRISH 1999

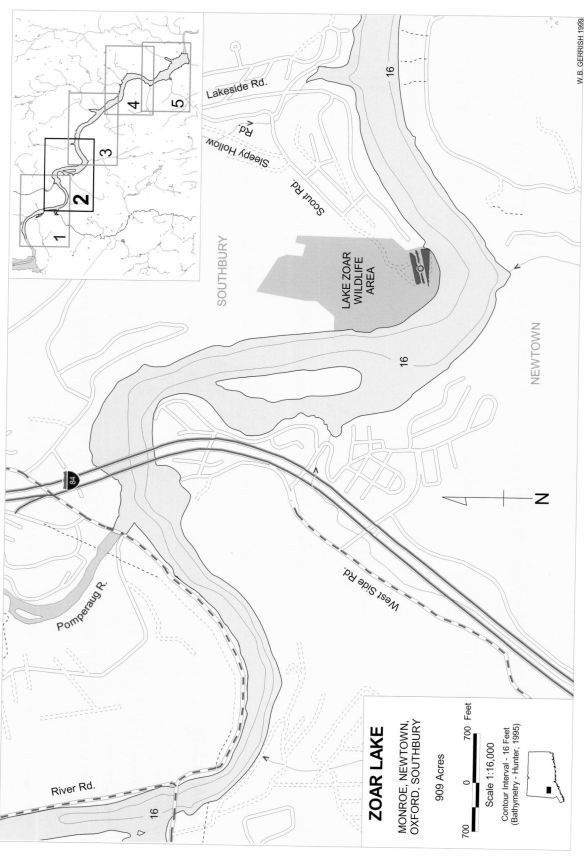

ZOAR LAKE

MONROE, NEWTOWN,
OXFORD, SOUTHBURY

909 Acres

Scale 1:16,000

Contour Interval - 16 Feet
(Bathymetry - Hunter, 1995)

700   0   700 Feet

W.B. GERRISH 1999.

N

SOUTHBURY

NEWTOWN

Lakeside Rd.

Sleepy Hollow Rd.

Scout Rd.

LAKE ZOAR WILDLIFE AREA

West Side Rd.

Pomperaug R.

River Rd.

16

84

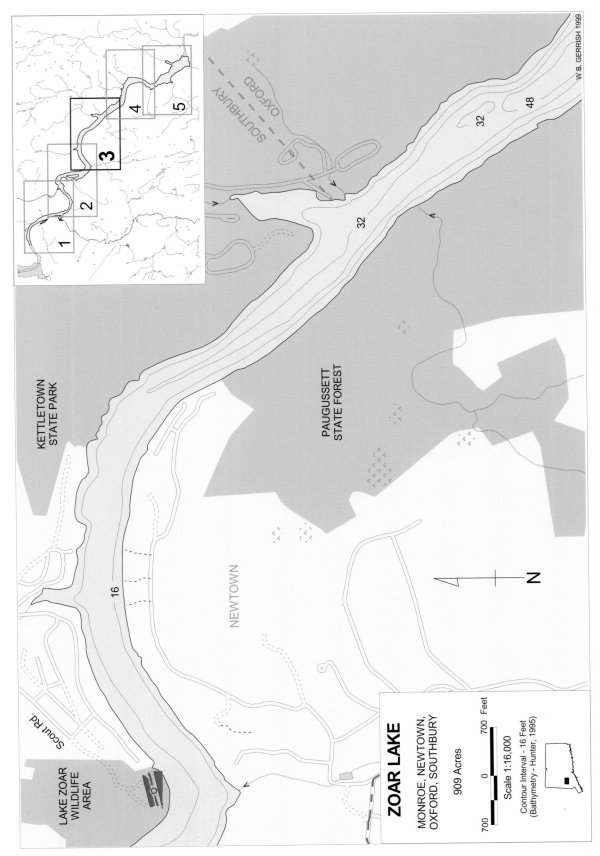

ZOAR LAKE

MONROE, NEWTOWN,
OXFORD, SOUTHBURY

909 Acres

Scale 1:16,000

Contour Interval - 16 Feet
(Bathymetry - Hunter, 1995)

700   0   700   Feet

W.B. GERRISH 1999

KETTLETOWN
STATE PARK

LAKE ZOAR
WILDLIFE
AREA

Scout Rd.

NEWTOWN

PAUGUSSETT
STATE FOREST

SOUTHBURY
OXFORD

N

16

32

32

32

48

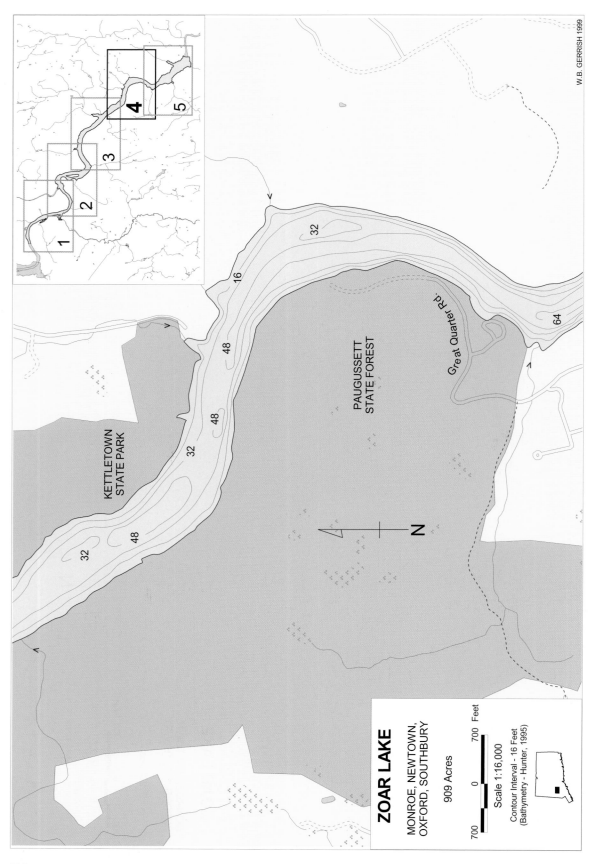

ZOAR LAKE

MONROE, NEWTOWN,
OXFORD, SOUTHBURY

909 Acres

Scale 1:16,000

Contour Interval - 16 Feet
(Bathymetry - Hunter, 1995)

700   0   700   Feet

KETTLETOWN
STATE PARK

PAUGUSSETT
STATE FOREST

Great Quarter Rd

N

W.B. GERRISH 1999

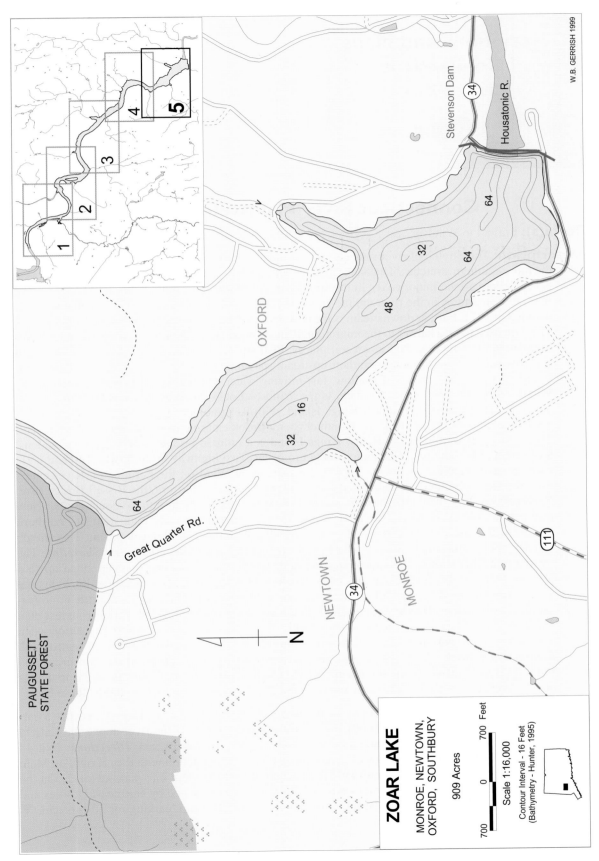

ZOAR LAKE

MONROE, NEWTOWN,
OXFORD, SOUTHBURY

909 Acres

Scale 1:16,000

Contour Interval - 16 Feet
(Bathymetry - Hunter, 1995)

700   0   700 Feet

W. B. GERRISH 1999

PAUGUSSETT
STATE FOREST

OXFORD

NEWTOWN

MONROE

Great Quarter Rd.

Stevenson Dam

Housatonic R.

N

Descriptions and Maps of Connecticut River Sites

Connecticut River Mainstem (North)

Town(s): Enfield to Windsor

Description: This stretch of river runs almost due south and is narrower (max. width 1,500 ft.) than the more southern stretches. The banks are characterized by shallow, sandy flats with some woody debris. There are no major coves in this area of the river. Heading south from the Mass. line, the first large structures in the river are the concrete footings of the old Rte. 190 bridge that was dismantled in 1971. Further downstream is the new Rte. 190 bridge and beyond that the Enfield Dam. The dam used to be a barrier to the migration of anadromous fish. Over the years the dam has deteriorated and is now breached in several places. Fish still tend to congregate below the dam, but can now easily swim through it on their upstream spawning runs. Below the dam are the Enfield Rapids, a three-mile stretch of shallow, fast-moving water. On the western shore, running from Windsor Locks to just above the dam, is the Windsor Locks canal, which was built in 1829 to transport cargo around the rapids. Kings Island, with its prominent jagged cliffs, is located just north of Windsor Locks outside the mouth of Stony Brook entering from the west. Boats can navigate both sides of this island. Below Kings Island is a railroad bridge — here the river widens, the current slows and tidal fluctuations begin to occur. Two highway bridges (Rte. 140 and I-91) span the river in Windsor Locks. Further downstream at Windsor, the Farmington River enters from the west, obscured by a long narrow island. Just north of Hartford, the Bissell Bridge (Rte. 291) crosses the river. *Watershed:* 6,318,745 acres that stretch into Massachusetts, New Hampshire and Vermont. The land immediately surrounding the mainstem in northern Connecticut is mostly residential with some agricultural and industrial development. This stretch is fed by the Scantic and Farmington Rivers plus numerous small tributary brooks. *Shoreline:* The riverbank in this stretch is characterized on both shores by a moderate to steep slope up to a plateau. Much of this higher land has been developed for agricultural (tobacco fields), industrial and residential purposes. The immediate shoreline is lightly wooded or open with little or no residential development. *Depth:* This reach of river has not been charted. Depth varies from less than a foot to greater than 10 feet in some holes and is subject to seasonal variation. Use caution when navigating. *Transparency:* Up to 6 ft.; more turbid after rain. *Productivity:* High (eutrophic). *Bottom type:* Rocky ledge; sand and silt in slow-moving areas. *Vegetation:* Tapegrass and Eurasian water-milfoil are the dominant species, which create large beds in some areas to depths of 4 ft. Coontail, mud-plantain, curly pondweed and waterweed are common amidst these beds.

Access: There are three public boat launches in this stretch of river: 1) A town-owned launch is located in the **Thompsonville** section of Enfield on the eastern shore of the river above the Enfield Dam. Facilities at this site include a paved ramp and parking for 30 cars. *Directions:* Exit 48 from I-91, Elm St/North Main St west, continue 0.4 miles past junction with Rte. 5, right on Main St. for 0.2 miles, first left after railroad bridge, right at first stop sign into parking lot. 2) On the eastern shore in Enfield, just north of **Kings Island** is a launch owned by Northeast Utilities and managed by the State. Facilities at this site include a concrete ramp, parking for 20 cars and ▼

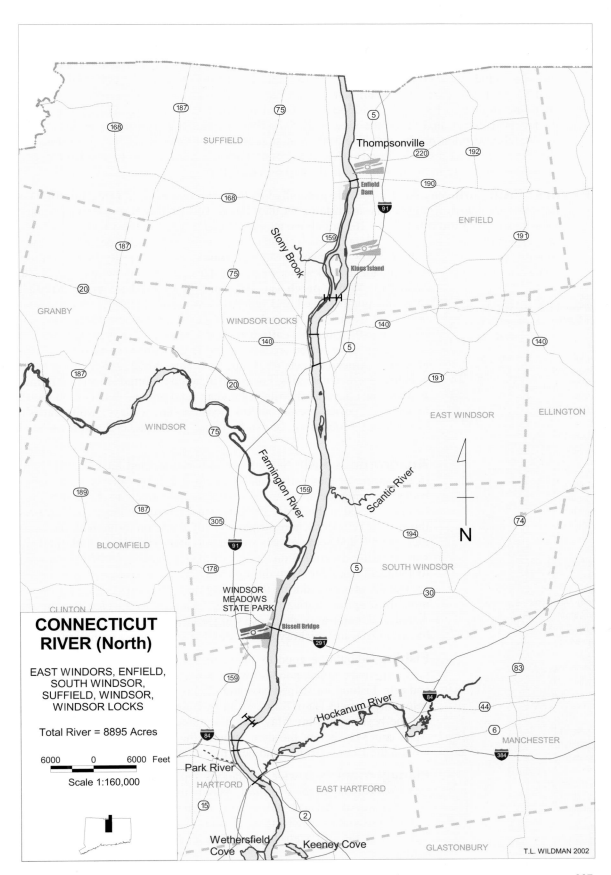

CONNECTICUT RIVER (North)

EAST WINDORS, ENFIELD,
SOUTH WINDSOR,
SUFFIELD, WINDSOR,
WINDSOR LOCKS

Total River = 8895 Acres

6000   0   6000 Feet

Scale 1:160,000

T.L. WILDMAN 2002

chemical toilets (seasonal). *Directions*: Exit 46 from I-91 to Rte. 5 north, bear left on Bridge Lane, left on Parsons Rd., launch is on right. 3) A state-owned launch is located directly under the **Bissell Bridge** (Rte. 291)on the western shore in the Wilson section of Windsor. Facilities at this site include a paved ramp, parking for 18 cars and chemical toilets (seasonal). *Directions*: Exit 3 from I-291 to Rte. 159 south, left on East Barber St., launch is at end of road. *Shore*: The shoreline around the Enfield Dam is popular for shad and striped bass fishing in the spring. It can be accessed from Canal St. on the west side of the river. Other popular areas along this stretch are Warehouse Point on the east side at the junction of Rte. 140 and River Rd., 1.25 miles of shoreline on the west side in Windsor Meadows State Park just north of the Bissell Bridge, and along the east shore in South Windsor at the end of Vibert Rd.

Resident Fish:
Northern pike densities are generally low in this section of river. **Largemouth bass** densities are below average in the mainstem, but they can be very abundant in backwater areas. Densities of **smallmouth bass** to 16" are above average. Smallmouths in the 13-16" size range are especially common. Very large bass (greater than 18") of either species are rare. **Yellow perch** are present at below average densities. **Crappie** to 12" (mostly black crappie, some white crappie) are abundant in backwater areas, but densities are below average in the mainstem. **White perch** can be abundant in the late spring. **Sunfish** (bluegill, pumpkinseed and redbreast) are more common in backwater areas, but even there are below average in abundance. **Rock bass** are common to 9". **Channel catfish** are fairly common, but their densities are not as high as in lower sections of the river. **Common carp** to 36" are abundant. **American eels** to 26" are common. White suckers are present at below average densities. Forage fish include spottail shiners (extremely abundant), juvenile herring (abundant) and golden shiners (common). Other fish species present at low densities are walleye, white catfish, brown trout, brook trout, brown bullhead, redfin pickerel and tessellated darter.

Anadromous Fish:
School size (15-18") **striped bass** are abundant in the spring as they follow and prey upon herring (alewives and bluebacks) that migrate upstream to spawn. Large stripers to 40 pounds may be encountered at this time. There is also a fall run of large adult stripers through November. School stripers remain common throughout the summer and fall and some remain over the winter. **American shad** numbers vary annually depending on the size of the run. They are usually common to abundant from late April through May. Alewives and blueback herring are usually abundant during their spring runs. Gizzard shad are also common from spring through fall. Other anadromous species present are Atlantic salmon (rare), shortnose sturgeon (rare and endangered), sea-run brown trout (rare), hickory shad (rare) and sea lamprey (common).

Fishing:
Should be good to excellent for largemouth and smallmouth bass, carp and crappie; good for white perch and fair for catfish, rock bass and eels. Fishing for striped bass and shad is seasonally good to excellent below the Enfield Dam. Stripers can be caught from spring through fall, but the best months are May and June. Shad fishing is best during late April and May below the dam, around the bridges in Windsor Locks, around the Bissell Bridge, and near the mouth of the Farmington River.

Management:
Statewide regulations apply for most species (see current *Connecticut Anglers' Guide*). Minimum length for northern pike is 24". Taking of Atlantic salmon or shortnose sturgeon is prohibited. Striped bass and river herring regulations change frequently. Read posted signs, check the DEP website or call Marine Fisheries (860-434-6043) for details.

Conn River Mainstem (North)
Fish Species and Abundance

	ALL SIZES	BIG FISH	GROWTH
Gamefish			
Largemouth bass	C	C	> Avg
Smallmouth bass	A	C	Fast
Brown trout	R	R	
Brook trout	R	R	
Northern pike	U	U	
Walleye	R	R	Fast
Channel catfish	C	C	
White catfish	U	U	
Panfish			
Black crappie	C	C	Avg
White crappie	U	U	
Yellow perch	C	C	Fast
White perch	C	C	
Brown bullhead	R	R	
Sunfish			
Bluegill	C	R	Avg
Pumpkinseed	C	R	< Avg
Redbreast	C	R	> Avg
Rock bass	C	C	Fast
Anadromous (Abundance seasonal)			
Atlantic salmon	R	R	
Striped bass	C	C	
American shad	A	A	
Alewife	A		
Blueback herring	A		
Gizzard shad	C		
Shortnose sturgeon	R*		
Sea lamprey	C		
Other			
Redfin pickerel	R		
Tessellated darter	U		
Common carp	A		
Golden shiner	C		
Spottail shiner	A		
White sucker	C		
American eel	C		

A=Abundant, C=Common, U=Uncommon, R=Rare
*State and federally endangered

Boating: Speed limits for most of the year are 25 mph nights, 30 mph weekends and holidays and 45 mph weekdays (see current *Connecticut Boater's Guide* for specifics).

Comments: Some areas in the northern river may not be accessible to motorboats during times of low water. The northern river is popular for bass tournaments, with 11 events launching annually from this area. The State Record American shad (9 lb. 4 oz.) was caught at Windsor in 1981. The Connecticut Department of Public Health has issued a consumption advisory on carp and catfish in the Connecticut River and its coves due to PCB contamination (see current *Connecticut Anglers' Guide* for details). Many of the backwater areas are popular for waterfowl hunting in the fall.

Connecticut River Mainstem (Central)

Town(s): Hartford to Portland

Description: This area of the river becomes slower, deeper and more meandering. Just north of Hartford is Riverside Park, a major city-owned access area. Here the river is shallow with a large sand bar near the eastern shore just south of Riverside Park. Three bridges span the river at Hartford: the Bulkley (Rte. 44), the Founders (I-84) and the Charter Oak (Rte. 5). Below the City of Hartford, the river narrows, meandering between the towns of Wethersfield, Rocky Hill and Glastonbury. The Army Corp of Engineers maintains a dredged channel through this stretch for tankers and barges to navigate as far north as Hartford. Between the towns of Wethersfield and Glastonbury is the entrance to Wethersfield Cove (to the west), the Putnam Bridge (Rte. 3), and the mouths of Keeney Cove (to the east) and Crow Point Cove (to the west). Farther south is the Glastonbury-Rocky Hill Ferry (Rte. 160). South of Rocky Hill is Gildersleeve Island in Cromwell. The channel runs along the eastern side of the island, but small boats can navigate both sides at high tide. South of Gildersleeve Island and just north of Middletown is Wilcox Island, which hides the mouth of the Mattabesset River flowing in from the west. The water to the west of Wilcox Island is very shallow and only navigable near high tide. Just below Wilcox Island, the Arrigoni Bridge (Rte. 66) and a railroad bridge span the river between Middletown and Portland. This area is highly urbanized with some industrial development along the shoreline. Heading downstream, the river turns due east. In this area is the entrance to Wright's Cove along what is now the northern shore. The river then passes through an area known as The Straits, where it narrows slightly and cuts through hills of metamorphic rock. Five miles downstream from Middletown on the west side of the river is Dart Island, an undeveloped state park. The western end of Dart Island is now almost completely silted in, forming more of a peninsula. The long, narrow cove on the western side is very shallow and may not be navigable at low tide. At the East Hampton town line the river turns south again and passes Hurd State Park on its eastern bank. *Watershed*: 6,578,134 acres that stretch into Massachusetts, New Hampshire and Vermont. The land immediately surrounding the mainstem in central Connecticut is mostly agricultural land and undeveloped woodland with two highly urbanized areas in Hartford/East Hartford and Middletown/Portland. Three major rivers (the Hockanum, Mattabesset and Park) enter the Connecticut in this stretch along with many smaller streams. Although its tributaries are above ground, the entire length of the lower Park River flows through an aqueduct beneath the City of Hartford. *Shoreline*: Is mostly wooded north of Hartford and becomes heavily developed around the City of Hartford with skyscrapers, a sewage treatment plant, a trash-to-energy plant and Brainard Airport all visible from the water. South of Hartford, the shoreline is mostly wooded flood plain and marshland. South of Rocky Hill, the shoreline becomes hilly and wooded. *Depth*: Channel depth ranges from 20-35 ft. *Transparency*: 4-5 ft.; more turbid after rain. *Productivity*: High (eutrophic). *Bottom type*: Primarily sand and silt. *Vegetation*: Tapegrass and coontail are the dominant species and create large beds in some areas to depths of 4 ft. Eurasian water-milfoil, mud-plantain, curly pondweed and waterweed are common amidst these beds.

Access: There are five public boat launches in this stretch of river: 1) The launch at **Riverside Park** is open to the public for a fee. It is owned by the City of Hartford and operated by Riverfront Recapture, Inc. Facilities at the launch include a double ramp with a docking pier, parking for 30 cars and chemical toilets (seasonal). *Directions*: Exit 33 from I-91, east on Jennings Rd., first right on Leibert Rd., left into Riverside Park, follow signs to launch. 2) The **Great River Park** launch is owned by the Town of East Hartford and is open to the public for a fee. Facilities at the launch include a concrete slab ramp, parking for 20 cars, and chemical toilets (seasonal). *Directions*: Exit 4 from Rte. 2 west, left at end of exit ramp onto East River Dr., the park is 0.5 miles on left. 3) **Charter Oak Landing** is open to the public for a fee. It is owned by the city of Hartford and operated by Riverfront Recapture, Inc. Facilities at the launch include a paved ramp, parking for 26 cars and chemical toilets (seasonal). *Directions*: From Exit 27 off I-91 south – left on Airport Rd., left on Brainard Rd., left on Reserve Rd., Charter Oak Landing is on right. From Exit 27 off I-91 north – left on Brainard Rd., follow previous directions. 4) **Wethersfield Cove** ▼

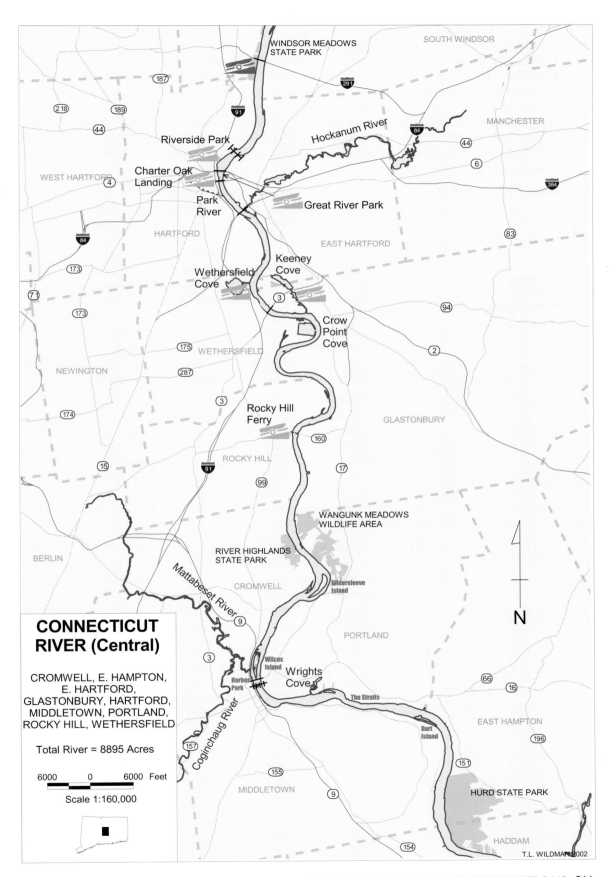

CONNECTICUT RIVER (Central)

CROMWELL, E. HAMPTON,
E. HARTFORD,
GLASTONBURY, HARTFORD,
MIDDLETOWN, PORTLAND,
ROCKY HILL, WETHERSFIELD

Total River = 8895 Acres

6000   0   6000   Feet

Scale 1:160,000

WINDSOR MEADOWS
STATE PARK

SOUTH WINDSOR

Riverside Park

Hockanum River

MANCHESTER

Charter Oak
Landing

Park
River

Great River Park

WEST HARTFORD

HARTFORD

EAST HARTFORD

Keeney
Cove

Wethersfield
Cove

Crow
Point
Cove

NEWINGTON

WETHERSFIELD

GLASTONBURY

Rocky Hill
Ferry

ROCKY HILL

BERLIN

WANGUNK MEADOWS
WILDLIFE AREA

RIVER HIGHLANDS
STATE PARK

Mattabeset River

CROMWELL

Gildersleeve
Island

PORTLAND

Wilcox
Island

Harbor
Park

Wrights
Cove

The Straits

Coginchaug River

EAST HAMPTON

Dart
Island

HURD STATE PARK

MIDDLETOWN

HADDAM

N

T.L. WILDMAN 2002

has a town-owned launch that is open to the public for a fee (see Wethersfield Cove for details). 5) Next to the **Rocky Hill Ferry** slip is a town-owned launch that is open to the public for a fee. Facilities at this site include a paved ramp, parking for 30 cars, and chemical toilets (seasonal). *Directions*: Exit 24 from I-91, Rte. 99 south to Rocky Hill center, left (east) on Rte. 160. Follow signs to ferry slip. *Shore*: There are many shore access points along this stretch. Popular areas are around each of the boat launches, around the ferry slip on the east side in Glastonbury, the Wangunk Meadows Wildlife Area 0.5 miles north of Wilcox Island in Cromwell on the west side, Harbor Park on the west side in Middletown, Paper Rock on the east side off Rte. 66 in Portland, and Hurd State Park on the east side in East Hampton. Canoe camping is available at Hurd State Park during April-September (call 1-877-668-2267 for reservations).

Resident Fish: **Northern pike** to 32" are common. **Largemouth bass** are locally common in backwater areas, but densities are generally low in the mainstem. **Smallmouth bass** densities are slightly below average for all size classes. **Yellow perch**, **crappie** (mostly black, occasional white), and **white perch** are common to abundant in the coves during the spring and fall, but typically more sparse in the mainstem. **Rock bass** and **sunfish** (mostly redbreast, some bluegill and pumpkinseed) are present at less than average densities. **Channel catfish** to 24" and **white catfish** to 16" are common. **Common carp** to 30" are abundant. Small **American eels** (less than 12") are abundant, but larger ones are less common. White suckers are abundant. Forage fish species include spottail shiner (extremely abundant), juvenile herring (abundant), golden shiner, fallfish and banded killifish. Other fish species present at low densities are brown trout, brook trout, walleye, redfin pickerel, tessellated darter and central mudminnow.

Anadromous Fish: The same anadromous fish species that are found in the northern stretch of the river are found in this area although most are just passing through *en route* to upstream spawning areas. School and larger **striped bass** are common in the spring and fall and can be present throughout the year. **American shad** are common to abundant, but are seldom caught by anglers in this area because they pass quickly through on their way upstream. Alewives and blueback herring are usually abundant during their spring spawning runs. **Hickory shad** occasionally move this far up into the river in the fall.

Fishing: Should be good to excellent for catfish, carp and white perch; fair to good for pike and bass; and fair for panfish. The bridges around Hartford are popular sites to catch channel catfish up to 8 pounds. Striped bass fishing is good to excellent during the spring, particularly around the bridges in Hartford and adjacent to coves and river mouths south of the city and along the trash-to-energy plant in Hartford.

Management: Statewide regulations apply for most species (see current *Connecticut Anglers' Guide*). Minimum length for northern pike is 24". Taking of Atlantic salmon or shortnose sturgeon is prohibited. Striped bass and river herring regulations change frequently. Read posted signs, check the DEP website or call Marine Fisheries (860-434-6043) for details.

Boating: Speed limits for most of the year are 25 mph nights, 30 mph weekends and holidays and 45 mph weekdays. There are no-wake zones (steerage speed only) in the areas of the Rocky Hill Ferry and south of the Arrigoni bridge (Rte. 66) in Middletown (see current *Connecticut Boater's Guide* for specifics).

Comments: The central river is very popular for bass tournaments, with 43 events launching annually from this area. The State Record carp

Conn River Mainstem (Central) Fish Species and Abundance			
	ALL SIZES	BIG FISH	GROWTH
Gamefish			
Largemouth bass	U	U	
Smallmouth bass	C	C	Fast
Brown trout	R	R	
Northern pike	C	C	Fast
Walleye	R	R	Fast
Channel catfish	C	C	
White catfish	C	C	
Panfish			
Black crappie	C	U	
White crappie	U	U	
White perch	C	C	Avg
Yellow perch	C	U	Fast
Sunfish			
Bluegill	C	R	Avg
Pumpkinseed	R	R	
Redbreast	C	U	Fast
Rock bass	C	U	Avg
Anadromous (Abundance seasonal)			
Atlantic salmon	R	R	
Striped bass	C	C	
American shad	A	A	
Hickory shad	U		
Alewife	A		
Blueback herring	A		
Gizzard shad	C		
Shortnose sturgeon	R*		
Sea lamprey	C		
Other			
Tessellated darter	U		
Common carp	A		
Fallfish	R		
Golden shiner	U		
Spottail shiner	A		
Central mudminnow	U		
Banded killifish	U		
White sucker	A		
American eel	A		

A=Abundant, C=Common, U=Uncommon, R=Rare
*State and federally endangered

(38 lb. 8 oz.) was caught at Hartford in 1995. The Connecticut Department of Public Health has issued a consumption advisory on carp and catfish for the Connecticut River and its coves due to PCB contamination (see current *Connecticut Anglers' Guide* for details). Sewer overflows in Hartford occasionally discharge untreated sewage into this section of the river during rainstorms. At Hartford, the tidal fluctuation averages approximately 1 ft. and is 4.5 hrs. behind Old Saybrook.

Wethersfield Cove

Town(s): Wethersfield   **90.2 acres**

Description: Wethersfield Cove is a backwater cove located at River Mile 45 on the western side of the river. The mainstem used to meander through this area; however, a big flood in 1692 cut the present, more direct channel to the east of the cove. Entrance to the cove from the river is via a culvert that passes under I-91 (25 ft. clearance). This channel and a large central area of the cove were dredged during the construction of I-91. There are shallow flats along the northern and western shores. Numerous private boats are moored in the cove throughout the boating season. There is one private marina located on the western shore. *Watershed*: 4,005 acres of dense residential development. The cove is fed by Folly Brook and the Connecticut River. *Shoreline*: The northern shoreline is part of the Folly Brook Preserve and is mostly wooded. The western shore is mostly an open grassy area. The eastern and southern shores are dominated by a large paved boat ramp and a town park. *Depth*: Max 17 ft., Mean 10 ft. *Transparency*: Turbid; 1-3 ft. *Productivity*: High (eutrophic). *Bottom type*: Mostly sand, mud and silt. *Vegetation*: Submerged vegetation is relatively sparse overall, but more dense near the inlets. Dominant species are Eurasian water-milfoil and tapegrass. Water-nymph and mud-plantain are also present.

Access: There is a town-owned boat launch on the eastern shore of the cove that can be used by the public for a fee. The cove can also be accessed via a channel from the river. Facilities at the launch include a large paved ramp, docking pier, parking for more than 50 cars with trailers and chemical toilets (seasonal). The launch may be inaccessible during flood conditions. *Directions*: Exit 26 from I-91, turn west from exit ramp, right on Marsh St., right on Main St. to end, launch is on left. *Shore*: The most accessible areas are the boat launch, the eastern and southern shorelines, and the southern side of the channel leading to the river.

Resident Fish: Northern pike to 32" are common. **Largemouth bass** densities are average for all size classes. **Walleye** to 10 pounds are occasionally present. Densities of smaller **crappie** (mostly black, some white) are average, but numbers of larger crappie (10-12") are above average. **Yellow perch**, **white perch**, **white catfish**, **channel catfish**, **brown bullhead** and **sunfish** (mostly bluegill and pumpkinseed, some redbreast) are all present at below average densities. **Carp** to 30" are common. **American eels** to 18" are abundant. White suckers are common. Forage fishes include spottail shiner (extremely abundant), juvenile herring (abundant) and golden shiners. Other fish species present at low densities are smallmouth bass, rock bass, tessellated darter and goldfish.

Anadromous Fish: Schools of **striped bass** will occasionally enter the cove on feeding forays. River herring (alewives and bluebacks) spawn in the cove and can be extremely dense during their April-June runs. Gizzard shad are also common. **Hickory shad** occasionally move into the cove in the fall.

Fishing: Should be fair to good for pike, crappie, carp, white perch and eels; and fair for largemouth bass.

Management: See special regulations within central mainstem description.

Boating: See general boating restrictions within central mainstem description.

Comments: Tide is approximately 4.5 hrs. behind Old Saybrook.

Wethersfield Cove
Fish Species and Abundance

	ALL SIZES	BIG FISH	GROWTH
Gamefish			
Largemouth bass	C	C	Avg
Smallmouth bass	U	U	Fast
Northern pike	C	C	Fast
Walleye	U	U	Fast
Channel catfish	U	U	
White catfish	U	U	
Panfish			
Black crappie	C	C	Avg
White crappie	U	U	
White perch	U	R	Avg
Yellow perch	C	U	Avg
Brown bullhead	U	U	
Sunfish			
Bluegill	C	U	< Avg
Pumpkinseed	C	U	Avg
Redbreast	U	U	Fast
Rock bass	R	R	
Anadromous (Abundance seasonal)			
Striped bass	U	U	
Alewife	A		
Blueback herring	A		
Gizzard shad	C		
Hickory shad	U		
Other			
Tessellated darter	U		
Common carp	C		
Golden shiner	C		Avg
Goldfish	U		
Spottail shiner	A		
White sucker	C		
American eel	A		

A=Abundant, C=Common, U=Uncommon, R=Rare

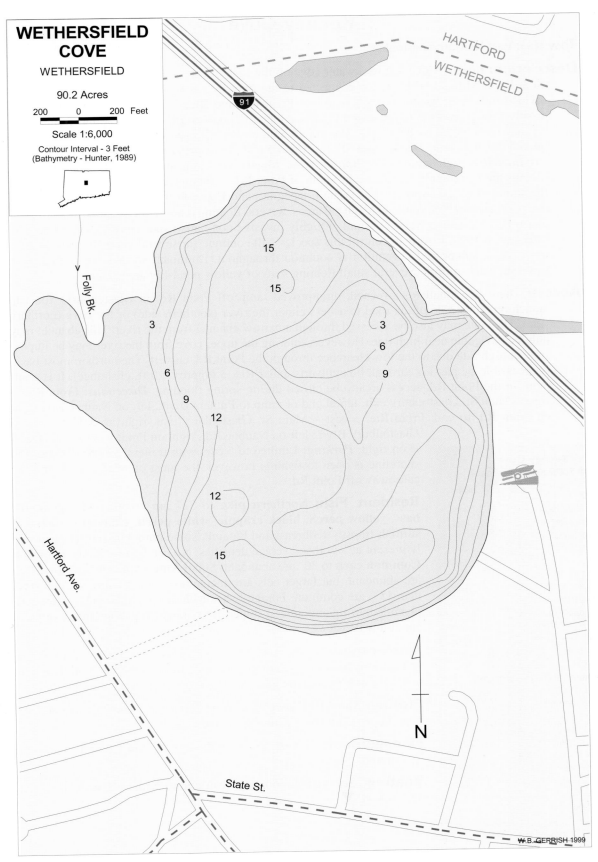

WETHERSFIELD
COVE

WETHERSFIELD

90.2 Acres

200   0   200 Feet

Scale 1:6,000

Contour Interval - 3 Feet
(Bathymetry - Hunter, 1989)

HARTFORD

WETHERSFIELD

91

Folly Bk.

15

15

3

3

6

6

9

9

12

12

15

Hartford Ave.

N

State St.

W.B. GERRISH 1999

Keeney Cove

Town(s): East Hartford/Glastonbury

73.6 acres

Description: Keeney Cove is a backwater cove on the eastern side of the Connecticut River located at River Mile 43. The cove is connected to the river by a narrow and shallow channel. It is divided into three basins by culverts under Point Rd. and Rte. 3. *Watershed:* 11,388 acres of mostly residential land to the east and undeveloped floodplain and open meadows to the west. Keeney Cove is fed by Pewterpot, Porter and Salmon Brooks. *Shoreline:* Wooded with no residential development. *Depth:* Max 27 ft., Mean 5.6 ft. *Transparency:* Turbid; 2-3 ft. visibility. *Productivity:* High (eutrophic). *Bottom type:* Mostly sand, silt and muck. *Vegetation:* Algal blooms are common in late summer. South of Point Rd. – Submerged vegetation is dense along the shore. Dominant species are coontail, tapegrass and Eurasian water-milfoil. North of Point Rd. – Vegetation is common in localized areas. Several floating mats of yellow pond-lily are present in isolated areas. Water chestnut, a highly invasive non-native species, was found here and removed in 1999. Efforts to control this species will continue for several years. In the northernmost basin, submerged vegetation is common throughout. Dominant species are coontail and Eurasian water-milfoil. Several small floating mats of yellow pond-lily are present.

Access: There is a small town-owned, unimproved ramp off Point Rd. in Glastonbury. You can launch on either side of the road to access either the river (southern side) or the cove (northern side). The cove may also be accessed through a narrow channel from the river. This channel may only be navigable near high tide. However, entering the upper cove from the river may be impossible at high tide due to the low clearance through the Point Rd. culvert. The northernmost basin is accessible by passing through box culverts under Rte. 3 (approx. 10 ft. clearance). It is common for the Point Rd. access area to be closed during spring flooding. *Directions:* From Rte. 3 west – Main St. Glastonbury exit, left at end of ramp to Putnam Blvd., left on Naubuc Rd., right on Point Rd. to end. From Rte. 3 east – Main St. Glastonbury exit, right at end of ramp to Glastonbury Blvd., left on Naubuc Rd., right on Point Rd. to end, launch is on right. *Parking:* Limited to 5 cars with trailers. *Shore:* Most of the shoreline is open to fishing; however, the most popular site is from the causeway off Point Rd.

Resident Fish: **Northern pike** to 32" are common. **Largemouth bass**, **yellow perch**, **black crappie**, **white perch**, **channel catfish** and **sunfish** (mostly redbreast and bluegill, some pumpkinseed) are generally present at less than average densities, but can be seasonally abundant. **Common carp** to 30" are abundant. Small **American eels** (less than 13") are abundant, but larger eels are uncommon. Small white suckers (less than 15") are common. Forage fishes include spottail shiner (abundant), juvenile herring and golden shiner. Bowfin and hogchoker are also present at low densities.

Anadromous Fish: Alewives and blueback herring are common to abundant in the spring when they migrate through the cove on their way to spawn in tributary streams.

Fishing: Should be good to excellent for carp; and fair to good for pike, largemouth bass, white perch and catfish.

Management: See special regulations within central mainstem description.

Boating: See general boating restrictions within central mainstem description. ▼

Keeney Cove
Fish Species and Abundance

	ALL SIZES	BIG FISH	GROWTH
Gamefish			
Largemouth bass	C	C	Avg
Northern pike	C	C	Fast
Channel catfish	C	C	
White catfish	U	U	
Panfish			
Black crappie	C	C	
White perch	U	U	Avg
Yellow perch	C	U	Avg
Brown bullhead	U	U	
Sunfish			
Bluegill	C	U	Avg
Pumpkinseed	U	R	< Avg
Redbreast	C	U	Fast
Anadromous (Abundance seasonal)			
Alewife	A		
Blueback herring	A		
Other			
Common carp	A		
Golden shiner	C		Avg
Spottail shiner	A		
White sucker	C		
American eel	A		
Bowfin	R		
Hogchoker	R		

A=Abundant, C=Common, U=Uncommon, R=Rare

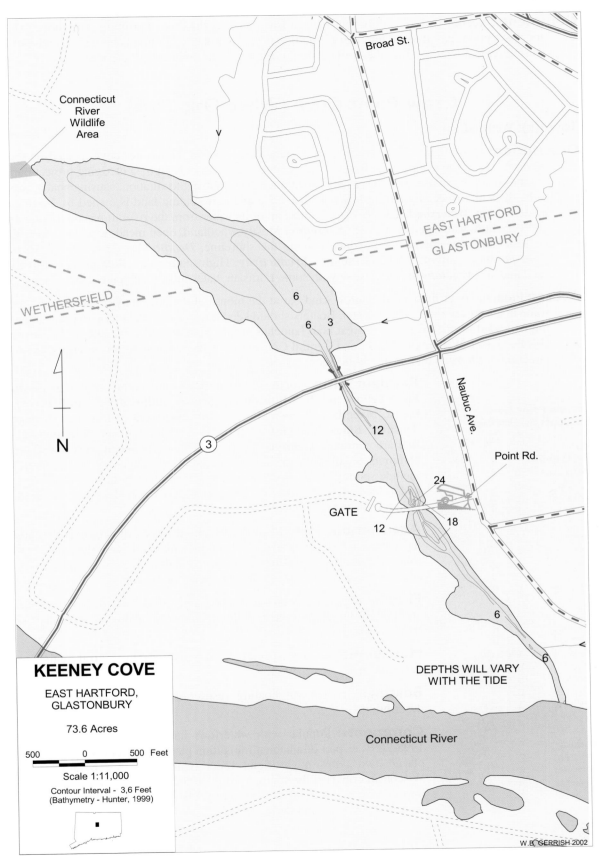

Connecticut
River
Wildlife
Area

Broad St.

EAST HARTFORD
GLASTONBURY

WETHERSFIELD

6

6   3

N

3

12

Naubuc Ave.

24

Point Rd.

GATE

12   18

6

DEPTHS WILL VARY
WITH THE TIDE

6

Connecticut River

KEENEY COVE

EAST HARTFORD,
GLASTONBURY

73.6 Acres

500   0   500   Feet

Scale 1:11,000

Contour Interval - 3,6 Feet
(Bathymetry - Hunter, 1999)

W.B. GERRISH 2002

Comments: Keeney Cove had only been electrofished once by the time of printing. The above fishery description may thus be imprecise. The tide is approximately 4.5 hrs. behind Old Saybrook. During typical winters, only the northern basin of the cove is covered by safe ice.

Crow Point Cove (White Oak Cove)

Town(s): Wethersfield   **84.7 acres**

Description: Crow Point Cove is a roughly rectangular, artificial, backwater cove located on the western side of the Connecticut River at River Mile 42. It was created by a dredging project during the construction of I-91. It has a narrow entrance that is subject to siltation, causing boat access to be difficult, especially during low tide. The cove and surrounding land is owned by National Eastern Corp. *Watershed*: The cove gets almost all of its water from the river. It has no tributaries and very little watershed of its own. *Shoreline*: Mostly woodland, open meadow and marsh with no residential development immediately along the shoreline. *Depth*: Max 23 ft., Mean 16 ft. *Transparency*: Turbid; 2.5 ft. in summer. *Productivity*: High (eutrophic). *Bottom type*: Mostly sand and silt. *Vegetation*: Very sparse with some Eurasian water-milfoil and emergent coontail

Access: From the river by boat. A shallow sand bar at the mouth of the cove may prevent access for some boats during times of low water. Boaters should keep track of the tidal phase to prevent getting stranded in the cove. The nearest boat launches are in Wethersfield Cove and at the Rocky Hill Ferry (see Wethersfield Cove and Central Connecticut River Mainstem for descriptions and directions). *Shore*: There is no public shore access.

Crow Point Cove
Fish Species and Abundance

	ALL SIZES	BIG FISH	GROWTH
Gamefish			
Largemouth bass	C	C	Fast
Smallmouth bass	R	R	
Northern pike	C	C	Fast
Channel catfish	C	C	
White catfish	R	R	
Panfish			
Black crappie	A	A	Fast
White crappie	C	C	
White perch	U	R	Fast
Yellow perch	C	U	Avg
Brown bullhead	U	R	
Sunfish			
Bluegill	C	U	< Avg
Pumpkinseed	U	R	Avg
Redbreast	C	U	Fast
Anadromous (Abundance seasonal)			
Striped bass	U	U	
American shad	U	R	
Alewife	C		
Blueback herring	A		
Gizzard shad	C		
Other			
Tessellated darter	C		
Common carp	C		
Golden shiner	C		Avg
Spottail shiner	A		
White sucker	A		
American eel	C		

A=Abundant, C=Common, U=Uncommon, R=Rare

Resident Fish: Northern pike to 32" are common. **Largemouth bass, yellow perch, white perch, brown bullhead** and **sunfish** (redbreast, bluegill, and pumpkinseed) are all present at less than average densities. **Black and white crappie** to 13" are abundant. **Channel catfish** are common. **Common carp** to 32" and **American eels** to 24" are common. Small white suckers less than 13" are abundant. Forage fishes include spottail shiner (extremely abundant), juvenile herring (abundant) and golden shiners. Other fish species present at low densities are smallmouth bass and tessellated darter.

Anadromous Fish: Schools of **striped bass** will occasionally enter the cove on feeding forays. Juvenile herring (alewives, bluebacks and shad) are common to abundant at times. Adult and juvenile gizzard shad are also present. Alewives probably spawn in the cove.

Fishing: Should be good for crappie and catfish; fair to good for pike; and fair for largemouth bass, yellow perch, carp and eels. A popular ice fishing spot.

Management: See special regulations within central mainstem description.

Boating: See general boating restrictions within central mainstem description.

Comments: Popular with waterfowl hunters during the fall. From 1998-2001, as part of a habitat mitigation plan, Riverfront Recapture, Inc. placed two types of artificial reefs (Christmas tree pyramids and Wisconsin cribs) off the southern shore of the cove. As of this writing, the impact of these artificial reefs has not yet been evaluated. Tide is approximately 4.5 hrs. behind Old Saybrook.

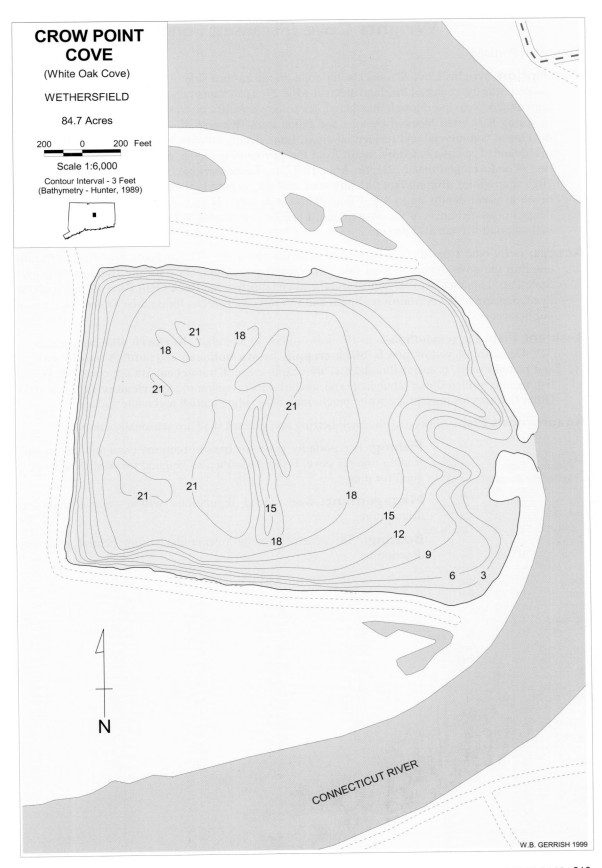

CROW POINT
COVE

(White Oak Cove)

WETHERSFIELD

84.7 Acres

200   0   200 Feet

Scale 1:6,000

Contour Interval - 3 Feet
(Bathymetry - Hunter, 1989)

N

CONNECTICUT RIVER

W.B. GERRISH 1999

Wrights Cove (Pecausett Pond)

Town(s): Portland   **34.2 acres**

Description: Wrights Cove is a backwater cove on the eastern side of the Connecticut River. It is located near the center of Portland at River Mile 27. The channel entering the cove is narrow and convoluted, weaving through marshland. It can be very difficult to navigate during low tide and in spring it is often blocked by logs and fallen trees. *Watershed*: A mixture of woodland and developed commercial and residential areas. Immediately surrounding the cove is undeveloped marshland. The cove is fed by runoff from the surrounding marsh. *Shoreline*: The entire shoreline is undeveloped marsh. *Depth*: Max 10-12 ft. *Transparency*: Turbid; 1-3 ft. *Productivity*: High (eutrophic). *Bottom type*: Mostly sand and silt. *Vegetation*: Submerged vegetation is very dense in water depths up to 8 ft. Coontail and waterweed are the dominant species. Fanwort is dense in isolated areas of the eastern end. Eurasian water-milfoil and scattered floating mats of yellow pond-lily are also present.

Access: Is by boat from the river through a narrow channel — larger boats may have difficulty entering the cove except at high tide. The closest public launches are the Haddam Meadows State Park Launch (10 miles south) and the town launch at the Rocky Hill Ferry (9 miles north). See Connecticut River Mainstem South and Central descriptions for details. *Shore*: There is no public access.

Resident Fish: Largemouth bass to 19" are common to abundant. **Northern pike** are common to 32". Densities of **yellow perch**, **black crappie**, **brown bullhead** and **sunfish** (mostly bluegill and pumpkinseed, occasional redbreast) are near average. **Channel catfish** are common. Forage fish include golden shiner (abundant) and spottail shiner (common). **American eels** are abundant. Other fish species present are white perch, rock bass, white catfish and white sucker.

Anadromous Fish: Alewives, blueback herring and gizzard shad are seasonally common.

Fishing: Is reportedly good for bass in both the cove and the channel leading into the cove. Fishing should also be good for panfish and fair to good for pike.

Management: See special regulations within central mainstem description.

Boating: See general boating restrictions within central mainstem description.

Wrights Cove Fish Species and Abundance	ALL SIZES	BIG FISH	GROWTH
Gamefish			
Largemouth bass	A	A	Fast
Northern pike	C	C	Fast
Channel catfish	C	C	
White catfish	U	U	
Panfish			
Black crappie	C	C	> Avg
White perch	U	U	> Avg
Yellow perch	C	C	> Avg
Brown bullhead	C		
Sunfish			
Bluegill	C	C	Fast
Pumpkinseed	C	U	Fast
Redbreast	U	R	
Rock bass	U	R	
Anadromous (Abundance seasonal)			
Alewife	C		
Blueback herring	C		
Gizzard shad	C		
Other			
Golden shiner	A		> Avg
Spottail shiner	C		
Common carp	C		
White sucker	C		
American eel	A		

A=Abundant, C=Common, U=Uncommon, R=Rare

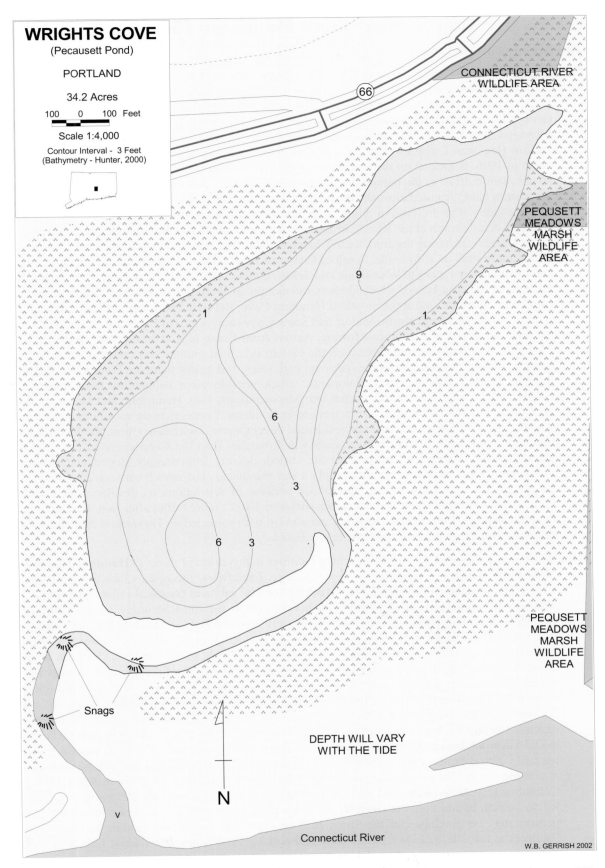

WRIGHTS COVE
(Pecausett Pond)

PORTLAND

34.2 Acres

100   0   100 Feet

Scale 1:4,000

Contour Interval - 3 Feet
(Bathymetry - Hunter, 2000)

66

CONNECTICUT RIVER
WILDLIFE AREA

PEQUSETT
MEADOWS
MARSH
WILDLIFE
AREA

9

1   1

6

3

6   3

PEQUSETT
MEADOWS
MARSH
WILDLIFE
AREA

Snags

DEPTH WILL VARY
WITH THE TIDE

V

N

Connecticut River

W.B. GERRISH 2002

Connecticut River Mainstem (South)

Town(s): Haddam to Lyme

Description: As you travel closer to Long Island Sound, the river becomes wider and more estuarine in nature. Tidal influences can be as much as 3 ft. in this section with saltwater moving up as far as the Rte. 82 bridge during periods of low flow. Following Hurd State Park, the river passes George D. Seymour State Park on the eastern bank, Haddam Island State Park, and Haddam Meadows State Park on the western bank. The water on the western side of Haddam Island is very shallow (less than 1 ft. at low tide). The Connecticut Yankee nuclear power plant, which was shut down in 1996, is located on the eastern shore opposite Haddam Meadows State Park. Below the power plant outflow is the entrance to Salmon Cove and the Salmon River State boat launch on the eastern bank. A mile below the cove is the Rte. 82 bridge, one of the oldest turnstile bridges in the country. On the eastern shore is the Goodspeed Opera House and the village of East Haddam. A mile south of the Rte. 82 bridge are two small islands on the western shore (Richs and Lords Islands) sheltering the entrance to Chapman Pond. The water to the east of these two islands is extremely shallow at low tide. South of Chapman Pond on the eastern bank are Gillette Castle State Park, the entrances to Whalebone and Selden Creeks, and Selden Neck State Park. Opposite the Park is Eustasia Island, which shelters the mouths of Pratt and Post Coves. South of this is Brockway Island located at the mouth of Hamburg Cove. Between Hamburg and Essex the mainstem is narrow and deep. North, Middle and South Coves are located in Essex and are well known for their white perch and tomcod fishing. Across from Essex is Nott Island. Below this point, where the river widens, Lord Cove is on the eastern side. Just south of this cove is Calves Island near the eastern shore, which is navigable on both sides. Just below there are Ferry Point and the Baldwin Bridge with its many abutments, which provide great habitat for large gamefish. *Watershed*: 6,733,622 acres that stretch into Massachusetts, New Hampshire and Vermont. The land immediately surrounding the mainstem in southern Connecticut is mostly undeveloped woodland with some agricultural and residential development. Two major rivers, the Salmon and Eightmile, and many smaller brooks, creeks and marshes feed the Connecticut in this stretch. *Shoreline*: The riverbanks in this area are varied, ranging from steeply sloped undeveloped woods and ledges to undeveloped flood plain and marshland. The stretch between East Haddam and Essex has retained a natural appearance because of restrictions on development. *Depth*: Channel depth ranges from 20-48 ft. *Transparency*: 4-6 ft.; more turbid after rain. *Productivity*: High (eutrophic). *Bottom type*: Mostly sand and silt with some ledge. *Vegetation*: Not surveyed. Wide patches of eel grass in shallows below Essex.

Access: There are three state-owned launching facilities in this reach of river: 1) **Haddam Meadows State Park** launch is located on the western shore. Facilities at this site include a double ramp with concrete slabs, two docking piers, parking for 100 cars and chemical toilets (seasonal). A parking fee is charged on weekends and holidays from the third Saturday in April through Columbus Day. *Directions*: Exit 8 from Rte. 9, left (east) on Beaver Meadow Rd. for 1 mile to end, bear left across the bridge, then right onto Jail Hill Rd. for 0.8 miles, left on Rte. 154, state park entrance is 1 mile on right. After entering park, bear right to the launch. 2) **Salmon River** launch is located on the eastern shore at the entrance to Salmon Cove. Facilities at the site include a double ramp with concrete slabs, two docking piers, parking for 60 cars and chemical toilets (seasonal). This launch is subject to spring flooding. A parking fee is charged on weekends and holidays from the third Saturday in April through Columbus Day. *Directions*: From the junction of Rtes. 149 and 82, Rte. 149 north for 1.5 miles, access road on left. 3) **Baldwin Bridge** launch in Old Saybrook is located on the western shore under the I-95 overpass. Facilities include a double ramp with concrete slabs, a docking pier, parking for 75 cars and chemical toilets (seasonal). A parking fee is charged on weekends and holidays from the third Saturday in April through Columbus Day. *Directions*: Exit 69 from I-95 south, Exit 1 (first exit) off Rte. 9, right on Ferry Rd. to launch. In addition, the **Deep River Town Landing** is open to the public for a fee. Daily permits may be purchased at the Town Hall on weekdays and at the landing on weekends. Facilities at this site include a paved ramp and parking for 30 cars. *Directions*: Exit 5 from ▼

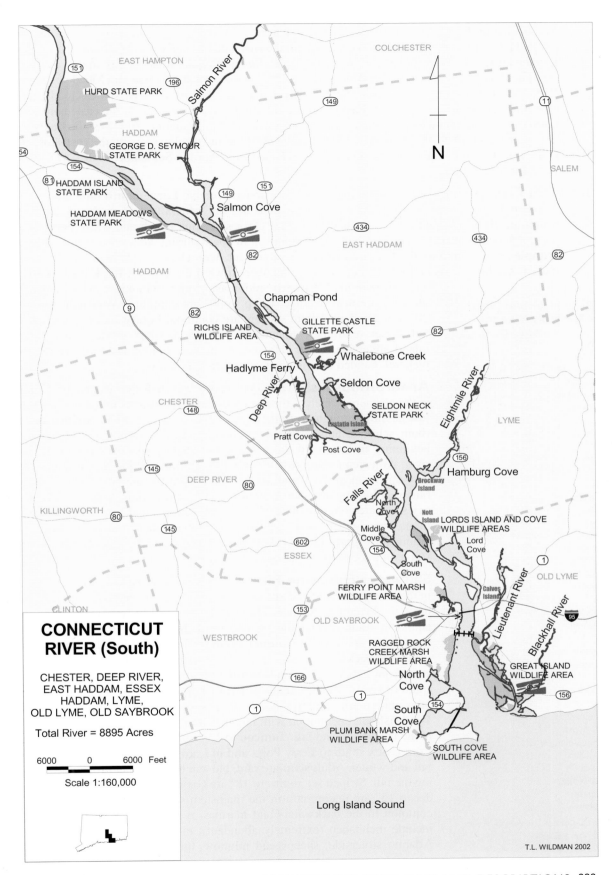

CONNECTICUT RIVER (South)

CHESTER, DEEP RIVER,
EAST HADDAM, ESSEX
HADDAM, LYME,
OLD LYME, OLD SAYBROOK

Total River = 8895 Acres

6000   0   6000 Feet

Scale 1:160,000

T.L. WILDMAN 2002

Rte. 9, east on Elm St./River St. for 1.4 miles, launch is on right. There are also car-top access points just north of the Rte. 148 ferry landing on the east side of the river in Hadlyme and on the Lieutenant River just east of Rte. 156 in Old Lyme. **Shore:** Popular areas in this stretch of river are: The mouth of Swain Johnson Brook off Rte. 154 on the west shore, Haddam Meadows State Park and launch on the west shore; Salmon River State Launch on the east shore, Goodspeed Opera House on the east shore in East Haddam; Gillette Castle State Park on the east shore just north of Rte. 148, Selden Neck State Park on the east shore 1 mile south of Rte. 148, the Baldwin Bridge launch under I-95 on the west side, and the DEP Marine headquarters on the east shore in Old Lyme. Canoe camping is available at Selden Island from April to September (call 1-877-668-2267 for reservations).

Resident Fish: Densities of **Northern pike** to 32" are above average. **Largemouth bass** are locally common in coves and backwater areas, but densities are generally low in the mainstem. **Smallmouth bass** densities are average for all size classes. **Yellow perch** and **white perch** are present at below average densities, but can be abundant in coves during winter and spring. **Black crappie** are uncommon. **Catfish** are common to abundant, with channel cats being more common in northern areas and whites increasing in numbers toward the estuary. **Rock bass** to 10", and **sunfish** to 7" (mostly redbreast, some pumpkinseed, occasional bluegill) are near average. **Carp** to 30" are common. **American eels** to 20" are abundant. White suckers are common. Forage fish include spottail shiner (extremely abundant), juvenile herring, golden shiner and inland silverside. Other fish species present at low densities are redfin pickerel, banded killifish and central mudminnow.

Anadromous Fish: The same anadromous fish species that are found in the northern stretch of the river are found in this area although most are just passing through *en route* to upstream spawning areas. **Striped bass** (both schoolie and larger size) are sporadically common to abundant beginning in late April through the fall. Some bass over-winter in the river. **American shad** pass quickly through this section of river on their way upstream in April and are seldom caught by anglers. Alewives and blueback herring are abundant during their spring runs. Schools of **hickory shad** are common during late spring, summer and fall. Other anadromous species present are alewife (abundant), blueback herring (abundant), gizzard shad (abundant), Atlantic sturgeon (rare), shortnose sturgeon (rare) and sea lamprey (common).

Saltwater/Estuarine Fish: A number of marine fish species arrive in the lower river after the spring floods cease in July and typically remain through November. Snapper bluefish less than 12 inches are common to abundant south of Hamburg Cove**.** Adult **bluefish** to 36" are common from Essex southward. **Summer flounder** to 20" are locally common in coves and backwater areas, but densities are generally higher in the mainstem from Essex south. Adult **Winter flounder** to 18" are below average south of Essex. **Blackfish** are generally rare, but can be common in rock piles and marina pilings south of Essex, especially during the fall. **Weakfish** are uncommon with larger fish to 32" occurring at Ferry Point in the late spring and fall. **Tomcod** to 14" are common in backwater areas from Essex south to Ferry Point and in Lord Cove, especially during the fall and winter. Adult **scup** are rare, but can be found near rock piles during the fall. Striped sea robins to 18" are common and windowpane flounder to 15" are uncommon in the mainstem south of Essex. Toadfish are common in the backwaters and marinas of the lower river. Forage fish include menhaden (extremely abundant), mummichog, striped killifish, Atlantic silverside, sheepshead minnow, three-spine stickleback, white

Conn River Mainstem (South)
Fish Species and Abundance

	ALL SIZES	BIG FISH	GROWTH
Gamefish			
Largemouth bass	C	C	Fast
Smallmouth bass	C	C	Fast
Northern pike	C	C	Fast
Channel catfish	C	C	
White catfish	C	C	
Panfish			
Black crappie	U	U	
White perch	C	C	Fast
Yellow perch	C	U	Fast
Sunfish			
Bluegill	R	R	
Pumpkinseed	C	R	
Redbreast	C	C	Fast
Rock bass	C	C	Fast
Anadromous (Abundance seasonal)			
Atlantic salmon	R	R	
Striped bass	C	C	
American shad	A	A	
Hickory shad	C		
Alewife	A		
Blueback herring	A		
Gizzard shad	C		
Atlantic sturgeon	R*		
Shortnose sturgeon	R*		
Sea Lamprey	C		
Other			
Redfin pickerel	U		
Common carp	C		
Golden shiner	C		
Spottail shiner	A		
Central mudminnow	U		
Banded killifish	U		
Hogchoker	C		
Inland silverside	C		
White sucker	C		
American eel	A		

A=Abundant, C=Common, U=Uncommon, R=Rare
*State and federally endangered

mullet and juvenile herring. Other fish species occasionally present at low densities are exotic marine visitors, including yellow jack, jack crevalle and inshore lizardfish. Other rare species are Atlantic mackerel and cunner.

Fishing: Should be good for pike, catfish, white perch (spring and fall) and eels; fair to good for bass and carp; and fair for sunfish and rock bass. Fishing for striped bass is good to excellent, especially during the spring and fall. Fishing for hickory shad is good in the late spring, summer and fall. Hotspots are the area between Deep River and Hamburg Cove and immediately downstream of the East Haddam bridge. For marine species south of Essex, fishing should be seasonally good for snapper and adult bluefish and fair to good for tomcod and summer flounder. Hotspots are the areas around Essex, Lord Cove, Ferry Point, and the mainstem between the bridge and Nott Island.

Management: Statewide regulations apply for most species (see current *Connecticut Anglers' Guide*). Minimum length for northern pike is 24". DEP Fisheries manages pike spawning marshes at Haddam Meadows that have led to an increase in abundance of northern pike in this area of the river. Taking of Atlantic salmon or shortnose sturgeon is prohibited. Regulations for marine fish, striped bass and river herring change frequently. Read posted signs, check the DEP website or call Marine Fisheries (860 434-6043) for details.

Boating: Speed limits for most of the year are 25 mph nights, 30 mph weekends and holidays and 45 mph weekdays. There are several no-wake (steerage speed only) zones in the lower river (see current *Connecticut Boater's Guide* for specifics).

Comments: Boating traffic (anglers and recreational) can be very high during the summer months. The southern river is very popular for bass tournaments, with 45 events launching annually from this area. Crabbing (blue crabs) in the lower river, particularly in the coves and backwaters during June through November, is excellent and large crabs are common. The Connecticut Department of Public Health has issued a consumption advisory on some fish species for the Connecticut River and its coves due to PCB contamination (see current *Connecticut Anglers' Guide* for details). Many areas are popular with waterfowl hunters during the fall.

Salmon Cove

Town(s): East Haddam

Description: Salmon Cove is at the mouth of the Salmon River on the eastern side of the Connecticut River at River Mile 16. The entrance to the cove is a deep channel that runs up to Cones Point. Thereafter, the cove widens and becomes shallow (less than 1 ft. at low tide) except for a difficult to follow channel (avg. depth approx. 8 ft.) that weaves back and forth across the cove. Beyond the cove, small boats can continue with difficulty up the Salmon River to the Rte. 151 bridge. *Watershed:* 95,346 acres of mostly undeveloped woods with light residential and agricultural development. The cove is fed by the Salmon and Moodus Rivers and by a small stream flowing out of Dogwood Pond. *Shoreline:* Mostly wooded with very little residential development. There is a moderate to steep slope along the northern shoreline of the cove. Areas near the entrance of the cove are marshland. *Depth*: At low tide, the average depth of the channel is 8 ft. with the rest of the cove being less than 1 ft. *Transparency:* Fair; 5-7 ft. *Productivity:* High (eutrophic). *Bottom type:* Mud and silt. *Vegetation*: Common throughout with submergent tapegrass, coontail, waterweed and Eurasian water-milfoil being the dominant species. Floating mats of white water-lily and yellow pond-lily are scattered throughout. Much of the cove is fringed with tall stands of wild rice.

Access: A large state-owned boat ramp is located at the entrance to the cove. See mainstem south for description and directions. *Shore:* Limited to the mouth of the cove at the state boat launch and the Echo Farm property (walk-in access area) off Rte. 151.

Resident Fish: **Northern pike** to 28" are common. **Yellow perch** densities are average with above average numbers of larger (10-11") fish. **Largemouth bass**, **black crappie**, **white perch**, **rock bass**, **brown bullhead** and **sunfish** (redbreast and pumpkinseed) are all present at less than average densities. **Catfish** (mostly whites, some channels) commonly enter the cove from the mainstem. **Brown trout** can also be found in low numbers, either as sea-runs moving upstream to spawn or stocked fish that drop down from the Salmon River upstream. **Carp** are common. Small **American eels** (less than 13") are abundant, but larger ones are uncommon. White suckers are very abundant. Forage fishes include spottail shiner (extremely abundant), juvenile herring (abundant) and golden shiner (common). Tessellated darters are also present.

Anadromous Fish: **Striped bass** are common, especially during May and June. A number of anadromous fish species run up the Salmon River in the spring to spawn. Many pass through the state-owned Leesville Dam Fishway located just upstream of Rte. 151. Species include Atlantic salmon (rare), **sea-run brown trout** (uncommon), alewives and blueback herring (abundant), rainbow smelt (uncommon) and sea lamprey (abundant).

Fishing: Should be fair to good for pike, yellow perch and carp; occasionally good for catfish; and fair to poor for other fish species. Striped bass fishing can be good during May and June. White perch fishing can be good in the river above the cove during early spring.

Management: See special regulations within southern mainstem description.

Boating: See general boating restrictions within southern mainstem description.

Comments: Salmon Cove had only been electrofished once by the time of printing. The above fishery description may thus be ▼

Salmon Cove
Fish Species and Abundance

	ALL SIZES	BIG FISH	GROWTH
Gamefish			
Largemouth bass	C	C	
Northern pike	C	C	Fast
Channel catfish	C	C	
White catfish	C	C	
Panfish			
Black crappie	U	U	
White perch	U	U	Fast
Yellow perch	C	C	Fast
Brown bullhead	U	U	
Sunfish			
Bluegill	R	R	
Pumpkinseed	C	U	Fast
Redbreast	C	U	Fast
Anadromous (Abundance seasonal)			
Atlantic salmon	R	R	
Brown trout	U	U	
Striped bass	C	C	
Alewife	A		
Blueback herring	A		
Rainbow smelt	U		
Sea lamprey	A		
Other			
Tessellated darter	C		
Common carp	C		
Golden shiner	C		
Spottail shiner	A		
White sucker	A		
American eel	A		

A=Abundant, C=Common, U=Uncommon, R=Rare

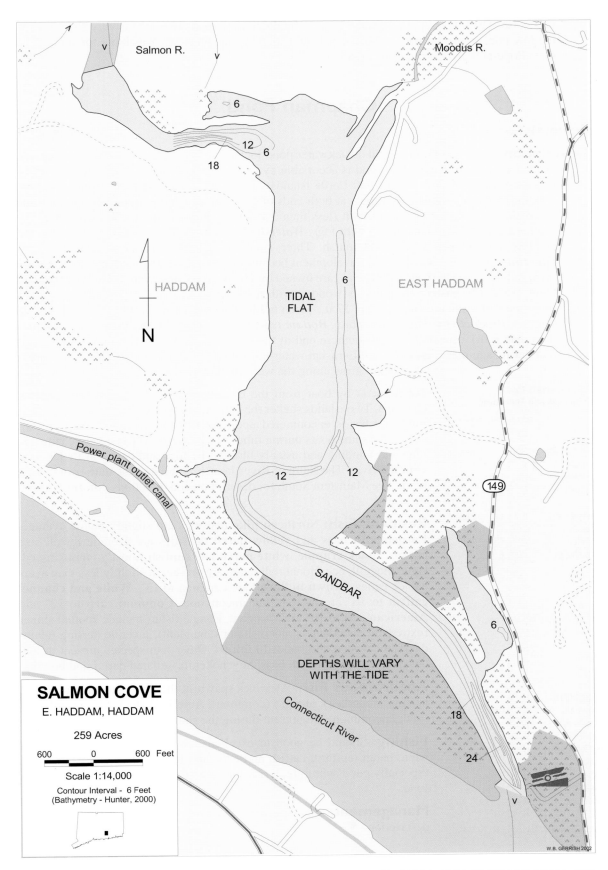

Salmon R.

Moodus R.

6

12 6

18

HADDAM

6

EAST HADDAM

TIDAL
FLAT

N

Power plant outlet canal

12   12

(149)

SANDBAR

DEPTHS WILL VARY
WITH THE TIDE

6

Connecticut River

18

24

v

SALMON COVE

E. HADDAM, HADDAM

259 Acres

600   0   600   Feet

Scale 1:14,000

Contour Interval - 6 Feet
(Bathymetry - Hunter, 2000)

W.B. GERRISH 2002

imprecise. The tide is approximately 2 hrs. behind Old Saybrook. The cove is very shallow during low tide, at which times larger boats should stick to channel areas. Watch out for submerged logs. Popular waterfowl hunting area in the fall.

Chapman Pond

Town(s): East Haddam   **51.9 acres**

Description: Chapman Pond is a tidal backwater pond located at River Mile 14 on the eastern side of the Connecticut River. The pond is accessible by two narrow channels. One is to the east of two state-owned islands (Richs and Lords Islands). The other enters the pond from the south, winding through a marsh. Tidal flats at both ends of each channel and surrounding both islands can make access to the pond difficult (less than 1 ft. deep) during low tide. The mouth of the southern channel is often choked with logs. *Watershed*: The land immediately surrounding the pond is undeveloped woods and marsh. Three small brooks feed the pond from the east. *Shoreline*: There is no residential development because most of the floodplain and upland areas surrounding the pond (nearly 800 acres) are owned by The Nature Conservancy and East Haddam Land Trust. The eastern shoreline is wooded with a moderate to steep slope and the western shoreline is marshland. *Depth*: Max 17 ft., Mean 6.9 ft. *Transparency*: Turbid; less than 3 ft. in summer. *Productivity*: High (eutrophic). *Bottom type*: Organic muck. *Vegetation*: Shallow areas (less than 8 ft.), especially in the southern end of the pond, are choked with submerged vegetation during summer. Tapegrass and Eurasian water-milfoil are the dominant species. Large areas of coontail grow along the western shoreline.

Chapman Pond
Fish Species and Abundance

	ALL SIZES	BIG FISH	GROWTH
Gamefish			
Largemouth bass	C	C	Fast
Smallmouth bass	R	R	Fast
Northern pike	C	C	Fast
Channel catfish	U	U	
White catfish	U	U	
Panfish			
Black crappie	C	C	Fast
White perch	C	C	Fast
Yellow perch	C	C	Fast
Brown bullhead	C	C	
Sunfish			
Bluegill	C	U	Fast
Pumpkinseed	C	U	Fast
Redbreast	R	R	Fast
Anadromous (Abundance seasonal)			
American shad	U		
Alewife	C		
Blueback herring	A		
Gizzard shad	U		
Other			
Tessellated darter	U		
Common carp	A		
Golden shiner	A		Avg
Spottail shiner	A		
Banded killifish	U		
Hogchoker	U		
Menhaden	U		
White sucker	C		
American eel	A		
Bowfin	R		

A=Abundant, C=Common, U=Uncommon, R=Rare

Access: Is by boat from the river via either of two shallow, narrow channels. Two islands shelter the entrance to the northern channel. A shallow sand bar is encountered upon entering the cove that may prevent access for some boats during times of low water. The southern channel is long and winding and usually blocked by logs and debris at its junction with the river. The Salmon River launch is the nearest state-owned boat ramp. See Mainstem South for description and directions. *Shore*: No public access.

Resident Fish: **Northern pike** densities are slightly below average. **Largemouth bass** and **yellow perch** densities are average for all size classes. **Black crappie**, **white perch** and **sunfish** (mostly pumpkinseed, some bluegill, occasional redbreast) are present at slightly less than average densities. **Brown bullhead** are common to 13". **White and channel catfish** to 16" are present, but uncommon. **Common carp** to 32" and **American eels** to 16" are abundant. Forage fishes include spottail shiner (extremely abundant), golden shiner (abundant), juvenile herring (abundant), menhaden and banded killifish. Other fish species present at low densities are smallmouth bass, hogchoker, tessellated darter and bowfin.

Anadromous Fish: Alewives spawn in the pond. Juvenile blueback herring (abundant), alewife (common), American shad and gizzard shad (both uncommon) are present during the summer and fall.

Fishing: Should be good to excellent for carp; fair to good for bass, white perch (spring), catfish and eels; and fair for pike and panfish. An especially good spot to bow-fish for carp during their spawning period in June.

Management: See special regulations within southern mainstem description. ▼

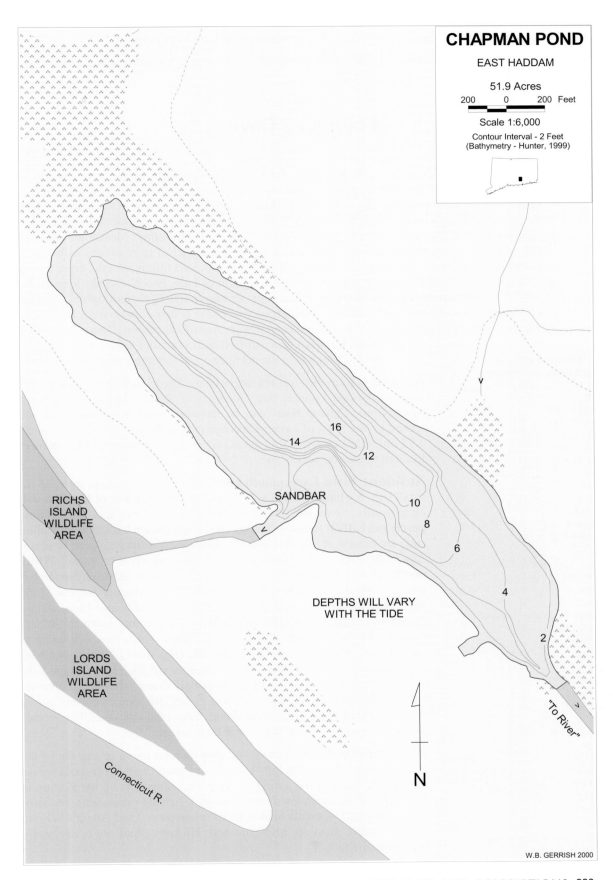

CHAPMAN POND

EAST HADDAM

51.9 Acres

200   0   200 Feet

Scale 1:6,000

Contour Interval - 2 Feet
(Bathymetry - Hunter, 1999)

RICHS
ISLAND
WILDLIFE
AREA

LORDS
ISLAND
WILDLIFE
AREA

SANDBAR

16

14

12

10

8

6

4

2

DEPTHS WILL VARY
WITH THE TIDE

"To River"

Connecticut R.

N

W.B. GERRISH 2000

Boating: See general boating restrictions within southern mainstem description.

Comments: Popular waterfowl hunting spot in the fall. Tide is approximately 2 hrs. behind Old Saybrook.

Hamburg Cove

Town(s): Lyme   **164 acres**

Description: Hamburg Cove is at the mouth of the Eightmile River on the eastern side of the Connecticut River at River Mile 7. Although the mouth of the cove is wide, it is very shallow (1 ft. deep) except for a narrow 8 ft. wide channel that is usually marked by stakes. *Watershed*: 39,937 acres of mostly woods with some residential and agricultural development. In addition to the Eightmile River, the cove is fed by Tisdale and Falls Brooks. *Shoreline*: Mostly wooded and steeply sloped with overlooking bluffs. There are a moderate number of large estates with docks, primarily along the southern shore. Numerous moorings are located throughout the cove during the boating season and a private marina is located just north of Falls Brook. *Depth*: Max 18 ft., Mean 7.3 ft. *Transparency*: Turbid; 4 ft. in summer. *Productivity*: High (eutrophic). *Bottom type*: Mud and woody debris. *Vegetation*: Submerged vegetation is dense and covers 15-80% of the shallow water throughout the cove. Marked channels are free of vegetation. Dominant species are tapegrass, Eurasian water-milfoil and coontail. Floating mats of white water-lily are common in the north end and scattered in the cove areas.

Access: Is from the river for larger boats. The closest state launch is the Baldwin Bridge Launch (see Connecticut River Mainstem South for description). Car-top boats can be launched from an unimproved site owned by the town of Lyme. *Directions*: Exit 70 off I-95, Rte 156 north 4.75 miles, left on Cove Rd., access is on right before the bridge. *Shore*: Limited to car-top access site.

Resident Fish: **Largemouth bass** densities are less than average for small fish, but larger bass (13-20") are common. Schools of **bluefish** will occasionally move into the cove during the summer and fall. **Yellow perch** and **catfish** (mostly channel cats, some brown bullheads and white cats) are present at less than average densities. Yellow perch can be abundant in the early spring when they move into the cove to spawn. **White perch** over-winter in the cove and can be very abundant from November through May, but are at less than average densities through the rest of the year. **Sunfish** (mostly pumpkinseed, some redbreast and bluegill) are common, but larger sunfish (greater than 7") are rare. **Carp** to 30" are common (a 38" individual was electrofished which was estimated at greater than 30 lb.). Small **American eels** (less than 13") are abundant, but larger eels are uncommon. White suckers are abundant. Forage fishes include golden shiner (abundant), spottail shiner (abundant), juvenile herring (common) and banded killifish. Other fish species present at low densities are northern pike, smallmouth bass, chain pickerel, black crappie, rock bass, tessellated darter and hogchoker.

Anadromous Fish: Schools of **striped bass** move in and out of the cove from spring through fall. A number of anadromous fish species pass through the cove in the spring on their spawning runs up the Eightmile River. These include alewife and blueback herring (abundant), sea lamprey (common), **sea-run brown trout** (uncommon) and Atlantic salmon (rare). Gizzard shad are also common. **Hickory shad** are occasionally present in the fall. ▼

Hamburg Cove Fish Species and Abundance	ALL SIZES	BIG FISH	GROWTH
Gamefish			
Largemouth bass	C	C	Fast
Smallmouth bass	R	R	
Northern pike	U	U	
Channel catfish	C	C	
White catfish	U	U	
Bluefish	U	U	
Panfish			
Black crappie	R	R	
White perch	C	C	Fast
Yellow perch	C	C	Avg
Brown bullhead	U	U	
Sunfish			
Bluegill	C	U	Avg
Pumpkinseed	C	U	Fast
Redbreast	C	U	Avg
Rock bass	U	R	
Anadromous (Abundance seasonal)			
Atlantic salmon	R		
Brown trout	U		
Striped bass	C	C	
Alewife	A		
Blueback herring	A		
Gizzard shad	C		
Hickory shad	U		
Other			
Tessellated darter	U		
Common carp	C		
Golden shiner	A		Slow
Spottail shiner	A		
Banded killifish	U		
Hogchoker	U		
White sucker	A		
American eel	A		

A=Abundant, C=Common, U=Uncommon, R=Rare

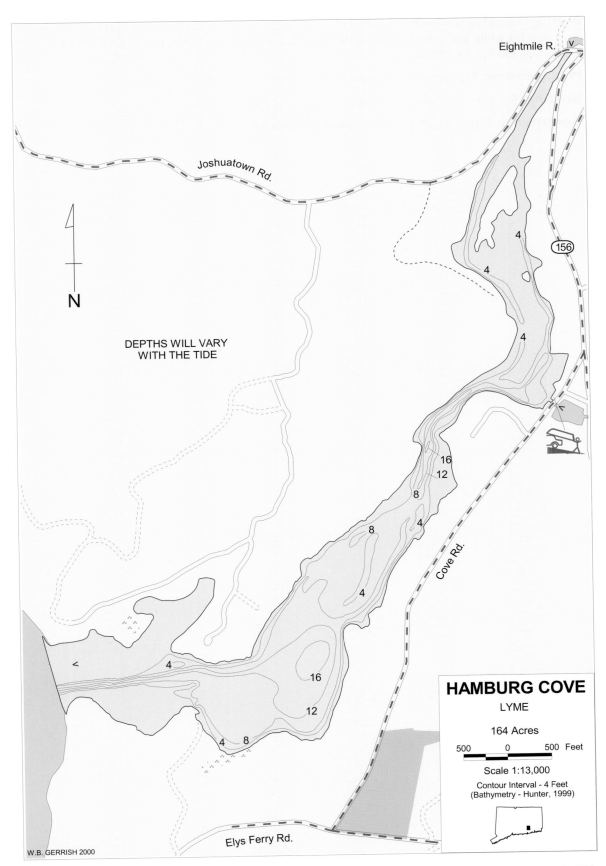

Eightmile R.

Joshuatown Rd.

156

DEPTHS WILL VARY
WITH THE TIDE

4

4

4

16
12

8

8

4

4

Cove Rd.

4

16

12

4 8

HAMBURG COVE

LYME

164 Acres

500   0   500 Feet

Scale 1:13,000

Contour Interval - 4 Feet
(Bathymetry - Hunter, 1999)

Elys Ferry Rd.

W.B. GERRISH 2000

Fishing: Should be seasonally good at the mouth of the cove for striped bass. It is also good to excellent for white and yellow perch in the fall through the early spring; fair to good for largemouth bass; and fair for catfish.

Management: See special regulations within southern mainstem description.

Boating: See general boating restrictions within southern mainstem description.

Comments: Tide is less than 1 hr. behind Old Saybrook.

Glossary of Scientific Terms

The following is a list of selected aquatic and fisheries terms used in this publication. In an effort to make them understandable to the lay person, many of the definitions are over-simplified from a technical standpoint.

< — Mathematical symbol meaning "less than." Example: <15" reads "less than 15 inches."

> — Mathematical symbol meaning "greater than." Example: >15" reads "greater than 15 inches."

Adipose fin — A small, fleshy protuberance on the back and toward the rear of some fish species, notably trout and salmon.

Algae — Aquatic plants that are often single-celled and microscopic. Some algal species are colonial or filamentous. Many types of algae float in the water column of lakes.

Algal bloom (or algae bloom) — A dense growth of algae that can severely reduce water clarity and give lake water a greenish color.

Anal fin — A fin on the bottom of a fish, set back near the anus.

Balance — A balanced fish population is one with high densities of fast-growing, large predatory gamefish and low to moderate densities of small fish. An imbalanced fish population has too many small fish (which leads to slower growth rates) and too few large predatory gamefish.

Barbel — A fleshy, protruding taste sensor near the mouth of some fishes (example, catfish "whiskers").

Bathymetry — Lake-depth data, usually expressed as equal depth contour lines.

Benthic — Living on the lake bottom.

Broadcast — Refers to the scattering of eggs over a wide area.

Caudal fin — Tail fin.

Crustacean — A class of mostly aquatic invertebrates that have a hard outer shell (examples, crayfish, shrimp, crabs).

Dissolved oxygen (or "DO") — The quantity of oxygen that is in solution in water, usually expressed as parts per million (ppm) or milligrams/liter (mg/l).

Dorsal fin — A fin on the back of a fish. Many warmwater fishes, such as members of the sunfish and perch families, have two dorsal fins — a "spiny" dorsal (with spines) followed by a "soft" dorsal (with no spines). Others, such as those in the minnow and pike families, have a single soft dorsal fin.

Eutrophic — See Trophic classification.

Fingerling — Small, juvenile fish older than the larval or "fry" stage.

Forage species — Fish and other animals that predatory fish feed on (for example, alewives are forage fish).

Fry — Fish in their larval stage.

Holdover — A term applied to trout that survive either the harsh summer or winter seasons.

Invertebrate — Animals lacking a backbone (for example, crayfish, worms, insects).

Lateral line — A series (line) of organs on the sides of fish that can sense vibration in water.

Laterally compressed — A common body shape in fishes that is narrower when viewed from the top and wider when viewed from the side.

Limnology — The study of lakes.

Macrophytes (or macrophytic plants) — Large multicellular (many-celled) aquatic plants.

Mesotrophic — See Trophic classification.

Mollusk — A group of invertebrates that have a soft body and a hard shell (examples, snails, clams, mussels).

Nutrients — Organic chemicals such as phosphorous and nitrogen that aquatic plants need to live and grow.

Oligotrophic — See Trophic classification.

Omnivorous — Eating a variety of plants and animals.

Pectoral fin — A pair of fins on the sides and toward the front of a fish's body.

Pelagic — Living in the open water away from structure.

Pelvic fins (or ventral fins) — A pair of fins on the bottom and toward the front of a fish.

Photosynthesis — The process by which plants convert organic chemicals (nutrients) and the energy from sunlight into plant tissue.

Phytoplankton — See Plankton

Piscivore (or piscivorous) — A fish or other animal that eats primarily fish.

Planktivore (or planktivorous) — A fish or other animal that eats primarily plankton.

Plankton — Small to microscopic plants and animals that live in the water column of lakes and form the base of the food chain for fishes. Phytoplankton refers to plant plankton and zooplankton to animal plankton.

Ppm — Parts per million.

Productivity — **Fish productivity** refers to a lake's potential for producing fish. **Lake productivity** refers to a lake's capacity to support plants and animals (see also Trophic classification).

Put-and-Take — A management strategy where catchable size fish are stocked for immediate harvest by anglers.

Recruitment — The relative number of fish that are born and survive to adult size.

Slot length limit (protected slot) — The size range of fish between which they may not be kept. Anglers may keep fish that are above or below the protected slot length range. For example, in the case of a 12-16" slot limit, anglers may keep fish smaller than 12" or greater than 16", but not between 12" and 16".

Stockpiling — An accumulation of one size group of fish in a population. In this publication, a stockpiled fish population refers to one that has too many slow-growing, small fish and relatively few large ones. Stockpiling is usually caused by excessive fish recruitment and/or low densities of large predatory fish, which causes young fish to become overabundant (see also Balance).

Stratification — A process where lake water separates into distinct layers by depth that differ in temperature and/or dissolved oxygen.

Stunting — A term applied to fish that grow so slowly that they never reach a size typical for mature adults.

Thermocline — A layer of water in lakes during summer that becomes suddenly colder with depth.

Trophic classification — A system to classify lakes into categories of productivity. It is based on the relative amount of chlorophyll-a, phosphorous, nitrogen, water transparency and aquatic vegetation present in lakes. Trophic classifications are (ranked from least to most productive): oligotrophic, early mesotrophic, mesotrophic, late mesotrophic, eutrophic and highly eutrophic.

Vascular plants — Describing plants that have ducts in their tissue that transport fluid and nutrients. Analogous to an animal's circulatory system of arteries and veins. Non-vascular plants include algae and fungi.

Ventral fin — See Pelvic fin.

Winter kill — A fish kill that occurs when heavy ice and snow cover causes oxygen in a shallow pond to decline to lethal levels.

Zooplankton (or zooplankters) — See Plankton.

Appendix

Appendix 1.

Cutoff points used to describe growth rates of common fishes in Connecticut lakes and ponds. Growth is defined here as how long (in years) it takes each fish species to reach "quality size". For example, largemouth bass that take 3.4 to 3.9 years to reach 12 inches in length are considered to have "average" growth; whereas bass that take 4.5 to 4.9 years to reach 12 inches would be considered "slow". For non-game species (alewife and golden shiner), growth is the length (in inches) attained by age two. (The symbol < means "less than"; > means "greater than".)

		AGE AT QUALITY SIZE						
SPECIES	QUALITY SIZE (IN)	VERY FAST (>Fast)	FAST (Fast)	FAST TO AVERAGE (>Avg)	AVERAGE (Avg)	AVERAGE TO SLOW (<Avg)	SLOW (Slow)	VERY SLOW (<Slow)
Largemouth bass	12	<2.6	2.6-2.9	3.0-3.3	3.4-3.9	4.0-4.4	4.5-4.9	>4.9
Smallmouth bass	12	<3.4	3.4-3.7	3.8-4.1	4.2-4.7	4.8-5.2	5.3-5.7	>5.7
Chain pickerel	15	<1.6	1.6-1.9	2.0-2.3	2.4-2.9	3.0-3.5	3.6-3.9	>3.9
Yellow perch	8	<2.4	2.4-2.9	3.0-3.4	3.5-4.1	4.2-4.5	4.6-5.3	>5.3
White perch	8	<2.0	2.0-2.1	2.2-2.5	2.6-3.1	3.2-3.5	3.6-4.3	>4.3
Black crappie	8	<2.0	2.0-2.3	2.4-2.7	2.8-3.3	3.4-3.7	3.8-4.1	>4.1
Rock bass	7	<3.0	3.0-3.5	3.6-4.1	4.2-5.1	5.2-5.7	5.8-6.5	>6.5
Bluegill sunfish	6	<2.6	2.6-2.9	3.0-3.3	3.4-3.9	4.0-4.5	4.6-5.3	>5.3
Pumpkinseed sunfish	6	<2.8	2.8-3.3	3.4-3.8	3.9-4.4	4.5-5.3	5.4-6.1	>6.1
Redbreast sunfish	6		<3.1	3.2-3.9	4.0-5.0	5.1-5.9	>6.0	

		LENGTH (INCHES) AT AGE 2 YEARS						
SPECIES	QUALITY SIZE (IN)	VERY FAST (>Fast)	FAST (Fast)	FAST TO AVERAGE (>Avg)	AVERAGE (Avg)	AVERAGE TO SLOW (<Avg)	SLOW (Slow)	VERY SLOW (<Slow)
Golden shiner		>6.9	6.5-6.9	6.1-6.4	5.5-6.0	5.1-5.4	4.7-5.0	<4.7
Alewife		>8.6	7.1-8.6	6.3-7.0	5.1-6.2	4.3-5.0	<4.3	

Appendix 2.

State average length-at-age (in inches) for common Connecticut warmwater fish species sampled during the Statewide Lake and Pond Electrofishing Survey (1988-95). To read the table, for example, largemouth bass average 3.9 inches at age 1, 7.3 inches at age 2, 10.8 inches at age 3, etc.

SPECIES	Oldest fish aged	AGE (Years)													
		1	2	3	4	5	6	7	8	9	10	11	12	13	14
Largemouth bass	17	3.9	7.3	10.8	12.9	14.5	15.8	16.9	17.7	18.5	19.4	19.8	20.4	20.9	21.4
Smallmouth bass	15	3.7	6.5	9.0	11.2	12.9	14.3	15.7	16.8	17.5	18.3	18.9	19.3		
Chain pickerel	8	7.8	13.1	16.0	18.4	20.5	21.5	24.2							
Black crappie	11	3.0	6.0	8.3	9.7	10.7	11.4	12.2	12.5	12.8					
Yellow perch	13	3.5	5.5	7.1	8.2	9.1	9.7	10.3	10.7	11.2	11.6	11.9			
White perch	14	3.9	6.6	8.5	9.7	10.4	10.9	11.6	11.9	12.4					
Bluegill	12	1.8	3.6	5.2	6.4	7.1	7.6	7.9	8.1	8.3	8.5				
Pumpkinseed	14	2.0	3.6	4.9	5.9	6.5	6.9	7.2	7.4	7.8	7.8				
Redbreast	9	2.0	3.4	4.6	5.6	6.2	6.6	6.8	7.0						
Rock bass	13	2.2	3.9	5.5	6.7	7.5	8.1	8.6	8.8	9.0					
Alewife	6	4.0	5.7	5.9	6.9	8.6									
Golden shiner	11	3.8	5.7	7.2	8.1	8.6	9.1	9.3							

Appendix 3.

A list of freshwater and anadromous fish species sampled from Connecticut lakes and ponds and the Connecticut River (1988-2000). Numbers indicate the percent of sites containing each species (for example, Atlantic sturgeon were found in none of the lakes and ponds, but were found in 10 percent of Connecticut River sites). (* = Native species, ** = Native only as an anadromous form.)

FAMILY NAME COMMON NAME	SCIENTIFIC NAME	LAKES AND PONDS	CONNECTICUT RIVER
Acipenseridae			
* Atlantic sturgeon	*Acipenser oxyrhynchus*	-	10
* Shortnose sturgeon	*Acipenser brevirostrum*	-	30
Amiidae			
Bowfin	*Amia calva*	1	10
Anguillidae			
* American eel	*Anguilla rostrata*	58	100
Atherinidae			
* Inland silverside	*Menidia beryllina*	-	10
Catostomidae			
* Creek chubsucker	*Erimyzon oblongus*	15	-
* White sucker	*Catostomus commersoni*	55	100
Centrarchidae			
* Banded sunfish	*Enneacanthus obesus*	1	-
Black crappie	*Pomoxis nigromaculatus*	72	100
Bluegill	*Lepomis macrochirus*	96	90
Green sunfish	*Lepomis cyanellus*	6	-
Hybrid sunfish	*Lepomis sp.*	59	20
Largemouth bass	*Micropterus salmoides*	97	90
* Pumpkinseed	*Lepomis gibbosus*	96	70
* Redbreast sunfish	*Lepomis auritus*	38	90
Rock bass	*Ambloplites rupestris*	34	50
Smallmouth bass	*Micropterus dolomieu*	50	70
White crappie	*Pomoxis annularis*	-	40
Clupeidae			
** Alewife	*Alosa pseudoharengus*	35	100
* American shad	*Alosa sapidissima*	-	60
* Blueback herring	*Alosa aestivalis*	-	100
Gizzard shad	*Dorosoma cepedianum*	-	70
** Hickory shad	*Alosa mediocris*	-	20
Cyprinidae			
Bluntnose minnow	*Pimephales notatus*	1	-
* Bridled shiner	*Notropis bifrenatus*	15	-
Common carp	*Cyprinus carpio*	16	100
* Common shiner	*Luxilus cornutus*	3	-
* Fallfish	*Semotilus corporalis*	8	10
Fathead minnow	*Pimephales promelas*	1	-
* Golden shiner	*Notemigonus crysoleucas*	88	100
Goldfish	*Carassius auratus*	7	10

FAMILY NAME COMMON NAME	SCIENTIFIC NAME	LAKES AND PONDS	CONNECTICUT RIVER
Cyprinidae (continued)			
Grass carp	*Ctenopharyngodon idella*	1	-
* Spottail shiner	*Notropis hudsonius*	17	100
Tench	*Tinca tinca*	1	-
Cyprinodontidae			
* Banded killifish	*Fundulus diaphanus*	47	40
* Mummichog	*Fundulus heteroclitus*	-	10
Esocidae			
* Chain pickerel	*Esox niger*	88	30
Northern pike	*Esox lucius*	7	70
* Redfin pickerel	*Esox americanus*	5	20
Gasterosteidae			
* Fourspine stickleback	*Apeltes quadracus*	1	-
Ictaluridae			
Black bullhead	*Ameiurus melas*	1	-
* Brown bullhead	*Ameiurus nebulosus*	91	70
Channel catfish	*Ictalurus punctatus*	1	80
White catfish	*Ameiurus catus*	16	70
Yellow bullhead	*Ameiurus natalis*	17	-
Moronidae			
** Striped bass	*Morone saxatilis*	-	60
** White perch	*Morone americana*	27	100
Osmeridae			
** Rainbow smelt	*Osmerus mordax*	3	30
Percidae			
* Swamp darter	*Etheostoma fusiforme*	5	-
* Tessellated darter	*Etheostoma olmstedi*	26	-
Walleye	*Stizostedion vitreum*	6	30
* Yellow Perch	*Perca flavescens*	90	100
Petromyzontidae			
** Sea lamprey	*Petromyzon marinus*	-	30
Salmonidae			
** Atlantic salmon	*Salmo salar*	-	30
* Brook trout	*Salvelinus fontinalis*	17	10
Brown trout	*Salmo trutta*	52	20
Kokanee	*Oncorhynchus nerka*	3	-
Rainbow trout	*Oncorhynchus mykiss*	46	-
Soleidae			
* Hogchocker	*Trinectes maculatus*	-	30
Umbridae			
Central mudminnow	*Umbra limi*	-	20

Appendix 4.

List of aquatic plants found in Connecticut lakes and ponds with notes on their status in the state.

PLANT FAMILY SCIENTIFIC NAME	COMMON NAME	STATE STATUS
Alismataceae (Water-plantain Family)		
Alisma	Mud- or water-plantain	
Sagittaria	Arrowhead, Arrowleaf	
Sagittaria engelmanniana	Acid water arrowhead	
Sagittaria graminea	Narrow-leaved arrowhead, Grass-leaved sagittaria	
Sagittaria latifolia var. *latifolia*	Common arrowhead, Duck potato	
Sagittaria montevidensis	Mississippi arrowhead	
Sagittaria subulata var. *subulata*	Hudson sagittaria	Special Concern
Araceae (Arum Family)		
Peltandra virginica	Arrow-arum, Tuckahoe	
Callitrichaceae (Water-Starwort Family)		
Callitriche heterophylla	Water-starwort	
Cabombaceae (Water-shield Family)		
Brasenia schreberi	Water-shield	
Cabomba caroliniana	Fanwort	Non-native Invasive
Ceratophyllaceae (Hornwort Family)		
Ceratophyllum demersum	Coontail	
Ceratophyllum echinatum	Coontail	
Characeae		
Chara sp.	Musk grass	
Nitella sp.	Stonewort	
Compositae (Composite Family)		
Megalodonta beckii	Water-marigold	Threatened
Cyperaceae (Sedge Family)		
Dulichium arundinaceum	Three-way sedge	
Eleocharis sp.	Spike-rush	
Scirpus sp.	Bulrush	
Scirpus acutus	Hardstem bulrush	Threatened
Scirpus subterminalis	Water club rush	
Scirpus torreyi		Threatened
Scirpus validus var. *creber*	Great or softstem bulrush	
Elatinaceae (Waterwort Family)		
Elatine sp.	Waterwort	
Eriocaulaceae (Pipewort Family)		
Eriocaulon parkeri	Parker's pipewort	Threatened
Eriocaulon aquaticum	Pipewort, White buttons	
Gentianaceae (Gentian Family)		
Nymphoides cordata	Floating-heart	
Haloragaceae (Water-Milfoil Family)		
Myriophyllum sp.	Water-milfoil	
Myriophyllum alterniflorum	Slender water-milfoil	Endangered
Myriophyllum exalbescens		

PLANT FAMILY		
SCIENTIFIC NAME	COMMON NAME	STATE STATUS

Haloragaceae (Water-Milfoil Family) (continued)

Myriophyllum heterophyllum	Variable-leaved water-milfoil	Non-native Invasive
Myriophyllum humile	Low water-milfoil	
Myriophyllum pinnatum	Pinnate water-milfoil	Special Concern
Myriophyllum tenellum	Leafless water-milfoil	Special Concern
Myriophyllum verticillatum	Whorled water-milfoil	
Myriophyllum spicatum	Eurasian or European water-milfoil	Non-native Invasive
Proserpinaca palustris	Mermaid-weed	

Hydrocharitaceae (Frog's-bit Family)

Elodea sp.	Waterweed	
Elodea canadensis	Common waterweed	
Elodea nuttalli	Free-flowered waterweed	
Ergeria densa	Brazilian waterweed	Non-native
Vallisneria americana	Tapegrass	

Isoetaceae (Quillwort Family)

Isoetes sp.	Quillwort	

Juncaceae (Rush Family)

Juncus sp.	Rush	

Lemnaceae (Duckweed Family)

Lemna sp.	Duckweed	
Spirodela polyrhiza	Greater duckweed	

Lentibulariaceae (Bladderwort Family)

Utricularia sp.	Bladderwort	
Utricularia biflora	Two-flowered bladderwort	Special Concern
Utricularia cornuta	Horned bladderwort	
Utricularia fibrosa	Fibrous bladderwort	Special Concern
Utricularia geminiscapa	Mixed bladderwort	
Utricularia gibba	Humped bladderwort	
Utricularia radiata	Floating bladderwort	
Utricularia intermedia	Flat-leaved bladderwort	
Utricularia minor	Lesser or small bladderwort	
Utricularia purpurea	Spotted or purple bladderwort	
Utricularia resupinata	Resupinate bladderwort	Endangered
Utricularia vulgaris	Common or greater bladderwort	

Lobeliaceae (Lobelia Family)

Lobelia dortmanna	Water lobelia	

Lythracaeae

Decodon verticillatus	Water willow	
Lythrum salicaria	Purple loosestrife	Non-native Invasive

Marsileaceae

Marsilea quadrifolia	Water shamrock	

Najadaceae (Naiad Family)

Najas sp.	Naiad	
Najas flexilis	Northern water-nymph	
Najas gracillima	Slender water-nymph	
Najas guadalupensis	Southern water-nymph	Special Concern
Najas minor	Eutrophic water-nymph	Non-native

| PLANT FAMILY | | |
SCIENTIFIC NAME	COMMON NAME	STATE STATUS
Nymphaeaceae (Water-lily Family)		
Nuphar sp.	Yellow pond-lily	
Nuphar variegatum	Yellow pond-lily, Bullhead-lily, Spatter-dock	
Nymphaea odorata	White water-lily	
Onagraceae (Evening-Primrose Family)		
Ludwigia sp.	False loosestrife	
Ludwigia alternifolia	Seedbox	
Ludwigia palustris	Marsh- or water-purslane	
Ludwigia polycarpa	Many-fruited false loosestrife	Special Concern
Ludwigia sphaerocarpa	Round-pod water primrose	Endangered
Polygonaceae (Buckwheat Family)		
Polygonum sp.	Knotweed, Smartweed	
Pontederiaceae (Pickerelweed Family)		
Heteranthera dubia	Mud-plantain, Water stargrass	
Pontederia cordata	Pickerelweed	
Potamogetonaceae (Pondweed Family)		
Potamogeton sp.	Pondweed	
Potamogeton alpinus var. *tenuifolius*	Red pondweed	
Potamogeton amplifolius	Large-leaved pondweed	
Potamogeton bicupulatus	Threadleaf pondweed	
Potamogeton confervoides	Alga pondweed	Special Concern
Potamogeton crispus	Curly pondweed	Non-native Invasive
Potamogeton diversifolius		Special Concern
Potamogeton epihydrus var. *epihydrus* and var. *ramosus*	Ribbonleaf or paddleleaf pondweed	
Potamogeton foliosus	Leafy pondweed	
Potamogeton friesii	Fries' pondweed	Special Concern
Potamogeton gramineus	Variable pondweed	
Potamogeton hillii	Hill's pondweed	Endangered
Potamogeton illinoensis	Illinois pondweed	
Potamogeton natans	Floating-leaved pondweed	
Potamogeton nodosus	Longleaf pondweed	
Potamogeton oakesianus	Oakes' pondweed	
Potamogeton obtusifolius	Bluntleaf pondweed	
Potamogeton ogdenii	Ogden's pondweed	
Potamogeton pectinatus	Sago pondweed	
Potamogeton perfoliatus	Perfoliate pondweed	
Potamogeton praelongus	Whitestem pondweed	
Potamogeton pulcher	Spotted-stem pondweed	
Potamogeton pusillus var. *pusillus*	Slender pondweed	
Potamogeton pusillus var. *gemmiparus*	Slender pondweed	Special Concern
Potamogeton pusillus var. *tenuissimus*	Slender pondweed	

SCIENTIFIC NAME	COMMON NAME	STATE STATUS
Potamogeton richardsonii	Richardson's pondweed	
Potamogeton robbinsii	Fern pondweed	
Potamogeton spirillus	Northern snailseed pondweed	
Potamogeton strictifolius	Straight-leaved pondweed	Special Concern
Potamogeton vaseyi	Vasey's pondweed	Special Concern
Potamogeton zosteriformis	Flatstem pondweed	
Primulaceae (Primrose Family)		
Hottonia inflata	Featherfoil	Special Concern
Ranunculaceae (Crowfoot Family)		
Ranunculus sp.	Crowfoot, Buttercup	
Ranunculus flabellaris	Yellow water-crowfoot	
Ranunculus longirostris	White water-crowfoot	
Ranunculus subrigidus	Stiff white water-crowfoot	Special Concern
Ranunculus trichophyllus	Common white water-crowfoot	
Scrophulariaceae (Figwort Family)		
Gratiola aurea	Golden-pert or yellow hedge-hyssop	
Limosella subulata	Mudwort	Special Concern
Lindernia dubia	False pimpernel	
Sparganiaceae (Bur-reed Family)		
Sparganium sp.	Bur-reed	
Sparganium americanum		
Sparganium androcladum		
Sparganium angustifolium		
Sparganium chlorocarpum	Green-fruited bur-reed	
Sparganium eurycarpum		
Sparganium fluctuans	Floating bur-reed	Endangered
Sparganium minimum	Least bur-reed	Special Concern
Trapaceae (Water-chestnut Family)		
Trapa natan	Water-chestnut	Non-native Invasive
Typhaceae (Cat-tail Family)		
Typha sp.	Cat-tail	
Typha angustifolia	Narrow-leaved cat-tail	
Typha *latifolia*	Common cat-tail	
Umbelliferae (Parsley Family)		
Lilaeopsis chinensis	Lilaeopsis	Special Concern
Zannichelliaceae (Horned Pondweed Family)		
Zannichellia palustris var. *major*	Horned pondweed	

Appendix 5.

Best Fishing Lakes by Species. The following tables show average densities (number of fish caught per hour of electrofishing) of fish sampled from public lakes by the DEP Fisheries Division. Lakes are ranked by densities of legal size or "quality size" fish caught (first column). Notice that lakes rank differently when considering densities of larger size fish (second column). Only lakes that were sampled more than once are included in the lists.

Top 40 Largemouth Bass Lakes

RANK	LAKE	>12 INCHES	>15 INCHES
1	Wononscopomuc L.	53.6	16.1
2	Ball P.	46.8	30.5
3	Rogers L.	45.8	20.4
4	Wyassup L.	43.3	7.0
5	Quinebaug L.	41.5	10.1
6	Waramaug L.	40.4	15.2
7	Pataganset L.	39.1	17.5
8	Congamond L.	38.0	23.8
9	Saltonstall L.	37.4	27.1
10	Bashan L.	37.2	11.2
11	Halls P.	35.5	12.2
12	Mudge P.	34.8	11.8
13	Uncas L.	33.4	16.5
14	Mamanasco L.	33.0	8.3
15	Batterson Park P.	32.8	18.1
16	Crystal L. (Ellington)	30.4	8.0
17	Beach P.	30.1	21.1
18	Squantz P.	29.1	16.7
19	Alexander L.	27.7	3.7
20	Amos L.	26.7	15.5
21	Coventry L.	26.6	6.3
22	Mansfield Hollow Res.	26.1	5.8
23	Bolton L., Lower	25.5	5.3
24	Billings L.	24.9	5.1
25	Mashapaug L.	24.6	13.0
26	Highland L.	24.5	12.6
27	Black P. (Woodstock)	24.2	8.0
28	Moodus Res.	23.3	4.6
29	East Twin L.	23.0	5.9
30	West Side P.	22.3	4.5
31	Pickerel L.	21.1	4.1
32	Dog P.	20.9	6.1
33	Powers L.	20.6	14.1
34	Kenosia L.	20.0	4.9
35	Quonnipaug L.	19.9	9.2
36	Candlewood L.	19.6	9.4
37	Quaddick Res.	19.5	5.8
38	Chapman P.	19.1	7.9
39	Bolton L., Middle	19.1	1.5
40	North Farms Res.	18.9	9.3

Top 20 Smallmouth Bass Lakes

RANK	LAKE	>12 INCHES	>15 INCHES
1	Mashapaug L.	22.1	3.4
2	Gardner L.	17.4	3.7
3	McDonough L.	15.7	7.7
4	Conn River (Enfield area)	10.7	4.8
5	Shenipsit L.	9.4	0.6
6	Bashan L.	8.8	1.9
7	Coventry L.	7.8	1.2
8	Saugatuck Res.	7.2	2.7
9	Colebrook Res.	6.1	2.2
10	Candlewood L.	6.0	2.7
11	Squantz P.	5.9	1.6
12	Wyassup L.	5.9	1.5
13	Highland L.	5.6	2.3
14	Housatonic L.	4.6	0.5
15	Lillinonah L.	4.5	1.0
16	Rainbow Res.	4.3	1.3
17	Zoar L.	4.0	1.2
18	West Branch Res.	3.7	0.8
19	Conn River (Haddam area)	3.7	0.0
20	Conn River (Hartford area)	3.3	1.0

Top 20 Chain Pickerel Lakes

RANK	LAKE	>15 INCHES	>18 INCHES
1	Silver L.	15.6	0.4
2	Amos L.	12.9	6.5
3	Dog P.	11.1	0.4
4	Powers L.	9.2	5.3
5	Wononscopomuc L.	8.6	4.6
6	Halls P.	8.6	0.9
7	Pataganset L.	8.1	2.3
8	Hayward L.	8.0	1.6
9	Mudge P.	7.8	3.0
10	Quinebaug L.	7.2	3.9
11	Waramaug L.	7.0	4.1
12	Quaddick Res.	6.4	1.2
13	Long P. (N. Stonington)	6.2	3.4
14	Bashan L.	5.9	2.6
15	Wyassup L.	5.4	2.8
16	McDonough L.	5.4	1.9
17	Bantam L.	5.3	1.8
18	Mansfield Hollow Res.	4.9	1.4
19	Rogers L.	4.8	1.1
20	Black P. (Meriden)	3.9	2.2

Top 20 Black Crappie Lakes

RANK	LAKE	>8 INCHES	>10 INCHES
1	Conn River (Enfield area)	33.4	15.0
2	Mamanasco L.	32.4	2.9
3	Lake of Isles	24.3	8.2
4	Silver L.	18.6	6.5
5	Aspinook P.	15.8	0.7
6	Dog P.	15.2	0.0
7	Bolton L., Low.	14.2	7.1
8	Quinebaug L.	14.2	5.5
9	Halls P.	13.3	2.3
10	Glasgo P.	12.3	3.5
11	Wethersfield Cove	11.8	7.0
12	Kenosia L.	10.7	3.0
13	Highland L.	9.4	6.4
14	Crow Point Cove	9.4	4.1
15	West Thompson Res.	9.2	3.5
16	Pickerel L.	7.4	1.8
17	Shenipsit L.	7.3	4.7
18	Black P. (Meriden)	6.9	0.6
19	Coventry L.	6.8	3.7
20	Rainbow Res.	6.1	1.1

Top 20 Yellow Perch Lakes

RANK	LAKE	>8 INCHES	>10 INCHES
1	Tyler L.	250.7	10.5
2	West Side P.	207.2	28.0
3	Coventry L.	147.0	16.0
4	Park P.	132.0	12.6
5	Bolton L., Lower	130.4	72.3
6	Bashan L.	93.7	12.3
7	Wyassup L.	92.3	17.6
8	Bolton L., Middle	85.5	10.8
9	Mudge P.	79.7	23.1
10	Colebrook Res.	77.5	1.4
11	Bantam L.	77.3	12.8
12	Wononscopomuc L.	75.8	29.0
13	Housatonic L.	68.9	24.5
14	Black P. (Woodstock)	66.2	20.1
15	Dog P.	57.5	6.2
16	Rogers L.	53.2	12.0
17	Hayward L.	52.8	6.3
18	Gorton P.	49.8	7.8
19	Gardner L.	48.7	24.8
20	West Branch Res.	48.6	0.5

Top 20 Sunfish Lakes

RANK	LAKE	>6 INCHES	>7 INCHES
1	Waramaug L.	351.1	100.0
2	Quinebaug L.	345.5	228.7
3	Mamanasco L.	345.1	146.9
4	Hayward L.	224.9	155.1
5	Amos L.	206.5	34.0
6	Bashan L.	205.1	129.5
7	Billings L.	198.0	52.6
8	Mudge P.	195.0	135.0
9	Quaddick Res.	193.2	99.7
10	Bolton L., Lower	172.8	120.0
11	Kenosia L.	166.5	17.8
12	Crystal L. (Ellington)	165.9	72.6
13	Bolton L., Middle	165.2	101.9
14	Highland L.	161.6	66.6
15	Ball P.	157.4	24.5
16	Halls P.	155.0	5.6
17	Pataganset L.	152.8	48.6
18	Wononscopomuc L.	143.4	77.2
19	Black P. (Meriden)	143.2	34.4
20	Rogers L.	141.3	28.2

Top 20 Brown Bullhead Lakes

RANK	LAKE	>9 INCHES	>12 INCHES
1	Ball P.	27.5	3.0
2	Congamond L.	22.8	2.8
3	Black P. (Woodstock)	20.5	10.7
4	Quonnipaug L.	20.3	0.6
5	Gardner L.	20.1	6.0
6	Mudge P.	16.6	10.2
7	Mamanasco L.	16.2	11.0
8	Tyler L.	15.1	8.6
9	Glasgo P.	14.6	0.0
10	Rogers L.	14.4	7.3
11	North Farms Res.	12.7	5.9
12	Amos L.	12.1	2.6
13	Avery P.	11.1	0.8
14	West Side P.	11.0	4.9
15	Billings L.	10.4	0.8
16	Waramaug L.	9.8	7.5
17	Chapman P.	9.8	3.7
18	Dog P.	9.8	1.2
19	Silver L.	7.8	1.7
20	Lake of Isles	7.7	4.4

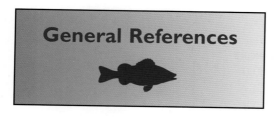

General References

Anonymous. 1982. Trophic Classifications of Seventy Connecticut Lakes. Conn. Dept. Environmental Protection. Bull No. 3. 364p.

Anonymous. 1991. Trophic Classifications of Forty-nine Connecticut Lakes. Conn. Dept. Environmental Protection. Bureau of Water Management. 98p.

Anonymous. 1998. Trophic Classifications of Twelve Connecticut Lakes. Conn. Dept. Environmental Protection. Bureau of Water Management. 24p.

Borton, M. C., B. E. Becker, T. Scannell, and G. Mitchell, eds. 1990. The Complete Boating Guide to the Connecticut River, 2nd Edition. Embassy Marine Publishing, Essex, CT. 239p.

Canavan, R. W. IV and P. A. Siver. 1995. Connecticut Lakes: A Study of the Chemical and Physical Properties of Fifty-six Connecticut Lakes. Conn. College Arboretum, New London, CT. 299p.

Crow, G. E. and C. B. Hellquist. 1983. Aquatic Vascular Plants of New England: Parts 1 - 8. New Hampshire Agricultural Experiment Station, Univ. of New Hampshire, Durham.

Dowhan, J. 1979. Preliminary Checklist of Vascular Flora of Connecticut. Conn. Geolog. & Nat. Hist. Surv. Investigations Rep 8. 176p.

Gleason, H. A. and A. Cronquist. 1991. Manual of Vascular Plants of Northeastern United States and Adjacent Canada. New York Botanical Garden, Bronx, NY. 910p.

Jacobs, R. P. and E. B. O'Donnell. 1996. An electrofishing survey of selected Connecticut lakes. Final Rep. 1995. Federal Aid in Sport Fish Restoration. F57R. Conn. Dept. Environmental Protection, Hartford. 190p.

Knoecklein, G. 1999. Ecological Assessment and Impact Evaluation of Wetland Habitats in Vicinity of Alexander Lake, town of Killingly, CT. Northeast Aquatic Research, LLC. Mansfield Center, CT. 65p.

Scott, W. B. and E. J. Crossman. 1973. Freshwater Fishes of Canada. Fish. Research Bd. Can. Ottawa. Bulletin No.184. 966p.

Werner, R. G. 1980. Freshwater Fishes of New York State: A Field Guide. Syracuse University Press. Syracuse, NY. 186p.

Whitworth, W. R. 1996. Freshwater Fishes of Connecticut. Second Edition. State Geological and Natural History Survey of Connecticut DEP, Bulletin 114. 243p.

Wilde, C. W. 1959. A Fishery Survey of the Lakes and Ponds of Connecticut. Conn. State Bd. Fish. and Game Rep. 1. Hartford, CT. 395p.

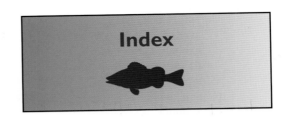

Index

A

Access, fishing, 56
Adipose fin, definition, 333
Aging fish, 53
Algae, 1-5, 9, 14, 19, 335
   definition, 333
   blooms, 3, 14, 29, 30
      definition, 333
   filamentous, 11
   toxic blooms, 19
Alewife, landlocked, 13
   as forage, 22, 23, 27, 48
   negative aspects, 7, 13-14, 23, 26, 27, 40
   average growth, 336, 337
   life history, 49
Anal fin, definition, 333
Apex predators, 33, 36
   definition, 33
Aquatic vegetation (see also algae,
   macrophytes, plankton), 1-4, 12-13, 19, 27,
   34-37, 41-43, 45, 47, 48, 51
   control of, 9, 28-30
      drawdowns, 29
      grass carp, 29-30, 51
      harvesting, 29
      herbicides, 29
   endangered, 12
   as fish habitat, 7-9
   identification, 9-12
   introduced, 12-13
   list of Connecticut plants, 340-343
   preventing invasives, 15
   as primary producers, 4
   survey methods, 55

B

Balance in fisheries, 4-7, 13, 15, 21, 24, 31,
   33, 54
   causes of imbalance, 5-7
   definition, 333
   effects on lake ecosystems, 5
Banded sunfish (see sunfish)
Barbel, definition, 333
Bass, 2, 4, 5, 7, 9, 13, 21, 25-27, 30-32
   largemouth, 13, 21, 24, 28, 338
      average growth, 336-337
      habitat requirements, 8

      life history, 33-34
      top 40 lakes, 344
   smallmouth, 13, 24, 26, 31, 338
      average growth, 336-337
      habitat requirements, 8
      life history, 33-34
      top 20 lakes, 345
Bathymetry, 54
   definition, 333
Benthic, definition, 333
Black crappie (see crappie)
Bluegill (see sunfish)
Boating, 56
Bowfin, 13, 338
Broadcast, definition, 333
Brook trout (see trout)
Brown trout (see trout)
Bullhead (see catfish)

C

Carp, common, 13, 21, 27, 338
   life history, 50-51
Carp, grass, 29-30, 339
   life history, 51
Catfish, 45-48
   black bullhead, 48, 339
   brown bullhead, 13, 46, 339
      habitat requirements, 8
      life history, 47
      top 20 lakes, 347
   channel catfish, 339
      habitat requirements, 8
      life history, 46
   white catfish, 13, 339
      life history, 47
   yellow bullhead, 13, 47, 339
Caudal fin, definition, 333
Chubsucker, creek, 13, 52, 338
Coldwater fish and fisheries, 2, 13
   definition, 7
   habitat requirements, 8
   management, 22-24
Contaminants in fish, 19-20, 126, 186, 202,
   266, 298, 300, 309, 313, 325
Coolwater fish, 24
   definition, 7
   habitat requirements, 8

Crappie, black, 13, 32, 338
    average growth, 336-337
    habitat requirements, 8
    life history, 41
    top 20 lakes, 346
Crappie, white, 41, 308, 312, 314, 318, 338
Creel limits, 21, 31
Crustacean, definition, 333

D
Depth, maximum, 56
Depth, mean, 56
Dorsal fin, definition, 333
Drawdown of lakes, 9, 27-29, 82, 96, 112,
    282, 300

E
Ecosystems, lake and pond, 4, 5, 7, 9, 13-15,
    21, 28, 30, 33, 47
Eel, American, 13, 338
    life history, 51-52
Electrofishing
    effects on fish, 53-54
    field methods, 53-54
    statewide survey, 6, 24-26, 54
Endangered animals and plants, 12, 30, 340-
    343
Epilimnion (see also stratification), 2
Eutrophic (see also trophic classification), 3,
    27, 38
    definition, 335
Eutrophication, 3, 9

F
Fertility (see productivity of lakes)
Fingerling, definition, 333
Fish, list of Connecticut fish, 338-339
Fish kills, 2, 18-19, 28, 29, 210, 240, 296
    Winter kill, definition, 335
Fishing quality, 56, factors affecting, 6, 7, 15,
    21, 22, 24-25, 27, 31-32
Food chains (webs), 4, 9, 12, 13, 20, 28, 29,
    33, 40
    definition, 4
Forage fish (see also predator/prey relationships),
    4, 5, 7, 13, 14, 17, 22, 23, 25, 27, 48-50
    definition, 334
    introductions of, 27
Fry, definition, 334

G
Gamefish, definition, 33
Genetics of fishes, 6, 15, 23, 25
Golden shiner (see shiners)
Goldfish, 13, 338
    life history, 51
Green sunfish (see sunfish)
Growth of fishes (see also aging fish, life

histories of fish)
    average growth rates, 336, 337
    density-dependent growth, 5-7, 13, 21,
        24-28, 31, 32

H
Habitat of fishes, 4, 6-9, 12-14, 22, 25, 35, 38
    habitat alteration, 8-9
    habitat limitations, 6-7
    habitat management, 27-30
Harvest of fish, effects of, 5, 6, 21-25, 27, 31,
    32, 38, 39
Herbicides (see aquatic vegetation)
Holdover (see trout)
Hypolimnion (see also stratification), 2

I
Introduced animals and plants, 7, 12-15, 21,
    23, 25-27, 29-31, 338-339
    benefits vs. dangers of introductions,
        13-15
    preventing spread of invasives, 15
Invasive species (see introduced animals and
    plants)
Invertebrate, definition, 334

K
Kokanee (see salmon)

L
Lateral line, definition, 334
Laterally compressed, definition, 334
Largemouth bass (see bass)
Length limits (see management)
Limnology, definition, 334

M
Macrophytic plants (macrophytes), definition,
    334 (see also aquatic vegetation)
Management of lake and pond fisheries, 21-
    32, 56
    aquatic vegetation control, 28-30
    artificial structure, 27
    creel limits, 21, 22, 31
    closed seasons, 21, 22, 30-31
    coldwater fisheries, 22-24
    history of, 21
    forage fish introductions, 27
    introduction of new predators, 26
    length limits, 7, 21, 22, 24, 31-32
        minimum length limits, 32
        slot length limits, 32
    regulations, 30-32
    stocking, 13, 15, 21, 22, 24, 26, 27,
        29-30, 35-36, 38-40, 46, 49
    stocking warmwater fish, 25
    trout, 22-23
    warmwater fisheries, 24-32
    water level manipulation, 27-29

Mapping of lake depths, 54

Mesotrophic (see also trophic classification), 3, 335

Metalimnion (see also stratification), 2

Minimum length limits (see management)

Mollusk, definition, 334

Mortality (see fish kills and harvest)

N

Native fish, 7, 12, 13, 21, 338-339

Nutrients in lakes, 1, 3, 4, 6, 8, 9, 14, 19, 28, 29
  definition, 334

O

Oligotrophic (see also trophic classification), 3, 334

Omnivorous, definition, 334

Oxygen, dissolved, 1-3, 7-9, 14, 18-19, 22, 24, 28, 38, 335
  definition, 333

P

Panfish, 5, 6, 13, 24-28, 31, 32, 40-45
  definition, 40

Parasites of fish, 15-18

Pectoral fin, definition, 334

Pelagic, definition, 334

Pelvic fin, definition, 334

Perch, yellow, 9, 13, 28, 36, 339
  average growth, 336-337
  habitat requirements, 8
  life history, 41-42
  top 20 lakes, 346

Perch, white, 7, 13, 21, 26, 339
  average growth, 336-337
  life history, 42-43

Photosynthesis, 2-4, 9, 19
  definition, 334

Phytoplankton, definition, 334

Pickerel, chain, 4, 7, 9, 13, 25, 26, 28, 31, 40, 48, 49
  average growth, 336-337
  habitat requirements, 8
  life history, 36-37
  top 20 lakes, 345

Pickerel, redfin, 13, 339
  life history, 37

Pike, northern, 7, 24, 26, 27, 339
  habitat requirements, 8
  life history, 36

Piscivorous, definition, 334

Planktivore, definition, 334

Plankton (see also algae),
  definition, 334
  zooplankton, 4, 5, 7, 9, 13-14, 23, 29, 38-40, 49

Plants (see aquatic vegetation)

Pollution, 3-4, 19-20

Predator/prey relationships, 4-7, 13, 14, 16, 24-28, 31, 33, 48

Prey species (see forage fish and predator/prey relationships)

Productivity (fertility) of lakes, 2-4, 9, 21, 27, 28, 56
  definition, 3, 334

Pumpkinseed (see sunfish)

Put-and-take, definition, 334

R

Rainbow trout (see trout)

Recruitment, definition, 334

Redbreast (see sunfish)

Regulations (see management)

Reservoirs, water supply, 6, 24, 31, 37, 54

Rock bass (see sunfish)

S

Salmon, Atlantic, 13, 21, 40, 339

Salmon, Kokanee, 14, 22, 23, 339
  life history, 39-40
  management, 23

Shiners, 4, 25
  golden, 9, 13, 28, 338
    average growth, 336-337
    life history, 48
  spottail, 49, 339

Slot length limits (see management)

Smallmouth bass (see bass)

Smelt, rainbow, 14, 22, 339
  life history, 50
  management, 23

Spottail shiner (see shiners)

Stocking (see management)

Stockpiling of fishes, 5, 24-25, 31, 32
  definition, 335

Stunting (see also growth of fishes), 5, 7, 25, 26, 28, 40, 43
  definition, 335

Stratification of lakes, 1-2, 56
  definition, 335

Sucker, white (see also chubsucker), 13, 27, 338
  life history, 52

Sunfish, 2, 7, 19, 33, 40, 43-45
  habitat requirements, 8
  top 20 lakes, 347
  banded, 12, 144, 338
    life history, 45
  bluegill, 7, 8, 13, 338
    average growth, 336-337
    life history, 43-44
  green, 13, 338

life history, 45
pumpkinseed, 7, 13, 338
    average growth, 336-337
    life history, 44
redbreast, 13, 338
    average growth, 336-337
    life history, 44-45
rock bass, 13, 338
    average growth, 336-337
    life history, 45

T

Tench, 49, 72, 339
Thermocline (see metalimnion)
Transparency (water clarity), 56
Trophic classification (see also productivity
    of lakes), 2, 3, 56
    definition, 335
Trophic levels, 4
Trout, 1, 2, 7, 13, 14, 25, 27, 29, 38-40, 49,
    50
    habitat requirements, 8
    holdovers, 13, 22-23, 38, 39
        definition, 334
    management, 22-24
    brook trout, 13, 339
        life history, 39
    brown trout, 339
        life history, 38
    lake trout, 13, 24
    rainbow trout, 339
        life history, 38-39
Turnover, spring and fall, 1

V

Vascular plants, defintion, 335
Ventral fin, definition, 335
Vegetation (see aquatic vegetation)

W

Walleye, 7, 14, 24, 26, 49, 50, 339
    habitat requirements, 8
    life history, 35-36
Warmwater fish & fisheries, 2, 5, 7-8, 13, 33,
    36, 40, 54
    definition, 7
    growth of, 336-337
    habitat requirements, 8
    management, 24-32
Watershed 3, 56
    management, 3-4
Water supply reservoirs (see reservoirs)
White perch (see perch)
Winter kill, (see fish kills)

Y

Yellow perch (see perch)

Z

Zebra mussels, 13, 14-15, 29, 134, 290
Zooplankton (see plankton)